PLANNING COMMUNITY SERVICES FOR CHILDREN IN TROUBLE

PLANNING
COMMUNITY SERVICES
FOR CHILDREN
IN TROUBLE

BY ALFRED J. KAHN

Foreword by Eleanor Roosevelt

COLUMBIA UNIVERSITY PRESS
New York and London

Dedicated to the memory of
Adele Rosenwald Levy
friend of all the children

FOREWORD

ADELE LEVY, to whom this volume is dedicated, was one of the
great friends and protectors of all our children. Her accomplishments and her contributions have already been recognized and
described elsewhere. This book is in harmony with the tradition
she established. Because she cared about children Adele Levy
wanted to know that agencies and institutions created for them
were equipped to achieve what they promised to do. In the terms
of this book, she would not have accepted services rendered as a
substitute for tasks accomplished.

I wish to call attention to another of Dr. Kahn's themes, one
which inevitably attracts the attention of a person who has watched
the slow, yet vital, growth of the UN. It is understandable that
organizational prerogatives and specialized concerns tend to dominate services at one point. People who serve in courts see the
task of working with children in trouble from a special perspective.
School people have their own preoccupations as do workers in
community agencies and the many others on whom effective efforts
depend.

Perhaps that is as it must be while specialties develop, skills are
perfected, and social interests are formed. Is it not, however, a
sign of general maturing, of social advance, to become aware also
of interdependence? No nation is an island—nor is any social agency.

I am therefore interested in this book's attempts to develop the
notion of a community system of services, mutually interdependent,
seeking to locate, evaluate, and serve the interests of families and
children in trouble. The concepts of accountability and respon-

sibility, advanced and illustrated here again and again, provide the motive power for some sacrifice of traditional prerogatives in the face of community objectives. The problems of delinquency and neglect are large and seem to require new energies, sparked by new ideas. Dr. Kahn's studies, conducted with the active participation of the Citizens' Committee for Children of New York, a most unusual group of informed laymen and highly competent professional experts who work with children, offer lessons which would seem to deserve serious attention everywhere.

New York City
September, 1962

PREFACE

LIBRARIES are well stocked with standard descriptions of agencies concerned with delinquency, and publishers' lists promise substantial additions. This volume will be justified only if its readers agree that it has moved away from the merely descriptive and has begun to suggest the characteristics and scope of a community *system* of services for coping with the *delinquencies* and the *neglects*.

I have long been convinced that community programs have failed on two scores: (1) They have been built on the assumption that the administrative labels "delinquency" and "neglect" denote populations to be dealt with as though all their members were relatively similar. Only recognition of the range and heterogeneity subsumed under each of the labels will permit realistic planning. (2) Too many communities have been willing to accept the agency and institution as the planning unit. Examination of experience discloses that effective intervention is so complex a process that it is doomed to failure unless all agencies are part of a truly integrated, carefully planned network.

These conclusions have been reinforced again and again in a series of studies of individual agencies and programs, as well as in studies of the impact of the total process of public and voluntary agency services on families and children. It was this which led to the decision to attempt an approach which asks how a *community* must equip itself to deal with serious problems of unacceptable deviance in children. What are the tasks to be done, the *functions* to be organized? What values are crucial? What philosophy should permeate the system?

A discussion of these questions (in Part A) precedes examination of the ways in which tasks may be divided among agencies and institutions. Given the concept of a community intervention network, in fact, it becomes possible to identify the boundaries of existing social institutions and the need for new forms of provision (Part B).

Most crucial, however, are the orientations and mechanisms for coordination and integration within the community system. While objectives and philosophy are presented in Part A, more detailed exposition of provision for accountability and responsibility is reserved for Part C.

More than half the chapters deal in general principles and national trends. Where relevant, however, some of the chapters (especially V, VI, VII, IX, XI) turn to specific New York City and New York State "case examples." Apart from the fact that these areas include about 8 percent of the elementary and secondary school age population of the country, this attention to New York is justified by the desirability of testing proposals against the realities of a specific area. The author and others have studied all parts of the New York service network, making possible the formulation of system-wide proposals. At all points, however, data are provided which give a picture of the situation elsewhere in the country—referring to specific agencies and programs and to general organization of services. The basic proposals developed and the fundamental principles arrived at are designed for broad application and adaptation. The future experience of those who seek to solve specific problems in a variety of urban areas will provide the only test of the validity of the approach and its efforts at generic formulations.

Mobilization of constructive forces in highly vulnerable communities, neighborhoods, and groups does not demand identification of any specific individual as needing help. In fact, to list employment services or youth programs—for example—as addressed to "delinquents" may in fact create undesirable self-identification and defeat the objectives. Thus, especially in the discussion of schools and local community organization, we shall be concerned with some levels of prevention.

Much else that would be relevant to prevention is not encompassed. This volume is concerned largely with control and treatment of undesirable deviance and antisocial behavior—rather than with primary prevention. As will soon become clear, however, the boundaries cannot be sharply drawn between case finding and situation finding at the level before there is an "official" problem —and what is often called prevention. Since a very large proportion of the daily police and court youth caseload consists of repeaters, the matters discussed in this work do involve what is generally called "secondary prevention." Successful intervention and treatment would substantially affect the volume of antisocial behavior.

The task of organizing for effective control and intervention once deviance has begun is itself a large task, and it deserves concentration, experimentation, and new organization. It is the central interest of this book.

The readers of this volume or of the studies which led up to it over a fourteen-year period will understand the author's considerable debt to many of the members and to the staff of the Citizens' Committee for Children of New York. While the total list of those who helped is too long to print here, the volume would be quite incomplete if it did not note the extensive contribution of Mrs. Trude W. Lash, Executive Director, or failed to record the author's deep gratitude to her.

Portions of this work have been supported at various times since 1948 by the generosity of the following: Marion R. Ascoli Fund, Dorothy L. and Richard J. Bernhard Foundation, the Field Foundation, the Ford Foundation, Milton A. Gordon & Company, Inc., Nathan Hofheimer Foundation, Inc., New York Fund for Children, and the Aaron E. Norman Fund, Inc.

A.J.K.

New York City
November, 1962

CONTENTS

Part A

PHILOSOPHY AND STRATEGY

The experts may list all sorts of causes. But they agree on one answer to why these conditions continue to exist: We permit them to.

EDWARD R. MURROW
"Who Killed Michael Farmer?"

CHAPTER I

WHY PLAN—AND FOR WHOM?

THIS is a volume about delinquent and neglected children and about those who seem destined to be so labeled unless there is effective community intervention. These labels do not, however, create a homogeneous group, even though charts, graphs, headlines, and statistical tables may tend to give a contrary impression.

For example:

Mission stabbed him and the guy he . . . like hunched over. He's standing up and I knock him down. Then he was down on the ground, everybody was kickin' him, stompin' him, punchin' him, stabbin' him, so he tried to get back up and I knocked him down again. Then the guy stabbed him in the back with a bread knife.[1]

Joan, a teen-ager in a prosperous suburban community, frequently was stopped by local police for minor traffic violations, but her father was well known and no tickets were issued. She received enough speeding tickets on the highway, however, so that her license was suspended for several months, less than a year after it had been issued. Then, one day, two weeks after the license was restored, while driving her sports car over 80 miles an hour on a parkway in mid-afternoon, she rammed the car of J.T., a salesman, from the rear. When he was extricated from his car, which had careened down an embankment, he was dead. Joan was hospitalized for a month before her court appearance.

Tony and Rico were stopped by a store detective as they walked out of a chain store and were taken to the manager's office. When the police arrived they were shown the small collection of items the boys had in their pockets: yo-yos, cap pistols, wallets, combs, flashlights. It was the third

[1] Columbia Broadcasting System, Inc., "Who Killed Michael Farmer?" as broadcast April 21, 1958.

time they had been found picking things up in this store. A call to the police records bureau disclosed a long list of informal complaints but no arrests. Now, however, they would go to court. In a day or two the court would know that Tony was in a class for children with retarded mental development and that Rico was a child in foster care.

Johnny, 10½, was brought to court by a police officer. He and three friends were charged with attempting to break into parking meters with a can opener. Johnny had been adjudicated delinquent and placed on probation a year earlier after breaking into an apartment and stealing a clock-radio. His mother reported that he was incorrigible and beyond her control. He was a chronic truant. Johnny said that his mother beat him severely. He wanted to be placed.[2]

Marie had been gone three nights before her stepfather called the police. While only 15½, she had a long history of truancy. Two years before a long series of unsuccessful attempts had been made to get her to attend a child guidance clinic regularly. A psychiatrist had called her "schizoid." Marie had told a social worker that the stepfather had made "advances" when the mother was out and that she did not want to stay there. The mother said this was a vicious lie. This was the third runaway for Marie and she would not be found for several days—nor would she be able to account for her time away: where had she slept; who had fed her; where did she get the new skirt?

Situations such as these soon involve the machinery of apprehension, detention, adjudication, investigation, and treatment: police, courts, detention facilities, training schools, clinics, voluntary institutions, private physicians, and clergymen. When case histories are assembled, we inevitably discover that years before the incident in the headlines or the event described in a court petition, others had prior reason for concern: parents, relatives, local clergy, teachers, physicians, social workers.

"He always ran away."

"She was terribly dull."

"I've never seen a child with such hatred for a mother."

"No one would play with him."

"Those children lived in twelve households in a five-year period."

"That gang always terrorized the neighborhood."

Why, if the signs are there, do things so often get worse? The

[2] Research Department, New York City Youth Board, *Delinquent Children under 12* (New York, 1960), p. 85.

cries of distress and signals of danger are sometimes heeded and at other times ignored. Most often there is a response, but it may be inept or inadequate. Delinquency rates rise; neglect increases; the child who is a "problem" today and a training school student tomorrow may well be a seasoned adult criminal in a decade.

Behind this situation are the gaps in knowledge and skill and shortages of qualified personnel which plague the work in this most difficult area. Also involved, very much involved, in our failures and half-failures, are major defects in the policies, philosophies, and organization of services for dealing with children in trouble. All of these represent the major concerns of this book.

THE POLICY VACUUM

At first glance, there would seem to be no problems in this realm which could not be solved by increased appropriations and assignment of additional personnel. For current literature in the fields of delinquency, child care, and mental health tends to converge in a series of widely accepted assertions in relation both to causes of the difficulties and to how services should be organized:

a) Causation is complex and must be studied from several perspectives.

b) Prevention and treatment efforts should take account of sociocultural as well as interpersonal and intrapsychic factors.

c) Treatment programs for children should be based on family diagnosis and should include adequate work with parents and other key figures and forces in a child's environment.

d) Careful interagency and interservice cooperation and coordination are essential if preventive and treatment efforts are to be effective.

e) Well-trained personnel should be assigned to this difficult and important work.

f) At times the group is the unit for intervention, but at other times it is the individual.

In addition to generalizations such as these, there are many volumes containing guides and standards for specific types of programs.

Unfortunately, scientific literature dealing with causes and professional literature specifying treatment orientations and methods do not always lead directly to soundly organized community efforts. There are many services, for example, in which treatment is organized around one factor or one aspect of the problem and in which data relating to other considerations are ignored. One might illustrate from the fields of child guidance, recreation, religious counseling, and health, without looking very far. How many clinics treat a boy's relationships in the family and ignore his problems with his peers? There are many programs which work with a child-patient as though he lived in no environment other than that of the room in which clinical treatment takes place.

Moreover, despite unusual individual instances of cooperation and expert coordination, the more typical situation seems to be one in which the potential effectiveness of services is seriously undermined by only partial implementation of announced philosophy, failure within a community to organize all necessary functions or services, quantitative or qualitative inadequacy of resources, and serious problems in communication.

To a substantial extent, in fact, the entire attack on delinquency may also be said to suffer from a policy vacuum. Some people want to lower juvenile court age while others wish to raise it. Some would introduce into juvenile courts more of the attributes of criminal court practice, while others see in these courts lessons for all court systems. Some expect settlement houses to cope with delinquency while others stress the role of clinics. There are, too, many public figures who would shame young delinquents publicly, disgrace them through the mass media, and have them fully disowned—and yet these same individuals claim to support expensive therapeutic services which are designed to facilitate readjustment, reintegration, and reacceptance.[3]

Far too often, a limited group of concerned citizens and professionals in this field have succeeded in passing legislation which creates needed programs or which authorizes essential personnel without ensuring adequate understanding by the officials involved or the public at large of underlying premises or objectives. The results are seen in inconsistencies in provision and practice and gaps in programs.

[3] Alfred J. Kahn, "The Policy Vacuum and Delinquency," *Federal Probation*, XXIV, No. 2 (September, 1960), 32–34.

With equal frequency, those who support or work on behalf of specific program objectives fail to think of the total implication of what they espouse. The illustrations might be multiplied./ Some people campaign for early school identification of children who need special attention (in fact, such campaigning is now a fad), but they do not help equip schools to make individualized case *evaluations* which might lead to remedial measures./ What is case finding not followed by evaluation? Others help their states to create good classification and diagnostic centers for evaluation of court-adjudicated delinquents—but they do not concern themselves about the fact that their states do not offer diversified networks of residences, clubs, treatment centers, and institutional resources at which to keep these well-diagnosed and ably classified children.

A final illustration: Are there not many states which dedicate their institutions and training schools to preparing young people for the idea that the community is ready to accept them? And is it not true that these very same young people encounter inflexibility and rejection in schools, in public housing, and in neighborhood agencies on their return? Failure on parole is sometimes the failure of the community as much as it is the failure of the parolee. Parole officers work with the client's attitudes: who works with community definitions of returnees? Sometimes, Buell comments, there is no policy except the open-ended objective of providing needed service. We need a problem-solving orientation to agency service, with defined objectives.[4]

Full debate about public policy toward children in trouble is unpleasant and difficult—whether it is carried on in national, state, or local forums. Such debate is nonetheless an essential prerequisite to the further development of programs, the statement of their objectives, and decisions about staffing. Without policy decisions which are deliberately made and widely understood, necessary public support and financing cannot be expected—and programs will continue to be far less effective than modern knowledge and skill might make them. Given widespread discussion and a core of consensus, communities could designate strategy and tactics for dealing with their problems. There would then be a basis for

[4] Bradley Buell *et al.*, "Reorganizing to Prevent and Control Disordered Behavior," *Mental Hygiene*, XLII, No. 2 (April, 1958), 155–94.

public and private bodies to establish the necessary planning and coordination machinery, lay and professional, and to expect it to do its job.

The fact is that the administrative label "delinquent" applies to many types of children and to an endless variety of offenses. Similarly, there are many kinds of parental neglect. These socially identified disorders must be dealt with in relation to many types of personalities and varied family strengths and circumstances. There is therefore no reason at all to expect effective public intervention except through a well-integrated, differentiated system of measures and resources, assured as a matter of public responsibility and administered by both public and voluntary agencies. Obviously, so complex a panoply would be little more than a costly, confusing, irresponsible improvisation unless it were guided by clear and consistent policy.

In addition to problems of policy, organization, and personnel, which result in substantial underutilization of current scientific weapons against these social problems in much of the country, we must also list the fact that knowledge and skill are not always equal to the task in all of its complexities. Thus, a way must be found, while defining policy and organizing services, to ensure the much-needed experimentation, flexibility, and change.

The present volume thus seeks to address issues of policy and of organization. With special attention to the large urban area it asks: How shall we view delinquency and neglect? What shall we strive to do? How must specific community services be organized for this purpose? How can they be coordinated? Our major themes are *responsibility, accountability, service integration,* and *coordination.* Their implications will become clear as we proceed.

While a good deal of work has been done to define ways of organizing specific services, not enough attention has been given to the community *system.* National agencies and standard-setting groups have developed some guides with reference to the work of juvenile courts, detention, police, probation officers, training schools, and other services within the scope of this discussion. It is certainly helpful to assemble these recommended standards and relate them to a context of policy and philosophy—as well as to practical problems of existing programs and to one another. It is desirable also to indicate their gaps and their strengths and to suggest alternatives. In addition, however, the interests of the community system require that there be developed that concept of function for each of the major services which seems to possess validity not only of itself but in relation to a *community-wide strategy* for dealing with a major social problem.

However, the requirements of a total strategy are hardly met by beginning only with existing services and current definitions of function and, then, striving for a better coordination as well as the strengthening of individual programs. Useful as such an approach may be, it allows the possibility of major gaps in service, serious deficiencies in day-to-day operations, and a failure to detect possible new models of organization. Thus, we propose, at one and the same time, an examination of *individual* programs (and how they might be made most effective) and the definition of *major elements in an integrated community* approach. The latter objective must play as substantial a role in determining how one examines existing programs as do the goals and standards formulated by national agencies and professional groups.

THE NEED TO PLAN

The emphasis on policy definition, coordination, and integration grows not out of theoretical considerations alone but out of examination of the status of services today. Listen to any group of administrators, top level supervisors, or skilled practitioners as they discuss their community efforts in the field of delinquency and one soon hears:

a) In many states, police and others detain children excessively, particularly as detention facilities improve. What kinds of admission controls are possible?

b) Agencies and institutions often have to render certain services by default, knowing that they are not equipped to work effectively with children having particular needs. What should they do?

c) In one community a child may be picked up by the police and offered service, although no arrest is made. Even though the service is technically "unofficial," he will have a "record." Should such practice continue?

d) In a large school system, cumulative school records designed to provide continuity of help for children in difficulty are often used to stigmatize children. Should they be eliminated?

e) Should a state construct residential treatment centers as part of its training school network? What is the current thinking about priorities in the development of institutional facilities for adjudicated delinquents?

f) A court has been planning a group therapy program but the local mental hygiene clinic has questioned the necessity for the venture. Should it continue?

A similar, but not necessarily identical, list could be produced in almost any community. As one pursues the questions further, they tend to fall into such categories as effectiveness, philosophy, coverage, methods, coordination.

The strongest case for a hard look at what we now do with children in trouble is also the most familiar: *our efforts are not sufficiently effective.*

The generalization holds as one examines national, state, and local data. While delinquency statistics are seriously limited in many ways, the evidence does nonetheless sustain the view that the delinquency increase since World War II, for example, has been substantially more rapid than the child and youth population growth and is probably only explained in part by more police activity, increased referrals from schools, or the creation of more facilities to work with delinquents (see chart on p. 30). For the country as a whole, between 1950 and 1961, the increase in delinquency exceeded the increase in child population annually except in 1959 and 1961. In New York State, our special focus, the delinquency rate per 1,000 children (Children's Court cases disposed of) rose from 5.5 in 1948 to 8.2 in 1958 and was 7.2 in 1961. The 25-year average is over 6 per 1,000. The New York City rate leaped from 6.4 in 1948 to 12.4 in 1961 (having declined briefly to 11.4 in 1959). The upstate rate for 1961 was 3.6.[5]

It may, of course, be argued that increasing delinquency tells us more about the broader society and its problems than about the

[5] U.S. Department of Health, Education, and Welfare, *Report to the Congress on Juvenile Delinquency* (Washington, D.C.: Government Printing Office, 1960), pp. 3, 20. New York data from the New York State Division on Youth.

effectiveness of services for dealing specifically with children in trouble. Such response is less valid, however, as we are confronted by data indicating the frequency of new offenses (technically referred to as recidivism) after agency services or institutionalization. This does not necessarily mean that the service has had no value at all for the repeaters. The basic fact remains, however, that we know from high recidivism rates that programs are not sufficiently effective. The expectation is that an agency or institution either will help toward rehabilitation, so that serious offenses against the community and severe personal disturbance will not recur, or will take steps to protect the community (usually through further institutionalization).

Thirty to 40 percent of youngsters who have been on probation are back in court in a few years. One fifth violate probation even before discharge. A representative group of state penitentiaries report that over half their inmates were training school graduates. Training schools note that 31 percent of their admissions during one year consist of youths returned to them as parole violators or for new offenses.[6]

It may be conservatively estimated that 50 to 60 percent of training school "graduates" are in new difficulty before their twenty-first birthdays. Follow-up studies conducted at child guidance clinics and elsewhere, where the population is not largely delinquent, and where the criteria refer to "adjustment," may show higher subsequent success rates; but even here the very substantial failure totals underscore the need to look at the adequacy of knowledge and skill and the appropriateness of case screening. Successes are, in fact, few with certain categories of delinquents.[7]

We fail, in part, because *resources are inadequate*. Concepts of humanitarianism and fair play and agency rehabilitative objectives

---

[6] *Report to the Congress on Juvenile Delinquency*, pp. 25, 43.

[7] See the summary in Helen L. Witmer and Edith Tufts, *The Effectiveness of Delinquency Prevention Programs* (Washington, D.C.: Government Printing Office, 1954), pp. 34, 40. Also see Louis Lehrman *et al.*, *Success and Failure of Treatment of Children in the Child Guidance Clinics of the Jewish Board of Guardians* (New York: Jewish Board of Guardians, 1959), as well as Henry S. Maas, in collaboration with Alfred J. Kahn, Herman D. Stein, Dorothy Sumner, *Socio-Cultural Factors in Psychiatric Clinic Services for Children*, constituting the entire issue, *Smith College Studies in Social Work*, Vol. XXV, No. 2 (February, 1955).

are given expression only through the acts of officials and agencies entrusted with the care and protection of children. It is unfortunately the fact that this is a field in which adequate facilities and personnel have not been made available on a scale to meet widely recognized needs. For instance, federal officials estimate that

   a) Except for the large urban centers, most juvenile courts are presided over by judges who devote the bulk of their time to other courts. There are few judges who may be considered truly specialized in children's court work.

   b) Of cities of 50,000–100,000, over one quarter have no special juvenile police officer and for cities of 25,000–50,000 the total is almost one half, despite agreement that such officers are basic to any community program for dealing with delinquency. Larger cities have such officers but are concerned at their lack of special preparation for the job. Smaller cities are seldom so staffed.

   c) Half of the counties have no juvenile probation service, the cornerstone of a special judicial approach to delinquency. While most probation officers are college graduates, only 10 percent have the social work training which is considered essential to effective work.

   d) Thirty percent of the state training schools have no social work staff at all, and almost half have no psychologists, even though such staff is basic to an effective program. Half the training schools are too large; half are overcrowded.

   e) 75,000 to 100,000 children are detained in jail annually for lack of suitable detention facilities.

From state to state and locality to locality the situation repeats itself: There are too few probation officers, detention facilities are overcrowded, courts lack clinical diagnostic resources, there are too few qualified remedial reading teachers, guidance clinics cannot recruit enough trained social workers, training schools are too large and crowded beyond recommended capacities, there are no casework treatment resources for highly disorganized families, and so on.

These data are not presented here to minimize the tremendous progress made in recent decades in expanding resources and providing needed facilities in most states and in many localities. Against the backdrop of the 1930s or even the early 1940s, we have gone far. The public investment in child care and treatment is substantially improved. These are, unfortunately, not adequate criteria. There was a time when "charity" and "welfare" efforts were justified largely by their value for the donors and participants; their adequacy or effect on recipients was not the main concern. Today, however, we plan social welfare, child care, and correctional services because we see the public stake in early and effective response to social deviation and disability. In such context, past progress is appreciated, but the effectiveness and coverage of the current effort must continue to be questioned.

One may nonetheless comment, as others have, that in this field we recognize problems only because we are making progress. As we try to develop appropriate services we appreciate how much more we need. When we try to work on all necessary levels, the available range of facilities and their current scope become less adequate to the needs as we have come to understand them.

It has been held that there is no point in introducing discussion of broad community strategy and of the interrelationships of programs as long as the total volume of service is inadequate and qualified personnel are in short supply. One proponent of this view has said: "You do not have enough services, so talk of reshuffling won't help."

Our own conviction is that it is important to go beyond the frequently echoed statements that we need more facilities and institutions, better trained personnel in larger numbers, higher levels of qualification, and means of ensuring staff stability and sound professional use of time. While constantly strengthening existing programs we must continue to ask where we need *more* facilities and where different *kinds* of programs. Would sound program decisions or realignments offer alternatives to continued expansion? What are the *priorities* as new resources become available? Recognition of crucial issues will prepare the way, eventually, for better functioning of our system of agencies and institutions as a whole.

Austin MacCormick has shown that the cost of building and operating a 1,200–1,500 bed medium-security prison would ensure the salaries of enough probation officers to work with 8,000 men at optimum caseloads of 25. The costs of services to children in institutions are three or four times those of the prison.[8] Do we not need to weigh our priorities?

If the current pattern of services is not sufficiently effective, close examination of weak spots and major problems is a useful preliminary to planning. Our own findings are confirmed by studies and reports from many cities and states.[9] They are not encouraging and may be summarized all too easily: Far too little is being done to ensure the right services for the right child—at the right time. Further, community services are not patterned or interrelated in a manner to ensure that we will be more effective in the future than we are now. Results will be no better than they have been unless something new happens.

More specifically:

Cases are found but opportunities are lost. Large proportions of the neglectful families or delinquent children who are of major community concern actually come to attention years before the final breakdown which leads to court or institution. Sometimes the family as a whole is known to need help; often it is one or another parent or one of the children.

Despite all the talk about the urgency of organizing for early identification of those who may need help, the problem does not in fact appear to be one of inability to establish contact with most families and children who will at some time be in serious trouble. Cases are "found" or make themselves known. Why then are *opportunities lost?* In dealing with families who are eventually known to

[8] Austin MacCormick, "Potential Value of Probation," *Federal Probation,* XIX, No. 1 (March, 1955), 3–8.

[9] Our own research is reported in Alfred J. Kahn, *For Children in Trouble* (New York: Citizens' Committee for Children of New York City, Inc., 1957), and Alfred J. Kahn, *New York City Boys Committed to New York State Training Schools in 1957 and 1958* (Albany: New York State Department of Social Welfare, 1959). In addition, see New York City Youth Board, *A Study of Some of the Characteristics of 150 Multiproblem Families* (New York, 1957), and New York City Youth Board, *Delinquent Children under 12.* Similar data are found in Community Council of Houston and Harris County, *Child Welfare Study,* Reports 1–2 (Houston, 1958–61). Also see Helen Hagan, *Relationships between Child Care Agencies* (New York: Child Welfare League of America, 1955), pp. 3–10.

courts and long-term institutions, agencies do not act—in fact are not *expected* to act—as representatives of an integrated community system. In most instances, the "finder" of the "case" hardly seems to consider that he is in a strategic position and that a valuable opportunity is before him. In most cases, there is a minimum of service as required by the agency's function (the giving of relief, the foster care placement of a child, the rendering of hospital social service). One finds only a handful of instances involving agency initiative—the going beyond a specified function: broad "family diagnosis," preventive planning, or concern for children other than those initially referred. These are outnumbered by cases in which relief checks are authorized regularly and no action is initiated despite obvious parental neglect of children, cases in which medical service is arranged but a subsequent handicap is not dealt with, cases in which one child in a family is placed in a foster care facility while others in the same family continue in a home recognized to be unsuitable or in which a long-term foster care arrangement is made even though termination of parental rights and adoption deserve consideration.

The extent of case "loss" varies somewhat with the "charge" of an agency and its place in the process. Police and courts may "hold on" more often because situations they deal with are already serious when encountered. Early case finders (when the problem is not yet acute) are most likely to let things drift. Not that all danger signs can lead to action unless intervention is clearly necessary to protect children. Under our conception of individual rights the client who does not accept service on a voluntary basis often cannot be led to do so. Analysis of practice shows, however, that agencies seldom strain the limits of their skills and sanctions, tending more often to recognize neither the opportunity nor the responsibility inherent in early case finding. At other times, caseloads, resource problems, or lack of machinery for agency collaboration are the sources of the failure.

Case plans are not made in accord with the best professional practice. Professional experience attests to the fact that one cannot choose between probation and institutionalization, foster homes and institutions, one institution or another, probation and an outpatient clinic, and so on without a systematic analysis and evaluation of a child's basic personality characteristics and strengths, his relationships to parent figures, their strengths and weaknesses, his relationships with peers, and his likely responses to various possible courses of action. Such formulation is more helpful for planning if it also includes information about the background and dynamic elements behind the problem situation or behavior which brought the child to attention.

Current thinking stresses the importance of presenting, where possible, a view of the total family situation and relationships, a "family diagnosis." Examination of records in a variety of agencies and courts discloses that in a considerable proportion of instances (the exact percentage varies) records have no adequate evaluations or contain evaluations which cannot in any sense lead to carefully considered disposition planning.

What, then, is the result? Some agencies merely *drift into dispositions:* habit, a realistic appraisal of the resource limitations, and the desire to be "harsh" with serious offenders lead to decisions. Thus, a probation violator may tend automatically to be committed to a training school, a pregnant girl to the one agency with facilities, and so on. Or, where the offense is the first one on record and the background is not too disorganized, superficially, the inclination is to allow a young offender a "second chance," without introducing the criteria which derive from social or psychiatric study.

The existence of a social case study does not necessarily change this. A judge may send a probation violator to an institution despite a diagnostic "case" for community treatment even though the probation period has only begun—and the probation "treatment" hardly tried.

Some of these patterns reflect community sentiment; others involve realistic assessment of what the resources are. Sometimes, "drifting" is rationalized in elaborate ways. Occasionally, a mother's courtroom tears, a child's manner of speaking set off a chain reaction which negates diagnostic studies and tests.

Dispositions arrived at often involve basic *community self-deception.* Well-intentioned staffs request the guidance of psychiatric hospitals, court clinics, or other facilities. They review the analyses and reports and, in good faith, arrange dispositions which they consider to be appropriate implementation of the recommendations. In fact, the clinicians who have made the studies have often named the agency selected for the referral as one possible way of meeting the client's needs. Yet, when the matter is explored in other contexts, those who know the facilities and are qualified to judge are often close to unanimous in their agreement that the treatment needs of clients cannot be met. Those who arrive at the dispositions often realize this; in their other capacities they may even seek to help strengthen the programs by additions of staff and enrichment of program.

The following illustrations will clarify this phenomenon:

a) A reformatory is selected where the recommendation is for "an institution for normal children, with facilities for psychotherapy and vocational guidance." None of these criteria are actually met.

b) A voluntary foster care agency is selected to provide "psychotherapy." There is no such program in the institution (even though it is specified in the exchange of correspondence).

c) A child is placed on probation on the assumption that there will be a measure of supervision and treatment; the reality often is one of occasional, superficial contacts with staff members who come and go.

d) A social agency closes a case because the police Juvenile Aid Bureau is in contact with the family and agrees to continue. It is widely known, however, that no treatment resources are thus made available.

Closely related to "disposition by self-deception" and often its cause is the related phenomenon of *resource location by shopping*. Shopping for resources is a major activity of probation officers, members of child welfare placement services, and others involved in planning for children. The success of the telephonic "shopping trip" often determines a child's future. Even though intra-agency and interagency competition may be controlled somewhat and the systems of placement or of clinic intake made somewhat more efficient, the problem will remain serious as long as resources are in short supply and intake criteria in foster care and clinics are not fully publicized or even completely consistent. It is almost impossible to overestimate the waste in professional resources resulting from these situations. It is even more difficult to overstate the damage wrought in the lives of children.

Agency definitions of function, procedures, and philosophies are not always consistent with the requirements of a community system of services. Successful work with children and families in trouble obviously requires more than occasional cooperation between various agencies. Case finding, evaluation, and disposition can hardly be effective unless the different agencies are part of a truly integrated effort. Yet the integration is seldom found and will be achieved only on the basis of substantial reconsideration of the philosophies and objectives of numerous agencies, their basic functions and procedures, and their relationships with other agencies.

The urgency of these matters is underscored as we note the poor service rendered the following family by a total system of facilities and realize that the problem is one of basic agency functions and philosophies as much as it is of unskilled personnel:

Peter is the oldest of three children who lived with their father and a housekeeper in a cold-water flat in a deteriorating neighborhood. His mother died when he was fourteen, but he was in Children's Court before that. He was known in school as dull, as a poor reader, and as a boy who stole, whose conduct was bad, and who truanted. When Peter was thirteen, he was found delinquent by Children's Court because he broke into an amusement park; he was put on probation. A few months later he was in court again for mischief on railroad property; probation was continued. The next court appearance was for shoplifting, and the judge decided on commitment to a voluntary children's institution since he saw no way to implement a psychiatric recommendation that a foster home be found for Peter "with a warm mother figure." He was described as severely disturbed emotionally.

Peter did not like the institution and ran away three times, stating that he would continue to do so. On one such occasion he was arrested for a series of burglaries. Thus, almost two years after the original commitment and two and a half years after the first court appearance, he was sent to the Training School. Frequent running away led to transfer to another training school and then to the newest training school program. There was some indication of improvement in the last few months, but staff reports were contradictory. It was known that the home situation was as poor as ever, and that Peter was uneasy about his return to the community. A few months after his release, he was arrested attempting grand larceny and sentenced to the Reception Center, having been denied the non-criminal "Youthful Offender" treatment.

This is a difficult situation at best, and we may not know enough to intervene effectively at such a late stage. It is clear, however, that the community took only token measures at a series of crucial points.

Too often the point of the procedure seems to be forgotten once the decision about institutionalization is made and the "machinery" begins to function to find a placement.

Terence needed treatment and could not remain at home. However, there was no space for him in detention or in the institution to which it was expected he would eventually go. He remained at home for nine months with the mother from whom it had been decided to separate him, for good diagnostic reasons; then, for lack of anything else, he was sent to a state facility which was not equipped to accomplish any of the purposes sought in the original plan.

One can only ask: Is the community less neglectful than the mother or less delinquent than the son?

Where children have been placed in institutions and do not get along, they are too often returned to the court, placed in detention or shelter, or sent to psychiatric hospitals for observation (depending on their categories), like pieces of mail incorrectly addressed. There seems to be little consideration of what it means to a child to be "returned to sender" as "too aggressive," or to be sent from a training school ("too disturbed") to an observation hospital ("not psychotic") and back to the training school ("we have no choice but to return A. to the community").

Examination of actual case situations with rehabilitative objectives in mind raises questions as to the justice of labeling children as delinquent, stigmatizing them, and closing to them certain treatment facilities provided for others known as "dependent" or "neglected." Children raised in foster homes, and neglected by foster parents and the agency which placed them, behave as they have learned they must behave to defend themselves and are then called "delinquent." A mother asks for foster care because she cannot manage to rear her children, but they remain on waiting lists over a year. In desperation, she requests that they wait in a temporary shelter. One of them misbehaves under these circumstances, reflecting his normal reactions to his problem, and is committed as a "delinquent" boy. The child's conduct may justify the label technically, but the categorization lacks either logic or justice as one examines it in depth. This problem is not within the scope of any one agency.

Among the orientations which must be questioned is the tendency, already mentioned, to assume that a new offense while a child is on probation or parole must lead to commitment to training school or reformatory. If the objective is rehabilitation, the meaning of the new occurrences requires exploration, and a strategy for effective work should be developed in the light of the understanding gained. Treatment decisions must be based on *diagnostic criteria* consistently; where community protection or "revenge" are the determinants (as they must, apparently, sometimes be) we have given up expectation of positive change and should do so honestly— with clear understanding of the consequences.

While shortages of resources, facilities, and personnel have major effect on the quality of case studies, on the types of dispositions made, and on the adequacy of treatment undertaken, another problem demands attention if the picture is to change: a deep and basic deficiency in community programs appears to be one in *responsibility and accountability.* The lack is a central one and transcends the practices of individual agencies and institutions. For example: A dependent child awaiting placement is referred by a temporary shelter to a psychiatric hospital for observation, is found to be not committable but "disturbed," and is returned home without further action. A clinic refers a disturbed child for neurological study and does not determine that the referral was never completed—despite obvious evidence in its record that this might occur. An institution returns a child to his home after a period and calls to nobody's attention the need for out-patient care. An agency does not pick up a "big sister" referral by the court, but does not report back. A clinic receives a case on referral and does not tell the referring source it has closed the case for noncooperation.

No one agency is at fault all the time—and no one agency is unusual in its failure here. We have not yet established the principle that a child who is in trouble and who is "found" must not be "lost"—because the community loses at the same time—or that an agency which has rendered incomplete or unsuccessful service has some obligations for assuring continuity of community concern when its own contacts end.

In a climate of continued responsibility and accountability, such strategically located agencies as a public welfare department, schools, and health agencies would inevitably define their obligations more broadly in instances in which they detected serious deviation while rendering their primary services. Agencies would think twice about transferring a "too aggressive" child from their institutions. Social service departments in hospitals, particularly in mental hospitals, would view the consequences of hospitalization and aftercare more broadly. There would be more uneasiness about the endless waiting lists which may eventually get a child to a needed clinic or institution, but often only after the child's problem has been much aggravated by a long stay in "temporary" shelter or detention or continued exposure to family pathology.

In a responsible community pattern of services, one would not meet so often a situation like that in which the father had a prison record, the mother spent two periods in mental hospitals, and all the children had been in foster care. Yet no one agency looked systematically at the family, pulled together the several facets of the problem, and offered help beyond that called for by the emergency of the moment.

Nor would agencies so readily close a case for failure to establish a contact, when several possible avenues (a protective agency or exploration of the school situation) might yield other results. Even in highly qualified agencies where the work with clients is usually and properly oriented to understanding the total family situation, the position of brothers and sisters in the family is at times not considered adequately. Similarly, considerable attention may be given to environmental and situational factors generally; but occasionally there is an apparent underestimation of how health, economic, and housing problems defeat any efforts to help with psychological or relationship difficulties.

Where there is a sense of responsibility and a view of one's agency as part of a community-wide program, a voluntary agency is prepared to depart from its usual procedures and to make use of court authority to meet a mother's refusal to permit psychiatric examination of her child and necessary placement planning. There is alertness, too, to the obligation to take the lead in coordinating resources, helping a family to use facilities, and providing direction to a community's efforts.

The sense of responsibility, at its best, seems to produce flexibility and sound improvisation as needed. There is a willingness to maintain a supportive relationship with a young man who needs it but who cannot enter into the usual, more formal, treatment relationship, for example.

In any but a relatively isolated rural area, full service to a family in connection with even one problem is seldom encompassed by any one agency of itself. At some point, if only in the initial referral, somebody else is usually involved. Planning must therefore become alert to those *problems of agency interrelationship* which may impede the most effective service.

First, there are a disturbing number of instances in which official agencies do not ask about the content of the records of other public or private agencies to which the families have been known (or clear with the Social Service Exchange), or do not cooperate actively with the efforts of such agencies. In a large number of cases, some units in the schools, for example, fail to ask for the contents of records in the files of other agencies, even though the case situation is such as to make it desirable to learn more about specific previous contacts.

There are also instances in which voluntary agencies do not seem to respect the public agency's role or to regard a probation officer, for example, as a colleague with whom one works cooperatively. The Juvenile Aid police have had great difficulty in learning from voluntary agencies to which referrals have been made when and why cases are closed. There are similar lapses in relationships between public services.

Instances of poor coordination always require careful attention, not because they necessarily characterize the majority of situations but because they highlight things in need of remedy. For example:

a) A court became involved in elaborate efforts to arrange psychiatric treatment without communicating with agencies with which the family was active—or (later) seeking to coordinate with them.

   b) An adolescent was on probation. When he was arrested by the Police Juvenile Aid Bureau because of a violation, they properly referred the matter to his probation officer. At a later date, having passed his sixteenth birthday, he was sent to the workhouse for a five-day term and completed it before his probation officer knew about the incident.

   c) A case finding agency had great difficulty in establishing contact with a very resistant family, yet no effort was made to obtain data about the family's prior experience with another agency, which might have shed light on the difficulties.

   d) A family long known to welfare, health, court, and school authorities continued in serious difficulties and there was no integrated interagency approach which might have relieved, in some way, the family's miserable plight and protected the children against serious hazards. The family was deemed ineligible for public housing, which they desperately needed, "because of a confused marital picture."

The problem is at times more complex than one of arranging cooperation, since *differences in values* stressed by various agencies may be at stake, i.e., belief in rehabilitation as compared with punitive values; belief in confidentiality in the individual therapeutic relationship as compared with community accountability.

At times a pace which is possible or acceptable to one agency is not permissible to another—as when a court took action to ensure placement at once while a child welfare staff worked slowly to deal, on a voluntary basis, with parental resistance to a necessary separation. At other times, action taken is understandable but illogical when the child's interest is considered—as when an interim foster care facility postponed accepting a child for a month and a half pending completion of certain dental work; the facility was not equipped to do the work and would not be reimbursed by the public welfare department if it sent the child out for it. The child then remained in temporary shelter for the dental work.

Major sources of *interagency tensions* are two phenomena described earlier. First, there is the tendency of certain foster home and institution agencies to retain undefined elements in their intake criteria and not to make readily available data as to space which they have at any given moment; the result is the frustrating "shopping" for facilities already described. Then there is the tendency of the clinic or psychiatric hospital to offer unrealistic recommendations to disposition agencies and to put them in the position of ignoring such recommendations completely (a foster home for an aggressively delinquent adolescent boy) or of convincing themselves that inadequate facilities actually meet the requirements, a phenomenon we have labeled as "self-deception."

There is evidence, too, that *unrealistic concepts of one's role and lack of knowledge of resources* sometimes conspire to block what might be useful contacts. Probation officers undertake service where the need is marginal, when the personal strengths are considerable, and where case dismissal or referral to a voluntary agency are clearly possible. The service given is then generally narrow and superficial. There are, too, judges who make personal appeals to agencies to find places for children who do not qualify by announced criteria. The results do not always prove the judge right.

Where agencies work well together, the results are apparent, especially if a practical agreement has been reached, even though not articulated, as to which agency is to coordinate the approach and interpret the plan to the family. There are many such instances observable in the community day after day, and their existence justifies the hope that they may become the general pattern.

These, to repeat, are universal problems. They are identified by workers in this country and in England, in child welfare and mental health—as well as in corrections. The implications would appear clear: much needs to be done so to organize services that

(1) agencies will cease to be so "hard to reach";

(2) the right clients will be served in the right places;

(3) cases will not be "lost" in the gaps between agencies or in the inadequacies of agencies;

(4) agencies will work together more efficiently, putting people before functions;

(5) necessary technical knowledge will be developed and taught to adequate numbers of personnel;

(6) sufficient resources will be available and, as a result, our community patterns of service will yield more effective and lasting results.

CHILDREN IN TROUBLE

Is it possible to reconcile a commitment to comprehensive planning with special concentration on a group vaguely defined as "in trouble"? Are the children adjudicated as delinquent and as neglected, or those who may be before long, in any sense a viable group from the perspective of the organization of community services?

Enough has already been said to suggest how blurred are the boundaries of a group so defined. Indeed, the field of child welfare has gone to considerable lengths to establish that the particular circumstances or symptoms leading to agency attention or intervention may in no sense define the service required, so that children known to a court as delinquent or neglected, to a child guidance clinic as emotionally disturbed, to a school as nonlearners, to parents as unmanageable, and to a community center as misfits may all require quite similar help. In fact, they may be the same children. On the other hand, any one of these settings may contain within its population children with a range of problems and needs, requiring many quite specialized and varied approaches.

It is also well established—initially through a series of studies by Bradley Buell—that there is a major degree of overlap of multiproblem families when community administrative problem categories are the basis of analysis.[10]

Why, then, single out a subgroup of troubled and troublesome children who in other contexts and perhaps at other times may be seen as in the domain of mental health services, education, public welfare, or other agencies? There is, first, the argument from

[10] The basic reports are Bradley Buell, *Community Planning for Human Services* (New York: Columbia University Press, 1952); Community Research Associates, *Prevention of Dependency in Winona County, Minnesota* (New York, 1953); Community Research Associates, *The Prevention and Control of Indigent Disability in Washington County, Maryland* (New York, 1954); Community Research Associates, *The Prevention and Control of Disordered Behavior in San Mateo County, California* (New York, 1954).

practicality: the programs of courts, police, institutions, attendance bureaus, detention facilities, youth boards, and related groups are in themselves comprehensive, complex, and deserving of considerable attention. To seek, at the same time, for example, to encompass adequately and in some detail foster care and Aid to Needy Families with Children, day care and parent education, child guidance and residential treatment centers for the emotionally disturbed would, inevitably, dilute some of the coverage and thus ignore the considerable need for full analysis and definition of goals.

There is, too, some logic to giving separate attention to situations which involve the formal intervention of the state (or the potential for intervention) to protect a child, the community, or both, through a variety of means, even to the point of compelling residence in detention or an institution, or other limitations on the person. The possibility or fact of such intervention immediately involves certain attitudes, problems, and potentialities which deserve special attention. It also requires particular concern for individual rights and due process, since treatment programs, accompanied by powerful sanctions, run the risk of substantial infringement on individual rights unless special efforts are made to guard such rights.

Finally, we might note, there is need to demonstrate to some members of the community that, logically, services to children in trouble must, in fact, be related to, and become part of, all child welfare services and that both must benefit from the philosophy and techniques which have developed in the mental hygiene movement. A volume which begins only with commitment to a humane approach and to the use of the best available professional experience and the findings of modern science may serve to establish the fact that community policy, so based, inevitably places services to children in trouble in a broader perspective for reasons of efficiency, cost, and effectiveness.

We might think of the special circumstances or needs of children which bring them to attention as a series of channels. One channel might uncover those considered physically handicapped; another might call attention to "severe mental retardation"; a third might direct for services the "emotionally disturbed children not involved in antisocial conduct." Through one series of channels the community learns of delinquent children, of the neglected, and

of those considered highly likely to become delinquent and neglected. They are directed into the channels in a variety of ways
and the community is sufficiently concerned about them to take
the initiative and to compel a degree of involvement, under certain
circumstances.

Once children arrive at the center of community attention, having
entered through a variety of channels, or by displaying a variety
of symptoms, there is the potentiality of offering to each the services
and facilities considered most likely to meet the need or to solve
the problem. Not that one finds universal agreement that, at this
point, the manner of entry is no longer relevant, and that only
individual needs and professional considerations should dictate the
approach. (We maintain special training schools for delinquents,
for example, quite apart from facilities for dependent children, and
many courts want their own psychiatric clinics.) The potential
for creating a unified system of services is obviously present, however, and it then becomes possible to discuss on their merits whether
or not legal-technical considerations or professional-treatment considerations require some degree of continued categorization at
the point of treatment.

This volume ultimately defends the view that programs would
be more effective if a child had access to the full range of community resources once it has been determined that he needs help,
whatever the portal of entry. Affirmation of this philosophy does
not, however, relieve one of the responsibility of demonstrating the
soundness of the view or of considering its possible complications
and implications, legally, administratively, and professionally. These
objectives may be attained in a volume which begins with focus
on children in trouble and moves out to the entire field of community services as they become—or do not become—available to these
children.

Thus we begin with a limited group and a broad perspective.
We seek that kind of guidance for organization of services which
may emerge from study of the consequences of current orientations,
from projections deriving from values yet to be specified, and from
experience in community organization and public health.

The phrase "children in trouble" as here used refers to delinquent and neglected children and is defined to include the "po-

tential" and "vulnerable" as well as the "adjudicated." Early case
finding and service before complex treatment is necessary is certainly a major objective of a community plan. The technicality of
adjudication may be determined, at any given moment, by the
vagaries of administrative policy or public attention.

We shall, therefore, be concerned with the deviant child, not
yet under agency care or receiving service, whose conduct is
believed to lead to delinquency. We shall talk, too, of those already known to agencies and who might well be found delinquent,
under the law, but who have not yet been to court—although they
may be later. We shall certainly wish to consider provisions for
antisocial deviant children coming to the agencies, whether or not
we are able to specify the likelihood of formal judicial labeling in
the future. The allegedly delinquent, already apprehended and in
court, will command substantial attention, as will those already
adjudicated.

Our broad concerns will encompass children categorized by law
into many subtypes of delinquency in various parts of the country.
All jurisdictions agree to the inclusion of behavior which, in an
adult, would be a criminal offense. There is substantial variation,
however, from state to state, in the specification of that unacceptable behavior which is considered delinquent in children, even
though there is no equivalent criminal offense for adults—for example, truancy, incorrigibility, staying away from home without
consent, habitual use of vile and obscene language, patronizing
public poolrooms, and so on.[11]

Statutes generally define neglect in terms of physical abuse or
lack of physical care and only in extreme cases do the agencies
and courts here under discussion deal with situations in which
the less obvious forms of emotional neglect and mistreatment are
at stake. These latter cases are not ruled out of the focus of this
presentation, but there is also the responsibility of admitting the
difficulty of locating all situations requiring attention and of noting
that in an era of overcrowded and inadequate foster care facilities,
community agencies have often refused to intervene when they
could only substitute community neglect for parental neglect.

[11] For a full listing, see Frederic Sussman, *Juvenile Delinquency* (New York:
Oceana Publications, 1959).

Where more community initiative is advocated, there are the dual
problems of specifying how resources might be developed and of
indicating how individual rights are to be safeguarded against
arbitrary intervention.

This book is not the place for systematic analysis of delinquency
and neglect totals and trends, but it is necessary to note that large
numbers of children are involved. Even limited and somewhat inaccurate statistics show that (traffic cases excluded) in 1960 approximately 514,000 delinquency *cases* involving 443,000 *children*
were handled by juvenile courts in the United States (see chart on
p. 30). In the country as a whole, almost half of all 1960 delinquency cases were dealt with unofficially, i.e., without the filing of
a court petition. In some states, the majority of cases received such
processing, in others only a few did. As has long been the experience, boys outnumbered girls in the ratio of 4 to 1. The 443,000
total represented 1.8 percent of all U.S. children between the ages
10–17 in 1960. Rates are higher in large urban areas than in the
rural areas. There is considerable interest in recent increases in
girls' cases and in general rates for suburban and rural areas.[12]

Excluding traffic offenses, about half of juvenile court cases are
accounted for by stealing (including auto theft, robbery, and
burglary), injury to persons, and sex offenses. The other half of
the court cases are based on allegations of acts of carelessness and
mischief, truancy, running away, ungovernable behavior, and
similar reasons.

The form in which data are cast would tend to suggest that
delinquency is largely an individual phenomenon, that most youngsters processed by police and courts are "loners." This is not at all
the case. Particularly as one excludes those delinquencies which
do not manifest internal family problems (i.e., running away or
ungovernable behavior, etc.), a large portion of children, whose
precise dimensions are unknown, carry out their antisocial activities
along with others.

[12] U.S. Department of Health, Education, and Welfare, *Juvenile Court Statistics, 1960*, Children's Bureau Statistical Series, No. 65 (Washington, D.C.:
Government Printing Office, 1961), and *Juvenile Court Statistics, 1957*, Children's Bureau Statistical Series, No. 52 (Washington, D.C.: Government Printing Office, 1959). Also, Federal Bureau of Investigation, *Uniform Crime Reports, 1960* (Washington, D.C.: U.S. Department of Justice, 1961).

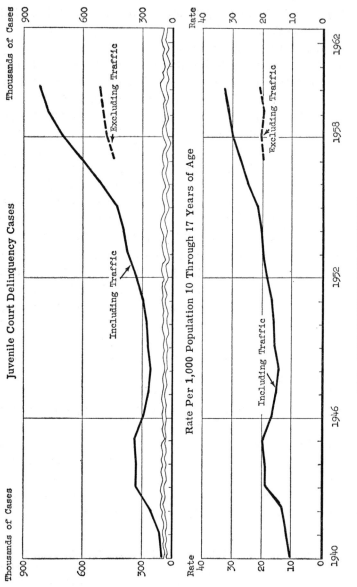

U.S. DELINQUENCY TRENDS

Source: *Health, Education, and Welfare Trends*

Although detailed trend data will not be summarized, the chart on p. 30 will serve to indicate a history of accelerated referral of children to courts—a history which has caused considerable public alarm, challenged all facilities, and resulted in substantial expansion.

Dependency and neglect statistics are subject to the same limitations as delinquency data. Moreover, national sampling procedures are not employed. About one fifth of the nontraffic cases reported to the courts are in this category; the 1960 national estimate was 131,000. Almost two thirds of these cases are processed officially, i.e., petitions are filed. Again, urban areas supply cases at a considerably higher rate than rural areas. The dependency and neglect case rates per 1,000 population under eighteen years of age are equal to only a fraction of delinquency rates, however, ranging from 2.7 per 1,000 in the urban areas to 1.3 per 1,000 in the rural areas.

All other national data represent the roughest of estimates and are mentioned only to suggest the numbers of children now of concern to agencies and institutions. The totals, of course, overlap; i.e., training school children come through courts, and so on. All are "in trouble," but many are never technically "delinquents."

Between 1,500,000 and 2,000,000 youngsters under eighteen come to the attention of the police each year because of allegedly delinquent behavior. (There is no estimate of "repeaters" in this total.) There are over a half-million arrests annually in this age group.

About 75,000 to 100,000 children are held overnight at least one night in jail (rather than in detention facilities meant for juveniles).

About 160,000 children are held overnight in juvenile detention for at least one night and sometimes for as much as many months.

Approximately 52,000 children are committed to youth training schools for delinquents each year (1958 data); about 36,000 were living in public training schools one day in mid-1958.

Should current court referral and police arrest rates continue, the normal population increase alone will bring approximately 760,000 juveniles to the courts by 1965 and 840,000 by 1970—and this assumes an end to the rate climb! [13] The implications for the

---

[13] Subcommittee to Investigate Juvenile Delinquency, Committee on the Judiciary, U.S. Senate, *Juvenile Delinquency*, Report of June 15, 1960 (Washington, D.C.: Government Printing Office, 1960), p. 4.

expansion and strengthening of services and facilities would seem to be clear.

One further point about the ramifications of the delinquency problem: it has become fashionable in recent years to begin each discussion of community provision with the reminder that 97 or 98 percent (or a similar percent) of children are *not* known to the courts. These are reasonable statements when *annual* rates are considered, if the community is reminded that rates in some sections are twenty or more times the rates in other sections of a city. There is also need to provide service to those who do not reach the courts. In addition, the best available estimates, based on careful research in large cities, suggest that 12–15 percent of all children (20–22 percent of all boys) are involved in at least one court delinquency case (traffic cases included) during adolescence. Twenty-two percent of all ninth-grade Minneapolis boys appeared before courts or police in a two-year period. Forty percent of Negro boys in Baltimore, ages 14–16, were in court in a four-year period. In Syracuse, 30 percent of all boys and 13 percent of the girls will probably be apprehended for delinquency before they become sixteen.[14]

THE DELINQUENCIES

Further discussion of the concept of neglect is deferred to a later point (Ch. IX). Immediately relevant is a brief summary of some of the major themes in current knowledge about children and families in trouble. For knowledge is of course a pillar of planning, policy, and operations. Especially important is the rationale for the view that there are *delinquencies,* not one delinquency—and that we must organize services so as to differentiate among them.

First, delinquency is not a phenomenon of one social class, ethnic or religious group, geographic area, or age group; but there are differential rates of reported delinquency which seem to reflect the extent of social disorganization, underprivilege, and "normlessness"

---

[14] I. Richard Perlman, "Delinquency Prevention: The Size of the Problem," *The Annals of the American Academy of Political and Social Science,* CCCXXII (March, 1959), 3–4. Also, Robert H. Hardt, *A Delinquency Profile of Syracuse and Onondaga County, New York, 1959–1960* (Syracuse: Youth Development Center, 1961), pp. 17, 18, and Thomas P. Monahon, "On the Incidence of Delinquency," *Social Forces,* XXXIX (October, 1960), 66–72.

in the family and community subgroup in which a child is reared.[15]

Second, various community subgroups (whether defined in economic, ethnic, class, or religious terms) have different ability or motivation to absorb and handle antisocial and deviant behavior within the group informally or by means other than resorting to official intervention or to agencies which see and respond to such behavior as reflecting delinquency or neglect. They may, for example, turn to private psychiatric help, "military" schools, or assistance from relatives who will permit a child to move in with them.

Third, there are certain forms of manipulative, aggressive, and evasive behavior (which may evolve into so-called white collar crime, tax evasion, etc.) which may be assets in the world of competitive business and to which children may be exposed in childhood as their values develop; it is not our custom to regard the development in children of such orientations as indicative of neglect or probable delinquency. Fourth, some of the behavior "which middle-class teachers, clinicians and psychiatrists regard as 'delinquent' or 'hostile' or 'unmotivated' in slum children is usually perfectly realistic, adaptive and—in slum life—socially acceptable response to society." [16] We might add that ethnic group or social group membership, rather than poverty or slum experience, may have similar consequences.

Administrative factors have considerable effect on whether a child who behaves in a given way is actually apprehended; this in turn affects delinquency rates. New police policy in relation to apprehension of children or bringing cases to court may, for example, change delinquency rates substantially. New court policy with

[15] The reader may wish to examine the excellent summaries of research and theory in Herbert A. Bloch and Frank T. Flynn, *Delinquency: The Juvenile Offender in America Today* (New York: Random House, 1956); Lucien Bovet, *Psychiatric Aspects of Juvenile Delinquency* (Geneva: World Health Organization, 1951); Negley K. Teeters and John Otto Reinemann, *The Challenge of Delinquency* (New York: Prentice-Hall, 1950). Also see Bernard Lander, *Towards an Understanding of Juvenile Delinquency* (New York: Columbia University Press, 1954), and Solomon Korbin, "The Conflict of Values in Delinquency Areas," in Herman D. Stein and Richard A. Cloward, eds., *Social Perspectives on Behavior* (Glencoe, Ill.: The Free Press, 1958), pp. 498–505.

[16] See Helen L. Witmer and Ruth Kotinsky, eds., *Personality in the Making* (New York: Harper & Brothers, 1952), p. 410.

reference to so-called unofficial handling obviously makes for major changes in official "delinquency." The presence of more police and other "case finders" in an area or in a city as a whole is in itself sometimes enough to explain apparent shifts in trends. Neglect statistics are similarly influenced by policy and by the availability of official and unofficial protective casework services. If a public or voluntary service, staffed by skilled individuals, is in a position to offer help and to meet resistance to help through a high level of competent practice, the number of situations requiring court intervention may be substantially reduced and official "neglect" statistics decreased.

The crucial point is that *delinquency and neglect are administrative rather than diagnostic categories.* A person's classification within either of the two classifications, or as between the two, is determined by the "rules of the game" not only for the community at large but for his specific subgroup, as well as by provision and availability of mechanisms for detection or case finding, committed to either informal or formal case processing (and to the use of the official sanctions available to the courts and related agencies at early or at late stages).

It is, therefore, no surprise, in examining cases so categorized, to discover a wide range of personality types, as well as considerable variety of social backgrounds, the latter range limited somewhat, however, by the selective factors already alluded to. A given pattern of deviant behavior may reflect one of many sources of motivation. At one extreme, and seldom met in pure form, are the individuals of completely "normal" personality whose coming to attention reflects their adherence to the norms of subcultures which teach and endorse behavior considered by the majority of the community as delinquent or neglectful. At the other extreme are those whose community, family, and peer-group influences are all clearly of a positive sort but who, nonetheless, display some form of personality disturbance which manifests itself in aggressive conduct or deviant behavior which is offensive in some other manner. Precision as well as clarity of research and planning would be advanced if we talked of the *delinquencies* and the *neglects,* to stress the many subcategories, variations, and causal patterns subsumed under each label.

For some purposes it is useful, although somewhat oversimplified, to introduce the concepts of adaptive and maladaptive delinquency. There are individuals who learn and practice delinquency in their families or intimate primary groups; there are others who strike out at the broader society because of frustrating experience and inadequate development of inhibition.[17]

For several decades, until the early 1950s, most social agency concern in this country was focused on the latter group, those delinquents whose misconduct might be understood as a product of personality disturbance. This emphasis was entirely understandable as a consequence of the tremendous impact of psychiatric knowledge about the dynamics of human behavior. It had suddenly become clear that deprivation of infantile needs, disturbances in family life, interference with adolescent requirements for growth and expression could, for example, cause personality consequences and behavior which might lead one to court as a delinquent child or, ultimately, as a neglectful parent.[18] Specific attention could, therefore, be directed at the special constitutional or developmental factors in the backgrounds of the several different personality types found among the delinquents and the psychological treatment approaches appropriate for each.

Bovet, for example, distinguishes unique etiologic patterns and prognostic potential for the following: constitutional psychopaths, mental defectives who are delinquent, delinquents with organic disease or disability, delinquents with superego defects, delinquents with partial retardation in development, psychoneurotics, psychotics. He nonetheless affirms that all these types have a "psychological common denominator . . . the feeling of insecurity to which any criminal tendency from whatever source gives rise."

[17] See formulation by Richard L. Jenkins in "Problems of Treating Delinquents," *Federal Probation*, XXII, No. 4 (December, 1958), 27–32. For illustration in relation to one form of antisocial behavior see the proposed classification in John M. Martin, *Juvenile Vandalism* (Springfield, Ill.: Charles C. Thomas, 1961).

[18] Harris B. Peck and Virginia Bellsmith, *Treatment of the Delinquent Adolescent* (New York: Family Service Association of America, 1954), p. 9. Also see Helen L. Witmer, *Delinquency and the Adolescent Crisis*, Juvenile Delinquency Facts and Facets, No. 11 (Washington, D.C.: Government Printing Office, 1960); Paul Goodman, *Growing Up Absurd* (New York: Random House, 1960).

A major pattern to which he calls attention is insecurity—anxiety—aggression—guilt—anxiety—etc. Even the socially determined delinquency in the psychiatrically normal individual should be looked at psychiatrically from Bovet's point of view because "if a social factor is to become a criminal force, it must set in motion a number of psychological processes." Moreover, the delinquency per se or the court experience may represent a psychological trauma converting the normal delinquent into one who needs personal psychological help.[19]

One of the most creative contributors to psychiatric theory in this field, Adelaide Johnson, has described how parents unconsciously initiate and foster antisocial behavior in children in order to experience gratification for themselves. What she calls "superego lacunae" are communicated in the context of the parent-child relationship.[20]

The psychiatric emphasis in treatment programs has been reinforced from time to time by research data indicating the very large, if varying, proportions of court and institution clients who have personality problems. From this, adherents of the clinical approach have concluded that the treatment goal is to resolve the psychic problems, with the expectation that a secondary effect would be changes in values and role performance.[21] The important point made by leading social scientists has often been lost: It is not

[19] Bovet, *Psychiatric Aspects of Juvenile Delinquency*, pp. 12–42, 20. One might, of course, cite many other diagnostic classification schemes developed to account for all delinquents, but our purpose here is illustrative only. A good deal of interest has been shown in the L. E. Hewett and H. L. Jenkins scheme, based on study of 500 Michigan Guidance Institute cases: (1) *the socialized delinquent* who rejects the broader community's value system (pseudosocial); (2) *the unsocialized delinquent* who has inadequate impulse control (psychopath or sociopath); (3) *the overinhibited delinquent,* the neurotic whose symptoms are compulsions leading to trouble. They note, however, that only 40 percent of their cases are readily accounted for in this scheme. "Fundamental Patterns of Maladjustment," quoted by D. V. Donnison, *The Neglected Child and the Social Services* (Manchester: Manchester University Press, 1954), pp. 42 ff.
[20] Mary E. Giffin, Adelaide M. Johnson, and Edward M. Litin, "The Transmission of Superego Defects in the Family," in Norman W. Bell and Ezra F. Vogel, *A Modern Introduction to the Family* (Glencoe, Ill.: The Free Press, 1959), pp. 623–35.
[21] Lloyd E. Ohlin and William C. Lawrence, "Social Interaction among Clients as a Treatment Problem," *Social Work,* IV, No. 2 (April, 1959), 3–13.

necessarily significant that many delinquents, like many other people, have symptoms of psychiatric disturbance; the real issue is whether and how the psychological disturbance is relevant to being a delinquent and/or whether and how it must be taken into acount in dealing with the delinquency.

While delinquency *research* in this country has long been dominated by sociology and, therefore, has not suffered from inattention to social factors, a recent discussion of the etiology and function of the delinquent subculture by Albert K. Cohen in a new classic, *Delinquent Boys*, has received widespread attention from those involved in *treatment* programs.[22] Writing at a time when the field had begun to reestablish a balance between attention to psychiatric dynamics and other elements relevant to the prevention, control, and treatment of antisocial behavior, Cohen both reflected and contributed to this new orientation.

Cohen does not pretend to be accounting for all delinquency with his sociological concept of the delinquent subculture, nor does he suggest what proportion may be involved. He seeks to attack the view that all delinquency is understandable as a simple function of the actor's problems of adjustment. There are, he feels, many idiosyncratic, personal, neurotic solutions to adjustment problems, and these may be analyzed, but the delinquent subculture represents cultural support and legitimation of certain particular solutions. The "purpose" of the culture, he hypothesizes, in sociological terms, is to help those of low socioeconomic position ("working class" in Cohen's sense) to deal with their experience of being denied status in respectable society or being unable to meet the criteria of respectable (middle-class) society because of the values with which they have been reared. The delinquency subculture offers a system of values, beliefs, codes, and activities which negates the larger culture's standards: *nonutilitarian stealing* (and a wide range of mischief) as a claim to status; *malicious activity* to bring discomfort to others; *negativistic behavior* which turns the generally accepted norms upside down; *short-run hedonism* as opposed to deferred gratification; *group autonomy* which accepts only its own

[22] Albert K. Cohen, *Delinquent Boys: The Culture of the Gang* (Glencoe, Ill.: The Free Press, 1955). For a critique see Marshall B. Clinard, "Criminological Research," in Robert K. Merton *et al.*, eds., *Sociology Today* (New York: Basic Books, Inc., 1959), p. 515.

internal restraints. New criteria of status are developed which these boys can meet.

Chein takes a related position in these terms:

> While the individual delinquent is probably motivated by many complex and mostly sub-conscious forces, the *spread* of delinquent behavior in a community is an expression of this community's *hospitality* to defiant behavior in general and especially delinquency.
>
> We further assume that this hospitality of the environment consists primarily (though not exclusively) in its failure to provide opportunities, directives and supports facilitating a successful transition from early adolescence to young adulthood; that is, the adolescent's chances for . . . learning a satisfying adult role in the legitimate environment are comparatively small. On the other hand, this type of environment usually also fails to provide constraints against defiant behavior and, at the same time, offers stimuli and opportunities for delinquent acts.[23]

Several scholars have shown how a rearranging of the elements in Cohen's hypothesis suggests another causal pattern: one participates in a gang and learns the delinquent subculture for any one of many reasons—the nonutilitarian, negativistic behavior which has been learned is met by formal, negative sanctions—all participants in this behavior share the resulting problems and then reject middle-class standards, emphasizing instead their status within the gang—the delinquent subculture norms are reinforced, etc.

Sykes and Metza also dispute Cohen's notion that most delinquents grow up without exposure to and some identification with the norms of the broader society. They maintain:

> The fact that the world of the delinquent is embedded in the larger world of those who conform cannot be overlooked. . . . Instead the juvenile delinquent would appear to be at least partially committed to the dominant social order in that he frequently exhibits guilt or shame when he violates its proscriptions, accords approval to certain conforming figures, and distinguishes between appropriate and inappropriate targets for his defiance.

The crucial point, according to these scholars, is that, for a variety of reasons, delinquents are able to "neutralize" the demands of society at large.[24]

[23] Dr. Isidore Chein, Research Center for Human Relations, New York University, Unpublished MS.

[24] Leslie T. Wilkins summarizes the alternative hypotheses, as suggested by Kitsuse and Dietrick, in his article "Crime, Cause and Treatment: Recent Re-

Dr. Franz Alexander, who has contributed much to the psychiatric understanding of criminality, acknowledges in the 1956 revision of his classic, *The Criminal, the Judge and the Public,* that whereas the volume was largely concerned with neurotic delinquents, there are many "normal" criminals who derive their codes from a special community in which antisocial behavior is acceptable. He does not choose between Sykes-Metza, on the one hand, and Cohen, on the other, although his orientation would be congenial with the "neutralization" notion. His main contention, from his new vantage point, is that one does not account for the behavior of a child only in terms of the internal structures of the "little society" system of which he is a part, i.e., the family, without reference to "the larger social system in which it is imbedded." The consequences of family membership depend on the social world outside the family since that social world conditions the experiences and problems of the family.[25]

While some of those who have been inspired by Cohen's work now concern themselves only with the social dimension, as others have accredited only psychiatric factors, Cohen himself does not ignore the need to understand how any given individual is motivated. He notes that several different "solutions" are available to an individual; choices may be understood in personality terms. For example, some reject delinquency and accept the rules of the larger (middle-class) society. In fact, when he speculates about middle-class delinquency, he points largely to psychological dynamics (stressing problems of masculine identification in middle-class adolescent boys).

Although there have been serious sociological critiques and modifications of Cohen's position, his work has served to give new and sound emphasis to sociological concepts and to accent the failure to give these appropriate attention in the recent past in either individual case diagnosis and treatment or in the planning of a service pattern. He has also reminded those who would deal with

---

search and Theory," a reprint from *Educational Research* (Britain), IV, No. 1 (November, 1961), 18–32. Also, Gresham M. Sykes and David Metza, "Techniques of Neutralization: A Theory of Delinquency," *American Sociological Review,* XXII (1957), 664–70.

[25] Franz Alexander and Hugo Staub, *The Criminal, the Judge and the Public* (Glencoe, Ill.: The Free Press, 1956).

children in trouble that to a very considerable extent they are dealing with a group-gang phenomenon and not with isolated-individual behavior.

In a more extreme position, Miller argues that the beliefs and ideas of the delinquent group arise not from status deprivation but, rather, as a "normal" adolescent version of "lower-class culture"—which values masculine "toughness," "sharpness," and so on. The fact that only a minority (albeit a large minority) of "lower-class" boys are delinquent seems to be ignored or denied. Others, from a sociological (Bloch-Niederhoffer) viewpoint, or a psychiatric perspective (Erickson), stress the special situation and coping problems of adolescents as a factor in delinquency.[26] Clearly, many of the theoreticians are accounting for different aspects of the phenomenon, for different *delinquencies.*

Sociologists and social workers have recently been offered a further elaboration of etiological (causation) theory as the result of the conceptualizations of Lloyd Ohlin and Richard A. Cloward.[27] They concern themselves with that delinquency (whose scope and volume is unspecified) which may be related to the prescriptions of delinquent subcultures rather than only to individual deviations and personally relevant motivations. Without going into detail, we might indicate that sociological theory about delinquency has been dominated by two strands of concepts. The Durkheim-Merton view (based on what is often called "anomie theory") has concerned itself with the consequences to the individual of "dis-

---

[26] These viewpoints are summarized by David J. Bordua, *Sociological Theories and Their Implications for Juvenile Delinquency,* Juvenile Delinquency Facts and Facets, No. 2 (Washington, D.C.: Government Printing Office, 1960). For more complete presentations see Herbert A. Bloch and Arthur Niederhoffer, *The Gang* (New York: Philosophical Library, 1958), and Helen L. Witmer and Ruth Kotinsky, eds., *New Perspectives for Research on Juvenile Delinquency* (Washington, D.C.: Government Printing Office, 1956), especially pp. 1–23. Also see Witmer, *Delinquency and the Adolescent Crisis.*

[27] This summary draws upon the following: Richard A. Cloward, "Illegitimate Means, Anomie, and Deviant Behavior," *American Sociological Review,* XXIV, 164–76; Richard A. Cloward and Lloyd E. Ohlin, *Delinquency and Opportunity: A Theory of Delinquent Gangs* (Glencoe, Ill.: The Free Press, 1960), as well as unpublished documents by Cloward and Ohlin. Inkeles comments in another context that objective factors of opportunity are inadequate to account for mobility. See Alex Inkeles, "Personality and Social Structure," in *Sociology Today,* p. 273.

junction between culturally prescribed goals and socially organized access to them by *legitimate* means." In Merton's view, particularly characteristic of the modern world is a situation in which many people internalize specific success goals to which they lack access. The result is widespread deviant behavior, the exact form varying with the "solution" to this situation which is adopted. (Merton does not attempt to account for all delinquency and crime in this way.)

The other theory, associated with the names of Shaw, McKay, and Sutherland, has focused attention "on the process by which persons are recruited into criminal learning environments and ultimately inducted into criminal roles." A particular finding of these researchers is that delinquency and crime are concentrated in certain portions of urban areas and that the behavior persists in these areas despite population movement.

Integrating these two streams of theory, Cloward-Ohlin call attention to the fact that, just as in a society there are differences in the degree of access which individuals have to legitimate, conventional forms of social attainment (varying with social class, ethnic group, sex, age), so is there variation in access to illegitimate means. Both legitimate and illegitimate ways of attaining the success goals considered highly desirable in our society must be learned. Moreover, the individual needs occasion to carry out the life pattern for which he has been prepared ("learning structures" and "opportunity structures").[28]

From the perspective of this theoretical approach, one considers, particularly in looking at underprivileged areas of a city, the relative access of young people to legitimate ways of attaining social goals (education, jobs, conventional agency membership), the factors which may block their access, the socially acceptable or unacceptable solutions adopted. One also notes access to illegitimate means (the "rackets" as a way of life, a career as a thief, etc.), as these offer alternatives, and particularly more accessible alternatives. Choices among alternatives in an area, variations as between individuals within an area or within a family, withdrawal from the major choices (some drug addiction, for example) would seem to

[28] Cloward, "Illegitimate Means, Anomie and Deviant Behavior," *American Sociological Review*, XXIV, 168.

demand (but the authors do not offer) individual psychodynamic interpretation, in the context of the particular social picture.

As yet, this line of theorizing has only limited, systematic research verification, and would not account for current middle-class delinquency and for the increasing suburban delinquency. Nor does it concern itself with that delinquency which does not, in the Cloward-Ohlin view, stem from participation in delinquent subcultures. It does seem, however, to encompass far more of the relevant group factors involved in much delinquency than does most prior sociological work and also permits a basis for the integration of individual psychodynamic theory with social science insights. In fact, it suggests the hypothesis that "retreatist" delinquency (such as drug addiction) may reflect either internal psychological dynamics or a "double failure" vis-à-vis both legitimate and illegitimate means. It also leads to such fruitful research as a study of the way in which different opportunity structures (a neighborhood organized around racketeering, as contrasted with a disorganized neighborhood, whose new arrivals have no access to legitimate or illegitimate means to success) may produce different types of juvenile gang structure (a "racketeering apprentice" type of gang in one area; a "conflict" gang in the other). The theory generates valuable research leads as well [29] and is guiding the ambitious delinquency prevention experiment of Mobilization for Youth, which may be described as an effort to change the opportunity structure.

Particularly valuable in the several new sociological perspectives is their tendency to affect not only research but also intervention. Ohlin and Lawrence point out that once delinquency is considered a social disorder, a product of group life, the intervention problem is one of how to change the delinquent's adherence to a deviant

[29] Cloward and Ohlin have prepared a 21-page (mimeographed) list of hypotheses derived from *Delinquency and Opportunity*. For a summary and critique of Cohen and hypotheses derived therefrom, see Harold L. Wilensky and Charles N. Lebeaux, *Industrial Society and Social Welfare* (New York: Russell Sage Foundation, 1958), Ch. IX. Also see Irving Speigel, "Types of Delinquent Groups" (Unpublished dissertation, New York School of Social Work, Columbia University, 1960). Four types of gangs are described in Subcommittee to Investigate Juvenile Delinquency, Committee on the Judiciary, U.S. Senate, *Juvenile Delinquency*, June 15, 1960, pp. 54–77.

value system.[30] One immediate consequence would be the likelihood of considering an approach to the gang or to the peer group, rather than to the individual. Similarly, Ohlin and Cloward believe that opening of new opportunities may lead gangs away from violence.

In summary, it is foolish to seek common backgrounds for all delinquents or common causes for all delinquencies. No one causation theory and no one treatment approach can possibly be relevant to so wide a range of phenomena brought together only by community policy criteria and administrative machinery.[31] Current knowledge thus underscores the generalization that if the community wishes to help, serve, intervene with, or redirect a child, a parent, or a group, there must be concern with the particular manner in which social-environmental factors and personality factors combine in the specific instance to create a course of conduct or a pattern of relationship.[32] Personality factors, in turn, are compounded out of constitutional-biological, intrapsychic, and interpersonal elements and experience.

Successful intervention must begin with an effort to develop understanding of the sources and significance of the difficulty for the individual or group requiring community attention. This will lead to clues as to which methods of intervention may be successful. A wide variety of approaches must obviously be available if there is to be success. Some children in difficulty may be reached through efforts to socialize their peer groups, whose antisocial norms lead to difficulty in school and neighborhood. Others may require removal from home environments in which emotionally disturbed parents subject them constantly to a form of tension which is re-

---

[30] Ohlin and Lawrence, "Social Interaction among Clients as a Treatment Problem," *Social Work*, IV, 3–13.

[31] Barbara Wooton, *Social Science and Social Pathology* (New York: The Macmillan Company, 1959).

[32] To use a technical vocabulary, one must seek to understand a "personality-situation manifold," i.e., the conditions under which a given motive (mobilized and directed energy, orientation of behavior) produces adverse effects. See Herbert A. Bloch, "The Inadequacies of Research in Delinquency Causation," *National Probation and Parole Association Journal*, I, No. 1 (July, 1955), 31–40. It is necessary to repeat with Bovet that "a factor cannot be a cause before it is a motive," *Psychiatric Aspects of Juvenile Delinquency*, p. 20.

lieved by delinquency. Others may be incapable of inner controls or responsible behavior unless they can have the benefit of a period of psychiatric treatment designed to reorganize certain basic features of their personality. Changes in the school environment may be all that is required to help some children, while others must be protected (while the community is also protected) by a period in a secure institution. Students of the problem are now trying to develop delinquency typologies (classification systems) and to link them through research validation to treatment typologies.[33]

Later sections of this volume will deal in some detail with the variety of service specializations which may be necessary to a community pattern. We should note, however, that just as our understanding of causation must include psychological and social dimensions, so do most treatment programs have such dimensions, with varying degrees of emphasis, strength, and value. That program which emphasizes helping an adolescent find his way to the community mainstream is as much part of the total picture as is the clinical effort to deal with disabling neurotic symptoms.

The fine task of selecting the appropriate facility for a given child is a prerequisite to conducting each program in a manner which will achieve optimum results with each child who is referred.

---

[33] For example, see California State Board of Corrections, *The Treatment of Delinquents in the Community: Variations in Treatment Approaches* (Sacramento: California State Printing Office, 1960). Also, Board of Corrections, *Inquiries Concerning Kinds of Treatment for Kinds of Delinquents*, Monograph No. 2 (Sacramento: California State Printing Office, 1961).

CHAPTER II

FIRST PRINCIPLES

MECHANISMS, structures, and designs come after values. Devices and instruments have no validity except in relation to goals. A community cannot be expected to support a program whose objectives are not understood or are opposed. And a practitioner, whether he be a judge, a probation officer, a school social worker, or a house parent in an institution, cannot implement a policy whose basic philosophy is confusing.

It thus becomes important, early in a work such as this, to specify our first principles, however obvious they already may be to some and however implicit they are in every paragraph already written and in the very organization of the book.

A modern approach to children in trouble has little validity if it does not organize itself to rehabilitate; rehabilitation, in turn, requires some individualization of measures. There must, in fact, be consensus at the beginning of program development that the objective is to treat those in trouble as individuals and to undertake that program which corrects, redirects, and restores them to useful family and community membership. We adopt this approach because it is consistent with our legal traditions (the very young are not responsible under law) and our knowledge of childhood (most of our delinquents are the products of a milieu and of family deprivation and could be expected to do little else). This approach is also in line with the moral traditions and religious convictions under which we tend to forgive and seek to restore the offender. The American ethic, moreover, allows the individual the right to have "another chance" and to win his own salvation by new efforts.

We do not wish, it might be added, to "waste" those who might be restored to productive functioning.

The Advisory Council of Judges of the National Council on Crime and Delinquency has, in fact, listed deterrence and *rehabilitation* as the two objectives of sentencing even in the adult field. Both are expected to prevent future crime but rehabilitation is considered "far more effective." [1]

Beyond all these positive reasons for favoring a rehabilitative philosophy is the simple fact, derived from long experience, that punishment does not work as the key to public policy. Discipline and punishment may have their role in the parent-child relationship but are effective only in the context of that relationship if effectiveness is to be gauged by the soundness of future conduct and adjustment.

There is no intention here to deny that a community must react swiftly and consistently to enforce laws and mores. Arrest by police, a period in detention, court processing, the requirement that one report to a probation office or spend a period in an institution—who would deny that these have the effect of deprivation of freedom and punishment on most of those who experience them? The crucial point seems to be that these programs seek (or might seek) other objectives as well: community protection, legal determination of facts, individual diagnosis, education, rehabilitation. The punishment is a secondary aspect of the procedure— at times a side effect—and not the be-all and end-all of public policy. The problem of conveying this intent to the offender of course remains a difficult technical one.

Centuries of experience have demonstrated that when punishment is the major remedy, the sole objective, it is largely ineffectual and creates a chain of undesirable secondary consequences. Punishment does deter some people, but only a small minority. "The deterring effects of punishment are best to be witnessed in the normal and not in the criminal population." [2] This should hardly

---

[1] National Probation and Parole Association, *Guides for Sentencing* (New York, 1957), pp. 1, 3.

[2] See, for example, Harry E. Barnes and Negley K. Teeters, *New Horizons in Criminology* (New York: Prentice-Hall, 1945), pp. 391 ff. The quotation is from Iago Galdston in New York County Lawyers' Association, *A Colloquium on Juvenile Delinquency and Its Socio-legal Aspects* (New York, 1948), p. 22.

be surprising. Children who are delinquent are in fact the most punished and deprived of children; they are not likely to respond positively to more of the same. Expanded opportunities which are responsive to their unmet needs and which seek to correct or undo unwholesome experience are more likely to establish for them a belief that the world can be a better place and that personal control, deferred gratification, and obeying the rules of the game are worth while.[3]

Because of the variety of social and personal motivations involved in delinquency and neglect, a "simple" formula (i.e., punishment) could hardly be expected to serve as a universal cure. There are some delinquents, for example, who know no other way of life. To punish them is to establish as true what they already suspect: that society around them is organized to their disadvantage and that they must strike out to protect themselves. Others face deep and vaguely felt drives which, in turn, create uncontrollable patterns of behavior of which society disapproves. No matter how convincing the punishment, it does not change many of these basic drives; as soon as physical restraint ends, the pattern may have to repeat itself. Where the delinquency reflects a character problem, a lack of inner social controls, stemming from basic deficiencies in early child-rearing, for example, only an approach which seeks substantial personality restructuring will hold any promise of long-term effect.

If, as already here suggested, one should really talk of the *de-*

Also see Harry Elmer Barnes, "Shall We Be Tough or Be Sensible in Facing the Increase of Crime?" *Federal Probation*, XXIII, No. 2 (June, 1959), 29–36, and Henry Weihofen, "Retribution Is Obsolete," *N.P.P.A. News*, XXXIX, No. 1 (January, 1960), 1–4.

[3] For a clear statement of this view, see the statement of the State of New Jersey, Juvenile Delinquency Study Commission, *A Coordinated Approach towards Preventing Delinquency* (Trenton, 1956), p. 16. More recently that commission affirmed its view with the statement: "The arguments favoring more 'old-fashioned punishment' for young people may have merit in normal non-delinquent situations but are fallacious when applied to most delinquents, whose social and emotional conditions are abnormally distorted." State of New Jersey, Youth Study Commission, *Helping Youth in Trouble* (Trenton, 1957), p. 2. For an outstanding statement and case illustrations see Justine Wise Polier, *Back to What Woodshed?* (New York: Public Affairs Committee, 1956). Also, on punishing parents, see Sol Rubin, *Crime and Juvenile Delinquency* (New York: Oceana Publications, 1958), Chapter II.

linquencies and the *neglects,* to emphasize the varieties of causation and motivation, it is perfectly obvious that remedial action requires a variety of approaches suited to the meaning of the difficulty. Anything short of this, whether the product of lack of knowledge or resources, or of readiness to go the whole way with our objectives, should be recognized as such.

Historically, an important step was taken in exchanging the inhuman severity of medieval punishment, which extended well into modern times, for the reform movement's insistence on precise fitting of the penalty to the wrongdoing. While certainly a mark of progress, this mechanical approach is behind current knowledge and objectives.[4] Its validity is particularly low in relation to children, who offer substantial promise of change and growth, given favorable treatment.

The public at large continues to find it hard to believe that a given young offender or neglectful parent is either ill or the inevitable product of a social environment he did not make—and should be dealt with as such. This is particularly true if the offense is especially vicious and well publicized in its details by press and other media. Such a situation only intensifies the need for a broad educational and informational effort—an effort necessary for many other reasons as well. The American public has supported progressive juvenile court laws and, in general, the enunciation of individualizing and treatment approaches. It has the right to fuller understanding of their bases, implications, and obligations. There will be more likelihood of wholehearted implementation and adequate financing as such understanding becomes widespread.

Those failures in rehabilitation which take the form of outrageous conduct by parole violators, institution graduates, or probationers are often used to raise doubts as to the adequacy of a rehabilitative outlook. We must admit, immediately, the serious limitations of current knowledge and skill, limitations which mean an inevitable percentage of failure and which may make it necessary to offer only long-range custody or supervision to some whom we do not know how to help. To this we should add, however, that a rehabilitation approach, like sound child rearing, requires a readiness to take

[4] Roscoe Pound in foreword to Charles L. Chute and Marjorie Ball, *Crime, Courts and Probation* (New York: The Macmillan Company, 1956), p. x.

risks; and with risks there are always some regrettable consequences even if services are of high caliber. As a group of wise and experienced judges has pointed out, no one can be improved, ultimately, except by himself; the degree of individual responsibility assumed by the offender of whatever age is therefore decisive. Yet "responsibility and freedom are inseparable." [5] Professional skill involves knowing how to make the proper amount of freedom available, how to help develop the responsibility. The method must vary with the individual in difficulty.

It is clear from all this that there is no logic to seeking the rehabilitation of a child through the punishment of his parents. To fine parents for the vandalism committed by their children is to introduce new sources of tension in what are usually disturbed relationships. To hold parents in criminal contempt, if they do not follow a course of conduct designed by a judge to prevent future unlawful activity by a child, is to deny all that we know about parents' inability to deal with certain courses of conduct in children, conduct resulting from personality disturbances, peer-group relationships, and social factors. In fact, to place parents under such "orders" is to ignore the fact that the very problem is often the parents' inadequacy and that one has merely established a new battleground for family conflict. To jail parents as negligent if they have not "corrected" and "reformed" their youngsters is to fantasy that personality inadequacy and extreme social pathology may be changed by mere act of will on the part of the least competent of our citizens. Experience shows, in fact, that if the parent whose cruelty or gross neglect is associated with his child's antisocial behavior requires institutionalizing, it is the mental hospital rather than the jail that is likely to be the appropriate setting.

Punishment, then, is not a sound central principle for public policy and not effective in relation to the ends sought. We undertake rehabilitation as humane, potentially economical of resources and manpower, and in line with our democratic and ethical traditions.

Despite all of this, community policy cannot deny society's need for protection. The objective of the total effort might be stated in these terms: *individual help and rehabilitation within a framework*

[5] *Guides for Sentencing*, p. 5.

of community protection. Police must be available to guard the individual against personal physical danger and to ensure against destruction or theft of his property. The offender must be detected and apprehended in a reasonable proportion of instances and with some speed. Moreover, there are those who must be locked up briefly, in detention, for their own or the community's protection pending case evaluation and disposition. Others must be institutionalized for longer periods until we can help them change, since unchanged they endanger themselves and the community at large. And, finally, there are some who must be deprived of their freedom because their antisocial actions provide cause before the law and because we simply do not yet know how to help them change or to reduce substantially the danger they pose for others. We should not pretend, as we outline a community plan to deal with those in difficulty, that our knowledge and skill are in all spheres adequate to create the ideal structure suggested by our values and objectives.

REHABILITATION IN SOCIETY

Early in the twentieth century this country sounded a slogan which was to become for many western nations a rallying point around which major child welfare developments were to take place: no child should be separated from his parents for reasons of poverty alone. It would be well, today, to add: no child should be separated from his parents for reasons of delinquency or neglect alone.

Where the objective is only punishment, the correct action is clear. The removal of a child from his community is, for most, a severe blow and certainly establishes society's dissatisfaction with the child and its power to do something about it. It may be an efficient way to ensure that his life will not be a successful one.

Where the ultimate goal is rehabilitation and social adjustment, the picture becomes more complicated. Institutions for juvenile delinquents everywhere are overcrowded, inadequately staffed, and poorly equipped by current standards. Many are effective schools for future antisocial behavior. Their graduates tend, at a disturbing rate, to move on to reformatories after appearances in adult courts. Foster homes for delinquents are not readily available. Similarly, group care facilities for the dependent and the neglected are, at best, high-risk environments for growing children.

Consideration, therefore, should be given to placing less emphasis in community strategy on institutional facilities and more on probation and community-based counseling services. This would perhaps be wise policy even if it were possible to reform the majority of the group care facilities but could hardly be implemented without substantial steps to expand and strengthen probation departments and clinics.

Dr. Querido has argued in even more basic terms for an emphasis on community services for the mentally ill, but one might substitute other categories of people in trouble:

> In the last analysis, the cure or the adaptation of the mentally disturbed can only be accomplished in society and . . . a successful stay in society is the only real test of any therapeutic endeavor. . . .
>
> Any removal of a mentally disturbed patient from his social background implies the sidestepping of the nucleus of the problem.[6]

This is not to ignore the fact that there are some children who cannot possibly be helped as long as they remain in their homes and neighborhoods—and that there are others whose presence represents a continuous source of danger to others too great to be tolerated. The community must be equipped to identify these children and to design institutional and foster home resources appropriate for them.

Such use of away-from-home facilities is, however, a far cry from the readiness to commit punitively. The point also applies, it might be noted, to the unnecessary use of detention. Those judges who would leave a child in detention for a few days "to teach him a lesson" would do well to ponder the personality effects of the first, punitively motivated, period of separation from family and exposure to the inmate culture of a detention facility.

A psychiatrist who has treated neglectful parents and their children has commented on the complexities of interrelationship and the possible implications of enforced separation:

[6] A. Querido, "Early Diagnoses and Treatment Services," in Milbank Memorial Fund, *The Elements of a Community Mental Health Program* (New York, 1956).

These children are often caught between the disturbed behavior of the parent and the hostility of the community which finds them part of the undesirable, dirty element. This serves both to drive the children back into any fragment of relationship to parents as well as stimulating counter-hostility toward the community . . . the ideal in treatment with these children would be rehabilitating the home. Even if the parent is grossly psychotic or has deserted the child and has to be placed, stabilizing the environment first is the primary goal.[7]

A legal scholar would appoint a responsible community "guardian" for each child under court protection, even one who is committed, so that his interests are not forgotten under the pressure of agency activities.[8]

It is necessary to add that, because the stigma of delinquency and neglect is so serious, and because the antisocial education in many facilities is so effective, we must be sure initially that the situation truly warrants bringing the court machinery into action. This is a matter of professional judgment, to be discussed later, but it is also related to the question of individual rights.

The case having being made, additional arguments are not necessary, but there is another one, a philosophical one. Modern society probably suffers from the excessive tendency to separate out the deviant at both ends of the continuum. Gifted children as well as troublesome children are given separate school facilities, and the "adjusted residue" conform in what is too often an unstimulating boredom. Social patterns and community institutions have found their ways of assembling homogeneities and limiting the exposure of their members to the unusual, the different, the challenging. Tension and discomfort are as essential to creativity as difference and stimulation. Let us keep our communities intact and even our delinquents in our communities, if there is any way to do so which is not destructive of them or of the larger community.

Mildred Arnold of the U.S. Children's Bureau draws upon experience throughout the country when she says:

[7] Irving Kaufman, "The Contribution of Protective Services," *Child Welfare,* XXXVI (February, 1957), 12.

[8] A. Delafield Smith, *The Right to Life* (Chapel Hill: University of North Carolina Press, 1955). A similar point is made by a social worker in Mildred Arnold, "Rehabilitation in Child Welfare," *Children,* IV, No. 6 (November–December, 1957), 208–12.

In the early days we said that children should not be placed in foster care for economic reasons alone. Now we are saying that foster placement can rarely be an answer to a child's need for a home and parents of his own. This means that child welfare agencies must assume greater responsibility for preventing family breakdown and for helping parents in their task of child rearing.[9]

Thus, the emphasis on rehabilitation in society also implies every possible effort to help the child in his own home. Despite the inroads made by social change on many of the functions of the family in an urban, industrialized environment, it remains the most central of all institutions in determining the value systems and personality structures of children. Indeed, as the family relinquishes many of its tasks to industry, to the service professions, to the schools, to churches, to community centers, its core function of early-life socialization and providing affectional satisfactions becomes accentuated. At its best, it is a major bulwark against impersonality and coldness in a society of high physical and social mobility and rootlessness. Clearly then, prevention and treatment efforts should reinforce the family role in every sense and offer substitutes only when they are obviously essential and clearly more likely to be effective.

INDIVIDUAL RIGHTS

Little is accomplished if planning is not carried out in the context of our concepts of individual rights and due process and in the spirit of the American cultural pattern which sees value and richness in diversity. In the words of the late Chief Justice Arthur T. Vanderbilt of New Jersey:

The indispensable elements of due process are: first, a tribunal with jurisdiction; second, notice of a hearing to the proper parties; and finally, a fair hearing. All three must be present if we are to treat a child as an individual human being and not to revert, in spite of good intentions, to the more primitive days when he was treated as a chattel. [Italics added.] [10]

Courts do not exist to impose treatment plans, however wise, on individuals not previously found to be delinquent or neglected in

[9] Arnold, "Rehabilitation in Child Welfare," *Children,* IV, 208–12.

[10] In foreword to Maxine Boord Virtue, *Basic Structure of Children's Services in Michigan* (Ann Arbor: American Judicature Society, 1953), p. x.

accordance with well-defined rules. Children may not be kept in shelters or institutions unless there is a basis, in law, for detaining them. It is not valid to undertake comprehensive social investigations of families or individuals and thus invade their privacy unless they have asked for help—and have agreed to the case study—or have been declared, after due process, to be under the care and protection of the court and subject to court disposition planning. Moreover, individuals must be helped to understand the court procedures and their own rights, must be permitted to challenge the facts, must be able to call upon counsel if they wish to do so, and must know how to appeal court action if they feel they have been wronged.

While these may seem to be commonplace observations, they are in order in relation to planning for children in trouble, because the professional person or public official dedicated to the welfare of the individual may tend to bypass that procedure and "red tape" which may seem to him to lie in the way of effective service. The fact remains that the individual has the right to resist all efforts of those who would improve his lot, however sound their motives or promising their methods. Only court action, following evidence of neglect, delinquency, or crime, evaluated in accordance with well-established procedure, can be the basis of external interference and compulsion. The caseworker, institution staff member, or psychiatrist must, of course, eventually help even involuntary clients to become involved if therapeutic efforts are to be successful.

When there is no basis for formal legal intervention, the community has access to all those methods which do not infringe on individual rights: offers of service, display of interest, and the less drastic sanctions available to schools and welfare departments.

The question is raised as to whether there is not an inherent contradiction between individualized treatment and equal treatment; this suggests that individualized treatment may not be completely just. The concern would be valid (and is valid) to the extent to which the individualization is really a matter of personal prejudice, capriciousness, and favoritism. Where, as in the context of this discussion, it means a scientific effort to weigh all factors and to arrive at the plan which available evidence shows is most likely to be effective, individualization can be equitable and just. For, as a group of judges have pointed out, under such circumstances cases which are relatively equivalent, in terms of needs, receive relatively equivalent treatment.[11] Limitations of knowledge and skill constantly qualify this generalization and suggest the imperfections of justice; despite them the interests of the offender receive better protection under a system seeking to equate needs and potential than under one which gives attention only to offenses and their degrees.

There is another aspect of individual rights which deserves mention, using the term "rights" now not to refer to court process but to a community's moral and legal obligations vis-à-vis an individual. Where a child has committed the equivalent of what would be a crime in an adult, there is little question about the community's need to intervene in some way in his life. Because of current philosophies, we hope that the intervention will be helpful. We have argued, from scientific knowledge and from goals, for early service which will rehabilitate. However, delinquency and neglect statutes permit intervention in the case of many forms of conduct which are entirely permissible in adults, or are ignored. They are not the equivalent of felonies, misdemeanors, or offenses. They represent, in a sense, the community's decision to contribute to sound child development and socialization. In these instances, a child certainly has a moral right to receive help and competent service. If confronted instead by gaps, lacks, waiting lists, outmoded practice, or incompetence he is both stigmatized by the contact and often harmed by the service. Here the community has organized itself in questionable fashion.

In a broader sense, this latter view should prevail for all children in trouble since, whatever the offense category technically, they are victims of the milieu in which they have been set. In deciding to intervene, the community offers them a new opportunity; to make the offer partial or to make the opportunity inadequate is to fail them once again.

[11] *Guides for Sentencing*, p. 4. On the broader question of rights and court procedure see Margaret K. Rosenheim, ed., *Justice for the Child* (New York: The Free Press of Glencoe, 1962).

DIVERSITY

The resulting pattern of services can hardly be expected to be neat and fully efficient. We need agencies and services for those who seek help voluntarily and for others who are found legally to require public intervention. We must have means of deterring, apprehending, evaluating, and disposing, on the one hand, and of publicizing services for voluntary clients, motivating potential clients, discovering those who have not yet been in serious difficulty, and offering appropriate services, on the other. And between these two "systems" are those intermediate agencies and facilities which must "reach" and deal effectively with those whose psychological and "cultural" resistance to help is deeply ingrained, whose personal disorganization and need is great, but who are not under court jurisdiction. A combination of professional skill, unorthodox procedure, and well-timed resorting to other than legal sanctions must be available for this latter group ("reaching-out," "aggressive," and "assertive" casework, etc.). Inevitably, these several "systems" will, and should, overlap in functions and in the clientele served.

The community pattern of services, in its diversity and necessary flexibility, should allow fullest development of the roles of both public and voluntary agencies. While the exact allocation of responsibility may vary with community and time in history, it seems reasonable to place in public agencies full responsibility in all those situations which involve the following: taking a person into custody in the first instance; arriving at a decision about adjudication as delinquent, neglected, youthful offender, wayward minor, or criminal; determining that a person shall not be returned to the community or supervising him in periodic contacts (probation or parole) on a basis in which defined courses of conduct are imposed and enforced. These are functions which must be under the aegis of legal and police machinery with built-in protection for individual rights; only a public program may be so characterized.

It seems reasonable to reserve for voluntary services those cases in which a function not legally possible for a public agency is involved, i.e., individual counseling requiring religious focus—or indoctrination. There are, too, the many services that develop out of meeting unusual needs through innovations and long-term obligations of a kind that public fiscal policy and administrative procedure generally keep outside of the public realm; for example: family service agency grants to permit a promising child to attend college, capital investment to reestablish a family in business, etc.

Between these two extremes are many services that might be offered publicly or privately. Historically, auspices have been a function of the time at which the program has developed, the traditions in a given part of the country, and availability of resources. (New York City voluntary child care has received state contributions since 1811 and city contributions since 1823. The present pattern of subsidy to sectarian institutions and agencies has existed since 1875.) Family agency services, traditionally under private auspices since their origins in the Associations for the Improvement of the Conditions of the Poor and the Charity Organization Societies, have seen their patterns of service adopted by progressive public welfare departments. Child guidance clinics are found under both public and private auspices, as are institutions and related treatment services. While there is no substantial evidence that one form of sponsorship or the other yields more effective or more economical programs, there seems to be a measure of agreement that it is within the realm of public obligation to ensure *availability* of basic services under some auspices. Expansion of public services appears to have been paralleled by a tendency toward public subsidization of a broader range of private agency programs, and there is need for clarification of the direction of public policy in this field. Certainly, when the public turns to the voluntary it should "purchase" well-defined services and enforce clear standards.

That this type of diversity is of value is seen in day-by-day experience. There are those delinquents, for instance, who are better able to accept and use service if court or probation department (or the police at an earlier stage) can suggest the availability of a voluntary agency clinic or institutional facility when it seems to be the appropriate medium of rehabilitation. Similarly, all those associated with voluntary agency services stress that they can identify, diagnostically, certain individuals who actually require a treatment setting publicly provided and with access to certain sanctions.

Sectarian content, which is possible for a voluntary agency, may also be a great asset and make services acceptable or attractive to some individuals in need of help.

In enunciation of the principle that a well-planned system of services has room for both public and private agencies, one should add that there must be evidence of readiness of groups of citizens, at times small and on occasion as large as a community-chest roster, to give of their energies, backing, and financial support to a voluntary program. The voluntary agency has meaning chiefly as the expression of the desire of members of a community to devote themselves to the creation of a special service and to set its fundamental policies or direction. In the absence of such leadership and some substantial evidence of voluntary financial investment (this does not in some fields preclude some public subsidy, purchase of service, or assistance toward expansion), there is no unique character in and little advantage to voluntary agencies.

There would be almost unanimous agreement at this point to what, early in the twentieth century, was a minority view: that public programs should not be "less eligible" than the private.[12] There may be real difficulties in attaining in all public programs in the near future the salary levels, job definitions, qualifications for appointment, pattern of supervision, and general professional atmosphere which are known to be associated with effective service. There is, however, no basis for setting the sights lower than they must be if programs are to achieve their objectives and to meet legally designated responsibility. Nor is there any defense for the countless direct and indirect actions or attitudes which in many communities serve to prevent gradual raising of public programs to a level of professional effectiveness. There are, of course, throughout the country, communities in which public agencies have developed high standards, have pioneered, and have shown major leadership. Similarly, there are many places in which programs under voluntary auspices have not kept pace with new knowledge, philosophy, and skill. The objective can only be high-standard programs universally, with no relegation of either to a backward role.

[12] Sidney and Beatrice Webb, *English Poor Law History*, Part II, Vol. I (London: Longmans, Green & Co., 1929).

Diversity of services also involves retention in both public and voluntary programs of the roles of volunteers and aides, as well as of professionally trained personnel and subprofessionals. It may take a highly trained caseworker to conduct an effective case study and formulate a recommendation in a complex court case. However, it is only the volunteer big brother or big sister who is in a position to provide the personal nonprofessional, supportive relationship and range of new experiences which some children and young people require. Similarly, the psychiatrist may be necessary for the psychotherapeutic services in an institution, but we ignore the heart of the program unless we plan for the cottage-parents or group leaders who live with the children from day to day and are available to them on a spontaneous, nonprofessional basis as a needed reality "touchstone."

As we think broadly of the variety of delinquencies and neglects we also come to appreciate that while the approach to planning for the individual must be oriented to him personally and to his unique needs, there may be situations in which the wisest disposition plan is community-oriented. Agencies may arrive at the conviction that only a massive effort directed at a total area will save its youth. We are only beginning to comprehend the preventive and treatment potential of local self-help projects and other neighborhood programs; they may prove to have as valid a place as do refined individual therapies (see Ch. XII).

The professions which help individuals directly, i.e., psychiatry, social work, psychology, education, etc., would do well to remember that, however much they are able to do with and for *individuals*, they cannot alone solve the total *community* problem of children in trouble. As already noted, causation is multiple and complex; some delinquencies are essentially explainable in social and cultural terms, while others have roots in personality disturbance, at least on an immediate basis; and both the social causes and the personality determinants—which are, of course, themselves interrelated—are rooted in the broader local, national, and even world arena. Basic economic trends, the prospects of war and peace, civil liberties and civil rights, the degree of morality in high office, and many other aspects of this broader picture may all be in some way involved. In this perspective, no one group can undertake full responsibility for designing community strategy, no single group can render the full range of essential services—and no limited group of professions can expect to be the major contributors to prevention.

PREVENTION—THE ULTIMATE, INTERMEDIATE, AND IMMEDIATE LEVELS

There is widespread evidence of the relationships between broad social change and social disorganization. Deviant behavior, particularly mental illness and delinquency, seems to increase with disorganization and the norm-vacuum which it implies. The individual may not know what the broader society expects by way of behavior, or may know it but have no reason to abide by it. Or, abiding by it, he may not have in the community around him the supports and props he requires if he is to rear his children as "adjusted," in society's terms.

This is true in the new industrial centers of underdeveloped countries, whose labor force is by definition made up of adults who have left the social supports of the "extended families" and village cultures which for hundreds of years assured belongingness, roots, and standards for successive generations. It is equally if less obviously the situation in American urban complexes in the post-World War II era. High population mobility, spurred by war and made part of the pattern of the age by industrial growth and expansion, has removed many Americans from their childhood homes and from the influence of relatives or long-known friends. What is more, mobility remains the pattern, so that many areas do not provide opportunity to develop the relationships and norms on which community controls, mental health, and values depend. The rush to urban fringes and suburban green-belts by the more prosperous and often more stable elements leave urban residues of the handicapped, the impoverished, the minority group members (people whose physical mobility is not associated with upward social mobility)—and the wealthy. If, as in the case of New York City, all space made available by the move to suburbs is rapidly filled by new migrants from the South or Puerto Rico, migrants without resources, subject to discrimination, and representing cultural differences which require bridging, the situation is complicated.

All of this has taken place in a social context which offers confused ideals and, even, questionable objects for emulation on the wider scene. Press, television, and radio provide the young, particularly our adolescents, almost daily evidence of the effectiveness of power and might, as compared with morality, on the international scene. From time to time, corruption in high places is charged to members of both major political parties, nationally, on a state level, and locally; there is enough evidence of the truth of some of these charges to create cynicism about public service. While to the businessman the line between illegal manipulation and clever business practice, between tax evasion and good planning, may be clear, the distinctions are often vague and questionable to a growing youth. Evidence that buildings collapse because inspectors are bribed, claims that even in prison racketeers obtain privilege, and conviction for fraud of the leaders of some labor unions hardly create desirable morality—nor do those incidents in which public officials use privileged information or contacts to promote their own interests.

What, then, is prevention? If Albert Cohen's thesis is correct about the way in which some delinquency meets the status problem of working-class youth in a society whose criteria of worth derive from middle-class values, preventive efforts shall perhaps be addressed to social stratification. Cohen himself is clearly at a loss in his speculations in this realm.[13] If the discussion about mobility, urban growth, minority migration, public morality, and international relations is sound, the problem of *basic* delinquency prevention is as broad and as difficult as the problem of general social change. It must deal with the world scene as much as with local communities to affect undesirable behavior. We enter here into the realm of political science, sociology, and social psychology to find that existing systems, explanations, and proposals are far from convincing.

The *ultimate* level of prevention (part of what public health people call primary prevention), the level having to do with the kind of world, country, and city-county in which we live, is the level thus most obviously outside the scope of a book addressed to services for children in trouble. When we turn to local delinquencies

---

[13] Albert K. Cohen, *Delinquent Boys: The Culture of the Gang* (Glencoe, Ill.: The Free Press, 1955).

and neglects and seek to deal with them, we must inevitably concern ourselves with that which is within the scope of local and state action.

Experience does suggest the reasonableness of the hypothesis that, despite negative factors in the world and national scene, a local community is in a position to *interpose* itself between the general social environment and the family or individual. In all of these instances the focus remains on the *whole* community, on *all* families, on avoiding that breakdown of values or of relationships which breeds maladjustment and deviation. Such types of prevention, not specific to delinquency or neglect, not designed only for the protection of children, must inevitably have only occasional mention in this book.

A city may, for example, be able to modify the "opportunity structure" experienced by the youth of a neighborhood (to use the formulation of the Ohlin-Cloward theories referred to in the previous chapter). Neighborhood self-help projects are one example of this. The "higher horizons" project, whereby schools seek to raise the cultural aspirations of members of underprivileged minority groups, is another. Educational, character-building, religious, recreational programs certainly belong on any list of influences within the scope of the community. To a considerable extent, too, this type of community prevention may also encompass many aspects of housing and intergroup relations as well.[14] All of these may be thought of not as "ultimate" prevention but, rather, as *intermediate* levels of prevention. In public health terms, this too is part of primary prevention.

Efforts such as these merge with the more *immediate* levels of prevention (secondary prevention to the public health worker), the efforts focused specifically on families known to be under special pressure or considered to be particularly vulnerable to difficulty, but whose members have not been reported as being in some way deviant or in trouble. One might refer here, for example, to what have become known as "special service schools," schools in disadvantaged neighborhoods with high concentrations

---

[14] For illustrations, see Helen L. Witmer, "Prevention of Juvenile Delinquency," a special issue of *The Annals of the American Academy of Political and Social Science*, Vol. CCCXXII (March, 1959).

of minority group children. They clearly require many special services, good teacher-pupil ratios, and creative programing if they are to help prevent some of the maladjustment and difficulties to which their pupils are vulnerable.

Parent education efforts, vocational guidance and placement facilities, language and acculturation programs in difficult areas, self-help and neighborhood improvement devices, aimed at the vulnerable, are here relevant. Programs which seek to reduce degrees of family disorganization for those on the public assistance rolls would be another illustration.

To fully outline intermediate and immediate prevention efforts would be to devote detailed attention to all services which touch on the lives of the disadvantaged members of the community. While we shall discuss the schools at some length because of their universal coverage, and shall touch on some of the other fields, it will not be possible to look at all services. Our objective here is adequate attention to those programs more directly, specifically, and narrowly concerned with young people in trouble.

Prevention programs on the intermediate and immediate levels will not be ignored here for another reason. Their coverage is broad and they meet many children in their normal routines who show signs of needing some special consideration and attention: a child begins to act up in school; a child in foster care begins to show withdrawal symptoms; a child in a settlement house program has trouble with his club members; a child whose family is in a public housing project seems out of control and destroys property. These agencies and programs may be in a position to do something about these difficulties. We would certainly expect them to recognize deviant behavior, not yet clearly classifiable perhaps, but behavior requiring some attention. If they do, that recognition may serve to initiate measures to assure that the problem will not be intensified. For planning purposes, it may be accurate and useful to think of these activities not as prevention but (Ch. III) as the *first level of case finding or case location.*[15]

[15] Bradley Buell prefers to talk of prevention through "organizing community treatment resources after pathological symptoms are suspected or detected." Bradley Buell, *Is Prevention Possible?* (New York: Community Research Associates, 1959), p. 7.

RECREATION

The general emphasis on recreation in programs of delinquency prevention and control makes it necessary to clarify a point of view about its place.

To those who would organize recreational endeavors to combat rising gang activity and delinquency, it is necessary to point out that the research and experience evidence is all in one direction, however unsatisfactory are many of the studies: *in and of itself* organized recreation will not prevent delinquency or cut delinquency rates to any significant degree.[16]

This finding can hardly be surprising. While it is true that recreational facilities may occupy leisure time and direct some energies, thus affecting the availability of certain young people for antisocial action some of the time, it is also true that the motives and drives behind deviant behavior are too strong to be so readily diverted.

Delinquents may come to recreation centers and shun the supervised portion of the program. They may, in fact, follow the practice of the gang which used Police Athletic League headquarters to plan an attack on another gang. Delinquent acts often take place en route to and from recreational facilities. Moreover, it need not be pointed out that it is possible to take part in boxing, basketball, or baseball without the game or activity having any effect on those core areas of one's life which promote antisocial behavior. Many delinquents are highly socialized and are excellent athletes.

None of this, however, suggests a basis for decreasing recreational endeavors. A well-planned community program of recreation is of itself an indispensable part of modern community provision

[16] For example: State of California, *Final Report of the Special Crime Commission on Social and Economic Causes of Crime and Delinquency* (Sacramento, 1949), p. 82. The literature is summarized in Herbert A. Bloch and Frank T. Flynn, *Delinquency: The Juvenile Offender in America Today* (New York: Random House, 1956), pp. 202–5. The Senate Delinquency Committee said, "Inevitably, most delinquencies are committed during the leisure time of children and in that sense do represent activities of unguided leisure, but this fact reveals nothing in relation either to the real causes of delinquency or to the effective methods of treatment and prevention." Subcommittee on Juvenile Delinquency, Committee on the Judiciary, U.S. Senate, *Juvenile Delinquency*, Report of March 4, 1957 (Washington, D.C.: Government Printing Office, 1957), pp. 100–102.

for both the young and the old. This remains the case even though the strongly antisocial delinquents tend to be kept out of some recreational centers or are not reached and affected by others. In the context of local community provision for young people, rather than as a specific preventive, recreation remains extremely important. Along with education, vocational choices, and health facilities, it is part of the opportunity picture which affects the way in which young people perceive and react to their social environment. Because they aim to serve all youth, most recreational programs, in fact, claim only that whatever their crime prevention potential, it is a by-product rather than a primary justification.[17]

In the organization of a neighborhood betterment program (which, among other things, might decrease deviance), one would certainly hypothesize that recreational programs might be both a point of motivation and a valuable component. Whether or not this is shown, however, we do know that the case finding potential of recreation programs is considerable, if only given appropriate staffing. It may also be possible to use a recreation program in a therapeutic way, as the platform on which to erect relationships and from which to introduce change. This, too, would require the kind of staffing and program not now commonly projected in recreation programs designed to decrease delinquency.

COORDINATION, INTEGRATION, ACCOUNTABILITY . . .
AND FLEXIBILITY

Coordination and integration of services, as forms of cooperation between agencies, will be discussed at a later point as crucial functions in a community pattern of services. They must, however, also be accorded mention in a review of principles and values. For the basic fact is that it is in the rare instance that any one agency can do the whole job which requires doing. It is therefore clear from the very beginning that the other values already discussed are in serious danger of being lost unless emphasis is placed in a total plan on agency interrelationships and their functioning as part of a community pattern of services.

[17] Joseph Pendergast in *Juvenile Delinquency: National Federal and Youth-serving Agencies*, Hearings before the Subcommittee to Investigate Juvenile Delinquency of the Committee on the Judiciary, U.S. Senate (Washington, D.C.: Government Printing Office, 1954), pp. 471–80.

In a sense, the premise of this entire discussion is that basic consistency of objectives, along lines outlined above, should characterize major agencies in the community but that this does not preclude flexibility, diversity, and variations to meet cultural differences. In the absence of reasonable consistency, the case referral, cooperative service, sharing of knowledge and resources, and all else implied in the phrase "concert of services" will be impossible. Since the objective is effectiveness, and not merely harmony, more than consistency is, however, required. A community also needs open channels of referral and regular interagency consultation. Much depends on the meeting and planning together out of which come mutual understanding of agency functions and ability to work cooperatively.

How can one expect independent agencies and specialized professionals to work together so as to achieve an integrated effort? What is to be the prime source of motivation? We suggest that each agency, service, and individual practitioner is *responsible* and *accountable* to the broader community in relation to the objectives, quality, and outcome of programs. Service to distressed families and to children in trouble is not private enterprise. Certain fields of activity are "reserved" for members of particular professions because they are pledged to given standards of service and to known ethics. Voluntary agencies are chartered to provide specific service; in their appeals to the public at large (or to the public treasury) for support, they undertake defined responsibility. This is why they deserve to be called *social* agencies. Public agencies also have clear roles and responsibility as defined by statute.

Because of these several types of responsibility, it is not possible to view any agency as an island or as a self-sufficient principality. Each is accountable to the community and each may be looked at in the light of community rights and community objectives. Were this not the case, any systematic planning effort within a community would be defeated at the outset. Specific administrative instruments, premised on agency accountability, are needed constantly to implement the responsibility of the agency and of the practitioner.

Assertions about the community pattern or about individual services must be modest; knowledge and skills are seriously limited. On what basis, then, is it possible to formulate any principles or to develop proposals? The fact is that while the areas of ignorance are important, the accumulation of experience and knowledge is also significant. Causal processes per se may be complex and obscure as they apply to some delinquents, but we know enough about surrounding conditions to plan preventive and treatment efforts. We may not know how to predict all deviance well in advance, but signs of much early difficulty are well known and recognizable. We may not always be sure about what is most effective in work with children, but we are certainly clear about many of the things which harm children or which are not effective. Precise training requirements for some personnel may not be defined, but fundamental knowledge, attitude, and skill for most of the key tasks have had preliminary and useful formulation.

As will be demonstrated in the remainder of this work, we are even able to outline the *major* elements of an over-all community strategy and to validate it against some experience and research, as well as against values and goals.

But because there is so much we do not know and are not sure of, claims remain modest and plans must be tentative. This entire book is, in a sense, a larger hypothesis, resting on current knowledge and skill, moving a little beyond, and in need of testing. We defeat ourselves unless the community pattern is flexible and experimental and unless plans constantly change and grow with new experience. Results must constantly be evaluated and measured. The individual practitioner, the single agency, or the community system of agencies will best play their roles if they see themselves as parts of a larger experiment, designed to indicate what would be best in the future. Those who will inherit the experience, in turn, should recognize that their efforts will have failed if they do not change, add to, and enrich the total effort.

CHAPTER III

A FRAMEWORK FOR
COMMUNITY PROGRAMS

AN AGENCY or institution serving families and children is not a self-contained entity. When it pretends to be, its program shows the consequences of isolation, and children suffer both from program inadequacies and from the gaps between programs. Voluntary and public agencies and institutions have long traditions of social responsibility and humanitarian concern and do not deliberately convert themselves into seemingly irresponsible, semi-isolated enterprises. Study discloses, however, that they tend to become such as a result of a variety of forces: built-in values; the "distance" between public and private programs and between those manned by trained and untrained staffs; the frustrations arising from resource inadequacies in the community and from the difficulties inherent in dealings with very disturbed persons; the unintended side-effects of bureaucratization and specialization which come with program "bigness."

Despite instances of close coordination and, in most quarters, a degree of accommodation, basic weaknesses in services are not overcome, and we are not nearly effective enough in work with children in trouble. It is doubtful that we shall be unless we are able to think deliberately and comprehensively not of the individual agency but of *a community system of services,* of *a community's program for children.* When we begin to give due attention to a community plan in this sense, each agency will be seen not only as an entity but also in relation to ways in which its policies, operations, and relationships contribute to community strategy—and how they might be further developed to play their role in an even more effective community endeavor.

All of this can be done without interfering with legitimate voluntary agency prerogatives and initiative, or with the special emphasis introduced by sectarian programs. It can certainly be accomplished without rigid central controls and authority. What is called for is a philosophy oriented to community strategy and integration of services, as well as that flexibility in practice which leads agencies to adapt themselves constantly to changing needs, knowledge, and values. A basic prerequisite is agency dedication to the best interests of the community as a whole and accountability of the individual practitioner not only for the *content* of his endeavors but, also, for their *consequences*.

The first and crucial step in clarifying long-range community strategy is the decision to emphasize *functions* rather than *agencies*. And functions make sense only when viewed in relation to one another, as parts of an *integrated approach* to children in trouble, rather than when seen separately. For the lessons of social welfare history and of recent experience are clear: where agencies do not operate as part of a larger whole and are not acutely aware of themselves as part of such whole, they inevitably become symptom or procedure focused, rather than client focused. Before long they may see nothing but one symptom and regard a problem as solved if (for example) truancy stops temporarily, a child is not arrested again, or the father regains his job. They may see only parts of people or parts of families and thus render partial service. Or they may perfect their own procedures and ways of working with no provision for those who cannot use the help as it is offered. We have already described the consequences.

What is needed, then, is an approach which will grow out of the needs of clients, in this case the children and their families, translating such needs and what we know about the total phenomenon of children in trouble into essential functions. Only as functions are defined and their interrelationships explored is it possible to look at specific agencies and at their roles.

The charges to agencies might then be regarded as flexible and changeable, responsive to the changing quality and volume of need, as well as to the appearance of new agencies and resources. In fact, even the listing and definition of functions essential for each community, the very basis for the assignment of roles to agencies, must have similar flexibility and responsiveness to new knowledge and new concepts. In this spirit, *there is continuity in planning, but never a final plan.* Moreover, one can outline the functions all communities seem to require in their approach to children in trouble in the light of current experience, but at the same time emphasize that the exact alignment of services and assignment of roles should reflect a particular community's size, rates of deviant behavior, and the many elements in the background which determine the availability and relationship of various public and voluntary facilities and resources.

This is not to say that any one agency must have only one function in an over-all approach. On the contrary, it may often be wise to have multifunction agencies. Various combinations of case location and evaluation, of diagnostic and referral services, of varied treatment approaches, may belong under one roof. Further, none of this is meant to suggest that clients must be considered responsible for understanding the pattern and getting to the right place. On the contrary, all social welfare agencies and many other public institutions must maintain some kind of more or less elaborate "intake," "screening," "advice," or "steering" service to answer inquiries, evaluate applications, and decide whether the agency's own services are most appropriate, or to assure a good contact with the appropriate resource. The community also requires, we shall maintain, a widely known general "advice" or "steering" center for those who are not aware of resources and who are too shy to make contact in what is obviously the "wrong" place in the hope of being referred to a source of help.

While every agency may need some intake and steering functions, and while a given agency need not be limited to one function, it is important that the functions which are assured be related to a total strategy and that the sum total of assignments undertaken add up to the full range of required activities. Otherwise, clients will continue to be lost in the gaps between agencies, or clients will remain on the rolls of agencies unable to be of any real help to them.

To put all of this in other terms: It should be possible to describe the total phenomenon of children in trouble in the community and to define the total approach to such children. Then, each agency should be expected to *find its place* as offering a specialized service or a combination of services to some children. Symptom groups or circumstances of detection should play the smallest possible role in the determination of function or of agency alignment unless it can be shown (and there are some instances in which it may be shown) that they contribute to efficiency, effectiveness, or sound organization.

The emphasis must inevitably be on the agency's *finding its place* or on community assignment of function as part of a mutual give and take. For the problem is not one of legalisms or of charters which can be revised once decisions are made. The situation is not necessarily helped by technicalities. What is crucial is clarity within the agency about what the community needs it to do and what it wants to do. The clarity should encompass administration, staff, and board—whether public or private.

The entire premise is, of course, that the community has assumed certain basic obligations for the welfare of its children and that these obligations extend even to those who are aggressive, antisocial, and destructive. In the broader national and state contexts there have been established certain minimum underpinnings for all people in the fields of employment security, housing, public education, public health, income maintenance, and social security. For children, all children, communities now affirm and, to varied degrees, seek to give full meaning to the right to competent health supervision from infancy to adulthood; opportunities for good education to the limits of one's potential; access to religious or moral training, as determined by parental background and wishes; adequate recreational facilities; vocational guidance and career planning with the assistance of skilled counselors. On this *foundation* and only on such foundation is it possible to talk of services which may be required by *some* children because of special problems. Among these are the "children in trouble."

INDIVIDUAL OR GROUP FRAMEWORK?

It may seem, at first glance, that the categories of functions suggested (i.e., case finding, referral, etc.) are so completely oriented to the individual as to preclude consideration of all of the suggestions previously summarized as to the possible significance of family, peer group, and neighborhood in the delinquencies and the neglects. This is not necessarily the implication, but the hazard continues to exist that long tradition will cause overemphasis on the individual and lack of imaginative group approaches.

Our sense of justice and our legal system demand that we avoid "group justice" or "group diagnosis," which in a courtroom can become little more than an exercise in group stereotyping. The protection of all therefore argues for a system which begins with case finding and evaluation on the level of the individual and his family. Where court adjudication is at stake, the unit must always be the individual. None of this should block out adequate attention in the evaluative process to neighborhood and peer-group aspects of a problem; possible intervention through group services or neighborhood programs rather than through individual treatment; treatment of a whole family rather than the original individual "client." Interesting current experiments in group "intake" deserve watching, of course. Most ultimate and intermediate (primary) prevention must deal with neighborhood and community.

Because a large proportion of agencies currently do tend to take an atomized view of the individual, there is need for constant stress on the fact that we are dealing with delinquencies and neglects and that the *level* of intervention must be determined by causal patterns and by what promises effectiveness. Ultimately, the community system should be evaluated by whether—following individualized differentiations and evaluations—the community is prepared with an armamentarium for intervention and treatment which includes family approaches, group methods, and neighborhood mobilizations. We shall attempt to give these attention in proper context.

PROTECTION

Before discussion of case location or of any of the other case-oriented functions which follow, it is relevant to stress the urgency of sound organization to guarantee the necessary framework of community protection. Only a secure community can support services and activities which are designed to help and rehabilitate.

A community which fears its antisocial and deviant elements tends only to attack and to demand revenge, refusing the financing which effective services require and not offering an atmosphere in which reformed offenders may return to community life.

A city, therefore, cannot consider the addition of probation officers, clinical staffs, or remedial teachers without also ensuring the adequacy of police services. Details of police functions are spelled out in Chapter VI but mention might be made of the need for adequate patrol work, detection, apprehension, and prosecution of offenders. If a low percentage of committed offenses are cleared by the police through arrests, some of the "leverage" for change is missing from the work with delinquents.

Similarly—and also to be elaborated subsequently—community protection demands adequate access to facilities for (a) the shelter of dependent and neglected children who would otherwise be endangered; (b) the detention (pending court disposition) of delinquents or alleged delinquents who endanger themselves or the community—or who may not remain available; (c) the institutionalization of those who are best helped in an institution or whose continued presence in the community courts danger for themselves or for others.

CASE LOCATION—THE FIRST LEVEL

To talk of "prevention" when the reference is to services for children already in trouble is to add to semantic confusion. We have suggested that there is an *ultimate* level of prevention, the level having to do with the kind of world, country, and city-county in which we live, and the influences they exert toward adjustment or maladjustment, toward social living or antisocial revolt. There is, too, what we have termed an *intermediate* level of prevention, the level concerned with efforts to interpose sound neighborhood, school, church, and other influences between all families and negative factors in the general social environment. (Both of these are called primary prevention in public health.) The more *immediate* prevention undertakings are the services and resources for vulnerable and disadvantaged families, families not in difficulty but known to have need for special backing if they are to achieve the standard of functioning expected of all. We have illustrated with reference to schools in the underprivileged areas or minority-group ghettos in our cities. Public health calls this secondary prevention.

Both the community protection function described above and the intermediate and immediate prevention activities demand that there be concern in many quarters about circumstances, influences, lacks, and conditions which may generate serious deviance and difficulty. This may be referred to as *situation finding*. It is discussed more readily after a review of case location.[1]

We turn first to those children already showing signs of deviant patterns and in need of attention. To work with them may be to prevent more serious problems, and this is why some employ the term "prevention." Functions become somewhat clearer, however, if this is considered the first line, or first level, of case location or case finding.[2] We refer here to:

(1) the child who is not getting along in school;
(2) the child who is "acting up" or doing peculiar things in the settlement house program;
(3) the child on the public welfare caseload who seems, on home visits by the investigator, to be particularly withdrawn;
(4) the group of boys in the housing project who are always breaking rules or ignoring requests by the manager;
(5) the children whose mother has just been hospitalized as an alcoholic and who remain at home with their father, but who seem to neighbors to be out of his control;
(6) the "gang" of pre-teen boys who seem to follow on the fringes of a "fighting gang" of older boys and who annoy the school custodian with minor pranks.

These cases are not in the channels of agencies specifically concerned with delinquent or neglected children, although investigation

[1] Although we shall use "case finding" and "case location" interchangeably, in accord with general usage, the former term would seem less precise. It suggests accidental "stumbling" over things where there should be deliberate organization and skillful perception.
[2] For a remarkably comprehensive earlier listing of the "basic pillars of a prevention and rehabilitation program," which includes many of the ingredients here discussed, see Cyril Burt, *The Young Delinquent* (1925), as summarized in Eva Rosenfeld, "Special Research and Social Action in the Prevention of Juvenile Delinquency," a paper (mimeographed) read before the American Association for Public Opinion, 1956.

might justify either label. Their problems may not be serious and may require little attention, or they may be very serious and may require psychiatric services, court concern, group programs, special school plans, or other help. The important thing is that there is already some sign of deviation, of adjustment problem, and that evaluation is needed. The community has been given some indication that these children may in some way be different and has reason to look at them and to see what the signal flares mean.

At this level, *case location is not specific* as to delinquency, neglect, mental illness, or anything else. Nothing is known to have been done by the child to require that certain channels (i.e., police) be used, and nobody has brought the case into specific service channels. The problem is one of ensuring that someone takes notice—so that there will be adequate evaluation and follow-up.

Where does responsibility for case location in this sense belong? The logical answer is in terms of opportunities available. Case location is most effective if it takes place in the social institutions in which children spend much of their time, where the behavior norms and expectations are clear, where deviance is readily noted, and where there is already a relationship which may be the basis for getting child and family to the spot where fuller evaluation will be made. We shall describe the opportunities for case location in the schools, health centers, the public welfare department, voluntary family agencies, hospitals, churches, courts, settlement and recreation centers, housing authorities, and spots at which children and families in trouble are encountered. We begin with a description of the nature of such opportunities and then turn to discussion of some problems and of preparation for case finders in settings such as these.

Case location in the schools. Many studies have found that schools are in a particularly strategic case location position because of the universality of their coverage and the duration of their relationships with children and parents. In many school systems, however, the typical teacher is not well equipped or not in a position to identify a child in need of help and may even (unintentionally, as a rule) mistreat a child so identified by others. In the New York City school system, where size leads to extremes of specialization, school resources for case finding and evaluation are at present thinly spread and fragmented among a Bureau of Attendance, a Bureau of Child Guidance, and the vocational and educational counseling program. There is obviously need in all systems to make it possible for the individual classroom teacher to play her strategic case finding role and to clarify the backing she requires from special services, resources, and programs.

In this connection, we might note that the group intelligence tests and achievement tests now widely used in schools are most useful as devices for identifying possibly deviant children requiring more individual attention and study. The possible language, cultural, and social biases in various devices require that teachers use them with caution and follow up only if there is behavioral confirmation of need to do so. There does not exist any device which can do case finding in the sense of specifying that a given child *must* have attention.[3] A child's need for attention is determined by the interplay of personality, family, environmental opportunity, and resources—and there is no way for any mass device to consider all these dimensions.

Whatever the efficiency of formal devices, however, the teacher's observations of the child as he learns, plays, interacts with others, studies, eats, meets aggression, and faces environmental demands offer unique case finding opportunity. Teachers are shown to be very sensitive case finders in study after study. A recent study has demonstrated, for example, that teachers actually identify personality traits differentiating graduates from early school leavers.

The main problem is one of encouraging and freeing our teachers to perform their case finding roles; the means for achieving this require detailed examination (Ch. V).

Child health stations and public health nurses as case finders. The criterion of universality of opportunity and of coverage suggests the importance of the child health station, which may not, at present, be an important case finding agency in many places. Dr. David Levy has demonstrated that the appropriate training of public health nurses and pediatricians will alert them to difficulties in early mother-child relationships, many of which may be dealt with at the time. In other instances, more intensive attention may be necessary, through case referral. Coverage of child health stations

---

[3] For discussion of delinquency prediction scales, see pp. 86 ff.

varies with many factors throughout the country and the basic health promotion assignment of such stations remains primary. Their case finding potential in a large city is major, however, as we recall their city-wide coverage and note that the vast majority of children not under care of personal physicians may be brought to such stations with some regularity in the first three years of life. Corrective efforts in such circumstances would normally be directed to the entire family.

The public health nurse has similar opportunities and a good deal of tradition in this field. The better training programs emphasize case location beyond the delimited medical spheres.

Case location through public welfare. The welfare department is second only to the schools in its potential in this area. Records reveal that public welfare department representatives encounter evidence of severe child neglect, parental brutality, serious parent-child conflict, the exposure of children to traumatic crises, and the beginning development of delinquent patterns. Although a public welfare department meets a smaller proportion of families than do the schools, its caseloads are made up in considerable measure of high-risk families and of the handicapped. By definition, the Aid to Needy Families with Children program is in contact with large numbers of children who are reared in broken families. It does not matter for this purpose whether categorical relief (i.e., Aid to the Blind, Old Age Assistance, etc.) and general home relief are administered by the same social investigators or whether caseloads are specialized, nor is it even important whether a department combines these responsibilities with the broader child care services (day care, foster care, adoption, homemaker services, etc.). What is important is the definition of the case finding roles of personnel in the first lines of contact with parents and children in all the programs, the preparation of these personnel for such a role, and the provision of necessary consultants and specialist backing. At present public welfare contacts are often "opportunities lost" as far as children in trouble are concerned.

Voluntary family agencies as case finders. Although the coverage of family service agencies may be relatively limited, the opportunities of such agencies are strategic. Large numbers of families in serious subsequent difficulty have been known at earlier points to sectarian family societies, to the Salvation Army Family Service, or to large nonsectarian family agencies. Moreover, these agencies affiliated with the Family Service Association of America nationally have high standards of personnel selection and practice. While at one time they may have regarded their methods as suitable only for those motivated to use help, there is an increasing tendency to understand cultural, social, and psychological factors in resistance and to "reach out" to clients, so as to make services more accessible. The family service field, in fact, has been discussing the possibility of a wider and larger "open door" than has prevailed in the past. One might even introduce the possibility (Ch. IV) of the family agency's potential as a general advice center.

Equipped as they are for competent social study and to obtain good psychiatric consultation service where needed, family agencies must certainly be listed as important case finders in this first line of community defense.

Medical resources and case location. By definition, medical facilities meet people when they face problems, at times quite serious problems. When a parent has to be hospitalized and there is need for social service help (in relation to arrangements for the family in the interim, posthospitalization planning, or patient and family reactions relating to the medical problem itself), the opportunity for becoming acquainted with the children and noting their need for special attention may be considerable. Currently, the emphasis more usually may be on the patient and the immediate problems confronting him or blocking the medical plan. All of this needs to continue, but the total community approach to children in trouble would also be strengthened by acceptance of the hospitalization crisis, which may be grave, as a possible opportunity for location of some children requiring additional attention.

There are, for example, children who respond to family medical crises by withdrawal or severe antisocial behavior. There are fathers who offer poor care in the mother's absence. Most often, it is a long-standing problem which comes to the fore under these special circumstances.

Many hospital social service departments are not adequately staffed for this kind of function as yet and little has been done to clarify the extent to which doctors and nurses might, in themselves, become in some ways involved.

Particularly troublesome is the evidence in hospital emergency rooms and medical wards that some children have been cruelly abused or seriously neglected. Yet, because the emphasis has tended to be on medical care and because the protective case finding potential of these situations is not defined, there is little clear statement of obligations or definition of suitable channels. Major new provision is needed for most parts of the country.

The out-patient clinic repeats the hospital experience in less intensive form and the crisis is generally not as great, since family separations are not under way. The clinic, however, does belong in the total case finding scheme; it is often, in fact, the center of work with families just before or just after hospitalization.

All of this applies, in even more emphatic terms, where the hospital is a mental hospital. In fact, current psychiatric research and theory suggest that much mental illness involves complex family group pathology which is not limited to the hospitalized member. Inevitably, the hospitalization or even out-patient treatment of a parent for psychiatric reasons means that the child or children in the family have probably been exposed to unusual, and perhaps destructive, experiences, which reflect themselves in all forms of personal deviation and pathology, from delinquency to psychosis. This is almost as frequently the case if the patient is a brother or sister. In these instances there is the obligation to look at all children in the family before determining that they do not require some special help despite such exposure.

Community child guidance clinics, while not attached to hospitals, would also do well to expand their case location activities. Since they are treating children referred to them because of specific difficulties, they quite naturally tend to give full attention to their child-patients and to work with or treat the parent(s) as their resources and philosophies dictate. In a minority of cases where other children in the family have also required child guidance services, clinics have taken the initiative and established a treatment contact. They have been limited in this, however, because of almost omnipresent waiting lists, as well as by their emphasis on client motivation for treatment. They have not recognized an obligation for some form of initiative where other children in the family present problems in need of evaluation, or seem to require other than child guidance services. Such initiative will be the product only of community-wide emphasis on case location, and the clarification of responsibility for recognition and the channels for evaluation and referral.

Churches and synagogues as case finders. Since churches do not list their contacts with social service exchanges and do not keep case records, there are no comprehensive statistical data as to their case finding potentials. Their broad relationships in every community and their direct service to many families in need of help make them major case finders. They may perform this service in various ways and in various degrees, of course, depending on the traditions and religious customs of a given group or sect. Their opportunity should not be underestimated, however, since like schools and settlements they are in the neighborhood, on the spot, and often able to see and feel emerging problems. Long-time relationships with individual families, sometimes over more than one generation, provide particular opportunity for balanced evaluation. They know of parents' concerns about their children and may be called upon to help when a child is arrested. Internal family crises are often called to their attention.

As with teachers, settlement workers, or police, the clergy have had to learn over the years which situations they can deal with directly themselves, offering religious counseling and other church services, and which require resources specialized in other ways. Most religious denominations have made important progress in these fields. Pastoral counseling courses and special psychiatry and social science offerings in theological schools have increased awareness of the implications of the problems children face and of the range of treatment possibilities.

Out of consideration of the problems of delinquents, a clergyman with special training writes:

The clergyman, through his relationships with parents, teachers, and young peoples' groups, and through his own direct relations with youngsters, can become aware very early of signs of disturbance in young people.

He must, however, know the signs of personality disturbances and also of possible future difficulty. He must have knowledge of the conditions and relationships most likely to give rise to such difficulties. He must know and respect his own limitations and be ready to solicit help for any problems which exceed his ability.[4]

The court's special case finding opportunities. The children in most serious trouble tend eventually to reach juvenile court as allegedly delinquent or neglected, if they are not sent to mental hospitals or placed in foster care through welfare authorities. These courts recognize their obligations for case study and disposition. What is too seldom understood, however, is that the courts which deal with adults, particularly those courts which are concerned with family problems, have special case finding opportunities. Similarly, it is not often the practice for a children's court or a youth court, dealing with one child in the family, to take notice, through its probation case study, of the needs of other children, and to initiate necessary follow-up.

All courts, in fact, have major case finding opportunity since the very contact reflects social or psychological causes of importance to all in the family.[5] Currently, many so-called family courts and support courts are not equipped to do much about their opportunities. The criminal courts, in particular, would need special facilities if they were to examine the status of children in a family when a parent or an older child is dealt with, since in this kind of case location there are no legal sanctions.

Recognizing the implications for children, New York State is now implementing a court reorganization involving the potential for creating a case finding apparatus in all family actions in which children are in some way involved. Other jurisdictions already have such facilities, but usually where the case volume is small.[6] Only fairly elaborate development of probation services in criminal courts

[4] Richard Vincent McCann, *Delinquency: Sickness or Sin?* (New York: Harper & Brothers, 1957), p. 126.

[5] Alfred J. Kahn, *For Children in Trouble* (New York: Citizens' Committee for Children of New York City, Inc., 1957), p. 39.

[6] New York State Temporary Commission on the Courts, *The Plan of the Temporary Commission of the Courts for a Simplified State-wide Court System* (New York, 1956). Also see Harriet L. Goldberg and William H. Sheridan, *Family Courts, an Urgent Need,* Juvenile Delinquency Facts and Facets, No. 6 (Washington, D.C.: Government Printing Office, 1960).

and a broader view of their opportunities would lead to more adequate case finding generally.

Settlements, mass recreation, and case finding. At their best and when they are most successful, settlement houses and community centers know their neighborhood children and families quite well. Several children in a family may take part in club activities or in recreational or crafts programs. The parents may also have some part in the program. Staff members are aware of what is going on in the neighborhood and may know of the special difficulties a child has encountered or the dangers he faces. It may be clear that clubs or boys or gangs, in and out of the settlement, are tending toward delinquency or drug use, or at least are not constructively motivated.

Under such circumstances, settlement houses have been and should certainly continue to be important case locators. Some, in fact, have staffed themselves with caseworkers, casework units, or clinic units to help in case evaluation or even to offer intensive treatment where a child is not getting along in the program or a gang is moving toward antisocial patterns. Others have offered themselves as outposts for family service agencies and clinics to facilitate case location and the transition to treatment.

There are, of course, settlements and community centers which are not strictly neighborhood-based and which place more emphasis on mass activities and on special events. They do not generally get to know many children well and are probably not better equipped than the large public recreation, park, and after-school recreation programs for much case finding. Impressive efforts have, however, been made in some instances to have a small number of group workers trained in social work available as consultants and to give special attention to individuals and groups. Where this is possible, even the mass recreation program has case location potential.

Case finding in public housing. Elizabeth Wood has noted the case finding potential of tenant relocation programs and of the public housing projects.[7] For a number of reasons not immediately relevant here there has been substantial self-selectivity in public housing. Public housing has high concentrations of racially-ethni-

[7] Elizabeth Wood, *The Small Hard Core* (New York: Citizens' Planning and Housing Council, 1957).

cally underprivileged groups, of relief recipients, of broken families, and of those who are in many other ways handicapped. Thus, a housing manager is in a position to do case finding in instances of open and violent marital conflict, below-standard housekeeping, and rent delinquencies, in addition to major misconduct of children or extremely questionable and hazardous parental behavior.

One should add, however, that public housing defeats its purpose, becomes further stigmatized, even more limited to those with recourse to nothing else, and thus even more abnormal as a daily living milieu if management is highly organized to pry into people's affairs and to interfere in their normal privacy and prerogatives. What is proper, however, is management alertness to the kinds of situations and circumstances to which all responsible citizens might react anywhere, as well as management's use of those opportunities which are routine in the management relationship: maintenance, rent collection, protection of premises, responding in emergencies to requests for help. Special social service units in housing developments or available to them may help to separate routine management from special individualizing functions.

Other case finders. It may be well to add, however obvious, that the logic which suggests case finding machinery in medical facilities is more than reinforced in all social welfare programs. Agencies responsible for foster care, those offering long-term or short-term care to the dependent and the neglected, family location agencies (in cases of fathers who desert), and those rendering many specialized services are already at work with families because it is known that problems exist or crises are being faced. Many now limit themselves to narrow interpretations of their functions. However, a family-oriented approach and a preventive outlook would dictate a degree of alertness to the implications of the problem for all family members and, therefore, a case finding role.

Certainly, agencies which already have children under their care in foster homes and institutions have major responsibility to contribute to their sound development and to ensure early detection and follow-up of signs of difficulty. To use such difficulty as the basis for returning the case at once to a court or to the original placement agency without efforts to cope with it as a parent might represents a reneging on primary child care obligations.

Advice centers—a new resource. The parent, friend, or neighbor is very often the very best case finder. He may refer himself, his relative, his child, or his neighbor, but he cannot be expected to know who is best equipped to evaluate the situation or to render service. Currently, the special attitudes and experiences of various ethnic groupings affect the choices of places to go for help; members of one group do not hesitate to turn to the police when they need help with their children; members of another group turn to the church; others may go to child guidance clinics or may have access to private psychiatric guidance.

None of this is in itself undesirable if channels are open and the initial steering is good. The problem is that our urban areas contain subgroups aware of no resources. Others know of facilities which they do not feel free to use. Still others turn to the unqualified—with disastrous consequences. The modern city needs a general advice center—widely known, with accessible branches—and with no intake criteria. Anybody should be free to enter for guidance and steering and feel that no stigma or disadvantages will result. Perhaps a special system of centers is necessary—or it may be that welfare departments, health stations, settlements, or family service agencies are able to expand their functions in these directions. Some possibilities are outlined in Chapter IV.

The complications of such case location. Agencies involved in case finding at this first level have not been established primarily for this purpose, and therefore have the task of protecting their central functions. For example, the classroom teacher must balance her basic educational function with her case finding obligations if her central role is not to change. The settlement worker loses members if the public image of the agency is dominated by the case finding. The general physician may discover that he loses patients if he raises questions about a family's child-rearing practices.

It is no small task for those agencies whose primary responsibility is not case finding and who operate at the level before there is identification of delinquency and neglect to balance for themselves and for their publics their basic, necessary (sometimes statutory) functions against a relatively broad focus. Yet these are socially created agencies, institutions, and programs, and socially responsible professional people. Community interest requires more than discharge of narrowly conceived functions: the child welfare worker cannot ignore family problems; the family agency worker must be alert to the problems of children; the child guidance worker must "see" the other children and parents.

Much depends on the inclusion in the education and training of the people who are to work in these settings of sufficient material about normality and deviance in family life and child development so that they recognize signals of distress even where their training does not equip them to diagnose such distress. Both psychological and cultural content belongs in this kind of training. Where the primary tasks are in other realms, personnel should be prepared to ask for consultation or advice. Ways must also be found through education and community organization to create that heightened sense of social responsibility which generates a broad exercise of one's opportunities. The need for this and the methods to be used must vary from group to group.

All case locators on the first level are most in need of information as to where situations may be referred for follow-up and evaluation, as appropriate to the particular setting. The teacher should have access to guidance personnel, school social workers, psychologists, or psychiatrists, while the policeman on the beat may call on a juvenile aid specialist or a clinical intake unit. Nurses and doctors need to know about school resources, social agencies, police facilities, and protective casework units—to mention a few. The family agency knows how to initiate proper referrals but is at a loss in certain situations if the community does not have a protective casework program. Members of the clergy require intimate acquaintance with all types of resources and how they may be brought into action. As already suggested, the settlement resident or club leader may have specialized personnel on the premises or may call upon other agencies—and what the housing manager does depends on whether a social service program is located within his own structure.

These are illustrative rather than all-inclusive statements. The method of first-level case location and the channels to which it should lead must be worked out specifically in a manner appropriate to a given agency, social institution, or profession. In subsequent chapters we shall deal with schools, police, welfare departments, and settlements in some detail in this regard.

CASE LOCATION—CHILDREN ALREADY IN TROUBLE

Not all case finding occurs when the child is not yet known to be involved in serious "trouble" and is not in specified authoritative service channels. There are many instances in which the children who are identified seem to be caught up in acts or circumstances of a kind which may require police or court action. In fact, in some of these circumstances or offenses (acts which would be crimes if committed by adults, etc.) there is legal assignment of an obligation to intervene.

Parents and any of the community personnel described in the previous section may initiate these cases, but the formal processing —the decision to ignore or proceed with situations—is largely in the hands of police, courts, attendance bureaus, and protective casework units. All of these have special responsibility for follow-through and all are ready to resort to delinquency and neglect petitions as necessary.

Before further examination of this level of case finding, however, it is necessary to comment about devices offered for the purpose of predicting delinquency and ensuring the early identification of children who will be in trouble—in advance of any overt difficulty.

Delinquency prediction. Considerable attention is currently being directed at the development and validation of devices designed to predict delinquency, chiefly as the result of the pioneer work of Sheldon and Eleanor Glueck.[8] A popular magazine responded to the early publicity with an article entitled "Criminals in the Kindergarten?" In the enthusiasm about possible future availability of a

---

[8] For a summary and comprehensive bibliography see Sheldon and Eleanor Glueck, *Preventing Delinquency and Crime* (Cambridge, Mass.: Harvard University Press, 1959). See, too, William C. Kvaraceus, "Forecasting Juvenile Delinquency," *Journal of Education*, CXXXVIII (April, 1956), 1–43, and Starke R. Hathaway and Elio D. Monachesi, "The Personalities of Predelinquent Boys," *Journal of Criminal Law, Criminology and Police Science*, XLVIII (July–August, 1957), 149–63. Expert consensus is reported in *Research and Potential Application of Research in Probation, Parole and Delinquency Prediction* (New York: Citizens' Committee for Children of New York and Research Center, New York School of Social Work, 1961, mimeographed).

device, there has been a tendency to lose sight of three important considerations: (a) whether the prediction instrument has been validated; (b) whether, if validated, it would be practicable; (c) whether it is socially desirable to use such a device in conjunction with a community's efforts on behalf of children in trouble.

The first of these questions need not concern us at any great length here. Although it has not yet been shown to exist, there is no technical reason why there should not eventually be available a prediction device with a known degree of accuracy, able to tell us how many in a given group are likely to be in trouble with the law and how many are not likely to be. The findings will be stated in terms of the "chances" of any individual in the group. All prediction is, by definition, in relation to group frequencies. Thus far, retrospective studies based on the Gluecks' device have shown that of those in difficulty most would have been properly identified had the instrument been used earlier—and had there been available at that earlier time the data used in the retrospective ratings.

There are not, as yet, any completed and convincing studies which use the Glueck scale to predict forward; the most elaborate such study, that of the New York City Youth Board, is inconclusive in its interim report. No current findings clarify, as yet, the rate of probable misprediction, a most important matter if a delinquency prediction instrument is to become an administrative device. There is some reason to believe that the Glueck scale would tend to over-predict delinquency in a normal school population.[9]

The New York City Youth Board is seeking to convert the Glueck scale into a practicable instrument. Such an instrument would have to be administered by teachers or other school-based personnel. The much-publicized Youth Board experiment involves ratings and judgments by specially qualified and trained personnel on the basis of data assembled by a special staff from three sources: home interviews with parents, interviews with teachers, collateral information from social agencies.

The third question, that relating to the desirability of a delinquency prediction device, takes one directly into the realm of social

[9] See Elizabeth Herzog, *Identifying Potential Delinquents,* Juvenile Delinquency Facts and Facets, No. 5 (Washington, D.C.: Government Printing Office, 1960).

policy. In developing ways of helping children before their problems are serious, should we seek devices to predict *delinquency* or to predict *maladjustment?* The Gluecks have written:

It is to be hoped that similar devices for early "spotting" or "screening" or early "identification" or early "diagnosis" not only of delinquent but of emotionally disturbed non-delinquent children will be developed by others, notably by psychiatrists and psychologists, who have access to extensive and intensive case materials.[10]

Concentration on a specialized delinquency prediction scale is reasonable where the purpose is to test a causal hypothesis; such experimentation with prediction is in the best of scientific tradition. A scientific "law" should enable one to predict. Where the emphasis is on community services, however, other considerations prevail.

Do we actually wish to stigmatize a kindergarten child or a first-grader with the label "will probably be a delinquent"? Have we the right to label, without due process; dare we label in the light of attitudes to delinquency? Are teachers, principals, and others able to deal completely objectively with a child said to belong to a group in which the delinquency likelihood is eighty chances out of one hundred? Do we not, in fact, run the risk of the self-fulfilling prophecy here, i.e., making the child delinquent because of the experiences we create for him through the labeling? To some degree deviance is a matter of self-definition.

It has been said that these negative consequences of a delinquency prediction instrument may be avoided by keeping the findings in the hands of such specialized personnel as social workers and psychologists. Experimentation along these lines is certainly justified, although it is difficult to see how such personnel could use knowledge of predictions, without informing others, in the absence of circumstances or behavior which would alert teachers. Would not the requirement that the device be used by specialists make it impractical for most school systems, except perhaps during special, short-term demonstrations?

Most important, however, if the purpose is to help children and

[10] Eleanor T. Glueck, "Identifying Juvenile Delinquents and Neurotics," *Mental Hygiene*, XL, No. 1 (January, 1956), 24–43. Also see Eleanor T. Glueck, "Efforts to Identify Delinquents," *Federal Probation*, XXIV, No. 2 (June, 1960), 49–56.

to avoid serious problems by early detection, attention had best be directed at the likelihood of deviation and adjustment problems in any areas; there is no special value to predicting delinquency per se. Those who would develop devices might invest their energies in this direction. As already indicated, the usual group tests of I.Q. and achievement are usable in this way to alert teachers and/or to supplement their observations. Glueck scale *items*, when validated, might be included in an all-purpose screening instrument.

Even the all-purpose prediction device cannot be introduced without recognition that being identified as a "risk" carries with it some potentially undesirable consequences: stigma in the eyes of some; being held up to standards more rigidly; being "typed," perhaps unjustly, in terms of expectation rather than performance. Prediction devices deal with group statistical probabilities and do not account for those who run contrary to the majority trends; some children are able to handle their handicaps or are influenced by factors not taken into account by the instruments.

In the light of these considerations it seems reasonable to suggest that the emphasis be on predicting "need for help," rather than "delinquency" (case location, on what we have called the first level), and that even such devices not be put into the hands of unqualified personnel.

In some school systems, skills and attitudes may be such that only clinical or guidance personnel should have access to the results of tests or screenings which identify individual children as needing help. In other systems, teachers may be adequately prepared for their use. Where there is no assurance of ability to control the consequences of a statistical prediction that a child is a "risk," it would be wiser policy to plan only for the identification of and attention to the child who already displays a problem or difficulty, however mild. Under any circumstances, there is no right to introduce pressure, formal or otherwise, for taking help, unless there is already a behavioral manifestation of its need. Parent or child could hardly be expected to be highly motivated as a result of actuarial information.

Predictions about the presence in a group of a considerable number of highly vulnerable children might lead to group programs, neighborhood programs, and community efforts—which need not single out any one child as a "risk." Emphasis on such predictions would be sound policy.

Major agencies for location of those in trouble. Repeated truancy is defined as "delinquency" by many children's court statutes. Further, countless studies of juvenile delinquents and adult criminals show that very large proportions were at one time truants and were thus identifiable through their truancy.

The school system's plans for coping with *unexplained* absence are thus part of the community's case location machinery for children who may already belong in the category "in trouble," in the sense of our discussion. Some truants are involved in stealing, vandalism, gang activity, running away, and sexual delinquency. Others are being severely neglected or brutally treated by parents who are inadequate, seriously mentally ill, or who are "lost" in a new and strange culture. On the other hand, unlawful absence may prove on investigation to result from school phobias or a variety of psychoneurotic problems, from situational school difficulties, or from environmental or economic pressures in the home.

Those who investigate unexplained absences are therefore major case finders, dealing with children in many kinds of difficulty and drawing on all possible community resources, including the courts. Whether a given school system requires a special attendance bureau or might integrate its attendance and general school social work and guidance services is a matter designated for more extended discussion (Ch. V).

The *police* are also major case finders, their volume of cases found being exceeded only by investigators of unlawful absence. This makes it necessary to define the relative assignments of all police and of juvenile aid bureau specialists. Should all youth cases be cleared with youth police, for example? The nature of the police case evaluation, the length of case contacts, the qualification of juvenile aid policemen become important questions. Answers must begin with the premise that the police *are* case finders and, therefore, must either make screening decisions or have help in making them (Ch. VI).

Family courts and *juvenile courts* (depending on the court structure) are also case finders in the sense of this section, i.e., they are often the first official agency to which the case is reported and are in a position to initiate formal proceedings, make referrals to a variety of resources, encourage family solutions without community help, discourage or encourage complainants and petitioners, give priority to delinquency or to neglect aspects of cases, and so on. The exact nature of the courts' "intake" or "screening" machinery which takes these actions is obviously affected by the total structure of community services. The extent to which the police do careful evaluation before coming to court is a major consideration. The existence of a case finding and social service program in the school conditions the court's procedures. Clearly, however, courts require some kind of structure and policies for handling situations not previously evaluated and not necessarily best served by formal processing. This kind of intake service may at the same time serve the important function of introducing those who will be dealt with in the court to the procedure and preparing them to view the experience constructively (Ch. VIII).

Where children are being grossly neglected or mistreated the situation is often called to the attention of *protective casework* units—protective casework sections in welfare departments in many places, child welfare workers in many counties, state-wide (in Massachusetts) or local Societies for the Prevention of Cruelty to Children elsewhere.

These units are in the same relationship to neglect cases as are police to delinquency. Some situations are acute, severe, obvious, and there is little choice but to arrange for immediate temporary shelter and to introduce court action which will lead to long-term plans for the children. Other situations require study and evaluation, since it may be possible to develop plans or to institute treatment under the auspices of the protective unit, or on referral from them, on a voluntary basis, or at least somewhat voluntary since the potential court petitions remain in the background. Further, just as a good number of complaints to the police about children require only brief notice that the community is concerned, a portion of the protective cases need not result in prolonged contacts or services. In fact, all such units must sort out a group of cases which are initiated by local eccentrics and cranks.

Every community obviously requires a case finding service of some sort which is particularly concerned with neglect and abuse of children. (Chapter IX is devoted to examination of current patterns.)

Community case finders. Families are, themselves, major case locators, as are friends and relatives. Depending on cultural attitudes, however, there are major variations in the extent to which members of different groups feel free to turn to the police, courts, schools, family agencies, and others to ask for help. Programs of education and interpretation may contribute to this process; helpful experiences for those who do go to the agencies are even more effective ways of advertising and opening the channels.

The special case finding unit. Community circumstances may dictate the creation of a special case finding unit or a system of such units. Thus, when the New York City Youth Board was launched and was committed to early case location and referral, a system of special Referral Units was designed as the necessary instrument in high-delinquency areas. After a period of experimentation as to the appropriate community base, these units were placed in the schools. Subsequently, they were moved out again because of administrative complications. Such units deal with the two levels of case finding we have differentiated.

Problems of case finders. Study of the case finding experience of special units and general agencies discloses that the case finder must solve many difficult problems if he is to work effectively. Some of them are problems peculiar to the service set up exclusively for case location, while others might confront any case finder.

For example, a Referral Unit worker may be making excellent progress with a family but must solve the technical problem of how far to carry a situation, once identified, before referral to the agency which will provide the long-range treatment. Even prior to this, the case finding agency must have on its staff professional personnel skilled in diagnosis and work with extremely complex case situations and with individuals resistive to community intervention on many grounds. This is no small consideration in the light of severe personnel shortages—as well as real gaps in knowledge and skill among the professionally prepared.

Particularly perplexing are the cases which are carefully studied, dynamically understood, but in which the parent wishes no help.

Systematic and skilled work to overcome resistance and to offer service on an acceptable level do not always break through parental refusal to have outside intervention in family situations. Then, unless a child gets into difficulty, thereby justifying more formal legal intervention, it is necessary to accept the fact that further efforts are not possible. Where staff are not skillful, these cases are inevitably lost.

All agencies meet situations in which parents "use" agencies to control or to punish their children. The parental petition or request for intervention is, at times, a desperate bid for help and at others a defensive measure against their own involvement. Considerable skill, of course, is required if the interests of all are to be considered and a helping process inaugurated. These are cases which are usually found none too early, but the agency must make its own assessment if it is to do something constructive. In some instances, the steps taken only convince the children that nobody cares about them; in others a real beginning is made in constructive directions even if the mother's initial demand for placement of a child has to be met.

Case finding may accomplish little if some one agency does not take responsibility for major help to the family and for relating other resources in a systematic plan (Ch. XII). Otherwise, a flurry of uncoordinated activity serves to confuse rather than to rehabilitate. Even where a case finding agency is oriented to continued responsibility, it often has no way under current patterns of assuring adequate reporting back by treatment agencies if referrals "do not take."

At their best, case finding agencies are characterized by a broad approach, systematic study, and careful planning. The possibilities are seen in a case such as the following:

The case was called to the attention of the Referral Unit by the school principal because Barney, age 11, was restless, wandered about, rarely completed his work, and had temper outbursts. Study disclosed that Barney was a member of a migrant family with many difficulties stemming from substandard living conditions, the need to adjust to a new culture and language, and the inability of the parents to cope with the needs of their seven children. During an eight-month period, the Referral Unit worker, who spoke the family's language, saw the father in weekly interviews, saw the mother occasionally (she was not well), and met with the boy. She conferred with the Department of Welfare investigator regularly until the family was helped to move to a larger apartment, obtain needed furniture, receive funds for clinic visits. At the end of the period, a referral was completed to a sectarian family service agency for continued help. Results were seen in a short time in the improved adjustment of the boy who was referred and of a sister who had also been having difficulty in school.

The right to intervene. Case location is not merely a matter of developing detection devices or of affirming the obligations inherent in those agencies which have contacts with many children under strategic circumstances. For the question remains: At what point does a community have the right to interfere on behalf of a child's future?

There are situations in which parents do not wish help and persist in their refusals despite all the efforts of caseworkers and others who use their skills to interpret a service and to overcome resistance. Where neglect or delinquency, as defined by statute, can be shown to exist, agency responsibility is clear. However, as we seek to locate cases early and to offer services to the deviant and to the vulnerable, we meet many situations in which, technically, there is no delinquency or neglect. Moreover, it would involve considerable stretching of both neglect statutes and current professional knowledge to hold that any parent who, under such circumstances, refuses to accept a referral is, by virtue of that fact, subject to court intervention.

While it is undoubtedly true that housing officials, schools, and public welfare authorities actually have access to certain sanctions, it is only proper to ask to what extent they have a right to seek to bring to bear services which are not part of their *primary* functions in the instance of the refusal of the parent to cooperate despite adequately interpreted offers of help. If these officials were to use their access to needed resources or their roles in the lives of children to bludgeon families into help which has been considered and rejected, we shall have changed the basic character of the social institutions they serve and undermined their primary functions. We also shall have seriously violated our concepts of individual rights. In the long run it would be wisest for the community to prepare to bow to the wishes of parents in these instances even if agency representatives are troubled about the consequences. Where experience shows repetitive circumstances in which this policy inevitably damages children, it may be time to consider amending the law with respect to delinquency and neglect. The Standard Juvenile Court Act, in fact, recommends a statement of neglect jurisdiction broad enough to include most circumstances in which there is evidence that a parental failure to offer or to accept service is truly injurious.

The large issue is not, however, one of offering services where there is no right to do so, but of professional competence and methods. Although many potential clients are initially resistive, their reactions are often found to be compounded of fear, lack of information, and cultural patterns which make it difficult to accept help. Many of the personal psychological obstacles can be overcome where the approach is skillful. Clients respond to the interest and psychological authority of teachers, welfare department representatives, doctors, ministers, and others. We need to alert personnel in many kinds of settings to the opportunities to help with developing problems, or with family situations out of which serious problems may spring. We also must equip staff to act appropriately and encourage a sense of responsibility about such matters in welfare departments, schools, hospitals, health stations, mental hospitals, courts, correctional institutions, voluntary family agencies, clinics, and other settings.

There may have to be legal clarification in some fields, and improvements in methods of service must certainly take place. These will tend to follow, however, as we advance the concept that to fail to identify those who need help early is to be responsible for their neglect and future difficulties. In the intimate, but isolated, interdependence of urban living, people cannot count on relatives and neighbors. They depend on community agencies in their need, and to miss the signs of desperation and helplessness is to fail in a major human obligation. To "find" a case is to locate an opportunity to save, to repair, or to prevent. And, since many undesirable consequences may follow from being labeled as a delinquent child or neglectful parent, to locate a case and not ensure adequate follow-through is destructive and punitive, whatever the intention or policy. A responsible citizen or a responsible community agency cannot permit the loss of what may be a child's last chance because of irresponsible service, a failure to follow up—or lack of community designation of some agency as responsible to help with a situation and to keep helping until there is either a satisfactory disposition or an irreparable and conclusive failure.

SITUATION FINDING

When charity organization societies (now family agencies) and settlements were at the height of their social reform interest at the turn of the present century, there was considerable alertness to the close relationship between case location and situation finding. The community loses opportunity for protective work, in the sense described above, and for immediate preventive planning unless this relationship is reaffirmed and reinforced by agency action in the present era.

To illustrate briefly: The settlement house staff, in discovering a number of members addicted to drugs, may become aware of channels of distribution in the community. A public welfare investigator's experiences, as checked against the experience of others, may clarify a special type of housing need—or may reveal a defect in housing legislation. Experience with families of several adolescents may suggest to a family agency that the community lacks adequate employment counseling and placement resources. Systematic attention to the pattern of complaints may alert a police officer to the fact that an empty school building is an "attractive nuisance" and encourages vandalism. Examination of delinquency data may reveal to a public official that social agency summer vacation shutdowns remove the props which keep some young people out of trouble.

In each instance, the step from case finding to situation finding is one involving generalization from case-by-case experience and is based on concern for community protection and prevention. At times, the agency's experience and knowledge of a situation are such that referral to the police or district attorney may complete the action. At other times, a given agency may be in a position to make a substantial contribution to the community through systematic study of a block of its cases or by assembling data from many of its clients—then reporting to the community at large about a hazard, a need, a problem, a resources gap.

While, typically, the situation finding by the individual agency is triggered by specific experience with one or more cases—leading to alertness, assembling of more data, perhaps to study and to generalization—all agencies may also at times be confronted quite directly, rather than through case materials, with evidence as to gaps or hazards. Police, particularly youth police, search for hazards during their patrol duties. Settlement workers and others in the neighborhoods become intimately acquainted with housing, recreation, and health needs, and with the economic problems of families. They often learn about racketeering. Public health nurses, to mention one other group, have direct experience too.

Again, some of this situation finding should lead an agency or a practitioner to report directly to the police, district attorney, public health officer, or housing official. At other times, it may initiate the type of study and exploration mentioned above. In fact, direct experience with apparent hazards may encourage an agency to turn to its case files to see whether the gaps or hazards are directly reflected in client experience.

The work of coordinating and city-wide planning bodies should reflect the initiative which derives both from members' and agencies' experiences with the individual case and from agency confrontation of a general hazard. These coordinating organizations are in fact under special obligation, by charge, charter, and role, to respond to the situation finding initiative of alert agencies and to consider carrying through the necessary study, planning, and action. They are well located, by function, to communicate information about hazardous situations to the general community. They should also undertake routine statistical analysis and periodic special studies relative to social breakdown, agency services, and unmet need—thus serving to pinpoint neighborhood and population subgroups exposed to many risks and helping to suggest service.

When the community machinery is working well, the discovery of local community situations which are hazardous to children and youth, and which will not be remedied by enforcement actions of administrative agencies (police, public health, etc.), or by the

addition of social services alone, should lead to special all-out resource mobilization and local self-help efforts. Settlements, neighborhood organizations, and community councils may be needed to
provide initiating force and guidance.

Case finders make major decisions all the time. The policeman
on the beat who sees two groups of boys in a fight may merely
"break it up" or may do something more. Except for those instances
in which his instructions decree that certain serious offenses must
lead automatically to arrest and to court petitions, he exercises a
measure of discretion about recording the situation at all, considering arrest, or making a referral to the juvenile aid police. The
juvenile aid officer, in turn, has access to a variety of dispositions:
to drop the case; to drop the case after a letter, telephone warning,
conversation with the parent, or interview with the child; to undertake full social study and to arrive at a plan that way; to make
a referral to a social agency or some other service; to file a court
petition.

Except in those cases where the particular offense automatically
leads to a formal court hearing under court rules or where the
petitioner demands such hearing, court intake workers may have
access to a similarly wide range of possibilities. Also, the attendance
officer in the home on an investigation of unexplained absence must
decide about next steps as he reacts to what he is told and sees.

Brief screening decisions. These *brief screening decisions,* as they
may be called, are a first level of case evaluation. They are the
routine separating-out in any agency assigned to deal with those
already in some trouble: courts, police, attendance, protective unit,
and so on. Public housing managers, clergymen, public recreation
workers have similar experiences. These are essential and unavoidable decisions if programs are not to be cluttered with trivial or
misdirected cases and if emergency or acute problems are not to
be lost in the mass of less urgent ones. Many of those involved in
what we have called case location on the first level are not called
upon to go further than the brief screening decisions in their case
appraisals.

At times, more systematic types of case evaluation are not undertaken where they should be, but the brief screening decisions are needed in their own right. They are inevitably made, because a client is there, in hand, and has to be sent home, sent elsewhere, or dealt with in the agency itself. There must be an exercise of some discretion at once, for better or for worse.

Far too often, the instructions under which personnel operate give them no choice but to make their screening decisions only in terms of the severity of the offense or the existence of a prior record of offenses. Where personnel are unprepared for the assignment, there is some protection for clients in this. Gradually, however, one might hope that all policemen on beats and receptionists in these agencies would have enough basic orientation to "the fundamental concepts of human behavior, including the need to consider the total person as well as any specific disorder," [11] so as to be able to exercise a greater degree of discretion in knowledgeable fashion. Community policy might still dictate that certain circumstances or offenses would lead directly to arrest or to the courtroom, but there would be more skill in determining when other matters might be completely dropped and when referral for study or fuller processing in the case finding agency was indicated.

Clergymen, housing managers, and recreation workers are increasingly exposed to influences and training which might guide their decisions, but they have need of consultation resources as well. An agreement with a family agency or a clinic which permits informal conversation as situations develop is extremely helpful and may lead to competent handling by the case finder or to initiation of an appropriate referral for more comprehensive evaluation or for service.

Even at present, however, it is reasonable to expect that juvenile aid specialists, attendance officers, representatives of child protective services, and other child care *specialists* will be equipped for such evaluation. One of the major contributions of such personnel, in fact, is made through their brief screening decisions

[11] From recommendation No. 8, Mid-century White House Conference on Children and Youth, 1950. It is necessary to add the caution that while learning to understand normal human development and its variations, professional workers in other fields must not give up their specialist roles to become psychotherapists. See C. A. Roberts, *Community Mental Health Services* (New York: Milbank Memorial Fund, 1959), p. 73.

and their orientation of the less-prepared personnel as to the basis for decisions.

All personnel involved in brief screening need to understand that knowing when not to drop a situation and lose an opportunity is neither more nor less important than avoiding community involvement where the family is capable of handling its own problems. Awareness of when to request full social or psychiatric study within one's agency, or at another appropriate place, is as necessary as ability to make immediate decisions in some cases on the basis of available data.

Disposition evaluations. The line between the brief screening decision and what might be called *disposition evaluations* is not too sharp in some settings but is very clear in others. Thus, the juvenile aid patrolman makes some decisions merely by looking at the report filed by the officer on the beat who received a complaint about a child; he may mail out a letter or call somebody in to be "warned." He may, on the other hand, decide that the case requires fuller consideration and may undertake (or another staff member may undertake) a somewhat more comprehensive social study leading to a disposition evaluation.

The better-known illustration is, of course, that of the probation officer whose defined task (except in treatment and supervision cases) is to conduct a social study so as to prepare a disposition recommendation. The detention social service staff, or a court diagnostic clinic, is also often designated to undertake social and psychiatric case study for the guidance of the court in its disposition planning. While it usually houses, in its probation bureau, what might be called a casework treatment service, the juvenile court is, in fact, the prime example of an agency organized around the process of disposition evaluation (adjudication and probation investigations) and case disposition making. Detention and clinic contribute their evaluations as arms of the court.

At a subsequent point we shall elaborate on the nature of the court's most specialized and unique form of case evaluation, *adjudication of status*. The probation study, which should be used only following adjudication, is in many respects similar to the case evaluations in many other types of setting and is designed to help the judge choose from among case discharge, community-based service, or institutionalization as dispositions after adjudication.

Diagnostic centers and reception centers are specialized facilities for case evaluation, set up to implement the Youth Authority notion of a centralized authority which makes differential treatment assignments—or to facilitate the functioning of a diversified network of services. Observed activities, tests, and individual case studies in such centers all contribute to the final evaluations. There has been considerable development of knowledge and skill in this work. Where diagnostic and reception centers exist, they are, in effect, allotted a portion of the court's disposition decision through statutory or administrative assignment.

Mention might be made of another type of disposition evaluation agency: there are places where a clinic is assigned statutory responsibility for determining whether a child of retarded mental development belongs at home, in a regular class, or in a specialized class.

The line between brief screening and the disposition evaluation ceases to be quite so sharp as one turns away from these specialized disposition agencies. There are, in fact, many gradations of evaluation—a necessary consequence of the variety of relationships which community agencies have with those whose cases are "found." For example, the schools' child health stations, welfare departments, voluntary social agencies, hospitals, clinics, and settlement houses do not meet all their obligations or make their full contributions through brief screening of all cases to which they are alerted. Our studies show that agency failures, the disappearance of cases in the gaps between agencies, the "opportunities lost" are sometimes traceable to instances in which agencies in this category do not follow their case finding with adequate case appraisal—because it is not dictated by their functions, narrowly conceived.

These agencies are often staffed by highly skilled personnel (the family agencies or child guidance clinics, for example) or by personnel whom it would not be too difficult to prepare for the necessary evaluations. Their relationships with families and their access to information is generally such that they are well situated to go beyond brief screening if the first, brief appraisal is not fully reassuring. This is not a proposal for anything as elaborate as a probation case study, since the client in question comes into focus at a point when the agency has a good deal of background data about the family or another of its members. Moreover, since the objects of the case finding usually do not, at this point, regard themselves as in need of service, they are not prepared to have their family's relationship with the agency formally converted into a case study process. What is possible, however, is the study of data already in the record and the systematic addition of available observations and reports. These become the basis for a sound referral decision or a decision, in the instance of the family service agency or guidance clinic, to offer service to a member of the family who is not the original "client."

Where the majority of staff are poorly prepared, as in many public assistance programs, or where the professional time allocated by a specialist is too limited to permit much time for this role, as in the case of the pediatrician in a busy child health station, the responsibility for evaluation and follow-through might be assigned a qualified social worker within the department. Case consultants or social service staff members, whatever their titles, undertake the agency's disposition evaluation where the brief screening of the original agency observer (case finder) indicates that it is necessary. School social workers are formally assigned this function, providing more complete evaluations of cases which the classroom teacher screens out.

Since it will probably be the situation for some time to come that there will be disposition agencies without access to staff capable of providing all the essential disposition evaluations, and since some disposition evaluations require quite specialized (clinical, medical) judgments, special facilities will continue to be necessary. New York City's Family Court, for example, makes use of social and psychiatric study reports prepared at the court's request in detention, psychiatric reports from its own clinic or (at times) community clinics, medical and psychiatric reports from hospitals with observation facilities, reports from social agencies and special school services. A sound community plan should certainly always ensure availability of such centers which, at the request of an agency with disposition responsibility, provide necessary case evaluations to guide disposition. Planning, however, should seek to ensure that an agency with a substantial disposition function is equipped with staff adequate to its primary task—even though it should not be expected to have all the specialized resources needed to appraise some of its cases.

As has been emphasized, recommendations appended to a case evaluation must be based on a realistic appraisal of facilities available.[12] One might add that this imposes an obligation upon those who prepare such evaluations and recommendations, as well as on legally constituted disposition authorities like judges, to keep personally acquainted with the resources on which they draw.

Two major problems cause concern in this field. First, far too many cases are disposed of without access to adequate case evaluations. Second, current disposition recommendations deal more adequately with personality dimensions than they do with sociocultural dimensions, or even medical factors, which should affect case planning. Before it can be solved, the former problem will require staff and resource expansion as well as changes in philosophy in many agencies. It will also demand certain administrative and professional-role decisions best discussed in the context of individual programs. (For example: The comprehensiveness of a probation officer's case evaluation is affected by what the judge routinely does with such evaluations; the likelihood that a home relief investigator will be concerned with the development of children will reflect agency philosophy.) The second problem, that of the dimensions of case evaluations, will be affected by the rate at which broader concepts of social deviance are incorporated into training programs and begin to be understood in their treatment implications.

Case evaluations to guide service and treatment. Complaints are often heard from clinics or institutions which accept referral cases to the effect that the disposition evaluation sent by the referral source was not adequate and that they have had to undertake their own intake studies. Or the referring agencies have reported that the agencies accepting cases for treatment have not respected them and their social studies and have duplicated the work. Such complaints are sometimes justified, but they are frequently based on

[12] Harris B. Peck and Virginia Bellsmith, *Treatment of the Delinquent Adolescent* (New York: Family Service Association of America, 1954), p. 23.

misunderstanding as to the nature of the case evaluation which guides an agency's services or treatment.

The children's institution must decide which cottage is appropriate for a committed child and must also assign him to a school or vocational program. Decisions must be made relative to possible casework or psychiatric plans and assignments as well. These are decisions which can be made only in the institution and on the basis of data assembled by institution staff acquainted with the prevailing treatment philosophy, bases for decisions, and current status of resources and workloads. Reformatories and prisons know that (depending on size) they require classification staff or classification units, to plan for maximum impact of program on inmates.

Similarly, a child guidance clinic which accepts a case on referral from the school cannot avoid some case study and evaluation as the basis for decisions which only it can make relative to case assignment, frequency of interviews, whether the parents are to be seen regularly and by the same staff member, whether group therapy is to be included in the program, and so on.

This suggests, then, that it is not only the case finding agency and the case disposition agency which must be staffed for case evaluation. Almost every service center, treatment agency, or institution must begin its work with a treatment-oriented case evaluation, incorporating the dimensions relevant to the program unless its peculiar relationships with the referral sources assure it of the required evaluation (as when a guidance clinic and residential treatment center are under one administrative auspices) or (as in the instance of Youth Authority programs) unless it is part of a system of facilities which receive their cases through one diagnostic and screening center.

Some comments on case classification. In a sense, the case evaluation process is one aimed at case classification, the assumption being that cases of a certain class are best dealt with in specified ways. While such classification may be too much to expect of some personnel at the level of the brief screening decisions, it is obviously the objective, the only reasonable objective, of disposition evaluations and of case evaluations made to guide service. Part of the difficulty in children's services today derives from the lack of an adequate case classification system, sometimes called case typology, to guide case evaluation. There has been some tendency to act as though psychiatric diagnostic categories might serve this purpose, but study reveals that (a) psychiatric diagnostic systems, particularly in the children's field, are terribly inconsistent and are very much in need of codification to permit reasonable communication; [13] (b) psychiatric diagnostic systems do not incorporate all dimensions essential to treatment decisions; children in a given diagnostic category might require a variety of disposition plans in view of factors not taken into account in the diagnostic labeling. This is not an unexpected finding, since diagnostic systems have, traditionally, been based in theory about etiology.

RESOURCE LOCATION AND CASE REFERRAL

In a responsible community system, case finding and case study must lead either to a decision that nothing more need be done or to the location of a resource which will intervene or offer service or treatment. Moreover, client and resource must be brought together (referral) in a fashion which ensures that something constructive may begin.

While this phase of service flows naturally after case evaluation, it requires special attention and deserves it own name because of its characteristic problems. In addition, there do exist agencies and bureaus which devote all, or substantial portions of, their resources to this effort, and they deserve notice, i.e., a children's placement division in a child welfare department or a placement unit in a probation department.

One cannot, with any conscience, end the process at the point of diagnosis or screening. Somebody (and more often than not it will be the case evaluation agency) must translate an appraisal into its service implications: Who can offer the help required? In the real world of waiting lists and shortages in all categories of

---

[13] *For Children in Trouble*, pp. 25–29 and footnote p. 29. Also, Alfred J. Kahn, "Some Problems Facing Social Work Scholarship," *Social Work*, II, No. 2 (April, 1957), 54–62; Group for Advancement of Psychiatry, *The Diagnostic Process in Child Psychiatry* (New York, 1957). Also, Samuel Finestone, "Issues Involved in Developing Diagnostic Classifications for Casework," *Casework Papers, 1960* (New York: Family Service Association of America, 1960), pp. 139–54, and Board of Corrections, State of California, *Inquiries Concerning Kinds of Treatment for Kinds of Delinquents* (Sacramento: California State Printing Office, 1961).

facilities, the problem becomes one of locating the resource which is available at the time needed and which meets the basic conditions specified in the case appraisal. A community—and there are far too many—in which shortages and gaps are so severe as to make this a hopeless process is, of course, not equipped for effective work with its children.

The service-planning agency or unit which closes a case or uses an inappropriate service because "no treatment resources are available" must immediately list the case as a community failure. Its minimum obligation is a regular report to the community on the frequency of such occurrences. Some agencies assume the broader obligation to help fill community gaps.

In work with deprived, troubled, fearful, and disturbed people, it is never enough to identify a resource and provide child or parent with a referral card. The agency has the obligation of working with those who are being referred until they understand the objectives of the referral on whatever level is possible and are motivated to establish the new contact. The client's perception should then be conveyed to the agency itself in an appropriate summary. Such preparation, often a function of skillful social casework, is equally necessary when a child, whatever his attitudes, will be taken physically to a new facility (an institution). Our institutions are full of those who "do time" and who perceive themselves as community exiles; they have not been oriented in advance to the potentials of the program and do not understand why they have been committed. In fact, misunderstanding is often so extreme or resistance so completely neglected by referral or committing sources as to make success most unlikely.

Where resources are in short supply, competitive "shopping" as between agencies or between staff members in one agency may become a serious problem. It can be dealt with appropriately only if *community* priorities are identified, through the work of planning and coordinating bodies, and are translated into agency policy. Centralized community child placement or assignment of centralizing responsibility within each of the major placement agencies (i.e., court) would seem to be an essential part of planning.

Service planning, resource location, and case referral are functional areas in which many of the current community problems lie. Solutions must be based on responsible use of resources and re-

sponsible relationships between agencies; adequate agency reporting of gaps and difficulties to one another, as well as to coordinating
groups and to the community at large; accountability of the agency
and of the practitioner for the individual case, until the transition
is made from case evaluation to necessary service.

INTERVENTION, SERVICE, TREATMENT

No one word encompasses the variety of action prescriptions to
which situation finding and case evaluation lead. Perhaps three
words may suffice to describe the range of possibilities: intervention,
service, treatment. At times, only neighborhood organization or
work with local youth gangs will do. At other times, a small group,
a child, or a family may need to be assured of service (vocational
guidance, a homemaker, etc.) or treatment (individual or group
psychotherapy, etc.).

The costly activities involved in large-scale case finding, court
hearings, social studies, diagnostic referrals, and the like may have
secondary "social control" functions, i.e., showing community concern for and reaction to certain behavior. Apart from police protective work, however, they cannot be defended solely as such.
The community's investment in these functions is not repaid unless this elaborate process, of finding problems and sorting those
to be ignored from those requiring attention, is capped by adequate
investment in well-used services and facilities. The skilled practitioner in these fields has no basis for satisfaction in the competence
of his performance unless his diagnosis and recommendations lead
somewhere. *Intervention* is a convenient generic term which suggests service, treatment, community planning, and social action.

To talk of a service and treatment armamentarium implies a
degree of necessary diversification to meet a variety of relevant
factors such as age, sex, degree of involvement, nature of causal
factors, special resources required, family and community strengths
and resources, a decision to intervene on the family, the peer-group,
or the neighborhood level, and the like. Inevitably, as skill and
knowledge develop, new methods are discovered (Ch. X) and new
considerations enter into the choice of form of intervention. A
community pattern of diversified service and treatment resources
is, therefore, an ever-changing and a never-completed pattern.

The following random illustrative list incorporates *some* of the

facilities and activities now important to an urban area as it seeks
to ensure, either under its own auspices, or through county and
state resources as well, the range of required interventions, treatment, and service specializations:

(1) family service agencies
(2) child guidance clinics
(3) general medical facilities and clinics
(4) homemakers and home helps
(5) mental hospital facilities and clinics, including so-called
day hospitals and night hospitals
(6) child welfare services
(7) foster homes of various kinds
(8) group day care and day care homes
(9) institutions of several kinds, including training schools
(10) residential treatment centers
(11) forestry and work camps
(12) youth residence clubs and hostels
(13) probation and parole
(14) big brother and big sister programs
(15) special school programs for children with handicaps or
particular needs
(16) vocational guidance and placement resources
(17) religious counseling
(18) recreation and group work facilities, as well as the variety
of resources in settlements and neighborhood centers
(19) summer camps of several kinds
(20) educational guidance resources
(21) local self-help programs and neighborhood "mobilizations,"
with a variety of primary objectives

Resources such as these are required by many children, normal
and maladjusted, not only those "in trouble" in the sense of this
discussion. Reasons of efficiency as well as cost dictate that there
not be separate systems of service in these categories (residential
treatment and educational guidance, to take two very different
examples). Whether policy or treatment considerations justify any
segregation by categories into treatment facilities (court clinics,
training schools for delinquents, institutions for the neglected) is
best examined in the context of discussion of the specific programs.

Our basic attitude is that the detection channels must be alert to categories and circumstances under which need arises, but that the intervention system should be one diversified system in which need and potential impact, not label, determine assignment to a facility.

Emphasis on the community's entire range of service equipment and its adequate diversification places an obligation on the individual agency, whether public or private, to identify its unique role and to relate that role to changing needs and knowledge. An agency asking for support from individual donors or out of tax funds surely has no right to perpetuate services unless they are constantly validated, in the sense of being shown to be needed in the community pattern and to be effective. An agency is called upon to define and publicize its special treatment or service offerings, so that it may be drawn upon as clients' treatment-service prescriptions dictate.

We do not wish to imply that an agency is, alone, in a position to relate itself to total need or to find its place in the community resource pattern. Planning and integration functions are essential to the community, and these will be discussed below.

REPORTING

Adequate data about clientele, their characteristics, their sources and dispositions, as well as caseload and staffing facts, should be regularly provided by individual agencies to the community and to other agencies. Some agencies have unfortunately been quite lax about this responsibility; others have sought to publish statistical reports regularly but have used outmoded systems, so that crucial questions are not answerable. Many large children's courts, for example, tabulate cases but do not tabulate the number of different children who appear before the court, do not record many kinds of data essential to analysis of clientele and operations, and use statistical methods which do not allow for analysis of interrelationships of factors which are tabulated (i.e., the relation between length of probation treatment and status at discharge).

The availability of statistical reports on a regular basis permits those concerned to keep informed of the size and characteristics of the problem faced and the resources being deployed to meet it.

Caseload data, data about overcrowding, waiting-list facts also serve to highlight some of the indications of unmet need and inadequate service. If the agency adds its own evaluation and analysis to this, the picture is enriched and the report makes significant contributions to community planning and improvement of services.

To all of this, however, must be added a new concept: the obligation in certain situations to report at the point of case-closing. An agency that has accepted a referral or commitment and thereby has become the community's representative in dealing with a person who may harm himself or others is accountable to the community. Some central registration source, or, in the absence of such source, the referring agency, must know that the case is being closed following a period of what is judged to be satisfactory service, or that a client has "disappeared," "refused to cooperate," or simply has not shown improvement. When warranted, designated steps should then be taken to initiate a new attempt, to watch the situation, or to agree that nothing more will be done.

More specifically, if a boy is discharged by a court because he has begun voluntary treatment at a guidance clinic, the clinic has no right to close the case subsequently, as a failure, without some community provision for returning the child to the court, informing the school, alerting the police, offering help through a community center, or making some other responsible plan for community protection and individual treatment. Similarly, particularly where legally constituted "authority" has planned treatment after adjudication, the record, in justice to the individual concerned, should report successful completion of a course of treatment.

While the concept seems clear, the development of practical mechanisms for reporting of this kind and for avoidance of undue regimentation of agencies or of individuals has not, to our knowledge, been undertaken for any large urban area. Some suggestions for accountability devices will be developed in further detail in Chapter XII. It must be said here that while special central registers have demonstrated their potentials for caseload analysis and community planning, they have not yet continued long enough or broadly enough for their full exploitation as instruments of case accountability.

MEASUREMENT AND EVALUATION

The entire discussion so far has presented the case for periodic evaluation of both the total pattern and single agency services, but brief remarks may be in order at this point. The ultimate test of the impact of a community pattern of services is the test of effectiveness. Research specialists agree that the establishment of controls and specification of all aspects of the service "exposure" pose formidable methodological problems.[14] There are consequently few significant studies that measure the successes of a single agency or of a community plan. The problem deserves and has achieved high priority status in agencies and research centers, however, and must remain in the forefront of attention.

While unable to do this kind of research, the typical agency has ongoing responsibility for self-evaluation, with particular attention to its flexibility in relation to changing needs, its staff qualifications, its relationships with other services, and its "failures" (in the sense described above). Beyond this, every community must, officially or by agreement, establish responsibility for constant review and appraisal of the total community pattern of services and its component parts. There is precedent for initiative in this area on the part of community chests and councils, public bodies, and independent groups concerned with child welfare. Using the methods most appropriate to the situation and the relationships involved, such evaluations reveal gaps, set the sights for the future, and help prepare public opinion for the expenditures involved in rendering service.

SERVICE INTEGRATION, PLANNING, AND COORDINATION

Tradition, law, chance, knowledge, and logic have in various combinations determined the individual functions of agencies. Some undertake case finding, evaluation, and treatment. Others are limited to one or another function or, at least, to emphasis on certain

[14] Elizabeth Herzog, *Some Guide Lines for Evaluative Research,* U.S. Children's Bureau Publication No. 375 (Washington, D.C.: Government Printing Office, 1959). Also see Paul Schreiber, *How Effective Are Services for the Treatment of Delinquents,* Juvenile Delinquency Facts and Facets, No. 9 (Washington, D.C.: Government Printing Office, 1960).

activities. There is little difference of opinion about the function or combination of functions of some agencies, whereas others are surrounded by confusion and controversy.

A community which is concerned with its approach to children in trouble must review the roles of its major agencies periodically. For example: What are appropriate functions for a juvenile aid bureau? Should a court clinic diagnose or also treat? Should "neglect" investigations be assigned the police, the welfare department, or a Society for the Prevention of Cruelty to Children? Is there a separate "attendance" function in a school system?

Even if well defined, for internal purposes, agency programs are not well interrelated unless there is community-wide understanding and unless coordinating devices are developed. What, for example, might be done to solve particularly perplexing problems in the field of child placement which result from information lacks, from poor coordination, and from undefined intake criteria?

Analysis of current community experiences gives emphasis to the need for the following:

(1) devices to *integrate* the services of one agency with the other so as to ensure a concert of services on the level of *case operations* and to eliminate gaps between agencies as they affect the individual case;

(2) means to interrelate agency functions and to *coordinate* their *programs;*

(3) provision for evaluation and long-range *planning,* so that agencies adapt and change their functions and functioning, and new services are created as required;

(4) *reporting* and *accountability* arrangements.

The necessary structures to implement these functions should be designed to ensure continued diversity of programs, flexibility, efficiency, and responsibility. The concept of the independent voluntary agency, sectarian and nonsectarian, belongs in the total picture, as does the basic public program. Professionals, volunteers, and semiprofessional technicians are necessary. Well-established and tried institutions have their contribution to make, as do the small, new, pioneer efforts. Research and demonstration play their parts, to ensure the charting of the future.

These, then, are the functions. A community plan requires the identification of essential functions, their assignment to agencies, and their coordination. How are such functions best distributed? Which agencies have major roles and how are they to be carried out? Our attention now turns to agencies and their tasks. Major emphasis will be on services traditionally designated for "children in trouble," but the logic of service planning and the fundamental orientation of our approach require that certain other institutions and services be considered as well. Accountability, service integration, planning, and coordination will be addressed in further detail in the concluding chapters, when their full implications may be described on the basis of concepts about the roles of specific services and the problems which are posed for them.

In the chapters which follow immediately no attempt is made to deal with all aspects of the services of schools, courts, institutions, or police—to cite a few. At all points, the concern is with the community system as an accountable, integrated network with defined goals. How is such a system to be conceived? What is each agency's contribution? Does the concept of system demand changes in agencies or new types of programs?

Part B

AGENCIES AND FUNCTIONS

CHAPTER IV

THE COMMUNITY
"OPEN DOOR"

THE COMMUNITY is not in a position to ensure efficient early detection of those who need help or to make such help available to those ready to ask for it unless there are available, in the system of agencies, institutions, and facilities, a series of "open doors."

Problems do not always neatly divide themselves up so that they are obviously in the provinces of particular community facilities. If a child needs a tonsillectomy, it may be clear that a hospital or a doctor with facilities in his private office needs to be involved. Grand larceny, when detected, leads directly to the court, at least initially. But what of the parents who cannot manage their fifteen-year-old daughter, who are worried about the enuresis of their eight-year-old boy, and who cannot manage financially on the irregular earnings of a father who is periodically depressed? Is there any one center to which this problem should automatically gravitate? If there were, could one expect the typical resident of a large city to know when he should turn to a hospital clinic, when to a child guidance clinic, when to the court, when to a family service agency, and when to one of a dozen other possible facilities? Further, if needed help is fragmented and lodged in a series of places, can we expect the pressured, below-par family to integrate the several services and to relate them to each other?

A recent national survey found that a significant proportion of those who reported that they could have used professional help, but did not receive it, were people who simply did not know of an appropriate professional resource.[1] Is the average citizen to be expected to know his way in a world of specialization in mental health, public welfare, health, education, and so on?

The "open door" has to do with the accessibility of an agency or facility to people who may not know where their problems belong and with the operation of such agency or facility so as to ensure an adequate overview of the problem and a transition to the appropriate service. It also involves the availability in the community of places to which people may turn for guidance if they do not have any notions at all as to the "channels" in which their problems belong. Exploration of the "open door" is thus an aspect of further elaboration of the case finding concept.

Those who fear the community around them because they do not understand it, because they consider themselves inadequate, or because they have acted aggressively and therefore expect to be greeted with hostility need the "open door." Those whose lives are in crisis and who may, as a result, not be functioning at their full capacities and with their best judgment need it too. Even the average, reasonably competent citizen cannot be expected at all times to find his way, unaided, in the forest of community bureaucracies.

Interest in the creation of a series of "open doors" is, of course, not limited to those who would provide for more effective work with children in trouble. The problems of the "opportunity lost" and of the client who "falls" in the gaps between agencies are general to the field of social welfare in its current state of expansion, professionalization, and incomplete coverage.

While our present discussion cannot encompass all of social welfare, it can stress that adequate consideration of planning for children in trouble is impossible without discussion of the "open door." We have referred to the need for a place to which an individual seeking help and guidance may turn, on his own initiative. The destinies of children are often involved in these situations. In addition, many of those case finders who are not part of professionally staffed agencies or who have little basis for initiative vis-à-vis those requiring help need access to a place which does not

[1] Gerald Gurin *et al.*, *Americans View Their Mental Health* (New York: Basic Books, Inc., 1960), pp. 348–50.

have rigid rules, inflexible procedures, or forbidding routines. It must be made possible for a storekeeper, a housing manager, a local physician, a policeman on the beat to say to Mr. X or to Mrs. X the equivalent of: "I see that you need help. I do not know exactly what is wrong or what help you need. I probably would be prying excessively if I tried to find out. Why not go down to the —————— center and see what they say?"

True, many neighborhoods have their storekeeper, clergyman, or senior citizens who advise and guide others. Unfortunately, population movements and the complexities of modern social services have substantially curtailed and decreased the adequacy of such informal help, although it should have all possible support and reinforcement. The established, advertised "open door" is one more instance in which social change demands organized community provision where once spontaneous human relationships filled a need.

This chapter deals with two aspects of the community "open door." First, there is the problem of how any large community service may make itself available for referral and steering—so that those in doubt may enter and be assured of more than an impersonal "You do not belong here." Then there is the question of whether a community needs a specialized, widely advertised "open door" facility, perhaps on the model of the Citizens' Advice Bureaux in England. Specific attention will be directed to three types of agencies which have relevant traditions, experience, or legal mandates: *public welfare departments, family service agencies,* and *settlements.* It is recognized that tradition and local initiative have created "open doors" under other auspices in specific communities (service clubs, churches, political clubs, for example) and that these should be encouraged. They do not, however, suggest a broadly applicable pattern. Nor do we deal here with health centers, which have a broad, case finding function but which, because of their primary functions, cannot generally play the role specified in urban America, although they may elsewhere. Schools are so important in their case finding, evaluation, and referral roles as to demand a full, subsequent, chapter.

In beginning this discussion it may be useful to refer to an instance in which an agency which cannot serve all possible community situations has ensured its accessibility to those who need it. The California Bureau of Social Work, which is the aftercare system for the state mental hospitals, has one person in the office on "office call" in each district, and assigns staff to this on a rotating basis. The "office call" worker handles situations presented by people who walk in, phone, or write in for help—but are not the department's patients. The worker on duty gives necessary information, often renders brief casework service, and makes necessary referrals. Thousands of people use this service annually.

As we turn to the agencies here in special focus it must be noted that we shall not undertake full analysis of the contributions and potentialities of public welfare, family service, or settlements. New, important service and treatment tendencies, for example, are reviewed in another context. Here the focus is on those activities and functions which make it clear to the community that an agency's door is "open" even to those not eligible for long-term service—or which create an all-purpose, specialized "open door" facility. General information about trends in these fields is provided only in so far as it is necessary and relevant background.

THE FAMILY SERVICE AGENCY

There are approximately 300 agencies affiliated with the Family Service Association of America, the national standard-setting organization in family social work. In a recent year they served over 300,000 families, many very briefly and some intensively. While a handful of the affiliated agencies are governmental, the typical member is a family service society under voluntary auspices which, in the main, devotes most of its resources to offering casework services to individuals and families with a wide range of personal and social adjustment problems. The help given may require social resources, personal guidance, or both.

Present-day family service agencies developed out of the charity organization societies of the late nineteenth century and the even earlier Associations for the Improvement of the Conditions of the Poor. While in their first several decades they undertook many activities (coordination, central registry, social legislation, courses and classes, penny banks, etc.), they increasingly devoted the bulk of their energies to granting financial assistance and to personal guidance and counseling. They played the crucial role in the gradual development and refinement of casework as a method of helping and did much to launch formal social work training. The present situation is outlined by the General Director of the F.S.A.A.:

During the past two decades, public welfare agencies have assumed the major responsibility for providing financial assistance and related welfare services for families in need. Voluntary family agencies now chiefly offer counseling services to families and individuals with problems of personal and social adjustment; they also provide a number of social resources, such as homemakers, camps, and nursery schools, and make available certain special services such as legal aid and vocational counseling.[2]

The "social resources" are not the major function. The family caseworker in effect has had to define his service in relationship terms and this definition has taken place in a period when the influence of psychiatry has been all-pervasive in social work.[3] As a result, there has been great emphasis on client motivation for treatment and a tendency to regard a client unable to meet treatment requirements in agency terms as "uncooperative" or "not accessible." Service has tended to be rendered through office interviews, and home visits have declined markedly. Technical casework has been preoccupied with the perfection of methodology for work with the psychoneurotic and near-psychotic patient—as has been the case with psychiatry per se.

While many of the leaders of the field stressed a balanced psychosocial approach,

in their enthusiasm to utilize psychological treatment means, caseworkers sometimes tended to negate the values of what had been achieved by social treatment means and the supportive relationship. This led them to move from the family as a whole to a preoccupation with the individual, from emphasis upon external factors and consideration of the influences of the social milieu upon the lives of the family and the individual to preoccupation with intrapsychic conflicts of the individual. . . . They

[2] Clark W. Blackburn, "Family Social Work," in Russell Kurtz, ed., *Social Work Year Book, 1957* (New York: National Association of Social Workers, 1957), p. 247.

[3] Alfred J. Kahn, "The Nature of Social Work Knowledge," in Cora Kasins, ed., *New Directions in Social Work* (New York: Harper & Brothers, 1954), pp. 194–214, and "Sociology and Social Work: Challenge and Invitation," *Social Problems*, IV, No. 3 (January, 1957), 220–28.

sometimes tended to overemphasize individual pathology and to under-estimate ego strengths. Sometimes social conditions as factors affecting family life came to be regarded as of secondary significance, and there was a tendency to regard social means of treatment as having little value.[4]

Improvements of method and redefinition of function vis-à-vis a subsegment of potential clientele have had the effect of converting the family agency from an all-purpose community center for help into a quite specialized facility, available to those prepared for the service offered, but not involved in the service to the remainder. In its extreme form (the minority), the family agency became an adult mental hygiene and personal counseling center—and thus a resource for the middle-class community, not for relief-eligible lower-class clients.

A systematic review found that a large portion of cases (perhaps 50–75 percent) in the typical family agency are in the "brief service" group, i.e., are seen less than twice or less than five times. In some instances, the service is completed in the one contact; in far more cases, steering or referral to another agency is called for. The third subcategory, which may be found to total from one third to almost one half of brief service cases, is of greatest concern: these are persons "who come to the family service agency because of problems of personal adjustment or interpersonal relations, but who do not respond to the offer of further service." [5] While many factors enter into these reactions, from the attitudes and motivations of the clients to the noncooperation of other family members, there is persistent evidence that one important influence is the inability of caseworkers to meet some clients on their own grounds. Perhaps, too, the form of help offered, a casework relationship through interviews, is not understandable and acceptable to members of all social and cultural groups and individuals of all possible psychological make-up.

The family agencies have not been unaware of issues raised by data such as these. Some have expanded their functions in the

[4] Esther Schour and Jennie Zetland, "The 'Open Door'—A Point of View," *Social Service Review*, XXIX, No. 3 (1955), 285–92. Quotation is from p. 286.

[5] Ann W. Shyne, "What Research Tells Us about Short-Term Cases in Family Agencies," *Social Casework*, XXXVIII, No. 5 (1957), 223–31; Leonard S. Kogan, "The Short-Term Case in a Family Agency," *Social Casework*, XXXVIII, Nos. 5, 6, 7 (May, June, July, 1957), 231–38, 296–302, 366–74.

direction of parent education and family life education or group therapy. Others have developed homemaker programs or special services in adoption or in connection with family courts, tenant relocation, disorganized neighborhoods, camps, or health programs. A few agencies have returned to earlier conceptions of their role, emphasizing situation finding, social policy, and social action. One or two have taken leadership in these realms and have also concentrated on research and on testing new methods. As a group they adopted, in 1953, a statement on the *Scope and Methods of the Family Service Agency*, recommended by an F.S.A.A. committee. This report defined the family agency's major roles both as providing casework services and as participating in community planning.

At the same time, the technical literature of the casework field has sought to reestablish the balance between psychoanalytic and sociocultural orientations in its study of, and service to, clients. A long-established view has been reemphasized and new concepts absorbed as the agencies have reaffirmed that they are psycho*social* in outlook. As part of this, some of the leading family agencies have sought to adopt and contribute to the new emphasis on "reaching out" to clients, variously called aggressive casework, assertive casework, generic casework. Under special projects they have assigned some staff members to deal with highly resistive, multi-problem clients in unorthodox ways if necessary; special efforts are made to meet resistance, establish treatment contacts, and bring service to clients. In such cases, home visits, for example, are once again common.

Also symptomatic of new developments is the appearance in the social casework literature of emphasis on work with clients diagnosed as character disorders. The discovery that many of the people in the community who need casework service are in this diagnostic grouping, while the caseloads are made up substantially of neurotics and psychotics, has not gone unnoticed. Casework teaching has also begun to reflect the new trend in its educational attention to these new diagnostic groups and to "reaching out."

It is these newer tendencies which provide the basis for considering whether the family agency may be numbered among the community "open doors"—whether, in fact, it should be considered as *the* major, all-purpose advice center. In their 1953 *Scope and Methods* the family agencies announced clear intent in this realm:

The agency should emphasize its willingness to offer consultation both to clients and other agencies or groups in the community. Agency procedures should be flexible and should be adapted to meet the needs of the particular situation. The procedures should include reaching out to clients or interested persons by means of home visits or conferences. This willingness to give individual consideration to client and community requests is sometimes characterized as an "open door" policy.[6]

Given present limited coverage by family agencies nationally, however, they cannot be proposed as the all-purpose advice center everywhere. Fewer than 10 percent of U.S. counties now have F.S.A.A. member agencies; since these are the largest counties, they contain half the U.S. population, but only a relatively small segment have access to service. Many applicants for service find that they live outside the designated area; many others encounter long waiting lists. Family agencies are financed through community chests and limited fees; they have not solved the problem of coverage.[7]

No perspective has been presented within the family field which would convert family agencies into the major advice and referral centers. Current ideologies do suggest, however, that they might become far more "open" to those who do reach them and might thus become valuable parts of the community case finding network. In some places they might even become all-purpose advice centers. Such development would be premised on broader definition of their responsibility and some relationship to a community accountability system.

This development would be strategic in the light of what is known about family agency clientele. In an interesting study of short-term family agency cases, Leonard Kogan of New York's Community Service Society demonstrated that the bulk of these cases (constituting the majority of present family agency cases) actually call for an advice and referral service, rather than extensive treatment.

[6] Schour and Zetland, "The 'Open Door,'" *Social Service Review*, XXIX, 285, quoting *Scope and Methods of the Family Agency* (New York: Family Service Association of America, 1953).

[7] Reginald Robinson *et al.*, *Community Resources in Mental Health* (New York: Basic Books, Inc., 1960), Chapter X.

Moreover, systematic referral (which includes interpretation, support, and follow-through) "takes" far more adequately than impersonal steering, which leaves next steps to client motivation.[8]

Experts in the family field have defined how the typical family agency might open its doors.[9] Some agencies already have. It is necessary, first, that all agree that *the family agency is responsible for a diagnostic service, regardless of the presenting request, to people applying or referred whose problems lie in the area of family relationships, interpersonal relationships and social functioning.* If family agencies were willing to undertake such evaluations (at times, brief screening; at others, full case studies), they could serve other case location sources which often have nowhere to turn: the courts, public departments, churches, housing managers, and others. They would tend to attract people who want to refer themselves or their neighbors and relatives. Such case location and evaluation must be on a "come one, come all" basis, not limited as to type of problem or treatment required. It defeats its spirit and its availability if limited to those who need the long-time treatment skills of the family agency.

In a family agency which would play this role, *the primary focus is on the family as well as on the individual client who makes application to the agency.* This is fundamental. A major present difficulty is the extent to which agencies note only their primary client, as the psychoanalyst often perceives the one who has come for treatment and forgets other family members. Individual diagnosis, out of family context, is inaccurate diagnosis; people are not understandable outside of the context of their relationship patterns and responsibilities and the mutual supports and attractions, normal and pathological, which are involved. Nor is it possible to help anybody except in relation to the social milieu in which he functions and will function.

Family-centered orientation would also ensure case location

---

[8] Kogan, "The Short-Term Case in a Family Agency," *Social Casework,* XXXVIII, 231–38, 296–302, 366–74. Also see Dorothy Fahs Beck, *Patterns in Use of Family Agency Services* (New York: Family Service Association of America, 1962).

[9] The italicized quoted generalizations in the paragraphs which follow are from Schour and Zetland, "The Open Door,'" *Social Service Review,* XXIX, 285–92. The elaboration and interpretation are ours.

where the child in need of help has not yet been called to any agency's attention. The family agency worker is in an excellent position to become aware of children beginning to show problems, as they are described by parents or older siblings who are being seen in the agency for study or for help.

Broadly based diagnosis is never simply intrapsychic (i.e., dealing with one's personality structure) or even interpersonal (i.e., concerned only with relationships). It notes economic, social, cultural, and other environmental factors which add to understanding and which may hold the key to successful work with a family member or the family as a whole. The professional literature of family casework is now unanimous in its call for family diagnosis and psycho*social* treatment.

It is now understood that any truly social agency *"takes responsibility for enabling the client to use its services."* This is, perhaps, the key. An effort to enable the client to use the services almost guarantees a broad approach in case understanding and service to clients and assures flexibility in admissions criteria. The recent experiences of agencies experimenting with "reaching out" have demonstrated that adequate agency initiative may overcome hesitation, confusion, and fear based on cultural patterns, psychological problems, or environmental pressures. A caseworker's constant readiness to help during periods of stress does much to reassure and to make it possible to "take" service which is otherwise inaccessible.

This does not mean that all cases are to continue in the family agency: *"Selection of cases for ongoing treatment is based on suitability for treatment by the skills and resources of family casework."*

If the family agency has an "open door" for advice, intake, and diagnostic study, its continued-treatment cases would be a small portion of the total load, selected because family casework is precisely the service needed. Some of these will be instances in which there is need for treatment aimed at "modification of the environment, help in handling critical life events, help in interpersonal relationships and social functioning in and outside of the family." [10]

Where the basic problem to be treated is the emotional disturb-

[10] *Ibid.*

ance, family agencies may be able to help through the casework relationship; there are some differences of opinion as to the diagnostic groupings to be included, the techniques to be used, and the point at which the service is in the province of the psychiatric clinic. It is to be expected that casework will here continue its clarification and technical growth and will not accept premature freezing of a field of service still in its youth.[11] It is to be hoped that the current interest in character disorders, and other clients who are the majority in the community caseloads, will continue.

The selection of a limited portion of cases for ongoing treatment does not meet the obligation to all others for whom the diagnostic service has been the main one. The family agency has responsibility for sound referral of such cases, and this includes preparation for referral, interpretation of the referral, establishing the contact, and following the case until it is certain that a transition has been made. In short, it should be part of an accountability network.

Treatment and service models must be flexible and varied: *"The family agency accepts cases with limited treatment goals compatible with diagnosis and the client's capacities."*

Improved social functioning within established patterns is as legitimate an objective as personality change. The maintenance of a precarious balance which thus avoids serious consequences to children is no less worthy than the effort to find new balances. In the selection of those with whom it is to continue, the family agency must conceive of a variety of goals, based on criteria appropriate to the family. The issue is essentially whether the skills and resources of the family caseworker are potentially helpful, rather than whether the client might one day meet certain stereotyped expectations in relation to insight and ability to verbalize.

In short, the family agency is in a position to fulfill certain basic functions in a community approach to children in trouble as referred to in the previous chapter: case finding on all levels; case evaluation of clients who come to it and at the request of other case locators; service planning and responsible referral; specialized

[11] See Florence Hollis's formulation of current techniques in "Social Casework," *Social Work Year Book, 1957*, pp. 525–31. Also see *Social Work Practice in a Family Agency*, constituting *Social Casework*, Vol. XV, No. 4 (April, 1959).

service and treatment where appropriate. Family agencies are already rendering such services and preparing to make themselves more available. Some may also be willing to become general, all-purpose advice centers and deserve support for such experimentation—although it is doubtful that there are the resources for much expansion in this direction.

Some in the family field have noted the resource problem and have affirmed the fundamental responsibility of government for large-scale restorative services to multiproblem families. Looking at its own city, for example, the largest family agency in the world found it necessary to declare: "It is apparent . . . that the present facilities in New York for family casework do not begin to meet the over-all need . . . immediate service for family problems is today practically unobtainable in New York." [12] This agency proposed that the public welfare department expand casework treatment services and that the voluntary family service stress social action and prevention and help to rehabilitate the less-disturbed through prompt provision of consultative, advisory, and treatment measures.

However useful this perspective it does not encourage one to expect community-wide "coverage" from a family agency. Clearly the door is opening but it is a relatively small one. There will have to be other provision as well.

SETTLEMENTS

Settlements have been called "experimental stations" in neighborhoods where there is need. Each settlement seeks to develop its unique program and combination of activities because no two neighborhoods are alike and "the neighborhood is their client." [13]

The original settlements began in this country late in the nineteenth century to help meet some of the most disturbing consequences of the rapid urbanization and migration which came with the post-Civil War industrial growth. They were an ideal channel for the humanitarian impulses of the time and also a vehicle for

[12] Study Committee, Community Service Society, *Searchlight on New York* (New York, 1960), pp. 60, 61.

[13] Lois Corke De Santis, "Settlements and Neighborhood Centers," *Social Work Year Book, 1957*, p. 512.

municipal and state social reform objectives. For those served they were often unequaled as centers of help, education, acculturation, and a variety of necessary services from day care to health. Their readiness to undertake new projects in response to local needs has been one of their major assets throughout. The closeness of staff to neighborhood was the other. (The early directors were called "residents" because they settled into and resided in the neighborhoods; some still do.) By definition, the settlement always sought to have an "open door" in the past and always aspires to one today. The specific individual and group programs, clubs, recreation, sports, crafts, dancing, classes, teams, concerts, camps, meetings, are seen as vehicles for helping the development of happy individuals and sound, democratic community life.

Like the family agencies, settlements have been affected by their times. Their movement has been joined by the neighborhood centers and community centers, many of which have been primarily recreational in staffing and outlook. Decreased immigration and upward social mobility or aspirations of original residents have also limited the extent to which local residents use some of the settlements as centers in the old sense. One neighborhood house was shocked when its survey revealed that very few people in the square block on which it was located knew of its existence or program. Others have continued their close local ties and services.

Professionalization of settlement work, while ensuring more skillful work generally, has had the consequence that professionalization often has in transitional periods: staff define their functions more rigidly and the most qualified are less accessible to the general run of members, often devoting themselves to administration and supervision.

Further, settlements set up by sectarian or ethnic groups which have improved their social positions and moved away often find it difficult to adapt themselves to new groups—or to be financed if they manage the adaptation.

These problems apart, settlements remain major community resources. The National Federation of Settlements and Neighborhood Centers, a coordination and standard-setting group, has 248 members operating 287 centers in 89 cities in 30 states; there are approximately 500 other "neighborhood centered type of agencies" in the

United States which are not affiliated.[14] As might be expected, the large cities, the older cities, have best coverage. Further, the more traditional settlements are heavily concentrated in underprivileged and deteriorating neighborhoods. Those in more desirable areas or in the new suburbs are more cultural and recreational in their orientations.

Despite their variations and flexibility, settlements have tended in several directions which make them especially valuable in the total community approach to children in trouble—and which suggest even greater possibilities. At present, they come closest to filling the essential roles for lower-class clients. They make less of a claim in middle-class areas.

Case location and situation finding. "Informal counseling and a neighborly type of home visiting" are carried on by almost every member of a settlement staff. The settlement is in a position to locate those in the early stages of difficulty as well as those in serious trouble and seeking help. The old-line settlements in underprivileged areas have deep roots and many contacts and they learn which families are in trouble. They often find ways to get to them. If the neighborhood ties are firm, settlement workers also know the informal groupings of children and the gangs, and are aware of those which are becoming or have become antisocial. The club activities, craft programs, dances, lounge activities, and other phases of settlement work provide ample occasion to identify those who are deviant and need to be looked at more carefully. Settlements are also, at their best, a place where a parent or adolescent child can find a staff member to talk to, share anxieties, express doubts, and ask where help might be available. Settlement workers can detect the prevalence of drug use, the existence of local racketeering, the development of tensions between youth gangs, the circumventing of housing laws by irresponsible landlords. They are thus *situation finders.*

While their coverage is never complete in any one neighborhood and certainly not in any one city, and while there are cities which are hardly touched, these opportunities make the fully developed

[14] Margaret Berry, "Settlements and Neighborhood Centers," in Russell H. Kurtz, ed., *Social Work Year Book, 1960* (New York: National Association of Social Workers, 1960), pp. 523–29.

settlement programs almost ideal case location and situation finding agencies for the neighborhoods served. They seek to remain such as "one of the few agencies in contemporary society that is not wholly formalized, bureaucratized, channelized . . . that offers a personal, face-to-face relationship in which a whole human being can be seen and talked to in something like his . . . life situation." [15] Staffs are already trained to be alert to problems and need only defined channels and policy. These often, but not always, exist. The help must be offered, not forced, available and not required. The very offer must be carefully timed and gradual—but the group workers and other settlement staff are qualified for this, or should be. Emphasis on this function and settlement tie-in to community accountability machinery or neighborhood coordination measures would add substantially to the effectiveness of the effort.

Case evaluation and referral. Some settlements employ caseworkers, psychiatrists, psychologists, and others and offer their own counseling and guidance services. Others serve as outposts for such services, i.e., offer space for extension centers. Still others simply make referrals or call upon agencies for consultation. Each pattern has its validity depending on the total community resource picture. It might be noted, however, that since it is known that many cases are lost in referral, there is no basic objection to having at least case study and diagnostic resources within the settlement, if there is no other community provision. Where there are no such resources, the settlement case locator ought to follow through to make sure that the request for case evaluation leads to such evaluation, and that the client is neither frightened nor discouraged. If his relationship is a close one, the settlement worker might also offer to participate in the transition to a treatment service.

Where the settlement house has its own direct service resources, it has the same responsibility as the family agency to select those clients who can be helped within its range of services and to ensure the transition into a treatment relationship of those who require referral outside.

Intervention-service-treatment potential. The settlement is a versatile treatment and service resource and may meet the needs

[15] National Federation of Settlements and Neighborhood Centers, *Neighborhood Goals in a Rapidly Changing World* (New York, 1958), p. 13.

of many in early difficulty and some in more serious trouble. By definition, it is a voluntary resource but its expression of interest and skillful efforts to make service available ensure it widespread receptivity.

There are, first, those who need intimate peer-group experiences under wise adult supervision, to enable them to grow, learn to handle personal relationships, and develop broader citizenship responsibilities. The group work programs of settlement houses are appropriate—or should be. Others need skills or hobbies of the sort they can learn in settlement programs, or opportunity to find their own way in the more "mass" social and recreational activities. Neighborhood centers and settlements have always provided these.

It may occasionally be appropriate for settlement houses to offer the equivalent of family agency treatment services or to house child guidance or adult mental hygiene facilities, but this can be determined only with reference to the total community resource picture and in cooperation with the responsible planning and coordination agencies. It is certainly appropriate for the settlement to house group therapy if not otherwise readily available. Nor are there many settings more suitable as a base for the "detached worker" who moves out into the neighborhood to locate and develop a relationship with the unsocial or antisocial gang, with the objective of bringing it into the community fold.

The settlement's most unique potential role and traditionally an important one is on the level of what we have called intermediate and immediate prevention—intervention in relation to dangerous local situations, serious community lacks, and generally unsatisfactory social environmental conditions. The specific methods and the sponsorship obtained vary with local circumstances, but the activities are generally encompassed under the headings of "citizen participation" and "interracial programs." Included are a variety of forms of neighborhood, block, and tenant organization of the self-help variety, urban renewal and tenant relocation activities, and neighborhood conservation programs.[16]

Some settlements have always been major centers for local neighborhood self-help efforts. Others have lost this function but would

[16] National Federation of Settlements and Neighborhood Centers, *Neighborhood Centers Today* (New York, 1960).

do well to resurrect it in those areas facing change, deterioration, and social pathology. The projects are per se important and have long-range preventive potential. It might also be conjectured that they have therapeutic impact on certain categories of individuals.

Coordination. Full evaluation of the settlement's coordination potential is best made in relation to other possibilities (Chs. XII and XIII). It is useful to record, however, that a settlement house which becomes a major case finding center and also the focus of local self-help efforts has a serious claim as the natural center for development of devices for case accountability, service integration, and coordination of services on the local level. Settlement leaders at a national meeting in 1958, in fact, gave special emphasis to the neighborhood center's role in the integration of social services.[17]

Well aware of the disparity between the number and resources of neighborhood centers and the size of their potential clientele, settlement workers are agreed that they must devote their resources to those sections of cities in which there are concentrations of low income families.[18] In seeking to fulfill the tasks they face and have undertaken, some settlements will have to correct major staffing deficiencies; others need to reestablish neighborhood ties. Many of the exciting innovations in programs and ways of working, which are now on the level of project, demonstration, and experiment, will have to be translated into more permanent activity.[19] All settlements must obtain considerably expanded resources.

There is evidence of enthusiasm and determination in the settlement field to meet the new needs of a rapidly changing world— and new support is being won. It may therefore be expected that where settlements exist a community concerned with children in trouble may count upon them to keep their doors "open." They may be seen as case finding and situation finding outposts, as case evaluation resources (in some instances), as referral channels, occasionally as instruments of service integration and coordination,

[17] *Neighborhood Goals in a Rapidly Changing World.*

[18] Berry, "Settlements and Neighborhood Centers," *Social Work Year Book,* 1960, pp. 523–29.

[19] *Neighborhood Centers Today* contains a large collection of impressive and promising "case" examples.

and as valuable intervention-treatment-service resources for individuals and neighborhoods. However, because the coverage of settlements is far from complete, either because settlements do not exist in many places or because there are many population elements who do not really enter settlement doors, the settlement will not of itself fill the *total* community need for a general "open door" facility.

THE PUBLIC WELFARE DEPARTMENT

There are many who would endorse strongly the view expressed by the U.S. Children's Bureau that "the major resonsibility for laying the groundwork of a sound system of community social services should rest upon the local public welfare department." [20] This would include responsibility to assure the availability of appropriate services under its own auspices as well as in schools, police departments, and courts. It implies concern with case finding and case evaluation resources as well as service and treatment facilities. As will be seen subsequently, the most enthusiastic proponents of this view also consider the state welfare agency as the logical coordinating agency for services to delinquents.[21]

The fact that the public welfare department is the only social service agency in half the counties in the country is of itself a strong argument for this view. The increasing tendency to develop comprehensive public welfare programs, emphasizing a variety of services, integrated through one state agency and concerned with prevention and case finding, suggests that it may be realistic.

The term "public welfare" is, of course, used in many ways but is clearest, for present purposes, if it includes (*a*) public assistance (Old Age Assistance, Aid to the Blind, Aid to Needy Families with Children, Aid to the Permanently and Totally Disabled, and general assistance); (*b*) assistance and services to such special groups as veterans, the mentally ill, Indians, or disaster victims, etc.; (*c*) child welfare services (adoption, licensing of institutions and foster homes, day care, foster family care, etc.); (*d*) other

[20] U.S. Children's Bureau, *Controlling Juvenile Delinquency* (Washington, D.C.: Government Printing Office, 1943), p. 19.

[21] Charles I. Schottland, "Public Welfare," *Social Work Year Book, 1957*, p. 481.

provision such as services for the aging, homemaker programs, medical programs.

Patterns of administration vary with special state and local conditions, as does the relative development of public and voluntary programs. Actual public welfare operations are performed locally either by local offices of a state agency or by county and local departments of public welfare. Several federal bureaus under the Department of Health, Education, and Welfare are involved.

The public welfare potential is underscored by the Bradley Buell findings in all the communities which he has studied intensively. A study of dependency in Winona County, Minnesota, disclosed that a close look at those who required community provision of the sheer necessities of life was, at the same time, a close look at many of those who suffer with ill health and maladjustment. In fact, about half of the families receiving service in connection with dependency were multiproblem in this sense. Maladjustment, defined to include delinquency, crime, and child neglect, was the *major* problem in 610 of 1,394 families classified as dependent; almost all of these families were receiving public welfare services and many had children known to be disturbed or antisocial.[22]

In Washington County, Maryland, where the point of focus was indigent disability (those "suffering from disabling physical conditions who must be cared for at community expense"), it was discovered that 81 percent of such families had other serious problems as well. In fact, 69 percent of the families receiving relief included one or more persons disabled in these terms. A very large proportion of the disabled required some form of public assistance or other public welfare service. A small but significant portion of these cases involved other social pathology and maladjustment.[23]

What the Buell group calls "disordered behavior" was the special project concern in San Mateo County, California (i.e., "overt behavior about which communities are compelled to take some kind of action"). It included what was previously classified in their

[22] Community Research Associates, Inc., *The Prevention of Dependency in Winona County, Minnesota* (New York, 1953).

[23] Community Research Associates, Inc., *The Prevention and Control of Indigent Disability in Washington County, Maryland* (New York, 1954).

work as maladjustment: "overt unsocial conduct, such as delinquency, child neglect, major and petty crimes or misdemeanors,
conduct requiring commitment to mental institutions . . ." but also
encompassed identifiable cases not a matter of official record. Forty-
four percent of the 5,456 "disordered behavior" families in San
Mateo were multiproblem (the figure was 56 percent in St. Paul).
Among the 1,267 families within this group who accounted for
all the family and juvenile unsocial behavior, 535 also were confronted by illness or economic need, or both. In fact, there were
very large numbers of cases (463 families) receiving relief who
had children with disordered behavior or other evidence of maladjustment (553 families).[24]

Although the Buell "disordered behavior" definition goes beyond
the "children in trouble" in the sense of delinquency and neglect,
incipient or detected, it does not in any sense exceed the first line
of case location as we have defined it: children showing early
signs of deviation. *The data serve to emphasize the opportunities
facing those who administer public assistance, child welfare, day
care, homemaker programs, and similar public welfare efforts.*

Wood found in a small New York City pilot effort dealing with
the most difficult families in public housing that half (in a not
necessarily representative sample) were known to the Welfare Department. Given adequate consultant and supervisor backing, relatively untrained social investigators serving as friendly visitors and
offering concrete services could work well with such families. The
Welfare Department was a logical and normal point of community
entry to these families whose children were already in some difficulty or exposed to considerable hazard.[25] Our own study and a
study by the New York City Youth Board dealt with more selective
groups, where the concern for the child was already quite serious,
but also gave emphasis to the Welfare Department's opportunity.[26]

[24] Community Research Associates, Inc., *The Prevention and Control of Disordered Behavior in San Mateo County, California* (New York, 1954).

[25] Elizabeth Wood, *The Small Hard Core* (New York: Citizens' Housing and
Planning Council, 1957).

[26] Alfred J. Kahn, *For Children in Trouble* (New York: Citizens' Committee
for Children of New York City, Inc., 1957), and New York City Youth Board,
Research Department, *A Study of Some of the Characteristics of 150 Multiproblem Families* (New York, 1957).

The evidence is conclusive that to render the minimum statutory service without attention to the total family situation is to defeat the general rehabilitative commitment of public welfare, and even to fail in the minimum service. In fact, Congress clarified in 1956 the authority of the federal government to participate in a state's costs in providing agency staff services so as "to maintain and strengthen family life" and to help needy people achieve increased self-care or self-support. Similar goals have long been clear in child welfare and related services. While all states have not uniformly moved in the direction encouraged by the 1956 amendments, the course appears to have been set and the pace accelerated by 1962 legislation. Most departments have ceased to limit their concern only to the granting of material assistance and have become "service conscious." Nonetheless, in most states, but not all, the social services which have been developed thus far are closely tied to the granting of material aid. Some would require local or state legislative action to change this policy. All would face serious staffing problems.[27]

In the light of these facts and trends, it is possible to discuss in general terms the view that the welfare department is the logical "open door" agency for a community. We can also outline the extent to which the welfare department might be expected to play its role in relation to the other major community functions essential in dealing with children in trouble.

Whether or not it becomes *the* all-purpose "open door" information and referral agency, the welfare department will continue a high rate of case finding. Public assistance cases will disclose serious marital problems, child welfare cases will contain elements of emotional disturbance, requests for homemakers will establish contact with children out-of-control, and so forth. And given such case finding, even a staff of subprofessionals cannot escape responsibility for *brief screening* evaluations as well. At present, situations are often ignored for lack of guidance as to how to exercise discretion— or for lack of qualified personnel available for consultation or to undertake more complete case study.

[27] Ellen Winston, "Public Welfare," *Social Work Year Book, 1960*, pp. 490–98, and Charles I. Schottland, "The Nature of Services in Public Assistance," in National Conference of Social Welfare, *Casework Papers, 1959* (New York: Family Service Association of America, 1959), pp. 5–19.

This is not a small or a secondary task. The 1956 and 1962 amendments, the emphasis nationally on prevention, and the data relative to the interrelation of dependency and other social problems add up to a major *case location* obligation for public assistance, child welfare, and other public welfare programs. Heavy caseloads, staff shortages, untrained staff do not decrease this obligation since only the welfare program has the opportunity. Case location in this sense is quite possible even for relatively untrained public assistance workers. In-service training and preappointment requirements might prepare them to recognize when children are living in hazardous situations. They can learn to sort out those indications of deviant or antisocial behavior by children which demand community follow-up. They must also become equipped to prepare a client for a referral, to know the resources to which to refer, and, failing successful referral, to call upon more competent specialists in a social services division or protective unit for help.

Might the local welfare center not also become the *general community information and self-referral center* already mentioned, the "open door" facility at which all might obtain advice and steering, whether or not they are in receipt of relief or other welfare services? This function is certainly encompassed within current, advanced concepts of public welfare. In fact, there are counties in which joint public welfare–public health centers are ideally suited for this kind of activity. There are already some counties which provide their community's only social service and which hear a case in intake whether or not there is an assistance or child welfare problem in statutory terms. The preventive task in public welfare opens the way to others.

Nonetheless, it is also true that the stigma attached to "welfare" closes the service to some, particularly in many large cities, and the present legal limitation of the public welfare service in many places to those who meet a "means test" makes it an unsatisfactory plan for others. One expert suggests that public welfare programs need an information service, but that the broader problems of community information should be solved on a community-wide basis by local community councils and public-voluntary cooperative bodies.[28]

[28] Schottland, "The Nature of Services in Public Assistance," *Casework*

The next several years will show whether the promise of the recent Social Security Act amendments is to be translated into preventive and rehabilitative social service not tied to a means test. To the extent that this occurs, and is supported by funds for staff training, one might expect a change in the public image of public welfare and a decrease in the stigma—which is probably a major deterrent to the present development of a welfare center as the all-purpose community "open door." In the interim, it is to be hoped that welfare centers will provide a broad service of this kind for their own clients, in all categories, and will cooperate with such other community experiments as the neighborhood service center (see Ch. XII) and, perhaps, advice bureaus (see below). In addition (Ch. IX), it is urgent in most communities that welfare departments offer to the general public a channel for complaints about child abuse and neglect. In fact, it may well be that as progress is made in the fuller integration of child welfare and assistance programs and as categorical boundaries are broken down, the conditions may exist for developing in the public welfare program the service which will make it an appropriate community "open door." [29]

While it may draw on psychiatric hospitals and out-patient clinics for clinical study, a welfare department will not do its core job unless it is staffed for social study involving possible neglect, the wisdom of child placement, the suitability of a foster home as compared to institutionalization, the possible need for day care or homemakers, etc. The public assistance case study, per se, may give priority to determination of eligibility in the light of limited statutory requirements, but *all* other public welfare services do, in fact, require case judgments of many kinds. A department must therefor strive constantly to equip its line practitioners in all programs for case study, case evaluation, and effective referral work. Where the front-line field staff cannot be qualified, better-trained consultants and supervisors might participate in this phase of case

---

Papers, 1959, pp. 14–15. Also, *Goals and Methods in Public Assistance* (New York: Family Service Association of America, 1956).

[29] Elizabeth Wickenden and Winifred Bell, *Public Welfare: Time for a Change* (New York: New York School of Social Work of Columbia University, 1961).

evaluation, drawing on data assembled by field staff and conducting interviews as necessary. In some instances the assignment of the limited number of qualified casework staff members to a family welfare service may be the way to protect the crucial decisions relating to child-parent separation, the type of placement, the point at which a home may be reconstituted, the need to take a situation to court, and the suitability of a foster home or adoptive home.

The welfare program (whether or not in one department) is, by definition, *a major service and treatment resource* in work with the families who produce many of the children in trouble and, in some instances, for the children themselves. We might simply list the minimum relevant services: emergency intake service; temporary shelter; stand-by emergency foster homes; foster homes; group homes; institutions; adoptions; group day care; day homes; homemakers and home helps; access to medical services.

The various case location and disposition agencies in the community, particularly the police, courts, schools, and voluntary agencies, must be free to draw on these resources. The department requires staff able to do the case evaluations appropriate to the work of the particular service and, of course, to administer these services.

In addition, the community resource pattern might dictate other responsibilities for a welfare department. For example: Where there are no adequate voluntary family service agencies or counseling facilities, the welfare department should also create such services and make them available to the community at large.

The final functions to be mentioned are in the fields of *planning and coordination*. Child welfare workers have for more than twenty years demonstrated their *community organization* leadership in helping create new facilities and promoting coordination. In many counties there are no centers around which planning and coordination efforts might develop except the public welfare structure. Broader coordination and planning roles are, however, possible even in larger urban areas which have community councils and other agencies with roles in this field: coordination of the work of agencies working with multiproblem families has been experimented with in a number of places. The use of the welfare department to house a case accountability register or to conduct case conferences which integrate service efforts are additional possibilities.

ARE ADVICE CENTERS NECESSARY?

If the "open door" cannot be created within and as part of existing community institutional resources, it may be necessary to consider innovation. At such time there should be examination of the experiences of the British Citizens' Advice Bureaux, created to fulfill a wartime need in 1939 and now expanded to over 420 units in nearly all big cities and many towns and handling over a million inquiries annually.[30]

The British local government act of 1948 permits grants by local authorities for the financing of this voluntary service, and most of the service is thus financed. Where grants are not adequate, supplementary voluntary fund raising is undertaken. In addition, the paid social work staff is supplemented in many bureaus by the services of volunteers. Although city staffs are generally paid, the volunteers are in the majority elsewhere. Even the city bureaus have some volunteer part-time help or legal consultation. Auspices are determined locally—with the most frequent sponsorship being provided by councils of social agencies. The national central organization is the National Council of Social Service. Whatever the sponsorship and pattern of financing, the bureaus are locally managed by local committees and there are actually several operational patterns. The advice is "independent and impartial . . . on any problem." It is also "confidential and free of charge to anyone."

The Citizens' Advice Bureaux seem to have solved the problem of stigma which would face an "open door" agency associated in this country with a welfare program or a court structure. The key to the solution would seem to be the readiness to provide simple information about laws, procedures, and channels (even visitor's information in a tourist center like Piccadilly), while at the same time serving as a case evaluation center and referral unit in complex parent-child problems or instances of considerable personal disturbance.

[30] National Citizens' Advice Bureaux Committee, *Pattern for Partnership* (London: The National Council of Social Service, 1959), and *Advising the Citizen* (London: The National Council of Social Service, 1961).

A substantial portion of a bureau's time and energy is devoted to interpretation of legislation. (Of about 1,000,000 inquiries in a recent year, 322,000 dealt with housing matters.) This kind of task is facilitated by an elaborate information guide prepared by the National Council and amended quarterly. Included are such topics as communications and travel regulations, educational facilities and opportunities, employment legislation, social insurance, health services, housing–taxes–town planning, installment purchases, veteran issues. Each unit also receives monthly circulars outlining the latest laws, rules, and policies. Where complex, new legislation is passed, there is a one- or two-day training institute for clarification, and it may be followed up subsequently with another institute for the sharing of problems.

The experience of interpreting legislation to the public is paralleled by the responsibility to help interpret client problems and circumstances to government departments. In addition, when a government agency finds that correspondence will not suffice in dealing with a citizen about a complex matter, it may ask the bureau to help with explanation.

Inevitably, these roles give the bureaus a strategic vantage point for assessing the effects of new legislation, for making policy recommendations to local and national government, and for advising on the preparation of many types of leaflets and pamphlets to be issued by government departments.

Despite the measure of service to the instrumentalities of a complex welfare state, the bureaus have an independence and objectivity which prevents their identification as an arm of government or of any specific voluntary service. People of all walks of life seem to feel free to use the information services. Many turn to the bureaus with personal problems. (In 1958 there were 225,000 inquiries involving family, personal, and matrimonial matters.) Parents may come in because their adolescent children are "out of control" and they are not sure whether to turn to the police or a social agency. Young people arrive announcing that they have "run away." Doctors turn to the units in relation to their patients' social problems. Referrals may be made to family agencies, to the local children's offices, or to probation—to cite several major possibilities.

While the typical information inquiry involves one contact, complex personal problems may call for a series of exploratory interviews. Or, as is the experience in any case finding agency, the bureau worker may have a series of interviews before the recommended referral can be initiated and carried through successfully. An occasional case may remain in the bureau in this fashion for a year; others come back several times for further clarification or for what may be described as reassurance and support. Often such a relationship begins when an individual comes in for help in filling out a complex governmental form.

Part-time legal volunteers are needed for screening and referral services in many units because of the volume of inquiries with legal implications. Where legal service is needed, a referral is made.

The British experience with these bureaus has been extremely positive as evidenced by their growth, public and voluntary support, volume of service to individuals and government, and firm place in local social welfare provision. Not that there is full satisfaction with all phases of the work. Closer partnership is being sought with legal advice machinery; efforts are being made to encourage more use of the service by doctors; attention is being devoted increasingly to problems arising from credit buying. Here, too, there remain some "unreached" people. In the words of the chairman of the National Citizens' Advice Bureaux Committee, "If these people are to be helped, we have to insure that to the local people the C.A.B. of the district is as well known as the local cinema, the local football ground, the post office, the pub." [31]

Although this chapter has suggested several possibilities and not chosen between them it is clear that any given community must make specific choices, depending on total resources and public attitudes. The following sums up the exploration to this point:

Major community agencies such as family agencies, settlements, and public welfare must keep their doors "open" to all who would approach them and must be staffed for considerable case finding and situation finding.

These agencies should be part of an as yet unspecified community accountability network so that the opportunities encountered are not lost.

[31] *Patterns for Partnership*, p. 4.

In some cities or parts of cities, each of these agencies has the potential for serving as a general community "open door" information and advice center.

None of the three major systems mentioned—family agencies, public welfare, settlements—is likely to be available and in every sense accessible to all elements and segments of the population in many parts of the country. For this and other reasons, some cities would do well to experiment with variations on the British Citizens' Advice Bureaux. This would be an excellent field for voluntary initiative, although public participation would eventually be required.

CHAPTER V

SCHOOLS AND CHILDREN WHO NEED SPECIAL HELP

BECAUSE of the major social changes of the past century, society has delegated to the modern school an unprecedented degree of responsibility for the education and socialization of the young. Much that was once in the province of family and neighborhood has been turned over to this institution of almost universal coverage. And precisely because of the scope and salience of its influence and its extended contacts with children, a school which does not understand and respond to the needs of children may create problems and contribute to maladjustment.[1]

Of primary importance, of course, is the fact that the successfully organized school can do much for the technical preparation of children for roles in the adult world and for their healthy and sound growth. The task is constructive and creative. In addition, however, for the very same reasons of prolonged and significant contact with children, schools have a unique opportunity for early case location and an unmatched potential for offering a wide variety of services and resources designed to cope with problems early and eliminate them where possible.

[1] Eli M. Bower, *A Process for Early Identification of Emotionally Disturbed Children*, constituting the *Bulletin of the California State Department of Education*, Vol. XXVII, No. 6 (August, 1958). Also, Samuel M. Brownell, "The Unique Position of the Schools in the Prevention and Control of Delinquency," in Subcommittee to Investigate Juvenile Delinquency, Committee on the Judiciary, U.S. Senate, *Juvenile Delinquency* (*Education*) (Washington, D.C.: Government Printing Office, 1955).

This discussion deals, largely, with the latter roles—school provision for children in difficulty. It is, however, impossible to discuss organization of services and assignment of responsibilities without some view of the kind of school in which it is possible to develop effective services. It will come as no surprise that the type of school which can make such provision would also seem to be a school so wholesome in its atmosphere and creative in its program that it tends to keep the numbers needing specialized help to a minimum.

Thus, the chapter begins with an examination of the characteristics of such schools.

AN ATTITUDE TOWARD EDUCATION

Jacques Barzun has reminded us that "education comes from within; it is a man's own doing, or rather it happens to him . . . sometimes because of the teaching he has had, sometimes in spite of it." [2] Society requires well-educated men and women and must concern itself both with the kind of *teaching* which will contribute to their education and with the nature of the *total school system* most conducive to personal development and growth. One of the sound directions, therefore, is the move away from thinking only of groups to be taught and "bodies of subject matter to be learned" and toward "planning education to meet the needs of the individual and of the community in which he lives." From this perspective, it has been said, the "entire school staff have but one purpose, that of helping each individual discover his potentialities and apply his energies to the end that he achieves the best possible placement and adjustment in the classroom, in curricula and in community activities, in his personal living and in an occupational area." [3]

To this, an expert panel adds: "A free society nurtures the individual not alone for the contribution he may make to the social effort, but also and primarily for the sake of the contribution he may make to his own realization and development." [4]

[2] Jacques Barzun, *Teacher in America* (New York: Doubleday Anchor Books, 1954), p. 10.

[3] Federal Security Agency, *In-Service Preparation for Guidance Duties* (Washington, D.C.: Government Printing Office, 1950), pp. 2–3.

[4] Rockefeller Brothers Fund, Inc., *The Pursuit of Excellence: Education and the Future of America* (New York: Doubleday and Company, Inc., 1958).

It may, perhaps, be important, in the light of current educational controversies, to note that the preceding paragraphs talk of *community* needs as well as those of the individual, that they assume the importance of subject-matter learning and of occupational skills, and that they imply an individual contribution to the social effort.

Whatever one's educational philosophy, it is hardly possible to ignore the social changes which have brought larger segments of the population into school, have decreased responsibilities carried by the child's own family, and have therefore made it essential for the school to carry on its essentially group activities with awareness of individual needs and potentialities and alertness to the total social context of the educational experience. This is not an argument for "social life . . . adjustment for everyone [as] the first aim of public education" as opposed to concern with competence, knowledge, and understanding, nor is it a deliberate attempt to preempt for the school roles best carried by recreational facilities, churches, social agencies, and homes. Further, attention to the whole child does not involve the assumption that "all parts are equally important and it is possible for the school to train them all." [5]

Our emphasis is on preparation of a child for active mastery of his world and not for passive minimal adjustment. The school can and does influence personality: "To the extent that the child is helped in school toward a fuller sense of accomplishment, greater self-realization and eventual integrity, he will be better equipped both to understand and to deal with the complexities of our modern culture." And, we might add, to contribute as a skilled citizen, trained to do a job. The family and other influences certainly play their major part in the development of personality and creation of motivation, but—in addition to its specific teachings—the school is in a position to do much to ensure the emotional satisfaction of achievement, to arouse desirable goals and values, to offer adult models after which a child might pattern himself. It can, equally,

[5] John Keats, *Schools without Scholars* (Boston: Houghton Mifflin Co., 1958), pp. 91–93. Also see James Bryant Conant, *The Child, the Parent and the State* (Cambridge, Mass.: Harvard University Press, 1959); Carnegie Foundation for the Advancement of Teaching, *Education of the Academically Talented* (New York, 1959).

damage the child, distort and negate sound values, and cause him to turn to undesirable models.[6]

The school uses a variety of methods but, for the most part, they are oriented to organization of group experience and teaching in group situations. What is sought is a means of individualizing within that group method and group process so that the experience itself has maximum effectiveness. Indeed, it would appear from some pioneering research endeavors that only successful "liberation" of able individuals from the demands for conformity inherent in group participation will produce truly creative persons.[7] The relevant point in the present context is that the individuality of the child can be developed, encouraged, and built on, without seeking to convert the school into something which it is not and cannot be: a therapeutic institution or a center of individualized services.

A U.S. Senate subcommittee heard testimony that "the social responsibility and moral fiber of tomorrow's children will be strengthened or weakened not only by their experience in the classrooms of tomorrow, but by the experience of their parents in the classrooms of today." The committee was also told that "delinquency or any other social ill is the resultant of the entire network of forces acting upon the individual . . . the school by itself does not make or unmake delinquents." However, those children who come to school not motivated by family influences to perform as the school would want them to, and those who are not personally able or equipped to take part in the accepted programs and activities, have serious adjustment problems and may find antischool and antisocial solutions.[8]

Training in a range of subjects, freedom to grow and develop,

[6] Sheldon and Eleanor Glueck, *Unraveling Juvenile Delinquency* (New York: The Commonwealth Fund, 1950), p. 135. For a more complete view of the school as a social institution, see Robert H. Herriott and Ann E. Trask, *Theory and Research in Sociology and Education,* a special issue of the *Harvard Educational Review,* Vol. XXIX (Fall, 1959). See, particularly, Neal Gross, "Some Contributions of Sociology to the Field of Education," pp. 275–87, and Talcott Parsons, "The School Class as a Social System: Some of Its Functions in American Society," pp. 297–318.

[7] "Creativity," *Quarterly* (Carnegie Corporation of New York), IX, No. 3 (July, 1961), 5.

[8] Subcommittee to Investigate Juvenile Delinquency, Committee on the Judiciary, U.S. Senate, *Education and Juvenile Delinquency* (Washington, D.C.: Government Printing Office, 1956), p. 19. Statement by Harold L. Clapp. Also pp. 50–60, statement by Albert K. Cohen.

encouragement in active mastery of the world, attraction to sound values, and creative, democratic goals—these are the schools' potential contributions to every child. Technical competence, in fact, is attained by a large proportion of students only in a school system so oriented and not one which sees science and mathematics or the achievement of any specific skills as alternatives to full educational opportunity.

Goals of this sort will be achieved only as the school organizes to gauge capacity, recognize differences, and offer opportunity and encouragement for every student. Where there is faltering, the school should be prepared to help children to meet obstacles. We speak, in brief, of a school dedicated to supporting, stimulating, teaching, and inspiring those who will make tomorrow's world.

The school, we repeat, should be neither clinic nor therapeutic community. Most of its children are psychologically healthy and its program rests on that assumption. This does not invalidate the view that the mental hygiene field has learned much about child development which can serve to help equip school personnel for their tasks. Some clinicians, too, have integrated child development data with material relevant to the dynamics of groups in a way which may be of help to teachers in classroom management and curriculum development. Beyond this, of course, personnel who have clinical backgrounds can play major roles in the diagnosis of difficulties, in the planning of remedial measures, and in the carrying out of treatment.

The structure and administrative ties of these services are better viewed against a backdrop of an educational philosophy for a school system concerned with all the children.

A teacher in a classroom—the basic educational pattern. The goals outlined are best achieved through the influence that has always been the central one in education, the relationship and response of the teacher to each child, an influence which develops despite the fact that the classroom is essentially a group situation. This, by and large, has been recognized by our school systems and they have not brought subject-matter specialists in, except for the occasional music or dance expert, until junior high school, where departmentalization is the rule, and high school, where it is an urgent necessity.

A completely impersonal school structure is impossible for any school child, no matter how good the specialists. Even though there would seem to be some sacrifice in foregoing subject-matter specialization in the early grades, it is probably more than made up for by the advantages of a sustaining relationship with one potentially inspiring teacher, who may be of great emotional and intellectual influence over an entire academic year. (A variety of interesting experiments are currently testing departures from the traditional pattern.) Where the teacher is effective, a relationship can develop significantly even in the limits of that one academic year; where the child-teacher combination is not good, there is the hope that next year's shift will be more successful.

The good teacher is, of course, a master of relevant subject matter and teaches it well. The three R's may be taught creatively and in the spirit of that modern education which stresses understanding and trying things out, rather than the memorization of unconnected facts and ideas.

A Public Education Association group reported after extensive observations: "We found that superior teachers stress the relationships among various subjects, showing their classes how one topic leads logically to another . . . always, where possible, subjects are introduced in terms of the children's own experience or daily activities and interests. Where experience is lacking, the teacher tries to provide it." [9] The experience should deepen, not dilute, the teaching of content, however, lest the point be lost in the process.

It is too often assumed that where something must be done about a behavioral deviation, it is, from the start, out of the realm of competence of the classroom teacher. Social workers, guidance counselors, or attendance officers who are available or are sought for schools are considered essential. Even where the teacher carries on alone, for lack of such behavioral specialists, he is too often thought of as making-do until resources are found. This is unsound. Educational goals are lost unless we prepare the teacher to retain his basic responsibility as educator in the broad sense, and as the one best acquainted with the child. Certainly, school systems require guidance specialists, but such specialists are meant to bolster the

[9] Public Education Association, *Look at Your Schools* (New York, 1951), p. 12.

teacher's understanding of children and their needs, to offer special services, and to be available where specialization is necessary.

These are not unusual or minority views. They are expressed and endorsed in numerous educational documents and in reports of major school systems. Nor does the typical teacher see the demands of this kind of role as excessive. In fact, it is clear that good teachers are eager to accept such responsibility. They cannot carry it out, however, unless they have been selected as suitable in personality for such an assignment, have basic subject-matter competence, and really care for and understand children, being dedicated to their healthy development. Teacher training should include content about child development and personality dynamics. The responses of children to teachers who like children and like to teach are marked and gratifying.

No, good teachers do not recoil at this role. However, when classes are oversized, curriculum is overrigid, and the supports by school administration are inadequate, teachers are frustrated and soon become discouraged. These conditions can be widespread at times of tremendous demands on schools for expansion, as in the current era of high birthrates. They are doubly complicated where population mobility and ethnic concentrations create, in parts of cities, school districts heavily made up of underprivileged and impoverished families, whose children face many more than the usual adjustment problems and inevitably bring them into the classroom.

School, neighborhood, and home. At any given moment, the teacher has in the classroom a cross-section reflection of what is going on in the community at large and in the pupils' homes in particular. No one would claim that all tensions or problems should be resolved in the classroom, but there are school systems which have played leading parts in helping citizens to deal with their community problems and there are some which have helped parents, personally, through courses and discussion groups. What is basic, however, is (*a*) the teacher's need for knowledge of home and community if effective education is to take place and (*b*) the participation of the community in basic educational policy decisions for its schools. Only the first of these is relevant at this point.

The way in which a teacher learns about home and community may have to vary with a school system and its particular circumstances, but certain fundamental possibilities are already well known and require consideration whenever planning is done. First, it might be said, the school for very young children should be neighborhood-based if at all possible. The child who begins school needs familiar surroundings and classmates. For the teacher, it is easier to grasp, understand, visit, relate to, and work with a cohesive local neighborhood than a widespread unrelated population. Numerous factors may, it is true, block this kind of prime consideration, among them the following: (a) the school may be rural or private or parochial and have to draw on a broad geographic area; (b) public policy may dictate giving up some aspects of neighborhood districting even for the quite young in order to achieve school racial and ethnic integration, which is accorded short-run priority over the neighborhood school objective.[10]

Second, the neighborhood and parents should be brought into the school as much as possible, and the school's representatives must find ways to be in the neighborhood and, where desirable, their pupils' homes. P.T.A. groups, parent activities of various kinds, and the use of school facilities by the community are widespread and valuable. In slum areas and transition areas, unfortunately, there is not the leisure or way of life necessary to such parental participation: it requires adequate arrangements at home, suitable clothing, funds, and a sense of relaxation to become a regular P.T.A. member or to join in other school or neighborhood programs.

It is common practice in suburban areas or in the economically more privileged areas of cities for teachers to visit their pupils' homes, on invitation, for luncheon or tea. School-wide picnics and other events also acquaint teachers with families and with the group with which they are working. School administration should encourage this type of activity wherever possible, by appropriate control of total job-load and provision of facilities. The child whose family lives in filthy, dilapidated, and condemned housing may not wish his teacher to visit, however, and a visit could be very difficult for a mother caring for several children on a marginal in-

[10] New York City Board of Education, reports submitted to the Commission on Integration by the following subcommittees: Educational Standards and Curriculum, Guidance and Educational Stimulation, Physical Plant and Maintenance, Teachers Assignments and Personnel, Zoning (1955 and 1956, mimeographed).

come—or for another mother who rapidly must get dinner for the children en route to a part-time job.

Thus, while it is sound to say that in an ideal school system a classroom teacher would be a regular visitor in the community, so that a visit at the time of some difficulty would be natural, it is also realistic to add that this will not be possible where classes are too large, teachers are overburdened, and families themselves are not enjoying reasonably stable lives. Neighborhood groups, nonetheless, should constantly seek means to bring parents into the school and in contact with teachers—with full regard for local customs, problems, and ways of life. Even under difficult circumstances, teachers must be ensured time to invite parents to school for periodic reports on their children's progress and for broader discussion of the program ("open school week," etc.)—as well as for special conferences when the occasion demands it. In certain situations, where it will be viewed as a token of interest or be the only way a parent can be seen (a handicapped person, a mother with young children), teachers even in crowded school systems must have time for some home visits. Finally, there are instances of unexplained absence or severe school maladjustment in which home contacts are required and in which failure of parents to respond to letters and telephoning requires efforts at home interviews despite all other considerations; whether this is the responsibility of the classroom teacher or a specialist such as a school social worker or an attendance officer will vary with the size of the school system and its resources.

All teachers have recourse to other kinds of devices to get to know their pupils' communities. A study of local population data, available through analysis of census tracts and surveys by community councils and others, is very helpful. Discussion with local leaders, professional persons, and other teachers who have long known the community is valuable. Analysis of the records of the total class is often quite revealing. Health cards, class grades, and material in cumulative records, when taken together and compared to data for the total school system or for the community at large, may clarify for the teacher the nature of the group with which he is at work.

Teachers who have grown up in the neighborhoods of their pupils find all of this easier, at least in one sense. Those who derive from other backgrounds, particularly middle-class teachers who seek to work with children in slums, or teachers of one ethnic background who work with other groups, need to assemble basic facts, consider their implications, and even do some reading or studying to ensure adequate understanding—and, thus, to promote education. They also need to prepare to master their own blind spots and prejudices.

The reason for identifying the backgrounds of children is, of course, to equip the teacher to free pupils to develop to their capacities, not to stereotype them and limit the offerings and encouragement accordingly. While none would advocate such policy directly, a number of major reports have concluded studies of the backgrounds of "slum" children and their problems in "middle-class" schools by implying the need for schools so rooted in slum culture as to handicap their pupils throughout life.

A diversified educational offering. All children are not equal in their potentialities nor are they made equal in their motivations or abilities, even by the best of school systems. A good school system, however, must offer equal opportunity to all and, then, ensure that there is available to each an educational offering in some way suited to individual needs and abilities. The "tyranny of the average" is a real problem in school systems and there is need to offer a variety of directions, emphases, and paces to meet varying needs and potentials. Equality of opportunity also implies, to use the phrasing of a recent report, opportunity for the "pursuit of excellence!" Motivations do respond to stimulation.

A large danger is that of placement on the basis of inadequate evaluation, or premature assignment of a child to an educational "track" from which there is no "switching." Parents are not always in a position to help their children to make wise choices. It is simply not true that the offspring of unskilled laborers are invariably best suited for a vocational program, even if their parents accept the suggestion. Scholarship offerings of all sorts and expansion of public facilities provide opportunity to the qualified, whatever their social classes or racial-ethnic backgrounds. The classroom teacher at his best tries to clarify, with students and their parents, the issues and the choices to be made. Preliminary decisions are often made at the junior high school level, although many educators feel that is too soon. Even if this cannot be avoided the system should permit one to try things out, to shift plans, and to make new decisions later. "Ability grouping" in major *subjects* has been suggested as an alternative to a system of several educational "tracks." [11] Particularly at the junior high school level, disadvantaged children should be assured experiences which will open "higher horizons" to them. Guidance resources should be concentrated on helping people make wise decisions; parental and community involvement should be sought to the maximum degree possible.

Test results are often very helpful in the making of educational decisions, but there is need to guard against possible social class and language biases which distort results. A variety of studies have demonstrated, for example, that social class membership affects motivation and values in a way which is reflected in group test scores. Others have shown that language and cultural factors affect outcome in achievement as well as personality tests. Specially designed instruments and real evaluation of potential as revealed in daily performance should be drawn upon, as appropriate, in the decision making.

If the choice between college preparation, a vocational program, and one limited to basic reading, writing, and social skills is based on true assessment of individual potential, each program is in a position to develop into an effective educational instrument and a desirable specialization. Assignment to such programs should not be made too soon, however. All students have a right to a comparable basic education and only the truly retarded may need to be separated. The others can be stimulated to learn to their capacities through a combination of good grouping and classroom individualization and through systematic efforts to open new doors and possibilities for children of deprived background.

This general approach would end those situations in which highly important vocational schools become in effect "dumping grounds" trying to serve a heterogeneous group in no way viable educationally: capable students with college potential who have been improperly steered because of the social class bias in selection; those suitable for and interested in vocational training; those who have

[11] James Bryant Conant, *The American High School Today* (New York: McGraw-Hill Book Co., 1959).

rejected school and are "doing time" until eligible to leave; those unable to meet minimum demands of any current secondary curricula. The school is challenged to create good programs for a variety of well-defined groupings. Some will be en route to college. Others can use full-time vocational preparation, which includes basic skills courses, relevant theory as well as skills training—leading perhaps to some technical school work beyond high school. Still others are able to use an educational experience which includes a part-time apprentice responsibility on one of many levels. For a few, a terminal "skills" curriculum may be appropriate.

The detailed requirements of these offerings are not immediately relevant here and need development and modification with experience; nor is it necessary to enter into the debate as to whether some vocational courses are too trival to be included in a school curriculum. A school system dedicated to offering the best possible program to each child, in the light of his special needs and capacities, will invent new patterns and will assess, responsibly, whether students' full capacities are being challenged.

As already suggested, specialization or concentration should be deferred until there is a basis for choice and until it is absolutely necessary. Nor need concentration lead to complete separation or segregation. Children ought to share their educational experiences with many kinds of children; otherwise, no matter how able they may be, they are deprived of the full stimulation and challenge which come from having to cope with variety and from seeing others who have different interests and capacities. There is, too, a gap in their lives if they do not come to appreciate ways in which some members of society make what are essentially nonintellectual contributions. To ensure both diversity of experience and flexibility of programs, many educators favor comprehensive high schools which do include all the children in one building. Conant defines the comprehensive high school as one whose programs correspond to the educational needs of *all* the youth in a community.

Some large school systems may find comprehensive schools impractical, particularly if they have large investments in buildings, or they may argue for a greater degree of group homogeneity for maximum learning. Many systems consequently separate children in junior high or thereafter. Intermediate and small systems are able to find some activities and experience in which all may participate.

The classroom teacher as case finder. In the kind of educational system here conceived, the teacher is alert to manifestations of distress in a child, whether the symptom is a sudden change in behavior, a nervous habit, inability to learn, or unexplained absence. This is often case finding in the earliest possible stages of a problem. It may uncover both mild problems and serious emotional disturbance, difficulties already taking their tolls in children, as well as parental neglect in the early stages. Inevitably, the first attempt to understand the difficulty and what we have called the brief screening evaluation must be made by the teacher. Requests for outside help and referrals come later, if needed.

Many recent reports have shown that, with the increased absorption of mental health concepts into teacher training, teachers have proven able to identify the withdrawn and unhappy child in need of attention, as well as the annoyingly aggressive or defiantly antisocial child. To supplement their observations, teachers may follow the clues obtained in the reports on group psychological tests.[12] Special rating devices to predict which children may need attention should be used with caution, and only if addressed to the problem of finding deviant children who may need help; the device to predict specifically who may become delinquent should not be introduced into the classroom lest it create a self-fulfilling prophecy (see Ch. III). Both teachers and experts overpredicted delinquency in the well-known Cambridge-Somerville Youth Study.[13]

From their preparation and experience, teachers must learn which kinds of situations can be managed in the classroom through special attention, or through discussion with the parent and adjustments of program. The very decision as to which things to notice, which to explore further, which to ignore, represents an unavoidable and highly desirable kind of screening by those in a position to know children well and to see them against appro-

[12] Bower, *A Process for Early Identification of Emotionally Disturbed Children.*

[13] Edwin Powers and Helen L. Witmer, *An Experiment in the Prevention of Delinquency: The Cambridge-Somerville Youth Study* (New York: Columbia University Press, 1951), p. 290.

priate norms. Training for basic understanding of personality growth is thus essential to teachers. They also need opportunity to discuss case situations with specialists, when they require help, and thus to learn general principles from their specific experiences.

A given school system will also find it necessary to acquaint its teachers with school and community resources for both case evaluation and service-treatment, and to make sure they have general comprehension of the criteria for referral. The use of a resource is determined by many things, including the extent of demands made upon it; the individual teacher is therefore not in a position to be a wise case screener without being helped to see the total picture and unless the picture is kept current. In large school systems, the actual referral process may have to be delegated and centralized to a degree.

A mental hygiene orientation to supervision and administration. A school system which seeks to emphasize respect and freedom for the individuality of its children must offer as much to its principals and teachers. It is obviously not appropriate for central authorities to decree educational experiments and to plan building repairs without consultation with local principals or assistant superintendents whose own priorities may have validity and even be economical. Teachers are more likely to concern themselves with the individual capacities and needs of children if they themselves are treated as unique individuals by their supervisors, principals, and administrative superiors. While they need over-all direction and must know and adhere to curriculum and policy, they also require opportunity for experimentation, variation, and initiative.

Where teachers feel free to handle problems with some ingenuity and where they receive help rather than censure from principals, they are more willing to accept responsibility. Easier staff relationships, constant sharing of experiences, a true interest in the suggestions of all teachers "on the line," and a conscious avoidance of an atmosphere which reduces all to the "least common denominator" of compliance and following prescribed routine—all this is needed to free the best in teachers. A mass educational system finds it easier to organize impersonal and mechanical handling of its teaching staff, but this can be done only at the sacrifice of the very qualities which make good teachers. In cases where a more individualized working relationship between teachers, administrators, and supervisors has been tried, the results have been excellent. Large systems will not be able to achieve any of this without a degree of decentralization.

A school system, of course, has the obligation and right to assure itself of the qualifications of teachers from the point of view of general content mastery and teaching skill before it turns its classes over to them. Civil service or merit system examinations are clearly in order, as are periods of internship, apprenticeship, and probation on the job.

School systems also should have some confidence in the personality suitability of those to whom they turn over their classrooms. Unfortunately, research in the field of personality assessment for teaching and utilization of personality data in job assignments is as yet in its early phases, and validated personality guides or "tools" are not available. What is more, most school systems have such great difficulty in recruiting sufficient numbers of teachers, during the present period of school expansion, that they dare not introduce another level of sifting, once teachers are found technically competent and seem, in interviews, to be acceptable. When, in the future, supply begins to meet demand, it would be wise to place greater emphasis on the development of devices for weeding out the unfit early in teacher training and for assigning the others where they can make optimum contributions.

Specialized services for children with learning and adjustment problems. The classroom teacher, even in a school system with diversified educational offerings, requires the buttressing, support, and supplementation of special services. Sometimes these simply undertake tasks for which the teacher lacks time. In other instances, they bring to bear specialized technical knowledge and skills. The extent of special services and their subdivision into special bureaus and divisions will vary with community size and resources.[14]

It is important to note in introducing this subject that special services are not a substitute for sound curriculum policy, diversified

---

[14] For another approach to services, which stresses the school in coordination, see William C. Kvaraceus, *Juvenile Delinquency and the Schools* (Yonkers: World Book Co., 1945). Also, William C. Kvaraceus, *The Community and the Delinquent* (Yonkers: World Book Co., 1954).

offerings, reasonable class size, and program flexibility. A school system which finds that a sizable portion of its pupils needs "special services" has cause to ask whether fundamental policy and administrative reform is not in order. The school system as a whole, not guidance services for the deviant and programs for children in trouble, should be prepared to meet the special requirements of the large numbers of children from underprivileged backgrounds who are not prepared for the regular curriculum.

The following listing of *functions and facilities* would seem to have some general validity in a system of specialized services; the order does not indicate priority rating:

(1) *Group testing.* While teachers may administer and even score group I.Q. and achievement tests, the school system ought to have consultants available for more complete examination, evaluation, and interpretation of deviant test performances, whether the deviation is in the direction of exceptional ability, inadequate capacity, or mixed results.

(2) *Individual testing.* The "unusual" or "exceptional" child, whether identified through group tests, which have a high degree of inaccuracy, or through observation, should be tested by the more precise, individual methods. School systems require qualified psychological staff for this function.

(3) *Individual educational and vocational guidance.* Whether one's educational philosophy stresses dedication to subject-matter competence alone, or calls for a broader concept of the role of the school, there is agreement that the school of today must offer programs for youth of a variety of competences and limitations. The "pursuit of excellence" or the preparation for minimum life-skills both assume a teacher with competence in educational guidance as well as (in larger systems) school specialists in this function. Pre-high school and college counseling are major assignments. Where there are no appropriate community resources, the guidance programs may include job placement. Inevitably, the guidance program is important to children in difficulty since symptoms of personal maladjustment in school often raise the question of school placement or program readjustments. The professional base of the guidance program is education, but it draws on child development knowledge and skills.

(4) *Personal guidance.* A school system, even if relatively small, requires some combination of school social work, psychological counseling, and personal guidance services. The function includes:

   a) Consultation services for teachers, principals, and administrators in relation to adjustment problems of children in school.

   b) More complete social and psychological study of the child and the home situation in the above instances, where required.

   c) Brief-contact casework or psychological counseling with children and their parents, to help with problems of school adjustment.

   d) Suggestions for school program adjustments and special placements of children in difficulty.

   e) Participation in, or conduct of, mental health training of teachers.

   f) Participation in, or conduct of, special discussion programs of classes for parents, work with local P.T.A.'s and participation in school-community projects.

(5) *Psychiatric evaluation and study.* Where problems seem to be complex and fundamental, more complete evaluation is needed. The essential resources include psychiatric staff and adjunctive psychological and social work services. This service is not necessarily located in the school system proper. It may, however, be related to the school social work program.

(6) *Investigation and handling of unlawful absence.* Whether this function requires independence or integration with personal counseling and social work services is an important issue, reserved for discussion below.

(7) *Special classes* for those handicapped and retarded children unable to meet the requirements of normal classroom routine.

(8) *Special classroom facilities* in detention, hospitals, and institutions if required by the local situation. Children have a right to continued education even if away from home temporarily.

(9) *A system of liaison* with community groups, social agencies, courts, police, churches.

(10) *A program of mental health orientation and education* for teachers and a forum for teacher-administrator discussion of children.

(11) *An administrative structure* to ensure that all of these

programs back up the classroom teacher and serve the individual child with maximum effect. This assumes combinations of these functions and facilities, as appropriate.

(12) Provision for the *coordination* and *integration* of these varied resources. The degree of formality and complexity of this structure will vary with the school system. The issue of who coordinates is a controversial one in educational-guidance circles, since many of the professions affected are very much in transition.

A listing of this kind is, unfortunately, only a starting point in development of a system of school services for children in trouble. As Krugman has pointed out so clearly:

One can find support for the thesis that the functions of the psychiatrist in schools is to diagnose and treat disturbed children as well as for the position that the only functions of psychiatrists in schools are consultations and mental health education for teachers; that child guidance clinics should be integral parts of the school system, and that they should by no means be integral parts; . . . that teachers are poor diagnosticians, and that teachers are superior diagnosticians; . . . that disturbed children should be educated and treated in special classes, and that disturbed children should, as far as possible, be educated in regular classes.[15]

Choices must, of course, be made at any given moment and should be based on the realities in the typical school, the orientations and specializations of the professions involved, and the weight of experience. Rather than discuss these in the abstract, we shall give attention to the major issues in the context of discussion of the New York City system and its provisions. Here, sheer size and the inevitable resulting specializations tend to bring issues into sharp focus and to dramatize the consequences of inadequate choices. We shall seek to outline an approach which gives some assurance that essential functions are performed with maximum effectiveness and basic school objectives are advanced. The question of combinations of bureaus, services, and functions to ensure administrative efficiency and effective case integration will also be relevant.[16]

[15] Morris Krugman, ed., *Orthopsychiatry and the School* (New York: American Orthopsychiatric Association, 1958), Preface, pp. x–xi.

[16] For more detail see Alfred J. Kahn, *New York City Schools and Children Who Need Help* (New York: Citizens' Committee for Children of New York, Inc., 1962).

Some of the facts about the New York City school system will provide necessary background.

Under any circumstances schools in large urban areas share what is intrinsically a particularly complex task. In this "age of acceleration" the social and cultural "distance" between generations is greater than ever. The problems of teacher-child communications are profound. There seem to be great chasms in perceptions of the world and value-systems as between teachers and those they would teach. The personal educational experience of the teacher is not adequate for his student, since the world is basically different; in many fields there have been major breakthroughs in knowledge. If all of this is compounded by differences of ethnic background, the problems of transition from rural to urban living, and the tendency toward deterioration of the "inner city," the process of establishing a basis for communication is difficult indeed.

New York City ranks high as compared with the remainder of the country both in its *scholastic* achievement averages for the system as a whole and in the accomplishments of its *best* pupils. Outstanding academic, technical, and vocational high schools in New York City have earned their reputations as offering almost unmatched educational opportunity.

Despite outstanding schools, classes, and pupils, however, it is inevitable that the system as a whole, when measured against the ideals set forth at the beginning of this chapter, should be lacking in many ways. To say this is merely to acknowledge that the city, along with many other metropolitan areas, has not yet solved a most difficult and perplexing series of problems which reflect its social character and housing patterns and which cannot be completely solved in the schools. Like the rest of the country, New York will require time fully to adapt its educational system, particularly its secondary schools, to all of the demands of the modern age and to all of the consequences of present urban living.

Educational decisions in New York City affect tremendous numbers of children. Programs, if they are to have impact, must be on a large scale. The public day schools enroll about one million children who are taught by a staff of approximately 40,000. There are over 800 separate schools in the system: elementary, junior high, high, and special schools.

The city's schools face more than a problem of size, however. As have other metropolitan centers since World War II, the city has experienced unusually high rates of population mobility. Pupil turnover in a school within a given year may be extremely high. Furthermore, a pattern of immigration from the rural South and from Puerto Rico, combined with a movement to the city outskirts and suburban areas of many in the middle class and in upper income groups, plus housing shortages in all but luxury areas, has left many parts of the city with large concentrations of the economically underprivileged or of disadvantaged ethnic and racial groups. Income ceilings and other aspects of public housing policy have converted many of the housing projects into similar concentrations.

All of this naturally has been reflected in the schools. Schools with a preponderant registration of underprivileged children, and there are many, face problems which may be overwhelming: large numbers of non-English speaking children; many tired and unmotivated children who do not have enough to eat, are poorly dressed, or are in many ways neglected; members of antisocial gangs who have rejected the prevailing codes and see no real reason to accept educational restrictions and obligations in return for the proffered long-term personal gains and advancement.

Many of the larger urban centers face a similar situation, despite variations in detail, according to Conant.[17]

For well over a decade after World War II New York was one of a significantly large group of American cities which did too little in equipping schools for their new tasks. Schools with large proportions of relatively inexperienced teachers and substitutes had to cope with large numbers of nonreaders and children difficult to teach. Standards were inevitably lowered and offerings became meager. Many of these schools were reduced to holding operations in which discipline became the primary consideration. In fact,

[17] James Bryant Conant, *Slums and Suburbs* (New York: McGraw-Hill Book Co., 1961). Also see Frank Riessman, *The Culturally Deprived Child* (New York: Harper & Brothers, 1962).

many principals and teachers found themselves so concerned with vandalism, delinquency, unmanageable children, and gangs as to be unable to give concentrated attention to basic educational matters.

In New York City, educational leadership, the Board of Education, and civic groups have gradually evolved the outlines of a program and a policy. Its components are: (a) a variety of efforts to speed school racial integration where housing concentrations have created *de facto* school segregation; (b) major efforts to raise the standards of schools in which there are concentrations of deprived children (more guidance, more adequate administration, smaller classes, classes for the non-English speaking, better-qualified teachers, etc.); (c) a speeded-up program of school construction and building renovation; (d) efforts to stimulate the less-motivated and culturally deprived young people.

Following an impressive demonstration in one school of the extent to which cultural enrichment affects school holding power, learning, and the objectives of underprivileged students, the "higher horizons" program (which might more appropriately have been called "broader horizons") gradually has been extended on a substantial scale.[18] Other cities are now duplicating the approach with federal and foundation encouragement. Yet to be dealt with systematically and on a large scale in New York is the reorganization and revitalization of vocational and technical schools, vocational guidance and counseling, and the context of motivations and orientations in which they function. These will not be discussed here. Major strengthening of these phases of the program is an essential component of the updating of all urban school systems today.[19]

All who are involved recognize that despite encouraging beginnings the task is a long and complex one. There are schools which show no progress at all. The process has been complicated by differences of opinion as to the extent to which the racial inte-

[18] See Board of Education of the City of New York, *Toward Greater Opportunity: A Progress Report from the Superintendent of Schools to the Board of Education Dealing with Implementation of Recommendations of the Commission on Integration* (New York, 1960). Also, Demonstration Guidance Project, *Progress Report, 1957–1958* (New York: Board of Education of the City of New York, 1958). Also, J. Wayne Wrightstone, "Discovering and Stimulating Culturally Deprived Talented Youth," *Teachers College Record*, LX, No. 1 (October, 1958), 23–27.

[19] Conant, *Slums and Suburbs.*

gration objective should supersede the general preference for the neighborhood school. Moreover, since not many teachers have been won over to the notion of volunteering for service in difficult schools which need experienced teachers, a variety of secondary motivations and assignment policies have had to be introduced. Also, the school system has sought to deal with all these matters while, at the same time, responding to the national call for raising academic sights and enriching offerings for gifted children.

Especially handicapping to this general effort in an era of rapid school expansion is the nationwide shortage of teachers. Thousands of substitutes and teachers not regularly licensed for the classes to which they are assigned must be called upon to take over classes. Personnel shortages also affect psychology, social work, and guidance—fields counted on in a major way for special programs.

NEW YORK CITY SCHOOLS AND CHILDREN IN TROUBLE—AN OVERVIEW

How does this large system deal with children in trouble? To a considerable extent, the programs, bureaus, and services have developed in response to specific problems and crises and not in relation to any over-all strategy. In this sense, New York City is typical. It assigns over 1,500 professional persons (or in some cases their equivalent in teacher-time) to services called child guidance, educational and vocational guidance, or attendance. The total would be substantially larger were we to include special teachers in what are called "600" schools or junior guidance classes. Expansion in all categories of service has been most rapid in the last several years. Yet the universal cry of principals, assistant principals, and teachers is that they do not have access to adequate individualized help for children who disrupt the classroom or are so disturbed that they cannot benefit from the educational program. The reader of reports soon discovers a complex maze of undefined and overlapping functions, fragmentation of personnel, and gaps in service. Obviously, New York's school system must redeploy resources and develop long-range plans. What is desirable and possible? What strategy would increase effectiveness?

Clearly the answer is not "pilot" projects or "demonstrations." For, it must be added, this large school system defers many problems and pressures by setting up "pilot" projects, "demonstrations," and "experiments." These are often creative innovations or solutions to important problems, and they are promulgated in good faith, because there is conviction about a new plan, a desire to test an approach, or a readiness to allow a method not too well defined to be clarified and demonstrated. The system is a large one, however, and its administrative layers are many. To convert a demonstration project into city-wide practice is complex and costly. The system (no one person is here guilty or responsible) thus often absorbs and swallows special units and special projects even though it credits and publicizes their accomplishments. The creation of a pilot project is not, then, necessarily a step toward meeting city-wide needs. It may even be a detour. A design is necessary, roles require definition, and priorities must be set. The issues and alternatives are in no sense peculiar to New York.

Included in two divisions within the New York system are a variety of special programs which are here relevant: the Bureau of Educational and Vocational Guidance, a School-Court Liaison Program, the Bureau of Child Guidance, the Bureau for Children with Retarded Mental Development, the School-Community Relations Program, the Health Education Program, a Program for Physically Handicapped Children, Classes for the Blind and Sight Conservation Classes, Schools for the Deaf and Hard of Hearing, a Home Instruction Program, "400" schools (i.e., for the physically handicapped), "600" schools (i.e., for the maladjusted and "difficult"), a Bureau of Attendance (including job certification).

Of the agencies and programs in this listing, the following, all in the Division of Child Welfare, are particularly strategic in the community provision for dealing with school children in trouble: the Bureau of Child Guidance, the Bureau of Educational and Vocational Guidance, the Bureau of Attendance, and the "600" schools. Analysis of each may serve to clarify the functions it might carry in a total school plan and the ways in which it might relate to other agencies and services. This review may shed light on issues faced in all large school systems: the functions of schools in relation to children in trouble; the respective roles of attendance, social work, and guidance within the system; the place of "special" schools.

SCHOOL SOCIAL WORK OR A CLINIC—THE CASE
OF THE BUREAU OF CHILD GUIDANCE

It is widely agreed that schools need a social work service but two models prevail: some would have a school social work program; others would adopt what was long the Bureau of Child Guidance (BCG) objective in New York City—a child guidance clinic *within* the school system. The bureau itself is in transition. The largest agency of its kind, the BCG has grown steadily and impressively since its establishment in 1931. Its size and scope would be adequate to meet the needs of most school systems but it has made only limited impact in New York City. To a considerable extent the problem has derived from the size of the school system, but the BCG concept of its role was not an unimportant factor. To recognize this is not to ignore the fact that

uncounted children have found a way out of their difficulties that otherwise would not have been open to them. Uncounted teachers have come to know children more deeply, and to deal with them more understandingly. In their services to pupils with problems, a dedicated Bureau staff have amassed a fund of experience that is unparalleled anywhere in the world.[20]

While some positions are generally vacant, the BCG is authorized to employ almost 200 social workers, 150 psychologists, 30 psychiatrists, plus clerical and administrative staff. It has been formally charged with several of the major functions identified in our discussion of the school's role; in addition it has developed programs in a number of related areas on its own initiative. The total program includes: (*a*) consultation to teachers in relation to their problems with individual children and referrals to the community where needed; (*b*) social work and psychological services to children in schools, in the manner of school-oriented social work programs; (*c*) child guidance diagnostic and treatment service; (*d*) specified services, usually involving psychological testing, to children with designated problems and handicaps, i.e., the mentally retarded, problem children assigned to special schools, children in speech im-

[20] Board of Education of the City of New York, *The Bureau of Child Guidance in the New York City Schools: A Survey* (New York, 1955), p. xiv.

provement classes, aphasic children, etc.; (*e*) enrichment of general educational practice, from a mental hygiene perspective, both through in-service training and the involvement of teachers in services to individual pupils; (*f*) parent education; and (in a more limited way) (*g*) research and training.

A school system soon discovers that establishment of a charge so broad as to swamp its staff leads to gaps, inconsistencies, and problems. The BCG found by the mid-1950s that over half of its resources were required for many of the "specified" services. To meet the needs of individual children from the general run of schools there was improvisation, arbitrary exclusion, and very limited coverage. The "model" of service was full diagnosis and treatment in the manner of a guidance clinic, but it could be offered only to several hundred cases each year. Consultation service to teachers and principals often became the less-desired alternative. The schools did not have enough social work help in locating needed community resources and making referrals out of the school system. Courses were a major vehicle for reaching teachers with mental health concepts—and not collaborative work with individual case situations.

A detailed survey which documented all of this and more made it all too clear that the BCG's qualified and dedicated staff members could not render the services needed, nor would they obtain their optimum professional satisfactions, if they continued to straddle two roles which required basically different administrative structures, professional interrelationships, and emphases: (*a*) the school-oriented social work and psychological counseling service; (*b*) the semidetached clinic.[21]

Our earlier discussion of the role of the school and the ways in which it might handle deviance would seem to supply a clear basis for choice: a school social work and psychological counseling program (with access to clinical services) is essential to any school system. Even the most competent and the most experienced of teachers occasionally require access to specialized services. For example, they may need advice and backing in their efforts to deal with a variety of classroom behaviors. They may need help in under-

[21] *Ibid.*

standing children, suggestions as to classroom adjustments, assistance from a worker who will do a more complete social study *in the home if necessary* and who will arrange for referral to community resources. From such contacts teachers learn general principles which make all their own efforts more effective. Experience with specific cases prepares them for discussion groups or special classes conducted by school psychologists and social workers.

If such service were generally available, cases located would not be so readily lost or sidetracked, nor would cases be assigned limited treatment resources on the basis of chance, pressures, or locally determined criteria. Social casework help on a short-contact basis, oriented to the home and available to children and their parents, would be part of this service, as would be the diagnostic testing and counseling by psychologists in instances of learning problems. Personnel rendering these services—psychologists and social workers—must be in a position to bring to bear the specialized clinical orientation which is basic to their professional training. They must, therefore, have access to psychiatric consultation. They should also have had supplementary training, experience, or orientation in the field of education if they are to function realistically in schools.

There is, in a sense, no choice here. Teachers deal with what they are able to in the classroom and do better if backed by a guidance program as the first line of support (see below) and by a clinically oriented school social work and psychological counseling program available to all schools and based in the schools, not in central units. When they need help, teachers must either turn to the principal and leave the next step to *many* local determinants, or count on the availability of specialists prepared to take the next step. If a clinic is to continue in the picture, it requires the referral structure and screening activity of a school social work program whose personnel have clinical backing, or it will only serve a heterogeneous, poorly selected population whose priority claims on the limited resources are not clear.

Such a program requires administrative arrangements which will place staff in the local school and free it to work in the home, ensure psychiatric consultation resources and psychological services as needed, and assign responsibility and leadership to school-oriented personnel. Informality and accessibility are prime prerequisites in developing the place of such services in the school; the major service must be to the classroom teacher or through the classroom teacher (perhaps with the guidance counselor as intermediary). The school social worker's and school psychologist's work routine, office, referral procedures, conferences, and discussion group schedules must all reflect this commitment. The traditional clinic "team" is not the work unit in such a service.

This kind of emphasis is not easily achieved, since the status accorded clinical service and the clinical team as a unit influences the professional self-images of affected personnel. It is what the situation requires, however. Emphasis on ties to the local school and on services to the classroom teacher is the general direction now taken by the BCG as the result of staff consideration and the policy directives of present leadership. The full implications of the new approach have not yet been evolved, however, and probably will not be without a period of experience. Also, although the BCG's resources have been increased somewhat, they are far from adequate to its tasks.

Currently, a portion of the city is served by what is now called a "school clinical service." Under this pattern a BCG team consisting of a social worker and a psychologist, with access to psychiatric services, is assigned exclusively to two schools. The remainder of the city, which includes the vast majority of schools, is covered by what would appear to be a makeshift, the "area clinical service." A central borough intake staff receives referrals, offers tests and mandatory services, carries out intake studies, makes referrals, and offers a limited amount of ongoing service in the clinic pattern. Under both plans the basic service is rendered by social workers and psychologists. Psychiatrists offer consultation, some diagnostic service, and a very limited amount of treatment.

A major justification for the school-based pattern as opposed to an area service or a central clinic is summarized in a recent BCG report:

It has been found that there is more opportunity to further the integration of mental hygiene and education if the social worker and/or the psychologist work intensively in a school. Consultation with teachers, division of therapeutic responsibility between school and clinic, cooperative study and treatment of a child—are all possible when school principals, teachers and clinicians can meet frequently around their common interest in particular children who need help.[22]

As much as one third of staff time in the school-based service may be devoted to consultation under this concept. The new manual places first emphasis on the need of the BCG team member to understand and relate to his school base. All referrals, for example, must be cleared through the principal of a school, since such involvement ensures the principal's participation in setting priorities for bureau services.

Further, in deciding whether to continue with a child in its own treatment services or to seek resources elsewhere in the community, the choice is often determined by whether the problem is school-focused and whether its solution would also have mental health educational value for school personnel. In line with this, parent-referred or agency-referred cases are more likely to be referred by the bureau, in turn, to other community resources, whereas it gives high priority, in the choice of treatment cases, to referrals from within the schools.

Consideration of school system needs would seem to lead to the conclusion that the school-based pattern should become the typical one, with the amount of staffing varied in accord with a given school's situation. An area system is only justified if the service model is that of a child guidance clinic. Should a city consider this as an alternative? What of the efforts, dating back to 1931, to create a clinical facility, a full child guidance clinic, in the New York City school system?

There is one point of view which holds that a school should never house a treatment clinic:

Psychiatric treatment functions cannot be properly carried out in school settings, especially since the symptoms which manifest themselves in the school are expressed through clashes with the value system. . . . The value oriented school setting, in which judgments are quite properly being made, is not an appropriate one for an individual psychiatric investigation.[23]

[22] Board of Education of the City of New York, *Annual Report: Bureau of Child Guidance, July 1, 1955—June 30, 1956* (New York, 1956, mimeographed), pp. 3–4.
[23] W. T. Vaughan, Jr., "Mental Health for School Children," *Children*, II, No. 6 (November–December, 1955), 203–7. Also see Gerald H. J. Pearson,

A school-based clinic is inevitably labeled as dealing with "bad boys," a description hardly appropriate for the range of children needing services.[24] There is, too, a widespread view that a child guidance treatment function belongs under medical auspices.

There are those who comment, in response, that while it is generally true that psychiatric treatment functions cannot properly be carried out in school settings, patience and skill have made New York an exception. After intensive study an expert group recommended that the bulk of the BCG resources be devoted to a school social work service because the traditional clinic cannot offer the basic on-the-spot services a school requires. More specifically:

a) "School referrals (to a school-based guidance clinic) are not usually based on the child's need for psychiatric treatment but on the school's need for help in relation to the child's problems." Clinics best serve a highly selected group. School personnel need a resource to which they can turn on the basis of the seriousness, to them, of the problem they confront.

b) "Referrals from principals and other school personnel do not always assure the kind of parental interest and cooperation which is important for treatment." While one must work with resistive parents and find ways of getting to them, it is true that a clinic would find that its resources, even if expanded, would not go very far if this were its responsibility. Handling the resistance to the point of referral would still require a school social work program as the basic service.

c) "Teachers and school administrators are not trained to deal with and cannot as a rule utilize clinical findings." The clinic's setting is medical, its interest is in pathology and its orientation is to the individual patient. The teacher's main interest is in constructive growth potentials. Even where a clinic is to be used, in school or community, an intermediary is needed. A school-oriented social work and psychology program could handle referrals and translate and adapt in both directions. A school-based service would

"The Most Effective Help a Psychiatrist Can Give to the Teacher," in Krugman, *Orthopsychiatry and the School.* He argues that a therapeutic unit in a school system is as much an anomaly as a medical clinic would be; many of his arguments are administrative and financial, however.

[24] Vaughan, "Mental Health for School Children," *Children,* II, 203–7.

see education, not medicine (psychiatry), as its "host" and would not be directed by psychiatry, yet it would have clinical origins and ties. It would become part of the school, master educational concepts and interests, and learn to meet school needs.[25]

A guidance clinic could operate successfully in the schools "only if it had such complete control of its intake and functional and administrative policies as to make it practically an independent unit."

These considerations would seem to be basic for a school system. Some would argue in favor of a small clinic in relation to staff training and recruitment needs,[26] but these problems have other possible solutions.

Since the focus of the present discussion is on basic roles and functions, some of the facts which may affect short-range New York City policy decisions or staff expansion will not be reviewed. Nor shall we turn to the considerable current staff allocations to special projects, mental health training, agency liaison, research, and special schools. Important for present purposes is recognition of the need for a local school-based social work staff, oriented to a school service and prepared to accept home-visiting obligations. All else is supplementary, secondary, and of lower priority. In such a program, psychiatrists carry out consultation and some emergency and diagnostic services. This plan appears to be evolving in the BCG. It has long been accepted in many smaller school social work services.[27]

EDUCATIONAL AND VOCATIONAL GUIDANCE—FROM CATCHALL
TO DEFINED PROFESSIONAL SERVICE

Expanding rapidly along lines which, in at least some ways, parallel the direction of the BCG is another of the major bureaus in the New York City school system, the Bureau of Educational and

[25] *BCG Survey*, pp. 23–24. The quotations are from the survey; the interpretations and inferences are mine.

[26] *Ibid.*

[27] National Association for Social Workers publishes the following: *Social Work in the Schools* (1960), *Helping the Troubled School Child* (1959), *School Social Work Practice*, ed. by V. Quattlebaum (1957), *Administration of School Social Work*, ed. by John Nebro (1960). Also see Nathaniel Bernstein, "Counseling and Psychotherapy," *Pathways in Child Guidance*, II, No. 4 (June, 1960), 3–6. Here a school psychiatrist seeks to define the guidance, attendance teacher, and BCG roles.

Vocational Guidance (BEVG). When, some year ago, the BEVG projected a ten-year expansion plan for a guidance staff of over 1,000 counselors, it was far from clear that budgetary allocations on such a scale would be forthcoming. However, the subsequent decision to expand guidance rapidly in all those schools in which children were considered to be receiving less-than-adequate education and the assignment of guidance personnel to a variety of new functions in connection with school suspensions of delinquents, early identification of troubled children, and the broadening of educational "horizons" for the underprivileged have all accelerated the development of this service. Although people within the program have their own clear vision of objectives, an outside observer must comment that roles are far from sharply defined and that the boundaries between these and related services (BCG, Bureau of Attendance) are not satisfactorily drawn. It is often far from clear whether this is a focused professional service or an administrative catchall. Nor is adequate coordination assured.

School systems everywhere tend to face similar problems as they try to step up vocational guidance, special education, career counseling, personal counseling, and delinquency prevention amid the conflicting programs, proposals, and claims of personnel trained in education, educational counseling, or one of a variety of specialties in psychology.

The Bureau of Educational and Vocational Guidance began as a high school vocational guidance program to assist those who were not going to college. Soon it was clear that assisting students to find employment was not enough; they needed help in preparation for a vocation. Educational guidance was thus developed, out of necessity.[28] The program remained relatively small and coverage was quite sporadic in the New York City school system until recent plans to ensure complete coverage in all types of schools. Licensed guidance counselors, members of a new, emerging profession, are being sought.

Review of the fundamental ideas and statements of objectives being advanced in the guidance field discloses that this is more than an educational and vocational service in the narrow tradi-

[28] Morris Krugman, "Guidance and Mental Hygiene Services in the New York City Schools," *Journal of Educational Sociology*, XXIV (May, 1951), 517–27.

tional sense. In fact, one must ask whether, *in some respects,* this does not tend to become the very school-oriented service we have urged in the discussion of the future of the Bureau of Child Guidance (although it does not, of course, render a significant home-visiting service).

The standard guidance manual for the elementary schools lists and elaborates the following basic concepts:

Guidance includes personal and social as well as educational and vocational areas.

Guidance must be related to a functional curriculum to meet children's needs.

The guidance point of view must pervade the training of the personnel of the school. It involves

attitude toward children,

emphasis on growth and development,

development of mental health concepts.

Sound guidance is based upon knowledge of children and an interest in learning about them.

Guidance is based on the recognition of the child as an individual.

Guidance takes into consideration the emotional needs of children, and as far as possible, implements these needs.

Guidance is inseparable from teaching.

No single technique of guidance is effective under all conditions.

Guidance is concerned with causes as well as symptoms.

Development problems are normal.

Guidance, to be successful, must have direction by the head of the school.

The aims elaborated include the following: to prevent the development of emotional disturbances; to offer assistance where there is learning difficulty related to emotional problems; to help detect children with difficulties and to assist in making referrals in the school system and to community agencies; to facilitate home-school communication; to help in orientation of children to school as well as in their transition to high school; to provide information about schools and vocations; to orient teachers to a testing program; to provide individual counseling sessions for children needing assistance as well as for those needing educational and vocational information; to help teachers learn guidance techniques; to aid in the placement of children in appropriate schools.[29]

[29] Board of Education of the City of New York, *Guidance of Children in Elementary Schools* (New York, 1956), pp. 2–7.

Apart from the educational-vocational guidance, in the narrow sense, and the basic task of helping place students in the appropriate schools, this selfsame statement of concepts and goals might well have been made by the Bureau of Child Guidance. In fact, a report of the BEVG says that counselors are "doing a competent professional job in the area of case work." Traditionally, as these two systems of service were growing, they were considered to be (a) a *clinical* guidance service (BCG) and (b) a *developmental* guidance service (BEVG).[30] The distinction, whatever its exact implication or earlier validity, has tended to be blurred or even lost as the programs have developed. The elementary school manual asserts that "the belief held by many that guidance need be only educational and vocational in nature is erroneous." Children face numerous adjustment difficulties during their school careers which may be reflected in learning, behavior, or relationship problems. Most require the kind of help which the classroom teacher is prepared to render. Some may be helped through "individual interviews, group guidance, consultations with parents, referrals to specialists . . . conferences with members of the administrative staff." [31]

A school system which plans an integrated system of helping services must obviously examine the resources and strengths of the BEVG, as it has the BCG, and must seek that kind of deployment and redeployment of resources, and that kind of administrative structure, which will guarantee the functions and services necessary. To plan the improvement and expansion of each separately is hardly a guarantee of efficiency or good coverage. Nor is it defensible in the light of the major resource shortages. As will be seen, we shall argue that the system requires *both* services and each has a *unique* contribution to make to the whole. We shall also hold that neither should preempt (but both should contribute to) the areas of school policy, curriculum, or administration—provinces also claimed by some enthusiastic guidance advocates who do not distinguish services for those needing special attention or individualized care from general programing.

Elementary schools. The BCG has tended to emphasize elemen-

[30] Krugman, "Guidance and Mental Hygiene Services," *Journal of Educational Sociology*, XXIV, 517–27.

[31] *Guidance of Children in Elementary Schools*, p. 2.

tary schools but the BEVG has turned to them only recently. In fact, there are still many who hold that in elementary schools all guidance should remain with the classroom teacher.

Educators stress that elementary school teaching should certainly be geared to child development concepts and should be alert to needs, aptitudes, interests, and disabilities. The consensus now appears to be that this broad task should be supported by guidance specialists able to orient teachers in their individualized and group work with children and to support specific action if more specialized help is needed.

Specially qualified staff has become available only recently in New York. Elementary school guidance began with "district coordinators" who were consultants and developed special projects. Gradually, coverage has been provided for individual schools where possible; first, through interested teachers with specialized courses and then through holders of a guidance license who have teaching experience plus specialized graduate courses. This does not, of course, provide the more intensive preparation and self-discipline of the field-work internship of either social casework training or of advanced clinical psychology training. On the other hand, it is noted that requirements such as these pose no serious recruitment problems, ensure staff well oriented to work in schools, and permit later acquisition of skill through experience and in-service training (at least by those of suitable personality). Until the number of authorized, licensed counselors is increased, however, most of the guidance work will be done by experienced teachers not yet licensed. Over half the schools do not yet have any coverage except that provided by a district coordinator.

Junior high schools. The guidance field and the school system see the junior high school as an "exploratory" institution which should seek to understand a child's capacities and offer him a variety of experiences. This does not, of course, minimize the need for basic learning in this period. Guidance toward a specific occupation would be premature, but a child should be provided opportunity to sample segments of the activity of the world of work; perhaps the area of choice can be narrowed.[32] High school program decisions

[32] Krugman, "Guidance and Mental Hygiene Services," *Journal of Educational Sociology*, XXIV, 517–27.

are made. In this sense the junior high school is basically a guidance-oriented institution and requires guidance staffing to attain its objectives.

The heavy guidance emphasis in junior high schools has made another type of service pattern necessary. The licensed educational and vocational guidance counselors serve as specialists, consultants, and coordinators. Although initially coverage was spotty, the number of counselors authorized was gradually increased and New York City now has such staff in all junior high schools. The work is supplemented by teacher-counselors (the school guidance committee).

The teachers are prepared through special courses, meetings, and institutes; they carry responsibility for the counseling of pupils in their grades. The ninth-grade teacher-counselor helps with high school applications, which are checked by the licensed counselor, who may interview pupils if necessary. The licensed counselor also carries on the personal guidance functions already described: accepting case referrals from teacher-counselors and others, serving as liaison with social agencies, and guiding teacher-counselors. The BEVG hopes eventually to have a licensed counselor for each 300 students in a junior high school.

Academic high schools. At the beginning, the academic high schools, which launched the guidance program, sought only to help find jobs for those who did not go to college. Educational guidance, when added, was the province of classroom teachers. The program is now elaborate and includes testing, interviews and program planning at admission, keeping cumulative records, periodic planning interviews, and special attention to maladjusted pupils. Group guidance courses for children are now also general and include attention to both educational-vocational opportunities and common personal-social problems. A full-time dean, administrative assistant, or guidance chairman coordinates the work of teacher-counselors, many of whom specialize in such fields as college advising, truancy, testing, personal guidance for the maladjusted, special programs. There is one position for 500–600 pupils.

Standards for teachers in this assignment have risen somewhat as the state has established minimum requirements for the guidance assignment, as local college courses have attracted many high school teachers for guidance training, and as special courses were developed in specific schools. The license for administrative assistants includes guidance training. Without doubt, however, the system would have a more effective program if the "equivalent-time" positions could become, instead, full-time licensed counseling assignments. The BEVG calls attention to the specialized content of the job. It has decried the tendency to use the bulk of guidance time for disciplinary functions in the province of administration and has called attention to the lack of personal guidance. It recommends a counselor per 300 students.

Vocational high schools. As might be expected, vocational schools weight their programs to vocational guidance. They concentrate much of their effort in the first year, which is designed for exploration, but continue throughout the four years. They have little specialized staffing for this task or for placement, and the entire program is under review. Classroom teachers render valuable service by remaining with a group throughout the course—but more specialized services are also necessary. A recently prepared manual projects a broad program which would include testing, home room and grade orientation and exploration, help for those who do not adjust, close integration with health services, job placement help, and steering of some to college or to advanced technical schools.[33] It also lays claim to a function which may be in the domain of the personnel of a school social work–psychological counseling program:

The understanding of the significance and severity of behavior deviations of pupils is one of the responsibilities of the guidance counselor. The counselor should have sufficiently good insight into a problem to be able to determine whether the school itself can work out a therapeutic program, whether agency help alone can be effective, or whether a combination of both is the best plan. When other agencies are called on, the counselor is expected to supply a good case history.[34]

Other activities. As in the instance of the BCG, it is not necessary to review all the other BEVG commitments except to note that they make heavy demands on personnel and tend to obscure the

[33] Board of Education of the City of New York, *Guidance in Vocational High Schools* (New York, 1955).
[34] *Ibid.*, p. 31.

issue of core function. Among other things, the BEVG is involved in court liaison, early identification projects, "higher horizons," attendance coordination, services to special groups of handicapped children, placement, and some group thereapy. This is an expanding and enthusiastic program in need of role definition, staff expansion, and the raising of staff qualifications.

The future. Obviously, "guidance" now is and could be many things. One of the major issues to be settled is whether the *personal* counseling function is so different, qualitatively, from the *educational and vocational* guidance as to invalidate the basic premises of the BEVG program. Those who hold this viewpoint begin with the assumption that *all* children need the educational-vocational guidance service, while the personal counseling is for the *troublesome and deviant.*

As seen from the various quotations above and the description of BEVG program direction, there is a contrary view. It holds that there is a continuity between these two aspects and that while there may be need for specialists in testing, job placement, and school assignment, the typical guidance counselor should be able to render a service in which the educational-vocational guidance is child-development-oriented and the personal guidance is school-based. Moreover, a guidance counselor who is trained and experienced as a teacher is in a position to demonstrate teaching methods and to help teachers and children on the classroom level.

While the school social work literature outlines a broad, school-centered liaison and direct-service role for *social casework* personnel, guidance authorities see the *guidance counselor* in a direct-service and coordinating role at the core of what they call the pupil personnel program (psychology, social work, psychometrics, physical and mental health, attendance, registration, remedial work, counseling). They would relegate social work to home-community relationships.[35]

Although the present guidance personnel situation nationally is called "discouraging," the employed counselors in the United States

[35] Arthur M. Hitchcock, "Guidance in American Education," in *Supplement to Reference Papers on Children and Youth* (Washington, D.C.: 1960 White House Conference on Children and Youth, mimeographed). Each article is separately numbered.

(qualified in a variety of ways and on many levels) outnumber trained school social workers several times over.[36] Recent federal legislation, oriented to assuring high quality of education and conserving human talents, places considerable stress on the training of guidance personnel and supports significant expansion of training opportunities.

The New York State Commissioner of Education, who stresses guidance on the secondary school level, supports a broad concept of the role. He has listed the objectives of guidance in this way:

(1) to assist, at as early a time as possible, *all* pupils in making appropriate and satisfying educational, personal, social and vocational adjustments and plans, (2) to assist teachers, other school staff members and parents in understanding better the needs and problems of each pupil, and (3) to assist administrators, staff members and the community in understanding needs and problems of pupil groups.

One proposed element in a guidance program to accomplish these objectives is "counseling." [37]

Guidance would seem to have considerable potentiality for expansion but its personnel are generally not adequately prepared in the clinical realm and for tasks involving self-awareness. This would tend to support a concept of function which would under any circumstances seem conceptually sound for a large school system: A system should seek enough guidance counselors to render both the educational-vocational and placement services needed and the *front-line, first-level consultation to teachers, referral, and individual counseling.* The guidance field is, in fact, rapidly moving in this direction. Because the education is often a matter of evening supplementary courses and lacks the field work or internship of social work and psychology, a system of supervision and professional controls will have to be developed. Personnel will have to become clear as to just what their courses in child development and their experience in guidance and education prepare them for

[36] Golden Anniversary Conference on Children and Youth, Inc., *Focus on Children and Youth* (Washington, D.C.: The Conference, 1960), pp. 107–8. Also see Reginald Robinson, David F. De Marche, Mildred K. Wagle, *Community Resources in Mental Health* (New York: Basic Books, Inc., 1960), Chapter VII.

[37] James E. Allen, Jr., "Good Guidance and Enough of It," Board of Education of the City of New York, *Guidance News*, Vol. X, No. 3 (March, 1958).

—and what one does not do without clinical training and "controls," or psychiatric consultation. If such clarity could develop, it would gradually eliminate confusion as to roles and the inevitable tensions which emerge when personnel not qualified for clinical tasks undertake clinical functions.

A third bureau, which has its counterparts in many school systems, the Bureau of Attendance, must now be discussed. It will then be possible to return to the BCG and the BEVG and to face definition of the functions for which each bureau is most suited and the ways in which these interrelate.

THE BUREAU OF ATTENDANCE

Truancy and unexplained absence offer unique case finding opportunities. A good deal is now known about these phenomena and about what an attendance program can and cannot accomplish:

1. Most children eligible for school attendance seem to go to school regularly when well. Most parents seem to want their children to go to school and cooperate in assuring attendance.

2. In spite of "attendance pressure" on school personnel, attendance rates have fluctuated but have changed relatively little in actual percentages since 1900.

3. Constant expansion of an attendance bureau is not accompanied by a corresponding improvement in attendance rates.

4. The majority of absentees reported to the Bureau of Attendance are either ill or absent for other legal reasons. Among the supposedly physically ill or lawful absentees may be children from unstable homes or disturbed children whose parents help them disguise the real nature of the absences.

5. Attempts to learn from the statistics of the Bureau of Attendance about causes of non-attendance, especially of unlawful absence, were largely unsuccessful, as these statistics are not focused on discovering causes or on finding the meaning of unlawful absence.

6. There is, however, an accumulation of evidence in some studies that the school situation is often a decisive factor in determining attendance rates and unlawful absence. It has been suggested by educators that crucial needs are: smaller schools, smaller classes, understanding, interested teachers and principals, more flexible curriculum.

7. Special studies and case observations show clearly, too, the role of social and economic deprivation among the causes leading to unlawful absence. More systematic research is needed.

8. If one eliminates casual non-attendance, the pranks of normal adolescence, the normal, periodic, independent searching for new experi-

ences, one finds a core of truants and other absentees who represent a wide range of school inadequacy, family disruption, social factors and emotional disturbance and who need to be identified and helped. Truancy for these children is not the heart of the maladjustment but only the symptom which calls to our attention the need for study and help.

9. Many (probably most) truants are not and never become delinquents, but many delinquents first manifest their difficulty in truancy. If such children can be understood and help can be given early, more serious trouble might often be avoided.[38]

Since absence, whether of the lawful or unlawful kind, is caused by physical illness, difficult family problems, strong personal drives, and serious maladjustments—as well as by the weather—it is not surprising that a limited stimulus, such as the efforts of an attendance bureau, does not change basic attendance trends. Nor can a typical attendance program of itself overcome economic, social, and cultural factors which affect the way in which the school, as an institution, is seen by specific parents and children and, thus, the emphasis placed by them on regularity of participation in the school program. New York City is not unlike the rest of the country in this regard.

Is it wise to look at all of the children unlawfully absent or truant as though they will eventually be involved in even more serious violations of law? Legally, children's court statutes often classify habitual truancy as delinquency, i.e., the child has been sent to school by his parents but does not attend, without suitable reason. Moreover, the defiant truant who remains out of school despite rules, parental urging, teacher urging, or threats arouses a good deal of anger and a desire to punish. Study shows, nonetheless, that while more truants than nontruants are potential delinquents, many (probably most) truants are not and never become involved in other serious problems.

Recent studies do suggest the case finding potentials of programs concerned with truants. Dozens of sources might be cited. For example: The Passaic study showed a 6.8 percent truancy rate among the general population and a 34 percent rate among delinquents. Even larger proportions of delinquents were found to have been truants in sample studies by Healy and Bronner (60

[38] Trude W. Lash and Alfred J. Kahn, *Children Absent from School* (New York: Citizens' Committee for Children of New York City, Inc., 1949), p. 30.

percent), Fenton (52 percent), Bartlett (46 percent), several New Jersey studies (29–66 percent).[39] The Gluecks reported that two thirds of 1,000 juvenile delinquents had been truants, while the Cambridge-Somerville Youth Study showed that the bulk of the most serious delinquents in the group had been truants.[40] Army soldiers with AWOL records showed serious truancy histories.[41]

The other lesson from all available data is that persistent non-attendance, whether or not technically truancy, may reflect a series of interrelated causes which are quite complex. It must at times be met by an approach to ethnic or social *subgroups* not motivated to have their children educated (or who do not see attendance in available schools as advancing educational ends), at times through *school* changes, and at times through work with *individuals*. All three may be necessary at one time. It would seem clear, then, that the case finding opportunity offered by repeated nonattendance and truancy must be followed by adequate case evaluation and differential decision making. This has tended to become the major specialized function of an attendance service.

New York City's Bureau of Attendance has made substantial progress in the past decade in the transition from an old-fashioned "hookey-cop" agency to a combination of elements of the BEVG, the BCG, school social work, and a protective service. A brief description may serve to define issues of function and place in the total system.

More specifically, the bureau was created by the New York State education law in 1914 to carry out the provisions of the compulsory education law and other duties imposed by statute and Board of Education assignment. Its early policing and enforcement emphases were natural and proper products of their time. The assignment was a "continual round of ferreting out truants from their hiding places or in chasing them about the streets." The problem was seen as the need to "close . . . the loopholes by which the child or his parent may escape the fulfillment of a statutory requirement."

[39] Kvaraceus, *Juvenile Delinquency and the Schools*, p. 145.

[40] Sheldon and Eleanor Glueck, *After-Conduct of Discharged Offenders* (London: Macmillan and Co., Ltd., 1945). Also Powers and Witmer, *An Experiment in the Prevention of Delinquency.*

[41] Samuel A. Stouffer and others, *The American Soldier* (Princeton: Princeton University Press, 1949), I, 133.

In all of the above, New York City was neither ahead of nor behind the times. Its attendance program reflected the prevalent views of truancy and was identified as an instrument of enforcement, not as a helping service. Those truants who could be compelled to go to school or helped to go by simple material aid were assisted by such an approach; those whose absences required more subtle handling remained away and were reported to the attendance officer time and again but were not aided.

Gradually there was applied to the truancy problem the more profound understanding of the personality of the child which was to affect basically all education and mental hygiene work. Note was taken too of the cultural changes in which most people recognized the need for education as preparation for successful adulthood. Educators, psychiatrists, psychologists, and social workers developed a new understanding of truancy and a new viewpoint toward the school attendance program. They knew that resistance to school had special economic, cultural, or personality causes which could and should be understood.

The professional literature, including some of that contributed by members of the New York City Bureau of Attendance, began to reflect some of this new understanding and the new viewpoints. However, the New York City program itself, looked at after World War II, was basically the pre-mental-hygiene enforcement effort, in which a policing approach was primary. Gestures in the direction of casework and individualization were consciously limited by policing concepts, narrowly conceived. Routine and empty field visits, district and division hearings offered little that was geared to modern objectives. Unexplained absence was followed almost immediately by a visit, but two thirds of the visits disclosed lawful absence. At the same time, little that was effective was done in cases of serious problems in the social or emotional realm.[42]

Many attendance bureaus have not moved from this point but the New York City bureau has changed in many ways in the past decade and there are indications of significant progress. Both social casework and educational-personal guidance philosophy and methodology have clearly influenced the attendance field and the bureau.

[42] Lash and Kahn, *Children Absent from School.*

The 1954 *Manual of Regulations for Attendance Staff*, for example, stresses these points:

The Bureau sees its goal as the furnishing of a treatment service for the school absentee that meets the needs of each child and which is based upon the principles of mental hygiene, sound human relationships, social work findings, and the principles of modern education.

. . . The Bureau of Attendance seeks to provide a technical help that will permit a recognition and diagnosis of problems.

. . . The attendance officer, through his knowledge, ability, and sympathetic understanding, seeks to discover the causes of maladjustment not only as this is manifested in school absence but as it can be determined from an assessment of the child's total personality and behavior.

Personnel qualifications have improved, and modern educational and mental hygiene concepts have made some headway. Journals and professional conferences in the attendance field seek to integrate a guidance and casework philosophy with some of the older attendance concepts.

Some attendance officers have taken part-time and some full-time social work training; several of these have reached district and division leadership levels. Many others have taken evening work toward the M.S. degree in education, psychology guidance, or related fields. Some are enrolled for higher degrees. One social work school established a training unit in an attendance office for use in general student field work and also to permit a work-study plan. A local school of education has also provided a specialized undergraduate and graduate attendance training program.

In recent years basic educational requirements have been raised so that no attendance workers are now appointed without college degrees and certain relevant professional courses (some of which may be taken after appointment). While they do not have practice teaching, their other requirements match those of teachers, and recent legislation permits attendance officers to qualify at a higher level of education and experience for the title "attendance teacher" (a B.A., two years of experience plus thirty semester hours of specified courses) and to be paid in accord with teacher salary scales. The vast majority of the attendance officers are so qualified.

The upgrading of qualifications and salary has been accompanied by an internal procedural and professional reorganization which seeks to combine what to an observer would seem to be a "policing" and an "assertive casework" organization. Routine hearings have been discontinued. The work is now carried on in four phases:

    (1) A small group of *consultants* work out of the offices of assistant superintendents, seeking to develop programs within the schools to encourage regular attendance.

    (2) A ten-man *Mobile Unit* patrols stores, entertainment areas, parks, and so on to pick up truants and to win the cooperation of managers in excluding children who belong in school. Some of those picked up are taken to court, some are referred for follow-up by local attendance staff.

    (3) Most of the staff devotes most of its time to the traditional *home follow-up of school-reported, unexplained absence.* Most of the cases are processed rapidly and generally superficially in the light of the home response.

    (4) A smaller number of cases are dealt with on a *more intensive basis* in one of two ways: (*a*) The district office staff members who do the routine follow-up also select a number of cases for what is called the "case process," more sustained supervision and service. The staff concentrates on this program during the summer. (*b*) Three *casework units* within the Bureau of Attendance (one of which is a field training unit for a school of social work), staffed with approximately twenty attendance officers who have completed graduate social work training, accept cases on referral from district offices for more intensive casework help.

These roles are in the process of evolution and choices will have to be made. One might predict movement toward concentration on the "case process" for the district staff as qualifications rise and as the validity of routine visiting in all nonattendance cases comes into question. The alternative would seem to be the creation of more casework units and relegation of the remainder of the staff to the routine visits.

Statistical reports at this point suggest the need to face this issue directly. Cases of unlawful absence are routinely referred to the bureau on the fifth day. Visits show that 65 to 70 percent are lawful. Of about 188,000 children served, 60,000 are unlawfully absent, of whom the truants total approximately 40,000. Only 2 percent of these get to court. Neglect petitions are often filed as more appropriate than an allegation of child misconduct.

Great emphasis is still placed in the school system on immediate reporting of unexplained absences and the assumption continues that a rapid home visit by an attendance officer is the most effective action and a necessary step. Officers are under pressure to make endless numbers of these visits and, as a result, most of these visits are routinized, rapid, and lead nowhere if reasonable though superficial explanations are offered. In part this "statistics anxiety" is explained by a not fully satisfactory formula for state financial aid to localities, a formula in which average daily attendance is a major element. To some degree, too, it reflects the philosophy of function. No staff can be required to make so many thousands of routine home visits, most of which merely establish the legality of the absence, and continue to retain an alertness to case finding possibilities and case screening issues. It is even less likely that the same staff will be able to undertake direct casework services of a more intensive kind.

There is considerable testimony to the effect that despite load and obstacles some of the new bureau emphases are being reflected in responsible, persistent, and helpful work by individual attendance officers. There is no doubt that increased efforts are being made to use the interviews with the parents in diagnostic fashion. Most attendance officers try to understand the problems of absentees and to inaugurate helping measures. This does not, however, create a fully satisfactory program and does not resolve all the issues. A partial emphasis on casework does not obscure basic questions about core function. And the nature of that function requires more complete integration of the bureau and the BCG and BEVG.

It is no longer possible to defend a one-symptom basis for the organization of services and *nobody does*. How, then, shall non-attendance be handled? It will be recalled that the discussion of educational principles, of child guidance as well as educational-vocational guidance, led to the view that the teacher's concerns must be broadened to permit, in the classroom, competent case finding and child helping activity. The teacher must be backed by school-based and school-oriented guidance and social work–psychological counseling programs. All that we know about serious non-attendance and its many possible meanings reinforces the view that it is just one of many symptoms which should lead to use of the general counseling service once the classroom teacher feels that the next level of help is necessary. A modern school helping service needs a basic program for children who are meeting adjustment problems and who need help. Segregation by symptoms leads to inaccurate stereotyping and does not permit development of a viable professional assignment.

New York City's program has been gradually moving toward full integration of the guidance and attendance programs and the process would now seem to require completion. This can and should be carried out in such a fashion as to ensure that serious non-attendance would not be neglected.

In a classroom situation conceived in the terms outlined, the teacher would be alert to all manifestations of distress in a child, whether the symptom is a sudden change in behavior, a nervous habit, inability to learn, or unexplained absence. It also follows that the first opportunity to understand the difficulty would be the teacher's. Referral and requests for outside consultation or help would come later, if needed.

If a child were absent without explanation, the first steps taken might be telephone calls, letters, postcards. Most absentees return after a few days even where the absence is truancy; where the absence is symptomatic of serious trouble it is likely to be repeated. When the child returns, a good teacher, by conversation with the child and by asking the parent to come in, will attempt to assess the meaning of the unexplained absence and decide whether it suggests the need for such next steps as school program change or referral for outside aid. At this point principal or counselor might participate in the planning by seeing child or parent, or through consultation or help with resources.

When the school picture permitted, and if the total situation suggested it as wise, teachers might themselves make some home visits in truancy cases (but it is recognized that current school system pressures make this an unreasonable expectation in the immediate future). If the teacher's work with a child, whether because of nonattendance or any other reasons, led to decision to bring the social worker or school psychologist in for service, home visits could and should be made as necessary. Visits would certainly be made by these personnel in cases of repeated non-attendance and parental failure to respond to calls and to notes. Where a child was known to be a truant or in special difficulty, they could visit immediately, much as does the attendance officer now. The difference is that this would be part of a normal case-work or counseling routine, diagnostically focused and carried out by staff trained for casework treatment, counseling, service of various kinds, and referral.

While it is possible to be quite clear about principles and func-tions, strategic decisions are needed as to the implications of this approach for a Bureau of Attendance per se. This is best discussed in the context of a total integrated pattern. How, in short, are school social work–psychological counseling, guidance, and attendance to be interrelated? What is the core task of each?

AN INTEGRATED PATTERN

BEVG personnel receive their training from guidance departments in schools of education, while BCG personnel are trained in social work, clinical psychology, and psychiatry. Nonetheless, their activ-ities have tended to overlap and to merge as the BCG has recognized that most of its operation belongs outside the clinic and as the guid-ance program has extended into personal guidance. In planning for a sound pattern, one should not ignore the basic expertness of the trained guidance counselor in rendering the school environment conducive to optimum student development; nor should one under-estimate the value of the special treatment focus of social workers and psychologists who have a clinical background—particularly if they work in home and community and use all possible environ-mental resources, including those of the school.

Writing in 1955, a survey team concluded that each of the two orientations has something necessary to contribute and that the delimiting of functions should derive from working together in the field. There is need for full and free communication on all levels. Eventually, there might be "coalescences and realignments on the basis of changed training and experience, and strict delimitation of function for each group." [43] In recent years, the BCG has accepted

[43] *BCG Survey*, p. 75.

the general principle of reorienting its base of operations toward the school. It recognizes that it cannot be an isolated, protected clinic simply housed in the school system. At the same time, the BEVG has expanded very substantially, has projected even more expansion, and has been turned to by the school system as a possible way of handling a wide variety of problems growing out of neighborhood change, the need for racial integration, and the desire to upgrade academic standards. Its manuals, plans, and some of its programs do not clearly separate it from the BCG function.

Thus, while the principle is sound that detailed operational patterns should be worked out by teachers, guidance counselors, BCG staff, principals, and superintendents in the field, it is hardly possible to delay general clarification of mission, roles, interrelations, and administrative alignments. Millions of dollars of annual expenditure are involved and even more is proposed. It is doubtful that the city is obtaining optimum returns on its investment. Nor is the *basic outline* obscure; it has already developed out of experience.

If there were no shortages of personnel in any of these fields, if length of training were no consideration, and if it were possible to wipe the slate clean for a fresh start, the case might be made for a new hybrid practitioner who would have the theoretical and field work training of the social caseworker, the diagnostic and testing training of the clinical psychologist, the educational training and experience of the guidance counselor. One could then envisage a school-based counseling service staffed by the hybrid and fully qualified to deal with all contingencies.

All realities considered, it seems wiser to encourage what has been developing and to consider structuring the schools' helping services on the assumption that the guidance personnel and the clinically oriented social work and psychological personnel will remain as two groups, one essentially rooted in education and child development and the other in social work–clinical psychology. The task is one of organizing school services for efficient use of both. The following seems desirable:

a) Classroom *teachers* must continue to assume important responsibility for educational, vocational, and personal guidance at all levels, and their formal education as well as in-service training should seek to add to their qualifications in this sense.

b) Guidance personnel should continue to render their *vocational-educational guidance services*. The "line" practitioner should have responsibilities in this field as well as in the personal counseling field, as indicated under (*c*), since the two responsibilities are closely intertwined at the first level of service after the classroom teacher. Children requiring intensive service because of problems in the educational-vocational realm or in personal behavior would be referred to the social work service. One might assume the need for considerably expanded vocational-educational guidance in light of current stress on enriched educational programs and conservation of talent.

c) *Specialized (licensed) guidance personnel* should also provide *personal guidance*, i.e., the first line of counseling: case finding, brief screening, consultation to teachers, help with classroom situations, referrals to community agencies at all school levels. They should not undertake clinical functions or functions which demand clinical background. They are, however, the child's "friend in school" even during clinic contacts and for the aftercare period.

d) *School social work and psychological counseling personnel* should be the next line of service, dealing with children who need more intensive help and clinical evaluation personally, or whose parents need intensive casework services related to a child's school problems. They should perform all the functions described above in the discussion of the BCG (i.e., psychological testing and counseling, social case study, referral, brief casework service, and preparation for clinical treatment). They should be ready and available to undertake home visits on a scale not now characteristic of the BCG, seeing their major identifications in school work, not in the office-based work of the psychiatric clinic. They should be the ones who clarify the need for long-term clinical treatment and be the channel to the clinics, thereby ensuring wise use of resources. The psychologists should give individual tests, as needed. The service must include psychiatric consultants for consultation to staff, diagnostic interviews as needed, and to handle psychiatric emergencies which arise in the schools.

e) Detailed working patterns should be evolved in the individual school and might vary somewhat in accord with local needs and preference. While all these specialized personnel require central supervision, direction, in-service training, and policy guidance, the schools would be served best if there were in each individual school an *administrative officer* responsible for unifying the effort. Otherwise, the schools might find, too often, that a series of part-time specialists come and go and are not used to maximum effect. The person given this assignment would not necessarily be the same type of person for elementary, junior high, and high schools. Principals would, in theory, be the ideal persons to carry such responsibility, but their many other preoccupations would not permit it. Assistant principals, administrative assistants, or high school deans would appear to be the most suitable. They would require new preparation for this, but it would be in line with current developments in formulating their qualifications.

Assistant superintendents might provide leadership in their districts to these school-based administrative officers seeking to integrate the efforts of guidance and social work–psychology specialists in each school. Centrally, the program would have its professional base and leadership in the Division of Child Welfare.

To sum up the "personal" guidance and counseling aspects of these proposals in terms which would seem valid for all schools, one might suggest the following propositions: If a child cannot be "brought into a condition of learning," from the teacher's perspective, there is need for some specialized help. Guidance is the first line of help, emphasizing support of classroom changes and adjustments. School social work and psychological counseling are the next line, giving special attention to problems within the child and the home situation. In those instances in which the child's internal processes are involved in a manner which is disturbing to motivation, discipline, and roles in the school, the treatment may have to be referred outside the school to a clinic or agency.

This, then, is the outline of a structure which might emerge out of current New York City developments, given clarification of responsibility, administrative reforms, and needed personnel expansion. In many respects it is currently being demonstrated in those schools in which BCG and BEVG personnel are now working to-

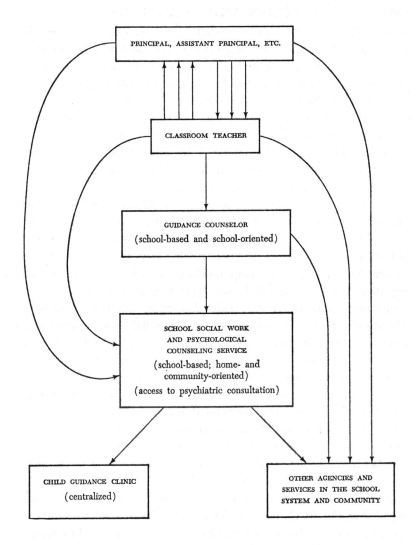

PROPOSED PATTERN OF TEACHER-INITIATED REFERRAL AND
CONSULTATION IN BEHALF OF CHILDREN MANIFESTING
DIFFICULTY

(*Arrows indicate direction of referral and consultation*)

Note: Although principals, teachers, and school social work–counseling are
shown as making referral to other agencies and services in the school system
and community, they would not refer to the *same* services. This more specialized channel should be used where social work and clinical judgments are
needed about the referral or in carrying it through.

gether with younger children in what is known as the Early Identification and Prevention Program.[44] It has implications for the Bureau of Attendance as well. Clearly, at the point at which attendance problems or other problems need more than the attention of teacher and principal, there is reason to draw on a school-based next line of service. This we have defined as the province of the guidance staff. In a smaller number of cases the help must move to the third line of service, characterized by clinical competence and channels as well as a focus on home and community. This is generally seen as a school social work service.

A fully integrated system in any city would thus tend to deploy attendance staff in accord with individual competence so as to strengthen guidance and school social work services; these services, in turn, would encompass situations arising from nonattendance and ensure "reaching out" to help families as well as the taking of initiative in court as needed. New York City's situation as a large center with substantial caseloads also offers another possibility. The Bureau of Attendance defines itself as a field-home-community service, something which is very much needed. The BCG, it will be recalled, has not become a complete school social work service. Moreover, the Bureau of Attendance has now moved somewhat from its one-symptom emphasis and undertakes home and community studies where they are needed in connection with classroom discipline problems or district hearings in connection with school suspensions. However, most of the bureau staff are not qualified by training for intensive social casework. If the core role of the bureau is to be casework the bureau's history and strengths offer a new possibility worthy of some consideration. Within one division, paralleling the BCG, the Bureau of Attendance might provide a specialized protective school social work service, oriented to home, community, and court. Such service would have to be closely integrated with the remainder of the school social work and would be prepared, aggressively and skillfully, to "go out" to cases in which

[44] Board of Education of the City of New York, *Report on the Early Identification and Prevention Program* (New York, 1960, mimeographed). Also, Bureau of Educational and Vocational Guidance, *Annual Report, 1959–1960* (New York: Board of Education, 1960, mimeographed), pp. 24–36, and Bureau of Child Guidance, *Annual Report, 1959–1960* (New York: Board of Education, 1960, mimeographed), pp. 8–9.

children's school problems manifest abuse, neglect, extreme family disorganization, and uncontrolled behavior. Referrals would come from the teacher, principal, guidance counselor, or school social worker. Since attendance officers are peace officers, they could take on this role, maintaining close court liaison but stressing the strengthening of the home. Protective casework is a complex, specialized task and the attendance staff would need retraining and continued upgrading for it. Given broader concerns, the bureau would cease to function as an attendance staff but would become *a specialized protective bureau in a school social work program.*

THE "600" SCHOOLS—AN OVERDUE EXPERIMENT

The basic elements of the school's program for children in trouble have now been dealt with and suggestions outlined. One basic program remains, and it may be introduced with a question: Do we need special schools for delinquents or those considered to be headed for delinquency? If all else that has been proposed is carried out, is the pattern incomplete without such schools?

In the past, many of the large urban school systems created special schools for delinquent boys or truants, often calling them "parental" schools. For the most part, however, whatever their names, these schools were custodial enterprises and they were offered as solution to the problems of the majority of pupils and teachers whose routines and learning suffered because of the interference of a minority of aggressive or noncooperative pupils. Few of these special schools could pretend to have educational or therapeutic programs, despite some gestures in the direction of vocational courses, training in basic skills, or activities designed to "build character." New York City, too, had its parental schools.

A modern educational system can propose conducting a custodial school whose only purpose is to comply in a minimal way with the requirements of compulsory education laws on one basis and one basis alone—the admission that it has exhausted the range of possible variations in basic educational approaches and is nonetheless unable to meet the needs, interests, problems, or potentials of a certain group of pupils. It would then have to ask whether such individuals perhaps did not require the institutional facilities of the state department or agency providing services for the mentally ill. Further, before condemning a child to a number of years in a school which is only custodial, because it has no confidence in or success with its educational offerings as applied to certain children, such a system would have to ask itself whether it was not abusing its prerogatives under the compulsory education law. Should a child be in custody, even if he returns home at night, without court proceedings? If the court decrees custody, should it not be in an institution designed to educate or to treat?

Not many cities have experimented imaginatively with variations and adaptations of the education program for children such as these. There is, therefore, no basis for a view that schools harbor substantial populations whom we have a right to condemn to custody until they are old enough to be released. New York City thus abolished its parental schools which had a history going back into the nineteenth century, and which had developed from places of confinement and labor into "day" disciplinary settings for truants and unmanageable children. The "truant" school of 1919 became the probationary school of 1927 but still lacked a suitable program for the group, in the sense of the new educational thinking. Therefore, when a new director began to emphasize curriculum and services designed to help boys to adjust in the academic and the social sense, school authorities became interested and the "600" schools were launched in 1947. Included in this new administrative structure and designated by numbers in the "600" series were also the schools associated with detention facilities (i.e., for children awaiting court action or arrangement of placement), the schools associated with psychiatric facilities in city hospitals, and schools which are part of the program of long-term institutions. There are now 25 such schools in the New York system. Our attention here is limited to the *"600" day schools for boys,* 13 in number, and the one school recently opened for girls. These accommodate approximately 2,300 children beyond the fifth grade. They have been organized as part of the schools' program for dealing, in the community, with children in trouble.

The intent. The school official who proposed the "600" schools was quite clear as to objectives. This was not to be a custodial or punitive instrument:

My purpose was to discover and develop from such a program the administrative, supervisory and other educational techniques which would make it possible to handle emotionally disturbed children in a school setting. Therefore, it is my belief that the "600" schools should be striving to "put themselves out of business" and not to expand. I think this tendency to increase the numbers of "600" schools is not a healthy one. Rather, more emphasis should be placed upon efforts to determine ways and means of detecting youngsters in our elementary and junior high schools as early as possible in their school careers who need special help and then provide for these in the school setting. If such plans were successful there would be a decrease in the numbers who would need our present "600" school program. It is my considered opinion that this trend, namely, of making the services of the "600" schools less and less necessary, is the one that should be striven for and not increasing them.[45]

This philosophy places emphasis on early case finding, enrichment of the general school curriculum, and keeping children in the mainstream where possible. Separating-out is not advocated as a basic solution to anything. The schools were to accept boys "with an I.Q. of 75 or over presenting grave emotional and behavior problems and for whom current procedures in the elementary or junior high schools have been unsuccessful." [46] The objective was to "return the pupils to the schools which they would normally attend as soon as their adjustment therein seems fairly assured." [47]

An experiment of this sort requires clear *criteria* for selection of participants; appropriate admissions *procedures;* well-defined experimental stimuli (in this instance, the plan, *the program,* the special facilities, and the teachers); *discharge policy;* tools of *measurement.* For one reason or another all of these were in some degree lost until recently. The city's official research agency in this field concluded an evaluation with the recommendation that

the "600" day school program be made and kept continuously experimental, not only to assure the best available provision for the special needs of the pupils in these schools but also in order to devise and de-

---

[45] Dr. Frank O'Brien, in charge of the Division of Child Welfare, in a letter, when the suggestion was made that a "600" school be established for girls.

[46] Board of Education of the City of New York, Division of Child Welfare, *Circular,* No. 4, December, 1949.

[47] Meeting of the Board of Education of the City of New York, as reported in the *Journal* of the Board, I (1946), 2052.

velop such approaches and modes of treatment as may be applicable to problem children in the regular schools.[48]

Earlier efforts. It is inherently difficult for a large organization to maintain a systematic experiment and the New York school system is no exception. And given an area in which knowledge is limited, the situation becomes completely unsatisfactory. Thus, despite widespread interest and some support and despite individual work of a high quality by some gifted staff, the "600" schools as a system were not meeting expectations by most criteria. While they were no less satisfactory than comparable efforts elsewhere, the expectations were high and the scrutiny constant.

Classes were small and managed good attendance records but the buildings were dilapidated, heavily screened, and unattractive outside. There was inadequate auditorium and play space. The only referral criteria stated that the boys should have "grave emotional and behavior problems," but referral procedures gave way to pressure arising out of emergency or desperation. The BCG and BEVG were often not involved.

Despite pronouncements as to therapeutic intent, these were essentially custody schools with heterogeneous groups having many needs. Curricular resources were limited. Efforts at orientation, work with parents, and remedial instruction were swallowed by the pervading preoccupation with discipline—an inevitable consequence of certain program and staffing lacks. The schools "contained" boys successfully but did not rehabilitate or return them to regular schools.

The subsequent history of studies and debate is not immediately relevant. Expansion took place and a "600" school was created for girls despite the limitations of existing "600" schools, because some teachers, principals, and others felt the need for relief from a difficult and tense situation in some schools:

The behavior pattern of these pupils ranges from serious anti-social behavior (violence, extortion, threats of bodily harm, gang fights, vandalism, theft) to disruption of normal school procedures and routines

[48] Juvenile Delinquency Evaluation Project of the City of New York, *The "600" Day Schools* (New York, 1957), pp. 29–30, and Juvenile Delinquency Evaluation Project of the City of New York, *Students and Their Progress in the "600" Day Schools* (New York, 1957)

(obscenity, disruption of classes, interference with fire drills, truancy, cutting of class). It must be borne in mind that the anti-social careers these young people are developing are destructive of their own well being as well as of that of the school. It is also well established that even a small group can (a) disrupt school routines, (b) interfere with normal procedures, (c) cause the expenditure of an inordinate and excessive amount of time to be devoted to them by teaching, guidance, and administrative personnel—which professional time of necessity must be at the expense of the great majority of students, (d) act as stimulus to influence other young people towards similar behavior, thus further undermining school procedures.

To date no adequate facilities have been located for these children. It has been apparent that the schools cannot cope with these children. When they occasionally appear before the courts, even though the obvious disposition in many cases, in the view of the Judge presiding, should be institutional care, they are placed on probation and returned to the schools because there is no space available in an appropriate institution. Thus, they remain in the public schools to continue their disruptive and self-destructive activities.[49]

Local studies and state requirements offered assurance of substantial improvements almost immediately. All who were concerned stressed the need for adequate criteria for assignment, strengthening of curriculum, adequate guidance and related services, remedial facilities, adequate physical facilities, and necessary professional supervision. The city set about to improve the "600" schools in the summer of 1958 and considerable progress has been made. Steps were taken to strengthen the administration of individual "600" schools and of the total "600" system. Soon the per-pupil expenditure in a "600" school was about two-and-a-half times that in a regular school. Each "600" school now has a full-time remedial teacher and one full-time guidance counselor from the Bureau of Educational and Vocational Guidance. All of the schools have some service by BCG teams. Much-improved physical facilities have been made available for some of these schools. Board of Education authorities in art, music, and physical education have helped plan curriculum enrichment. More teachers have been recruited for the expansion (the salary incentive continues) and the School Superintendent feels that the level of qualification is high.

[49] The New York Teachers Guild (AFL-CIO), *The Guild Program for the Establishment of Special Pilot Schools on the High School Level* (New York, 1957, mimeographed), p. 1.

When pressed to create "600" schools for younger children, the School Superintendent has stressed not only the undesirability of transporting children under ten to schools out of the neighborhood but also the importance of maximum guidance, counseling, and efforts to help children in the individual schools. The "600" schools are to be seen not as *the* program for children in trouble but as part of a total program. In this connection note might be made of the very recent, but quite promising, beginnings with a limited number of experimental special "junior guidance" classes in neighborhood schools. Based on earlier experiments, these classes now exist in fifty schools and offer BCG-BEVG services, small classes, experimental methods.

Present and future. Does all of this mean that the function, the role, the program of the "600" schools is now clarified and that their place in the total school system need no longer be questioned? Should other school systems copy the plan? More careful probing reveals that this is not the case. First, facilities and program have been improved and may be improved further. Especially to be noted are the smaller classes, the guidance and child guidance services, and the curriculum enrichment. However, the programs, as we shall see, are hardly adequate as yet to a rehabilitative effort.

Second, admissions criteria continue to be unclear because of conflicts of motivation within the school system. School authorities have stated that, apart from helping to relieve the regular schools of the problem of handling extremely difficult youngsters, the "600" schools have rehabilitative objectives. However, during a period of great publicity relative to school problems, an administrative hearing became the major instrument for decisions. Disruptive pupils were simply referred to the hearings. Gradually the more qualified of the superintendents modified the hearings so that they lost their semijudicial character. Presentations by attendance officers, BEVG counselors, and occasionally BCG personnel were incorporated into the process.

There are those within the school system who would continue to refine definition of the children who shall be referred to "600" schools. Their thinking incorporates several notions. Children in grades 5–10 should be referred, assuming that there is a history of disruptive and aggressive behavior which is dangerous or seriously interferes with classroom routine; the intelligence level is not "re-tarded"; they are not sex deviates, pyromaniacs, psychotic, or too seriously withdrawn. However, referral should not be made unless the home school has made extensive efforts toward help which have failed.

Not all referral sources accept these limitations, however, nor do they agree to the proposal that the BCG provide clinical evalu-ations in a considerable number of circumstances related to referral. (They are not staffed to evaluate all admissions.) For, from the point of view of certain teachers and principals, the main function of the "600" school remains to relieve the classroom of the ex-tremely disruptive child or of the child who endangers himself and others. From this perspective, rehabilitative objectives should not affect referral criteria. Thus, the debate remains stalemated and the policy issues are unresolved.

Pronouncements of objectives will not alone resolve these issues unless there is far more follow-through of the implications of a rehabilitative objective. For it remains necessary, at this late date, to ask: *What is the specialized nature of the program, and for what children, therefore, is it appropriate?* Guidance, remedial reading, enriched programs are all excellent, but the program is validated as each of its parts becomes a planned segment of a total effort, which has defined its emphasis and orientation and which directs the roles of its several major parts. To use an analogy: The criteria thus far suggest that a child needs medicine, but they do not tell us what the nature of "600" school medicine is. How can one know, therefore, which children should be referred?

Thus, one might grant that the "600" schools are being made more attractive; but there remains the likelihood that, for many or most of these pupils, their function as presently implemented will remain custodial. A hint as to recognition of this fact is seen in the failure to make adequate plans for transfers of significant numbers of the pupils from "600" schools back to regular schools. In fact, the schools' routines, incentive systems, and programs are not designed to support return to "regular" schools. This is terminal education for all but a minority.

Should the school system and the community, then, devote fur-ther efforts to the strengthening of programs and definition of the mission of the "600" schools? Should referral criteria and evaluation procedures be improved? Some continue to take the negative view.

There are educators and others who continue to hold that children having trouble should not be brought together, in special classes or in special schools, because to assemble them and permit the development of mutual support in their antisocial attitudes is to make their reeducation even more difficult. These are children who have often experienced parental rejection and have grown up on social islands which do not provide motivation to learn in school. Exposure to better-motivated youth might help them (given other supports as well). Segregation with others like themselves encourages a system of mutual encouragement and reinforcement.

In all likelihood, if the concern were only for the child having trouble, special schools or classes would not be developed. If capable of continuing in the community (rather than requiring institutionalization) such pupils would remain in the regular schools. However, the school system must face the fact that some children are too disturbed or disturbing to be contained in regular schools, if one is concerned, as one has to be, with the education of the vast majority. The development of special schools for difficult children, i.e., the "600" schools, must be seen in this context: (a) they are necessary because we must protect the education of the majority; (b) they must not be custodial because a school system has no right to deprive any child of the best education he can absorb; (c) they must therefore be developed with optimal educational and treatment services. Much therefore remains to be done, experimentally, to clarify just *what* these schools can become—and for *whom*.

From this point of view, special classes in neighborhood schools deserve priority. Reintegration into normal classes would seem more possible when a child is not moved into a new school. Rigorous formulation of plans and experimentation is warranted. The system would perhaps do well to include "senior guidance classes" for children above the fifth grade as an alternative to "600" schools and as an expansion of its growing "junior guidance classes" system.

Those associated with these programs as referral channels or as personnel responsible for the operations of special classes or "600" schools should also avoid the inevitable tendency to assign to such resources children too disturbed for community adjustment. There are some children who cannot be contained even in classes of four or five no matter how skilled the teacher, and they require home instruction, institutionalization, or exemption.

ONE PROGRAM

This discussion of guidance, school social work, and special schools has not dealt with all efforts within a school system relevant to the prevention, location, and treatment of disturbing deviance. The focus has been on major, specialized case finding, evaluation, referral, and service resources. The total school system is, of course, involved in primary and secondary prevention and there are many additional specialized services.

It is necessary to stress, in concluding, that the New York City "case history" would tend to suggest that creativity, large-scale investment, and dedication are not enough: roles must be defined, services integrated, the total pattern coordinated. Experience in other cities confirms the view. Just as a city must see all of its agencies as cooperating segments of one network, so must a school system provide administratively for one well-integrated effort.

Central administration reorganization and integration of policy and programs will not be enough, however. The central offices may provide professional leadership, supervision, training, and promotion, but the local field superintendent should be allowed considerable leeway in deploying and structuring resources allocated to him. In a large and complex community districts do vary considerably. One may wish to give priority to a "600" school, while another prefers an elaborate community program. Educational guidance may be the primary need in one area while individual clinical services may be found more urgent elsewhere. A central office cannot work out all of these details. It should certainly not assign projects and special programs without consultation.

A school system must face the fact that the handicapped or the outstanding child, who may occasion many of the special services and facilities discussed, may be responsible for higher expenditures than the average. It is also true that in today's world there is no alternative to prolonged education as a reasonable preparation for the complex demands of citizenship and the occupations. And, in making school attendance compulsory, the public takes on a moral obligation to provide for those who are exceptional.

CHAPTER VI

THE POLICEMAN AND
THE CHILD

OUTSIDE the schoolroom there are few public servants who meet as many young people on intimate terms as do the police. The national estimate is that there are probably almost two million *recorded* contacts—and this is a fraction of the total. Three quarters of juvenile court delinquency cases and 20 percent of neglect cases channel through police departments. More detailed data might be cited from many cities: a careful Syracuse study found that nearly three fourths of all first offenders and a substantial portion of all offenders are handled exclusively by police agencies before being released to parents. California reports are similar.[1] In New York City, the Police Youth Division is the first-contact agency for more children in trouble and alleged delinquents than all other agencies. More than half of all children reported to the New York City Youth Board Register in 1955 were first known to the Juvenile Aid Bureau. There are comparable findings from other cities.

On the front line in work with the most antisocial and vicious of young delinquents, police are intimately acquainted with the outrageous detail of specific offenses and depredations. Some will tend toward punitive policy as the result. A spokesman may sound a responsive note when he says:

It is not your job to become bemused with the vagaries of the "why-oh-why" school of causation. Your job is simply to enforce the law—with

---

[1] Statistical estimates by U.S. Children's Bureau. Also see Robert H. Hardt, *A Delinquency Profile of Syracuse and Onondaga County, N.Y., 1959–1960* (Syracuse: Youth Development Center, 1961), p. 29.

no nonsense about it. . . . Let others attempt the long-range approach of trying to wean young thugs from the traits of homicide, assault or rape.

The patrolman on a corner beat must know whether his particular police department has adopted a general "get tough" policy which precludes individualized measures. He must balance aggressively worded speeches against the oft-expressed view that police must evaluate cases, refer to direct-service agencies, and cooperate closely with social agencies and clinics.

Yet, despite some debates and differences of opinion, most police circles are agreed that there is, in fact, little choice for the police in definition of their core role with young people. That is dictated by the nature of the opportunities which are theirs alone. There may be differences in organization and administration which depend on community size, staffing, and social agency resources. There may be shifts in emphasis which reflect the delinquency situation and community mood. But the police have a clear task—and they need a juvenile service if they are to accomplish it.[2]

POLICE FUNCTIONS IN WORK WITH CHILDREN

It often has been said that police assigned to work with young people should do police tasks while avoiding the roles of social workers, teachers, clergymen, and recreation directors. But the crucial question is, "What *are* police tasks?" What responsibilities are inherent in the police assignment in work with youth, and how must police be equipped to fulfill their responsibilities?

Police are and should, of course, remain police, not doing more than is appropriate for them. Police certainly cannot play all roles in dealing with children in trouble. There is, in fact, basic agreement as to the appropriate functions for the police, despite some variations in views about police programs in recreation and community organization, at one end of the spectrum, and intensive treatment, at the other. The discussion which follows deals with police roles in any large urban area.

[2] This following formulation was evolved in connection with two earlier reports on the police juvenile program. See Alfred J. Kahn, *Police and Children* (New York: Citizens' Committee for Children of New York City, Inc., 1951), and Alfred J. Kahn, *The Crisis in the New York City Police Program for Youth* (New York: Citizens' Committee for Children of New York City, Inc., 1959).

Police are in contact with many children and young people. They meet children as they walk about on patrol, or stop their patrol cars, or when they direct traffic at school crossings. They warn young people, take complaints about them, or apprehend them as regulations are ignored or offenses are committed. Sometimes police intervene to block gang fights or to break them up. Many feel the impact of police activity and policy, either because of something they personally have done or because of activity meant to affect all youth in the area.

Protection, determent, and enforcement of regulations. Basically, the police are counted on by the community to protect it against offenders. People have a right to feel that their streets are safe, that they can relax in their parks, that their children will not be molested in the playgrounds and on the bike paths. If these conditions do not prevail, they feel that the police are failing, or that enough police have not been provided. Movement out of neighborhoods and even out of cities follows when basic protection is not assured.

Because the protective function is so important, it must dominate police training and affect the deployment of forces. Foot and car patrol, good distribution of precinct stations, emergency telephones, radio communications—these are the ingredients of a public protection program.

When the police are organized to protect the community, we say that they are fulfilling their determent function. The assumption is that most people in a society know and obey most laws (although there are many accepted and widely practiced evasions). However, some people are prepared to break the law but hesitate to do so if they are likely to be caught and punished. Thus, motorists drive far more comfortably because they know most drivers obey traffic rules, if only for fear of "tickets." Most storekeepers lock and leave their stores and feel relatively secure at night because police patrol most areas, and potential thieves know they face the risk of being caught.

This function is different from primary prevention because it assumes that people have arrived at a point where they are prepared to break the law. The police officer, as society's guardian, represents a warning that transgression may be costly. This may be enough to halt certain possible delinquencies. It hardly can be expected to halt all delinquencies since some are caused by deep and complex motives; there are even delinquents who, unconsciously at least, wish to be caught and stopped, or punished. Other delinquents know that only a very small proportion of crimes against property are followed by detection and arrest.

The enforcement of regulations is one special aspect of protection and determent. There are many regulations, ranging from traffic rules to park restrictions, considered essential to the safety and rights of the public in general.

To the sociologist, these activities are all part of social control, society's self-preservation mechanism. The psychologist adds that the existence of a body of social rules with sanctions and the presence of officers of enforcement are apparently necessary in society if individuals, as they grow up, are to incorporate as part of their own personalities, standards of the "good," the "right," the "permissible." There must be laws and police who represent outside "enforcement," it appears, if subsequently the growing child is to develop his own "internal" laws and controls (his conscience). To the typical citizen, these activities are the assurance of reasonable community order, safety, and protection.

For the most part, these activities are directed for and at the public as a whole, and there is no youth specialization involved. Possible exceptions are the traffic safety programs for children, centered around going to and from schools, and the youth squads which may respond to calls about impending gang activity or incidents actually under way. General police officers or youth specialists give special attention in enforcement of regulations and protection of youths to patrol rounds—which include taverns and bars, poolrooms, dance halls, certain candy store "hangouts," and other entertainment centers.

Adequate performance of these functions requires a police force sufficiently large so that it is readily seen and can respond to calls. Its officers must be honest and impartial so that the law is not easily circumvented. Its leaders must be alert to the development of tensions and dangers and able to react rapidly with such measures as will block potential lawbreakers.

Case finding, detection, and apprehension. Police are major case locators; they are also major channels for the members of the public concerned with reporting situations they have encountered but about which they are not sure where to turn. Police are, in fact, always on duty and are the most available of public servants. People therefore turn to them for many emergency services unrelated to crimes. In fact, only a small portion of police involvement with the community is in relation to traditional crime, as such.

These are not tasks for "specialized" police. Every policeman should be prepared to hear a complaint about a child severely beaten or to notice youths running out of the "5 and 10" with the manager in pursuit. Similarly, the desk officer in the precinct must listen to the mother who enters, in her desperation, to say that she is worried about her son, who defies his parents and is acting strangely.

Where an offense, serious or minor, is committed in the view of an officer or called to his attention, his responsibility for *apprehension* is clear. Other offenses require *investigation* and *detection* before apprehension is possible. These are the specialized police forms of case location.

The size and composition of a police department determines the degree of specialization within these functions. All policemen are responsible for some detection and apprehension, just as all are inevitably part of case finding where there is no real crime but where people need help. These functions develop normally and naturally in the course of patrolling for protective and deterrent purposes. All police in the department should know, understand, and adopt the content and the philosophy of the juvenile court law, which justifies the intervention in alleged delinquency and neglect. General police regulations, procedures, and practices should be in harmony with over-all community delinquency policy. All police should have necessary orientation and training in relation to the rights of young people during questioning and other phases of investigation and community practice in use of detention facilities.

Larger police forces may choose to assign special police or detectives for investigation of the more serious of the undetected offenses and to apprehend offenders. Detective Youth Squads, for example (later affiliated with the Youth Division of the New York City Police Department), had such responsibility for a long time.

These are important functions, not to be minimized in work with youth or others. A police force is not a deterrent unless evasion or flouting of the law is frequently followed by apprehension. Thieves must be caught, murderers brought to trial, speeding motorists given tickets, runaways located. For some offenses the apprehension rates are always low and offenders are not found, but the department's "average" must be good, or the community may expect further outbreaks. Quite properly, then, much police effort is devoted to increasing efficiency in this field and there have been important scientific developments.

Evaluation and referral. The issue is not whether police should do screening and exercise some discretion but rather how much they can and should do. For, in fact, all police officers use discretion about arresting and thus have some criteria for screening. Even in the system which defines the officer's role as detection and determent he uses judgment. He gives minor offenders "a second chance"; he decides that certain actions are the results of momentary impulses or accidents; he agrees to let parent, teacher, or clergyman effect reform. Surely the desk sergeant or police officer on post who responds to a neighbor's complaint or a parent's plea for help is making major decisions as far as a child's future is concerned.

This *brief screening* is an inevitable function of all policemen and policewomen and not only of youth specialists. It will always remain part of their responsibility, since they cannot possibly bring all situations they encounter into the office for screening by somebody else.

How, then, must they be equipped for this? When the issue is only "Has Tom broken the law?" the problem is relatively clear-cut (although the evidence may be quite complex). The officer gathers all available evidence. If it tends toward an affirmative answer, he either arrests or reports Tom. He will then be instructed to get more evidence or to drop the matter. On the basis of the strength of evidence, legal action will or will not be taken. Police departments have stressed mastery of the penal law by each police officer, since it certainly ensures appropriate screening of situations involving adults. In the instance of offenses by youths in which arrest is mandatory, such knowledge also clarifies next steps.

In addition to this, no matter what the total plan in a given police department, every officer on the beat needs some further preparation for brief screening in cases involving children and youth. He must get to understand juvenile court law; he must know about the state's protective obligations in neglect; he requires at least minimum knowledge of local social agency services and of how to steer people to them; and he should have a core of orientation to mental health. Given these, he should be able to answer inquiries and exercise that degree of discretion which is inevitable even in a department without a juvenile aid division.

Children's court statutes encourage community intervention in many situations involving children which are not the equivalent of adult crimes. In its "protective" role, the state is concerned if a child is out of control of his parents, runs away, engages in unacceptable sexual activity, frequents questionable places, truants, or is severely neglected or mistreated. Such cases are a large proportion of delinquency totals. The court (and the police as agents of the court) is prepared to accept and consider petitions alleging these "less serious" violations because it has a helping and rehabilitative role. The police officer who enters a situation where he cannot decide whether to take the case to court or not, simply in the light of a penal code law about the seriousness of the offense, therefore needs some additional basis for deciding whether the court should be called upon in a protective role.

For example, the evidence to prove that John broke into the bakery may be weak, yet the police officer, if instructed and qualified to do so, might note numerous indications that something is wrong with the boy and that he needs further attention. Perhaps further exploration would, in fact, show that the parents are extremely abusive and neglectful.

Jean may come to the officer's attention because she is a minor and is in a cocktail lounge, but a skilled person might also note signs that she is mentally ill and needs help.

Decisions about such cases require some examination of the situation to separate the apparently accidental offender from the deliberate one; the child in a normal family which is able to handle its problems from the child in the disintegrated family; the responsible parent from the obviously disturbed; the family in a neighborhood with many positive influences from the household influenced by the antisocial attitudes of a cultural subgroup; the child with personality strengths and stability from the one with signs of serious disturbance; the presence of sound ethical and moral standards from their absence. These factors do not have to do with legal evidence, with penal code considerations—but do provide the basis for the exercise of discretion in instances where arrests and court petitions are not mandatory. Unlike the *brief screening*, which is undertaken by every policeman on the spot, this kind of decision should be based on relevant social data and experience. To assemble and judge such material, what is generally called a *case evaluation*, requires a certain amount of professional knowledge.

If police are to be assigned this latter kind of screening they clearly need good understanding of human personality, of environmental problems, and of the causes of deviant behavior. They must be capable of rapidly reviewing individual and social circumstances; they need sufficient objectivity and maturity so that the decision is based on both community interests and the child's needs, rather than the officer's sentiments or prejudices.

Sometimes, it is true, police departments, large and small, have in their patrol forces wonderfully intuitive men who can decide which minor offenses and complaints require more intensive attention and when a word of advice or warning or a bit of humor will do. They have also been able to use good judgment and persuasive power where the complaint was relatively serious but where it was clear that corrective measures would be arranged without formal police or court intervention. Men such as these could undertake both brief screening and more complete case evaluation.

Case evaluations based on specialized knowledge or preparation cannot be expected of every patrolman on the beat, however. If departments are to undertake case evaluation regularly, they require appropriately prepared staffs—specialized juvenile police. While it is generally agreed in this country and abroad that police departments need some personnel of this kind, one group of police officials questions the view.

Where police do seek to become organized for evaluation and referral, the pattern of service varies from the assignment of youth police specialists to all police offices or precincts with the requirement that all youth cases be brought directly to them for processing, to the creation of centralized or districted youth programs and the definition of distribution of functions as between them and the general police on the beat. As already indicated, many of the small communities are not staffed for this role but would like to be, and many large communities are understaffed or consider their youth police in need of additional preparation.[3]

Brief screening and more complete evaluation and case *referral* are part of the same process and require the same basic qualities and attitudes. Proper referrals, whether to a guidance clinic for personality help, to a settlement for club contacts, or to a court as a preliminary step toward institutionalization, also presuppose a good working knowledge of community resources and agencies, the services they offer, and their methods of operation. Hospitals, family welfare agencies, public assistance programs, guidance clinics, clubs and centers, camps, religious programs—these and many other possibilities exist once it is decided that the contact requires some next steps. Yet the value of the referral depends on good selection of the agency, clear interpretation of the child and his needs to the agency, by way of preparing the ground, and adequate work with the child and parents so that the referral will be used. Agency records are full of the comment, "Did not cooperate," after referrals which were poorly prepared.

The concept of referral is certainly nothing new to the police. Police officers have always known where to send an evicted family for help or a homeless man for lodging. However, the types of referral described above require more than this. The full knowledge of community resources involved and the understanding and ability to work with all kinds of people in need or in trouble have not been traditional equipment of all police officers.

As police departments seek to prepare all of their officers for maximum public service, they will want to ensure that each has basic information and the orientation necessary to answer inquiries and to steer people to community resources. Increased understanding of the complexity of many referral situations will lead to provision of youth specialists equipped for case evaluation and referral and interested in following up until certain that the referral has led to service or to a decision that service is inappropriate or impossible. Since police cases by their nature represent a high proportion of

[3] U.S. Department of Health, Education, and Welfare, *Report to the Congress on Juvenile Delinquency* (Washington, D.C.: Government Printing Office, 1960), pp. 8, 26, 45–46.

serious "risk" from among child and family situations, departments need *accountability* systems of their own or should be tightly integrated into any general community system (see Ch. XII).

Police and prevention. Great value is attached in our society to what are called *prevention* activities, and this is not surprising in an era in which scientific public health work has made miraculous strides. Unfortunately, the understandable desire to acquire this particular halo has led to some ambiguity in the term itself and some confusion in the concept.

As already suggested, to prevent crime is to keep some people from feeling that unlawful means are their best sources of support and to keep others from reaching a point where they engage in social aggression as a result of confused moral values, frustration, or one of a variety of kinds of personal disturbances, including the need to be caught and punished. In this sense, a prevention program is one that concerns itself with the status of different groups in society, parent-child relationships, housing, family incomes, recreation facilities, education—and with the kind of communities and world in which we live.

On the next level, prevention is that which seeks to interpose positive local influences between the individual or family and the broader social forces. Then there is the prevention program which deals with so-called vulnerable children who have as yet developed no difficulties or maladjustments but whose life situations are disordered, so that trouble is possible. Their family status and neighborhoods or the discrimination they suffer may be a source of danger.

The police are involved in the above-described levels of prevention to only a vary small degree, if at all. They become somewhat more involved if they seek to use precinct councils or youth councils as general *community organization* instruments, thus to affect the total quality of neighborhood life in its impact on children. However, it is generally agreed that community organization is a specialized activity and police are not prepared for it. It is questionable, in fact, whether a public department, particularly an authoritative one, can or should staff local improvement and self-help activities. Police actually have rarely done so; they have sought, more often, to develop precinct councils so as to support recreation programs or to offer informal help to those in trouble; they have usually not seen themselves as initiators of broader community organization.[4]

The decision about the police role in *recreation* is somewhat more complex. A recent national survey conducted by the International Association of Chiefs of Police showed that the majority agreed that police should not conduct recreation programs. There was overwhelming agreement that recreation or park departments should sponsor group recreation. Despite this, it was also found in this study, and in an earlier one, that the police are heavily committed in recreation. More than half the departments may have programs.[5]

This discrepancy is explained in part by the widespread view that police should convey the fact that they are friends of youth by getting to know young people and becoming known to them in the midst of pleasurable activity. It is noted, for example, that the Police Athletic League presents itself as a PAL. To this argument is added the statement that in their work with young people police become aware of major resource lacks and feel prompted to supply recreational facilities when needed. Finally, it is said, policemen as a group represent a reservoir of attractive and physically fit men who are capable of conducting athletic programs.

These views have historical validity but, to most police authorities, are not adequate to justify continuation of police athletic programs in the future. The image young people will have, and should have, of police depends on what they do in their official roles in the neighborhood, on traffic duty, responding to alarms, and investigating complaints. Second, the recreation field has made major progress in recent decades. Many cities have recreation departments or other agencies to conduct large programs, and the leadership of these programs is, or should be, in the hands of personnel prepared particularly for the assignment. On the other hand, those police who wish, because of athletic ability, to serve as volunteers or part-time

---

[4] The Committee on Juvenile Delinquency of the International Association of Chiefs of Police recommended in 1956 that the police cooperate with such councils, but not actively conduct or sponsor them. Stephen P. Kennedy, Chairman, *The Role of the Police in Juvenile Delinquency: A Preliminary Report* (New York, 1956, mimeographed). Also see the committee's report, *Interim Report on the Role of the Police in Work with Youth* (1951).

[5] *The Role of the Police in Juvenile Delinquency: A Preliminary Report*. Also see U.S. Department of Health, Education, and Welfare, *Police Services for Juveniles* (Washington, D.C.: Government Printing Office, 1954), p. 53.

recreation workers would generally be welcomed by settlement houses and public recreation centers.

The late Bruce Smith, an outstanding authority in the police field, gave this advice to one department and it has general application: "The crime prevention task of the police department in general and the Juvenile Aid Bureau in particular is big enough, without undertaking this collateral responsibility for administering a separate and absorbing recreational program." He added that there was little evidence that the police athletic program really prevented delinquency. Specifically, "the hard fact remains that PAL does not easily attract or hold the interest of delinquents, while the predelinquency status of many PAL members must always reside strictly in the realm of opinion, with no demonstrable basis for asserted relationships." [6]

Even proponents of police recreation efforts agree that police participation should grow out of broad community planning and should ensure provision of trained recreation supervisors.[7] Such qualifications would rule out many current programs and give emphasis to the opportunity of police to report recreation needs to the community and to participate in the planning for needed services.

If the police have an important preventive role, it derives from their opportunity in *situation finding* which parallels their case finding. Their patrol and investigation functions bring them naturally to community conditions and situations which, uncorrected, are hazards to the development of youth. Dr. Howard Lane put it this way in a report to the mayor of Detroit:

In crime prevention, the police department will act in the field of personal and social behavior as does a department of health in the realm of sanitation and care of the sick. It will note and call for correction of unhygienic conditions such as: children without space; gang-aged children with no wholesome place to gang or be with their friends; neighborhoods of inadequate homes, providing no decent opportunities for boys and girls to play freely, to date; excessively quarrelsome neighbors; neighbors devoid of friendliness toward children; exploitation of children by adults. The Youth Bureau will find those situations through a modern conception of "patrol" and report them to appropriate agencies for correction.

[6] Bruce Smith, *The New York Police Survey* (New York: Institute of Public Administration, 1952), p. 31.

[7] *Police Services for Juveniles*, p. 55.

Whether this valuable role should be called prevention or alert patrolling is a matter of taste, of course. It is without doubt appropriate for all police and would benefit by the availability of police youth specialists assigned responsibility for special investigation in this field.

The *curfew* as a preventive device also requires mention here. Its use is widespread, but data are almost nonexistent about its consequences as a law enforcement measure or as a policing measure—and its results in attitudes toward law. Smaller cities are apparently most convinced about it. Large police departments see enforcement as most difficult. Many curfews are not enforced or are enforced selectively.

The objections range from the fact that most juvenile offenses do not occur in curfew hours, to the unfairness of regulating the lives of the vast nondelinquent majority of the youth population. Since all curfews permit some legitimate exceptions, they lead to the need for identity cards and the accouterments of a "police state" for youth. The curfew interferes with parental prerogatives as well.

The main argument for the curfew seems to be that it gives emphasis to the seriousness of the total community situation and simplifies enforcement by decreasing the numbers of youth in the streets. While the latter may or may not be true, the curfew itself poses major enforcement problems; thus, its validity, if any, is as a short-range dramatic gesture. It certainly solves no long-range problems and does not contribute to the kind of community life most conducive to sound child development.

Treatment. Shortages of casework and clinical treatment facilities and difficulties in making referrals to such agencies have led some police departments to create service units or treatment units for work with youth. Most departments recognize, however, that they are not staffed for intensive, long-term treatment and are glad to be relieved of the function if resources can be made available. Few would argue that a police office is an appropriate treatment center.

On the other hand, there are some less intensive relationships of the big brother–friendly visitor variety, or the brief social casework possible in a referral unit, which are both more common and more strongly defended. They seem to have validity if (a) associated with preparing a case for effective referral or (b) undertaken where only very brief services are required. If the police department is staffed with juvenile aid units capable of good case study and able to make disposition plans, the selfsame staff will in some instances quite properly continue with short-term casework, perhaps of some weeks' duration, while the appropriate helping agency is selected and the child is made ready to use the help offered. The unit may also be able to help, under some circumstances, with practical problems, i.e., medical services, special school program, family housing plans, recreational resources, etc.

Police should render these brief casework services, if at all, only to children who need not be taken to court and who are not referrable immediately for one reason or another. Since there will have been no court adjudication, everything necessary should be done to clarify the voluntary nature of the service. Where there is a "case" to be made for delinquency or neglect, the police, of course, have the right to turn to court, should the client not use the service voluntarily. Obviously, only a well-qualified juvenile staff could offer brief casework services.

For lack of other community services, many police units offer what is called "unofficial probation." Such programs raise serious doubts, since there has been no court action to determine that there is a legal basis for public intervention. Yet young people are being required to report regularly, listen to "lectures," and follow certain rules. A "big brother" or "friendly visitor" relationship may help certain youngsters, but it is doubtful that a police staff without competent case evaluation resources can locate those who need such service. If service is offered, the child and his parents must know that it is voluntary, or his rights are being ignored. "Unofficial probation" is not an appropriate status in a police department or a court. Further, big brother groups have developed a fund of knowledge about working with boys and supervising the volunteers. It would therefore seem wiser for police to carry out their case evaluations rapidly and refer to such agencies as appropriate. Individual police officers may wish to volunteer as big brothers, as will others engaged in a variety of occupations.

THE PROGRAM OF THE NEW YORK CITY
POLICE YOUTH DIVISION

As it became clear that wise decisions on behalf of children required diagnostic skill as well as an ability to use a variety of criteria going beyond the offense itself, standard-setting groups urged that all police officers receive instruction in the handling of juveniles, as part of their basic police training. They added that each police department in an urban area should have a special unit with major responsibility for work with juveniles. In a small community, the department should assign the responsibility to a special officer.[8] Police departments soon began to create specialized juvenile units for the task. Such names have been used as Juvenile Aid Bureau, Juvenile Bureau, Crime Prevention Bureau, Juvenile Control Bureau, Youth Aid Bureau.

The spelling out of duties was modest: (a) these officers and divisions should perform their functions with understanding of the special needs and characteristics of young people; (b) they should have sufficient understanding of child behavior to handle the child constructively; (c) they should know how to refer appropriately for official action or informal guidance; (d) they should control community conditions harmful to children; (e) they should give consultation to other divisions or officers. The responsibilities assume some special training and selection on the basis of personal fitness and capacity to work with children or youth.[9]

A recent survey found that no city department doubted the need for a special juvenile unit.[10] The very large cities (over 500,000) all have such units and the cities of 100,000–500,000 generally do; coverage is far less complete for smaller cities. There is, in fact, some

[8] Consensus as stated by the U.S. Children's Bureau, National Council on Crime and Delinquency and National Advisory Police Committee on Social Protection (Federal Security Agency). Summarized in U.S. Department of Health, Education, and Welfare, *Recommended Standards for Services for Delinquent Children* (Washington, D.C.: Government Printing Office, 1953). Also see Henry J. Mulhearn, *Handbook for Police Youth Bureaus* (Albany: New York State Youth Commission, 1958). For a full description of California's well-developed specialist juvenile programs in police and sheriff offices see I. J. Shain and Walter R. Burkhart, *A Study of the Administration of Juvenile Justice in California* (Sacramento: California State Printing Office, 1960).

[9] *Recommended Standards for Services for Delinquent Children*. The National Conference on Delinquency Control (1952) and the White House Conference on Children (1950) took these positions.

[10] Kennedy, *Role of the Police in Juvenile Delinquency*. Also see *Report to the Congress on Juvenile Delinquency* and *Police Services for Juveniles*, pp. 38, 67. Also see Bernard Greenblatt, *Staff and Training for Juvenile Law Enforcement in Urban Police Departments*, Juvenile Delinquency Facts and Facets, No. 13 (Washington, D.C.: Government Printing Office, 1960).

coverage in 89 percent of the cities of over 100,000 population but only 41 percent of those over 10,000 population. It is variously held that 2.5 to 7.5 percent of police personnel should be assigned to juvenile work, but surveys show many communities with one officer, part-time juvenile specialists, or staff too small for the population involved. In a recent national study, 60 percent of the departments responding cited the need for more youth specialists. Those departments which do appoint so-called specialists often fail to require special qualifications.[11]

There are great variations in the current educational requirements for these posts, and this has caused national concern and emphasis on the importance of selection and training. Programs are staffed by policemen (57 percent), policewomen (24 percent), and civilians (under 10 percent), according to a recent poll.[12]

As a department seeks to move from intention to administration in this field it must solve many problems both theoretical and practical. New York City's experience may serve to explain why some have made only partial progress and to suggest some next steps.

Backgrounds. In New York City the new children's court philosophy in work with youth, stressing the need to separate children from adults and to protect and help, began gradually to influence police work.[13] The city set up Junior Police in 1914 in a forerunner of the PAL, and stressed "admonition and warning" as well as protection of youth. A year later, welfare lieutenants were appointed and assigned a protective and educational function. In 1930 the Police Department created a Crime Prevention Bureau, taking a fresh and comprehensive approach which was a major step forward for the time. A staff of police officers, policewomen, and twenty-five social workers undertook a program of determent, "adjustment" of minor incidents, and more complete treatment when needed. Emphasis was placed on controlling community conditions contributing to delinquency and on social investigation of cases, followed by referral. An experienced social worker headed the bureau. A police officer commanded each local unit, but there was a social worker to supervise casework. It might be noted that the PAL recreation pro-

---

[11] *Police Services for Juveniles,* and Greenblatt, *Staff and Training,* pp. 11–12.

[12] Kennedy, *Role of the Police in Juvenile Delinquency.* The other positions are supervisory and apparently filled by police officers.

[13] A more detailed history appears in *Police and Children,* Chapter I.

gram grew naturally out of needs recognized by the Crime Prevention Bureau but was considered as a temporary demonstration.

The Crime Prevention Bureau was reorganized under police leadership as the Juvenile Aid Bureau (JAB) in 1934. The JAB placed new emphasis on reporting "potential" delinquents, and caseloads grew; the case lists were made up largely of those matters considered in themselves relatively trivial but nonetheless important to deal with for preventive purposes. Neighborhood councils (later precinct coordinating councils) were established to help with local needs and to support the recreation program, PAL, which became a major part of the whole. Cases were screened according to the seriousness of the offense; the civilian caseworkers were concentrated in a Service unit for treatment of the more serious cases. They gradually became an isolated civilian island in the force until the unit was abolished in 1942, not to be reestablished until after the war, this time with police staff.

More recent developments are presented in the context of discussion of issues raised about the program.

The Youth Division assignment. In 1957 the New York City Police Department unified its JAB and its detective Youth Squads to form a Youth Division. The division now consists of a Youth Patrol Bureau in seven units, a Youth Investigation Bureau in twelve field units, a Youth Records Bureau (responsible for a central file, a gang file, statistics, research, training), and 77 precinct youth patrolmen. Approximately 225 men are assigned to investigation, over 200 to patrol, and over 50 to records and related functions. Each bureau has its commanding officer, and an inspector is the line officer for the total division. He, in turn, reports to the Chief Inspector. There is a special civilian deputy commissioner in charge of the youth program and precinct youth councils.

The *Youth Patrol* units, staffed by detectives-in-training, respond to calls in squad cars. They patrol high delinquency areas, seek to halt gang fights, apprehend violators of the law, inspect premises where there may be violations or trouble. Theirs tends to be a relatively traditional police emphasis on community protection and the apprehension of violators.

The *Investigation* units have a broader task. Over the years the Police Department has developed procedures governing the disposition by patrolmen on the beat of situations, incidents, and complaints which they witness or which are brought to their attention. In general, where the allegation is that the youngster has committed what would be a felony or a serious misdemeanor in an adult, arrest and a court appearance become automatic. Where the involvement of the child does not constitute a crime in an adult, the patrolman on the beat fills out a standard form which is routed to the Investigation Bureau through the local precinct. Some complaints of this sort reach the bureau through the local precinct—which is open to any citizen—or come directly to the Investigation Bureau unit office through social agencies or citizens. However, the less serious misdemeanors and offenses constitute a shadow area in which specific decisions must be taken as between arrest or referral to the Investigation unit. At one time the decision was made by the JAB. Today it is made by the desk officer in one of 77 precincts.

The *precinct youth patrolmen* staff the local precinct youth councils and support PAL programs. Some of the councils carry out local projects and recreational activities. Other are defunct. The department is now seeking to revive and expand the activity. Plans were made at one point fully to integrate the youth patrolmen into the Investigation unit structure but this has not eventuated. Their activities vary considerably, being generally classified as "prevention." They report to the local captain.

The *Records Bureau,* open twenty-four hours a day, provides case clearance for all units and maintains a gang file.

The Youth Division charge covers all youth to age twenty-one. The nonarrest cases are, inevitably, largely in the under-sixteen group. In recent years close to 34,000 cases in this category have been processed annually—while there have been over 11,000 arrests of those under sixteen. Of the nonarrest cases, 14–17 percent are reported for the equivalent of misdemeanors (petty thefts, malicious mischief) in adults. At least three quarters are minor situations legally speaking (disorderly behavior, malicious mischief).

Thus, in New York City, as elsewhere, most "first contacts" with youth are made not by specialized policemen but by police on all beats. Cases get to the Youth Division Investigation Bureau in a number of ways, but as has been seen, other police are a major source. They referred 73.7 percent of 33,599 referrals in 1959, a typical year. Transit police, in fact, accounted for about 14,000 referrals, mostly for minor offenses. While a large proportion of all police referrals probably arise from community complaints, the important point remains that the overwhelming number of Investigation unit (nonarrest) cases come through the police. The officer on the beat or the subway transit officer is a case locator and a major screener of "less serious" matters.

Some of the nonarrest cases are closed at the point of receipt; others after letters are sent to parents or after home and neighborhood investigation by Investigation unit patrolmen; still others are continued with the unit; some are referred for help or service elsewhere in the community.

Thus, most situations are dealt with completely within the Investigation unit itself. About 35–45 percent involve only a precautionary letter and a third are cases closed to the parents following the home study. Most of the other cases are closed as already known and being handled in courts or social agencies. About 2,000 new referrals to court and social agencies actually emerge out of the some 34,000 nonarrest cases annually.

Clearly, the investigation arm of a police youth division has a serious case evaluation objective if something constructive is to occur before new events bring these cases automatically to court. Since most of the children in this latter group will remain in the community —in fact, since most nonarrest cases in police hands will be processed by taking notice, giving advice, and warning—the police must somehow be staffed so as to know when this will be enough and when they must go further. And if help is needed, they must be equipped to offer suggestions or to initiate that service which would be most constructive under the circumstances.

OPINIONS AND COUNTERPRESSURES

All of this would seem to have clear implications. What, then, is at issue? Where are the problems? The New York Youth Division history and experience elsewhere suggests the following points of difficulty even where youth divisions exist and are reasonably well staffed: (a) police departments may not be willing to permit youth police to screen and evaluate all discretionary cases; (b) the investigation unit staff may not be adequately qualified for the evaluation and referral; (c) the case evaluation and referral process may not be adequately accredited within the department and thus comes to lack support, cooperation, and personnel; (d) youth police work may not be a formally recognized police career and a path to promotion; therefore, youth patrol officers and investigation unit staff may lack incentives to take relevant specialists training; (e) the patrol function—because it produces arrest and "clearance" statistics —may take the lead and the youth police philosophy (i.e., the juvenile court statute philosophy) may not be visible within a department.

Since the New York City Police Youth Division has been studied and reported on frequently, it provides considerable data to illustrate these possibilities.[14] In general, it has created a large investigation staff and has invested in their training and orientation. Staff are usually recruited at the college-degree level. Referrals for treatment on the basis of case evaluations are stressed. Basically, however, the patrol function and the arrest function are evaluated as more important, the Patrol units are of higher status than the Investigation units, and there is no recognized youth police career. A small core of well-trained personnel are well used for training, research, and special projects and their contributions are respected, but there is no likelihood of major upgrading or expansion for highly qualified staff. Youth police do not usually affect the handling of youth by general officers.

All of this requires further illustration and elaboration.

It is clear that the Investigation Bureau of the New York City Police Youth Division has made major contributions in its modernization of police work with youth. Except where arrests are made, young offenders are referred by all other police to these special police. Children are not to be in police line-ups or subjected to the "third degree." Processing is meant to help to greater adjustment.

---

[14] See footnote 2. Also, Mayor's Committee on Juvenile Delinquency, *Report on the Juvenile Aid Bureau and the Prevention of Crime and Delinquency,* (New York, 1944, mimeographed); Juvenile Delinquency Evaluation Project of the City of New York, *The Police Department* (New York, 1956); Juvenile Delinquency Evaluation Project, *The Police Department: One Year Later* (New York, 1957); Jacob Chwast, "The Selection of Personnel for a Police Juvenile Service," *Journal of Criminal Law, Criminology and Police Science,* LI (1960), 357–62.

Thus, the very existence of a police youth program represents a major and not sufficiently emphasized contribution. Many communities have yet to make such provision. This is very good planning for crime determent, enforcement of the law, detection and apprehension of those who break our laws. The Youth Division is a counterpart of children's court laws.

A community needs the special skills exemplified by the youth officer or JAB patrolman who knows his neighborhood very well, is acquainted with many children and is considered a fair friend, knows which premises may be breeding places of trouble, recognizes and does something about tension situations or lack of recreational facilities. The job of observing, patrolling, inspecting, escorting youth to court, and interpreting the law is a major job for police devoting themselves to youth. And, if a specialized youth officer or any other policeman recognizes or hears about a situation involving youth and requiring some evaluation or looking into, it is proper that such responsibility should rest with the Youth Division Investigation Bureau.

This phase of the work continues to be capably handled. In one type of situation, a child who is loitering in a hallway at an improper hour is picked up and taken home. Only the police can do this, and it is an important assignment. In another situation, the police show to a child and his family that people must be held to account for what they do. If windows in a school have been broken, somebody finds the offender and calls at the home. Youth Division staff let it be known that the community has police and courts, and that action can be taken. This does not require understanding a child's personality or family problems on a deep level but is rather an aspect of creating respect for law and order.

The case evaluation and referral aspect of the work are more difficult to organize and plan despite intentions and dedication. Studies over the years have confirmed that where arrest is not mandatory preliminary case screening decisions are often based almost completely on the offense. Many errors can be made in such dispositions. Cases are closed as "adjusted" and letters sent or parents warned or given advice, sometimes appropriately and sometimes because the offense is the first one, the superficial picture of the family is satisfactory, or the promises are convincing. The inadequacy of such processing is seen in the frequency with which the "adjusted" cases reach the courts again and again.

And where the effort is more extensive, it may not be wisely directed:

A trial and error series of environmental manipulations is often undertaken to see if any of them will help. These are usually a matter of habit and formula with a given officer. Referral to other agencies may derive from a full understanding of a client's needs and frequently is just another manipulation. Seldom, however, is the client adequately prepared so that referral and agency activity are a focused and continuous treatment or helping process.[15]

For more than a decade the JAB and, now, the Investigation unit have worked to improve the situation, although there was a period of marking time during the term of a police commissioner who did not approve of the basic function when located within a police department. The strategy has in part involved raising staff qualifications so that almost all have college degrees, some have graduate training, and a small group are trained in social work. More basically, a series of in-service efforts have striven to communicate a family-centered type of case evaluation. Staff have been taught how and where to refer cases. A police treatment unit not qualified for intensive casework (the Service unit) was abolished on the basis of criticism and the evaluation-referral task of the investigation staff stressed. Liaison with all public and voluntary agencies has been improved to facilitate referral and policies have been clarified.

However, all of this has had to take place against considerable odds. At certain times youth squad (later, Patrol unit) philosophy has been at variance with that of Investigation units and has stressed an aggressive approach toward gangs and more frequent recourse to courts. Only community focus on the large proportions of court-dismissed cases and the reassertion of police philosophy modified the situation somewhat. The Investigation and Patrol units continue out of separate offices and are unified largely through top command, directives, and essential training.

The efforts have also been affected by continually rising youth caseloads. A police department with many commitments has taken the understandable short-range path of increasing patrol forces as-

---

[15] *Police and Children*, p. 34. See this report for detailed case illustrations.

signed to youth whenever crises threatened, leaving the Investigation arm too overburdened for effective work with much of the load.
In the face of staff shortages, the Investigation unit has not been able
to support proposals that all discretionary cases now reviewed by
precinct desk officers be processed by youth specialists as they once
were. However, the importance of desk officer clearance with the
Records Bureau to learn of previous records and consultation with
any Youth Division personnel who are in the precinct at the time
has been reiterated. Heavy caseloads have drained inadequate local
agency, clinical, and center resources, discouraging officers who
seek help for young people.

A small, loyal cadre of social work-trained youth police have
shared their knowledge and contributed to policy and training. However, while one would certainly not seek social work or related
training for the bulk of the staff, it would be desirable to have one
well-trained person on duty in each unit at any one time for such
tasks as intake, case consultation, or complex referral. The trained
staff is not adequate for this purpose and few opportunities exist for
full training. Nor are there present those incentives which would
attract more social workers or encourage more on the staff to obtain
graduate training on their own in this and related fields; expertness
in youth work offers no advantage in traditional police promotion
examinations. Indeed, an officer who becomes a sergeant and then a
lieutenant will be used in a variety of police tasks. This is the way
police careers are built.

At some point this latter problem will require resolution en route
to an expansion and strengthening of police youth work. The then
New York City police commissioner told a U.S. Senate subcommittee
in 1957:

It is . . . important the police effectively exercise a dual responsibility: first, that the potential delinquent act is discovered. Second, the
police must handle each offense so that a recurrence can be prevented
if it is possible. This dual responsibility demands that a police department
provide both intelligent law-enforcement facilities to prevent crimes and
*a corps of skilled investigators trained to arrive at the best disposition
of each case involving a youth.*
Having thoroughly investigated the case, the police should follow
through. In an appropriate case, this is accomplished by referral to the
public or private agency best equipped to handle the problem from that

point on. *Police agencies can and should initiate the rehabilitative process,* but they are not equipped, and should not be expected to engage in re-habilitation of children. [Italics added.]

The logic of this view demands an ultimate policy which permits a career in youth work in a police department, promotions for suc-cessful work, and a guarantee that upward mobility does not mean a new assignment. It requires, too, over-all departmental consistency as between police on the beat and in precincts, patrol units, and investigation units. Precinct patrolmen should be integrated into the whole and used to best advantage in the program. Enough staff must be available to do the job. And, finally, community agencies must recognize, respect, and cooperate with police as community protec-tors, as first-level case finders and case screeners, and as accountable representatives of public concern for young people in trouble.

CHAPTER VII

WHEN CHILDREN COME
TO COURT

IT IS OFTEN said that the children's court *idea* is one of the great achievements of the twentieth century. Occasionally, the public is also reminded that the juvenile court movement, which seeks to implement this idea, is at "dead center," that the "whole works" is at a "dead stop."[1] Since no community is well organized to deal with children in trouble without a good juvenile court, because a weak court may undo the efforts of many effective services in the pattern, and because a court which confuses its functions may throw the total network of services off balance, several vital but complex questions must be explored in some detail:

(1) What is the children's court idea and wherein lies its significance?

(2) How may the court's principles and objectives be translated into procedures and services?

(3) How should the court fit into a *pattern* of community services?

(4) How and why are courts so often in difficulty?

(5) What are the strategic points for community action in strengthening a court?

In brief, the core of the children's court is a basic, revolutionary concept which is suggested as a guide for work with those who of-

[1] Tully McCrea, "Juvenile Courts and Juvenile Probation," *National Probation and Parole Association Journal,* III (October, 1957), 389–90. Also see William S. Fort, "The Juvenile Court Examines Itself," *National Probation and Parole Association Journal,* V (October, 1959), 410, and Sol Rubin, "The Child in the Juvenile Court," in *Crime and Juvenile Delinquency* (New York: Oceana Publications, 1958).

fend, attack, or seek to destroy the larger community or some of its members. The concept is simply this: We ought to recognize that the offender is really somebody whose very offense is a sign of needed help. Our response, therefore, should be to understand the specific meanings and causes of the antisocial or anti-individual outbreak and to offer help and remedies suited to the etiology and to the individual. Not "to make the punishment fit the crime"; but "to make the assistance and remedy suit the offender." Not "to do something *to* a child because of what he *has done*"; but to do "something *for* a child because of what he *is* and *needs*." [2]

All of this did not spring, fully developed, from the convictions and experience of the early experimenters in a number of cities, nor was it completely elaborated by the Chicago pioneers who actually phrased and won backing for the first full juvenile court law in 1899. The philosophy itself, and ways of implementing it, may be said to have evolved over a long period. At times, in fact, pragmatic considerations predominated, only to be followed by humanitarian and legal rationale. There were thus both ancient ideas and recent experience behind the formulation by the committee of the Chicago Bar Association when it said:

The fundamental idea of the Juvenile Court Law is that the State must step in and exercise guardianship over a child found under such adverse social or individual conditions as develop crime. . . . It proposes a plan whereby he may be treated, not as a criminal or one legally charged with crime, but as a ward of the State, to receive practically the care, custody and discipline that are accorded the neglected and dependent child, and which, as the Act states, "shall approximate as nearly as may be that which should be given by its parents."

Behind this was long tradition in the criminal law of what was called "age of responsibility," i.e., children of certain ages were not considered able to understand the consequences of their acts and therefore were not punishable for them. The dividing line varied with the century and the culture, of course, and there were certain "optional" age groups for whom a prosecutor could seek to prove understanding and responsibility.

Another stream of influence (about whose importance there is

[2] The last quotation is from Edward F. Waite as cited by Francis A. Allen, "The Borderland of the Criminal Law: Problems of 'Socializing' Criminal Justice," *Social Service Review*, XXXII (June, 1958), 116.

some controversy), relevant originally to neglect and dependency but applied later to delinquency, could be traced to the medieval assumption by the crown of supervision over the estates of minors. Transferred later to so-called chancery courts, this responsibility evolved into the notion that king or state, as *parens patriae*, acting as "a wise, affectionate and careful parent," assumed the protection of all infants—or at least saw to it, as A. Delafield Smith has said, that they were "parented" or cared for. In modern times the state became the guardian of social interests.[3]

The origins should not be depicted only in legal terms, however. In the eighteenth and, particularly, the nineteenth century, religious and humanitarian reformers had begun to provide special and separate institution facilities for children, as it became clear that the mixed almshouse was a hazardous environment for child development. They were influenced, particularly late in the nineteenth century, by the obvious inaccuracy of considering child victims of parental misfortune or mistreatment as, themselves, unworthy and degenerate—a characterization of other almshouse residents. Special institution programs led to foster home placements and aftercare services. Then Massachusetts pioneered in providing visiting agents to supervise the way in which children so placed were treated. It was natural to add, in 1869, that agents could appear "in behalf of children" when there was a court hearing to commit a child.[4]

Separate institutions, supervision, and aftercare were soon followed in a number of places by provision for separate trials and (later) separate detention. The earlier unofficial probation services of the 1840s could now become specialized and incorporated into law—as a natural evolution from the legal tradition of the use of the suspended sentence in its several variations.

Thus, there were current, at the end of the nineteenth century, in the form of social objectives, legal philosophy, court procedure, and community practice, the components of the major reform represented by the first juvenile court law. The participants in this great innova-

[3] For a more detailed review of juvenile court origins and philosophy, see Alfred J. Kahn, *A Court for Children* (New York: Columbia University Press, 1953), Chapter II. Also see Herbert A. Bloch and Frank T. Flynn, *Delinquency: The Juvenile Offender in America Today* (New York: Random House, 1956), Chapter 12. Both of these sources contain documentation and bibliography.

[4] Bloch and Flynn, *Delinquency*, p. 309.

tion had invented the idea of a nonstigmatizing, noncriminal status and the word "delinquency" (already in use) was soon applied to it. It seemed reasonable to hope that the separation of children from adults and a sincere effort on the part of judges to be helpful, in themselves, would be effective. It should cause no surprise that these pioneers did not foresee all of the organizational, administrative, and professional problems yet to be faced by the juvenile court movement.

Because the complexities of delinquency were not yet well understood, the problem of criteria for disposition did not loom large, and the invention of adequate helping and reformative devices seemed a reasonable task. Because social work, psychology, and psychiatry were just beginning, their relationships to the court and the best structure for teamwork were hardly issues. Since the early atmosphere was quite legal and formal, and because social welfare services in modern form were little developed, the concern that the court might ignore due process and become a social agency was yet to be faced. And because there was, as yet, little experience with success and failure, it was not yet realized that the choice of judge or probation officer could be crucial in the implementation or defeat of the court's objectives.

With hindsight, the problems were of course inevitable. The "criteria" for justice can be much clearer if the judge is to apply rules which are meant to suit penalty to offense than if he is charged with finding a helping plan appropriate for a given child. His task is complicated further by the assumption that the child's rights are always protected. As we have noted, this must ultimately mean that similar circumstances result in similar treatment, but how is this to be achieved while knowledge is so incomplete? Courts eventually came to see that psychological and psychiatric clinics might add to the social investigations of probation officers and contribute to dispositions. As the treatment needs were clarified, the standards of probation were raised and access to a variety of institutions and community treatment facilities also became important. Where such facilities did not exist, courts were tempted to create them, not always foreseeing that the court might thus become an administrative and treatment agency which had not yet adequately integrated its legal function.

This latter trend was accentuated by the lack of social welfare services in many counties throughout the country early in the twentieth century. As child welfare programs were created (particularly so-called mothers' pensions or widows' pensions), it seemed natural to turn to courts to administer them. Programs for handicapped children were also so assigned. On the one hand, this emphasized the court's helping orientation and nonpunitive role. On the other hand, and too often, it unnecessarily converted a request for social services into a court process, a stigmatizing process. The later development of broader social welfare programs confronted courts with the difficult problem of deciding which of their activities were central to their roles and which were historical accidents, better reallocated. Inevitably there were those who would now convert the children's court to a judicial agency, narrowly defined, while others were convinced that the court would never meet its responsibilities unless certain minimum diagnostic and treatment activities were assured under its own aegis.

THE NATIONAL PICTURE

Juvenile courts now serve approximately 400,000 to 800,000 cases annually, depending on whether traffic matters are included in the tabulation. The totals are for children ages 10–17, an age range most appropriate for national statistics, even though courts do work with younger children and do not end children's court jurisdiction at the same maximum age. More than half the courts, in fact, have jurisdiction until the eighteenth birthday, while some stop at age 16 and others at 17. The trend, nationally, is to raise the age limits of juvenile court jurisdiction. A few states include youths to 21 within the scope of children's courts, but the jurisdiction is concurrent with criminal courts.[5]

Cases may be processed either "officially" or "unofficially," the exact point of differentiation varying with the state; most crucial, perhaps, is the fact of formal adjudication in the "official" cases. Approximately half of all cases, nationally, are handled officially and half unofficially. Rural areas tend toward a somewhat higher

[5] Frederick B. Sussman, *Juvenile Delinquency* (New York: Oceana Publications, 1959). Also, National Probation and Parole Association, *Standard Juvenile Court Act* (New York, 1959), p. 330, and Fort, "The Juvenile Court Examines Itself," *National Probation and Parole Association Journal*, V, 408.

ratio of official handling, semirural areas to a slightly higher ratio of unofficial service. The urban areas are between the two.

All states have some form of juvenile court and there is basic similarity of philosophy and outlook in statutes despite differences in age jurisdiction, specification of offenses included as delinquency, and assignment of types of jurisdiction affecting children and families, other than delinquency and neglect. It is far too seldom noted, however, that only a minority of these children are, in fact, served in courts which are exclusively children's courts or juvenile courts (as they are more often called). Three states have state-wide juvenile court systems providing complete coverage (Utah, Connecticut, Rhode Island); eighty other counties have special judges for children, only half of them full time. The remainder of the some 3,000 counties in the United States are served by judges whose children's court responsibilities are discharged on a part-time basis within the framework of another court. These judges have the task of adapting their methods and outlook to this special setting as they move into it.

A report to the 1960 White House Conference on Children listed as serious problems confronting juvenile courts the lack of judges who are truly specialists in juvenile matters, the prevalence of part-time judicial service in these courts, and the tendency to excessive workloads.[6]

There is general agreement that juvenile courts should have jurisdiction over those offenses committed by children which would be crimes in adults, i.e., felonies, misdemeanors, or other offenses. In some instances adult courts are given concurrent jurisdiction in felony cases, or juvenile courts may transfer to adult courts. In others, particularly where the punishment might be death or life in prison, criminal courts may be required to waive their rights before children's court procedure is permitted. This is, of course, one index of incomplete commitment to the juvenile court idea or a compromise to meet what some consider to be community sentiment.[7]

Court jurisdictions are far from uniform in regard to those of-

[6] Golden Anniversary, White House Conference on Children and Youth, Inc., *Information Sheets on Children and Youth* (Washington, D.C., 1960), Workshops 191–194, p. 2.

[7] Fort, "The Juvenile Court Examines Itself," *National Probation and Parole Association Journal*, V, 408–9.

fenses labeled as delinquency not because they are crimes in adults but because they are deemed as antisocial or indicative of inappropriate development and, thus, of need for public intervention; specified lists of offenses vary from state to state, and a situation considered as indicative of delinquency in one may suggest neglect to another. All courts also have provision for jurisdiction over children not adequately cared for or not provided with basic necessities owing to parental or guardian failings. Here, too, definitions vary widely, particularly with reference to the relative emphasis on physical abuse alone as contrasted with the failure to provide specific forms of care and service. Some courts, under dependency jurisdiction, in effect administer social services and authorize expenditure of welfare and health funds.

Many states include in their statutes broad provision for jurisdiction over adults who "contribute to the delinquency or neglect of a minor." This is a provision which might be used in a variety of ways but is often not called upon at all; serious acts which would "contribute" to delinquency are, in fact, also in the realm of criminal courts. Transfer to such courts is to be preferred both to avoid overloading children's courts with criminal cases and because individual rights are better protected where there are specific charges (assault, cruelty, etc.) which go beyond the difficult-to-establish allegation about "contributing to delinquency." Where children's courts do act in these cases, standard-setting groups consider it sound for them to limit their jurisdiction to offenses committed against children by adults with a continuing relationship to them.

In addition, in every state one court or another has jurisdiction over appointment of guardians, termination of parental rights, adoption, custody of mentally ill children, support, separation, divorce, paternity determination, intrafamily assault, and so on. These jurisdictions are usually dispersed in probate courts, county courts, circuit courts, and elsewhere. Some of the jurisdictions may be assigned to juvenile courts. While these matters are beyond the scope of our present discussion, it is relevant to note that the Standard Family Court Act of the National Council on Crime and Delinquency proposes that all such jurisdiction, including marital actions, be placed in one family division. Obviously, any assignment of such jurisdictions should facilitate close ties between children's court work and the proceedings involved, since the evidence is overwhelming as to the close interrelationship between broader family problems and child delinquency and neglect.

As we have already suggested, the national juvenile court picture is not encouraging in many respects: personnel inadequacies, staff shortages, resource lacks, structural defects, procedural problems, statutory limitations. These difficulties have many origins. First, the task is basically complex and both knowledge and professional skills are far from complete. Next, there are the honest differences of opinion as to the proper emphasis and direction for the court. Third, some communities are simply not able to solve the problems of financing and staffing which are involved in strengthening a court. In fact, the national increase in court caseloads has inundated some courts and led to compromises.

Despite all of this, and on the positive side, the juvenile court goal is not being abandoned. Higher courts consistently support the basic constitutionality of the approach. Some states have made notable progress in increasing the qualifications and numbers of professional staff. Nationally, juvenile court judges, on the one hand, and probation leaders, on the other, have been working to supply the knowledge and skill which have been lacking. Increasing support has come from a variety of professional groups and from the federal government. Recently formulated statements of standards and goals are particularly helpful. Finally, and most important, the juvenile court idea remains consistent with our basic heritage and attitude toward children; the reforms which are proposed tend to fit within the farmework of juvenile court philosophy.

Given this situation, it seems appropriate (a) to seek more specific definition of the place of a court in the community's total approach to children in trouble, and then (b) to examine each phase of the court process and structure with a view to specifying the direction and conditions for reform. The remainder of the chapter is devoted to these tasks.

A CHILDREN'S COURT IN THE COMMUNITY PATTERN

Enough has already been said of the history of juvenile courts to suggest the reasons for an excessively expansive concept of their functions. These courts developed where other social services did not exist and they had to create such services in order to do their own jobs. Inevitably, they were then turned to when new programs had to be housed. Their judges, influential and highly respected public servants, as well as leaders in the efforts to secure facilities, often became the initiators, planners, or coordinators of broad community efforts.[8]

Historical perspective does not, however, justify perpetuation of an unbalanced view which sees the juvenile court as the *hub* or *nexus* of community services to children. Far too often, community efforts at prevention and treatment are organized from the court's perspective and guided by its needs, whereas sound planning would demand another vantage point.

First, the court is not primarily a preventive agency and should neither be credited with a decrease in delinquency nor held to account for its increase. Enough has been said in earlier chapters to make the point that the causation of delinquency is, basically, a matter of the world and the national scene, community atmosphere, family life, peer-group experience, and individual personality dynamics. While a court has some part in social control, it cannot affect basic causal factors of this kind in significant fashion. The evidence suggests that it is not even a major deterrent.[9]

Nor should we expect a judge's lecture from the bench to modify a child's value system or to alter a personality pattern which is rooted in lifelong experience. Therefore, it is no reflection on the competence or dedication of juvenile court judges to suggest that the courtroom per se is not a rehabilitation center. For, although it may become a traumatic experience, the courtroom hearing is generally brief and transitory and, to the child, part of a total process which includes a variety of new and salient exposures, including arrest, detention, and parental reactions.

What, then, are the court's appropriate functions? Why the view that the community system of services has an unbridgeable gap unless it includes a strong and soundly employed children's court?

The core role of the court. Most deviant behavior in a community

[8] For detailed discussion see Alfred J. Kahn, "Court and Community," in Margaret K. Rosenheim, ed., *Justice for the Child* (New York: The Free Press of Glencoe, 1962).

[9] Harry Elmer Barnes, "Shall We Get Tough or Be Sensible in Facing the Increase in Crime?" *Federal Probation,* XXIII (June, 1959), 29–36.

is absorbed in or handled by the family, schools, churches, and medical facilities. Some is assigned to the special channel of the court, as a matter of policy, because action is contemplated which seriously affects the child's status and may deprive him of liberty. Such action is contemplated in instances of behavior so dangerous and disruptive as to cause public concern (conduct defined as illegal or criminal in adults); when a child's behavior is considered a likely precursor of such illegal conduct; or (in so far as children are involved) when the behavior causes serious damage to self, family, peers, or community. The last category, in particular, is a flexible one reflecting the status at a given time of the community's evaluations of deviant conduct in children and of the need for public intervention. It is the schools and the child care, child protection, medical, and religious agencies which are the major forces in conveying to court and to legislature the status of such evaluations and, thus, their priorities as to court concern.

Two questions are foremost in the minds of agencies and community institutions as they seek to define when and how they wish to use the court:

(1) Are we dealing with phenomena which are beyond the scope of a service lacking access to potent sanctions?

(2) Since our service to this particular case demands some infringement on custody, guardianship of the person, or parental rights, what legal procedural measures are necessary both to assure our right to arrange the service and to protect the child's legal rights—avoiding unnecessary and arbitrary infringement?

Part of the definition of the place of a children's court in the community pattern is based on consideration of what shall occur before the decision is made that there must be legal recourse in order to render a service to a child. The remainder of the definition involves the situation after the court's intervention.

A juvenile court is inevitably involved in both levels of *case finding:* the kind which is concerned with early deviance not yet in the defined province of any particular service as well as the kind assigned to it by statutory directive. In fact, citizens, teachers, police officers, representatives of child care agencies, and others often come to the court for the purpose of clarifying whether a situation

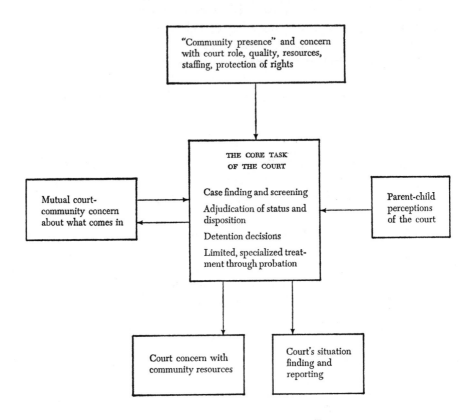

CHILDREN'S COURT IN A COMMUNITY SYSTEM—
RELEVANT DIMENSIONS

is—or should be—in the former or the latter category. Obviously, the court may contribute to the necessary processing at that point only if it has an adequate intake structure. While the nature of the legal, social work, and psychological skills on which intake must draw will be elaborated at a later point, it is appropriate to note that, like all case finding, intake may lead to the giving of information or advice, to referral, to brief service, or to complete court processing. Located, so to speak, in the court "vestibule," it should be a brief service. And, situated in the pre-judicial phase of the court's work, its direct service should remain *voluntary* and should not involve formal judicial decisions.

An alert judge or intake worker is also well located for that case finding which is a by-product of the work on the case at hand. Thus, a delinquency hearing may disclose the health problem of a sibling, or a neglect procedure may produce evidence of the delinquency of a neighborhood boy. These matters should obviously be channeled to the appropriate agencies—again, on a voluntary basis.

Case finding is also accompanied by *situation finding*. Probation officers and judges will become aware, constantly, of gaps in community provision, of problems in the educational system, and of conditions hazardous to child development. It is difficult to accept the notion that a court should be an isolated, judicial, decision-making mechanism which ignores such things. Rather, most courts would agree to the need for a pattern of organization which permits assembling of data and experience, ensures periodic internal assessments of such material, and provides for prompt reporting of observations and concerns, as appropriate, to police, government officials, schools, health services, churches, and the public at large.

Case evaluation accompanies all of the court's case finding, whether it is of the brief screening variety which determines that the family should go elsewhere or the more complete evaluation which guides brief service in intake or leads to the courtroom. Information desk and petition-writing personnel have responsibilities for some of these functions, although major responsibility belongs to probation and other intake personnel.

Court intake asks, primarily, "Should the case be referred to the courtroom, helped here, or referred out?" The determination may be routine (certain cases must get to the courtroom) or very complex.

The judge in the courtroom is called upon to answer another kind of case evaluation question, "Does the court have jurisdiction?"

We have, elsewhere, referred to the case evaluation in the courtroom as

the special skill of the court, the monopoly of the court and, indeed, its *unique* function in the total community system of services. The reference is of course to adjudication—which is largely a legal evaluation and involves both issues relating to jurisdiction and issues relating to facts.[10]

Unlike those situations in which people may be offered and will accept service on a voluntary basis and those others in which total context creates some built-in sanctions (the relief investigator and his client), there are some human circumstances, we have seen, in which society adopts the right to impose measures whatever the attitude of the individual. The applicable circumstances are defined by statute as interpreted by court opinions. It is the special purpose of adjudication to determine whether situations as alleged and as defined in the statute prevail and whether social measures may therefore be initiated. So crucial, so unique, and so valuable is this special prerogative of the court that no true advocate of juvenile courts could fail to concern himself with legal definitions, court procedures, and the full preservation of legal rights. To do so is to ignore the special contribution of a court to the total pattern.

The court's *service planning* after adjudication demands a more comprehensive *case evaluation* in the form of a probation case study. This study, where appropriate, should be supplemented by clinical reports. It is our view that a social study of this kind, involving considerable invasion of privacy, should follow only after adjudication. We shall defer the question of whether the judge should (*a*) do all the service planning; (*b*) limit himself to the decision of whether or not a child is to remain in the community or be committed; (*c*) turn the planning over to a treatment authority.

In what sense is the court also a *treatment or direct service* agency? Children and families before the court may require services as varied and diverse as any that a community can provide. No court would seek to meet all—or even most—of the needs. It does have in probation, however, the potential of a unique service, especially suited to it. We have already defined the probation task in intake

[10] Kahn, "Court and Community," in *Justice for the Child*, p. 225.

and in case evaluation prior to disposition. The service-treatment role in probation should also be quite specific; not the endless, meaningless "reporting" and checking up which it is in many places but, rather, a defined form of intervention appropriate for a definable subgroup within the court population. The "helping" professions have described some young people in trouble as most likely to be reached if served by a community treatment facility which has direct and immediate access to sanctions—in this instance, the right to commit. It is these young people who should be placed on probation. Others may be assigned this disposition because there is conviction that they should be followed up for a period and reevaluated carefully prior to discharge.

In a later section we shall have occasion to discuss in further detail the probation role and the qualifications which an individual should bring to it. Particularly promising are several new group approaches and the "reporting center" idea. We shall also, subsequently, consider the relationship of probation to court clinical services. For the present we might stress that a qualified probation structure would seem to be the best way to incorporate into treatment method the court's particular advantages as an authoritative agency. Clinical skill and personnel might be included within probation for a variety of purposes. It would be difficult to make a convincing case for a separate clinical structure. It may be appropriate in a large community to create a probation office which is administratively independent and which serves several courts.

In general, a court is not the agency best equipped to manage or operate institutional or general therapeutic services, unless the community is small and the social welfare structure undeveloped. Where possible, even detention should be administered as part of a system of facilities which includes shelters, youth residences, boarding homes, and so on. This does not preclude court control of detention intake and social service, clearly a necessity for efficiency of operation, protection of individual rights, and to avoid unnecessary use of detention. Where local conditions suggest the desirability of court administration of detention because of the close tie of detention to its core role, this should be seen as a justifiable exception, rather than reason for excursions into more extensive direct-service areas.[11]

[11] The principle would appear to be sound despite the fact that large- and medium-sized probation departments in California successfully operate deten-

What comes to the court. Having looked, briefly, at the heart of the court's task and at its unique role in a community system, we must hasten to add that a court cannot implement that role in isolation. It requires close ties to all major social institutions so as to be sure that there is clear understanding of what it is ready to do. It also needs these ties so as to be in tune with community evaluations of juvenile conduct. There is no system of law which can fully determine for all time the "cut-off points" for community concern about deviance in children. As part of the mainstream of community life a court must remain in tune with the culture in relation to those statutory provisions implying evaluations of the consequences ot given behavior.

To discharge its responsibility in effecting what comes into court, the court needs formal ties to voluntary and public agencies and civic groups through public and voluntary coordinating and planning bodies (Ch. XIII). Its judges and probation leaders must also be active in many phases of civic life in their personal capacities.

What the community offers. Judge O. W. Ketcham of the Washington, D.C., court, using a helpful literary device, has talked of the juvenile court as a court-community compact. Certain criminal court protections are given up in the juvenile court on the "promise" that court intervention into his life "will enhance the child's welfare." [12] A court can hardly discharge its obligations without constant attention to what the community resources on which it draws are like and what they do.

Judges and other court administrative personnel may meet their responsibilities in part through participation in planning and coordinating bodies, as suggested above. But more is involved. At the time of appointment and periodically during a term of office, top court personnel require the kind of in-service training and orientation which will acquaint them with the resources which exist and with reasonable expectations which may be held. A court should regularly receive, study, and respond to reports on the size, staffing,

---

tion, forestry camps, and local treatment facilities. It hardly contributes to the development of balanced community provision to accept a view as expansive as Stark's. See Heman Stark, "Standards for Juvenile Halls," *Federal Probation*, XXIV, No. 1 (March, 1960), 36.

[12] Orman W. Ketcham, "The Unfilled Promise of the American Juvenile Court," in *Justice for the Child*, p. 26.

and effectiveness of agencies and institutions on which its own effectiveness ultimately depends, and it should plan periodic visits to such organizations.

In reacting to community needs, reporting about serious gaps, and urging new provisions a court is discharging functions which we have identified as *reporting* and *accountability*. These are responsibilities which a court holds in common with many other community agencies rather than unique roles. Implementation of accountability requires both conscientiousness and particular discipline for a court, however. Since it intervenes in individuals' lives in what is often extremely drastic and strategic fashion, the court carries the heavy responsibility of being informed about the status of agencies and programs. It must seek constantly to assure itself and the public that public intervention is followed by constructive experience rather than by community-sanctioned mistreatment and neglect. Yet, despite its interest, its visiting, and its reporting, the court must not convert itself into a supervisory body or into the guiding force in the community system. As soon as it does, its core role is distorted and the pattern suffers a major gap because it ceases to be primarily a court, albeit a special kind of court, for children.

The "community presence." The "compact" of which Judge Ketcham speaks involves two parties. A court must remain alert to the status of community values, objectives, and resource provisions. A community must constantly keep informed about the quality and operations of its court.

There is need for citizen advisory committees to the court, "watchdog" bodies of citizens, periodic over-all reviews by scholars, legislative bodies, or bar groups. Furthermore, within the limits of protecting privacy and not affecting procedures, qualified responsible officials and citizens should visit the court and express their interest in its work. Representatives of the press and mass media should also visit in order to gain understanding of the court and to reflect community interest in its work—again, only upon assurance that names will not be used and the procedure and atmosphere not interfered with.

The client's perception of the court. A discussion of the court in the community system of services is far from complete without mention of the perception of the court on the part of children and their parents who are brought to it—or who should use it. To what extent are the philosophy and objectives of the court translated into a public image which reinforces the work? Do court structure, procedures, and dispositions convey the purposes and objectives which the court holds? Do young people before the court see it as perceptive and helpful or as naïve and foolish? Do parents regard it as a potential ally or as a threat to their families? [13] The factors which will determine the answers are best outlined in a more detailed examination of issues of court structure and procedure.

LOOKING AT A COURT

An institution as complex as a large juvenile court must ultimately depend for its success on its ability to create a pervasive philosophy and to bring many types of roles and individuals into harmonious activity. This fact must be kept in the forefront as we move from broad generalizations to consideration of specific aspects of court role, jurisdiction, organization, procedure, and administration.

In what follows, we shall seek to document and to specify this point by (a) drawing upon available guides and standards, especially the Standard Juvenile Court Act and the *Standards for Specialized Courts Dealing with Children;* (b) reporting national and local developments and opinions; (c) using illustrations drawn from the New York City court. This court has been reported on regularly and in some detail in recent years by observers who are agreed basically as to the court's status and needs. Our own materials have been kept current since publication of *A Court for Children.*[14]

[13] Elliot Studt, "The Client's Image of the Juvenile Court," *ibid.,* pp. 200–216.

[14] Juvenile courts and legislators framing statutes have always received major aid from the Standard Juvenile Court Act (henceforth referred to as Standard Act), a model statute which embodies the ideas of the outstanding experts in the field. In recent years, an extremely valuable set of guidelines has appeared in the form of *Standards for Specialized Courts Dealing with Children* (henceforth referred to as *Standards*). See Children's Bureau, U.S. Department of Health, Education, and Welfare, *Standards for Specialized Courts Dealing with Children* (Washington, D.C.: Government Printing Office, 1954).

New York City analyses are found in Alfred J. Kahn, *A Court for Children,* Walter Gellhorn, *Children and Families in the Courts of New York* (New York: Dodd, Mead, 1954). Also, Juvenile Delinquency Evaluation Project, *The Judicial Process: Its Impact on Youth* (New York, 1960), and *The New York City Probation System* (New York, 1959). New York's 1962 unified Family Court Act, which became effective September, 1962, elaborates its rationale.

Our fundamental purpose, where we present New York material, is not evaluative. The New York court's jurisdiction, services, and structure are in the process of major reorganization, as this book appears, as the result of unification of probation in three lower courts under an up-graded independent office of probation and the creation of a comprehensive, statewide Family Court. Nonetheless, the illustrative material may be used to suggest a degree of detail not reported upon for most courts, making it possible to move from standards to real situations and to visualize the requirements for any urban area seeking to create an effective facility.

As background for the illustrations, it is useful to record that the Children's Court in New York had traditional delinquency, neglect, and related jurisdiction prior to the 1962 changes and was loosely tied to a support court called Family Court. Since September, 1962, children's jurisdiction is incorporated into a Family Court with comprehensive coverage, except for the exclusion of matrimonial actions. The term "delinquency" is limited to the equivalent of crimes and offenses in adults. There is broad neglect jurisdiction. A new category, children in need of supervision, covers many of those matters previously included under delinquency but not the equivalent of crimes or offenses in adults. As did the old court, the new court has an upper age limit of sixteen for original, exclusive delinquency jurisdiction, with exclusions at fifteen for crimes punishable by death and life in prison. In the neglect and in-need-of-supervision categories the upper age limit is sixteen for boys and eighteen for girls, in a compromise effort to include the "wayward" group, while a legislative committee reviews the general problem of youth jurisdiction for ages 16–21.

A total of 17,586 new delinquency and neglect petitions were processed in the New York court in 1961. The court operates in five borough branches. There are twenty-four judges who rotate among the branches and between the adjudication and disposition "parts" and the family and children's work in each. Judges are required under the new law to have ten years of legal experience. The bench will be increased to absorb the expanded family jurisdiction and new "parts" are being created.

The largest court of its kind, it inevitably requires structure and procedures more complex than those of smaller cities. It is this elaboration of structure and procedures, however, which makes the New York court a useful one to observe in relation to issues and problems. These may be obscured but are not eliminated in smaller communities where there is less specialization and more consolidation.

According to *Standards,* individualized, nonpunitive, remedial justice requires:

1. A judge and a staff identified with and capable of carrying out a nonpunitive and individualized service.
2. Sufficient facilities available in the court and the community to insure:
    (a) that the dispositions of the court are based on the best available knowledge of the needs of the child.
    (b) that the child, if he needs care and treatment, receives these through facilities adapted to his needs and from persons properly qualified and empowered to give them.
    (c) that the community receives adequate protection.
3. Procedures that are designed to insure that two objectives are kept constantly in mind, these being
    (a) the individualization of the child and his situation, and
    (b) the protection of the legal and constitutional rights of both parents and child.[15]

While the subject of "sufficient facilities" is for the most part explored in other chapters, we shall concern ourselves here with both the staffing and the procedural requirements of a children's court. And it is necessary to stress at once that there is more to court impact on children and parents than the organized plan of the manuals, rules, and routines developed by those in authority. Attitudes conveyed by the manners and mannerisms of personnel are an important part of the atmosphere as it affects those who must use the court. The gossip and mood of the waiting room may influence responses as much as the instructions of a judge. The "low-down" as communicated to a child in the bus en route from detention to a court hearing has much to do with how he interprets a court disposition. In the language of the social scientist, concern for strengthening court operations demands attention to factors of informal, as

[15] *Standards,* pp. 1–2.

well as formal, organization, to staff and client culture as well as to rules and procedures.

An institution such as a children's court begins to make its impressions from the moment a parent or child enters the building. The desperate parent who has arrived determined to take some definitive action after years of difficulty with a child, or the community member who has a complaint about a neighbor, receives many of his cues and forms many of his expectations in the first few moments. It is these expectations, in turn, which condition the manner of participation in the court process.

Apart from the physical appearance of the building itself (many court buildings are certainly not designed with their tasks in mind), the behavior of "doorway" personnel can be most important. If a court is to be truly accessible to those who must use it, the information function must be conceived as an important one and the desk must be staffed by personnel who know the court well and can refer appropriately within it, as well as answer more general inquiries. The court, along with other major health, welfare, and police services, must also be prepared to be used as a general information center by citizens who may not need court services but do not know where to go. Information desk personnel therefore require reasonably good knowledge of major community agencies and their functions and must be prepared to "clear" with other information sources when they cannot answer inquiries. Information desk staff need preparation to listen to inquiries by distressed, confused, and anxious people, and to handle them with understanding and reassurance.

The New York court has been aware of the importance of its information desk and has on occasion offered consultation advice to information desk personnel through the probation department. Special orientation has been given at times. However, staff turnover, clerical shortages, the need to use these personnel in other capacities as well have generally defeated the efforts made. It is doubtful that a court's doorway is as "open" as necessary or can render the required service until information desk personnel become part of a general intake staff in a unified Bureau of Applications (i.e., a complete intake service). Some courts have achieved such a plan.

Many courts have recognized that there are case situations which may be settled through referral, without formal court action, or which may require a brief informal discussion and advice and little more. The latter may take the form of a family conference at which agreements are reached about visitation by a separated parent, a child's allowance, "coming in" time at night, or return to a clinic. The *Standards* recommends such service in a court; this kind of service accounts for many of the "informal" cases in the delinquency and neglect statistics reported by the Children's Bureau.

Appropriate as such activity may seem to be, courts are often concerned lest they renege on some of their primary obligations and offer steering or a conference with a probation officer in an intake unit when the complainant or child has the right to legal, not social, guidance and the attention of the judge himself. According to *Standards,* this may be achieved by provision of legal advice for the intake worker—who is usually a probation officer. In addition, any person should have the right to appeal to the judge from any action or decision in an intake unit. Nor should any person be deprived of the right to file a petition on any specific issue to which he is a party.

Most observers agree that New York tended in the past excessively to limit the intake function to a point where the courtroom was unnecessarily overburdened. The court created a pioneer Bureau of Adjustment in 1936, but set up a series of rules which limited the service to less than 10 percent of court cases—those cases considered "less serious." It was widely recommended that the bureau become part of a broad court intake service, offering informal, brief-contact help in some instances and serving as a channel to the courtroom when appropriate. A complete intake structure would also include the *petition desk*, which, in the New York court, has in the past been under supervision of the clerk of the court and not always attuned to the basic philosophy of the whole. Cases which did not go to the Bureau of Adjustment began their processing at the petition desk, and those bureau cases requiring petitions were also steered there. According to a recent report, "Despite efforts by the administrative officers . . . to standardize the procedures involved in preparing petitions, there is no uniformity of quality or practice. Some clerks prepare excellent petitions; others are verbose, use archaic legal expressions, include irrelevant allegations, and even make glaring errors of fact." [16]

[16] *The Judicial Process: Its Impact on Youth,* p. 8.

Equally crucial is the fact that the discussions of petition clerks with police officers, parents, other petitioners, and children necessarily emphasize details of the offense, the item stolen or destroyed, the circumstances of sexual misconduct. For all participants, this creates a criminal atmosphere and orientation contrary to the court's purpose. The objectives are, of course, appropriate: a desire to follow correct judicial procedure and establish which allegations are to be proven before the court assumes jurisdiction. It is relevant to inquire, however, whether these ends might not be achieved in a manner more suited to the nature of the court. For, whether they come through a Bureau of Adjustment or its equivalent, or are required to go almost directly to the courtroom, all children and parents about to go before the court require preparation for the significant experience and an indication of what to expect. They need to know about procedures, legal rights, possible dispositions, the meaning of remand. They often require considerable reassurance that their rights will be respected, their story heard, and their wishes seriously considered. The court's helping intent needs to be explained time and again. Currently, the petition procedure, in this and many other large courts, is not expected to provide any of this. While it is understood that, except for the judge at the hearing, no one can properly enter into a determination of the truth of the allegations, there are serious grounds for concern that a completely clerical conception of the responsibilities assigned to, or assumed by, petition clerks may, at its doorway, negate the very intent of a children's court.

The *Standards*, the Standard Act, and all other guides are agreed that a court for children requires a comprehensive intake service. In delinquency and neglect the intake department should receive all complaints and conduct "investigations to determine whether (a) the court or its staff should take action, and, if so, what kind of action, or (b) the matter should be referred elsewhere." An intake service needs consultation with or the participation of legally trained personnel to assure the accuracy of petition writing and the screening out of cases not within the court's scope. It needs skilled probation staff, with access to clinical consultation, so as to render its brief service skillfully, oriented both to legal and to social-psychological diagnostic considerations. Its social appraisals are appropriately brief-screening inquiries to determine the court's apparent right or need to intervene, whether more might be accomplished by "informal" agreements and adjustments or through referral to another agency, the type of court proceeding apparently called for, the need for detention or emergency psychiatric observation pending ultimate disposition. Where a court appearance is to follow, preparation (in the sense described above) is a major responsibility. Where the service required may be completed through "brief service" by the intake staff, this would seem to be desirable, provided that the voluntary nature of participation is kept clear. Extensive "unofficial casework" or "informal probation" would not seem to be a sound function for a court, despite some differences of opinion and contrary practice.[17] New York's reorganized court is evolving a comprehensive intake service as this volume goes to press.

A JUDGE IN A COURTROOM

A children's court cannot be expected to have the atmosphere of a theater lounge or even a school play yard. The children present are frightened, confused, disturbed, and anxious. Petitioners from the community are often angry or hostile, and police officers may show the insensitivity of long exposure to misery. Family tensions may erupt into arguments as next steps are discussed in preparation for the hearing. In the midst of it all, lawyers confer with clients, young children cry at their discomfort, and attendants call out names on the calendar and demand order and attention.

Surely, adequate provision for reasonably attractive physical surroundings is a minimal requirement. The fact that waiting rooms are often small, crowded, improperly furnished, and not well decorated is evidence that the atmosphere of the court anteroom has not had adequate attention. Nursery rooms to care for young children exist in some court branches and are essential everywhere, since young children should not be present at neglect hearings or at the delinquency hearings of their siblings.

Even if waiting rooms are drab, however, and if court buildings are designed to inspire dignity rather than confidence and relaxation, personnel may do much to convey the respect, individual attention, and helping purposes of a court. Again, if this is appreciated,

[17] *Standards,* p. 43; *Standard Act,* p. 352.

attendants and matrons are indoctrinated in court objectives and shown how they may advance them. If it is not fully understood, or if the court is overburdened and understaffed, the court attendants only add to the general anxiety and confusion, and unintentionally undermine the best of judge and probation officer efforts. People are herded into the courtroom, more apprehensive than their normal reactions would make them; even the most talented of judges finds it difficult to overcome the formality insisted upon by those attendants who hold criminal court concepts of client courtroom behavior. Whether or not the judge does overcome all of this and conveys another mood during the hearing, attendants may undo much of what he communicates by their brisk ushering of people out. The objective may be to speed the calendar, but the consequence is a mood which again poses needless obstacles as the probation officer's work proceeds.

The New York City court has not fully conquered the task of converting many types of personnel into a unified, consistent staff; many other courts are similarly unsuccessful. Nor has this court as yet found ways of building courtrooms appropriate to court functions and to the mood it seeks to establish. In some boroughs, the bench is no higher than an ordinary table, but in others the judge is as high and as distant as judges ever are. Some of the rooms do lend themselves to disposition conferences, but instead the tendency is to arrange the tables and chairs as though there were a formal "bench" available. Even the judges who seek to undo this and to communicate more intimately with those before the court for disposition discussion find the atmosphere forbidding: in addition to personnel who must participate in the conference and the attendants, who do not try to be unobtrusive, clerical workers, translators, and a group of waiting probation officers, who are not sure when they will be reached to present cases or to confer with the judge, convert the hearing into a rather public occasion. This may be inevitable to a degree in the adjudication phase, where the court must decide whether or not a finding is to be made and must consider all those involved in an incident as well as witnesses—but even here one should guard against unnecessary paraphernalia or ceremonial which confuses or intimidates. A public occasion is very far from the objective at the disposition hearing, however, where there is need to talk, understand, explain, and reassure.

The *judge* is the leader of the court "team" and his qualifications and characteristics do much to make a children's court, or to disappoint those who believe in its potentialities. In the language here being employed to describe basic functions essential to a total community plan, the judge may be said to have extremely important parts in the following:

a) *Community protection:* He may place a child in detention pending long-term disposition. He may commit an adjudicated child to an institution or hospital if the child's presence in the community is a hazard.

b) *Case evaluation:* He decides whether a community has the right to exercise authority.

c) *Case disposition:* Drawing upon the data and recommendations of specialists (probation officers, psychiatrists, psychologists, educators, detention personnel, etc.) as well as his own observations and evaluation, he decides what the court's "plan" for a case will be.

d) *Referral:* The judge makes the first attempt to interpret the plan, encourage optimum use by child and parent of the service offered, and, at times, ensure agency understanding of the client and the reason the disposition was made.

e) *Reporting:* The judge may be alert to shortages or inadequacies of facilities and may communicate these to responsible bodies and to the community at large.

The judge does not carry out treatment, since a treatment relationship requires time to develop and frequency of contact. His courtroom statements to parents and children may serve to communicate community opinion or to encourage maximum use of treatment opportunities.

A sound definition of role for the judge requires a balancing of legal knowledge and method with the basic knowledge and ability essential to understand reports of specialists, to choose from many alternatives, and to convey encouragement and support as he selects and interprets a disposition. He must be able to question skillfully, observe courtroom behavior, and draw inferences from it. In addition, he must know how to respect the contributions of personnel in all categories and integrate all the court's parts into an effort on behalf of children.

Protection of rights is as vital as sound dispositions, since the court may not plan where it has no jurisdiction. Judges must explain the allegations, inform parents of the right to adjournment for counsel or to summon witnesses, and avoid disposition considerations prior to adjudication.

Procedural details will not here be reviewed. The separation between *adjudication* (the judicial determination as to whether the allegation is true and, if so, where the state shall assume some responsibility) and *disposition* may be achieved by the division into two parts, or by an adjournment for probation study between the two phases. New York City uses both these methods. Some courts blur individual rights by ignoring these two separate phases.

Creative judges are able to make excellent use of their courtroom assignments. In many jurisdictions, judges are only in children's court part of the time. Others, although full-time, may be neither dedicated to the court's objectives nor qualified for its complex demands. Thus, in all juvenile courts there are judges who overemphasize the offense and lose its significance, or fail to note clues which indicate how they may help. Many lack sufficient understanding of individual behavior or skill in relating and communicating to translate an honest desire to help into effective action. Some are basically too insensitive to work with troubled people and they hurt many who come before them through ridicule, rudeness, or failure to understand and to feel with those in court. There are, too, those who are unfamiliar with educational, social welfare, and mental hygiene resources and who do not seek to equip themselves with the knowledge their task requires.

Most judges suffer to a degree from the occupational hazards involved in extreme power over others, unchallenged by defense counsel in most cases and seldom reviewed by higher courts.[18] A few succumb in extreme form and prefer their own hunches to the reading of probation or psychiatric reports or referral for treatment. Or, if they make referrals, they precede them with long lectures or impose behavior requirements designed, in their minds, to be the

[18] For illustrations, see *A Court for Children*, pp. 104–6. The matter of counsel is discussed on pp. 100 ff.

important factor in change. They may "play to the gallery" as well, as though audience ratings were a gauge of court effectiveness.

There are judges who are best equipped to deal with adjudication and others gifted in the disposition phase. In contrast to outstanding judges who give leadership to community child welfare efforts, there are those who simply do not seem to know or to care.

Honest differences of opinion are current about the judge's role, but it is clear that some of the patterns ignore the court's objectives or at least fail to contribute to their realization. This situation will change only as the result of clearer court and public agreement as to the behavior which is not desirable and the qualifications to be sought—as well as the establishment of an appointment or selection procedure to protect against obviously inappropriate choices.

Many strong opinions are held as to the superiority of election, appointment, or their several variations as a mode of staffing courts. Investigation discloses no preponderance of evidence in favor of any one plan. One can cite outstanding judges derived from all possible selection procedures, and at the same time point to some among their colleagues who are hardly assets to court work. Many court reformers currently support a plan whereby a highly qualified citizen-bar panel nominates a roster of qualified candidates from which either an appointing official (mayor, governor) or party nominating conventions might make selections.

Whatever the procedural format, however, it is clear that there is need for candid legal and civic appraisal and the placing of qualifications (rather than prerogatives) in the forefront.[19] Nationally, there is need for law schools to add to the reservoir of those potentially qualified for this role by filling some of the gaps in training in this area of what is at times called sociolegal jurisprudence. They might consider the proposal of the late Judge Jerome Frank that judicial training become an advanced law school specialty. If this is too far from any immediate reality, institutes, seminars, and in-service orientation for those selected for these courts might help convert interested and qualified attorneys into judges for children.

[19] Citizens' Union of the City of New York, *Towards Better Judges* (New York, 1960). Also, Eleanor Roosevelt, John Warren Hill, Walter Gellhorn, and Alfred J. Kahn, "Judges for Children," *The Record of the Association of the Bar of the City of New York*, II, No. 1 (January, 1954), 8–19. *Standards*, pp. 83–85.

The National Council on Crime and Delinquency has given considerable leadership to these efforts in recent years.[20]

CASE EVALUATION IN PROBATION

Court intake personnel of all kinds make brief screening decisions. The court also requires more comprehensive case evaluations, adequate to guide a decision about intervention, i.e., so-called disposition evaluations. Because a substantial number of cases remain in treatment in the court as probationers, the disposition evaluations must be designed so as to guide the work of the probation officer in the early stages of contact (i.e., serve as a case evaluation to guide treatment). What has been traditionally called the "investigation" role of the probation officer is thus seen as a case study which should draw on the best available professional knowledge and skill. Despite earlier differences of opinion, the probation field and standard-setting groups now see the assignment as belonging within the scope of social casework and seek to adapt case evaluations, as prepared by caseworkers, to the particular needs of the court. Courts are recruiting trained social workers wherever possible, or are introducing social work concepts and methods into their in-service efforts.[21]

The case evaluation study, designed to contribute to disposition planning, as well as to facilitate the launching of probation treatment where probation is the disposition selected, requires a psychosocial emphasis. *A Court for Children* stated it thus:

Such study must concentrate on the child's social environment and personality, in an attempt to comprehend the significance of the current situation to him and to his family. Understanding of this kind derives from careful review of social history, current social setting, personality, and interpersonal relations. It makes possible, and should ultimately be formulated in, a case evaluation, "a diagnosis," and is prerequisite to the inauguration of helping measures. Whether these are wisely selected depends

[20] See, for example, National Council on Crime and Delinquency, *Procedure and Evidence in the Juvenile Court* (New York, 1962).

[21] For the backgrounds of probation and documentation of this view see *A Court for Children*, Chapter VI. Note, too, the files of the *Journal of the National Probation and Parole Association*, now *Crime and Delinquency*, and the files of *Federal Probation*. Also, William V. Chudd and Agnes A. Donnelly, "Characteristics of the Investigation Process in a Children's Court," *Social Casework*, XL, No. 5 (May, 1959), 262–68. Also, *Auxiliary Services to the Courts of New York City* (New York: Office of the Mayor, 1961).

on: the ability of the probation officer to understand the child, to evaluate the case data assembled, and to make valid recommendations; the willingness of the judge to consider the probation officer's formulation carefully, without necessarily being bound by it; and the extent to which "disposition" is regarded as a treatment plan based on case study and courtroom observations. The formulation finally accepted may be that of judge, probation officer, psychiatrist, supervisor, or the product of a conference. It may utilize reports of social agencies, examinations, tests and observations by other groups, as well as the court's own data. To achieve the court's aim, all these aids to understanding must be employed in a unified strategy for rehabilitation.[22]

These requirements indicate the possible sources of inadequate studies or studies inadequately employed. First, probation officers may not be equipped to conduct good case studies. Course work and experience under capable supervision are necessary if one is to learn adequate social study. Second, the study may be made but the position of the probation officer vis-à-vis the judge may be such that he does not end it with an evaluation, an appraisal—as well as a recommendation. Third, judges may, for various reasons, ignore the contents of studies or not even read them. (For example, following a recent incident in which the public was outraged after a gang stabbing in one city, all the "under sixteen" boys involved were committed to a training school at once.) Fourth, judges may read the reports but not be equipped to make wise use of them. Fifth, all may function well but community and court facilities may be in such short supply as to render the activity almost futile.

All of these situations prevail in a large court system and are not readily conquered. Far too often case study is a matter of mechanical filling out of headings by partially trained probation officers who have mastered professional devices superficially. Facts are assembled, but there is little analysis to provide a dynamic, living picture of a child in trouble. Plans may be proposed—yet often the rationale is not given. Recommendations may be avoided or the standard proposal made that there be psychiatric study, thus reflecting the probation officer's insecurity.

Little more should be expected in any court system with inadequate job qualifications, salaries too small to prevent rapid staff turnover, poorly trained supervisors, and caseloads too heavy to

[22] *A Court for Children,* p. 145.

permit sound work. The job definition, in fact, is often attuned to these realities and does not demand more.

Governmental and probation leadership in New York and elsewhere has dealt seriously with these problems in recent years in many ways. Higher examination requirements, matched by better salaries, have attracted more people. Where possible, graduate social workers are sought. Supervisors are released for social work training in a work-study program. In-service efforts are made. Unfortunately, constantly growing court caseloads, reflecting the general rise in delinquency, and a rate of expansion and recruitment not equal to the caseload rise have not given many major courts opportunity to consolidate, plan, or train staff.

A staff which is not sufficiently large, or is not adequately qualified or used, is a weak link which defeats the total logic of a system of service. For example, partially trained and, therefore, insecure probation officers are ready to follow most of the recommendations from court clinics, psychiatric hospital observation wards, and detention. Frequently the probation officer's only recommendation (often on the basis of little study) is that there be psychiatric study. Yet one hardly requires a full probation case study of two to three weeks' duration to arrive at the decision that psychiatric observation or study is necessary. The intent of the law, of course, is that the probation officer take responsibility for final weighing of formulations and recommendations from all sources and that he have expert knowledge of available resources. He can then make recommendations to the court independently. However, wherever probation officers are less equipped, technically, than clinic or detention personnel, funds will continue to be expended on pointless repetition.

Because clinic recommendations are, as a rule, accepted, the probation officer's job is, in fact, gradually redefined under circumstances such as these. A large portion of the officers avoid any major responsibility for suggesting a long-range disposition by recommending clinical diagnostic study unless they feel that a "minor" offense, "deserving" probation or discharge, is involved—or unless there has been a pattern of recidivism, so that commitment to a training school is considered inevitable. The consequence may well be an excessive use of court clinics and detention psychiatric facilities. Without doubt, more responsible probation case studies, with opportunity for psychiatric consultation to the officer, would simplify the procedure, speed up processing, and be more economical of psychiatric time—with no less satisfactory results.

There is determination almost everywhere to improve this situation. Increased recruitment of social work graduates and provision of in-service training and work-study opportunity must accompany administrative reform and job redefinitions.

THE DISPOSITION FORMAT

We shall hold at a later point (Ch. XI) that case disposition in a children's court is a technical matter and that the judge should perhaps limit himself to the decision as between commitment and service in the community. The choice from among the variety of community-based services or away-from-home treatment facilities may be variously assigned.

Many judges do not accept what they would define as a truncated role; others agree in principle, but point to the lack of treatment "authorities" or fully qualified probation staffs. These realities make it necessary to discuss the court's disposition format. Even where the disposition specifics are assigned elsewhere, the judge probably will retain primary responsibility for the choice as between a community-based or a residential service. Structure and procedure for decision making are therefore of considerable interest.

To begin: Disposition planning must follow adjudication. A court has no right to assume jurisdiction in order to arrange treatment. When the court plans a service, it should use its rights and prerogatives. It should not, however, permit any of its functions to be undertaken without formal procedure and order.[23]

Given clear agreement that it is the judge who makes the disposition decision, a conference format would seem to be most desirable.[24] A case conference procedure at the disposition phase would both create the informal atmosphere which is sought and permit more adequate exchange of views between those who contribute to disposition than the current, more formal, plan. It could encourage real discussion among judge, probation officer, psychiatrist (if needed

[23] *Standards*, p. 44.
[24] A possible format is outlined in *A Court for Children*, pp. 301–9.

for the case), counsel (if one is involved), parents, child, representatives of other agencies concerned. A conference will not develop, of course, if the judge considers himself as *the court* rather than as a team leader who wants to understand and consider all relevant views and data. In contrast to adjudication, which requires considerable procedural structure in order to guard individual rights, the disposition conference, while a hearing, should be quite informal and should take place only in the presence of those who must be involved. The decision making is the judge's and he has the right to interview a child privately, to ask people to come and go as the progress of the conference requires, to permit attorneys to examine certain relevant materials, without disclosing medical-psychiatric data, so that they may understand the ways in which the plan is meant to help. Most important, the conference permits discussion with parents and children under reasonably good conditions so as to interpret and initiate disposition plans with them.

CASE TREATMENT IN PROBATION

The probation officer who does not complete adequate case studies for the reasons already given is hardly qualified to make maximum use of the court's decision to assume protective supervision over a child. It takes dynamic understanding of a child, as well as ability to develop and control a relationship in a helping way, if one is to use the probation period to promote sound growth and change. There must be good knowledge and use of community resources and services as well, and this, too, is founded on both case appraisal and skill in referral.

A friendly, big brother approach, which is possible for the well-meaning layman who likes young people, was once all that was sought in probation. Despite all of the advantages and the usefulness of such an approach in appropriately selected cases even today, the probation field came to understand that it is not enough. The personal and social pathology in the backgrounds of children in the court often defies all but the most skilled workers who bring specific professional preparation to the task. This view is bolstered by the recognition that the probation officer, unlike the worker in many agencies, must grapple with the problem of changing people who, initially at least, must see him unwillingly. Moreover, he must impose certain rules and limits to protect the community, whether or not these advance individual rehabilitative objectives.

It is these considerations which give emphasis to the view that the decision to assign a child for probation treatment must be based on case understanding rather than on that misdirected generosity which employs it not as the treatment of choice but as a "second chance."

The probation field is clear about these views and has made remarkable progress in the past decade in adapting social casework to treatment in the probation setting. A chief U.S. probation officer in Illinois has put it this way: "The . . . most important role of the probation officer is that of friendly counselor, caseworker or guidance officer. To fulfill it he must . . . be equipped to serve as caseworker. . . . The trend is towards the methods of social casework." [25]

Even earlier, the National Conference on Prevention and Control of Juvenile Delinquency expressed broad consensus in stating:

Probation treatment . . . is essentially a task of reorientation, reeducation, a process of guidance and reconditioning in which the *relationship* between probation officer and child is the vital element which effects the changes or modifications in attitudes, habit, and environment needed to bring him into closer harmony with the requirements of society.

As the probation field has matured professionally there has been increased understanding of the central place of that relationship between probation officer and child. Lectures and even concrete services have little effect without it; advice has meaning only in the context of a relationship in which it is given; and concrete services do not contribute to rehabilitation unless the probationer can "participate in the solution of his own problems. He becomes able to deal with difficulties constructively only by dealing with them, not by blindly following the advice of others." The probationer may need emotional support and help in expressing his fears, his likes and dislikes, at one point in the helping process, while he may require tangible and concrete services at another.

Yes, much progress is being made, but probation bureaus are

[25] Ben S. Meeker, "Probation and Parole Officers at Work," *National Probation and Parole Association Journal*, III, No. 2 (April, 1957), 99–106.

everywhere understaffed and qualified personnel are in short supply. According to a recent survey, while 85 percent of probation officers are college graduates, only 10 percent meet the accepted standard of graduate social work training. Large cities (population 500,000–1,000,000) have the highest proportion of trained staff—17 percent—with graduate degrees in social work. The training level is lowest in smaller communities; in areas of less than 50,000 population, only 50 percent of probation officers are college graduates. Yet probation officers are the "treatment agents" for three fifths of court-adjudicated cases. At present, 30 to 40 percent of cases so served are back in court in a few years.[26]

Some courts have lagged in their concept of probation as well, and have not provided the supervision, consultation, clerical and office facilities essential to good work with individuals. At times, rules for probationers have dominated the scene; at others, counseling efforts have been sincere but inept. Probation is, however, the court's unique treatment instrument and there is commitment to its sound development. It must refer to Big Brothers and to friendly volunteers those boys ready for such help, but it seeks to be something else. Similarly, it must refer to clinics, as needed, but does not thereby give up its own special helping method.

Heavy caseloads and a tradition of probation as policing and supervision in the narrowest sense result in an unsatisfactory situation in many cities. Many children "on probation" are seen five to twenty minutes a month, from one to four hours a year, in brief "reporting" or checking-up sessions. They are asked a few routine questions about school, church, recreation, family, and avoidance of codelinquents and are sent away until the next time. Reporting dates are often missed. Few have any sort of relationship with their officers and many are not even known to those to whom they are assigned. In exceptional cases, a favorable probation officer–child combination may lead to a warm relationship and protective supervision. Some cases reveal friendly big brother or big sister work at its best. In a good number of cases, valuable referrals for services of other

[26] U.S. Department of Health, Education, and Welfare, *Report to the Congress on Juvenile Delinquency* (Washington, D.C.: Government Printing Office, 1960), pp. 25–26. Gladys M. Krueger, *Survey of Probation Officers, 1959*, Juvenile Delinquency Facts and Facets, No. 15 (Washington, D.C.: Government Printing Office, 1960).

agencies are made (too often unskillfully and unsuccessfully). The officer at times serves as an instrument of community control.

New York City is now one of several large communities seeking to encourage more complete development of probation as a specialized service whereas, at present, formal structures and inadequate status convert it, too often, into the instrument of the local judge. New York's integrated probation office will no longer in fact be administered by the local court. Whatever the administrative details, which must be suited to local situations, it is unlikely that probation anywhere will have its necessary professional flowering and play its full role unless its leadership is accorded high status in the court and is dedicated to developing effective probation services. To the extent that a judge or a board of judges feels equipped to make decisions about probation policy and procedure, decisions not central to the function of the judge and not deriving from his training, the program cannot evolve to make its full contribution.

Five states (New York, Indiana, Ohio, Washington, Colorado) have begun modest state subsidies toward improved probation services. Others hope to do so. A variety of educational plans are also under way. It is understood that administration, job definitions, and professional qualifications need as much attention as caseload size.[27] As probation treatment standards are raised, it should be possible to offer probation as the treatment of choice far more often. New York City selects probation as the postinvestigation disposition for about half the cases. An enthusiastic probation advocate estimates that, for the country as a whole, about 90 percent of delinquents might be placed on probation in their first court experiences and 50–75 percent on the second or third appearance. Given high quality services, he would expect a success rate of 75 or 80 percent.[28] This is, of course, a desirable goal in view of the many obstacles to successful institutional treatment and its relatively high costs as compared with even the best of probation.

[27] Sol Rubin, "Developments in Correctional Law," *National Probation and Parole Association Journal*, VI, No. 1 (January, 1960), 85. Also note Ernest Reine and Martin Warren, "Special Intensive Parole Unit," *National Probation and Parole Association Journal*, III, No. 2 (July, 1957), 222–29.

[28] Austin MacCormick, "The Potential Value of Probation," *Federal Probation*, XIX, No. 1 (March, 1955), 3–8.

Many courts have used afterschool reporting as a rather hollow checking-up device, usually on a weekly or biweekly basis. For some years now, the Citizenship Training program under the Boston juvenile court has sought a somewhat stronger impact by requiring, as a condition of probation, that boys between the ages of twelve and seventeen report five days a week from 3:30 to 5:30 P.M. An educational-counseling-recreational program is conducted. A recent ten-year study was encouraging.[29] Other cities have borrowed the plan.

More recently, there has been interest in a promising intensification of this approach, which is being subjected to careful study. It should be said, by way of background, that the application of group methods to probation is not new, and that there have been a variety of encouraging reports since shortly after World War II. The Provo, Utah, program, under the leadership of Professor LaMar Empey, represents an introduction of a group therapeutic approach into the reporting center idea.[30] Boys are brought directly from school on weekdays. Originally, there was emphasis on crafts, recreation, and meetings which might broaden one's perspectives and give some realistic information about the ultimate outcomes of a criminal career. Later the program was modified under the influence of the theory followed at Highfields in New Jersey (see Ch. XI).

In brief, under the Highfields plan, boys reside in a home with very few facilities and no program to divert them from focus on themselves and one another. The daily work is routine. Life is concentrated on the five-day-a-week evening "guided group interaction sessions," a sociological modification of group therapy. Groups of ten meet for an hour and a half. The group "culture" shapes a "social system" in which there is a constant process of mutual interaction and evaluation. Evaluative studies show impressive results.

It occurred to Professor Empey that a nonresident version of

[29] Citizenship Training Group, Inc., *Annual Reports* (Boston). Also, L. Maglio, "The Citizenship Training Program of the Boston Juvenile Court," in Sheldon Glueck, ed., *The Problem of Delinquency* (Boston: Houghton Mifflin, 1959), pp. 634–39.
[30] LaMar T. Empey and Jerome Rabow, "Experiment in Delinquency Rehabilitation," *American Sociological Review*, XXVI (October, 1961), 679–96.

Highfields might be valuable and his program has been reshaped in this direction. A rigorous research design provides for assignment of boys on a random basis from among two categories: those who would ordinarily be committed to institutions and those placed on probation. The boys are brought to the center (a house) five days a week and, although there are some facilities, the program is kept unstructured—to encourage spontaneous interaction. Half of the daily three-hour period is devoted to a "guided group interaction program." A Saturday work project and a summer daily work program, with the work in each instance followed by a group meeting, repeat much of the Highfields approach, on a less intensive basis, without the residential unit.

Nationwide interest has been aroused by this program, which is now being replicated in several places, and several programs which reflect aspects of both the Boston and the Provo programs have also developed (Washington, D.C.; Minneapolis, Minnesota). Traditional probation is so structured that it tends to be individually oriented, often intrapsychically. This is often necessary. Group therapeutic approaches add diversification. Given a range of diagnostic types and social meanings inherent in the delinquencies, the reporting center would seem to be a particularly promising program for those whose delinquency is related to neighborhood and peer-group culture—a major subgroup before the court. At the same time, present research may also disclose certain psychiatric-diagnostic subgroups who may respond to a program of group interaction which focuses on the ways in which one copes with the rules, demands, and values of the broader society. The program also promises—and this is no small consideration—to avoid exposure to the negative consequences of institutionalization where it is not necessary. Since all-day reporting is also possible (one New Jersey variation) the reporting center offers considerable community protection.

It is not yet clear whether a reporting center always should be administered by a probation department; the Highfields advocates are convinced that some authoritative auspices are essential for their programs.

A COURT'S MENTAL HEALTH SERVICES

When Chicago's juvenile court recognized that no judge alone could encompass all the skills and knowledge essential to case appraisal, it called upon Dr. William Healy (1909) to establish the first court psychiatric clinic. Other courts followed. At first devoted largely to diagnosis, such clinics gradually took on treatment responsibilities as well. Their methods and emphasis, based originally on the early psychiatry and psychology of the turn of the century, soon reflected the development and application of dynamic mental hygiene.

Today, in the light of broader community planning concerns, we must face issues which did not exist for court clinic pioneers—issues which still are not real to many American communities which lack any clinical resources and which cannot afford to be too concerned about auspices and context of what becomes available. Let us again illustrate with reference to New York.

The New York City Children's Court Bureau of Mental Health Services began in 1916 before the court had its present form. It was essentially diagnostic and sought originally to identify mental defectives. With the growth of the mental hygiene movement, its diagnostic skills were deepened, but it did not evolve its treatment role until 1937. In fact, this phase of the work was developed by a voluntary group and was not fully supported by public funds until 1942.

Despite severe limitations of resources, the New York court's Bureau of Mental Health Services has played a pioneering role in its field and over the years has demonstrated how modern psychiatric and psychological knowledge might be applied to diagnosis of delinquent children and their parents, as well as in cases of neglect. Its staff has contributed to the development and adaptation of social work treatment methods for this group. Valuable experiments were conducted in the use of group therapy with parents and children, and there were innovations in group "intake" interviews and remedial reading. A special project tested ways of introducing clinical skills into court intake and of offering consultation services to judges in emergencies.[31] The research and writing of bureau staff members had broad influence. There were periods, too, during which the

[31] See A Court for Children, Chapter VIII. Also, Harris B. Peck et al., A New Pattern for Mental Health Services in a Children's Court (Springfield, Ill.: Charles C. Thomas, 1958). Also see Harris B. Peck and Virginia Bellsmith, Treatment of the Delinquent Adolescent (New York: Family Service Association of America, 1954); Harris B. Peck, "Principles and Techniques in the Integration of Psychiatric Services in a Juvenile Court with a Community Pro-

clinical staff contributed significantly to the in-service training of probation staff.

However, for many years this clinic has lacked resources and personnel for more than a small portion of the service sought by the judges. It has also faced fundamental questions about its role. Coordination within the court has always been difficult. For this court and all courts must ask:

  a) In a city with a variety of courts, should each court develop mental health services or should there be one system serving all courts? Should the clinical system perhaps also serve the adult jail, penitentiary, and detention facilities?

  b) Should court clinics limit themselves to diagnosis and consultation, or is treatment an essential function for them?

  c) What relationships should be developed between court-serving clinics and the hospitals or health departments?

  d) In what manner should probation and clinical services be interrelated?

These are certainly relevant questions as one takes a fresh look at courts, from the perspective of total community interests. Particular doubts are raised about the efforts to create treatment clinics in a children's court. There are those who hold, for example, that the close relationship with the court represents an obstacle to the progress of treatment, since parent and child remain suspicious of court intent, hesitate in forming relationships, and are not free in their expression. Proponents of this view note the evidence that staff in this and other clinics have often tended to isolate themselves from the court program and to separate themselves, in the minds of clients, from court authority. This seemed to be a condition of effective work.

Others add that the presence of a court clinic in which the bulk of treatment is actually rendered by social workers tends to divert attention from the need to convert probation into an effective casework treatment program. Probation officers may limit themselves to emotional support, encouragement, advice, or concrete environmen-

gram," *American Journal of Orthopsychiatry,* XXII (April, 1952), 277. Dr. Peck's concept of the clinic role is also seen in Government Consulting Service, Institute of Local and State Government, University of Pennsylvania, *Summary Report, Survey of the Juvenile Division of the Municipal Court of Philadelphia* (Philadelphia, 1956, mimeographed), Part 7.

tal services and tend to recommend case referral if a more intensive service is required.

The proponent of a court-based treatment clinic cites the experience in rendering successful treatment in authoritarian settings; he holds that a child or parent should be treated under the auspices of the authoritarian agency responsible for him. Such a patient should know that nonparticipation or failure may have certain consequences. But this type of logic would lead to the creation of treatment clinics in all courts and protective agencies as well as in schools —hardly the efficient way of organizing community resources. It is our view that a community would be wiser to develop a community-wide public clinical service to which courts, schools, and correctional agencies would have easy access in making referrals for *clinical treatment*. These clinics should be medically based—in a health or hospital department.

This view of treatment services does not preclude other clinical service and impact in a court. An experiment in the Bureau of Mental Health Services and subsequent experience in the New York court suggests that the mental health program in a court should be organized primarily as a diagnostic and consultative service.[32] Such service ought to be available in connection with court intake, when necessary, or as requested by the judge at hearings. It should meet psychiatric emergencies which arise in the court. It should be accessible in connection with disposition conferences. Organizational considerations might suggest a city-wide division with units assigned to individual courts.

Given present tendencies to ask for psychiatric studies in too routine a fashion, guides for referral will have to be developed. One experienced judge reports that he asks for clinical study in the following types of situations:

(1) where there is homosexuality or a severe sexual problem (the probation officer will require guidance to deal with the case)
(2) where the child's behavior has had such serious consequences that he requires help with his guilt
(3) where the child's conduct seems to reflect serious emotional disturbance, so that diagnostic guidance is necessary

[32] *A New Pattern for Mental Health Services.* Also several staff documents at the New York City Community Mental Health Board.

(4) where a parent shows a history of serious mental illness or psychopathology

(5) where an institution requires a psychiatric report before considering admission of a child

(6) where help is needed in evolving an appropriate placement plan

The availability of a clinic service as part of the intake machinery, prepared to consult with the judge or to conduct interviews and tests as needed, on the spot, would certainly equip a court for more effective service. Indications of the need for clinical advice could lead immediately to study efforts and to emergency action, as required. For other cases, a regular diagnostic service would still be important, prepared to accept referrals considered necessary in the course of court hearings or probation contacts. Clinic personnel, for their part, need to work closely with judges and probation officers so as to suit their reports in form, language, and content to the functions of these central court personnel. They must be alert to the status of community resources so that recommendations may be realistic and meaningful.

This recommendation does not necessarily preclude clinical impact in court treatment. We have already described the probation service as rendering that direct treatment, individual and group, which takes special advantage of the authoritative nature of the court's setting and the sanctions available to it. Well-trained probation workers obtain a core of clinical knowledge and technique which guides their service. Given access to psychiatric consultation, and reasonable workloads, a probation department may duplicate that portion of the work of a Bureau of Mental Health Services which is within the province of a social worker. That portion which is more appropriately medically based, or which demands the psychiatrist's intervention, would be referred to the community-based clinics.

VOLUNTARY AGENCIES IN CHILDREN'S COURT

Early in the history of children's courts, voluntary social agencies provided the only available probation services. Later, when full-time publicly employed probation officers became part of usual court staffing, these agencies sought to adapt their programs to the new situation. They recognized that, depending on their own staffing and auspices, they could offer specific advantages to the court for cases appropriately selected:

  a) They could supply volunteer "big brothers" and "big sisters" who could offer friendship, sound models for identification, individual attention, recreation, and personal help—services requiring a warm, interested adult and not a professionally trained caseworker.

  b) They could serve as a channel to social service programs in the community, acting as a generalized intake for all Catholic or all Jewish family and children's agencies, for example.

  c) They could serve as a channel to religious guidance and counseling if sought by clients, or voluntarily accepted by them. The court cannot, as a public agency, offer direct religious services.

  d) They could be friends and supporters of the court, understanding its problems and needs and interpreting them to the community. All of the above types of activity would, of course, provide a vantage point for this role.

There has been a tendency in recent years to add casework treatment resources and accompanying psychiatric consultation to all of the patterns. This increases the adequacy of evaluation and the skill in referral by voluntary programs. The particular pattern of organization in a given court has tended to reflect community factors and the sectarian group involved.[33]

A long-range look at the total community pattern requires that sectarian voluntary services, whatever the immediate advantages of these programs (and none doubt the value of the service rendered), be considered in relation to the whole. From such a perspective, a plan whereby a sectarian agency provides intake and treatment for its coreligionists does not represent a desirable plan, and its most effective agents are very clear about this. All clients before the court have a right to the service currently available only to the minority in some courts: the competent assembling of background data and the preparation of clients for the courtroom, access to consultation, and careful planning of interim and long-range dispositions. The development of adequate court intake services and raising of the quality of probation case studies would, of course, achieve this.

[33] *A Court for Children.* pp. 240–45.

The liaison function for voluntary social agencies, big brother and big sister programs, and religious counseling remains appropriate and necessary. In some instances it requires considerable expansion to assure necessary coverage. The liaison workers might be professional or lay, depending on the specific service.

Several cautions remain necessary. It is important, first, to stress that voluntary services should not be used as though any voluntary agency offers something superior to probation. Probation treatment needs strengthening but is not inferior to some voluntary agencies. The disposition decision to be made is whether a given child is best served through a court-based relationship with a probation officer, by a caseworker in another public agency, or by a representative of a voluntary agency. The case evaluation may also suggest the desirability of a referral to an outside service (i.e., a big brother) and concomitant probation status and contacts. Legal or treatment reasons may make the case for continuing a relationship to the court after adjudication. If it is considered desirable to ask voluntary agency representatives to assume full responsibility, client and agency should be clear that this is an alternative to a court-based service and that while agency representatives may bring cases to court, they do not function as probation officers. Especially important is the guarding of rights in referrals to religious counseling or sectarian programs. Parents have a right to choices here, constitutionally, and must understand their rights to refuse referral, to choose other sectarian or nonsectarian groups, and to be served under public auspices, if they prefer.

A DREAM?

A successful children's court is the product of agreement and clarity about function, availability of qualified personnel, and access to a diversified system of resources. Our comments on the New York City court in 1953 would apply to a large portion of such courts today.

This study has found that the New York City Children's Court, considered by some as an illustration of what a successful court should be, has only begun to move in the expected direction. A minority of children are served with both kindness and skill by those judges, probation officers, and other staff members who have understood the purpose of a children's court, are equipped to perform their tasks competently, and have at the same time had available to them needed community resources. The majority of children before the court, however, receive service which does not reflect the juvenile court movement's aspirations or the kinds of help that fully qualified personnel with adequate community resources at their disposal would be able to provide. For some of the children, the court represents a well-intentioned but inadequately prepared, pressured group of individuals who cannot achieve what they strive to do. For many, it is the insensitive instrument of an indifferent or hostile social world. Thus, in most instances, the Children's Court in New York City fails to act as a "good parent" or as a skilled counselor; far too often it does not even appear as a kind friend. Indeed, it is as though an ambivalent society created a new institution and then, not being sure about what it had wrought, permitted old practices and failings to continue and provided so few new resources that the institution could not flourish.[34]

Despite the prevalence of difficulties there is widespread agreement that a community service network requires a strong juvenile court. Hence the consensus that the obstacles must be faced directly. Nor is there major controversy about the steps to be taken.

Clearly, a powerful tribunal of this kind is justified only if properly staffed and equipped. Localities, states, and professional schools are involved in a variety of efforts to improve the availability and qualifications of court personnel. Federal assistance through the support of training programs is proposed. In addition, much is being done and more will need to be done to assure the adjunctive services and the social resources on which court effectiveness depends.

There are, however, some critics who feel that this is not enough.[35] A court is not fully successful, they remind us, unless it carefully sorts out cases in which it has no right to intervene and unless it

[34] *Ibid.*, pp. 264–65.

[35] Paul Tappan, *Juvenile Delinquency* (New York: McGraw-Hill Book Co., 1949), Chapter IX, particularly p. 210. Also see Subcommittee to Investigate Juvenile Delinquency, Committee on Judiciary, U.S. Senate, *Juvenile Delinquency: The Effectiveness of the Juvenile Court System* (Washington, D.C.: Government Printing Office, 1959), p. 17. Also, Monrad Paulsen, "The Delinquency, Neglect and Dependency Jurisdiction of the Juvenile Court," Jack Elson, "Juvenile Courts and Due Process," Paul Tappan, "Judicial and Administrative Approaches to Children With Problems," all in *Justice for the Child*. But also note the view that children do not have the same rights as adults in Paul W. Alexander, "The Fable of the Fantastic Delinquents," *Federal Probation*, XXIV, No. 1 (March, 1960), 13–18, and "Constitutional Rights in Juvenile Court," in *Justice for the Child*.

guards rights constantly while imposing treatment through use of sanctions of various degrees of severity. This remains important even though this is, by definition, a civil and not a criminal tribunal. For these critics assert, in the words of Roscoe Pound, that the court's nonadversary procedure, confidentiality, informality, flexibility, and rehabilitative aims may convert it into a "star chamber." Although the past responses to warnings and to illustrations of arbitrariness have tended to take the form of reassurance and denial, the problem does deserve serious attention. There are few appeals from a children's court. Private lawyers do not often appear and have not generally learned to play a useful role. What occurs is not known to many people except the agencies concerned. Should we not seek to determine, through adequate experimentation, whether there are ways of using public defenders in children's courts without, at the same time, converting the judge into a prosecutor or requiring the assignment of one? Certainly, whether or not defenders are provided, all in the court have the right to counsel and should be so informed. New York's new law ensures legal aid to all who need and request it.

Whether or not a public defender is assigned, the concern for individual rights also will lead more courts to such procedural safeguards as notice, the right to adjournment for witnesses and counsel, separation of adjudication from disposition phases of the process, the right not to serve as a witness against oneself, the right to cross-examine witnesses, the right to appeal.

Is it necessary, as well, to restate the court's jurisdiction in a form which will make it more specific? The *Standards* does urge clear delineation in each statute of the conditions under which the state is empowered to intervene and that "whenever the State seeks to intervene, it should be required to show that those conditions do in fact exist . . . and that its intervention is necessary to protect the child or the community or both." This does not necessarily require differentiation between "delinquent" or "neglected," since the latter distinction is often a matter of chance, depending on the time or the point of case discovery and the perceptiveness or attitude of the petitioner. One third of the states now avoid labels and the Standard Act would end labeling; it suggests a list of circumstances under which a juvenile court shall have exclusive jurisdiction.

Tappan would go beyond all of this: holding that court methods are hardly suited to a broad program of child welfare activities concentrated upon optimum child development, he would limit juvenile courts to jurisdiction over that behavior which would be unlawful for adults. All else would be in the province of social agencies. In our view, this type of policy would, however, leave the community poorly equipped. Much child behavior is serious, dangerous, and a cause for community concern even though it has no adult equivalent. At certain points, community experience with children and their parents demands authoritative intervention and potent sanctions. Given statutory spelling out of conditions and behavior known as threats to the community and to a child's well-being and procedures which require objective evidence of the existence of such conditions, it is entirely proper to find that a child requires the care and protection of the state. He need not be labeled as offender or as delinquent. This does not mean that courts should retain a type of jurisdiction (such as that over dependency or the physically handicapped) which is merely a matter of the administration of a social service.[36]

In fact, a case is readily made for court jurisdiction where there is the equivalent of adult crime and offense, where there is a course of conduct so deviant as to occasion concern, and where a child is endangered, neglected, or abused by parents or guardians. A statute might spell these out in detail as circumstances possibly demanding the care, protection, or cognizance of the state and therefore justifying the taking of jurisdiction by the court, requiring both (a) that one of the specified situations be shown to exist and (b) that the taking of jurisdiction be shown to be necessary in the interests of child or community.

The British Inglesby Commission recently proposed raising the age of criminal responsibility to twelve. Where younger children require court intervention it would be, in their terms, for protection or discipline, not for delinquency.[37] While it would be difficult to

[36] Thomas D. Gill, "The Legal Nature of Neglect," *National Probation and Parole Association Journal*, VI, No. 1 (January, 1960), 15.

[37] Sol Rubin, "Legal Definitions of Offenses by Children and Youth," University of Indiana, *Law Forum* (Winter, 1960), pp. 512–23. Also, *Standard Act*, Sections 8 and 24.1. Also, Home Office, *Report of the Committee on Children and Young Persons* (London: Her Majesty's Stationery Office, 1960), pp. 30–33; *Recommendations for Changes in California's Juvenile Court Law*, Report of the Governor's Special Study Commission on Juvenile Justice (Sacramento: California State Printing Office, 1960).

win wide acceptance of this view, since many very young offenders are involved in considerable offenses and neglect adjudication does at present carry some implication of parental "guilt," the purposes of the Commission are admirable. American experience would suggest as a more basic objective the giving up of labels altogether, while continuing to specify circumstances for the taking of jurisdiction.

A tendency is noted, also, to limit the courts' "remedies" in accord with the offense. In fact, the 1959 revisions of the Standard Act reserve for those involved in law violations all institutions designated for "delinquents" and include in their neglect listing a child "who is beyond the control of his parent." Recent California legislation limits commitments of certain types (Youth Authority facilities) to situations in which young people are involved in the equivalent of adult crimes. Other resources are available for the "less-serious" delinquents (county camps) and the neglected (voluntary agency institutions). New York does not permit assignment of "children in need of supervision" to training schools under its 1962 Family Court Act.

This type of legislation is well motivated. It would avoid punitive sanctions where the child is placed under the court's jurisdiction for protective reasons—not for the equivalent of crimes. Basically, however, the approach misses the objective of the court: to assume jurisdiction under specified circumstances and to suit the treatment to the child's need, not to his act. Inadequacies in institutional provision make this an attractive avenue of reform but it does not achieve long-range objectives. Statutes should not limit the flexibility of dispositions; reformers might concentrate more energetically on the suitability of the treatment network. A training school should never be conceived of as the equivalent of an adult prison.

CHAPTER VIII

DETENTION FOR CHILDREN
BEFORE THE COURT

THE DISTANCE yet to be covered if the juvenile court's protective and rehabilitative ideal is to be achieved is nowhere more clearly seen than in the detention field. The Chicago framers of the very first juvenile court law formulated the objective of keeping children (then up to twelve) out of jail and separated from adults. Judges, probation officers, social workers, psychiatrists, criminologists, and others have, since that time, developed reasonable consensus about detention's functions and requirements. Yet Congress was told in 1960 that over 2,500 of some 3,100 counties in the United States have no detention for children but the county jail. Over 100,000 children awaiting juvenile court hearings are annually incarcerated in jails and police lockups for lack of detention facilities. There are fewer than 200 special detention homes in the entire country. Furthermore, many of the children who are being detained "could just as well be home while awaiting a hearing." [1]

The methods of selection for detention and the programs of many facilities which are currently used give evidence of only a partial commitment to individualization, protection, and help. Despite the universality of sound statements of principle in law, the prevailing

[1] U.S. Department of Health, Education, and Welfare, *Report to the Congress on Juvenile Delinquency* (Washington, D.C.: Government Printing Office, 1960), pp. 26–27, 41. Also, Sherwood Norman, "Juvenile Detention," in *Crime and Delinquency Treatment, National Probation and Parole Association Journal,* III (October, 1957), 392–403. For an earlier report see Herbert A. Bloch and Frank T. Flynn, *Delinquency: The Juvenile Offender in America Today* (New York: Random House, 1956), p. 268.

concept is often clearly the view that a delinquent act calls for retaliation, and that detention is an instrument of punishment. Where
jails are not used, detention homes may be operated around adult-
controlled routines in which conformity is secured by deprivation of
privileges or threat of isolation. If such abuses are avoided, little
may be offered except physical care and custody.[2]

None except the most punitive opponents of rehabilitative programs would argue in favor of jail for children who must be kept in
secure custody pending court disposition. The laws of the various
states protect children against criminal procedures, and jails are part
of the accouterments of criminal justice. Clearly, too, jails spell defeat and failure rather than the help and guidance intended by
juvenile court law. If they offer separation from adults, jails must
place children in isolation and provide questionable physical facilities. The therapeutic value of "shock treatment" is yet to be demonstrated, particularly where it involves unprotected exposure to adult
derelicts and criminals, inadequate food and sanitation, physical
beatings, and absence of supervision or isolation.[3]

Inadequate provision of detention and failure to end, for all time,
jail detention for children are, however, only two of the ways in
which detention is a *mirror* of the status of the entire community
program for children in trouble. No matter how modern the detention building and how forward-looking the staff, the detention operation is intimately intertwined with all the agencies serving these
children. Where the court is not well staffed or well run, decisions
as to the need for holding children are not wise. If there are not
enough foster boarding homes or shelter facilities, children are
detained who should not be. Where diagnostic resources are in short
supply, children may be sent to detention who belong at home during case study. Crowding in long-term foster home and institution
facilities, particularly in state training schools, may make it necessary to keep children in detention too long and to convert the program into one caring for some children for months at a time.

*Thus, to develop juvenile detention and to ignore court opera-
tions, child welfare services, probation, diagnostic or treatment*

---

[2] Norman, "Juvenile Detention," *National Probation and Parole Association
Journal*, III, 392–403.
    [3] *Ibid.*

clinics, or the institutional picture is to be shortsighted. On the other hand, without a good detention program, properly integrated in the whole, a community is only partially equipped to deal with children in trouble.

There is some encouragement in a recent appraisal of the situation by the National Council on Crime and Delinquency, an organization which has conducted three major nationwide detention surveys since 1932, has completed many individual surveys, and has offered an outstanding consultation service. Looking at the past dozen years, the NCCD reports five significant developments:

(1) A clearer definition of detention, as differentiated from shelter care, has become generally accepted.

(2) Juvenile courts are now giving appropriate attention to the establishment of detention intake controls.

(3) A new type of architecture for detention is being adopted or has been used in a good deal of recent construction.

(4) Detention objectives are being reformulated to go beyond "care and custody," and the staff requirements of the new programs are being understood.

(5) Regional detention is gaining ground where the geographic unit is not large enough to sustain or require its own facility.[4]

These developments have provided the foundation for a new statement of detention standards, a statement which will serve as a guide in coming decades.[5]

FUNCTIONS, PHILOSOPHY, AND PRACTICE

Modern detention fills two major functions in the community's system of services for children in trouble. First, the more traditional function: protection. A detention facility ensures secure care of those likely to harm others, or themselves, pending a court plan. The sec-

[4] National Probation and Parole Association (now National Council on Crime and Delinquency), *Standards for the Detention of Children and Youth* (New York, 1957), Preface, p. xvii.

[5] *Ibid.* The current statement derives from the N.P.P.A.'s 1946 *Detention for the Juvenile Court*, which was later reformulated in a major California survey (1954), analyzed at a Children's Bureau Conference in 1954, and then carefully studied by a special N.P.P.A. Advisory Committee on Detention and Shelter Care and the committee revising the Standard Juvenile Court Act. The *Detention Standards* contains only practices in use, although not all practices are found uniformly in one jurisdiction, according to the Preface.

ond function is a more recent development and many facilities are not yet equipped for it: case evaluation. *A detention facility should not be regarded as a study home in the sense that children should not be required to remain in secure custody in order to be studied.* However, if the court decides that they require such custody pending disposition, the detention facility offers excellent opportunity for the kind of case evaluation which contributes substantially to disposition planning. In fact, the observations of the child in detention by house parents, counselors, teachers, social caseworkers, recreation personnel, and others are, themselves, extremely helpful, quite apart from the findings of the more formal medical, psychiatric, psychological, and social work studies.

Confusion has entered the detention field on occasion because of the tendency of some enthusiasts to assign to detention a third function: systematic treatment. Obviously, an intensive psychotherapeutic effort, using individual or group helping methods, is hardly possible in a setting designed to house children for very brief periods of time and at the height of anxiety as to what the court's disposition will be. In fact, even an educational program which is based on extensive projects or ambitious syllabi would be out of place. The detention facility, however, does make its *contribution* to treatment through *preparation* for rehabilitation.[6] An atmosphere attuned to understanding and acceptance, personnel who see the children as individuals and who are not punitive, recognition of the role of peer groups and an effort to break through peer-group definition of the experience, a program which emphasizes confidence that the court's plans will launch a joint effort of child and treatment agency to get to the roots of the trouble and to end it—all of these certainly make possible an easy transition to the treatment program, whether clinical, institutional, or probational, to which the court will assign the child. Detention's function, then, is not to offer treatment but to prepare the child for it by offering an experience in acceptance and an atmosphere which disapproves of antisocial conduct but not of children.

[6] Heman D. Stark, "Standards for Juvenile Halls," *Federal Probation*, XXIV, No. 1 (March, 1960), 35–41, and Department of the Youth Authority, *Standards for Juvenile Halls* (Sacramento, 1958). Also, L. Leslie Bailey and Arthur B. Carfagni, Jr., "The Other Two Hundred Hours," *Federal Probation*, XXIV, 41–45.

Standards for the Detention of Children and Youth [7] points out that, whatever the nature of the provision, children are being detained as long as they are restricted physically.

Detention is the temporary care of children in physically restricting facilities pending court disposition or transfer to another jurisdiction or agency. If detention is used properly, these are children who have committed delinquent acts and for whom secure custody is required for their own or the community's protection.[8]

There are of course delinquents who do not require physically restricting facilities but do need substitute care while the court conducts its study and seeks disposition resources. They may, therefore, be placed in shelters or boarding homes. There is often confusion about this point and a failure to make use of shelters for delinquents. In part, it derives from a desire not to expose the (often younger) dependent and neglected children in shelters to the influence of delinquents. To some degree, however, there is a failure to appreciate the possibilities of nonrestrictive shelter, as appropriate, for some delinquents. Classification within a shelter facility to separate out the more aggressive or more disturbed older children, even among the allegedly neglected and dependent, is necessary under any circumstances. The tendency of shelters to be closed to delinquents provides one more illustration of the undesirable consequences of labeling.

The *Detention Standards* notes, along these lines, that the shelter facilities for children before the court on delinquency petitions, who need to be housed away from home but who are not security risks, may quite properly be temporary foster homes or boarding homes. One might add that such homes are less likely to be a feasible plan in large urban areas with heavy shelter caseloads, but the maximum available number should be located and used if appropriate. Under any circumstances, these homes are not adequate detention, even if special window screening and doors are provided: "Adolescent youngsters who comprise the majority of detained children need vigorous activity and constructive group life. Neither the jail nor the boarding home can supply these." [9]

Intake controls. The misuse of detention is one of the major na-

[7] Henceforth referred to as *Detention Standards.*
[8] *Detention Standards,* p. 1.   [9] *Ibid.,* p. 3.

tional problems in the field of services to children in trouble. Children who need not be exposed to undesirable influences, through the association with others in detention, or who need not experience the trauma of enforced separation from family, are the victims of inadequate admission control. At the same time, the community thus expends, unnecessarily, large sums of money which might have rehabilitative impact in the form of probation or casework services. Finally, to use detention continuously in lieu of more appropriate facilities (i.e., a treatment institution) is to continue to mask basic needs and the gaps in the total effort.

The *Detention Standards* provides a clear and usable listing of those *who should be detained;* the objective is to protect child and community from danger:

(a) Children who are almost certain to run away during the period the court is studying their case, or between disposition and transfer to an institution or another jurisdiction.
(b) Children who are almost certain to commit an offense dangerous to themselves or to the community before court disposition or between disposition and transfer to an institution or another jurisdiction.
(c) Children who must be held for another jurisdiction; e.g., parole violators, runaways from institutions to which they were committed by a court, or certain material witnesses.[10]

Children should not be detained where the court intake service is of the view that "casework by a probation officer would be likely to help parents maintain custody and control, or would enable the child to control his own behavior." If children are detained who should not be, the purpose of detention is distorted, children are harmed, and court philosophy is negated. Among the children who do not belong in detention are the following:

(a) Children who are *not* almost certain to run away or commit other offenses before court disposition or between disposition and transfer to an institution or another jurisdiction. . . .
(b) Neglected, dependent, and non-delinquent emotionally disturbed children, and delinquent children who do not require secure custody but must be removed from their homes because of physical or moral danger or because relationships between child and parents are strained to the point of damage to the child.
Detention should *not* be used as a substitute for shelter care.

[10] *Ibid.,* p. 15. This is the major source for the remainder of this section.

(c) Children held as a means of court referral.
Detention should *not* be used for routine overnight care. Release to parents after twenty-four or forty-eight hours usually indicates that the child need not have been detained had the court intake procedure functioned earlier.
(d) Children held for police investigation or social investigation who do not otherwise require secure custody.
Detention should *not* be used as merely a convenient way to hold a child for an interview, or for an investigation into his unsubstantiated connection with other offenses, or to facilitate the apprehension of suspected accomplices unless he himself is involved and the situation is serious.
(e) Children placed in or left in detention as a corrective measure.
Other state or local facilities should be used for corrective purposes. The court should not permit a case to be "continued" in order to "teach a child a lesson." Detention should *not* be used as a punishment or as a substitute for a training school.
(f) Psychotic children and children who need clinical study and treatment and do not otherwise need detention.
Detention should *not* be used as a substitute for a resident clinical study and treatment center.
(g) Children placed in detention because of school truancy.
Truancy is a school problem which should be handled in the school system through social services and special classes or schools when necessary. The court should cooperate with the schools, but detention should *not* be used as a control for truancy.
(h) Children who are material witnesses, unless secure custody is the only way to protect them or keep them from being tampered with as witnesses.
Normally, if a child material witness must be held, he should be sent to a shelter facility.

Detention should thus not be designed as punishment for the law violator or for the child who does not keep to the conditions of probation. While a child may interpret the detention as punishment, it should be used not in retaliation but as part of a diagnostically developed plan.

Enforcement of these standards would, incidentally, end much of the present overcrowding of detention facilities. It is also the only means of stopping the oft-noticed phenomenon whereby new and good detention centers are filled as soon as they are built, even though capacity has been carefully estimated on the basis of previous experience and of population trends. The NCCD's Advisory

Council of Judges has estimated that, typically, a community should not detain more than 20 percent of those referred for probation study; some communities have kept the rate to 10 percent. Methods of estimating needed detention capacity in a community have been developed.[11]

The protection of children against undue detention and the assurance of detention as needed may be achieved through assignment to the juvenile court of responsibility for detention admissions and length of stay. Only the court has legal right to decide that a child should be held. The court (judge or judges) should see therefore that machinery is established for effective admission control. Such machinery might consist of agreements with law enforcement agencies and a policy that no child will be admitted to detention unless authorized by an on-duty or on-call probation officer. If admission must take place when the court is not in session, a judge should review all such cases as soon as possible. The person who authorized detention should have to answer to the court why the child was not released to his parents and the answer should not be in terms of the offense alone. A court, to repeat, is legally empowered to deprive children of their freedom through detention and should be recognized as the agency accountable for the use or misuse of detention. Intake and discharge controls should be organized to implement such accountability.

There are many who believe that consistency of approach and integrated operations are best assured if detention is completely administered by the juvenile court. Judge Alexander of the Toledo court argues strongly for a court which operates all of its own adjunctive services, including detention, and thus meets its basic responsibilities.[12] In California, where large- and medium-sized probation departments administer treatment institutions and camps, detention (called juvenile halls) is also provided through the pro-

---

[11] *Ibid.*, pp. 16–18, and also see Edgar W. Brewer, *Detention Planning*, Children's Bureau Publication No. 381 (Washington, D.C.: Government Printing Office, 1960), pp. 21–41. Also, National Council on Crime and Delinquency, "Survey Guide for Determining the Capacity of a New Detention Facility" (Unpublished manuscript, n.d.).

[12] Judge Paul W. Alexander, in Maxine Boord Virtue, *Basic Structure of Children's Services in Michigan* (Ann Arbor: American Judicature Society, 1953), pp. 288–89n.

bation department.[13] Courts hold special hearings to review detention decisions as rapidly as possible after the fact.

The *Detention Standards* states realistically that administration should be by the agency best able to meet standards and to secure funds and personnel. Local welfare departments, private agencies, and state agencies may be the best auspices under some circumstances, while courts or probation departments are, under others. Assignment of such administrative responsibility does not, however, relieve the court of its obligation to formulate local detention standards and procedures and to make, or review, all detention decisions.[14] At present, courts and probation departments do administer facilities providing half of all detention care.

Ideally, the community (court) might assign intake responsibility to the children's court intake service, staffed by the most competent of probation officers. When court is in session, all cases screened by the unit and found to require detention might be reviewed by the judge, either in the course of an immediate initial hearing (particularly if the offense is denied) or preliminarily, until the hearing can be held. (There may be a delay to call parents in, call witnesses, obtain counsel, etc.) If the need for detention arises during the night or a weekend, when court may not be in session, an intake service authorized to act for the court, in the interim, provides maximum protection.

Philadelphia's modern and well-designed Youth Study Center houses much of the staff of the Juvenile Intake Unit of the Philadelphia Municipal Court. The director of probation supervises the program. An intake desk in the court building itself serves nondelinquency cases and some cases in which delinquency is alleged. A recent study saw the need for certain administrative and organizational changes in the Philadelphia program in order to increase effectiveness and to ensure all-night coverage. The study proposed that the initial detention decision made by the intake interviewer be strengthened, through clarification of criteria and administrative improvements, and that the intake section of the court have full control over the status of children in detention.[15]

[13] Stark, "Standards for Juevenile Halls," *Federal Probation*, XXIV, 35–41.
[14] *Detention Standards*, pp. 30–33.
[15] Government Consulting Service, Institute of Local and State Government,

Police officers in special juvenile units may be prepared to make decisions where there is no court intake unit, but this is a second-best arrangement. Under no circumstances should there be prolonged detention without an order from an authorized court person (judge, referee, probation officer) or in the absence of a complaint or petition. The *Detention Standards* suggests twenty-four hours, excluding weekends, but this may be too long an interval in a large city. Release from detention always requires a court decision; since the issue is whether the child can safely return to the community, bail should be neither required nor accepted (except in areas where the child resides far from the court, away from its jurisdiction, and the court wishes to ensure that the parents will return with him). In fact, an offer of bail by parents is often an indication that the child might be released to them (under probation supervision) pending court disposition.

Parents, of course, require immediate notification if children are picked up by police in the midst of a violation and taken directly to court. Under ordinary circumstances, in fact, even questioning should be delayed until the parents arrive, if rights are to be protected. Detention intake staff should not accept a child at night if parents are reachable and there is evidence that they are able to return to the court intake department the next morning and that neither the child nor community is likely to be exposed to danger if the child goes home.

Given adequate court probation staff for intake, study, and supervision functions, as well as adequate community facilities for serving children, detention should be relatively brief. Ten days is considered as an adequate average period if the court requires a case study but no clinical reports. More complete clinical work-up may extend the period to two or three weeks. Brief postdisposition detention may be required to arrange transportation and to meet the routines of institutions. However: "Post-disposition detention should not be allowed to extend to more than twenty-four hours. If a longer period is necessary for lack of institutional resources or other reasons, such detention should be considered expedient rather than legitimate."

University of Pennsylvania, *Summary Report: Survey of the Juvenile Division of the Municipal Court of Philadelphia* (Philadelphia, 1956, mimeographed), Parts 4 and 5.

Every effort should be made by the court and the community to correct the situation.[16]

As we shall see, this comment is appropriately directed at the New York City situation and New York is not an exception.

A program. The intake criteria outlined tend to make a detention facility a concentration point of disturbed, difficult, and aggressive children, most of them in the upper brackets of the children's court age group. Their detention may be seen by them as evidence of the hostility of the world to them or of their own inadequacy. The resulting anxiety may express itself by "extreme indifference, by open hostility, or by a veneer of cooperation." The acting out may make control difficult; the extreme withdrawal may resemble psychosis: "All properly detained youngsters show the effects of sociological and psychological damage and can be considered socially sick. This does not relieve them of the responsibility to get well, but neither does it relieve society of its responsibility to help them get well." [17]

They will not be aided by repressive or punitive methods, or by "giving them a good time," without efforts to help them face up to their problems realistically. Inconsistency in detention will only be a repetition of their previous experiences. Subjecting them to the tyranny of their strongest peers or to the rule of an unsound group culture tends to contribute to their delinquency.

A positive detention program must, then, be prepared to serve disturbed children and to weed out those who can remain safely in the community. Its program must ensure secure custody and physical care which fosters growth and minimizes the damaging effects of confinement. Children should not be held even for a few days, however, without providing satisfying and constructive individual and group activities, indoors and out, including school and a variety of recreational and creative activities. Since the court also needs a case evaluation prior to its disposition, detention must be even more than all of this. The presence of qualified staff will permit study and observation of the child to provide a professional report to the probation department and the court, with special attention to each youngster's potentialities. Observation is not helpful without a constructive program because it is not enough to know how a child responds to custodial care or enforced idleness. Finally, custodial

[16] *Detention Standards*, p. 27.   [17] *Ibid.*, p. 9.

and teaching staff require casework, group work, and clinic backing to help them understand their charges and to offer a "first aid" service when problems arise. Beyond this, the program should include "individual guidance through social casework and social group work to help the child use the detention experience to understand himself better and come to grips with his problems." This implies not a long-range treatment program but preparation for and introduction to treatment.[18]

The quality of the program is all-important; it demands constant focus on the purposes of detention and the state of the children. The school, for example, cannot hope "to keep the child up with his studies" but might aim to provide structure and content to the day in confinement, to create a more positive attitude to learning, to replace a pattern of failure with some real achievement, and to develop some understanding of why the child may have failed so completely in the general school.[19]

Crafts, music, shop, outdoor play, and other activities also provide opportunity for staff-child relationships in which a new view of authority is begun. At the same time, games, crafts, and leisure offer observational opportunities which contribute to diagnosis and evaluation. In this programing, as in all detention, "frugality is expensive, since it defeats the program of the detention home by curtailing staff, equipment, or supplies."[20] Youth-participation activities are appropriate to enrich program and climate, particularly in the airing of grievances, selection of materials, and some program planning. Children should not, of course, sit in judgment of one another or have authority.

Central to morale, a major determinant of the frequency of behavior incidents, and a key factor in deciding the effect of detention on a child is what the *Detention Standards* refers to as social climate.[21] The counselors, group leaders, and all other staff members who deal with children do much to create this climate in informal contacts, joint activities, program activities, the way in which authority is used with the group or with individuals, the conduct of individual or group interview sessions, and the dealing with disciplinary infractions. The recommended theme for the detention

[18] *Ibid.*, pp. 11–12.   [19] *Ibid.*, pp. 54–55.   [20] *Ibid.*

[21] Also, Stark, "Standards for Juvenile Halls," *Federal Probation*, XXIV, 35–41.

center is respect for the individual, even if his behavior is rejected: "We like you even though we do not like what you do and will not permit you to do it."

One cannot buy respect for authority, for bribery wins no respect from delinquents. Nor can one teach respect or gain it by punitive measures; this has been tried often at home and elsewhere with those who are detained.

A professionally qualified person may use an outburst or aggression in detention as a starting point in an effort to establish a relationship with a child; similarly, progress in understanding a child's need to erupt may contribute much to adequate evaluation and planning. A staff which creates an accepting climate and maintains it with consistency does much to provide a transition to a treatment program.

The *Detention Standards* places great importance on the availability of an adequate casework program. The casework staff has a major role in orientation and diagnosis. It is the liaison between detention, probation, and clinic. Observations of staff members in all phases of the program may be coordinated through and interpreted by the caseworker. The caseworker may also be the child's confidant and the one to deal with outbreaks, major infractions, and symptoms, to see parents when necessary, and to contribute to in-service training. It is the caseworker who must work with the child if desperate circumstances require that he be separated from the group.[22]

A program designed to provide all of these services requires staffing, adequate in size and qualified by background, training, and experience, for the following: administration, staff supervision and training, health services, social casework and group work, clinical diagnostic studies, physical care, school (preferably under the public school system), recreation, religious services, kitchen service, housekeeping and laundry, building and ground maintenance. In small detention facilities, the same staff members may perform many functions. Separate departments and divisions will be required in larger facilities. Philadelphia's Youth Study Center, with a capactiy of 175 beds, has departments devoted to children's services and program, clerical services, household, kitchen and cafeteria, maintenance, and medical-clinical-social services. The school

[22] *Detention Standards*, pp. 66–72.

program is furnished by the Board of Education; the Medical Department of the Municipal Court supplies psychiatric and psychological treatment; and the Police Department participates actively in intake.

Detailed qualifications for professional positions are outlined in *Detention Standards* and need not be reviewed here. Merit system selection, freedom from political interference, and assurance of personnel in a state of such physical and mental health as to permit their association with disturbed children and youth are stressed. The staff should, of course, be large enough so that children are never unsupervised or abandoned temporarily. Experienced detention personnel report that, except for small, family-type facilities, detention homes must have as many staff members as children (or at least three-quarters as many), teachers excluded, given a 40- or 44-hour work week.[23]

The building. The design and construction of detention facilities is a technical matter outside the immediate scope of this discussion. The National Council on Crime and Delinquency offers a published guide, a scale model, and expert planning and consultation service to communities without charge.[24] Brief mention may, however, be made of a few points outside the special sphere of the architect and builder.

First, there is the matter of size. In addition to suggesting, in some detail, how statistical projections might be made, the NCCD urges that the planning period be an occasion for an overview of all community provisions, so as to be sure that one is not providing for capacity which would not be needed if there were adequate probation staff, improved court intake, or better police policy. A California report echoes an oft-repeated theme in its assertion that there is "at least some evidence to support the idea that the capacity of a juvenile hall influences not only how many youngsters will be detained, but also to a certain extent the types that will be detained." [25]

A detention facility requires provision for reception and administration (including casework and clinic offices), as well as sleeping

[23] *Ibid.*, pp. 34–47.

[24] *Ibid.*, Part IV, and Norman, "Juvenile Detention," *National Probation and Parole Association Journal*, III, 403.

[25] State of California, Department of Justice, *Delinquency and Probation in California in 1959* (Sacramento: California State Printing Office, 1960), p. 93.

space, "general living" room for each group, school, activities, service and maintenance, and outdoor play. Experts urge a plan built around a series of "units" offering sleeping and "general living" accommodations for about fifteen children of the same sex. Philadelphia, Cincinnati, Kansas City, Des Moines, and a number of California counties (among others) have constructed "notable buildings."

Emphasis is placed on having the detention center on the same site the juvenile court or close to it, so as to conserve the time of probation officers, eliminate a transportation problem in getting children to court, and permit close ties between the court and detention. It is of course undesirable so to situate the facility that court and detention interfere with one another.

Regional detention. Earlier reform efforts in relation to detention stressed legislation forbidding the jailing of children; but some counties could do little more than to give the name "detention home" to private homes, courthouses, homes for the aged, mental hospitals, and children's institutions which had barred some windows, locked the doors, and offered only idleness. Other counties found that they could purchase detention on a per diem basis from neighbor counties. Standards might not be adequate, however, and the space might be reclaimed as needed locally. It did, however, suggest that travel to court is better than inadequate detention. Why should counties not pool resources, perhaps with state aid, and create a good facility, physically, as well as plan specialized services too expensive for any one county? Convinced that this might be the needed answer, the National Council on Crime and Delinquency began to recommend the approach nationally. It urged—and continues to urge—regional detention, despite the distance it creates, geographically, between detention and court.

Massachusetts was the first to build and operate regional units. Delaware and Maryland followed. Georgia has passed enabling legislation. Connecticut, which has a state juvenile court, is the one state which accepts full responsibility for detention; it has been free of juvenile jails for fifteen years. In several other states, counties are inaugurating regional detention on the basis of local agreements or state reimbursement policy.[26]

[26] Norman, "Juvenile Detention," *National Probation and Parole Association Journal,* III, 402.

The vast majority of counties in this country need detention for so few children that they would not be justified in constructing and maintaining separate facilities. Yet, if they persist in using this fact as justification for jail detention or equally destructive makeshifts, courts will continue to be hampered in their work and children will suffer. Regional detention planning would seem to be an answer for some 80 percent of the jurisdictions in the United States.

It is pointed out, with considerable validity, that detention planning should not be given priority over the strengthening of probation, for obvious reasons. Nor should there be regional arrangements without supervision of intake and personnel standard setting. Also, to avoid unnecessary transportation of children and for reasons of economy, some regional arrangements should also include plans for a maximum of twenty-four hours of local overnight care following apprehension.[27]

Age differentiations? It is assumed that the problem of age range in detention is solved by having dormitory or cottage groups based on age, among other criteria. The detention literature does not deal with a problem which confronts the visitor to many detention facilities throughout the country; namely, the fact that those states whose juvenile court jurisdictions may reach the age eighteen and beyond and who increasingly are also detaining large numbers of children at the minimum age have assembled a population which may not be viable.

Detention administrators, teachers, counselors, and caseworkers cannot create a constructive atmosphere and a vital program given too broad a range. The security requirements for the eighteen-year-old are inevitably somewhat different and may adversely affect the program for younger children. The need to protect the very young from some of the disturbed older children adds to the complications.

In a few instances, detention facilities have been divided into younger and older "sections," but they are not truly divided and observation does not leave one encouraged about the results. It may be that larger cities and counties in states with broad age jurisdiction in juvenile court should experiment with separate "child" and "youth" facilities—just as they arrange for age separation in camps

[27] *Detention Standards,* Part 5.

and institutions. The decision to cover older adolescents by a statute does not automatically make them the same as younger children.

PROBLEMS—AND BRIGHT SPOTS

A survey of the *Detention of Children in Michigan* disclosed that in 1950, of 2,860 children held in secure custody outside of Wayne County, 520 were detained in county jails. The jail was the only place of secure custody available to children in 63 counties, even those which had county detention homes or lockup facilities (county infirmaries for the aged, a barred room in a hospital, a courthouse basement, etc.). The two counties with specially built detention homes were said to be misusing them because of court policy or personnel inadequacies. There were major differences of opinion as to the use of detention throughout the state; there were few "programs" and supervision was minimal. Some youths were held for part of one day, others over a year. The study concluded: "The present method of detention of children in 'secure custody' as it exists throughout almost all of Michigan today adds to the problems of disturbed children and therefore should be eliminated entirely at the earliest possible time." The recommendations made emphasized the need to keep a clear distinction between detention and shelter. Regional detention centers were held out as a major solution for the state.[28]

The important detention and shelter study in California, a state which has done considerable path-blazing in the correctional field, set a similar pattern.[29] In the calendar year 1951, 35,622 admissions to detention were recorded of which 26,536 were to "juvenile hall detention" and 9,086 to jails (ages up to 18). Included were 2,100 admissions to juvenile halls for secure custody only, for lack of shelter facilities. The study noted that detentions equaled 41 percent of the total number of delinquent arrests, a very high total compared to practices elsewhere. Further analysis showed that many of the detentions were made by law enforcement agencies without subsequent petitions for delinquency or referral to probation intake.

[28] Sherwood Norman, *The Detention of Children in Michigan* (New York: National Probation and Parole Association, 1952).
[29] California Committee on Temporary Care, *California Children in Detention and Shelter Care* (Los Angeles, 1954).

Children were being detained for varying periods of time, the local averages ranging from 4 days to 30 days, the latter Los Angeles figure being larger than that in any major city. Extended stays for nondelinquents, changing probation practices, lack of detention intake policies, and insufficient probation staff were seen behind the long detention stays. Many resource shortages prolonged detention after commitment.

Two groups of children crowding many of the facilities were not seen as appropriate subjects for detention, according to the California study. There were, first, those admitted for police questioning or probation referral who might have been more appropriately dealt with by juvenile police specialists or through immediate probation screening. In addition, there were many children admitted for detention observation and study who should have remained at home during this period. There were others for whom plans had been made and who could not remain at home; their use of detention spaces would continue, despite the problems they created, until space could be provided in mental hospitals and private child care institutions, or until foster homes and Youth Authority facilities could become available more rapidly.

Many of the questions in practice were seen to derive from lack of juvenile court control of detention and the subsequent control by either law enforcement officers or by probation officers, but without court policy guidance. Statutes were interpreted in a variety of ways; detention hearings were often not held or were routine and children were detained without parents being informed. On the other hand, probation services were not staffed to provide adequate intake administration.

The California study made major recommendations for a legal framework to protect children's rights and clarify detention policy. It called for statutory amendments to define the court's jurisdiction as attaching from the time a child is taken into custody; such custody is not an arrest and children do not belong in jail. Parents do have a right to notice of a child's detention and to a hearing; an amendment to ensure this was urged. Provisions permitting bail were recommended for repeal, and a statute setting a two-year maximum for continuous use of jail detention was called for. Full recommendations were also detailed relative to the development of detention intake policy and its implementation; the provision of shelter facilities for children who do not require secure custody; and the general improvement in the building, staffing, and program planning for juvenile halls. Again, regional detention homes were suggested for counties too small to construct or maintain their own. Going behind some of the delinquency encountered, the study also called for protective casework services in county welfare departments as a means of reducing both family breakdown and the need for shelter and detention care.

A recent New York State survey by the detention consultant to the State Department of Social Welfare found the following:

Upstate counties have been meeting their need for detention services in a variety of ways. Ten counties, principally the larger ones, use detention homes of their own, of which four have physical plants that are unsuitable for the detention care of children. Sixteen counties purchased service on a limited scale from five of the existing detention homes. Three counties use their jails routinely for detention. The others use open-type boarding homes, various makeshift arrangements, and/or jail for overnight in emergencies, or they avoid the need for detention by holding a quick hearing and committing the child to a state training school.[30]

While none of the counties lacking a satisfactory detention home was found to have a sufficient number of children requiring detention to justify the construction and operation of a detention home, the upstate total of children unsuitably detained was 447 of 2,813 detained children. Some rapid, inadvisable training school commitments were traced to the detention lack, as well.

Interestingly, the study also found that the availability of open-type boarding homes for those not requiring secure custody decreases detention demands. In general, many listed as needing detention do not meet the criteria recommended nationally. Finally, poor detention may not be more economical than good detention. The survey proposed regional detention homes, particularly on the basis of "purchased service," plus local overnight facilities.

A recently published national survey illustrates the best of the practices suggested in *Detention Standards* and calls attention to contrary practice. While we shall not summarize the details from

[30] New York State Department of Social Welfare, *Child Detention Care in Upstate New York* (Albany, 1958, mimeographed).

many facilities, it may be appropriate to conclude this section with reference to several particularly salient generalizations.[31]

    a) There is clear warning that "construction of a new detention building usually results in a sharp increase in the number of cases in which detention is used."

    b) In some jurisdictions, less than 5 percent of the apprehended children are detained. In other jurisdictions, with the same police-to-court referral practice, over 50 percent are detained. Detention criteria are not interpreted uniformly.

    c) Twenty-four-hour court intake control, under which probation officers are "on call" after office hours, is used in many places to ensure consistent application of detention criteria.

    d) Staffing is improving in a variety of ways.

    e) Few detention homes have good medical programs, because such programs are not well defined and no assignment of responsibility is made in most places.

    f) Over-all advances are reported in the staffing, methods, and curricula of schools in detention.

    g) State responsibility to improve detention is being expressed in a number of ways: regional detention, standard setting, consultant services, intercounty cooperation, subsidies.

YOUTH HOUSE—DETENTION FOR A LARGE CITY

Youth House for Boys and Youth House for Girls, New York City's detention for children, have a record of sound philosophy, imaginative programs, and pioneering in method. At the same time, the constant problems of overcrowding and "backing-up" of committed children awaiting long-range care have decreased the effectiveness of what is attempted and have raised basic problems relative to the role of detention and its place in a system of services. The discussion which follows deals with those aspects of Youth House which have relevance to questions of administrative responsibility, intake controls, program, and plant. Issues which are transitory or only of local import are bypassed.

Some history. Reviewing the earlier history of privately operated detention in New York City, Bertram Beck concluded in 1949 that

---

[31] Sherwood Norman, *Detention Practice* (New York: National Probation and Parole Association, 1960), pp. iv, 9–10, 41, 58, 79, 165–77.

prolonged public financing of privately operated detention facilities ends
with the city paying for the operation of substandard institutions outside
of effective public control. Past history indicates that as long as such
public subsidy without public control exists no single public administrative organ is developed to insure standards, consistency, coordination and
planning in the particular field . . . action is taken on the basis of ex-
pediency, jumping from crisis to crisis, without sound planning and often
creating public dissension.[32]

Whatever the validity of the broader generalization for all time, it
certainly describes adequately the situation preceding the establishment of the unified Youth House program for boys and girls requiring detention in New York City.

Following emergency closing of inadequate private facilities,
Youth House for Boys opened officially in April, 1944, to serve allegedly delinquent boys from Manhattan and Brooklyn. The mayor
had accepted a plan under which the city would support the program
but a voluntary group would finance the diagnostic clinic. (This,
too, was taken over by the city after three years.) A board of eighteen
citizens, of the three major religious faiths, took responsibility for the
program, and continued as the Youth House Board.

Between 1944 and 1953, the city separated its allegedly delinquent
children from those considered neglected and dependent, closed
private facilities or permitted their closing, and provided opportunity and financing, under a "private" board, for a new detention
development.[33]

Children served. Certain facts should be looked at in the light of
the long Youth House history of crises arising from overcrowding,
the virtual closing of intake on occasion, and the considerable city-
state disagreement as to whether the resultant problems should be
met through an increase of state training school capacity, an increase in city detention space, or a review of practices and policies.
While the exact statistics and their ratios have shifted in recent
years with the increases in delinquency totals and the gradual rise
in both detention capacity and training school space (none of which

[32] Bertram Beck, *While Children Wait* (New York: Community Services
Society, 1949), p. 5.
[33] Youth House backgrounds are reported in Beck, *While Children Wait;*
Frank J. Cohen, *Children in Trouble* (New York: Norton, 1952); and in various
Youth House annual reports.

will be reviewed here in detail), the trends have been consistent for some time.

New York's Children's Court heard 13,243 new delinquency petitions in 1960. A total of 6,603 children were detained. The official, expanded capacity of Youth House for Boys is 365 and the expanded capacity of Youth House for Girls (a building scheduled for replacement) and its two temporary annexes is 224. For some time (until arbitrary "quotas" were established in 1962), each exceeded its capacity on daily census for most of the year. Expansion of the boys' facility by use of space intended for other purposes did not slow down this process, nor were the periodic girls' detention crises ended by the creation, first of one and then of two, temporary annexes. At one time the "crises" occurred only in the late spring and early summer, as training schools stopped discharges so that children might complete vocational courses or an academic year. Soon, winter crises were also common. A steady and impressive program of state training school expansion did not end this process. Youth House staff reported serious consequences for all phases of the program as a result of the overcrowding. Staff itself suffered vacancies and turnover too.

A Family Court judge arriving in the morning often was handed a slip telling him his "quota" for the day. All day long, as new cases appeared, he played "checkers" to find needed space: releasing a child to detain another. He regularly sent children home, concerned as to whether it was a safe action. At times, children were committed improperly to a hospital for psychiatric observation to avoid returning them to the streets.

When the court was not in session and facilities were filled to capacity, police precincts were informed by teletype. It sometimes occurred, for lack of alternatives, and contrary to law, that boys were detained overnight in station houses under the guard of police officers.

Examination of what is known about the characteristics of the detained children discloses that, while most detained children, like most alleged delinquents, are in the age group 14–16, there are a surprising number of the very young and their totals have increased. In a recent year, 10 percent of the boys and 3 percent of the girls were under 12.

Judges and police, at a 5:1 ratio, are the channels to detention. In recent years, the proportion of cases held on police request without a court hearing has declined. The court returns 40 percent of police detentions to the community after a hearing. A larger proportion of girls than of boys detained at police request are returned to detention after the first hearing. The average stay in detention is 24+ days for boys and 30+ for girls. Over the years, about 40 percent of the detained boys and two thirds of the detained girls have been committed to long-term institutions, foster care, institutions for the defective, or mental hospitals. In recent years, the rate of commitment from detention has decreased.

In contrast to the *Detention Standards* recommendation that not more than 20 percent of alleged delinquents be detained, the New York figure was 50 percent in the most recent year. Only systematic research would of course disclose whether the New York delinquent population is "different" enough to justify a higher rate—but this is doubtful.

What do these statistics suggest? The philosophy, standards, and nationwide experience, as reported in the previous section, would seem to lead to questions such as the following in response to the record of detention overcrowding in New York City:

a) Are detention criteria adequate, where the detention rate is so high?

b) Are committed children moved out of detention to training schools (state facilities) rapidly enough?

c) Is detention properly used when many boys under twelve are found in the population?

d) Are detention admissions criteria sound, where so many youngsters detained at police initiative are released after the court hearing?

e) Are detention admissions criteria sound, where so many are returned to the community after court disposition?

Intake controls. The problem of detention intake controls in New York City provides dramatic illustration of the interdependence of the entire network of services to children in trouble. Although some of the problems described may be en route to solution as these lines are published (see below), the lessons would seem to have general validity.

It will be recalled from the previous chapter that the Children's Court in New York City long had a very truncated intake service and that probation was understaffed, not highly developed professionally, and not accorded a role equal to its potential. The consequences for the court have already been described. They were also disastrous for detention.

Prior to recent reorganization, when the court was in session an arrest case would be brought in for an adjudication hearing the day of the arrest with no intermediate process except the filling out of a petition (apart from a limited group of minor cases, eligible for a Bureau of Adjustment). The judge made a detention decision on the basis of impressions in an adjudication hearing, without access to any reports, clearances, or background reports in most cases. In fact, if an adjournment to another day was requested to arrange for counsel or witnesses (or to reach the parents) the judge would make the decision on the basis of even less information.

Nor was probation staff involved in detention decisions after court hours or on weekends. Police brought children in at night or weekends and determined the readiness of parents to guarantee their return to court—or that they must be held. Caseworkers had no part in the decision. A member of the custodial staff took remanded children to detention after court hearings and returned them in groups —in buses or station wagons—when they were due.

California courts, by contrast, leave the initial detention decision to a probation intake worker, specifying a rapid detention hearing before judge or referee. This permits assembling of data relevant to the detention issue and their presentation. Structurally, the plan would seem to have merit since all cases move through probation intake under any circumstances in that court system, the probation officers being charged with review of the appropriateness of the petition making. Probation intake remains open all night and weekends. Also, a plan which for the most part has court and detention located in the same or adjacent structures simplifies probation access to children for social study.

It is of some interest to note, however, that in several of the large California systems observed directly, detention intake is no more likely to reject detention recommendations by police and sheriffs than are the Youth House staff in New York City. In part the explanation resides in the fact that well-oriented police and sheriffs avoid unnecessary use of detention in most instances. To some extent, however, it is also the case that mere formal assignment to probation of the detention intake responsibility does not solve fully the problems of status, community expectations, and achieving the point where judges will be ready to put aside all criteria for detention except the professional criteria described earlier in the chapter.

The Community Service Society found in 1949 that some New York City judges used detention punitively, and the finding has been repeated by others from time to time. Certainly, space shortages have protected some children in this regard. It is difficult, without up-to-date study, to know the extent to which such use of detention is a significant problem today. Known to be important is the well-publicized practice (for lack of other community provision) of detaining children to speed up psychiatric study. This is a misuse of detention in terms of the national *Detention Standards.* Especially questionable are those situations in which the purpose of the psychiatric examination is to meet the admissions routine of a voluntary agency. In general, a substantial portion of the detention crowding is traceable to the practice whereby referrals are made to a series of voluntary institutions, in sequence, before training school commitment. Only a very small percentage of those referred can be accommodated. Although placement is paid for out of public funds, the court has little influence and no control over the allocation of these limited spaces.

Nor has New York City, faced as it is with a "chronic" shelter care "emergency" and lacking foster boarding homes in sufficient numbers, been able to offer shelter to boys and girls who need to be away from home pending court action but who do not actually require secure custody. Included in this category are those quite young children who should not be in detention—or who require separate resources.

Two numerically small groups of girls who tend to remain in detention for long periods are of concern to Youth House. It has been pointed out repeatedly that detention is no place for pregnant girls. The program cannot meet their needs and they upset the program. Other community provision is essential. Similarly, girls in the prepuberty period, ages 9–11, who are sent to detention tend to be severely disturbed and to have difficult symptoms. Youth House annual reports stress that children in this group should not be exposed to older, acting-out delinquents. All discussions have also pointed to the girls in the "material witness" group; these are girls being held to testify at the trial of an adult. They are held to protect them, to avoid possible tampering with their testimony, and often because they have no place to go. Numerous delays in court calendars, intentional or routine, may keep them in detention well beyond the recommended maximum time.

An official city investigation recently replied in the affirmative to the following three questions:

1. Are children sent to Youth House who need not be sent there?
2. Are children kept too long at Youth House pending court disposition?
3. Are children kept too long at Youth House following the court's disposition? [34]

A variety of administrative-procedural solutions are being sought to these problems. Youth House social service and probation are to become one—as they are in much of the country—with the resultant efficiencies in deployment of manpower and strengthening of procedures.

As it reorganizes its court system, New York plans to strengthen probation services further, create extensive court intake services, and add to its adjunctive resources. It hopes to see a considerable decrease in its detention rate, length of time in detention, and overcrowding as a result.[35] All who are involved recognize clearly, however, that the situation will be perpetuated unless all elements in the system are dealt with simultaneously. For, to repeat, a decade of public focus on overcrowded detention, periodic crises, and evidence of poorly treated children accomplished little, each of the participants focusing on the failings of others. In addition to placing detention intake within a probation intake structure, other elements in the situation will have to be dealt with for these reasons:

a) Part of the problem clearly stems from a periodic shortage of

---

[34] *Detention Facilities for Children in New York City: A Plan for Management Improvement* (New York City: Division of Administration, 1962), p. 8.

[35] As this volume goes to press, data from the New York City Family Court reveal that the more extensive intake service and changed rules about detention have in fact decreased substantially the use of detention.

institutional space. *Detention Standards* urges, it will be re-called, that a committed child be moved from detention within twenty-four hours. This is in the area of state respon-sibility. Voluntary agencies provide part of what is required, aided by public funds.

b) Part of the problem is related to the intake policy and practices of voluntary institutions. As publicly supported bodies, these institutions should be willing to develop a more reasonable in-take system, related to the problems faced by courts and de-tention.

c) Part of the problem demands solution of the shortage of tem-porary shelters and boarding units, especially for younger children.

d) Part of the problem may be met by better use of court and community psychiatric diagnostic and consultation resources or expansion of such resources.

e) Part of the problem may be met through court speed-up of cases affecting material witnesses.

Only adequate planning and coordinating machinery of the sort mentioned briefly in an early chapter and described at length in Chapter XIII is able to deal with all such elements as needed in order to cope with overcrowded detention. Adequate accountability devices are also required so that young people will not remain in detention for excessively long periods—the exact duration deter-mined only by the degree of inadequacy of public provision. The accountability "machinery" should be able to ring a widely heard "bell" in the face of any case situation involving community abuse of its right to deprive a child of freedom in the course of a court study or while it evolves a treatment plan.

Program. Intake controls, better policy, and decreased overcrowd-ing would permit full development of what might become once again an outstanding program. At a time when "crises" had not become routine, Beck's evaluation said, quite properly, "The Youth House program has many extraordinary and praiseworthy features. . . . concepts often discussed in literature but seldom witnessed in prac-tice have been made part of a working program."

While the strengths of the program have tended to decrease com-munity concern about intake controls or lengthy detention, the fact remains that children who wait in detention for long periods while institutional space is being sought or while awaiting transfer to a state facility become disturbed and disruptive. Also, children who do not belong in detention and who are exposed to those who do cannot escape the harmful consequences. Gradually, thus, the program itself is undermined. It is in no sense as strong today as it was in a period of less pressure. Nonetheless, it deserves description, for what it may teach others and to define some of its needs. We turn, first, to Youth House for Boys. The description deals with elements of universal concern, not special local factors. Focus is on the characteristics of the program at its best, when the situation is stabilized and staff filled.

Youth House for Boys has successfully integrated caseworkers into all aspects of custody and administration, so that adjustment problems lead to efforts to understand and to help boys. Social workers orient all new admissions and do much to deal with initial anxiety. Children participate in formulating rules and regulations and participate, through self-government, in helping one another achieve controls and in offering advice as to the freedom which can be constructively used. All members of the staff contribute to diagnostic studies for the court, and the data obtained also govern the system of grouping in Youth House, school assignment, and other aspects of the program. Apart from contributing to diagnostic studies where requested by the court, psychiatrists see any child in the population if an emergency requires it. Well-qualified social work, psychology, and psychiatric staff teams are able to produce fifteen to twenty full psychiatric studies for court each week when all positions are filled.

The basic philosophy is expressed in the view that children in detention are helped only if understood and that they cannot strengthen their own controls if adult controls are externally imposed.

We must build toward the future by making use of the period of detention to help the child understand his own problems and some of the destructive ways he has been taking to solve them. We must help him to mobilize his ability to express himself in constructive terms.[36]

The permissive setting avoids imposing conformity but implies it, "helping a child to achieve control through the limitation of his own

[36] Cohen, *Children in Trouble*, p. 9.

action." The objective is to get the child to conform to the adult's pattern because he feels he belongs and is accepted by someone who cares. Acceptance, in turn, begins with understanding.

The key to much of what has been possible at Youth House is a group culture which seems to work on behalf of the program. The boys have been helped gradually to feel that the program is worked out for their welfare and that the interest in them is deep. The resultant group pressure taboos much undesirable behavior, ensures cooperation in "housekeeping" chores, and even means that others will make a bed for a boy seen as unable to mobilize himself for the task.[37] As is often the case, the culture is transmitted from "generation" to "generation" as boys come and go, since it satisfies real needs.

Years of experimentation have led to close integration of all departments and to a consistency of handling and objectives, in a context of diagnostic alertness. Staff seminars, interchange of reports, and ability to hold leadership personnel for an extensive period in Youth House for Boys have all contributed.

The nucleus of the day's activity is the school administered by the Board of Education. Teachers plan for work continuity "on an individual basis, at the level which each child has reached in the community school." A few children are given work assignments which permit close attachment to a staff member, if they are unable to adjust to school. An elaborate leisure-time program is focused by the group work staff on diversified recreation which allows choices at any given moment, thus creating situations to help each child gain self-confidence and permitting adequate recording of observations which will contribute to diagnosis and planning.[38]

Total personnel in all categories are equal to the bed capacity of the center, but this reduces itself to a ratio of one staff member to three children during any one shift. This compares well with recommended standards and is seen as adequate in daily experience. Rapid staff turnover and vacancies in many categories are a major problem, however; the work is difficult for professionals who find that knowledge is not always adequate to deal with this group.

So well do some detained boys seem to respond, in contrast to their earlier behavior in the community and their subsequent actions in

[37] *Ibid.*, pp. 30–32.   [38] *Ibid.*, Chapter IV.

the training schools and institutions, that there is some tendency to think of detention as important for all as part of treatment. As indicated, this decreases interest in intake controls. Youth House expresses this in a recent report as making "use of the detention period as a first step in the rehabilitation of the young delinquent." This is described as a fourth objective which emerged after formulation of earlier objectives: to minimize the detrimental effects of detention, to use detention positively, and to utilize detention for individual observation.

Youth House is clear, of course, that its major contribution to the child is in adequate study and reports and in "a start" in helping him to see himself and the world differently—and to make use of what will come next. In its inevitable identification with the children it gets to know, and its knowledge of how inadequate so many of the other facilities are, it may drift into the tempting trap of seeking to do more and more for children. What the community requires is translation of some of the interest into efforts on behalf of the other facilities, so that Youth House may relate closely to a well-staffed court and know that it transfers committed children to effective treatment institutions, able to pick up the work it has begun.

The girls. A public evaluation of New York City detention presents a similar picture of the nonpunitive but firm atmosphere in Youth House for Boys and of the pattern of easy consultation within the staff. It states, however, that

the spirit of the boys' institution and its smooth flow of communication have not been achieved at Youth House for Girls. Those staff members who have worked at both Houses attribute a difference in spirit to the high turnover in top level staff at the Girls' House, with a consequent lack of consistency in policy. . . . It has taken many years to build the spirit at Youth House for Boys. Since emotionally disturbed girls are even more difficult to serve than delinquent boys, there is an even greater need that the staff at Youth House for Girls not only be highly competent, but also maintain continuity of service.[39]

Others have evaluated Youth House for Girls in similar fashion. Efforts to strengthen the program through integration of the administration of both the boys' and girls' facilities have been ham-

[39] Juvenile Delinquency Evaluation Project of the City of New York, *The Youth House* (New York, 1956), p. 4.

pered by overcrowding and the extended periods of waiting in detention.

Nor should one underestimate the factor of emotional disturbance in girls who go to court and detention. One sees here far less of the socially determined group delinquency in relatively intact individuals than one finds among the boys. Girls before the court in recent years are characterized by a high percentage of emotional disturbance and sexual "delinquency." The community process which gets girls to court is more selective than with boys. The result is a population whose members come from difficult home backgrounds and who are themselves not easy to work with.

It is therefore not surprising that fewer of the girls brought to detention are taken home by their parents when notified; they remain in detention until the hearing. What is more, the court returns far more of the girls to detention after an initial hearing than it does boys brought to detention by police. Finally, a higher percentage of the girls in the group are ultimately committed to an institution.

Despite the fact that Youth House personnel have given some special attention to the characteristics of girls in detention and their differences from boys, it may be that all relevant factors have not been isolated. The major work describing the Youth House program notes that girls react to the delinquency with more emotional distress, since social disapproval is greater than in the case of misconduct in boys, particularly sexual misconduct. Parents, in particular, tend to ostracize delinquent daughters. Girls seem to react more to separation from home and possessions and have great need for a room and privacy. They seem to transfer to one another their disturbance at court plans for them—and to do so more rapidly and more often than boys, just as they exchange confidences more often. Group hysteria easily occurs in girls' detention. Individual work with girls may be required where a group approach succeeds with boys. Certainly, individuality in clothing and opportunity to maintain personal appearance seem important. A tendency to "pairing" may create special problems.[40]

Individualization of the approach to girls in detention may thus require added investment in staff time, physical facilities, and equip-

[40] Cohen, *Children in Trouble,* Chapter 11.

ment. Program modifications beyond those already made may be needed. Youth House, which has placed major emphasis on creative innovation in its work with boys and which embodies much of the philosophy of *Detention Standards,* will probably have to give new attention to girls to maintain its own objectives.

The physical plant. For some years the Youth House for Boys' program was handicapped by the completely inadequate plant. After years of community effort, the city authorized a new facility. A new Youth House (cost over $5 million) was opened in 1958. The bed capacity of 350, which was set in order to meet the projected future needs, was exceeded in a few weeks, and remained inadequate until intake controls were imposed under the Family Court reorganization in 1962.

The building is built in "wings" and there are outdoor playgrounds between wings. Each of ten dormitories provides separate rooms for 25 boys, to make a total of 250. (Most recent construction elsewhere has preferred units of 15; California has tended to plan for units of 20—with high staffing ratios.) If not overcrowded, the building permits grouping and classification. There is a reception wing accommodating 30 and another wing able to hold 20 disturbed boys. Fifteen hospital beds bring the total to 315. The larger capacity is obtained by having 50 boys double up in rooms. Pressure for beds has defeated plans for specialized use of the reception and "disturbed boy" facilities.

The building includes an indoor pool and gymnasium, dining rooms, recreation rooms, and a special services building with chapels, shops, conference rooms, arts and crafts rooms, a room for table tennis and pool, and space for probation officers. A main building contains two floors for the special school serving Youth House, administration and social work offices, an intake unit, and an infirmary.

Since late 1953 the main Youth House for Girls has been located in the East Bronx in a renovated three-story building close to the Youth House for Boys. When it opened it was far better than the building housing the boys or an earlier temporary facility for girls. Within the wall surrounding the building are trees and grass, athletic and playground areas, and a skating rink. The remodeled building is clean and modern. There is a smaller building for reception and an infirmary. However, despite the recognized need for private rooms for girls, there is an obsolete dormitory arrangement which places fifteen girls in one large room. There is no privacy. The excitable girl cannot relax until all are quiet. An immature twelve-year-old sleeps in the bed next to a pregnant fifteen-year-old. Hysteria spreads rapidly.

The building was not constructed for this purpose originally and does not have the modern devices which permit detention control, yet do not constantly confront the child with it. Locked doors are everywhere and are always under discussion by the girls.

Youth House for Girls was also soon too small for its assignment. The urgency of expansion of girls' facilities was clear by 1955; a situation was reached during which two thirds of the girls were being held for postcommitment periods for lack of training school space, some as long as six months, and "disturbances reached riot proportions for several weeks." In 1957 a temporary annex was opened on Welfare Island; new interim annex facilities were again needed by 1960. Plans are under way for new buildings which will meet modern standards and will reflect the Youth House philosophy. Their adequacy will depend on delinquency trends, alternative community provision, and intake controls. In the meantime, as overcrowding continued and the proportion of committed girls increased, new riots occurred in 1960 and 1962.

When New York City decided to centralize its detention in the late 1940s, it did so in the midst of an urgent need to close totally inadequate combined, privately operated shelter-detention facilities. As a result, the issue of centralization was not debated as such. Now a responsible planning body would do well to review its strategy as it proceeds to make provision beyond the existing relatively new building for boys. Courts exist in five counties and case volume is high. Many courts elsewhere in the country maintain detention in adjacent structures or in the selfsame building on the basis of caseloads smaller than the loads in almost all New York boroughs. Probation staffs in New York are decentralized. Would it not be wise to plan future building, as needed, so as to ensure detention space in each borough? Parental visiting certainly would be simplified at the same time that the probation task would be made more reasonable. A court is accountable for children it places in detention. A visitor to detention facilities throughout the country is soon convinced that a child is not left in detention for months on end if the probation officer directly concerned is on the grounds regularly—or if he is personally accessible to the detention superintendent and his staff. The probation case study benefits from access to the staff who supervise the child daily and see visiting parents.

Administration of New York City detention. Current reorganization integrates New York City detention social service operations into probation—the usual practice elsewhere—and the role of the voluntary board, long responsible for Youth House as such, is being reexamined. A historical accident placed Youth House under this board despite the fact of full public financial responsibility and public provision of the total plant. Two problems resulted. First, as already shown, detention intake did not become a court function and the entire use of detention was thereby affected. Second, community planning became confused as a board overburdened by a crowded facility proclaimed periodically that it would not take any more children into detention—while no other community body had responsibility or ability to provide alternate space.

On the positive side it should be said that the New York plan did create a unique program and attracted considerable talent at one point. The Youth House Board has shown a degree of dedication and comprehension seldom seen in any field. Also, the "voluntary" status, under public financing, freed the facility from certain civil service policies and procedures which complicate staffing in a period of acute professional shortages.

Important as these factors may be, they are not overriding. A public facility deserves an advisory board as good as the one of a "voluntary" facility publicly financed. The same citizens would not refuse to serve. Public personnel policies also must flexibly meet the staffing situation or no program will be adequate.

On the positive side, favoring full public operation of detention, it is necessary to note that if a court remands a child to secure custody through its machinery, and then makes the decision as to next steps (offering in the interim social and clinical services, education, recreation, and other aspects of a program fully financed by the taxpayers), it is difficult to see any reason for a residue of private operation. Since detention is an extension of public police power and assignment of responsibility for public protection, it is logical that it be publicly run. In fact, none of the conditions justifying private operation exist: this is not a sectarian program and it is not a service which a private group has undertaken to provide for the city. It is completely financed out of tax funds.

Given the decision in favor of public operation, preferably on a basis which would convert the present board into an advisory and visiting group, the city might consider either full operation by an expanded probation department or probation administration of professional services while the Welfare Department administers the plant (as it does several shelters). The city school system already operates the schools. Either of these plans should provide for a detention superintendent who could implement that concept of detention which gives it a balanced place in the total system of services.

CHAPTER IX

PROTECTIVE SERVICES: THE COMMUNITY RESPONSE TO ALLEGED NEGLECT

THE STORY has often been told of the church worker in 1874 who, while visiting an aged woman in a tenement, learned of the brutal mistreatment of a child by her foster mother. Already weak and ill as a result of long abuse, Mary Ellen was chained to a bed and fed only bread and water. However, the church worker found no way to intervene on behalf of the child. The police, the district attorney, and various agencies in the community could not, they felt, intercede where the primary rights of parent or guardian were involved. Long tradition of parental power over children and hesitancy about outside intervention remained dominant, even though the right to intervene had previously been expressed and legally justified.

There had been created in the previous decade, in Manhattan, an American Society for the Prevention of Cruelty to Animals, patterned upon an animal protective society established in England in 1822. The mission worker, in her concern, argued that surely a child was a member of the animal kingdom and merited protection, at least as much as a cat or dog. Thus, on petition of the Society for the Prevention of Cruelty to Animals, the suffering child was brought to court and the foster parents were jailed.

The American public took a new step in affirming the rights of children, as many other humane societies, originally founded for the protection of animals, began to intercede on behalf of children who were abused, mistreated, or cruelly neglected. Legislation was enacted protecting children and authorizing special societies to undertake the task. New protective societies were created to work on behalf of children, while others which had animal programs revised their charters to create children's divisions.

New York County's Society for the Prevention of Cruelty to Children, founded in 1875, was followed almost at once by similar societies in Portsmouth, San Francisco, Philadelphia, Boston, and other cities. The American Humane Association, created in 1877 as a general coordinating body in this field, added a Children's Division in 1887 (and has reactivated it recently).[1]

Early American efforts in the tradition of the English Poor Law had been designed largely to relieve the public of the financial burden of caring for children. Indenture and other forms of apprenticeship were the preferred means, and almshouses took care of the rest. Growing humanitarian concern and recognition that "acts of God" or uncontrolled environmental forces compelled many to seek aid finally laid a basis for enforcement of laws, already on the books, to protect children against cruelty and neglect and to strengthen such laws. Some agencies had sprung up to care for or to place neglected and dependent children, but they did not seek directly to promote or to enforce protective laws. Thus, the new protective societies, the S.P.C.C.'s, filled a gap in community provision.

Mary Ellen had played her dramatic role, but the functions of a protective program had to be developed in the twentieth century, as American social welfare, particularly child care, began to reflect a changing social scene.

The S.P.C.C.'s sponsored many progressive child protective laws and demonstrated in their daily actions that society meant to protect certain minimum rights of children over whom parents, even seriously disturbed or totally incompetent parents, had, until then, been supreme. Later, some S.P.C.C.'s became part of the general child welfare movement, often merging with other child and family agencies to develop social services which grew and changed along with social work as a whole. Others sided with the president of the first society, Elbridge Gerry, whose name became synonymous with

---

[1] Emma V. Lundberg, *Unto the Least of These* (New York: D. Appleton-Century, 1947), and Henry W. Thurston, *The Dependent Child* (New York: Columbia University Press, 1930)

S.P.C.C., in the view that "it is better to do one thing well." He held that since "child rescue work is a science," it is wiser not to link it to other aspects of "general scientific charity work," but rather to retain the S.P.C.C. in the form of its initial emphasis on law enforcement and rescue.[2]

In 1910 Roswell C. McCrea, teaching at the New York School of Philanthropy, put it even more strongly:

> The work has to be done in cold blood, so to speak, with a deaf ear to the pleadings and entreaties of mothers and fathers whose love for their children is never so strong as when they think their children will be taken from them. The best interests of the children, and not the feelings of those closely connected with them, have to be considered, and a trained charity worker is seldom qualified by his or her training to absolutely banish the spirit of "love for fellow-man" from his or her work. The SPCC worker, on the other hand, looks at the matter from a colder (a legal) viewpoint, and therefore the only training he should receive is such that will enable him to detect cruelty and apply the remedy, regardless of how the application affects those who are responsible for the cruelty. In short, SPCC is not, never has been and never will be charitable.[3]

Another note was struck almost from the beginning by some S.P.C.C. pioneers. Henry R. Jones, President of the Brooklyn S.P.C.C., said the following in his first annual report on October 31, 1881: "We have no wish to sever the sacred bond between parent and child, but rather to strengthen it by kind advice and counsel— and yet prevent cruelty at all hazards." By 1915 the Brooklyn S.P.C.C. had set up three divisions: investigation, law enforcement, family welfare. It sought to exert "more effort to bring about betterment in the home conditions of children and thereby avoid the necessity of breaking up families." In 1917 it stated that "only as a last resort do we remove children or institute adult prosecutions."

The two orientations have often merged, and concern with restoring the family has been deepened over the years. However, the New York County S.P.C.C. has remained loyal to Gerry's concept. At times, too, the pioneering "child saving" function of 1874 has seemed to take on the character of an end in itself, and a routine of remov-

[2] Roswell C. McCrea, *The Humane Movement* (New York: Columbia University Press, 1910), pp. 139–40.
[3] H. H. Hart, *Preventive Treatment of Neglected Children* (New York: Charities Publication Committee, 1910).

ing children from their homes and prosecuting their parents has left its mark on some agencies and personnel.

Today, to limit functions to investigation and rescue would ignore all that has been learned about why parents do not care for their children properly and about how people are most effectively helped. Child protective workers, generally, have understood this. A few have not, and the consequences may be the substitution of community-sanctioned cruelty for parental neglect and inadequacy.

NEGLECT—WHAT IS IT?

Our communities sometimes intervene in family life because of the allegation that a child is being severely mistreated, is endangered, or is not being given urgently needed medical attention, adequate food, clothing, and care, or educational opportunity. Even early nineteenth-century legal authorities, who had no way to implement their theory, saw this as entirely fitting: the rights of fathers, in fact, "result from their duties." [4]

The Standard Juvenile Court Act, which does not favor the use of labels, nonetheless suggests that the children's court have exclusive jurisdiction over any child "who is neglected as to proper or necessary support, or education as required by law, or as to medical or other care necessary for his well-being or who is abandoned." In addition, and unlike most statutes, it includes the child "whose environment is injurious to his welfare, or whose behavior is injurious to his own or others' welfare," and the child "who is beyond the control of his parent." Many states list the latter two as classes of delinquent children but students of the problem are giving serious attention to the Standard Act formulation.

The *Standards for Specialized Courts Dealing with Children* proposes original and exclusive jurisdiction over "children whose parents, guardian, or custodian, have allegedly failed to provide them with the care, education or protection necessary for their well-being as required by law." (Dependence on public assistance is not of itself construed as failure to provide for the child.) [5]

[4] James Kent, *Commentaries on American Law,* as quoted by Grace Abbott, *The Child and the State* (Chicago: University of Chicago Press, 1938), I, 51.
[5] National Probation and Parole Association, *Standard Juvenile Court Act* (New York, 1959) Art. II, Sec. 8, and Children's Bureau, U.S. Department of Health, Education, and Welfare, *Standards for Specialized Courts Dealing with*

The British Children's and Young Persons Act of 1933 describes neglect as "want of reasonable care—that is, the omission of such steps as a reasonable parent would take." [6]

In New York State a neglected child is a boy under sixteen and a girl under eighteen

(a) whose parent or other person legally responsible for his care does not adequately supply the child with food, clothing, shelter, education, or medical or surgical care, though financially able or offered financial means to do so; or

(b) who suffers or is likely to suffer serious harm from the improper guardianship, including lack of moral supervision or guidance, of his parents or other person legally responsible for his care and requires the aid of the court; or

(c) who has been abandoned or deserted by his parents or other person legally responsible for his care.[7]

The legal borders of neglect, as Judge Gill of Connecticut has noted, are far from clear. The state's right to intervention does, however, seem to stem from the *parens patriae* doctrine, under which the state is the ultimate guardian of every child. Neglect statutes are not penal and are not designed to vent community indignation on allegedly offending parents: "The sole purpose of the court's inquiry into the behavior of the parent . . . is the determination of what harm their behavior has caused, is causing, or if uncorrected can be reasonably anticipated to cause in the future to the child." [8]

Children's courts in this country usually have jurisdiction over neglect, but definitions vary and are sometimes indistinguishable from dependency. In general, neglect is taken to involve acts committed or omitted, while dependency or destitution has to do with inability to provide food and shelter for a child. As noted, however, the Standard Juvenile Court Act talks of neglect "as to proper or

---

Children (Washington, D.C.: Government Printing Office, 1954), p. 27. Also see Sol Rubin, "Legal Definitions of Offenses by Children and Youth," The University of Illinois, *Law Forum* (Winter, 1960), pp. 512–23.

[6] Women's Group on Public Welfare, *The Neglected Child and His Family* (London: Oxford University Press, 1948), p. 76.

[7] Family Court Act, 1962, Sections 311, 312, 313.

[8] Thomas D. Gill, "The Legal Nature of Neglect," in "Neglect," a special section in *National Probation and Parole Association Journal*, Vol. VI, No. 1 (January, 1960). Quotation is from page 8. This issue henceforth cited as *NPPA Journal*, "Neglect."

necessary support." Obviously the line between neglect and dependency becomes thin as one begins to understand pressures to which parents are subject and the motives behind their conduct. As suggested by many sources, in fact, the labeling as delinquency or neglect, i.e., as *child misconduct* or *parental mistreatment*, is often decided by the chance factor of time or the nature and circumstances of the case finding. One third of the states do not use the labels.[9] Some students of the problem would redefine as neglect all juvenile misbehavior now called delinquency which is not the equivalent of a crime in an adult (Ch. VII).

Whatever the details of definition, however, it is clearly wise public policy that children be "protected against the harmful effects resulting from the absence, inability, inadequacy or destructive behavior of parents, parent substitutes, or others."

The neglected child is one who is in need of such protection because of the impairment or threat of impairment of his health or welfare "as the result of a violation of or noncompliance with law or legal responsibility for the protection of children, their education, employment, health or welfare."[10] Many students of the court (see Ch. VII) would transfer all dependency jurisdiction to welfare departments but all agree that courts must continue to concern themselves with severe neglect.

One listing suggests that community concern justifiably begins under the following kinds of circumstances (the categories are obviously not mutually exclusive):

(1) when children lack essential food, clothing, and shelter;
(2) when a lack of care causes continuing emotional or physical illness, disability, or retarded physical development;
(3) when parental emotional disturbance interferes with or prevents proper child care;
(4) when lack of supervision endangers the child's development;
(5) when a community condition endangers the child and the parents do not seek to protect him even though remedies are available.[11]

[9] *Standard Juvenile Court Act,* Art. II, Sec. 8, and comment.
[10] Draft, *Model Act for Child Protective Services* (Denver: American Humane Association, 1958).
[11] Children's Division, the American Humane Association, *Report of the National Agencies Workshop on Child Protective Services* (Denver, 1957), p. 10.

Only Minnesota actually specifies emotional neglect as a reason for intervention ("who is without proper parental care because of the emotional, mental or physical disability, or state of immaturity of his parent, guardian, or other custodian"). Gill holds that general neglect jurisdiction permits action in cases of emotional neglect after adequate clinical evaluation.[12] Many experts would ask to see behavioral evidence of negative consequences of emotional problems.

It is possible to misuse society's right and need to intervene. American and British social welfare history has many examples of zealots who have sought to impose their own standards and rules upon others, and who have used their official status punitively and arrogantly against the weak and the ignorant. Such cases of overenforcement or even abuse of laws to protect children do not, however, justify reneging on a primary social obligation.

Even when there is good will and considerable competence, boundaries are difficult to define. How far is society to oversee child rearing? How much neglect (few parents are perfect) justifies intervention? Is the community to organize itself for intimate knowledge of how all children are reared, in order to protect them? Or, as is generally held, can an efficient system of case location operate within a framework which assumes the general competence of most parents, but acknowledges an obligation not to miss clues that certain children require active help?

A democratic society is defeated if it seeks to control family life for all children. Most parents are not neglectful, and the quality of family life is changed if it must be held up to public view to make sure that it is sound. However, a responsible society will not take this as justification for society to neglect the brutalized, the deprived, the starved children whose parents are incapable, for psychological or social reasons, of providing them with at least the minimum of essential care.

Particularly difficult is the question of how much consideration should be given to local conditions in evaluating a child's milieu. Specifically, does one hold up the objectives of the most recent White House Conference on Children, which are more often aspirations than standards, or should the criteria be the norms of the state

[12] Gill, "The Legal Nature of Neglect," *NPPA Journal,* "Neglect," pp. 11–12.

as a whole or the acceptable conduct in the geographic locality or social subgroup in which the child is being reared?

Social welfare agencies will certainly strive to raise community standards in the direction of national aspirations. Formal, authoritative public intervention at any moment in a family's life is obviously affected by court policy in adjudicating neglect. Court policy, in turn, usually reflects a broader community backdrop than the social or cultural subgroup, particularly a minority, underprivileged, or deviant subgroup. The court must ask whether the apparent or alleged neglect is, in fact, acceptable practice in another subculture. Given cohesive family life and evidence that other children grow up without harm under such circumstances, the court or agency should not wish to intervene. But intervention becomes necessary when a child is endangered (by the refusal to arrange medical attention, for instance), when the child clearly shows the undesirable consequences of such rearing, and when the parents' own mores have collapsed in the midst of the majority culture so that the family offers no cohesiveness and no framework for socialization.

TRENDS IN CHILD PROTECTION

Protective services and agencies are plagued by confusions in definition, by major differences of opinion as to appropriate organizational forms, and by historical residues. Standard-setting groups and individual agencies, however, are now making major efforts to give sound direction to future development. Facts are being assembled as to current provision; several national forums have been created in an effort to achieve consensus; experimental efforts have pointed to the potential of new professional approaches.

A 1956 national survey, under the auspices of the reactivated Children's Division of the American Humane Association, began by defining "child protective services" as a "specialized *casework service* to neglected, abused, exploited, or rejected children." The premise is that a protective service is preventive, is nonpunitive, and seeks the rehabilitation of the home. Characteristically, the service is "initiated on a complaint or referral from sources outside the family." The readiness to turn to the court when necessary and, perhaps, other factors give the agency a degree of authority in its approach. However, the agency may also render a variety of other child welfare services.[13] Thus, excluding the investigatory activities of police or other departments in relation to neglect, as well as court services in this field, the survey sought to determine, nationally, whether there was adequate coverage provided by public or voluntary casework programs. It was found that there was not.

Private agencies, the backbone of the original child protection development, do not exist in most communities. In fact, "32 states and the District of Columbia have no private agencies with a child protective function as defined by this study." There are 84 such agencies in the nation, but 40 of them are local branches of state-wide agencies: 5 offices in Connecticut, 21 in Massachusetts, 5 in Rhode Island, 9 in Maryland. Of the remaining private groups, 14 are found in New York State, 9 in Pennsylvania, 6 in New Jersey, 4 in Illinois, and one each in Indiana, Ohio, Kentucky, and Tennessee.[14] Thus, outside of the Eastern seaboard, few communities have private agencies, and even there such coverage is far from complete.

On the other hand, the study showed that in 35 of 48 states (in 1956) the social welfare law imposes general responsibility upon the state for child welfare services, including the protection and care of the "homeless, dependent, and neglected . . . and children in danger of becoming delinquent." In 22 states this responsibility is discharged by the state through supervisory or consultative services to the local welfare agency. A minority of counties have a specialized child protective program. A sizable minority have no program at all. The programs of many counties are severely limited by the size and qualifications of staff.

In 13 of the 35 states, the legal responsibility for child protective services is discharged through a direct service program (although coverage may be lacking in a few counties). Direct service is also

---

[13] Vincent De Francis, *Child Protective Services in the United States* (Denver: American Humane Association, 1956), p. 18. After several decades of inactivity, the Children's Division has sought to bring protective services' thinking up to date from the mid-1940s and has, during the past decade, sought to play a leadership role in formulating definitions, standards, model statutes, and educational materials. The U.S. Children's Bureau has recently begun a new national survey which should supply more precise data.

[14] *Ibid.*, pp. 35–38.

rendered in a limited number of instances in the 21 states where the pattern is generally one of supervision and consultation.

Eight states have neither public nor private child protection provision and no legal designation of responsibility.[15] Furthermore, many of the programs described above are only token efforts, according to the survey's director, since they depend on the federal child welfare program which until recently was limited to rural counties and areas of special need.[16] Large parts of the country thus lack casework services specializing in child protection.

The survey also disclosed that public child welfare personnel, whatever their varied levels of competence and training, seem agreed concerning their obligations: they must respond to reported neglect and abuse of children, evaluate the situation carefully, offer temporary shelter where required; they must seek to help the parents improve the home situation; they must refer the matter to court, if this is the only means of protecting the child, and arrange short- or long-term placement, with or without parental approval, if home conditions cannot be remedied.[17]

Private programs, on the other hand, range from social casework services which seek "to prevent cruelty before it occurs and to effect fundamental remedies after cruelty has occurred," to traditional law enforcement efforts concerned with apprehension and prosecution of adults guilty of cruelty to children. Some societies combine law enforcement and casework service.

The same basic dichotomy is discovered in England where a national voluntary group, the National Society for the Prevention of Cruelty to Children (N.S.P.C.C.), operating under a royal charter and through 220 local branches, is staffed by a group of almost 300, most of them male, for investigation and prosecution. Many on the N.S.P.C.C. staff are ex-police officers. The officer instructs parents

---

[15] For listings and a state-by-state summary, see *ibid.*

[16] Vincent De Francis, "Accent on Prevention," a statement before the House Subcommittee on Juvenile Delinquency, May 29, 1957 (Denver: American Humane Association, 1957).

[17] For illustration from Colorado, see "The Public Agency," a presentation by Marie C. Smith, Director, Child Welfare Division, Department of Public Welfare, State of Colorado, at National Conference of Social Welfare, May, 1957. Unpublished.

to end their cruelty and to ensure adequate care, food, and sleeping arrangements if they wish to avoid court.

The N.S.P.C.C. takes few cases to court (under 1 percent as compared to 5 to 10 percent in most U.S. programs for which data are available) but uses the threat of court frequently. When cases are brought to court, however, British law and tradition make the jailing and fining of adults for child neglect far more common than it is in the United States. In one of the cases cited in a recent study, for example, a parent had left a child with someone else for care, and the other person did not protect the child. Both the parent and negligent "baby sitter" were sentenced by the judge because he felt that the parent had acted irresponsibly and the "sitter" neglectfully.[18]

Modern psychological and social understanding has led to questions about the British protective program similar to those raised in the United States. One case-by-case study in England, for example, showed the neglectful mothers to be in poor health and without anybody who would help care for their children or relieve them, even briefly. The families were often broken, subject to extreme poverty, residing in poor housing, and suffering from mental defect or illness. Analysis suggested, in fact, that misfortune, rather than neglect, was a more appropriate designation for 50 percent of 234 cases studied intensively. Only 11 percent were considered to represent deliberate cruelty or willful neglect.[19]

The study concluded, as have all recent studies of the kind which make use of modern social welfare knowledge and principles, that neglectful families require social casework services which are reassuring and supportive, and which offer practical services as well as emotional help. In some instances, residential treatment may be required.

The N.S.P.C.C. began to devote more effort to improving conditions in the homes visited and hired women as "visitors" to supplement the work of the inspectors. It sought public funds to expand this phase of its work, only to find that the Home Office (the responsible department) preferred to devote its resources to a com-

[18] See *The Neglected Child and His Family* for general discussion of the British program and for the case studies.

[19] *Ibid.*, particularly p. 41.

prehensive local public child welfare program (under the children's officer of the local authority) which would include individual rehabilitative services in case of neglect.

A recent review comments that the N.S.P.C.C., despite its stress on the small prosecution percentage and its desire to do constructive work, actually continues to emphasize lurid aspects of family life in its literature and appeals and has not developed a modern preventive program. Moreover, agencies wishing to reserve for themselves a friendly and constructive role are willing to preserve the N.S.P.C.C. as a "police service for the authorities." [20] They ask whether casework and prosecution are ever effectively combined. They point, by contrast, to the creative possibilities of a dedicated casework program, like the voluntary Family Service Units, developed during World War II, whose approach to disorganized families corresponds somewhat to the "reaching out" casework programs in this country. Given public support, such units are expanding through much of Great Britain. Other British localities have assigned the function to "intensive" workers in the public departments.

It seems likely that the core of modern child protection development, British and American, will be in public child welfare departments. And like the British, we in the United States will have to determine whether it is wiser to preserve a limited number of voluntary S.P.C.C.'s with their original law enforcement emphasis, equipping them to provide modern casework services, or whether to encourage other types of development. If law enforcement and investigation are not to be voluntary functions (and this hardly seems likely, if only in view of the limited coverage of voluntary protective services) there is need for clarification as to where they are to be housed.

Also, clearly, we in the United States shall continue, as will the British, to introduce modern understanding and professional procedures into the law enforcement phases as well. In this connection, one might cite a recent report of England's National Association of Probation Officers, which urged courts not to dispose of neglect

[20] See Samuel Mencher, "The Relationship of Voluntary and Statutory Welfare Services in England" (unpublished D.S.W. dissertation, New York School of Social Work, Columbia University, 1957). Also, The Home Office, *Sixth Report of the Work of the Children's Department* (London, 1951).

cases without full social study, and which proposed creation of observation centers for remand of mothers with their children, if necessary, during the case study period, to permit observation, medical and psychiatric examination, as well as elementary training in child care.[21]

Those who approach protective programs in modern social welfare terms continue to face complex professional questions:

Child neglect is basically a social problem. In what way can it be dealt with through individual casework?

All are agreed that the protective agency cannot withdraw or discontinue service simply because the parent has refused or is unable to take help. Should the service also be organized so that the client is unable to withdraw, or is the potential court petition adequate authority?

Some emphasize the specialized skill in protective work, while others stress the individual agency or the community pattern. Which approach will yield the best definition of method and the most organized service?

At what point is a child in the purview of a protective program?

What organizational consequences follow from concern with individual legal rights?

Should all protective services be located under public auspices, or is a public-private pattern desirable?

In what sense should non-governmental agencies engage in direct law enforcement?

Should the protective service be a separate unit or part of a more general child welfare or family casework effort? [22]

Answers may be possible if we consider some of the essential functions and their best location, from the point of view of a total community pattern of services.

FUNCTIONS WITHIN A PROTECTIVE PROGRAM

There is no unified conception of protective programs. To some, protective services are functions divided among a variety of agencies and institutions. Others stress the social casework task of the child welfare agency with a protective specialization. Still others empha-

[21] National (British) Association of Probation Officers, "Cruelty and Neglect of Children," *Correction* (New York State Department of Correction), XX, No. 6 (June, 1955), 5–8.

[22] These and many more specific procedural questions are suggested by Isabel Stamm in an unpublished MS (1957). For consensus as to answers, see Child Welfare League of America, Inc., *Standards for Child Protective Services* (New York, 1960). This document is an authoritative source on professional philosophy and standards of practice. It deals with many issues beyond our present scope.

size techniques and essential skills. Any detailed examination of what the community requires seems to point to the first of these views: the protective responsibility is lodged in the whole community. In fact, "protective services to children [is] a total process involving a constellation of agencies, public, private and legal—any one or several of which may function at various times in the interest of the care of the child and help to his parents, to insure such care." [23]

The community as a whole is responsible for the adequate rearing of its children. To suggest that any one agency could undertake the entire protective function would be to move backward at least eighty-five years.

This view does not, of course, preclude assignment of specific functions and responsibilities to specialized agencies. Indeed, such assignment of specialized tasks is a necessity. For example, there is wisdom in the recommendation of the National Agencies Workshop on Protective Services to the effect that each state either provide or ensure provision by some agency of protective casework services and related functions.[24] The casework service, however, does not encompass the entire protective process.

Consideration of all the functions to be provided and staffed in a total protective process suggests that the pattern of organization should vary with size, type, and traditions of a community. No matter what the pattern of organization, however, the essential functions of a protective program are the same.

One premise needs emphasis before specific functions are reviewed. Protective services, which operate most effectively within a circumscribed area, cannot realistically aim at satisfying "all the needs of children" or at ensuring "all their rights." Many social institutions and social welfare agencies have a part in meeting children's needs and protecting their rights, including the family, the church, the school, the welfare department, and the court. The protective service moves into action only when socially defined minimums are not being met, or where children are in "clear and present danger." [25]

Case finding. The first step is to identify those families in which

[23] Stamm, unpublished MS.
[24] *Report of National Agencies Workshop on Child Protective Services*, p. 12.
[25] The phrase "clear and present danger" is suggested in this context by L. L. Geismar and B. Ayres in *Families in Trouble* (St. Paul: Family Centered Project, 1958), p. 139.

parents or parent-substitutes are not providing or arranging adequate care for their children and those not able to recognize and take action on their problem, thereby causing injury to the children.[26] Members of the community at large are in a position to notice and to alert official agencies to situations involving extreme neglect or mistreatment of children, not yet known to agencies. To do so, however, community members must begin to share growing professional knowledge about the consequences of abuse and deprivation upon children. They require, too, knowledge of resources to which they may turn.

Beyond this, however, all the case finding resources come into play: public health stations, police, welfare department staffs, schools, social agencies, doctors, public health nurses, hospitals and clinics, settlements, recreation centers, and so on. What these agencies must have, each according to its function and staffing, is clear information as to the kind of situation requiring intervention, and knowledge about how the community is organized to deal with neglect complaints.

When the problem goes beyond the internal family difficulties, inadequacies, or relationships, case finding may also involve *situation finding*, the discovery of what has been called "community neglect." Response to a complaint or exercise of an agency's normal functions may uncover the lack of "vital health and social welfare services," or community conditions which deny children the opportunities they should have, or which "affect children adversely." [27] While one would hope that all citizens would report such circumstances to proper authorities and would join in community action to correct undesirable conditions, such reporting and corrective action is clearly an obligation of any social agency. It is not the special province of protective work. This does not, of course, preclude the decision by any agency, including one rendering protective casework services, to devote itself to social action and legislative initiative in these spheres. Historically, voluntary protective societies in fact did much to end extreme child labor abuses.

[26] *Standards for Child Protective Services*, 1.1, and Elizabeth Elmer, "Abused Young Children Seen in Hospitals," *Social Work*, V, No. 4 (October, 1960), 98–102.

[27] *Standards for Child Protective Services*, p. 7.

Case evaluation and emergency removal of children. It is essential that the case finder or complainant about neglect know where in the community he may turn so as to ensure adequate evaluation of the situation. The case evaluation or case study function should, of course, be preceded by some measure of screening, to consider the possibility of hostile motivation or clearly incompetent sources. It is agreed, however, that unless the evidence is overwheming that the allegation is unfounded, the report should reach the agency designated for case evaluation; otherwise, children may be hurt.

Evaluation is a protective casework task. Within the protective casework field, it is called by various names: intake, substantiating the complaint, and so on. It is often a specialized assignment, even in departments which encompass protective casework within a general child welfare service. A national committee under the auspices of the Child Welfare League of America urged that each community have one known place authorized to receive complaints.[28]

It has been alleged that at one time the humane society representative would enter a home, inspect the premises, look at the child, perhaps talk to the parent, and decide, on the spot, to remove the child. Today, it is still agreed by all that the community cannot at any time permit children to remain in "situations of serious or extreme danger." Current concepts of individual rights seem to suggest that if such situations exist, it is the police who should enter, remove the children, and take them to a shelter for protection.

There are still some people in the protective field who would retain in voluntary protective agencies the police power originally assigned by statute or charter when there were no other protectors of children. They consider it the protective agency's duty to intervene and remove a child in danger. This seems increasingly to be an outdated view, however, inconsistent with either the expansion of juvenile aid police programs or the emphasis on protecting the rights of people in difficulty.

[28] In Minnesota, for example, all counties except one integrate protective services with general child welfare loads, but assignment is made to the most skillful workers. Some New York State counties have an intake specialization and all child welfare workers receive treatment cases. See Appendix A of American Public Welfare Association, *Preventive and Protective Services to Children, a Responsibility of the Public Welfare Agency* (Chicago, 1958).

There are S.P.C.C. leaders who, although they consider the child's removal as an S.P.C.C. responsibility, nevertheless favor having the agent summon a policeman to participate. No effective argument has been made against the view that parents have the right to the possession of their children until this right has been abrogated by the court. It is a law enforcement function to protect all individuals, including children, from personal harm and danger. In situations of danger to children, when immediate action must be taken to protect the child by removing him from the home, this action is the function of law enforcement officials. A court petition and provision for social study should follow at once. If the rights of a parent or child are to be limited in their own or society's interests, they can be limited only in accordance with due process of law and only to the extent and for the time necessary.[29]

Law enforcement officers need to be called in only occasionally—when a child's life or safety is in immediate danger, a crime is being committed, forcible entry is necessary, or when a child or caseworker needs protection against bodily harm.[30] Protective workers attest that few cases require immediate removal. It is now understood, in fact, that apart from the matter of parental rights, an unnecessary separation of child from parent may contribute to decreased responsibility and make permanent family disintegration more likely.[31] There was far less concern about this in the early days of protective work than there is today, when we know that few substitute arrangements match even marginally acceptable parental care.

Skilled investigation of complaints or case study is thus essential in all protective cases and is a major function in the protective field. This is hardly the place to outline the elements of such study in detail, in the manner of a manual, but some indications of the requirements are relevant as an aid in clarifying what the

[29] *Standards for Child Protective Services,* p. 12. A social agency shall act only in those rare circumstances "where humane considerations would obligate any citizen to act." *Ibid.,* p. 13.

[30] *Ibid.,* p. 13. For a description of how this may be developed see Dolores M. Schmidt and Betty Johnson, "Protective Services for Neglected Children in Denver," *NPPA Journal,* "Neglect," pp. 40–43.

[31] See, for example, Claire R. Hancock, *A Study of Protective Services and the Problem of Neglect of Children in New Jersey* (Trenton, N.J.: Board of Child Welfare, 1958), p. 29.

community must be prepared to staff in a protective casework service.[32]

The protective agency caseworker, as already indicated, is usually conducting the investigation contrary to the wishes of (or certainly without an invitation from) one or both parents. Furthermore, both he and the parents know that the situation may reach the children's court as a result of his findings, or if parental cooperation on some level is not forthcoming. Finally, the caseworker may not withdraw despite extreme parental hostility and resistance; in De Francis's terms, his is "a higher than ordinary degree of responsibility," since he represents an agency assigned a protective role through statute or charter. (It is doubtful that a protective casework service can exist without such formal assignment.)

The case evaluation process should reflect the fact that the protective field has shifted from "rescuing the child from the home," to preserving the home for the child wherever possible. This does not decrease the need to follow up a complaint immediately and thoroughly through several means: social service exchange clearance; clearance with agencies which have known the family; interviews with each parent (including a visit to the home); contacts with such other sources of information as the school, physicians, clergy, relatives; an interview with the children alleged to be neglected. Where possible, of course, there should be a prior interview with the complainant to evaluate motives as well as to obtain information. When complaints are made anonymously, as they often are, case studies must usually be initiated without such interview, especially when initial explorations reveal that the situation cannot be safely ignored.

The evaluation should have the full scope of a professionally competent social study, but may focus, in addition, on areas of parent-child relationship, child-rearing practices, household conditions, or other factors which enter particularly into the expressed concern about the child. Symptoms of physical neglect and mis-

[32] What follows relies most heavily on Stamm's unpublished manuscript; *Standards for Child Protective Services; Report of the National Agencies Workshop;* Elliot Studt, "An Outline for the Study of Social Authority Factors in Casework," *Social Casework,* XXXV (June, 1954), 231–38; and Vincent De Francis, *The Fundamentals of Child Protection* (Denver: American Humane Association, 1955).

treatment are noted, but there must be equal attention to the manner of functioning in major areas of life, evidences of normal growth or retardation, and the nature of interpersonal relationships in the family.

The caseworker conducting the study requires particular skill at evaluating parental personality strengths and problems and recognizing evidences of serious pathology. He must be equipped, too, to identify some practices as typical of cultural subgroups in the community and not harmful to normal development, even though different and, perhaps, annoying to some community members, including the complainants. Whether or not efforts will ultimately be made to deal with deep-seated personality and social deviance in neglectful parents, the difficulties must be explored, understood, and evaluated, as the basis for decisions which must be made as to the need for community intervention and the nature of the intervention.

Since the objective is both immediate protection and, if possible, long-range help to restore the family (recognizing that some evaluations will show that there is no neglect in the legal sense) all contacts must be carried out with professional skill and with respect for individual rights and dignity. Parents have the right to know the nature of the complaint and the objectives of the protective agency. They often also need help "to express their shock, fear, anger, resistance or hostility" at the complaint and at community intervention. The full problem, community expectations and concerns, possible sources of help, and what is involved in change, all require discussion in terms which have meaning to the parents during initial interviews and later. Clear expression of respect for parents and regard for them is a prerequisite to strengthening them, if possible, in a sound parental role.

The caseworker from a protective agency is described as equipped with authority, by law or charter, to intervene and evaluate the children's situation.[33] This concept requires some clarification, however. As Wilson McKerrow has pointed out, the protective worker must have "the right to be in the situation" on the basis of law or agency charter. This is not the same as the policeman's role, nor does it eliminate the need for a police role described above.

[33] *Report of the National Agencies Workshop*, p. 12.

Collaboration between protective workers and the police dates back to the early S.P.C.C. days.

If there is no acute emergency and danger, and if the parent refuses to participate in an investigation, allegations and limited data are assembled and the court is called upon to authorize more formal intervention. The protective caseworker does not use strong-arm devices, since they defeat his goals and are unlawful as well. Thus, the real authority in protective casework is not coercive, except in the sense that there is an announced readiness to appeal to the court and a socially assigned charge to be persistent and responsible. At a later date, the caseworker's judgment that the conditions involved in the neglect have changed will also have great effect.

The essence of the protective caseworker's authority, during case evaluation and in the subsequent period of work with people, is, perhaps, his professional and psychological firmness and consistency, which are based on his charge to take the initiative in the relationship with the parents. Agency policies and procedures and the requirements of the law, as used by skilled caseworkers, are the framework for a process of social reeducation. Studt has described the psychological authority which develops in the relationship between worker and client as deriving from the competence and expertness of the caseworker and an ability to help which is demonstrated and available to the client for dealing with his problem.[34]

The literature of the protective field and the standards of all national groups concerned concur in the view that case evaluation can be carried out with greatest competence by staff who are trained in social casework. They must be prepared to be confronted by hostility, resistance, and extremely disturbing situations, psychologically and socially. They must give special attention, in their professional preparation, to the use of legal and psychological authority.

The investigation and case evaluation function has been discharged by voluntary protective societies (the Massachusetts S.P.C.C. or New York S.P.C.C., for example), by voluntary children's agencies which include a protective unit (Buffalo Children's

[34] Studt, "An Outline for the Study of Social Authority Factors in Casework," *Social Casework*, XXXV, 231–38.

Aid and S.P.C.C.), by county and city public welfare departments, or by child welfare programs conducted directly under state auspices.

Adjudication of status, service planning, and referral. The case evaluation by the protective agency leads, as does any case evaluation, to conclusions, recommendations, and plans. In some instances, brief or extensive exploration supports the view that there is no neglect and no need for any kind of service. Sometimes a service may be called for even though no neglect finding can be made. Such service, usually a referral, should be voluntarily offered —and clearly labeled as voluntary. Much more often the difficulties are clear, and a skilled caseworker will be able to make, with the client, a gradual and natural transition from the case study to a casework therapy process. To illustrate at random, referrals for housekeepers, day care, or vocational guidance may be part of the service. The relationship should continue until there is mutual readiness to terminate it; the agency cannot do so unless convinced that the children will be cared for properly.

Experience reveals that a protective service is severely hampered unless it encompasses within its own department, or has available through referral, facilities for direct casework treatment, homemaker services, day care, foster home care, temporary shelter care, institutional care, adoption, and specialized pediatric, psychological, and psychiatric services.[35]

Sometimes the protective agency or somebody else in the community must turn to the court. A case cannot be dropped, for instance, only because the client refuses to participate in case study. On other occasions, commmunity members or public officials may be convinced that formal court action and perhaps child placement are essential. They may wish to exercise their rights to charge neglect formally and to request a court hearing.

Under still other circumstances, the protective agency case evaluation may conclude that only a formal court finding of neglect and subsequent court supervision or placement of the children will help or protect the family. This conclusion may not be reached until a later point, after a period of casework treatment and a variety of services are used under the initiative of the protective worker.

[35] Ellen Winston, "The Responsibility of the State Public Welfare Agency for the Neglected Child," *NPPA Journal,* "Neglect," pp. 59–62.

Most juvenile court statutes define neglect and permit a variety of court dispositions after a neglect adjudication. There is obvious need to clarify court functions in such cases in addition to adjudication, if any.

Major national agencies interested in this field of service agreed to differentiate between acceptance and investigation of complaints, on the one hand, and action on neglect petitions, on the other. They felt that all complaints should be referred to child protective agencies, whether or not originally brought to the court, so that there might be the full, skilled evaluation and the offer of appropriate service described above. Where the investigation leads to a decision to file a petition, or where a formal application is made to invoke the court's judicial authority, the matter should have court attention. The court may adjudicate, decide about separation of parent and child, make determinations about custody, and so on.[36]

This formulation may prove rather difficult in practice. To a considerable extent, the dividing line between a complaint and a request for formal adjudication is in the orientation of the intake worker, whether in court or protective agency. It should be possible, nonetheless, to reach agreements within a given community that court intake will make referrals to the protective casework service of all those situations not absolutely requiring immediate court process. This would not preclude brief service, which any intake renders to cases coming directly to court. Nor would it deprive complainants, or those alleged to be neglectful, of the right to court consideration if they wished it.

Where an agency's experience with a family points to the need for court action, the protective agency must enter as the petitioner, and the case data provided should be adequate to sustain the allegations. Witnesses may be summoned and counterevidence offered. The probation staff may be subsequently called upon for a supplementary social study, not to evaluate the evidence as to neglect, but to assist the judge in his disposition.

Once the court decision is made, the protective agency is *one* resource for treatment among many available to the court. If the child remains in the home and a period of casework help is considered essential, the court must decide whether to call upon its probation department for supervision and treatment or whether

[36] *Report of the National Agencies Workshop*, p. 19.

to refer to the protective casework agency or to another source of service. The agency's prior role and the character of its relationship with the client might be the deciding factor, assuming that both staffs are equally available and well qualified. The probation officer's orientation in such cases should certainly be no different from that of the protective agency's caseworker. Specific community resources and the desirability of close court surveillance of the treatment may determine the choice between a protective casework service and probation supervision.[37]

Casework treatment of parents and children. The correction of unsatisfactory parental behavior is *not* achieved through assumption of parental responsibility by a caseworker, nor through intervention between parents and children within the home, nor through holding the parents to a standard by direct supervision, which includes a concrete list of "musts" and a system of checking up.

The casework treatment in the protective situation makes use of all social work services and methods, but, carried out in the context previously described, is characterized by application of formal and psychological authority. The service turns to the court only under the circumstances described above. Treatment might be undertaken in the specialized protective casework agency, in the probation department assigned supervision following neglect adjudication, or in almost any casework agency aware of the problems of working with highly resistant and disorganized people and willing to undertake the responsibility on court referral or on request of a protective agency.

Severe character disorders and psychoses are often found in the parents in these situations, but the caseworker who seeks to treat the parents so that the family will become a safe place for the child must be prepared for almost every diagnostic type and social complication. One study puts it this way:

Through emotional immaturity, instability or mental illness, an adult is incapable of responding to the demands the child makes on him, and because of his inadequacy, escapes from the situation by neglecting or at-

---

[37] In a unique and somewhat controversial plan in Baltimore, a judge who adjudicates a child as neglected and in need of care must assign legal custody to the Department of Public Welfare which determines whether placement is needed and carries out other necessary measures.

tacking the child and so performs acts of cruelty. The child may be merely a scapegoat for his warped passions, or the focus and victim of his difficulties.[38]

Internal emotional conflicts as well as tension and violence between the parents may often be part of the picture. One parent is often the complainant in neglect cases.

Effective treatment is frequently based on long periods of simple, helpful, friendly service, with understanding of backsliding and with necessary firmness which is nonpunitive. There are many frustrations, particularly in the earliest phases:

To expect such a client to come to the office for help on any regular basis, especially in the beginning of treatment, is as unrealistic as expecting a person with a broken leg to walk to the orthopedist to have it set.[39]

One would perhaps aspire, in all situations, "to help the parents restore or enhance their capacities as parents to the fullest potential, and to modify situational factors so that their children may have the opportunity to develop into mature adults able to handle parental functions in their turn." The obstacles are so many, however, that more modest attainments are more common: sustaining the child in his own home without damage, correcting specific defects in parental care, correcting and alleviating the effects on the child of prior parental mishandling. Between the optimum goal of full restoration and enhancement of capacities and the minimum acceptable objective of correcting legally intolerable conditions is the effort to "help the parents resolve those problems and modify those patterns which prevented or inhibited adequate parental functioning." [40] Most protective caseworkers would aspire to this.

This type of service and treatment demands well-qualified personnel. Dr. Irving Kaufman, who has worked intensively with the most disturbed of neglectful parents, and who has studied treatment problems, says that one must begin through use of community authority and that it is essential to "go out" to these people, for,

[38] *The Neglected Child and His Family*, p. 63.

[39] Irving Kaufman, "The Contribution of Protective Services," *Child Welfare*, XXXVI, No. 2 (February, 1957), 8–12.

[40] The formulations of alternatives are Stamm's. For a full statement of possible goals see *Standards for Child Protective Services*, pp. 24–25.

"bewildered by the disruptive forces which have swept over them, many of these parents need the protection and reality framework supplied by the caseworker's firm but consistent hand." The work, he finds, is in two phases: (*a*) a "supervisory protective role" in which the parent is helped to identify with a more adequate parent figure and (*b*) a more definitive dealing with basic causes.

Techniques include going into the home and reviewing the daily routines of when the family gets up, what they eat, and so on. Help with practical planning is often a good beginning. Unless the caseworker is identified from the start as interested in the entire family's welfare, he may tend to "solidify the pathologic aspects of the parent-child interaction." [41]

In work with children in the family, caseworkers will seek chiefly to help both parents and children to understand the intervention on a basis which does not harm the child or the relationship between parent and child. Should removal of children from the home be necessary, through court petition or by voluntary action of the parent, all the child welfare knowledge and skills relative to support and preparation prior to separation from the parents will have to come into play. Referrals will be necessary in many cases for specialized help to repair the physical, intellectual, and emotional consequences of neglect.

A number of cities have become interested in the programs developed in Europe whereby "training apartments" in public housing are used as the setting for family reeducation or acculturation in circumstances where the problem is severe but the potential encouraging.

The distribution of functions. The total protective process thus requires:

(1) full support of community members, agencies, and institutions in case finding and situation finding;
(2) children's courts for adjudication, disposition planning, and some treatment;
(3) a variety of social, therapeutic, and medical services to accept referrals;
(4) agencies offering protective casework service for case evalu-

[41] Kaufman, "The Contribution of Protective Services," *Child Welfare*, XXXVI, 8–12. See the full article for a profound review of treatment tasks.

ation, for initiative in court proceedings, and for treatment of parents and children, as necessary;

(5) police readiness to enter for emergency protection and removal of children.

Protective casework is now generally defined either as a specialty within the scope of child welfare services or as part of the general child welfare job. Because of regional differences, it would be inappropriate to specify one organizational pattern. The protective casework agency may be public or voluntary, depending on the local situation. If public, the program may be administered by either the locality or the state. The state's obligation to ensure the provision of service by *some* agency has been widely recognized. Language for incorporation into existing state welfare and juvenile court statutes has recently been proposed in order to specify this obligation and to suggest objectives.[42] In an era of expanding public welfare and few new large-scale voluntary developments, it seems likely that the bulk of the specialized protective casework programs, or child welfare programs which include protective service, will be established by public departments. Most standard-setting groups favor this in principle.

Important federal support for the child protective effort began in fact with the 1935 Social Security Act. States enacted laws to conform with the federal law, and expressed their responsibility for "child welfare services for the protection and care of homeless, dependent and neglected children, and children in danger of becoming delinquent." Programs known as "services to children in their own homes" have been initiated under these provisions and have included protective casework within their scope.

Funds were originally devoted principally to rural areas, but recent amendments to the Social Security Act (1958) permit the expansion of urban child welfare services. Some public assistance funds have also become available. There has, however, been concern at the general lack of social services in Aid to Needy Families with Children and other assistance programs granting funds to families for millions of children. The Congress and the Department

---

[42] Children's Division, the American Humane Association, *Suggested Language for Legislation on Child Protective Services* (Denver, 1958). This is Part 2 of the *Report of National Agencies Workshop*.

of Health, Education, and Welfare launched measures in 1962 to remedy this situation and to ensure greater coordination between child welfare programs and public assistance programs involving children.[43]

ORGANIZING FOR CHILD PROTECTION

New York City is in transition from complete reliance on voluntary S.P.C.C.'s to creation of a public protective service in its Welfare Department which will share responsibility with the voluntary agencies. Review of what is involved in this change may serve to clarify in some additional detail the requirements of a protective program.

The programs today. New York County (Manhattan) houses the parent society of all voluntary child protective agencies. When created in 1875 by an act of the legislature, it was dedicated to "the prevention of cruelty to children and the enforcement of the laws relating to or in any wise affecting children." Similar societies followed in the other New York City counties: Brooklyn and Richmond S.P.C.C.'s in 1880, Bronx S.P.C.C. in 1915, Queens S.P.C.C. in 1920.

It was clear from legislative enactments, reinforced by court opinion, that the intent was to create quasi-public agencies and to vest in them powers ordinarily granted only to public agencies. The societies' agents, although privately hired and not subject to public control, were designated as peace officers, i.e., "A constable or police officer *must*, and an agent or officer of any incorporated society for the prevention of cruelty to children *may*, arrest and bring before a court . . . any persons offending [against children, and] . . . may interfere to prevent the perpetration of any act forbidden . . . A person who obstructs or interferes with any officer or agent . . . is guilty of a misdemeanor." [Italics added.]

The quasi-official status also derived from other assignments of responsibility. Although not necessarily attorneys, society agents were empowered to present evidence in court. Societies were given

[43] Elizabeth Wickenden and Winifred Bell, *Public Welfare: Time for a Change* (New York: New York School of Social Work, Columbia University, 1961). Also, State Letters Nos. 538–540, Bureau of Public Assistance, Department of Health, Education, and Welfare (Washington, D.C., 1961) and Public Law 87–543 (1962).

the right to investigate and make recommendations with reference to applications for appearances of children as entertainers, prior to action by the mayor on the applications.

Most important, special legal provision gave the societies the right to make complaints before the court about violations affecting children, to aid "in presenting the law and facts to such court, to become guardian of the person of a minor child and to accept court commitments and to receive the aid of all magistrates and peace officers in enforcement of laws relating to children." Subsequent provision in the Domestic Relations Court law specified the societies' rights to accept children in detention.[44]

The S.P.C.C.'s long stressed their law enforcement responsibilities. Their mission was to "receive . . . every child suffering from brutal treatment or living in degrading surroundings," and they did it with enthusiasm and dedication. Some of the societies seemed to lack understanding or concern for the parents, while others stressed the family unit from the beginning. Laws necessary for child protection were formulated and actively championed. The New York S.P.C.C. rejected supervision by the State Board of Charities on the ground that the S.P.C.C. "is not a charitable organization but a prosecuting instrument. It is an auxiliary government agency." This position was upheld by the Court of Appeals in 1900.

Transitions are often slow when there is long, traditional dedication to a way of doing things. However, modern social and psychological understanding began to reach some of the S.P.C.C. personnel. Personnel trained in social work schools entered some of the programs. The emphasis on preservation of the home where possible was proclaimed loudly at the first (1909) White House Conference, implemented in Mothers' Pension Laws, and adopted as a principle by the new U.S. Children's Bureau in 1912. This principle had great influence in all areas of child care. Correction and prevention became the objectives in work with parents, replacing the old assumption that one could protect children by punishing their parents.

[44] Documented in the Department of Investigation and Accounts, City of New York, *A Study of the Societies for the Prevention of Cruelty to Children in New York City* (New York: City of New York, 1936, mimeographed), pp. 1–18.

In New York City, the Brooklyn S.P.C.C. was one of the first affected by the new, humane concept and by the added knowledge. In 1930 it spoke thus of its past:

> The Society looked back on its accomplishments both with pride and sorrow. It was proud of the role it had played in furthering necessary protective legislation . . . it was proud that it had awakened a community consciousness for the welfare of its children . . . it was proud of its record of . . . protective service . . . and temporary shelter.
>
> Its sorrow stemmed not from anything it had wilfully done wrong, but rather from the things it had left undone or done inadequately, in the light of the knowledge it had gained in fifty years. In its early days too much emphasis had been placed on prosecutions and not enough on rehabilitation and prevention and only the most casual inquiry had been made into the causes of individual family breakdown—children were too quickly removed from homes that were labeled unfit. They were then placed in institutions or sent to foster homes about which little or nothing was known.[45]

The other New York City societies were not prepared to join Brooklyn in this kind of statement as early as 1930; some may not be yet. Brooklyn itself has lacked the resources and support essential to following all the implications of what it saw thirty years ago and has learned since that time.

The several different and independent S.P.C.C.'s in the New York area have evolved to varied stages of professionalization and skill. The Staten Island society is no longer active and all but Queens have ended their shelter programs. With one possible exception all face problems of limited resources and provide only part of the volume of service required in their counties. Because the sum total of all voluntary protective services in the city could provide only a very small portion of the obviously needed protective casework, New York City began to move in late 1961 toward a measure of public provision. Description of one of the most developed programs, that in Brooklyn, will serve as a point of departure for characterizing the voluntary provision and the manner in which public services may develop.

[45] The Brooklyn Society for the Prevention of Cruelty to Children, *Fiftieth Annual Report* (1930), as quoted in *Seventy-five Years of Protecting Brooklyn's Helpless Children* (New York, 1955), p. 4. For more detail about New York programs see Alfred J. Kahn, *Protecting New York City's Children* (New York: Citizens' Committee for Children of New York, Inc., 1961).

The Brooklyn S.P.C.C. has "law enforcement" and casework services. The former involves a publicly subsidized service in cases of sex offenses against children: emotional support to parents and children involved; advice to the district attorney relative to prosecutions; medical examinations; arrangements for prenatal care; efforts to speed the cases through court. The service is valued by the district attorney but it need not enter into basic issues of function; in most communities it might be rendered by well-staffed probation departments.

The casework service receives allegations of child neglect and abuse, approximately 1,700 to 2,600 cases annually over the past five years, involving six to seven thousand children. Cases get to the S.P.C.C. through parental referral (often a complaint by a separated parent), individuals in the community, relatives, schools, anonymous sources, and other agencies—in the given order of frequency. For lack of resources the Brooklyn S.P.C.C. discourages or rejects many potential cases. It refers to the Welfare Department all situations involving children already on the department rolls and turns over to the police all emergencies and anonymous complaints.

This is a casework service—despite difficulties in recruiting and holding an adequate number of qualified caseworkers. The staff uses casework methods in accepting complaints of neglect and in evaluating the extent of parental failure and parental capacity for adequate functioning. Where appropriate, direct casework help is offered or referrals are made. Even though parental resistance may be strong, the casework staff considers itself under obligation to stay with a situation until certain that the children will not suffer seriously. Where parents are not reached and children are endangered, a neglect petition is filed in court. Court is occasionally turned to when treatment considerations in a case suggest the need, despite overt parental cooperation.

Only a very small proportion of new cases are actually accepted for full study and (where needed) continued service by the casework staff. One third are found, following clearance, to be under the care of other agencies and are not served. Many others are referred immediately by the intake unit to other agencies to which they were not already known. Over one third require information and consultation service and nothing more, and about 1 percent are improper referrals. The intake unit responsible for this preliminary screening is staffed with the society's most experienced caseworkers. Because of its resource shortages, the Brooklyn society has done everything possible to encourage other voluntary casework agencies to increase their services in neglect cases so that they will refer to S.P.C.C. only cases requiring "more authoritative treatment." [46]

Cases assigned to the casework division beyond intake do not all involve intensive treatment. Following investigation, a good number of additional cases are referred for service to public or private agencies, or to court. Some cases show no basis for action and others are "adjusted" satisfactorily quite rapidly. Some cases are served over a longer period. The staff stresses home visits, work with community sources vital to the family, and a responsible "staying with the case" approach.

All other New York City voluntary S.P.C.C.'s are somewhat less developed in the direction of a casework division, because of problems of resources and staffing or (in the instance of the Manhattan society) because they do not accept the concept. Special attention to the latter aspect will clarify some issues in relation to the planning of services in the future.

The Manhattan society long stressed "law enforcement" and "rescue" work, narrowly defined, but was described in the 1930s as beginning to place more stress on the adjustment of children in their own homes and on the use of court as a last resort. It has nonetheless refused over the years to identify itself as a social agency and has persisted in the view upheld by the court years ago that it is not a "charity" and not subject to supervision by the State Social Welfare Department.

Annual reports do point to a philosophy of helping and rehabilitation and a readiness to do "field work," where other agencies may prefer office interviews. It is not clear how well the society is equipped to carry this out. Three phases of the work are identified: the handling of neglect complaints, prosecution of offenses (usually sexual) against children, and review of applications for child entertainers. Apparently the same staff members do the law enforcement work and handle neglect allegations.

[46] Brooklyn Society for the Prevention of Cruelty to Children, 79 *Years of Protecting Children* (New York, 1960).

Case totals are large—neglect complaints in a recent year involved the welfare of over 5,000 children. Referral sources are not specified in detail, but a little less than half of these cases originated in public agencies, probably Children's Court and the Welfare Department for the most part. A good number are cases in which evidence of neglect is noted in court and the judge merely asks the S.P.C.C. representative to serve as petitioner (on "information and belief") so that the case may be officially placed before the court for neglect. The New York S.P.C.C. took about 15 percent of its neglect cases to Children's Court in 1959.

While others would add to casework resources, the Manhattan S.P.C.C. continues to insist that the S.P.C.C. is and should remain a law enforcement service—not a casework agency:

The Society becomes active, generally speaking, when it is alleged that laws enacted to protect children against neglect or penal laws intended to safeguard them are being violated. It investigates complaints of neglect and initiates neglect proceedings before the Children's Court when indicated in the child's best interest. Such investigations are not merely routine inquiries. Specialized knowledge of the law and rules of evidence are essential. Where the child requires the protection of the Court, the investigation must develop sufficient admissible evidence to sustain the petition. Failure to fully develop and properly present evidence to the Court could result in dismissal of the proceedings which might be interpreted by the respondents as a license to continue the neglectful conduct and the child's plight would be worse than ever.

Although the facts developed by the investigation may not indicate present need for Children's Court action, the family situation may be such that it cannot be ignored. It may be expected to benefit from casework services. *The Society does not consider providing casework service to be its function.* It must seek to refer the family to an appropriate agency. Unfortunately, this is not always possible in view of intake requirements. Therefore, because of necessity rather than choice, it sometimes must keep open longer than it would like, cases more appropriately handled by casework agencies.

. . . . .

. . . it would be desirable if the Society could dispose of matters without undue delay by court action or agency referral. It is to be hoped that intake requirements of casework agencies will become more flexible and aggressive casework more available so that, when appropriate, successful referrals can be made in more cases.[47] [Italics added.]

[47] From a communication from Thomas T. Becker dated October 20, 1958; full text in *Protecting New York City's Children*, pp. 27–30.

Planning for the future. In short, New York City—like many other cities—faces a problem of systematic allocation and integration of protective *functions* and the assurance of adequate *protective case-work coverage.* Its voluntary S.P.C.C.'s are unable to meet the latter need because of problems of resources and, in at least one instance, concept of role. The serious community vacuum which results may be underscored with one specific illustration. The family doctor or the member of a medical group in a health plan is a potentially crucial case finder. Especially in middle-class homes, he sees evidence of neglect or physical abuse of children which will not come to an agency's attention. He notes which parents do not follow through prescribed medical routines, and he encounters extremely eccentric parental behavior. Today, the doctor who would do anything about these things find the prospect discouraging. He must search out the correct channels and be willing to submit and validate a statement of his concerns. Since he has not undertaken to do a comprehensive study, he is reluctant. If he is a private physician, he may hesitate to lose a patient as well, especially when there is no substitute for whatever service he has been able to give.

A community needs, but many do not have, a widely known agency or unit with sufficient staff to explore such situations on referral. Other professionals, like doctors, will begin to carry through their responsibilities only when they are clear about procedures, sure about follow-through, and have evidence of the competence of the protective service.

The New York State Social Welfare Law (which is typical in this regard) authorizes welfare commissioners and city public welfare officers to carry out relevant services. The applicable sections of the law in Section 398 read as follows:

2. As to neglected or abandoned children:
    (a) Investigate the alleged neglect or abandonment of a child and, if necessary, bring the case before the court for adjudication and care for the child until the court acts in the matter.
    (b) Receive and care for any child alleged to be neglected or abandoned who is temporarily placed in his care by a children's court pending adjudication by such court of the alleged neglect or abandonment; and receive and care for any neglected or aban-

doned child committed or discharged to his care by a children's court.

· · · ·

6. As to all foregoing classes of children:
   (a) Investigate the family circumstances of each child reported to him as destitute, neglected, delinquent, defective or physically handicapped in order to determine what assistance and care, supervision or treatment, if any, such child requires.
   (b) Provide for expert mental and physical examination of any child whom he has reason to suspect of mental or physical defect or disease and pay for such examination from public funds, if necessary.

Under these provisions, all counties in the state which do not have S.P.C.C.'s (i.e., all except Erie, Monroe, Westchester, Nassau, and four New York City counties) have assigned full protective casework responsibility to their child welfare departments. Occasionally, some specialized staff handles the work, but it is usually part of the child welfare task. Only Onondaga County has created a special protective unit.

New York City has come to recognize that S.P.C.C.'s cannot perform all functions in a total protective process and that a public welfare department must have a major role in the planning. Relevant, too, is the current concept that police powers are not in the domain of a private organization. New plans are being drawn. Inevitably such planning must consider both distribution of responsibilities and pattern of organization. Equally important, any plan made should ensure sufficient protective service and the necessary related resources, services, and facilities.

Case finding is everybody's obligation, and situation finding is a responsibility of every social agency. The juvenile aid police have particular responsibilities in their patrol assignments for detecting hazardous conditions and taking necessary steps. A special case finding and protective role in the schools has been outlined in Chapter V.

When children are in danger of personal harm, the matter should be reported to the Youth Division of the Police Department (or its equivalent). Police are legally equipped to remove a child from his home in such an emergency, and to get him to shelter or court, depending on the hour and the circumstances. They are trained to guard individual rights in the process. They can move rapidly. The police will, themselves, detect some of these situations; others will be reported by community members. Both police and social agencies have turned to S.P.C.C.'s in the past for such action, but it now seems clear that the peace officer role, though appropriate in its time and though still in the statutes, is incongruous in a modern city, equipped with a Police Youth Division or police Juvenile Bureau.

The police and district attorney are responsible, respectively, for decisions about arrest and prosecution in cases of sex offenses against children. If police are equipped with a well-staffed and capably led youth service it is both efficient and appropriate for all arrest situations involving alleged adult offenses against minors to be referred for immediate police exploration, screening, and advice. Police youth staff are, or should be, capable of the sensitive interviewing, emotional support, and clarification of procedures in these difficult and tension-charged cases. If appropriate, such cases might in turn be referred to a protective casework service.

When the case reaches court calendars, similar service should be rendered by the probation department. Cases of this kind belong not in adult courts but in a family and children's court equipped with a probation bureau able to provide necessary consultation to the district attorneys and service to the children and their parents.

The S.P.C.C.'s should thus be asked to give up their *peace officer* and *law enforcement* roles. There is no question about their backgrounds and legal rights in these fields, but changing times and the scope of existing needs suggest new arrangements. As responsible social agencies, S.P.C.C.'s will always want to retain the potential for *situation finding* and for initiating and supporting legislation relating to their concern.

The function that remains is *protective casework:* the intake, case evaluation, referrals, and casework treatment agreed by all to represent the core of services to safeguard children today.

Although the Child Welfare League calls for a public unit in each community and although most service of this kind is publicly rendered, some authorites hold that once the police task is assigned to the police, there is no absolute requirement that protective casework be lodged in a public agency. The National Agencies Workshop, it will be recalled, urged provision in the state's social welfare law for state responsibility to see to it that the service is lodged *somewhere*. From this viewpoint, local history and agency conditions determine which agency, public or voluntary, actually renders the service. Yet New York City S.P.C.C.'s—with one possible exception—are unable to render the necessary service without almost full public subsidy. In addition, the New York County society defines its role in terms quite different from the national trend or the need here described. Planning must also be affected by the answer to a key question: Can the right to pursue a complaint and to continue an interest in a family, in which children may be in danger, be lodged anywhere but in a department responsible to the public? Citizens understand legal authority delegated to a public department and also know that provisions exist to protect their rights. Most twentieth-century protective casework programs have developed in public departments for this reason. Also not to be ignored is the practical consideration that a large portion of neglect cases originate in families on public assistance rolls, families known to a public agency and more readily reached by an agency which has previous "leverage." In recent years a significant number of communities have created public-welfare-based protective services.[48] Recently, too, legislation has called upon welfare departments concerned with the suitability of home environments of the children in relief families to make referrals for protective service and court action.

For historical reasons which are understandable but which have had a variety of undesirable effects [49] state and local child welfare programs (the casework and service programs) have tended to be organized separately from and not to be well integrated with public assistance programs. The latter (Aid to Needy Families with Children in particular) contain the bulk of the cases of children

[48] Gus B. Lange, "Facilities for Neglected Children in the Portland, Ore., Urban Area," *NPPA Journal*, "Neglect," pp. 44–47. Also see Welfare Federation of Cleveland, "Report from the Committee on Protective Services to Children in the Case Work Council," (Cleveland, 1957, mimeographed). Also see *The Cleveland Story* (Denver: American Humane Association, 1959). Also, Elizabeth Cooper, "Pilot Study of Protective Services in Los Angeles," *NPPA Journal*, "Neglect," pp. 56–58.

[49] Wickenden and Bell, *Public Welfare.*

living under hazardous situations and in need of urgent services. Efforts are currently under way nationally and in many states to integrate these services, making child welfare casework available to assistance cases or creating well-staffed casework services for assistance cases needing intensive work. Protective programs are being expanded in this context in a variety of administrative patterns.

To illustrate: New York City's welfare program has tended in the past to view public child welfare services as residual provision, filling in gaps which could not be managed by voluntary agencies. The latter have had considerable public subsidy toward their work. In recent decades, however, changes in the volume of programs and the character of need have underscored the unsatisfactory nature of such provision and the extent to which many children remain, as the result, under "temporary" arrangements in shelter for many months and years—and the extent to which families in crisis lack needed casework help, homemakers, day care, and other resources. The city is now moving to remedy this situation by the strengthening of its public child welfare services through creation of an expanded decentralized program.

It is thus natural, as a first step in New York City, that decentralized protective services under public welfare be lodged in child welfare in this first phase. Plans are now under way along these lines.[50] Concurrently provision must be made to strengthen the role of public assistance workers in case finding and first-line service—to decrease the need for specialized protective services. Gradually, the city will have available a case finding network in public assistance, specialized decentralized offices able to accept allegations of neglect from all sources and to become involved in intake as appropriate, a system of protective casework, liaison with youth police for emergency purposes, and provision for protective service access to specialized resources which may help to preserve family life where possible: intensive casework, homemakers, medical service, short-range foster care.

Given such development, S.P.C.C.'s so qualified by staffing and orientation might continue to offer an intake service to those who

[50] Laurin Hyde Associates, *Protective Services for the Children of New York City: A Plan of Action* (New York, 1962).

choose to call upon them. More important, several might offer ongoing, intensive treatment services to disorganized, neglectful, "multiproblem" families. In addition, they have much to teach the new public service in a transition period about creating centers to which allegations will be channeled and about the early phases of case processing.

These general lines of development would seem to have broader applicability, the ultimate objective being a protective program in an integrated public welfare setup buttressed by police and school services on the one hand and voluntary agencies (including S.P.C.C.'s which are involved in treatment or situation finding and legislative matters) on the other.

Finally, it should be said, there are few general categories of cases more in need of an accountability system than cases of alleged abuse or neglect. The system established by the community to keep them in focus (Ch. XII) is an important part of over-all protective provision.

CHAPTER X

INTERVENTION, SERVICE, AND
TREATMENT IN THE COMMUNITY

IN GENERAL, the chapters in Part B have been organized to suggest the movement from case finding ("open door," "schools," "police") to evaluation ("court," "protective programs") to treatment. However, agencies may have several tasks and we have seen how schools, protective agencies, and courts develop specialized ongoing services appropriate to their institutional functions and relationships with people. This chapter and the next one concentrate on agencies and institutions with a primary service or treatment assignment.

Situation finding and case finding bring under the community spotlight a wide range of neighborhood, group, family, and individual phenomena. It is possible, quite frequently, to deal with the vulnerable, the exposed, those in clear danger at a point prior to the development of fixed antisocial patterns or personality symptomatology. But it is also necessary, and on a very large scale, to act with and on behalf of those whose lives are considerably disorganized, whose values may be distorted, and whose patterns of response and relationship are identified as forms of mental illness.

No one term describes adequately all the actions called for in the interest of the larger community, neighborhoods, groups, or individuals concerned. There are those who would talk of "planned change," a helpful concept if broadly defined.[1] Perhaps the word "intervention" is a most useful way of suggesting purposeful action

---

[1] Ronald Lippett, Jeanne Watson, Bruce Westley, *The Dynamics of Planned Change* (New York: Harcourt, Brace and Company, 1958).

to interpose new influences into an ongoing situation or to seek new directions. Some actions, particularly those involved with the provision of specific resources or facilities, are best encompassed by the term "service," whereas professional efforts to arrest, cure, or change pathological processes are called "treatment." These are hardly well-defined or mutually exclusive categories of action; indeed, the boundaries between them are not at all sharp and to an extent the terms refer to differences in perspective rather than in operations. Nonetheless, they serve to suggest that children in trouble and their families are served and helped in a multiplicity of ways by many types of program and many categories of people.

We have already presented (Ch. III) the range of required interventions, treatments, and service specializations which come to the fore following competent case and situation appraisal. Deferring, for the moment, the components of a diversified system of facilities for those children who must be helped away from home and noting that protective services have had special attention, there remains a long list which ranges from psychiatric clinics and family agencies to vocational guidance, group services, in-patient and out-patient medical care, probation, big brothers and big sisters, religious guidance, homemakers, foster care, public assistance, neighborhood self-help, and so on.

Clearly, the present chapter must be somewhat different from most of the others. We shall not be able to describe and to review current standards for all major forms of intervention, service, or treatment since this alone would require a full volume. Nor shall we be able to look at any one city's total service network as it affects clients and patients. A somewhat different approach is appropriate—and possible. We shall consider *the most promising currents in philosophy, theory, and method as they are relevant to the major programs serving those who are here in focus.* We shall illustrate from efforts throughout the country, not necessarily giving special attention to New York. That which is familiar, widespread, and traditional will not be mentioned—not out of negative evaluation but rather to conserve space for newer approaches which require description.

Particularly since World War II, new directions and emphases in a variety of agencies and programs have added considerably to the potency and range of the armamentarium available for coping with the problems at hand. In fact, to some degree, developments of the past two decades have for the first time led to definition of certain types of individuals, families, and groups as candidates for hopeful intervention, whereas they were once seen only as "hopeless" or "uncooperative." We shall, therefore, begin with a review of some of the new notes struck in professional philosophy and some of the more promising emerging components of theory and method which reflect this new attitude.

In a sense, of course, some of the relevant themes have already been sounded, if briefly, in discussion of such specific programs as probation or the "open door" in the family agency. There is place, however, for a more systematic review.

THE NEED FOR A POST WORLD WAR II BREAKTHROUGH

The developments here under discussion did not all begin at one specific point or in response to one specific influence. Some go back to earlier points in American social science or in the histories of social work, psychology, and psychiatry. Minor themes which once occupied only a few individuals or agencies found new support. Nonetheless, for the most part, it remains true that the approach in the 1960s to children and families in trouble is different from the approach in the early 1940s. As we outline the major sources of pressure for change and the components of the new approach, the strokes must perforce be broad and countercurrents and exceptions will not be given adequate attention. This may perhaps be justified in the interest of the main ideas which must be conveyed. The validity of the basic analysis is strongly confirmed by any review of professional literature of the past twenty years.

Psychoanalytic emphasis. Why, then, were changes inevitable? First, perhaps, because the "psychoanalytic deluge" of the period immediately after World War II offered a method of intervention not suitable to many of those who needed to be helped. Social work had welcomed psychiatry early and gained much from it, beginning in the 1920s. A variety of external pressures tempered the absorption of psychoanalytic concepts and methods into environmentally oriented services and methods: the depression, the refugee situation, the war emergency, the postwar adjustment. Nonetheless, by the end of World War II, the number of psychoanalytically trained social workers had increased severalfold, the supply of psychiatrists available as consultants or as team members had risen, and psychiatric clinic work or psychoanalytically oriented family casework was the high-prestige activity in social work. While there were many more untrained or partially trained workers dealing with clients than there were those who had full professional training, which included preparation for work in a clinical team, the professional literature, supervision, and role models reflected what must be described as a "deluge."

All of this certainly added to the effectiveness of work with neurotic patients, yet a large component in the public assistance caseload in times of high employment is a diagnostic group most recently called the "character disorders." "Character disorders" are also a predominant diagnostic group in families which abuse or neglect children and in which there are high rates of other disordered behavior.

Similarly, whereas the psychoanalytic emphasis added much to intervention with middle-class clients, it did not do as much for those in the working class, the source of the bulk of delinquency and neglect cases now in the courts and agencies. Psychoanalytic therapies had been shown to be valuable for the well-educated, but could they be expected to reach the new arrivals or those whose social or cultural patterns did not encourage them to talk about their problems, to formulate them in abstract terms, or to share them with outsiders?[2] Perhaps, most important of all, no matter how effective psychiatric service might be where delinquency or neglect was a matter of intrapsychic factors, it could not hope to reach—at least at a reasonably early stage—those many situations where group, neighborhood, and cultural factors were at work. Thus, there was need for a shifting of balance.

Individual emphasis. Some of the troubled and the vulnerable could not be served by the treatment emphases of the early 1940s because of the assumption that intervention is necessarily on the level of the individual. The entire structure of case finding, par-

[2] See August B. Hollingshead and Fredrich C. Redlich, *Social Class and Mental Illness* (New York: John Wiley and Sons, Inc., 1958). Also, Jerome K. Meyers and Bertram H. Roberts, *Family and Class Dynamics in Mental Illness* (New York: John Wiley and Sons, Inc., 1959); Gerald Gurin, Joseph Veroff, Sheila Field, *Americans View Their Mental Health* (New York: Basic Books, Inc., 1960).

ticularly that associated with individualized justice, is a force in this direction. If one tries to understand influences and motivations, while protecting fully the rights of each individual, one tends to emerge with a "remedy" oriented to the individual case and a methodology which is conceived in individual terms.

Yet certain *types* of problems, at specific *stages,* are not affected on this level. For example, the member of the teen-age antisocial gang who is not yet in the hands of the law has problems in the realm of values and goals which are probably best approached as part of an approach to the group. Later, perhaps, he may require individual help or guidance. Albert Cohen, to illustrate, has pointed out that the delinquent gang member he has studied finds it difficult to change without group support and is more readily reached as part of a change-effort directed at group values.

Similarly, even in the instance of intrapsychic problems, there may be specific age or diagnostic categories which respond best to interventions organized on a group basis.

Finally, it may be, as we shall suggest, that neighborhood "self-help" approaches are the method of choice even to change *individuals* under some circumstances.

Resistance as an intrapsychic problem. An emphasis on the individual under all circumstances and a psychoanalytic orientation combined to create a situation in which agencies and services tended to interpret most client nonparticipation, noncooperation, withdrawal, or hostility as a psychiatric problem in "resistance." Explanations would be sought in developmental and personality terms.

In one sense, this was an old "charity organization" moral evaluation in new dress. For the early nineteenth-century friendly visitor tended to differentiate the "worthy" from the "unworthy" poor in part on the basis of their ability to take advice and to follow prescribed courses of conduct. The "unworthy" were left to the "poor law authorities." Modern psychiatry provided diagnostic categories which offered no hope ("constitutional psychopath") and the "resistance" concept which placed the problem in the client rather than in the therapist. Or, at least, there were many who felt able to use the explanation "client will not cooperate" to mean that there was present a degree of client resistance beyond agency ability or responsibility to affect.

Not adequately encompassed by such formulation is information about the ways in which social, ethnic, and cultural factors influence perception and cognition, or about the ways in which background affects role expectations, ways of perceiving problems, manner of asking help, and so on. Clearly, the entire "resistance" and "noncooperation" concept required reanalysis.

Authority as precluding a helping relationship. On the level of ideology, the most serious obstacle to the adequate development of casework services in probation, parole, institutions, and juvenile police programs was a very limited concept of the role of authority in a helping relationship. This stemmed in part from an era of "passivity" in casework technique, a reflection of the early psychoanalytic influence in which the caseworker sought to facilitate client "catharsis." More basically, it was a natural result of a treatment model in which a voluntary, self-motivating client came in search of personal insight—and all deviations were taken as lacking the essence of treatment. It was assumed that casework could not be practiced in an authoritative setting and that the historical separation of "charities" from "corrections" had been wise. Caseworkers who persisted in probation work were considered to be outside of the professional mainstream.

But a few inventive workers refused to give up so vast a field of practice and insisted on looking at the matter as an unsolved issue: "Can casework be practiced in such settings?" they asked. Ultimately however, the concept of authority itself required analysis and reconsideration before the field could be opened up to hopeful work. Social work, psychology, and psychiatry had to learn that all professional helping relationships have authority components and that these must be understood and dealt with in specific ways.

Building-centered programs. Other types of breakthrough were also necessary. With some exceptions, the group services field had tended toward a building-centered approach in its programing. This was certainly not the tradition, since the earliest settlements had not been "houses" in the modern sense, and they had been characterized by broad experimentation. Yet professionalization had brought standardization of method and structure.

Group workers, the social work professionals in group service programs, were thus negating part of their professional tradition in permitting themselves to be tied in their programing to buildings. They were not taking account of cultural attitudes and ethnic attitudes to agencies controlled by a majority group bent on promoting acculturation and social control. And they were forgetting what they actually knew about adolescence and the tendencies of adolescents to want to "gang" away from adult leadership and to solve together some of the problems of the transition from childhood to adulthood.

The prefabricated clinic unit. Another, still potent, stereotype must also be mentioned among those undermining the effectiveness of agencies. Once the child guidance clinic became a unit with defined professional roles and some reputation for therapeutic success, the assumption gained currency that it could be attached in its one pure form to a variety of settings which would thereby become effective treatment centers: schools, courts, children's institutions. We have already discussed consequences in schools and courts. In the children's insitutions (see Ch. XI), social workers, psychologists, and psychiatrists acted as though they believed that daily life and education could continue on their own, in rather neutral fashion, while an occasional "fifty-minute hour" became the most salient of initiators of change. In daily reality, of course, the clinic was rendered very weak and ineffective by isolation from daily living. This, too, had to be taken into account.

FORCES ON THE SIDE OF CHANGE

The need for a breakthrough—or a series of changes—was inherent in the outmoded and inadequate assumptions and consequent problems of existing programs. It received its impetus, too, from the rate of failure, recidivism, withdrawal, and noneligibility for existing services—at a time that rates of reported delinquency, neglect, disorganization, and personality disturbance continued to rise and the public sought greater effectiveness in return for its increasing investment.

There were also a variety of other developments which contributed to change. Most important, perhaps, was the new impact of social science on social work and on psychiatry. This occurrence has been described and analyzed in other contexts.[3] For present pur-

[3] Alfred J. Kahn, "Sociology and Social Work: Challenge and Invitation," *Social Problems*, IV (January, 1957), 220–28. Also, "The Nature of Social

poses we might note that social work had been rooted in late nineteenth-century social science and had deserted it when, as social philosophy, it offered little by way of dynamic analysis of the clients' current situations and provided few clues to planned intervention and change. The social science to which social work could "return" after World War II had gone through a period of empiricism. It had been called upon to address itself to current realities. In some of its branches it was emphasizing concepts and levels of abstraction which made it useful to professional practice. Moreover, some of its most creative practitioners were willing to concern themselves with problems of social practice. To illustrate the new "availability" of social science we mention mid-century work in' social stratification, small groups, the family, organizational (bureaucratic) theory, urban sociology, contemporary cultures, criminology, and penology.[4] The emergence of functional sociology and anthropology offered an approach to theory familiar to those trained in Freudian psychodynamics. Strong support to this entire development came from the program of grants, internships, research, and publications of the Russell Sage Foundation, in particular, and later from other foundations and the National Institute of Mental Health. The psychometricians, too, began to serve clinical situations by the imaginative development of projective techniques. In general, social science could be integrated with rather than opposed to the dynamic psychologies.

Professional inventiveness during World War II, spurred on by manpower shortages, had led to a variety of types of experimenta-

---

Work Knowledge," in Cora Kasius, ed., New Directions in Social Work (New York: Harper & Brothers, 1954), pp. 194–214; Ernest Greenwood, "Social Science and Social Work—a Theory of Their Relationship," Social Service Review, XXIX (1955), 20–33; Herman D. Stein, "The Concept of the Environment in Social Work Practice," Smith College Studies in Social Work (June, 1960), pp. 187–210.

[4] Note, for example, the range of social science excerpts which could be reproduced in Herman D. Stein and Richard A. Cloward, eds., Social Perspectives on Behavior (Glencoe, Ill.: The Free Press, 1958). Other helpful volumes, to illustrate from several sources, are: Kurt Lewin, Field Theory in Social Science (New York: Harper & Brothers, 1951); A. Paul Hare, Edgar Borgetta, Robert F. Bales, eds., Small Groups (New York: Alfred A. Knopf, 1955); Robert K. Merton, Leonard Broom, Leonard S. Cottrell, Jr., eds., Sociology Today (New York: Basic Books, Inc., 1959).

tion with therapeutic groups. Inevitably, psychiatrists, psychologists, and social workers continued the pattern of innovation on their return to civilian life. Since these steps were now backed by strong social science underpinning, treatment would never again be conceived of only in individual terms.

There were other forces. Within "corrections" itself, there were impulses toward professionalization, as there were in many emerging fields in the modern world. Several disciplines were suggested as the base for this field of practice. After a period of debate, leadership groups, including the National Council on Crime and Delinquency (then the National Probation and Parole Association), defined probation, parole, and certain roles in the detention and correctional administration field as within the province of social work. Given such identification, and offered opportunity within the National Association of Social Workers and the Council on Social Work Education, a small group of well-equipped correctional personnel began to effect basic orientations toward this work and, in turn, all social work service. On the governmental level, after World War II, a special juvenile delinquency project in the U.S. Children's Bureau also supported and accelerated this development, eventually to be replaced by a permanent delinquency division which develops and publicizes standards, encourages innovations, and seeks to help solve personnel needs.

Within the field of psychiatry itself, there were internal dynamics which led to more attention to ego problems—a subject which might take us far afield. Important here is the fact that this, too, affected concepts of client and therapist role, goals, and methods and gave status to objectives which in an earlier era would have been defined as "too superficial." What is more, ego psychology provided a bridge between the psychoanalytic and the cultural, offering an approach toward the integration of the older clinical wisdom with newer social science emphases.[5] At the same time, these currents in theory and their own practice experiences were

[5] For a summary, see Isabel L. Stamm, "Ego Psychology in the Emerging Theoretical Base of Casework," in Alfred J. Kahn, ed., *Issues in American Social Work* (New York: Columbia University Press, 1959), pp. 80–109. In the same volume, the "rediscovery of social science" is summarized and documented by Alfred Kadushin, "The Knowledge Base of Social Work," especially pp. 58–65 and bibliography on p. 59.

leading some psychiatric practitioners to concentration on family dynamics where once the diagnostic and the treatment unit was the theoretically isolated individual.[6]

Ideas and creative leadership gave rise to experiments and demonstrations. Among the most influential have been the St. Paul Family Centered Project, the various innovations of the New York City Youth Board, the work of Otto Pollak at the Jewish Board of Guardians in New York, several "detached worker" experiments in major cities (Los Angeles, New York, Philadelphia, Chicago, Boston, Detroit, Cleveland), the Chicago Area Project and Hyde Park Youth Project, Nathan Ackerman's family therapy experiments, and a number of institutional programs.

PROFESSIONAL CURRENTS

Seen together, these new factors in the situation suggest new formulation of goals and pose new requirements. While we must be quick to admit that much of the thinking still requires validation through results and translation into method and professional training, the new currents can no longer be ignored. To the extent that their programs for children and families in trouble are organized only on the models of 1940, communities have reason for serious concern.

What, then, are the themes which have already established themselves as deserving attention and consideration? The variety of perspectives creates some inevitable overlapping. The following would seem to be a minimal list: (a) more adequate incorporation of the social dimension in diagnosis and intervention; (b) the use of "family diagnosis" and "family treatment" wherever relevant and possible; (c) adoption of a "reaching out" philosophy in serving those unable to meet agencies on traditional middle-class terms; (d) use of group methods as appropriate; (e) use of neighborhood methods as appropriate; (f) formulation of goals in "value change" and "means change" rather than "personality change" terms, where appropriate; (g) assurance of integration of services around the case where more than one service is involved; (h) attention to total

[6] For example, Nathan W. Ackerman, *The Psychodynamics of Family Life* (New York: Basic Books, Inc., 1958). Also, Group for the Advancement of Psychiatry, *Integration and Conflict in Family Behavior*, Report No. 27 (New York, 1954).

agency and institutional milieu; (*i*) assurance of a flexible and ex-perimental orientation to intervention. Several of these matters are best elaborated in subsequent chapters (service integration and the therapeutic milieu, for example), but the remainder may be briefly reviewed. We shall also discuss the much-publicized so-called multiproblem family.

The social dimension. In one sense, all of the professional tend-encies summarized in the remainder of this chapter reflect the new ways in which social science is being drawn upon by the "helping" professions. As we specify some of the current contributions which must be absorbed and built upon, however, the extent of adapta-tion and professional innovation will be noted.

The basic point is simple and, once made, inevitable: it is not valid to conceptualize only in intrapsychic terms causation of and intervention in a broad range of maladjustments, depredations, problems, and tensions. Current theory of delinquency has evolved in what may be a helpful manner (Ch. I). In seeking to intervene, one cannot ignore the social backgrounds, peer-group pressures, and value systems which affect aspirations, view of reality, attitudes toward constituted authority, presence or absence of guilt, and concepts of adequate family life and of parent-child relationships. Where ethnic derivation remains salient in family life, the case-worker or settlement worker, for example, must also take account of the ways in which Jewish, Italian, Negro, Puerto Rican, Irish Catholic, or Mexican family culture (to cite only a few) defines adolescent boy and girl roles and parent-child relationships.

Already a substantial body of professional literature, too exten-sive for summarization, has evolved to suggest and to illustrate how social factors should affect the helping professions. One col-lection stresses social science concepts in the following categories: family structure, ethnic patterns, social roles (age, sex, occupation, associations), values, social stratification, bureaucratic theory, theory of deviance as a group property.[7] In the most comprehensive effort to the present point, specifically to illustrate the incorporation of social science concepts in child guidance treatment, Otto Pollak has emphasized a limited number of concept clusters: family of orientation, i.e., growing up (to assure attention to the father, sib-

[7] Stein and Cloward, *Social Perspectives on Behavior.*

lings, relatives in the household, etc.), social interaction (to bring into focus all forces having impact on a child outside the therapeutic hour), social role (to contribute to realism in goal setting and to enrich family diagnosis), culture conflict (client culture and therapist professional culture both affect diagnosis and treatment).[8]

Concepts such as these lead to a reevaluation of the entire impact of "social environment" on the client—or what the psychiatrist would classify as "social reality." In an earlier era, the therapist would seek to neutralize negative impact of these "externals" or to achieve that environmental stability which would permit the intrapsychic change processes to work. Today we know that the very complex and many-faceted interpersonal, social, and cultural environment is relevant to problem identification, need for and interest in change, setting of goals, perception of self, perception of the helping profession and the agency, ability to participate, and mode of participation in a given kind of change process. Practitioners everywhere are now seeking to absorb fully the implications of these notions, while professional schools attempt to broaden the basic social science preparation of coming generations of workers.

The application of sociology, social psychology, and anthropology to the analysis of professional culture and organizational structures has yielded new perceptions of professional blind spots and of the ways in which *administrative and service structures* affect the usefulness of agencies.[9] Valuable insights are being derived relative to agency size, communication patterns, relationships between professionals from different disciplines, and the extent to which total agency impact rather than professional interview sessions alone is important in achieving the effects sought.

The emphasis on the *ego*, where treatment personnel were once preoccupied substantially with superego (conscience) and id (impulse) problems, has provided a way to conceptualize connections

[8] Otto Pollak, *Social Science and Psychotherapy for Children* (New York: Russell Sage Foundation, 1952), and *Integrating Sociological and Psychoanalytic Concepts* (New York: Russell Sage Foundation, 1956).

[9] Alvin W. Gouldner, "Organizational Analysis," in Robert Merton *et al.*, *Sociology Today*, pp. 400–428. Also, Robert Vinter, "The Social Structure of Service," in Kahn, *Issues in American Social Work*, pp. 242–69. See, too, Herman D. Stein, "Organization Theory-Implications for Administration Research," in Leonard S. Kogan, ed., *Social Science Theory and Social Work Research* (New York: National Association of Social Workers, 1960), pp. 80–90.

between the intrapsychic and the social reality realms. The ego serves this mediating and integration role for the individual. Some would, in fact, substitute the broader social science concept of interpersonal competence.[10] This total development has pointed to the validity of advice giving, educational approaches, and retraining—where these were once frowned upon as superficial techniques. Clarification of social realities, training which changes understanding and perception, reinforcement of skills for coping—all these have their substantial validity. As a result, new opportunity for experimentation and flexibility in program and method is opened up. Only beginnings are being reported as of this time.

To illustrate specifically, one might mention the "children who hate," a group whose problems are tied up with direct disturbance of ego functions. In some instances there is a deficiency and helplessness in ego functioning. In others, an overdeveloped ego "serves the wrong masters" and defends impulse gratification at any cost. These children are said to need a "supportive design to strengthen the deficient ego functions and a counter-delusional design to dissolve their defenses before any of the well-known channels of therapy can be tried on them." [11]

Social science concepts have provided the basis for a reanalysis of the nature of *authority* and the recognition that various intervention and social treatment situations are characterized by differences of degree of authority, rather than by mere presence or absence of it. This was a necessary development if serious progress was to be made in technique. Elliot Studt, who has given this subject special attention, points out that fully to understand an authority "event" one must look at the social organization in which it occurs, the two positions related by authority, and the two persons in these positions. Authority is, to her, "legitimized power"; in correctional settings, for example, the workers must make explicit what the client's subordinate role requires. In all settings, apart from the "power" deriving from statute and agency structure, the worker draws upon what may be considered professional "author-

[10] Stamm, "Ego Psychology," in Kahn, *Issues in American Social Work*, pp. 80–109, and Nelson N. Foote and Leonard S. Cottrell, Jr., *Identity and Interpersonal Competence* (Chicago: University of Chicago Press, 1955).

[11] Fritz Redl and David Wineman, *Children Who Hate* (Glencoe, Ill.: The Free Press, 1951).

ity"—the power deriving in a relationship from demonstrated competence. His effectiveness with a client probably increases as, in the course of a relationship, a shift occurs in the type of authority which predominates. For those who work with offenders of all ages, the authority relationship implies certain control over behavior and decision making which demands both skill and self-awareness.[12]

In relation to the last item, in particular, professional workers in authority roles are often tempted to avoid their responsibilities as unpleasant. The exercise of the role reflects personal history, broadly conceived. Given the view that many delinquents have had unfortunate experiences with authority figures, the case for providing a new and constructive type of relationship with authority is strong.[13]

The new social theories about deviance suggest new approaches to prevention and intervention, too. While these theories are being tested empirically, there would be validity to action research which seeks to determine whether changes in the legitimate opportunity structure will, in fact, decrease the frequency of antisocial gang membership or the forms of gang activity. Special attention is being given to vocational counseling and placement for youth in disadvantaged neighborhoods, community work projects, job training opportunities, well-led boys' club and center programs, ways of broadening and widening cultural horizons, and intergroup programs.[14] Similarly, constructive leisure-time programs assume new importance. While all of these approaches have existed in the past and while so-called character-building agencies have always represented themselves as important in delinquency prevention, the "opportunity" emphases may suggest special target populations for the programs and may help ensure sharp focus where there is now

[12] Elliot Studt: "Worker-Client Authority Relationships in Social Work," *Social Work*, IV, No. 1 (January, 1959), 18–28; *Education for Social Workers in the Correctional Field* (New York: Council on Social Work Education, 1959); "An Outline for Study of Social Authority Factors in Casework," *Social Casework*, XXXV (1954), 231–38.

[13] Dale Hardman, "The Constructive Use of Authority," in "Some Aspects of Authority," a special issue of *Crime and Delinquency*, VI (July, 1960), 245–54.

[14] See "Employment of Offenders," a special issue of *National Probation and Parole Association Journal*, Vol. VI, No. 2 (April, 1960), with particular attention to Lila Rosenblum, "Jobs for Youngsters," pp. 192–96. Also, *A Proposal for the Prevention and Control of Delinquency by Expanding Opportunities* (New York: Mobilization for Youth, Inc., 1962).

a diffuse "shotgun" offering. It is of interest that the Ford Foundation is currently supporting a variety of preventive programs which base themselves on an opportunity-enrichment strategy. In the words of a foundation spokesman:

> Successful prevention . . . means recognizing the increasingly frustrating conditions of life of low-income youth in our cities, and trying to provide more jobs, more educational possibilities, and more of the normal opportunities for recognition and achievement possessed by other youth. Experts are realizing that much gang activity results from the fact that youth in slum areas see little chance of achieving status and recognition except through antisocial activities.

Family diagnoses and treatment. The current family emphasis, at its best, is, in fact, a specific case of the return and deepening of concern for social variables. Florence Powdermaker has put it in these vivid words:

> No man is an island, no member of a family is free from the impact of all the other members. When we treat a child or young person, indeed any member of a family, we put all of the burden of change on him despite the fact that as he endeavors to change, he remains in the situation in which his problem arose and in which the impacts continue. Thus, while he is trying to modify the behavior that defeats him, members of his family often cannot sustain him. They are not aware that his behavior is frequently the result of an interaction with them and between them—indeed the patient himself may not know it in all its subtlety.[15]

Porter Lee said as far back as 1919 that "the individual members of a family cannot be successfully treated without treating the family." [16] However, the child guidance field continued to give lip service to the notion while working with the mother to a limited degree as "social environment" and almost completely ignoring the father's role. Even the family service agencies, presumably the center of a family orientation, were making individual diagnoses, were treating individuals, and had to begin to experiment with family-oriented diagnostic conceptualizations and family treatment procedures in the mid-1950s.[17] The process has only started.

[15] Bert K. Smith, *A Family Grows* (Austin, Texas: The Hogg Foundation, 1959), "Introduction."

[16] Quoted by Maurice R. Friend, "The Historical Development of Family Diagnosis," *Social Science Review*, XXXIV, No. 1 (March, 1960), 8.

[17] Pollak, *Integrating Sociological and Psychoanalytic Concepts*, pp. 177 ff. and pp. 24–26.

To some extent, the family diagnostic orientation has served to counter an excessively intrapsychic tack in case evaluation. Inevitably, it raises social role questions and calls attention to interaction within the family. It alerts one to the siblings as well as to the child who may have occasioned a referral. It may suggest the importance of grandparents who are in the home. It has certainly highlighted those ethnic and cultural patterns and values which may be at the core of interpersonal tensions or conflicts or which may block adjustment. It has shown how shallow are diagnoses which do not consider family factors. It has guided experimentation with family-oriented interventions.[18]

However, the decision for family diagnosis and treatment poses many problems. Is there any way to suggest boundaries and limitations? Obviously, every contact of an individual with a social service does not demand a family appraisal or involvement of all household members. When does it? There has been some tendency to defer this issue and to get on with experimentation: reestablishment of the importance of the home visit; diagnostic interviews with the family as a group; assignment of all family members for clinic treatment to the same professional worker where "case division" was once the norm; alternation of individual and two-parent interviews.

Helen H. Perlman proposes that social workers keep their professional footing by letting the "job for which we and the family have met" determine how one moves. One might be selective by looking particularly at the interaction "with the problem in the center of concern." She hastens to add that whereas the diagnostic value of family interviews has been shown, little is known about the treatment used or effectiveness of such interviews. Perhaps, she comments, increasing insight from the "small group" field may change this.[19] In the psychiatric field, too, it will require considerable imagination and innovation to move from conviction about a family approach to the formulation and teaching of principles and techniques.

Multiproblem families. Spurred on by the family diagnostic em-

[18] *Ibid.*

[19] Helen Harris Perlman, "Family Diagnosis: Some Problems," in National Conference on Social Welfare, *The Social Welfare Forum, 1958* (New York: Columbia University Press, 1959), pp. 122–34.

phasis as well as by social planning concerns, there developed, particularly through the 1940s and 1950s, a considerable amount of interest in what have variously been called multiproblem, hopeless, hard-core, or problem families. The development has both useful and misleading features.

The starting point is clear: since the time of organized social services and the compilation of administrative statistics it has been known that there are certain groups of families which make heavy demands upon community resources and facilities. It has also been known that within this group there are those particularly "resistant" or "unhelpable" families (to cite both American and British terms) who absorb services and funds but do not seem to change and who continue patterns of living which arouse community concern or fury, as the case may be.

In England, it is reported, there was heightened awareness of this group when the wartime evacuations and the resultant problems which arose occasioned considerable attention and the assembling of data. In this country, there was widespread interest in Bradley Buell's findings in a series of American communities that 6 or 7 percent of the families absorbed half or more of health and welfare services and that too often one could cite only "services rendered," rather than "problems solved."

Perhaps, inevitably, there has been a tendency in many quarters to act as though the multiproblem family is a diagnostic entity. Charity and social welfare have known the Victorian "undeserving poor," Booth's "submerged tenth" of the 1890s, and the "unhelpable" of the turn of the century—and there has always been some tendency to seek a unified interpretation of that condition, sometimes in moral and at other times in diagnostic terms.[20] Thus, it is not surprising to find in the professional literature of social work of the 1950s (some of it contributed by psychiatrists and social scientists) a substantial number of analyses which imply or accept the notion of group homogeneity and the existence of common psychiatric and social dynamics. Even the most sophisticated of professional workers have not been able to avoid the trap of discussing the characteristics and causes of what is assumed to be a real

[20] For useful background see A. F. Philp and Noel Timms, The Problem of "The Problem Family" (London: Family Service Units, 1957).

group.[21] It is as though study has revealed a new disease entity known as "multiproblemitis."

The amount of confusion which this has generated has been considerable. Moreover, the less sophisticated practitioners are given one more stigma-evoking label to overcome in rendering service. One is not surprised at the comment of a British health officer:

I never did like the term "problem families" and think that it has the most unfortunate effect upon the staffs of any Social Services, who have the habit of using it. . . . There is, of course, no clear-cut division between responsible citizens and those whose habits make them a nuisance and a burden to the rest of the community. . . . I should be glad if I never heard the term again.[22]

On the positive side, however, we must take note of the extent to which the "multiproblem" concept has contributed to much-needed professional innovation. To mention a few results, we might list the Family Centered Project in St. Paul, Minnesota; several Youth Board programs in New York City; Bradley Buell's Winona, San Mateo, and Washington County experiments; and (more recently) a long list of special efforts variously called "reaching out," "programs for multiproblem families," "operation outreach," "family-centered casework," and so on.[23]

The response to what has been learned about the multiproblem phenomenon has given particular support to family diagnosis and treatment, "reaching out" (see below), group treatment methods, experiments in combined individual and neighborhood work, and

[21] See Cora Kasius, "Family Disorganization and the Multiproblem Family," in 1960 White House Conference on Children and Youth, *Survey Papers* (Washington, D.C., 1960), pp. 233–41. This source contains a particularly valuable bibliography. Also see *Multi-Problem Families and Casework Practice* (New York: New York City Chapter, National Association of Social Workers, 1960, mimeographed).

[22] Philp and Timms, *The Problem of "The Problem Family,"* opening quotation. Also note Foreword by R. M. Titmuss.

[23] For example: Family Centered Project, St. Paul, Minnesota, *Casework Notebook* (St. Paul: Greater St. Paul Community Chest and Councils, Inc., 1957); Bradley Buell, *The Prevention and Control of Disordered Behavior in San Mateo, California* (New York: Community Research Associates, 1954); New York City Youth Board, *How They Were Reached* (New York, 1952), and *Reaching the Unreached Family* (New York, 1958); Ruth Chaskel, "Impact of Community Needs on Casework Policy," *Social Casework*, XXXII, No. 3 (March, 1951), 114–19.

AGENCIES AND FUNCTIONS

been brought together in a variety of cooperative undertakings. In
addition, having discovered that a very substantial proportion of
the families which make such heavy demands on community services are, in fact, already known to welfare departments, Community
Research Associates, the organization headed by Bradley Buell,
has undertaken to introduce a series of administrative, training, and
family diagnostic procedures. The outcome of many studies, including considerable attention to family diagnosis, these new procedures are now being tested on a large scale throughout Minnesota,
in San Francisco, in four Pennsylvania counties, and in Omaha,
Nebraska. It is expected that an emphasis on family diagnosis,
prognosis, classification by level of service needed, in-service training, periodic evaluation, and follow-up may increase problem solv-
ing, in contrast to mere continued service in welfare agencies.

The St. Paul Family Centered Project, which had considerable
influence, summed up its own special features as follows: (a) going
out to a family; (b) use of home visits; (c) use of social diagnosis
and an original profile for evaluation of family functioning; (d) the
caseworker as the coordinator of services. Especially interesting
in the context of discussion of increased attention to social dimensions of problems is a scale developed by the project for the
evaluation of family functioning. Attention is paid to such areas
of family functioning as child care; individual behavior; family
relationships; social activities; relationship to the caseworker; use
of community resources; family economic practices; health practices and problems; home and household practices. Many of these
categories were ignored in the earlier "all-psychodynamics" era.
In the most rigorous evaluative study as yet available in this field
(but lacking a control group) the project's research team found,
after two years of service, that there was some slight movement in
two thirds of the cases. This is an impressive record if sustained,
in view of the degree and complexity of pathology involved.[24]

Particularly heartening is the fashion in which the experiences of
special projects increase professional confidence in the potential for

[24] L. L. Geismar and Beverly Ayres, *Patterns of Change in Problem Families*
(St. Paul: Family Centered Project, Greater St. Paul Community Chest and
Councils, Inc., 1959), pp. v, 4, 5, 29.

accomplishment and change. Buell speaks with conviction of the potential for improvement in recidivist, multiproblem families. All of the St. Paul reports cite the evidence of strengths in deprived families. In the words of the manual: "Multi-problem families are far better treatment risks than had been assumed. We have learned that improvement in social functioning is possible even with serious personality limitations." [25]

Wiltse, who joins in the view that there is no such thing as a "hopeless" family, and who emphasizes that a variety of diagnostic entities are involved, nonetheless chooses to call attention to those families (many of whom are on public relief) who are completely controlled by events around them. They are too disorganized to be ignored but may not offer one major problem as a point of attack. The caseworker must often take on a "parenting" responsibility while developing a partnership with his client. The helping relationship demands teaching by precept and example, supervision and setting limits, offering both warm support and an ego ideal, mobilizing needed resources and facilities. In a sense, there is need for new "role training." Family diagnosis and work with the family as a unit are fundamental.[26]

Settlements, neighborhood centers, family agencies, and child guidance clinics are among those developing special programs for what are called "multiproblem families." [27] In addition, there are some beginnings in this country in the testing of a European approach, the development of housing units for the training and education of families in need of special help in adjusting to the standards and demands of social living in urban areas.

As one examines reports and surveys it becomes clear that the multiproblem concept has, in fact, had a variety of effects:

a) The tendency to think of this as a new diagnostic category

[25] Bradley Buell, Paul T. Beisser, John M. Wedemeyer, "Reorganizing to Prevent and Control Disordered Behavior," *Mental Hygiene*, XLII, No. 2 (April, 1958), 184. Also, Family Centered Project, *Casework Notebook*, p. 157.

[26] Kermit T. Wiltse, "The 'Hopeless' Family," in National Conference on Social Welfare, *The Social Welfare Forum, 1958*, pp. 135–53. Also see Alice Overton, "Casework as a Partnership," *Children*, II, No. 5 (September–October, 1956), 181–86.

[27] State Charities Aid Association, *Multi-Problem Families—a New Name or a New Problem* (New York, 1960); National Federation of Settlements and Neighborhood Centers, *Neighborhood Centers Today* (New York, 1960).

or social label has, among the less sophisticated, created confusion and promoted undesirable attitudes affecting both workers in the field and the public at large. One large city spoke hopefully of listing, "isolating," and quarantining the group.

b) The emphasis on multiproblem families has made it possible to win support from public authorities and community chests for a wide variety of new programs.

c) Many of the developments which we have already pinpointed as post-World War II professional breakthroughs have been promoted, accepted, and developed under the "multiproblem program" label (family approaches, reaching out, social science emphasis, etc.). In actual fact, however, these new orientations are not limited to work with any one client group or in any one type of program.

d) Most of the more elaborate case coordination experiments (service integration) win support as ways of dealing more decisively with these special problem groups.

"*Reaching out.*" The ideology of "reaching out" has provided the dynamic force behind a significant portion of the initiative and innovation associated with the work with "multiproblem" families, antisocial gangs, and disorganized neighborhoods. Such terms and concepts are associated with this approach as "aggressive casework," "assertive casework," "operation outreach," and "going out." The New York City Youth Board has played a leading role in demonstrating and publicizing this ideology in action.[28]

In the perspective of more than a decade and a half of experience, the basic theory is clear and obvious: Because of differences *among* the various cultural, ethnic, and social groups in need of social services, one cannot and should not expect members of all groups to conform to one model of the agency client. Furthermore, in view of the personality variations *within* each social-cultural-ethnic group among those in need of help, one cannot expect all to conform to one model of the agency client. The degree of introspection about one's problems and the tendency to "structure one's distress" in personal or interpersonal terms, for example, vary among the social classes. Self-referral and cooperative appointment-keep-

[28] See footnote 23. Also, New York City Youth Board, *Reaching the Group* (New York, 1956), *Reaching the Unreached* (New York, 1952), *Tri-School Study of Three Guidance Clinics* (New York, 1957).

ing at social agencies must be expected to vary with education, to take another illustration.

Social science insights, as already suggested above, thus lead to modifications of application procedure. They make it clear that the caseworker, at least under certain circumstances, must be willing to undertake a considerable amount of home visiting. Client "noncooperation" is seen to represent much more than psychological resistance related to treatment dynamics. The insights of ego psychology suggest ways of conveying an image of a helping person and developing a helping relationship appropriate to a person's situation and problem, not necessarily conforming to the hour-a-week-in-the-worker's-office pattern. Material help and guidance in relation to daily routines may be offered quite appropriately and actively not only to meet urgent family needs but also to develop a starting point for relationships on which future work may be built.

Similarly, if antisocial groups or groups of youth under high hazard are to be found on the street corners and not in the community centers, it becomes reasonable to assume that group workers, now "detached" from their buildings, will "go out" to them and will invent new ways of establishing contact and demonstrating the desire to be helpful.

"Reaching out" sometimes requires physically moving the service closer to the potential users. Economics and administrative dynamics have created a tendency toward centralization of social agencies in recent decades, but the new philosophy has counteracted this to a degree, stressing service outposts in settlement houses, new public housing, and store fronts.

For "operation outreach" assumes that if one analyzes the total social situation one comes to understand that it is often the agency, rather than the child or parent client, which is "hard to reach" or "self-defeating." Those doing this work are convinced that programs which are inventive and flexible can be effective. In fact, so varied are the current innovations that "reaching out" may best be characterized as an ideology supporting inventive and flexible approaches which seek to bring needed services to those who are not served by the more traditional agencies or professional workers.

A British effort with a particularly good record is a program which began during World War II. In 1942 a Liverpool pacifist service unit sought to help "hopeless" cases abandoned by existing services. The following description is of interest:

Conscious of their inexperience, they began by offering the humblest services and attempting to find a sound basis for their relationship to the families. . . . Cleaning, decorating, removing, repairing and disinfecting were the first forms of service and on this basis the rest was built. Friendship was made the foundation of the work . . . a relationship of mutual trust and respect as between equals.[29]

The experience of these units and their professionalization led to the creation of the Family Service Units in 1948. While it has continued to reflect the dedication and flexibility of the earlier units, the current effort has been fully identified as a social work program to be staffed by trained social caseworkers. Its philosophy and methodology have merged into the general "reaching out" approach to multiproblem families.

Faced by the need to work intensively and flexibly with the most complex and disorganized of client situations, both public and voluntary authorities have welcomed the Family Service Unit effort. Particular attention is given to those "unable to maintain proper standards of home and child care without proper assistance." The emphasis is as much on avoiding family disintegration as on comprehensive efforts at family rehabilitation. As the need for this work has been appreciated, public authorities in Britain have been willing to support expansion of the program through subsidy in many localities. By 1959 there were thirteen units throughout Britain plus four in London. Other authorities have assigned so-called intensive workers for similar work as part of the public social welfare program. It is not yet clear whether the program will remain under voluntary auspices or eventually will be fully absorbed as a public service. In the meantime, it continues to contribute to refinement of philosophy, theory, and method and to the development of content for training programs.

Of specific interest in the history of these units is the emphasis on neighborhood self-help to parallel work with individuals. To strengthen the spirit of friendship and identification between staff

[29] T. Stephen, ed., *Problem Families* (Liverpool: Pacifist Service Units, 1942), as quoted by Philp and Timms, *The Problem of "The Problem Family,"* pp. 42–43. See the latter source for a full British bibliography. For recent developments see the *Annual Reports* of the Family Service Units (London).

and client, the former are usually expected to live in the area, often in the center which houses the unit. While it is now rare for the workers to become involved in apartment clean-up and renovation, the heritage of that practice remains in the form of an emphasis on role training and concrete services as the point of departure.

There is some evidence, too, that the Quaker background of the program, the close neighborhood identification, and the group feeling in the staffs which is fostered in each unit provide even the fully professionally trained with a sense of "cause" which supports staff in innovation and persistence despite obstacles. A similar, almost missionary zeal was sensed in the group which originated New York's Services for Families and Children and the St. Paul Family Centered Project. Strong identification with a unit and staff stability are essential in this work also because of the likelihood that work with a given family must be long-term and requires a continuity of outlook. Thus, if the absence of a given worker or his departure means continuation with a unit member who is well informed, rather than a basic change in orientation, the service is more likely to be effective.

Although American programs have used the language of "reaching out" only since the late 1940s, the philosophy and practice did exist earlier. The well-known Cambridge-Somerville Youth Study, for example, found that relatively untrained staff, by today's standards, could establish relationships in all but 10 percent of the cases, whether or not invited in by the client, and could remain as long as the program objectives required.[30]

Current philosophy is expressed in a recent report:

To offer help through words may be a service that is incomprehensible to some families, while the offer of a practical service—be it a pair of shoes, a promise to visit the school or make a clinic appointment—may make concrete to the family what we mean by our abstract term, "relationship." . . . The goals we set for all families will be a reflection of our commitment to help, and not merely an opportunity to exercise our skills in treating in depth. The decision to meet the needs of the ever-increasing multiproblem families will be a reflection of our dedication to help people who need us, and not only those who meet our requirements.[31]

[30] Edwin Powers and Helen L. Witmer, *An Experiment in the Prevention of Delinquency: The Cambridge-Somerville Youth Study* (New York: Columbia University Press, 1951).

[31] *Multi-Problem Families and Casework Practice*, pp. 4–5.

Given this kind of commitment on the part of the caseworker, agency policy must support and encourage it. Thus, "we question selecting clients on the basis of the presence or absence of motivation or self-awareness."

It is artificial to carry on a discussion of "reaching out" without mention of the problems of ethics and authority. This entire tendency is premised on the professional resolution of conflict about authority which we have described in a previous section. "Reaching out" is possible only as the agency and staff members are prepared to assume a greater degree of responsibility and to exercise a greater degree of initiative when case appraisal shows this to be vital to family-child protection and rehabilitation. This is neither legally nor psychologically possible for a staff unless they are backed (as appropriate) by law, agency charter, or community values. Nor, given skilled "reaching out," must the client ultimately be deprived of the right to "close the door"; the agency is obligated to turn to the courts if that "closing" exposes children to hazard. Given an adjudication, the worker has new leverage to extend service.

While we shall discuss at a later point (Ch. XII) the approaches which may be taken to integrate services involved in a given case, it is of some interest to note the convergence in planning case integration of: a reaching-out philosophy, full understanding of the problems of so-called multiproblem families in many categories, and social science insights. Thus Buell, on the basis of the San Mateo effort, stresses the importance of the caseworker's "historic role" of mustering, focusing, and coordinating a multiplicity of special resources and services needed by a family in relation to the totality of family problems. At the same time, clinicians lead one to the view that both family psychodynamics and social science concepts establish the necessity for spelling out a method of case integration. Once the total interaction is understood, it becomes obvious that fragmentation actually defeats family and child welfare efforts.[32]

Group methods. We have already suggested above those limitations of an approach focused only on an individual and those potential advantages of group techniques which encouraged the post-

[32] Pollak, *Integrating Sociological and Psychoanalytic Concepts,* pp. 13–15.

World War II breakthrough. Psychiatrists, social workers, and psychologists who had experimented with group methods in the armed forces welcomed the opportunity to transfer their explorations to civilian settings. At the same time, a variety of impulses set in motion by the field of progressive education and by social science merged with casework development in social work to suggest new group methods.

1. *Group therapy:* Today, a wide range of interventions is subsumed under the general titles of "group therapy" and "group psychotherapy." Leaders in the field and writers in some of the professional journals make fine distinctions among the several approaches and define the requirements of sound practice. They are gradually evolving a system of theory, much of it based in psychoanalytic psychology.[33] Although small group research and group dynamics have yielded impressive laboratory-type findings, they have not for the most part been translatable into professional practice. One interesting approach, the Highfields "guided group interaction" and its nonresident derivatives, has been mentioned (Ch. VII) and will receive additional attention in the next chapter. While the rationale is sociological, the session-by-session process resembles certain psychologically guided group therapies.

The many concepts and applications of group therapy are now demonstrated in programs in child guidance clinics, schools, settlements, courts, family agencies, adult mental hygiene clinics, health centers, and elsewhere. At times the group therapy represents the total intervention; in other situations it is integrated with individual therapy or with a variety of social services. Among those served are young children, adolescents, either or both parents, entire families as a unit, tenant groups, and client groups in many social service programs. Staffing and leadership are found on a team basis

[33] Saul Scheidlinger, *Psychoanalysis and Group Behavior* (New York: W. W. Norton, 1952). Also, Saul Scheidlinger, "Group Process in Group Psychotherapy," *American Journal of Psychotherapy,* XIV (1960), 104–20, 346–63; "Group Psychotherapy," *American Journal of Orthopsychiatry,* XXIV (1954), 140–45. S. R. Slavson, *An Introduction to Group Therapy* (New York: International Universities Press, 1954). Marion Strahanan and Cecile Schwartzman, "An Experiment in Reaching Asocial Adolescents through Group Therapy," in Helen L. Witmer, ed., "The Prevention of Juvenile Delinquency," *The Annals of the American Academy of Political and Social Science,* CCCXXII (March, 1959), 117–25.

or in the hands of personnel who may be trained in psychiatry, education, psychology, social work, or social science. Many of the reports of specific therapeutic undertaking are impressive and encouraging.[34]

For present purposes, it might perhaps be appropriate to sum up with the observation that the experimentation with group therapeutic approaches has now reached the point of need for codification. Some methods must be more suitable than others, some professional workers best prepared for specific roles. However encouraging some of the anecdotal records reproduced in professional journals, more rigorous validation of programs should be sought so as to facilitate choices and planning. People live large segments of their daily lives in association with family members, peers, neighbors, and associates; there is every evidence that groups of various kinds, purposively formed and professionally controlled, are effective change media. However, the time has come to systematize criteria for group formation, techniques, and setting of objectives; not, it must be stressed, to "freeze" the field of group therapy but as a step toward rendering it more specific and responsible.

2. "*Detached workers*": "Reaching out," a group focus, and emancipation from the fixed building converge in the "street club" programs in large cities. Of all the program developments described, none has caught the public fancy as much as has the work with antisocial gangs, some on the verge of "rumbles." The stage, television, novels, the daily press, and popular periodicals have acquainted all Americans with the group worker who moves out to the "hangouts" of youth on corners, in poolrooms, and in candy stores, establishes himself as concerned with their welfare, offers certain direct services (for example, help in the search for work), and attempts gradually to introduce sound goals and direction. At times, as an interim objective, he attempts to bring an antisocial group into membership in a center, settlement house, or especially

[34] For example, note: Harris B. Peck and Virginia Bellsmith, *Treatment of the Delinquent Adolescent* (New York: Family Service Association of America, 1954), Chapter V; Robert H. Geertama, "Group Therapy with Juvenile Probationers and Their Parents," *Federal Probation*, XXIV, No. 1 (March, 1960), 46–52; Glenn J. Walker, "Group Counseling in Juvenile Probation," *Federal Probation*, XXIII, No. 4 (December, 1959), 31–38; Bernard M. Schiffman, "Effecting Change through Social Group Work," in National Conference on Social Welfare, *Social Welfare Forum, 1958*, pp. 71–77.

established teen-age lounge. Where street fights threaten, efforts are made to head them off; sometimes there is mediation between rival gangs.

Although public awareness of these programs is a matter of approximately a decade, they have a somewhat longer history. All the earlier efforts were sponsored by voluntary agencies. The roots are probably in the Chicago Area Project, launched by Clifford Shaw over twenty-five years ago. A number of variations, on a relatively small scale, emerged in several large cities which became concerned with antisocial gangs as World War II ended: Los Angeles, Cleveland, Detroit. Two small New York City programs were encouraging—the Central Harlem Street Club Project and the Tompkins Square Project.[35] When the New York City Youth Board was launched, it financed expansion of the former undertaking and sought to base a larger effort in a group of neighborhood centers. A variety of problems developed and the Youth Board decided to organize, supervise, and coordinate the program directly as a public program. Each major gang outbreak for a period of several years was followed by an expansion of this work. In the ten-year period from 1950 to 1960, the authorized staff grew to 120 field workers working out of the 10 units of the Council of Social and Athletic Clubs. There is liaison with many groups but workers are formally assigned to 130 groups with "membership" of 8,000. Approximately 40 of the groups are reported to be conflict groups of "considerable concern."

Most of the direct service in the New York City program is rendered by street club workers (a noncompetitive civil service category which has no educational requirements) and senior street club workers (who hold a social work M.S. degree, or some combination of other M.S. training or a B.S. plus relevant experience). There are well-qualified supervisors and coordinators and a program of in-service training.

The Youth Board reports an impressive record of "incidents averted," "mediations," social and athletic activities arranged, participation in lounge programs, referrals for medical-job-educational-

[35] New York City Youth Board, *Reaching the Fighting Gang* (New York, 1960), pp. 1–3. Also, Paul L. Crawford, Daniel I. Malamud, James R. Dumpson, *Working with Teen-Age Gangs* (New York: Welfare Council of New York City, 1950).

social services, and direct services rendered by its own staffs. It has also published a variety of descriptive reports which seek to clarify gang-member motivation and methods of intervention. It has not undertaken more rigorous measurement of effectiveness or systematic formulation of theory.[36]

The following capture the spirit of the street club worker's approach:

I was standing next to the orchestra when Shorty came over with a relatively large youngster whom I had never met before. There were two other kids behind him whom I didn't know. Shorty said, "I want you to meet our boss, the big man. This is Ringo." I had heard a lot about Ringo but had never met him. Ringo shook hands with me and then said, "I hear you're supposed to be working with us. I just got out of jail, but they told me down at the Tombs that somebody had been around." I told him that I had been around for the last month or two and that I had heard about him and I was very glad to meet him. Ringo said that if I were to take on his crew I would have my hands full because they were a bunch of wild kiddies, the roughest in all New York. I told him that that was one of the reasons why I had been assigned to the group. I told him that I didn't know many of the fellows and I was awfully glad to meet him because I was certain that I would have to get to know him. I then invited Ringo over for a soda and he introduced me to the other two fellows who didn't say anything, but just looked me over. One was Bobby and the other his brother, Walter. While we were having soda Bobby began to comment on some of the girls at the dance, calling them real bags. He did this good naturedly and pretty soon we were laughing and joking, and I suggested to Ringo that probably now that he was out of the Tombs he might need a job. Ringo said he was wondering if I could help him do that. I told him by all means I would be able to. I gave him my telephone number and told him to stop around the next morning if he could and we would see what we could work out. Ringo thanked me and I terminated the contact at this point because I didn't want to let it drag on too long.[37]

After the game we hung around outside the settlement shooting the breeze for a while until it was time to go. When I got back to my car it was in a mess. Somebody had taken a knife and ripped and cut the back seat so that the material was scattered everywhere. I was shocked. I went back to the settlement to see where the fellows were and the only one I

[36] *Reaching the Fighting Gang.* Also, Juvenile Delinquency Evaluation Project of the City of New York, *Dealing with Conflict Gangs in New York City* (New York, 1960, mimeographed), p. 25.

[37] *Reaching the Fighting Gang,* p. 129.

met was Abe. I told Abe about it and he came to the car and both of us cleaned it together and then I went back to the block. All the fellows were gathered around and there was a great deal of talk about it, wondering what the pitch was since nothing had been taken. I recall that Manny had not been at the game nor had I seen him around all day. I didn't think that this was the kind of thing in which someone I didn't know at all would be involved. After speaking to the supervisor on the phone, we both agreed that I ought to look up Manny. I left the fellows and walked up to Manny's house. He was standing on the stoop by himself with a funny grin on his face. I exchanged greetings with him and told him what had happened. He still didn't say anything; he sort of looked at me. I told him that the reason I had come over to see him about it was that I thought that he was the one who had done it, and if he had I wanted to find out why. Manny didn't say anything for a long while. I talked to him about the way his game was coming and we talked about girl friends and then I told him that frankly the car was three years old already and it could be repaired but it would cut down the amount of money I got when I traded it in. He then very quietly began to curse at me. He said that I was no good. He said that I thought that I was smart; he said I thought the sun shone only on me, that he didn't like the clothes I was wearing, the way I tried to con him all the time, the way I acted as if I could play basketball better than he could. In a word, he really tore into me and after a while he was no longer quiet, but was really very, very furious. I listened to him and then I began to get mad, because here Manny had destroyed the back seat of my car and I was being bawled out for it. So I lambasted him. I told him I thought it was a stupid, crazy, mixed-up thing to do and he should drop dead. Then he started to laugh as if he wanted to hurt me; he was glad I was mad. At that point I decided that this was getting a little bit complicated and I wasn't understanding all the things that were going on. So when he asked to see what the damage was, I consented, frankly because I didn't want to continue this kind of talk. We walked over to the corner where I parked the car. Manny looked at it and was still laughing. Then all of a sudden he stopped laughing and very seriously told me that he was sorry—that really, before I had come around, he had been crying. He didn't know what had gotten into him. He thought that one of the things he wanted to do more than anything else was to be like me and he said he didn't feel he had a chance at all. Then he got to the point where he just hated me for being what I was. He wanted to do something to hurt me, hurt me bad. Then we got into the car and drove around while Manny began to try to tell me why he did this and what it meant.[38]

Lerman has analyzed a similar pattern of work with what he calls "Youth in Conflict" in Chicago as demanding:

[38] *Ibid.*, pp. 234–35.

a) active communication that the worker cares about the group's problems;

b) active demonstration that the worker is nonjudgmental;

c) a willingness to sympathize with members' weaknesses and to support their strengths;

d) overt expectation that they can cope with their problems;

e) flexibility, openness, imagination in the role of the helpful adult;

f) the worker's coming to grips with his own system of values, his social class biases, and his own personality components.

Effective intervention also requires a worker who is trained to understand internal peer-group dynamics, the predominant surrounding value system of the adults who are significant to the group, the behavior and values of the sources of authority, and other salient social realities.[39]

While there are variations in the terminology, most sources report similar emphases and concepts. A conference group of experts called upon the staff member to analyze groups and their members from a variety of perspectives and to follow two general principles:

First of all he is a representative of adult society and he is obligated to uphold the code of ethics to which he subscribes as a member and representative of a law-abiding, democratic community. He knows that the code is imperfectly practiced. He also knows that the code was evolved over a long period of time and that it can be changed, but only by the efforts of people who can understand it and restrain their judgment while they work for change. The worker becomes the bearer of values to youngsters who have pretty good "hunches" about what is right and what is wrong but they want their "hunches" corroborated by an adult in whom they trust.

The second principle is that the worker sets limits and sticks by them. If such limits are interpreted objectively and enforced impersonally, yet consistently, the group members sense the conviction behind them and develop a feeling of steadfast support. They feel that the worker is saying: "I like you but I don't always like what you do. I meant it when I said I'd do everything I could to help you but if I can't get your cooperation then I can't help. If I know you have a gun, I'll have to call the police. If you have, use, or sell narcotics, I must inform the police. But, if you honestly try to change, I'll understand and we'll work things out together."

The street club worker transmits his values and set limits in a way that

[39] Paul Lerman, "Group Work with Youth in Conflict," *Social Work*, III, No. 4 (October, 1958), 71–77.

makes him different from other adults these youngsters have known. The worker is a "different" adult—one who represents something strong and solid. He has no need to punish them, to make them feel small, or to change them into replicas of himself.[40]

The worker's chief program objective is to help the group to undertake activities which would not be undertaken without his support. To the extent that they are able to perceive new possibilities in their lives, members are en route toward more successful adulthood.

In one of the most perceptive analyses of the type of work in the professional literature, Walter Miller describes the results of the Boston Special Youth Program, a three-year intensive, direct-service undertaking with corner groups. Seven groups received the intensive service and seven less intensive service. The workers' direct objective was that of "redirecting the energies of group members into constructive channels." Of special interest is the manner in which the arrival of the street club worker affected the relations of younger boys to older gang members and the relation of all the boys to influential local adults. Moreover, when the groups which had received the intensive service began to shift their value systems, so that "rep" derived from winning in sports, running dances successfully, and conducting legitimate enterprises, the "neglected" gangs began to attack. They were jealous of their rivals' successes. Miller notes the need to work with all groups in what he calls a "community relational system" if success with some is not to increase conflict initiated by others.[41] Workers in other cities have arrived at similar conclusions. Where conflict groups are involved, the New York City Youth Board finds it neces-

[40] Mary E. Blake, *Youth Groups in Conflict: A Report of a Conference,* Children's Bureau Publication No. 365 (Washington, D.C.: Government Printing Office, 1958), pp. 25–26. Also see bibliography in Mary E. Blake, *Selected, Annotated Readings on Group Services in the Treatment and Control of Juvenile Delinquency,* Juvenile Delinquency Facts and Facets, No. 3 (Washington, D.C.: Government Printing Office, 1960), especially Part III.

[41] Walter Miller, "The Impact of a Community Group Work Program on Delinquent Corner Groups," *Social Service Review,* XXXI (December, 1957), 390–406. Also, David M. Austin, "Goals for Gang Workers," *Social Work,* II, No. 4 (October, 1957), 43–50. The latter paper is based on the Boston project, of which Mr. Austin was director, and the Cleveland program. Also see Walter B. Miller, "Preventive Work with Street-Corner Groups: Boston Delinquency Project," in Witmer, "Prevention of Juvenile Delinquency," *Annals,* CCCXXII, 97–106.

sary to ensure liaison with all major fighting gangs and to establish an elaborate staff communication network to head off conflicts, end inflammatory rumors, and facilitate mediation.

The question may be posed as to whether at this latter point the street club program is not attempting to be, to do, and to promise more than it should. Its basic pattern of seeking out street clubs in the neighborhood, establishing relationships slowly, and offering program-guidance services is appropriate for the group workers assigned and for a social service. Beyond this, and the responsible reporting of information about danger, weapons, and antisocial activity, the street club program is in the realm of law enforcement. It cannot possibly have the city-wide coverage, the mobility, and the communications system essential to adequate community protection. While, in the short run, the public image of a force in readiness to protect the community may lead to support for the program, there must inevitably be disillusionment—which is not related to the sound core of the program.

In the early period of this work, staff members had considerable difficulty with the problem of maintaining their responsibility for cooperation with law enforcement authorities while seeking to develop a relationship of trust with group members. To some degree the problem still remains.[42] Nonetheless, major programs report that deep relationships may develop and effective work may be carried out while adhering to the fundamental principles:

1. That workers in implementing their role never consciously violate the law nor aid and abet anyone else in so doing.
2. That work with an individual gang member, or with a gang as a whole, is always done within the framework of the well-being of the total community and its members.
3. That in our work with individual gang members and the gang as a whole, when the well-being of the community, its members, the gang involved, and/or its members are in jeopardy. . . . we seek the active participation and assistance of law enforcement agencies in the community, including the police, the district attorney and the courts. At the same time, while working in consort with the above mentioned agencies, we continue to exert our own efforts to the fullest to control the anti-social behavior of the gangs and/or individuals involved.[43]

[42] Russell Hogrefe in an unpublished document.
[43] *Reaching the Fighting Gang*, p. 255.

On the basis of these principles, detached workers find it possible to prevent and control conflicts, remove dangerous individuals from the community, remove weapons from gang members, and, generally, to control dangerous situations so as to create a climate in which positive results may be achieved. Workers in many communities report that gang members welcome release from the need to fight. Los Angeles has, in fact, staffed its program with probation officers and reports that this does not impede the gang work; research evaluation is now under way.

The discussion may create the impression that all gangs in all cities are alike—and that professional workers are in complete consensus about the nature of teen-age gangs and the form to be taken by programs. This is far from the case. Some report elaborate gang organization and solidarity and a network of intermediate junior and "deb" groups associated with major conflict gangs. Other observers note gang instability and shifting leadership. To them the gang is only a "near group." Different age groups seem to provide the focus of antisocial activity in different communities. There are some observers who stress the threat of conflict gangs, while others see drug-using gangs as the major menace. A few observers call attention to gangs as channels of induction into adult rackets. Some consider the gang as "given" and to be worked with; others would break it up aggressively and would ridicule its leadership as "psycho."[44] Most serious workers favor working with the gang structure and leadership even if the ultimate purpose is gang dissolution—in contrast to an attempt through punitive tactics to compel a gang to "break up."

The discrepancies are not the result merely of differences in perception. Clearly there are many types and degrees of youth grouping. A large portion seems to be on the fringe of antisocial activity, occasionally stealing, destroying, or fighting. Others are

[44] *Ibid.*, Chapter II. Also, Miller, "The Impact of a Community Group Work Program," *Social Service Review*, XXXI, 390–406; Austin, "Goals for Gang Workers," *Social Work*, II, 43–50; *Youth Gangs in Conflict*, pp. 10–18; and Subcommittee to Investigate Juvenile Delinquency, U.S. Senate, *Juvenile Delinquency: Report of June 15, 1960* (Washington, D.C.: Government Printing Office, 1960), pp. 59–65. See, too, Lewis Yablonsky, "The Delinquent Gang as a Near-Group," *Social Problems*, VII, No. 2 (Fall, 1959), 108–17, and Yablonsky, *The Violent Gang* (New York: The Macmillan Company, 1962).

launched on well-organized delinquent careers. To the present point the evidence does seem to suggest that the general approach of the "detached workers" apparently has real merit—*if conducted on a sufficient scale and so as to have impact on the total youth life in the community.* There is agreement that qualifications of staffs should be raised and training intensified.

Of some interest too are the variations in the work developed on behalf of female gang members (the "debs") and younger boys whose gangs are on the fringes of delinquency. Inevitably, the "ganging" patterns of girls are somewhat different from those of boys and result in changes in method. A report of Boston and Roxbury experience, for example, notes less local tolerance of girls who violate the neighborhood "code," more "hanging around" in the home, the need for greater worker program initiative, and early and frequent invitations to meet the mothers.[45] Since there have been few reports of work with girl gangs elsewhere, generalization is difficult. New York City Youth Board reports describe some girl gangs as responsible for male gang fights but the evidence is limited.

There has been much interest in reports of work at the Henry Street Settlement in New York since 1956 with gangs of boys in the 8–13 year age range and with some girls as well. The Settlement has sought to break through the pattern whereby the juniors of a gang which is dissolved or the members of which end up in prison graduate to take over and continue the pattern. The unique feature this program is an emphasis in the early stages on developing cooperative relationships with parents so as to stimulate interest in and concern for their children. While the particular parents do not tend to join the usual settlement groups, it is found that through persistent work it is possible to get them to meet with other parents to consider situations affecting their children. This is a "mobilization" of neighborhood adult opinion against juvenile delinquency but not against juveniles. Custom-tailored group work programs for the children offer positive and acceptable status-providing experiences and a "socializing relationship with a group worker." One goal is to help individual children free themselves from overwhelming and unsound peer controls, so that they may

[45] Ethel Grumman Ackley and Beverly R. Fliegel, "A Social Work Approach to Street-Corner Girls," *Social Work*, V, No. 4 (October, 1960), 27–36.

pursue individual choices and preferences. The program offers a variety of forms of stimulation and direction.

In the words of the project director, "The children seem to thrive on the attention given them as the immediate adult community attempts to prescribe regularity and order. It would seem that when adults, particularly the parents, close ranks and stand together, the very ground these children travel from home to various parts of the neighborhood becomes more solid." [46]

So promising is this approach that a major foundation grant has now permitted its expansion to a sizable group of New York City settlement houses.

In concluding this section we might also note that many of the programs have, in fact, combined their group work with direct work with individual gang members. At times the group leadership has been in focus. In other situations the worker becomes an all-purpose counseling and referral service for youth on the corner. Where the worker is clinically trained, he may be able to offer a refined and subtle therapeutic service to a few, thereby shifting the gang balance.

Neighborhood self-help, planning, and therapy. The street club work thus must be tightly integrated at the one end with services to individuals and at the other with general neighborhood self-help efforts. We have already noted the Roxbury experience which demonstrated that one could not abstract a few gangs from an area and work with them while ignoring others. And we have cited the Henry Street finding that to heighten parents' concern for their children and to back them in their sense of responsibility is to begin to change the community value system and thus to affect the youth.

It has been pointed out that the main limitation of the St. Paul Family Centered Project was its concern with cases scattered throughout the city. The project could integrate community welfare service but could not concentrate services on one neighborhood as such. New Haven's Neighborhood Improvement Project seeks to remedy this.[47]

[46] *Neighborhood Centers Today,* pp. 127–40. Quotation is from p. 132. Also Ruth S. Tefferteller, "Delinquency Prevention through Revitalizing Parent-Child Relations," in Witmer, "Prevention of Juvenile Delinquency," *Annals,* CCCXXII, 69–78.

[47] Ludwig L. Geismar, "Three Levels of Treatment for the Multiproblem Family," *Social Casework,* XLII (March, 1961), 124–27.

The hypothesis is offered that "if new opportunity structures are opened. . . . violence tends to be relinquished."[48] The authors of this statement posit the theory that the form of gang which develops reflects the legitimate and illegitimate opportunity structures. One might broaden this hypothesis with the assertion that individual and family deviance is in part shaped by local neighborhood factors.

Although Clifford Shaw began his work in Chicago over twenty-five years ago, it seems reasonable to state that the serious, large-scale area and neighborhood work is only beginning in this country. In its largest dimensions and implications it is beyond the scope of our present volume: involved are all aspects of the attempt to make the metropolis viable and livable once again by reducing it to identifiable and unique neighborhoods with which people may become identified and which regain a form of stability and informal social control. This is truly a basic form of social reform and prevention which would affect rates of deviance. A *segment* of this general objective is the mobilization of local sentiment and energies in relation to specific needs, situations, and services which affect the young people or the character of family and neighborhood life. In this category one might list the Hyde Park Youth Project; the Chicago Area Project; New York City's LENA, "Neighbors United," or Riverside Youth Assembly; or many other similar undertakings throughout the country. Mobilization for Youth, a large-scale experiment, has begun operations in New York.

These are all beginning efforts, not in chronology but from the perspective of the size of the task, the need to develop professional methods, and the limited achievement. It is nonetheless fascinating to observe the convergence of group work and social planning and to note how self-help also becomes therapy. This requires explanation.

To begin with the Chicago Area Project, Clifford Shaw and his colleagues concluded in their studies that only a halt in neighborhood deterioration brought about through active involvement of residents would decrease delinquency. It was crucial, they felt, to reestablish spontaneous social control. They believed that local self-help enterprises of many kinds would create a sense of neigh-

[48] Richard A. Cloward and Lloyd E. Ohlin, *Delinquency and Opportunity* (Glencoe, Ill.: The Free Press, 1960), p. 175.

borliness and mutual responsibility, would increase resident concern about children, and would offer youth clear moral codes and much-needed controls. The self-help objectives result in a method which emphasizes local, "natural" leadership and as much local financing as possible. The work has been carried on in twelve areas. The neighborhood centers, which provide the core of the recreational and educational activity, do have both paid and volunteer professional staff; so-called indigenous workers are selected wherever possible, however. The project fosters and preserves the independence of local groups. The range of specific program content and form is as wide as that of the settlement. "Detached workers" have been included. Neighborhood committee members work with groups—but also work with individuals, seeking to "reincorporate" them into conventional groups. As the project is currently structured, much of the field service and research staff is supplied by public bodies, but the original private board remains in a coordinating role. Citizen groups and the Project Board raise close to half the annual budget.[49]

The program is so complex that exact measurement of results has not been possible. Close observers testify that (a) it is possible, successfully, to encourage resident self-organization in low income areas and to establish stable and enduring community organizations; (b) it is possible to mobilize local leadership in the interest of children's welfare; (c) large proportions of the boys and girls in the "target" population use the facilities of the neighborhood centers; (d) it is likely (but not proven) that all of this does both decrease delinquency and help the reintegration of training school and correctional institution graduates into the community.[50]

The Lower Eastside Neighborhoods Association (LENA) in New York, another large-scale self-help effort which has an impressive record of accomplishment, is described in Chapter XII.

[49] Helen L. Witmer and Edith Tufts, *The Effectiveness of Delinquency Prevention Programs*, Children's Bureau Publication No. 350 (Washington, D.C.: Government Printing Office, 1954), pp. 11–17; Solomon Kobrin, "The Chicago Area Project—a 25-Year Assessment," in Witmer, "Prevention of Juvenile Delinquency," *Annals*, CCCXXII, 19–29; Anthony Sorrentino, "The Chicago Area Project after 25 Years," *Federal Probation*, XXIII, No. 2 (June, 1959), 40–45.

[50] Witmer and Tufts, *Effectiveness of Delinquency Prevention Programs*, pp. 15–17.

The Harlem Interdepartmental Neighborhood Services Center, also mentioned there, is an experiment in case integration which added a community organization component out of treatment considerations. Ways had to be found to reestablish contacts between disorganized families and their neighborhoods and to win local support for client efforts at self-involvement in community life. Staff community organizers took on these specific objectives in close contact with the casework program, but did not assume a general neighborhood organization task. Almost all very large cities now have programs which accept the premises of the Chicago Area Project and which seek ways of "normalizing" neighborhood life in order to decrease antisocial activity and enrich the futures of their youth.

Hillman, who summarizes many such programs which have been initiated by settlement and neighborhood centers, distinguishes what he calls "practical aspects" (getting new facilities, city services, police protection, urban renewal) from what he calls "idealistic aspects," the personal growth and satisfaction in being more than a pawn in civic life.[51] He adds that it is "the practical side of citizen organization and action which accounts for the renewed current interest." There is substantial documentation of the expanded activity which includes many new types of endeavor. One wonders, however, whether the distinction between "practical" and "idealistic" is valid or whether the appraisal of their roles is correct. For, in broader perspective, these are aspects which are not only intertwined but also interdependent. All available theory and documentation suggest this. There are adequate, effective neighborhood mobilizations only as a community attains a sense of purpose and power—and none of the practical achievements are properly implemented and accomplish what is sought unless the new buildings, parks, street lights, and recreation facilities provide an environment for people who are becoming ever more self-directing.

If, to return to a term quoted in an earlier section, there are in the disorganized areas of our cities many "hopeless" families, then we may say that the mobilization for self-help is only successful as it achieves the material conditions for family rehabilitation—

[51] *Neighborhood Centers Today,* Chapter I.

but that it will not achieve this unless, in the process, the people themselves become better able to grapple with the factors affecting their daily environments. In this sense, then, *the self-help endeavor may be said also to have a therapeutic aspect.*

Astute observers of such programs all cite specific instances in which individuals have undergone major personal change as they have found useful roles in local action. Perhaps at some point in the future, in fact, we may be in a position to identify those types of people or situations for whom the self-help mobilization is the most suitable therapeutic medium, in contrast with individual or group psychotherapies. While noting this, we hasten to caution, however, that the mobilization has its own validity for all the "practical" reasons and that it does not achieve individual rehabilitation without accomplishing many of its practical goals simultaneously. Social welfare programs evolve from the custodial to the therapeutic to the preventive-social-planning phases.[52] Successful citizen action and planning is the heart of prevention and ultimately decreases the need for therapeutic interventions.

FLEXIBILITY AND EXPERIMENTATION

Despite the length of this chapter, we have identified only major professional currents and have illustrated with reference only to a very few of many pioneering efforts. It may be appropriate to conclude on the note that while the process is underway it is by no means completed. Much that is only now begun or which will emerge in the next several years may achieve levels of effectiveness not currently known. Many of the theoretical insights are not yet reflected in most practices. For the problems are complex, the goals demanding, and current failure rates high.

The relevant professional literature contains many additional insights, leads, and suggestions which would seem to deserve attention, yet full summary is not possible and codification is premature. To illustrate very briefly and not at all comprehensively, we might note, for example, the evidence that a social worker with both casework and group work training may serve a group while focusing on individuals, and may reach a gang by involving its leadership in

[52] Foote and Cottrell, *Identity and Interpersonal Competence,* Chapter IV, especially pp. 132–34.

casework services. Or, to cite another illustration, those who work with probationers would find helpful the suggestions as to how one makes them aware of the realistic consequences of behavior while conveying concern. The objective is to "be effective, not popular." The context of such treatment is the definition of intensive treatment as a privilege, not a right. Many therapists also now join in the view that the therapist cannot help a patient to adjust socially unless he himself has a definite, if not too rigid, set of moral values which he is willing to impose. For all treatment directed at enhancing social functioning contains social control elements; strict therapist "neutrality" is not possible. A skilled practitioner avoids imposing idiosyncratic personal, cultural, and class values, while continuing to stand for social norms.[53]

Many new treatment designs are needed, and the recognition of this will increase as the various subgroups among the delinquencies and the neglects are identified. The adaptive delinquent needs to be persuaded that he cannot, in fact, "get away with it indefinitely," while the maladaptive needs one of a variety of psychotherapies if he is not reached early enough on a preventive level.[54] For those "children who hate," who are "beyond the reach of education" but below the grip of the psychiatric interview, other approaches need to be invented. Many technical innovations are needed, such as the life-space interview, an on-the-spot confrontation in private which follows immediately on salient experiences as a kind of emotional "first aid" which may also be exploited clinically.[55]

Unless future results are negative, there is even validity in the pursuit of approaches which might seem at first glance to sacrifice indispensable values in the community posture vis-à-vis the offender. In this category we might include experiments in paying delinquents

[53] Melitta Schmiddeberg, "Making the Patient Aware," in "Some Aspects of Authority," a special issue of *Crime and Delinquency*, VI (July, 1960), 255–61. Also, Irving Weisman and Jacob Chwast, "Control and Values in Social Work Treatment," *Social Casework*, XLI (November, 1960), 451–56; Jacob Chwast, "The Delinquent's View of the Therapist," *Federal Probation*, XXIII, No. 4 (December, 1959), 26–31.
[54] Richard L. Jenkins, "Problems of Treating Delinquents," *Federal Probation*, XXII, No. 4 (December, 1958), 30–31.
[55] Redl and Wineman, *Children Who Hate*, Chapter VII, and David Wineman, "The Life-Space Interview," *Social Work*, IV, No. 1 (January, 1959), 3–17.

for "working" on a research basis, during which they become involved in treatment.[56]

Special encouragement should go to many treatment innovations which would seek to take advantage of the milieu and staffing of the hospital-institutional type of setting while avoiding the pathologies of "institutionalism." In this category one would include day treatment centers (the child goes home to sleep), day schools in psychiatric hospitals (a special type of classroom plus individual therapy), night centers (the child goes to a regular school but his residence is the hospital or institution), and their variations. Such programs are only effective as they include concern for peer groups and inmate cultures as dynamic forces, a subject elaborated in the next chapter.

Finally, and in another category, we may return to the need to be inventive about community opportunity structures, for preventive purposes and to ensure service resources. Particularly in the interest of adolescents it is vital to be concerned with resources which guide in the preparation for work, resources which record the availability of temporary and part-time jobs, and resources necessary to remedy physical defects. New opportunity camps and apprenticeship programs are also being developed to advance these ends. Especially encouraging in New York have been several small, voluntary employment placement and counseling programs which have adopted a "reaching out" philosophy in the face of the knowledge that many youths in underprivileged groups are too fearful to venture out to centralized services. New York State has begun to support an expanded, decentralized Youth Employment Service (YES). The U.S. Department of Health, Education, and Welfare and the Department of Labor have begun to take the lead in suggesting new counseling, retraining, and guidance approaches.

Progress in this field depends both on trial and error and on deductions from and applications of new theory. The former captures the energies and experience of creative practitioners, but sometimes fails to leap far enough forward. The latter is most fruitful if the social scientist will join in the task of translating his findings

[56] Ralph Schwitzgebel, "A New Approach to Understanding Delinquency," *Federal Probation*, XXIV, No. 1 (March, 1960), 31–35.

into service hypotheses. Otherwise the practitioner is tempted to work with what is clearest and at hand (the individual patient unit) and to avoid the vaguer, if potentially fruitful, challenge of dealing with family units, groups, interactions, and total situations.[57]

Perhaps the greatest challenge is one mentioned at several points throughout the book: the matching of type of person-situation to type of treatment. Current practice in selection of intervention methods is often dominated by unsubstantiated hunch and by folklore—with occasional validated findings. Systematic experimentation is required. Otherwise progress in intervention technology will not yield maximum returns.

A primary area of concentration in the first phases of this work must be clarification of just when a client or patient must remain in his own environment to be changed and when he must be moved. At times home and family pressures are overwhelming. At other times, only constant confrontation of an environment in which one's own responsibility for a problem is clear will contribute to change. These issues will be illustrated further in discussion of children's institutions.

[57] Pollak, *Integrating Sociological and Psychoanalytic Concepts*, pp. 24–28.

CHAPTER XI

CHILDREN WHO MUST BE COMMITTED

A RESPONSIBLE service network oriented to the interests of the child in trouble and ever-accountable in its decisions to the community as a whole will not want to make a commitment unless there are good reasons for doing so—and will seek early return of institutionalized children to the community if it is at all possible. Commitment will be made to facilities designed to accomplish defined objectives. However, because these readily defended principles are so difficult to implement, the realities often leave one uncertain as to what is actually intended. We turn, therefore, to a review of the status and determinants of programs for children who must be committed.

PERSPECTIVES

At its inception, the training school for delinquents was a humane innovation. It represented a move away from that earlier punitive practice which ignored the differences between children and adults.

Children had long been punished physically and cruelly, as had adults, for breaking the law. Then with the substitution of incarceration for physical retaliation, they were imprisoned in large institutions, along with adults. There were places, in fact, in which the mentally ill, the criminal adult, the dependent child, and the delinquent child (to use today's terms) all shared the same crowded, unsanitary facilities which were designed, as well, as "indoor relief" for the unemployed but able-bodied poor.

Thus, the "separation out" of the delinquent child and creation of the New York House of Refuge in 1825 as the first youth reformatory in the United States was a humane act. Humanitarian and religious concern was also involved in the founding of similar specialized facilities in Boston in 1826, Philadelphia in 1828, Massachusetts (the first state reform school) in 1847, and elsewhere later.[1] Similarly, one must regard as a progressive step the founding in 1851 of the New York Juvenile Asylum, a facility which could provide for the younger children in the group who had been sent to the House of Refuge.

The founders and supporters of these public and voluntary facilities, which existed throughout the country by 1875, considered work and rigid discipline as the route to individual salvation. While some portion of the daytime program was devoted to education, religious instruction, and household tasks, a system of contract labor was the center of these programs and determined many of their policies. After a while the "houses of refuge" were called "reform schools," then, industrial schools and finally, training schools. Eventually they gave up the contract labor. Yet, well into the twentieth century, the typical institution stressed almost exclusively the training value of hard work, offered only the most limited general education, and failed to approximate in any sense the family atmosphere which was posed as a goal.

Nonetheless, to those working on behalf of child welfare, to the reformers and the legislators who supported them, these institutions were an integral part of a progressive approach to children. They were in the spirit of the movement which created special courts for children, originated the probation concept, and eventually substituted individualized rehabilitation for punishment as the goal in dealing with delinquents. The plans for institutions were based on this philosophy.

If in today's perspectives the early houses of refuge and later training schools were punitive, harsh, and unable to rehabilitate, we must recall that, for lack of resources or facilities, many of the institutions did not actually implement the intentions of their

[1] For further detail see Grace Abbott, *The Child and the State* (Chicago: University of Chicago Press, 1938), II, 323–92. Also, Robert J. Pickett, "A Study in Social Action: The New York House of Refuge Movement, 1817–1825," *Correction* (New York), XXV, No. 1–2 (January–February, 1960), 6–14.

founders. Further, they all lacked more recently acquired understanding of children and their needs. It becomes more difficult,
however, to excuse what Albert Deutsch found in the late 1940s in
his journalistic survey of public training schools:

Austin MacCormick . . . while surveying a certain training school, no-
ticed a boy confined in a bleak basement cell, bare save for a coffin-like
wooden box which did for a bed. This was the institution's "bedwetter's
cell." In another training school, MacCormick saw a frail lad of thirteen
who had to make frequent trips to the toilet. . . . This sickly lad had
been sentenced to do more "knee dips" than any of his fellow students—
all because of his chronic eneuresis.

"Brick counting" is a form of punishment wherein the boy or girl is made
to stand erect for specified periods with his or her nose to the wall . . .
"rice polishing" means forcing a boy to crawl on his hands and knees
across a floor strewn with rice grains until bleeding starts or until suffering
is intense enough.

A boy who had offended his supervisors was taken down to the basement,
stripped naked, and forced to stand facing a bare wall. A high-pressure
fire hose was then played full force against his spine.

[Monitors] are authorized to beat up or otherwise discipline their fellow
inmates—to make flunkies of the weaker boys, to extort bribes, to inflict
sadistic punishments and even to force homosexual relationships.[2]

There are few forums before which even the most punitive-
minded today would defend conditions such as these. There is, too,
more widespread understanding that institution superintendents
must have qualifications beyond their political connections and
that the conditions under which even delinquent children are reared
should be under constant public scrutiny and brought into line
with minimum child care standards of the twentieth century.

Nonetheless, what is known generally about services and attitudes
throughout the country is not reassuring. There have been no recent
exposures of deliberate cruelty on a large scale, but not very long
ago a group of Negro boys, who had been left at night without
adult supervision, were burned to death in Arkansas in a training
school dormitory whose doors were locked from the outside. There

---

[2] Albert Deutsch, *Our Rejected Children* (Boston: Little, Brown and Company, 1950). Quotations are from the text in this sequence: pp. 147, 16, 20, 38.

is overwhelming evidence that state training school commitments are often made for punitive reasons rather than out of conviction that they offer the type of care which a given child requires. In other instances, while the judge who elects to send a youth to a training school may have ample evidence of the need for a group care facility, he must also know that the institution to which the commitment is made has so many negative features as to render it little more than a place to hold a child in custody. In general the tendency to use the language of rehabilitation, however sincerely, has not been matched by a readiness to provide essential resources. And also, it should be added, even the staffing of institutions in accord with current standards does not necessarily ensure effectiveness. For, as will be noted, even the well-equipped voluntary institution or training school is far from being a carefully designed therapeutic tool. Moreover, training schools tend to contain populations so heterogeneous and needing so many different types of help as to make unsatisfactory results with some committed children almost inevitable.

These facts are so well recognized as to require little documentation. One candid official survey, for example, looked at a state's Boy's Industrial School and reported poor food, permissible beatings, undesirable monitor and "citizen card" systems, and drab surroundings. "Training" amounted to little more than employment of the boys in maintenance operations. Even letter writing was severely limited by rule. Custody was the only real objective. The Girls' Industrial School was similarly repressive. Spanking was permitted. There were "Jim Crow" cottages. Neither institution could be said to have a treatment program and each had high recidivism rates.[3]

Because of circumstances such as these, 36 state penitentiaries found it necessary to report, in 1956, that 52 percent of their inmates were state training school graduates. From a third to a half of training school graduates reappeared in court within ten years. In addition, state training schools noted that one quarter of the children admitted during 1958 were returnees. Fortunately, the desire to improve this situation is almost general. The traditional

[3] H. Ashley Weeks and Oscar W. Ritchie, *An Evaluation of the Services of the State of Ohio to Its Delinquent Children and Youth* (Columbus: Bureau of Educational Research, The Ohio State University, 1956).

training school program based on a reeducative, retraining philosophy (which concerned itself largely with habit training, vocational training, and character building) has been affected by a new treatment emphasis. It is assumed that adequate implementation of new concepts will yield better results.[4]

Before examining this view more fully, however, it may be helpful to summarize some relevant facts about the national picture.

It is estimated that approximately 350 institutions in the United States serve adjudicated delinquent children. Of these, one is the federal training school, 132 are state training schools (almost 70 for boys, 50 for girls, 14 coeducational), 52 are county or city training schools, 11 are state reception or diagnostic centers, 29 are forestry camps, and 135 are schools under private auspices. The public institutions accommodate approximately 36,000 delinquent children at any one time (and about 72,000 in the course of a year), while the private schools house approximately 10,000. The average age of a training school student, nationally, is close to 16, but the range is from under 10 to over 18 depending on state statutes and policies. Seventy-five percent are boys; two thirds are white; 15 percent have been in training schools before. Forty percent of the institutions house over 200 children each (in fact, 15 institutions have capacities of 300–399 and 12 house over 400). Over half have capacities of more than 150 children. Many are overcrowded and are operating well beyond official capacity.

The staff totals are 12,700 and 4,000 respectively for public and voluntary training schools. Operating costs are estimated at $82,000,000 annually for the public facilities and well over $20,000,000 for the private. The average per capita expenditure for the public training schools in 1958 was $2,155.[5]

[4] Marjorie Rittwagen, Sins of Their Fathers (Boston: Houghton Mifflin Co., 1958), p. 192. Also U.S. Department of Health, Education, and Welfare, Report to the Congress on Juvenile Delinquency (Washington, D.C.: Government Printing Office, 1960), pp. 10, 25, 43; Robert L. Rowland, Statistics on Public Institutions for Delinquent Children, 1956, Children's Bureau Statistical Series No. 48 (Washington: U.S. Department of Health, Education, and Welfare, 1958), p. 1.

[5] For sources of the approximation see Statistics on Public Institutions for Delinquent Children, 1958, Children's Bureau Statistical Series No. 59 (Washington, D.C.: U.S. Department of Health, Education, and Welfare, 1960); Statistics on Public Institutions for Delinquent Children, 1956; and Donald G.

The U.S. Children's Bureau institutions consultant concluded in 1958 that "our training schools are swinging slowly but surely into well-balanced treatment-oriented programs and away from programs which serve primarily as a means of maintaining custody." He noted a trend to recognize each staff member, even maintenance personnel, as part of a treatment team and reported a consequent emphasis on good staff supervision and in-service training. Efforts are being made to improve staffing for clinical diagnosis and treatment for committed children. As group therapy and individual counseling gain, educational programs become more flexible. There is increasing involvement of the child's own family in treatment. The training school recognizes, too, that its own program requires a close and positive relationship with the local community. Older "control" methods, which diminished self-respect and self-confidence, are said to be giving way in favor of methods which build "self-respect, self-control, and confidence in others." Such practices as the eight-hour day have been adopted to make institution work more attractive but often leave the children without close ties to any adults and bring with them the problem of assuring twenty-four-hour coverage.[6]

This is a period of expansion of institutional facilities, reflecting the increase in the number of adjudicated delinquents. Flexible, functional architectural styles are appearing with greater frequency and, with some exceptions, the trend is to construction of cottages for smaller groups. Schools generally considered among the best in the country are shortening the period of stay (8–9 months for boys, 12–14 months for girls). The national average is 9.3 months for boys and 12 months for girls (1958). Most notable is the ex-

Blackburn, "Institutions for Delinquent Children," *National Probation and Parole Association Journal*, IV, No. 1 (January, 1958), 12. All the sources cited detail the inadequate professional staffing (3 of 10 with no full or part-time social workers, 4 of 10 without psychologists, etc.).

A 1958 study, which excluded camps and treatment centers, said that there were 196 public and 78 voluntary training schools and that 84 percent of the committed children were in the public facilities. See *Comparison of Expenditures and Estimated Standard Costs for Selected Juvenile Services,* Juvenile Delinquency Facts and Facets, No. 10 (Washington, D.C.: Department of Health, Education, and Welfare, 1960), p. 18.

[6] Blackburn, "Institutions for Delinquent Children," *National Probation and Parole Association Journal*, IV, 12–17.

pansion of forestry camps, which now exist in 15 states—in addition to the one operated by the federal government. This program trend has generated great enthusiasm but has not yet been systematically evaluated. Research interest has increased, however, and a number of potentially valuable research programs are reported. Aftercare services are receiving new and important emphasis, but apparently much remains to be done to make them adequate. Crucial is the fact that training schools now recognize that large proportions of their students are not "normal" in personality; training school leadership understands that the total program must take this into account.[7] As they seek to expand and improve programs, training schools and voluntary institutions encounter serious shortages of qualified staff in all categories.

Another authority adds to this review of trends the note that more centralized diagnostic facilities are being established to guide state-wide institutional placements. At the same time, where diagnostic centers do not exist, individual institutions are sharpening their own diagnostic facilities and skills.[8]

One of the important advantages and characteristics of the private institution has been its ability to control its own intake. This right is receiving even more emphasis as private institutions seek to take advantage of selectivity, greater homogeneity, and smaller size to create programs offering intensive treatment and varied aftercare services.[9]

Objectives. Appraisal of trends such as these and readiness to apply them to the institutional system of any one state must rest on some consensus about training school objectives. The U.S. Children's Bureau guide to standards and goals, *Institutions Serving Delinquent Children*, reminds us:

The general public expects the training school to control the child for the period of commitment without a recurrence of delinquent conduct and to provide some type of training that will enable him to become a contributing rather than merely a consuming member of society. They assume that the institution will have honest, efficient management by capable, responsible personnel who understand children and enjoy working with

[7] *Ibid.*, pp. 17–21.

[8] Abraham G. Novick, "Classification and Treatment," *National Probation and Parole Association Journal*, IV, No. 1 (January, 1958), 34.

[9] Henry J. Palmieri, "Private Institutions," *ibid.*, pp. 51–56.

them. Beyond this they are not seriously concerned, as a rule, with either the method or the means by which such a change in the individual is effected.[10]

The committed youngster sees the training school as concerned only with compulsion and restraint, at least initially. His own objective, generally, is to get out. The worker in the field of delinquency, however, has broader and more far-reaching objectives. Commenting on objectives, Alan Keith-Lucas notes that there are four possible views of the training school:

(1) Some see it only as a place to keep children out of trouble and out of the community. This is hardly an adequate objective today although many training schools can claim little more.

(2) For many others the training school (or voluntary institution) is a place in which a child may be held while he is getting individual therapy of some sort which will correct his delinquent tendencies. This very influential view is an outgrowth of the more traditional notions of individual treatment. It ignores the effect of daily living experiences on attitudes and on the therapeutic process. Of this, more later.

(3) There are others to whom the training school is a place where a child may live under reasonably favorable conditions while receiving vocational or social training. This concept recognizes the importance of daily experiences but limits its objectives by the assumption that the delinquent's problem is a lack of training.

(4) The fourth view, and to Keith-Lucas and many others the one closest to current knowledge of delinquency, sees the institution as "providing a therapeutic environment in which a child can relearn attitudes, can discover trust in adults and their world, and thus begin to accept their values." This formulation does not underrate individual therapy, good teaching, or consistent discipline, but adds, as an essential ingredient, the daily therapeutic experience through which new attitudes are learned.[11]

[10] Children's Bureau, U.S. Department of Health, Education, and Welfare, *Institutions Serving Delinquent Children: Guides and Goals,* Children's Bureau Publication No. 360 (Washington, D.C.: Government Printing Office, 1957), p. 1. While directed primarily to the public institution, this publication has relevance to voluntary institutions carrying similar responsibility.

[11] Alan Keith-Lucas, "The Role of the Houseparent in the Training School," *National Probation and Parole Association Journal,* IV, No. 2 (April, 1958), 156.

Obviously, positive objectives will not be attained unless commitment is wisely used. Having adjudicated a child as within court jurisdiction, the court requires psychological and social diagnostic data to support choice of the most suitable disposition possible. For example, the choice of institutionalization rather than probation or referral to a clinic, on the basis of the offense alone, may reflect a normal, emotional impulse but is hardly the way to promote individual change. Judge Gill has described the problem of properly protecting the community and serving its youth through wise decisions rather than on the basis of either pity or hostility. Commitments made in anger "inevitably leave to a perhaps applauding and impressed community a legacy of hostility and multiplying troubles." In making the decision about the use of the training school, he tries to consider the child's pattern of behavior—the seriousness and frequency of unacceptable acts—as well as his attitude toward the antisocial behavior, the need for community protection or protection of the offender against his own self-destructive tendencies (probation is often enough), and the question of timing in relation to the meaning of the disposition to the child. All these considerations, and the last in particular, assume the availability of substantial diagnostic data and social study to clarify which institution, if any, will be suitable.[12]

Others have elaborated the psychological-dynamic factors which may make institutionalization the disposition of choice, particularly for adolescents. Some children require placement because their total life situation is so lacking in emotional and social satisfactions and in growth opportunities as to make an adjustment at home impossible. There are instances in which one might consider a foster home, only to discover that the child, or his parents, cannot accept the idea of a foster home, or that a foster parent cannot tolerate the behavior patterns which the child develops in a close relationship.[13] The heart of a good institutional program is the potential for constructive relationships with adults and this is what some

[12] Thomas D. Gill, "When Should a Child Be Committed?" *National Probation and Parole Association Journal,* IV, No. 1 (January, 1958), 1–11.

[13] Harris B. Peck and Virginia Bellsmith, *Treatment of the Delinquent Adolescent* (New York: Family Service Association of America, 1954), p. 59. Also, Dale and Margaret Hardman, "Three Postulates in Institutional Care," *National Probation and Parole Association Journal,* IV, No. 1 (January, 1958), 22.

children require; but in contrast to the foster home, the relationships in the institution need not be intensive at first and may develop as rapidly as the child's emotional status permits. This is a decided asset, if understood and soundly exploited.

In sum, placement is best seen as a positive and therapeutic step in rehabilitation; the specific placement should derive from a child's status and needs. It defeats itself if undertaken either punitively or by default because nothing else is available. Sometimes the community resource situation may lead to a series of consequences for a child wherein only institutionalization becomes possible; even then, the concern with the *proper* placement may represent the difference between a helpful experience or a continued decline.

The program. Given objectives such as these and the ability to select, for commitment, children who may be able to use the group-centered training school, there is need for a program which will convert intent into actuality. *Institutions Serving Delinquent Children* reports current consensus of experts from all parts of the country about state training schools. The smaller residential treatment centers may pose added or somewhat different requirements.

Details regarding administration, physical plant, staffing, in-service training, educational program, food, and recreation are extremely important to the institutional program but need not be reviewed for present purposes.[14]

The central concept which has been winning wide support and which many are seeking to implement is as follows:

The word "treatment," as used in training schools today, means help given to the child—the total effort made by the school to rehabilitate the child and the after-care services in his home community. It denotes helping a child by providing a new and more satisfying experience in community living together with any special services that he may need. It includes a proper diagnosis of the child's problems and a plan of care based on that diagnosis. It implies providing an environment in which all activities are directed to getting the child ready for a successful return to community living. It covers every aspect of the child's institutional life and involves the total staff, as well as the neighboring community. Every staff member, including the cottage supervisor, teacher, clerk, maintenance

[14] See *Institutions Serving Delinquent Children,* and Blackburn, "Institutions for Delinquent Children," *National Probation and Parole Association Journal,* IV, 12–17.

man, cook, and nurse, has a definite and important contribution to make to treatment.

"Treatment" means more than "training". . . . We mean discerning what has caused the child's trouble and, on the basis of this knowledge, attempting to correct his difficulties.[15]

From this point of view, the traditional forms of habit training or vocational training are not adequate to the task of the training school. What has become known as "milieu therapy" is essential since almost all committed delinquents need to experience socially acceptable behavior if they are to mature and to revise their concepts of the surrounding world. Those too disturbed to benefit fully from the experience in such a controlled environment also require individual or group psychotherapy, involving the use of clinical personnel. Others may also need specialized medical help, remedial learning programs in reading and arithmetic, specific vocational training, orientation to the world of work, stimulation to unusual creative talents, religious guidance, or a traditional academic program—depending on their age, status, problems, preparation, and outlook.

The need to provide services on an individualized basis does not and should not obscure the point that the strength and value of the traditional training school (and its inevitable limitation) lies in its being essentially a group care facility. Because *some* delinquents are not effectively redirected in such a facility (which relies, primarily, on peer-group experiences, contacts with desirable adult behavior models, and educational-remedial-vocational programs) each community is faced with the need to provide a variety of alternative resources in its total network of out-patient and in-patient facilities, and in its child welfare and family services, both public and private. We have already discussed many of these. None of this, however, permits or justifies failure to give major attention to the strengthening of the training school per se, in its modern variations, along lines dictated by its characteristics as a group facility and by knowledge of what makes for a sound group milieu.

Principles. A rehabilitative objective does not preclude control or discipline. The training school is selected for a child, or should be, because, in addition to requiring care away from home, he

[15] *Institutions Serving Delinquent Children,* p. 5.

is in need of a degree of control for his own or for community protection. If this is not the case, he belongs in the community or in another type of institution, whether under public or voluntary auspices, but not in the training school.

Inevitably, then, the training school requires rules and regulations "to maintain orderly group behavior . . . [and to ensure] individual survival in a group situation. But there should be a minimum number of rules and regulations and they should be stated in positive rather than negative language." Constant reevaluation of rules is desirable in order to prevent that extreme regimentation and inflexibility which retards self-regulation and direction and only increases anxiety. The training school program should seek to provide a framework of clear, strong, necessary, and reasonable regulations within which a child can have the experience of functioning as a free and responsible citizen because sound group norms are pervasive—not because of fear of punitive devices.[16]

This is, of course, an objective often lost because of an endless variety of training school limitations or, as will be seen, because the training school serves a population too heterogeneous to benefit from one system of rules and regulations. Where disciplinary measures are essential because of violations of rules, they should follow soon after the offense, be appropriate to the child and the setting, and not undermine long-range objectives. The Children's Bureau stresses the need for consistency between various staff members; the undesirability of segregation rooms except where essential to the protection of child or group; the danger that extra work details as punishment may detract from the general dignity of work; the harmful effect of cruel and unusual punishment, corporal punishment, or measures which humiliate the child or punish the group for the acts of an individual; the carefully determined deprivation of special privileges as an institutional disciplinary device. The last-named has the advantage of keeping the child in the ongoing basic program for which he has been sent to the school.[17]

Positive relationships with a variety of adults who offer desirable models of behavior are, of course, central to the training school. It is now clear that the houseparent or group counselor generally is, in effect, the hub of the institution. Many authorities feel that a

[16] *Ibid.*, Section IX.   [17] *Ibid.*, pp. 100–104.

"houseparent couple" are essential and describe them, at their best, as wise, loving, mature individuals who do much to create the essential milieu. They are not to be confused with the psychiatrists, social workers, or psychologists on the clinical team; they make their contribution by offering the child warmth, patience, humor, love, and devotion. The general trend is to recognize their importance, pay better salaries, and, consequently, to attract ever more satisfactory personnel. Britain has, in fact, developed an impressive training program for houseparents. Some authorities have despaired of the possibility of recruiting adequate numbers of good houseparents for training schools in this country. One survey found that couples as houseparents are more usual in boys' training schools than in girls' schools: only 5 of the 42 girls' training schools had couples as houseparents.[18] The assignment of two women to a girls' cottage or two men to a boys' cottage may be the only staffing pattern possible. Various writers have noted that the cottage parent assignment is not considered an attractive one in this country, so that shortages are inevitable and the proportion of "misfits" attracted is high. The alternative often suggested is the group counselor, a subprofessional technician with high school or college-level education, in an assignment somewhere between that of the custodian in a correctional institution and the recreation leader or counselor in a camp or settlement house.

Those who favor the houseparent tend to stress the importance of developing a family-like atmosphere in the cottage or—more realistically—of providing an example of wholesome family relationships, something which is lacking in the lives of most training school children. The proponents of the counselor system consider it impossible to approximate a family atmosphere with a group of twenty or more. To them, the cottage is a carefully developed and directed peer-group experience. The counselor is a supervisor, group leader, and, for some children, an adult model.

There is no clear evidence that one or another of these approaches is the more effective. Both will probably continue. Both are predicated on the assumption that all institutional staff members are identified with basic objectives and have been so selected and

[18] Muriel Evelyn Jenkins, "The Administration of a State Training School for Girls" (Unpublished M.S. Thesis, Atlanta School of Social Work, 1957).

oriented as to ensure consistency in attitudes toward committed children and the availability of a variety of sound adult models. This includes cooks, maintenance personnel, drivers, painters, electricians, clerical personnel, and other employees of the institution.

Clinical programs. The training school clinical programs are now in transition. They developed originally as aids to classification in an era when educational, vocational, and habit training as well as work-production dominated the institutions. In the last several decades, both the general rise in status of psychiatry, social work, and psychology as rehabilitative disciplines and the recognition of high failure rates in training schools which sought to "educate" and "train" in the traditional sense led to the decision to add clinical staffs to institutions in order to render individualized services. In actual fact, few institutions have professional staffs adequate to offer much more than a program of orientation of new arrivals, classification, and help with severe personal problems which arise. A few have managed to provide for systematic casework treatment during institutionalization or even, in rare instances, for individual treatment by a psychiatrist.

However, despite these realities, a large proportion of the training schools have set for themselves the *model* of the residential treatment center, usually under voluntary auspices, in which a relatively large staff is able to offer a full clinical team service, involving weekly or more frequent casework sessions, diagnostic and progress interviews with the psychiatrist, diagnostic and other tests by the psychologist. Such a model spells inevitable frustration for a training school. There is, first, the harsh fact that few states have been willing or able to staff training schools for this kind of function. More basic, perhaps, is the fact that the concept of the training school as an institution which merely contains children physically while the "treatment" takes place in a clinic building on the institution grounds is clearly unrealistic; it is giving way to the view that the change in the child is the product of the total living experience. This is particularly the case if the commitment system selects for the training school those "socialized" delinquents capable of functioning in peer groups and of benefiting along with other members of their group from sound reorientation of values and from living experiences which will help them reevaluate their earlier appraisals of the adult world. Those too disturbed, emotionally, to make use of such a program, it is now understood, should not be in training schools, even well-staffed training schools. Public and voluntary institutions of other kinds are necessary. Even the psychiatrically directed residential treatment centers now stress the total milieu and try to avoid isolating the clinic.

This kind of thinking has led to new formulation of the responsibilities of the clinical and social service units in training schools. The term "intensive treatment services" has been suggested for those institution programs other than the education, recreation, cottage life, and religion departments. The psychiatrists, psychologists, or social workers in the intensive treatment services (or child guidance, or clinical services) are in a position to contribute to the total milieu through their understanding of the causes of behavior and of how pathological or objectionable behavior is changed. As consultants, supervisors, and co-workers, they can extend their influence from the one-to-one relationship of the clinic to the program as a whole.[19]

Recognition of this potential has led to a series of experiments; no one pattern is clearly superior. For example, under one plan, all children in a given cottage are assigned to the same caseworker, who also has a supervisory relationship to their cottage parent. Under a related plan, both caseworker and cottage parent report to the same supervisor, whose training is in casework and who is responsible both for the individual work which may be done with the child and for the nature of the home or cottage experience provided.[20]

Under both plans and their variations, the *caseworker* is charged with ensuring, through all phases of the program, that each child is seen as an individual. He assembles data relevant to diagnosis and periodic appraisal, helps interpret the child and his behavior, works intensively with the individual as problems arise in the daily living experience or in relation to obstacles preventing discharge, and is either in touch with families and community to prepare for the postdischarge situation or is the liaison to the caseworker whose

[19] *Institutions Serving Delinquent Children,* pp. 50 ff.
[20] Novick, "Classification and Treatment," *National Probation and Parole Association Journal,* IV, 34.

responsibility that is. While some children will require frequent contacts, others will not. Each should be assigned to a caseworker, however. *Institutions Serving Delinquent Children* states that a training school with this view of the role requires one caseworker for each thirty children.

Also essential are *psychologists,* who undertake diagnostic testing, educational and vocational classification, remedial teaching, occasional individual therapy, group therapy, research, and in-service training. The *psychiatrists* have major diagnostic and treatment-planning roles, are extremely valuable in in-service training, and are now broadening their interests so as to apply their specialized perspectives to general policy formulation in the institution. To a limited extent they may offer individual treatment in addition to handling psychiatric emergencies. For the most part, however, the training school is not, per se, a psychiatric treatment institution.

The increased emphasis on the group aspects of the training school experience has led to employment of *group workers* (not the traditional recreationist, who has another task). Knowledge of group process facilitates the development of a group atmosphere conducive to the achievement of training school objectives. The group worker, trained in social work, may play a responsible role in the cottage life program, may participate in program planning and scheduling, may participate in developing sound groupings and cottage placement of students, may supervise volunteers in the leisure-time program, and may work directly with small groups of children requiring special attention. He may or may not be the group therapist. More and more institutions are coming to realize that the type of boy or girl who needs training school commitment may very well benefit substantially from a group therapy experience. In a sense, group therapy provides opportunity to hasten, channel, articulate, and strengthen the positive peer-group experience which can be the constructive core of the training school milieu.

Since group therapy is in a preliminary exploratory phase, there are inevitably many types of programs based on a variety of theories and conducted by many types of personnel: psychiatrists, caseworkers, social group workers, psychologists, sociologists, educators, clergymen. A period of continued experimentation is justified but each institution must assure itself of the qualifications of the personnel involved, within their own disciplines, and of the necessary professional controls and evaluation procedures.

Vocational and educational programs. Vocational and educational programs are coming back into their own in a new and sounder form in today's training schools. They are no longer—or should not be—seen primarily as ways to meet state costs, since it is by now recognized that the demands of production for the market introduce criteria not appropriate to rehabilitation. Nor do the institutions under qualified leadership assume, as they once did, that mere exposure to work routine or to the discipline of a school program is certain to be helpful. In fact, it is understood that the group values, attitudes, problems, distortions, and lack of "coping skills," which may have been involved in a child's difficulties in school and community, will inevitably be intensified if the program merely re-creates the educational experience of the community or offers a vocational plan not adapted to individual interests, motivation, and opportunities.

For too long, without the goal of rehabilitation, the slogan had to be: "Use the children for the work instead of the work for the children." That slogan is still appropriately applied to the more backward institutional systems. Some of the state schools committed to rehabilitation, however, have given all of their attention to creation of responsible and sound attitudes to work and to learning. Under such an objective the major emphasis of a vocational program is prevocational and exploratory. The program is not primarily designed to develop skills. Since the fact is that a large proportion of training school graduates do go from training school directly into the job market, the appropriate objectives would seem to be the development of sound attitudes toward work and interest in specific occupations, as well as the attainment of skills appropriate to first jobs. Institution vocational programs thus need personnel equipped to teach salable skills as well as to individualize and to motivate. Programs require modern equipment and adequate materials. Where children are employed in institution maintenance and repair tasks, the assignment should be on the basis of sound classification criteria and related to the individual's total educational-vocational program. This again gives emphasis to the need to select and orient even maintenance personnel in accord with institutional objectives.

Many training school children are retarded in reading and arithmetic. Educational programs therefore require strong staffs equipped for remedial work. Classes must be small, instructional materials individualized, and programs suited to the capacities of students. It is essential, too, that a training school have educational resources adequate to the needs and potentialities of all its students. Some schools lack sufficient classroom space and supplies. Others are so oriented to considering training school pupils as educational failures that they do not offer adequate opportunity to children capable of meeting diploma requirements. All phases of the educational program should ensure personal relationships which support the general institutional objectives. Since committed delinquents have often been school failures, the organization and staffing of the school and its integration into the institution are basic to the entire program.

Obviously, an institution dedicated to a sound living experience will also make available, on a voluntary basis, opportunity for religious instruction, guidance, celebration, and observance—in accord with a given child's faith and his parents' wishes. Training schools require part-time or full-time *chaplains*, depending on the size of the population and its religious distribution. In fact, clinically oriented chaplains are able to make a significant contribution to the planning of an institution's total milieu.[21]

Recreational and leisure-time programs. Such programs might, of course, be discussed at some length. For present purposes we shall merely stress that they are salient aspects of individual and group experience in an institution and that they offer valuable opportunity for constructive adult leadership, sound channeling of group energies, individual creative satisfaction, diagnostic observation, and flexibility of programing. Staff require careful selection and sound leadership. Volunteers under trained leadership can make an important contribution to the program. In relation to the latter, the comment has been made that "the volunteer program brings an

[21] Harold E. Davidson, "The Chaplaincy in the Juvenile Institution," *National Probation and Parole Association Journal*, VI, No. 1 (January, 1960), 69–74.

ingredient to residential treatment which cannot be supplied by staff: the living communication of community responsibility to children under care." [22]

Peer culture. Recent research and writing have stressed the considerable impact of the peer culture in an institutional setting. Concepts originally developed as relevant to adult prisons are found to be applicable to institutions for juveniles as well.

Adolescents tend, even in normal community situations, to "gang" together for mutual support in the difficult transition from childhood dependence to adult independence and responsibility. To this the institution adds the fear of many unknowns, powerlessness in the hands of adults who make the eventual decisions about release, the fear of certain aggressive institution inmates, the desire for material things (cigarettes, candy, etc.) and for privileges and experiences not formally provided. Moreover, many youths seem to become convinced in the course of the court and detention experience that their commitment represents an irrevocable branding as community outcasts. They band together for mutual support. Small wonder that the peer group becomes, for most, the strongest force in the institution.[23]

Based as it is on the premise of public rejection and offering substitute satisfactions and security, the peer culture often convinces the young people that one should not really participate sincerely or wholeheartedly in the treatment and educational programs or seek to be rehabilitated. Nor does it tolerate the conformity of those who try to participate. In some ways, as already suggested, this is not unlike adolescent "gang" behavior. In still other ways, this is related to the gang's perpetuation of the delinquent subculture as the vehicle whereby, through collective rejection and destruction, some lower-class youths solve their problem of in-

[22] Joseph F. Phelan, Jr., "The Role of the Volunteer in a Residential Treatment School," *Federal Probation,* XXIII, No. 3 (September, 1959), 13–20.

[23] Lloyd E. Ohlin, "The Reduction of Role Conflict in Institutional Staff," *Children,* V, No. 2 (March–April, 1958), 65–69; Lloyd E. Ohlin and William C. Lawrence, "Social Interaction among Clients as a Treatment Problem," *Social Work,* IV, No. 2 (April, 1959), 3–13; Howard W. Polsky, "Changing Delinquent Subcultures: A Social-Psychological Approach," *Social Work,* IV, No. 4 (October, 1959), 3–15. Also, Howard Jones, *Reluctant Rebels* (New York: Association Press, 1960); Howard W. Polsky, *Cottage Six* (New York: Russell Sage Foundation, 1962).

ability to attain middle-class standards. There is here, however, the crucial added factor of the use of the informal group organization to meet the special institutional situation. Trent found that, at admission, a good many boys had goals and norms not too different from those of the training school administration. The differences increased, with the boys moving further from institutional norms as they continued in the program.[24]

Institutional administrators tend to drift into acceptance of this informal organization since a degree of accommodation to inmate wishes ensures the "cooperation" which maintains discipline and is consistent with the humanitarian philosophy which prevails.

As Ohlin and Lawrence point out, the traditional correctional institution borrowed the clinical model, which assumes that the delinquent is deviant because of internalized conflicts and which stresses treatment through a controlled relationship aimed at resolving the psychic problem and, incidentally, the value and behavioral manifestations which follow. They offer the sociological alternative, which regards delinquency as a social disorder, a product of group life, and they pose the treatment problem of changing the antisocial attitudes, beliefs, and goals of the group members. From this point of view, the delinquent subculture of institutional inmates must be dealt with not only to permit access to the individual requiring casework or psychiatric help but also because it is, in a sense, the core problem leading to the commitment.

This kind of analysis, while tentative and hypothetical, suggests a variety of possible directions for action, most of them in need of testing. Some, in fact, still require translation from theory into imaginative action designs. For example: If inmate organization could be turned toward constructive tasks, where now it "fights" the goals of formal institutional organization, it might use its strong hold on the young people for constructive ends. Or, should this not be possible, ways might be developed (in line with current knowledge of small group behavior) to dissolve strong peer groups which block rehabilitation. Efforts might also be made to break the chain

[24] Study summarized in a basic report and four supplementary volumes by Daniel P. Clarke, Bettina Warburg et al., Report of the Warwick Child Welfare Services Project (Albany: New York State Department of Social Welfare, 1959), 5 vols. (mimeographed).

of indoctrination wherein each "generation" of institution inmates teaches new arrivals that opportunities for rehabilitation and re-acceptance in the community are actually very few.[25]

While details are obviously to be developed through testing and experimentation, it already seems possible to suggest that the large congregate care institution, which seeks to transform itself into an institution rendering individual psychotherapy, might direct its program instead in a more realistic direction. Knowledge of peer-group formation in institutions poses the possibility of an institution organized to make constructive use of peer relationships (perhaps along some of the lines proposed above), while offering reme-dial educational courses and continued school work, as appropriate, as well as vocation-oriented training for those who need it. Edu-cators have a good deal to say about value changes which may not have had adequate attention in institutions oriented toward clinical treatment. Casework and psychiatry would play diagnostic and supportive roles in such a program and would have major re-sponsibility for help in the transition to the home community. The core program, however, would be based on a guided kind of group living experience, not on clinical treatment. Many training schools are tending toward this kind of formulation.

To achieve this, an institution would have to become somewhat smaller than the traditional training school (200 maximum?) and would have to rethink the roles and responsibilities of cottage per-sonnel, counselors, and other staff members as well. Most crucial, of course, would be the definition of the types of boys for whom this kind of program would seem to be appropriate and the manner in which they are to be identified. Those requiring more intensive, individual social work or psychiatric treatment, either because the delinquency is traced to personality disturbance or because they cannot tolerate the group experience, should be sent to institutions equipped, in staff, structure, and size, to do the task.

It is already clear from studies of informal organization and peer culture that careful orientation programs must be built into train-ing schools, in an effort to communicate objectives clearly and to

[25] Ohlin and Lawrence, "Social Interaction among Clients as a Treatment Problem," *Social Work*, IV, pp. 11–13. Also see Robert D. Vinter and Roger M. Lind, *Staff Relationships and Attitudes in a Juvenile Correctional Institution* (Ann Arbor: School of Social Work, University of Michigan, 1958).

launch a newly arrived child in a constructive way. During the orientation period, a diagnostic and classification process permits the pooling of expert knowledge and judgment for the purpose of placing a child in an appropriate group and cottage, under the best possible houseparents and counselors, with a plan for such educational-vocational experiences and individual clinical and remedial help as offer the greatest promise of successful correction. In addition, individual medical and dental services are scheduled as needed, and the work of postdischarge planning and family counseling is begun.

Aftercare. Whatever their theories of delinquency, all who believe that rehabilitation of delinquents is possible are agreed as to the importance of the aftercare program. In fact, the U.S. Senate delinquency subcommittee reported in 1958 that this was one of the most vulnerable points in the entire antidelinquency effort. It cannot be said too often that *rehabilitation must, ultimately, take place in the community.* Institutionalization is, at best, a successful period of removal from the community in order to help the individual equip and prepare himself for his return. The proponent of psychiatric treatment notes that even a very successfully treated patient is faced by a reactivation of all prior problems unless environmental pressures are eased and he is helped to cope with them on his return to the community. The criminologist who stresses the effects of antisocial delinquent subcultures as causative factors notes that the child helped in the training school faces irresistible community pressures when he returns unless strong supports are also present, in the form of aftercare services, to reinforce the values which the institution represents and to help the individual cope with some of the extremely difficult problems involved in return to family and neighborhood, readjustment to school or job, and establishment of healthy new friendships and group associations.

There is expert consensus to the effect that the very decision to return a child to the community should, in fact, be based on both an estimate of the progress made in the institution and the strengths and limits of the community situation. Aftercare programs require qualified social work staff, who are in every sense members of the rehabilitation team and who work in continuous contact with the training school from the time of a child's commitment. During this same period, work with the family must prepare the way for the eventual return.[26]

Aftercare services have been organized in a number of ways: [27]

a) Service by a state agency, usually through strategically located regional offices. To many, this is the preferred plan.

b) Service by the casework or parole staff attached to the training schools. This would seem desirable and possible in a state which is not too large, geographically; otherwise, travel would be prohibitive.

c) Service by the juvenile court. The aftercare function hardly seems appropriate for a probation staff.

d) Service by a public or private casework agency, often a child welfare department. Unless the agency reserves adequate time and specializes in this function, staff may not be able to discharge it satisfactorily.

e) Service by the adult parole staff. This is not desirable for all the reasons which dictate specialized juvenile courts and treatment facilities. The entire approach in youth work is different.

f) Service provided by the judge. This is possible only in very small rural counties.

g) Service by volunteer organizations, such as the Big Brothers. While this is a valuable supplement, it is not a substitute for state responsibility.

Each of the plans has its proponents and all are to be found in active use. While it is possible to specify circumstances under which some would not work, systematic comparative data are unobtainable. U.S. Children's Bureau data for 1956 show that the institution itself or the parent agency (i.e., the department supervising the institution) provided about two thirds of the aftercare, while other state or local departments, courts, or community agencies accounted for one third. Parent agencies provided almost three times as much aftercare supervision as institution staffs.

Aftercare programs in several parts of the country (Oregon, Washington, New Mexico, for example) are said to have developed

[26] Frank L. Manella, "Aftercare Programs," *National Probation and Parole Association Journal*, IV, No. 1 (January, 1958), 75–76.

[27] *Ibid.*, pp. 76–77. Facts cited below about proportions of parent agencies, other agencies, and institutions providing aftercare supervision are in *Statistics in Public Institutions for Delinquent Children, 1956*, p. 9.

extensive, successful foster care resources. Residence clubs, halfway houses, and a variety of other facilities are also essential.

A large state certainly needs administrative decentralization to provide state-wide coverage and a plan ensuring close integration with the training school programs.

It may be expected that future organization for aftercare will reflect the new emphasis on the problem of establishing for the dischargee an environment in which community adjustment is possible—and is even supported. Aftercare was too long defined only as the problem of dealing with the parent-child attitudes involved and was approached through preparatory interviews with each, and occasional supportive contacts after discharge. Then, as the complexity of the interpersonal pathologies was revealed, more intensive treatment was sought for some parents while the child was being helped in the institution. Today there is more realistic appraisal of the deficiencies of some family situations, the poor prognosis for change, and the danger of recidivism if the child goes home. Therefore, foster homes and (even more frequently) residence clubs become the great need. Communities have barely begun to develop what is here required.

Recent sociological analyses suggest the need to devise ways to go even beyond this, however, though specific methods have not yet been proposed. If, as has been held, the experience of commitment and institutionalization results in a definition of self as rejected by the controlling powers in the community, and if this merely confirms a self-image previously developed and indicating that one cannot, legitimately, succeed in the large society, then the aftercare program must demonstrate (as must the institution program before it) the possibilities of community acceptance and success—and help the youth attain the necessary knowledge, attitude, skills. Methods for accomplishing this will have to be developed experimentally.

On the basis of findings on inmate culture in a study of a voluntary institution and a training school, the Ford Foundation is backing an exploration focusing on methods for influencing institutional inmate cultures. Several investigators are trying to understand more fully the problem of reintegration into the community after discharge. It seems likely that group therapy, group residences, vocational counseling, and placement will have great importance in such programs, but a variety of community organization efforts may require emphasis. In this connection, one might note the suggestion that the core role of the aftercare worker of the future (except where he is the individual psychotherapist in the institution continuing his work) may be a form of community organization concerned with providing the means and conditions essential to reintegration in the community. He must discover and help to create essential resources and must deal with community receptivity to the returnee—as much as he must offer counseling and guidance to former inmates.

The concept of a diversified system. From all that has gone before, it is clear that constant refinement and strengthening of the traditional training school will make it a more effective social instrument—but one appropriate for a more limited group of boys and girls than generally assumed.

The clarification of objectives, development of program, and assignment of staff along the lines outlined above should make the training school more than the place of custody—in fact, place of punitive custody—that it has often been. For its "typical" student, the "typical" training school today is a center which reinforces antisocial attitudes and proves to him the impossibility of rehabilitation. Only through greater understanding of the boys and girls, their problems and their attitudes, and through provision not only of program content but also of a milieu capable of molding their group culture will the typical training school be converted into an agency of social reintegration. However, in order to become more effective, the training school must become more focused and somewhat more specialized. As already suggested, this tendency would seem to make it most suitable for relatively socialized delinquents (not "isolates")

(1) who can benefit from a group experience without excessive exploitation of others and without being personally victimized;

(2) who do not require intensive psychiatric treatment;

(3) who need a measure of secure custody outside the community for their own and community protection;

(4) whose exposure to a sound milieu (through a well-directed

group experience) gives promise of a reorientation of values and attitudes;

(5) who may be able to benefit from exposure to sound adult behavior models;

(6) who may require new attitudes to the world of work and an educational-vocational experience which will equip them for first jobs or future training after institutionalization;

(7) who may need short-term psychiatric, social work, and psychological help, relative to their institutional adjustment and postcommitment plans.

There are many delinquents who do not meet this description but who need help away from home. Many of them are now in training schools. There are those who are capable, personally, of continuing in the community but who must be committed to an institution which substitutes for the lack of enough foster homes or foster homes of the type required. Some of these cannot remain at home because of family circumstances or facts connected with their offenses. Others may be particularly suited for a group experience in a more open setting in which the total group is smaller, the relationships with adults closer, the specialized program resources fewer, and the stay perhaps briefer (i.e., the *forestry camp*). Among these would be boys who must leave the community but for whom a relatively rapid return is possible, who are capable of the controls necessary for intimate living in an open setting, and whose basic values seem capable of redirection through a socializing experience, without need for intensive individual counseling.

There are other delinquents who are mentally ill, emotionally disturbed, or mentally defective and who require a variety of specialized facilities, including the small, psychiatrically directed, residential treatment center, the state hospital, specialized institutions for defectives, and the like.

Where continuation of school and job ties in the community seem desirable but the child must leave home and/or the immediate neighborhood (and cannot sustain the intimacy of a foster home relationship or no foster homes are available) a residence club-hostel type of facility may be appropriate. Individual guidance and, perhaps, intensive casework or psychiatric treatment may be provided in the residence or by an agency or clinic in the community.

These are not the only alternatives, but they serve to underscore the current emphasis on diversification of treatment resources for children who need help away from home. *If the "traditional" training school is to be effective, it must be strengthened for one group and not required to include those whom it cannot be expected to help.*

Diversification has not developed as a concept in the abstract. It has evolved through experience. Historically, as the old "orphan asylums" were needed less and less with improvements in health services and the advent of social security, many voluntary institutions began to serve neglected and dependent children. Some opened their doors to court-committed delinquents who seemed relatively normal in personality, but who required care away from home. Some sectarian groups designed institutions to provide treatment for children who needed institutional care whatever their legal category (dependent, neglected, delinquent).

A variety of emphases developed out of this experience: some institutions tended toward the type of group-oriented programs described above for training schools, with supplementary treatment and educational-vocational resources. Others sought to develop intensive individual clinical treatment programs, occasionally in relatively large settings but most often of late in small facilities. Several types of community-based treatment centers were developed. New experiments also emerged out of medically based programs. Children with a variety of "labels" were of course served. A current illustrative list would include such voluntary and public facilities as the Langley Porter Clinic (California), the Grove School (Wisconsin), Orthogenic School (Illinois), Southard School (Kansas), Sweetser Children's Home (Maine), Child Study Center (Maryland), Neuro-psychiatric Institute (Michigan), Bellefaire (Ohio), Child Guidance Home (Ohio), Ryther Child Center (Washington).

In the first phase of the development described above, variations were often undertaken by voluntary agencies (sometimes with public subsidies) while the public department provided only training schools in most states. There were some exceptions. Because there were not enough voluntary resources, or out of conviction as to their responsibilities, some states began themselves to offer alternatives. They saw that the training school could not work as a heterogeneous catchall. The forestry camp became the most common alternative. In New York, city and state funds were granted to small, intensive-treatment, residential centers under voluntary auspices.

In a few instances, large voluntary sectarian federations saw the need to diversify facilities under their own auspices. One federation undertook studies in 1947 and 1956 in which experts outlined a diversified network of treatment resources, described the characteristics of the children considered most suitable for each facility, estimated the number of children requiring each on the basis of a case sampling, and reported the number currently "misplaced" by such criteria. The gap between actual practice and an abstract "ideal" pattern underscored the extent to which current practice may not be in tune with changing knowledge, even in agencies in the forefront of professional development and relatively fortunate in their resources.[28] Similar data for typical state programs would be most disturbing.

Today the move toward diversification is well under way. The following principle would seem to encompass present thinking and to take account of policy variations in different parts of the country: *A state which assumes jurisdiction over delinquents and commits them with a view toward their rehabilitation should provide a diversified range of treatment facilities either under its own or under private auspices.*

There is much evidence that valuable developments have taken place and that more will come. We shall illustrate briefly and at random.

States such as *California, Washington,* and *Minnesota* operate diagnostic-reception programs, upon which hinge efficient diversification. Careful observation and study is a preliminary to assignment. Such centers depend on competent staff and on statutory authority to make the decisions.

Maryland stresses forestry camps in its diversification program begun in 1953. It rejects the "traditional view that the care or treatment for children in institutions depends upon training them in vocational pursuits" in favor of a "mental hygiene concept of causa-

---

[28] Philip Klein, *Institutional Placement Needs for Children Served by Agencies in Federation* (New York: Federation of Jewish Philanthropies, 1947), and Martha K. Selig and Blanche Bernstein, *To Serve the Children Best* (New York: Federation of Jewish Philanthropies, 1956).

tion and treatment . . . [under which] the child is reeducated for community living . . . by helping him to assume responsibility for belonging in the free community in accordance with the prevailing mores and the laws of society." [29] The Maryland forestry program, available to youths up to eighteen, was established through the joint planning of the welfare and conservation departments; its per capita costs are substantially below those of a training school. The Maryland Commission for the Prevention and Treatment of Delinquency also proposed a "children's village" for boys and girls under fourteen, with a program emphasizing general education, remedial education, recreation, a good deal of parental participation, and much home visiting.

California's Youth Authority has pioneered in the development of a diversified, integrated, state-wide system of facilities anchored in the diagnostic clinics of its two reception-classification centers for children and youth. In addition to having the services of the reception centers, each of the institutions has classification counselors who follow the progress of the boys, recommend specific programs for them, and, where necessary, refer children back to the reception centers for more study or to the parole board for hearings. The reception centers do not hesitate to recommend parole if it seems appropriate (most states fear this as an infringement on judicial prerogatives), and they may refer for mental hospital observation those children considered possibly committable. These centers provide orientation as well as diagnostic study and refer to a reasonably diversified range of resources including, of course, the pioneering system of camps.[30]

It is of some interest to note that California has found it useful to operate two systems of camps: camps for the 13–15 age group are school-centered, but offer the opportunity for part-time work; camps for the 16- to 18-year-olds have a substantial work-forestry component, but also include a school program. Both groups receive remedial courses and preparation for work (tool handling and first-aid instruction) in the reception centers.

California counties operate a system of camps-ranches-schools

[29] Raymond L. Manella, "A Troubled Boy and the Forest," *Child Welfare,* XXXVI, No. 2 (February, 1957), 25–31.

[30] Heman G. Stark, "Central Reception and Diagnosis in California," *National Probation and Parole Association Journal,* IV, No. 1 (January, 1958), 28–33.

for the less-serious offenders, while the more-serious offenders are committed to Youth Authority.

Concerned with the constant need to add new facilities and the accompanying costs and staffing problems, California is planning two multiple-institution "constellations" near universities and cities and tied in to local utilities and sewerage systems. These constellations will have space for standard units. While the system will mean giving up California's emphasis on camp and forest facilities, it is expected to simplify expansion and administration and to make it possible to have small institutions which are not too costly. At the same time, great stress will be placed on community treatment alternatives.

One might cite a wide variety of innovations and the development of programs which seem particularly suited to a comprehensive diversified system. *Portland, Oregon,* reports a valuable foster care program for the under-twelve group, operated by the court for lack of community provision, but more appropriate to a child care agency.[31] A *Wisconsin* group has experimented for several years with the use of small group homes for the placement of selected juvenile parole cases. Each home is licensed to care for six youngsters whose return to the parental home from the training school would be damaging and who are not considered able to meet the emotional demands of a relationship to foster parents.[32]

World-wide interest has been aroused by the *New Jersey Highfields* experiment, whose effectiveness is attested to by an evaluative study. New Jersey has opened two more facilities for boys as well as for girls (Allaire); New York has opened two and is planning others. There is a facility (Southfields) at Louisville, Kentucky. A nonresident version at Provo, Utah, has been described (Ch. VII). One of the New Jersey units is also nonresidential.

Highfields traces its origins to the residential treatment centers as well as to the forestry camps. It offers a routine work experience, mainly on state hospital grounds. Its unique factor is an intensive program of daily "guided group interaction" sessions conducted by a sociologist, in a new version of group therapy. Highfields holds

[31] Gladys I. Kellar, "Court Foster Home Program," *ibid.,* pp. 57–65.
[32] Lester E. Wogahm, Edith Sommer, and Lawrence Larsen, "An Experiment in Group Placement of Juvenile Parolees," *ibid.,* pp. 66–73.

a small group of 20 boys ages 16 and 17 on probation status; it has few rules and few facilities. There is a staff of 4–6. Everything possible is done to avoid institutional routine in the traditional sense. Some critics have, in fact, questioned the lack of classes, reading matter, organized recreation, religious program, or more rules about personal hygiene, appearance, and behavior. Its advocates stress the importance to the program of concentrating all attention and energies on the group sessions and on individual relationships to the group. They maintain that more facilities or program would dilute this.[33]

Highfields does not purport to provide psychiatric treatment for boys who require it. Nor can it deal with "hardened criminals" or serious runaways. Its program stresses reorientation of values in the direction of greater understanding of the value system of the majority of society, or at least attainment of skills which will promote conformity to social demands—so that no matter what one's problems or core beliefs, it becomes possible to avoid trouble. It may be seen, perhaps, as teaching adjustment and "coping" skills through an intensive socialization experience in which both one's peers and the group leader constantly point up one's defects and vulnerabilities. Here rehabilitation becomes the boys' objective; in most institutions it is a staff goal, not an inmate goal.

Particularly interesting is Highfield's economy (its costs are only a fraction of training school costs) and brief "terms" (average stay about four months).

Highfields and other treatment facilities sometimes shock those accustomed to rigid controls, severe discipline, and outward order. Howard Jones's dictum is here useful:

It is not the behavior of the child in the institution that really matters, but his behavior when he goes out into the world again. There is no reason to believe that taking away responsibility for self-discipline by imposing discipline upon him externally will make him more capable of unaided self-control when he does leave.

British Approved Schools and probation hostels may also hold useful lessons for states interested in diversification. Since 1942 the

[33] Lloyd W. McCorkie, Albert Elias, F. Lovell Bixby, *The Highfields Story* (New York: Henry Holt and Company, 1958). See also H. Ashley Weeks, *Youthful Offenders at Highfields* (Ann Arbor: University of Michigan Press, 1958).

British have used so-called Classifying Schools for observation and evaluation prior to assignment to one of the variety of Approved Schools. Because of the strong Approved School tradition of vocational training, classification for *such* training is quite refined in the English scheme. Particular stress is also placed on a point to be emphasized below: "definition of the functions of the various schools and the shaping of methods for selecting appropriate boys." [34] This is, of course, the foundation stone of a system of diversification.

The *British probation hostels* are also worthy of further attention as possible resources. Residence in the hostel becomes a condition of probation, but only for the probationer who accepts it voluntarily. The probationer who remains a year, but whose program is reviewed after six months, works and contributes to costs in accordance with a sliding scale. The hostel warden becomes the primary person in contact with the youth, but a probation officer retains contact on behalf of the court. One group of hostels serves the 15–18 age group and another the 17–21; there are over twenty hostels for boys and ten or more for girls. There are also approximately twelve probation homes which provide work on the premises. Those associated with the program stress that it is suitable only for an appropriately selected group, not for the failures of other institutions and certainly not for the very disturbed or extremely immature.

A variety of American cities have developed halfway houses to serve in the transition period between institutionalization and full-fledged community independence, but these programs are very small. *Austrian apprentice work homes* under public, philanthropic, and union auspices contain many interesting program notions, as do several of the *French semi-liberté institutions* and *Italian focallari*. Clearly, modern cities need many residence clubs for adolescents as a substitute for institutions and as a postinstitutional resource. Certain of these are also needed for youth who do not get into trouble at all.

Diversification, it should be noted, does not necessarily require population homogeneity in any one facility. The success of certain programs may in fact require heterogeneity to accelerate constructive interaction. This, then, is the core of the challenge: *It is neces-*

[34] John Gittins, *Approved School Boys* (London: Her Majesty's Stationery Office, 1952).

sary both to identify the essence of the treatment impact of each major type of program and to specify the range of children for which it is suitable. The complexity of the task is not to be denied; it is unavoidable once we make the decision to help and to treat, not merely to hold or to punish, children who offend.

NEW YORK STATE—SOME ISSUES IN PLANNING

We have described in detail elsewhere the progress to date in achieving a degree of institutional diversification in New York State and the problems yet to be solved.[35] Unless the efforts of a variety of public and voluntary bodies can be organized to create an integrated system of facilities, large investment may continue to yield only limited results. The obstacles in the way of such integration and the issues posed are not unique to New York.

New York State training schools have long demonstrated their interest in strengthening treatment programs and have often been in the forefront of national development. Nonetheless, state traditions have given priority in commitment decisions to the voluntary institutions—particularly those conducted by representatives of a child's religious faith. This is in accord with public policy and statutes going back to the nineteenth century. Thus, during 1914, 70.6 percent of the delinquency commitments in the state were to privately operated institutions. There was a brief decline for several years, and then the proportion reached 81.9 percent in 1918, remained over 75 percent until 1924, and began a gradual decline thereafter. Not until 1937 did the private "share" of commitments fall below 60 percent in any year. Until 1950 it fluctuated in the 50–61 percent range, gradually settling in the low 50s. Between 1950 and 1960 the proportion of admissions to voluntary institutions declined quite rapidly, so that by 1960 one third of all commitments were to voluntary institutions and two thirds to training schools.

The committed population census of about 3,500 at any given moment does not find the voluntary and public facilities quite so far apart, the difference being 300–500 children. The public facilities absorb many more commitments since their average period of institutionalization is briefer. Voluntary institutions did decrease their

[35] Alfred J. Kahn, *When Children Must Be Committed* (New York: Citizens' Committee for Children of New York, Inc., 1960).

capacities in the 1950s but have recently returned to their 1949 levels. The state has added substantial new space to accommodate the increases since 1955. A small number of delinquent children are also committed to hospitals or specialized institutions as psychotic, as mental defectives, or as drug addicts.

Study of New York commitment statistics and trends suggests several additional generalizations relevant to over-all planning:

    a) Despite the tremendous concern with delinquency and the strongly expressed view that many troublesome young people should be removed from the community, the institution admission *rate* for delinquency, per 1,000 children in the child population of the state, has changed very little for the approximately twenty years for which data are available. In fact, it has fluctuated between .9 and 1.1 per 1,000 except for the period 1943–46 when it was 1.2 and 1.3. Members of the general public and those concerned with finding institutional space for children sometimes forget that the pressure and shortages experienced in recent years may reflect the vastly increased child population rather than a major change in the rate or character of delinquency. As in the construction of schools, our resources tend to lag behind population growth. The stability of the rate has obvious potential for projecting needed capacity in relation to population growth.

    b) After twenty years of gradual decline, the total institutionalized population began to rise a decade ago. Nonetheless, commitment totals have not reached the volume of the period between World War I and the 1929 depression. Probation services have expanded during this period and reservations about institutions have become more widespread.

    c) Since commitment rates are affected by both the volume and the nature of the court's petitions, variations may reflect such factors as the prevalence of multiple petitions (i.e., a child may appear on several), the philosophy of individual judges, police activity, case dismissal rates in Children's Court, availability of space, and community sentiment at a given time.

Questions have been raised from time to time as to whether there is not too much reliance in the state on institutionalization. New York City's Juvenile Delinquency Evaluation Project, commenting that institution life is abnormal and should be resorted to only if absolutely unavoidable, noted that a large proportion of the girls at the State Training School had been sent away without any prior effort at probation treatment.[36] A study conducted for the New York State Department of Social Welfare of a sample of boys committed in 1957 and 1958 showed that, in fact, the training school was a preferred resource for approximately 20 percent of the boys; it was the court's first choice in even fewer cases. However, because of family and personal circumstances, the majority of boys in the sample needed some alternative form of living arrangement, and the training school was often selected for lack of such resources.[37] While institution officials are able to point to sizable proportions of their populations (often 5 to 20 percent) as unsuited to the particular programs available, they do not label so large a number of children as being in need of community-based rather than residential treatment.

As various states experienced the postwar rise in delinquency, they adopted their own solutions to the problem of providing additional institutional space.

a) State A met its commitment increases by adding dormitories and buildings until a facility designed for 400 housed 1,500. Barbed-wire fences, guards, and motor patrols have not ended the resultant riots, runaways, and assaults on staff.

b) State B avoided institution overcrowding by creating a "revolving door." Once capacity is reached, a boy is released as soon as one is committed. The average stay is less than four months. There are no aftercare services.

c) State C avoided these alternatives by establishing county commitment quotas and "freezing" intake when capacity was reached. It is not known what occurs when a county uses up its space.

New York rejected these alternatives and chose to add to its in-

---

[36] Juvenile Delinquency Evaluation Project, *Three New York State Training Schools* (New York, 1957), and *The Institutionalization of Young Delinquents* (New York, 1958). Also, Alfred J. Kahn, *For Children in Trouble* (New York: Citizens' Committee for Children of New York, Inc., 1957), p. 65.

[37] Alfred J. Kahn *et al.*, *New York City Boys Committed to State Training Schools in 1957 and 1958* (Albany: New York State Department of Social Welfare, 1960).

stitutions so that at present only California has a larger public program. The total state program is impressive: Hudson, for girls, with a branch in operation and an annex under construction; Industry; Warwick; Annex; Otisville; Highland; New Hampton. Fifteen million dollars have gone into new facilities and an equal sum into expansion and repair. Further expansion is under way.

Nonetheless, New York State Department of Social Welfare leadership and staff face serious obstacles as they strive to provide institutions which are more than adequate custodial facilities. *First,* although training schools now accept two thirds of all committed delinquents, the implications of the fact are not fully absorbed by courts, agencies, legislature, or public. For a long time these were "residue" institutions, to be called upon in those instances in which voluntary institutions lacked space or regarded a child as unmanageable and in other ways unsuited for their programs. The law states that if there is commitment to a voluntary institution it should, when practicable, be to an institution of the child's own faith. Some judges take this to mean that all sectarian commitment possibilities should be exhausted before training schools are considered!

Two consequences have followed: public institutions have had little control of their populations, quantitatively and qualitatively; public institutions have been compelled to serve populations too heterogeneous to permit viable programs and without adequate professional resources.

Thus, despite devoted work and good leadership, training schools must necessarily fail with some of the types of problems and situations they face because of basic public policy. They strive to improve things while constantly under public pressure; as we have seen in the detention discussion, individual bed space has not kept up with commitments and the wait while voluntary institutions process applications creates a difficult bottleneck. *Second,* the expansion must continue even though methodologies are only partially developed for translating new knowledge of peer culture and the components of a total milieu into specific agency programs and into a general strategy for diversification. Thus far boys' institutions are differentiated by age, offense, and management problems and there are additional dimensions emerging. Further progress is being made with girls.

Third, planning for better training schools is complicated by misconceptions about voluntary institutions for dependent, neglected, disturbed, and delinquent children—misconceptions prevalent in several sections of the country in addition to New York. The facts are known and documented but have not been widely publicized or fully absorbed in their planning implications.

Voluntary institutions. Institutions under voluntary auspices, some of them sectarian, continue to absorb about one third of New York's delinquency commitments. They receive substantial public reimbursement for the service. Several of these "institutions . . . are constantly engaged in thinking, planning and experimenting for the improvement of their services. They convey a sense of vitality. . . . There is no standing still at any point. . . . The basis of this service is the clear recognition that the delinquent child must be viewed as a total personality." [38] While the conceptions of treatment and the orientation of leadership among these institutions may vary somewhat, the better ones all understand the importance of integration of the several facets of program (daily living, recreation, education, work, clinic, aftercare) into a whole, guided by sound philosophy, adequate knowledge, and appropriate skill. They have not grappled fully, any more than have the training schools, with the problem of peer culture and informal organization—but limited knowledge makes this inevitable.

The voluntary institutions are not by any means all identical in quality or in program. They cover a very substantial range. They include what were once large, congregate facilities which emphasized education, training, and vocational preparation and which are now seeking to develop social work and psychiatric treatment programs. In the manner of the training schools, several of these larger facilities will have to wrestle with the issue of whether their treatment emphasis is to be on individual psychotherapy, with the other program content offering support, or whether they are to develop group treatment programs around which all else revolves, on the assumption that they are seeking value-attitude changes rather than personality restructuring. Obviously they all need not, indeed should not, make the same decisions about this matter. Various gradations and combinations may be desirable.

Also included within the voluntary institutions, at the other end

[38] Juvenile Delinquency Evaluation Project, *Three Residential Treatment Centers* (New York, 1958), p. 41.

of the range, are small, experimental centers for psychiatric treatment and research. While attention is or should be given to the total milieu, the objective here is to create a milieu which supports the psychotherapy. The issue has become whether these should be regarded as residence programs under social agency auspices or as medically directed in-patient psychiatric treatment resources. It has been urged that a distinction be made between those situations in which children receive psychiatric care while living at home, in foster homes, or in nonmedical institutions and situations requiring in-patient psychiatric hospital treatment.[39]

Special mention should be made of the extent to which a number of the voluntary institutions have been able to develop outstanding school programs, in cooperation with the New York State Department of Education. By special legislation, several of these institutions are public school districts and receive state educational aid. They also receive state grants for special education. Several of these programs and programs in other voluntary institutions have been particularly inventive in the interrelation of educational and clinical programs and have been able to report remarkable progress in learning for some children. Since some children arrive at the voluntary institutions (and most arrive at training schools) as "educational casualties," the significance of these efforts and the need to study and to expand them cannot be overemphasized. Obviously, the specific form of the educational program should vary with the type of institution, much as should all other aspects of program.

The voluntary institutions have had the advantage of controlling their intake of court-referred delinquents in both type and volume. The larger treatment-oriented institutions may reject four or five children for each one accepted. The residential treatment centers accept only 15 percent of the children deemed eligible by their referral sources. (Rejection rates reflect referral policy as much as intake policy. An institution may be approached as part of a carefully made plan or in the course of random "shopping for a bed.")

Voluntary institutions in general have tended in some instances to accept a narrower range of children than those committed to train-

<hr/>

[39] J. Franklin Robinson et al., Psychiatric Inpatient Treatment of Children (Washington: American Psychiatric Association, 1957). For description of social agency experience, see Herschel Alt, Residential Treatment for the Disturbed Child (New York: International Universities Press, 1960).

ing schools. Some of the larger institutions, which in other respects are much like the training schools, have avoided the more disturbed, disruptive, and difficult-to-reach youth. Application pressures have militated against homogeneity, however. Unlike the training schools, the voluntary institutions accept dependent and neglected children, too—as well as children admitted on parental initiative because of their need for treatment of the sort offered. The issue for these institutions is often the degree and type of disturbance in the child rather than the administrative category. The welfare departments are major referral sources to these institutions.

Control over intake and, at times, an ability to pay for and to attract somewhat better qualified personnel are the main differentiating factors between several of the larger voluntary institutions and the public facilities. Considering both groups as wholes, there is no absolute qualitative difference in the basic treatment approach. A few voluntary facilities are more custody- and security-minded than the training schools. (Los Angeles County's Las Palmas, a girls' treatment center under the Probation Department, compares favorably with so-called residential treatment centers under voluntary auspices elsewhere.)

Confusion about differences between voluntary institutions and training schools has been compounded by use of the designation "residential treatment center" which has gained increasing popularity and status among the voluntary institutions but has become so loose a description as to be devoid of clear meaning. The term now includes both intensive residential treatment centers and those larger voluntary institutions accepting delinquents which meet certain staffing and intake criteria.

The courts are so desperately in need of commitment resources and the system of application-allocation is so lacking in central policy and control that children are not clearly separated in accord with need and then assigned to institutions with the most suitable programs. The objective is placement, and the courts use the best facility available at a given moment. While placement authorities may want a facility offering treatment, the treatment is a secondary consideration under the pressure to find a bed. The courts in particular make multiple referrals in their search for placement, often sending the child's case summary for consideration "to institutions having different intake criteria and different programs. There is evidently little precision in the matching of the child to the therapeutic instrument." [40] Scarce resources are not, then, allocated in accord with any wise strategy; circumstances and pressures of the moment tend to govern. The designation "emotionally disturbed child," used originally to characterize the child thought to need residential psychiatric treatment but not in a psychiatric ward in a hospital, has gradually become an almost useless phrase to planning purposes or in the referral-intake process.

It is not surprising to learn, under these circumstances, that the small residential treatment centers contain populations showing substantial diagnostic heterogeneity: "Children of all diagnostic categories are being placed in both training schools and mental hospitals," [41] even though the proportions may not be equal.

Although, to training school personnel, the voluntary institutions generally seem to be well financed and equipped, this is not always the case. With a few notable exceptions, they continue to face financial difficulties as they seek to organize themselves to render good clinical service while providing wholesome daily living experiences, education, and recreation. Several are in serious financial straits despite public subsidy considerably above three fourths of operational costs! All lack resources for capital expansion. It thus seems likely that public funds will continue to provide the bulk of the new institutional resources, and public planning would appear to be both necessary and possible.

It is generally assumed that the voluntary institutions are more effective than the training schools since they are less crowded, house diagnostically more homogeneous populations, tend to have better qualified staff, and reject those considered to have poor prognoses. However, definitive data relative to effectiveness are not available. Several of the institutions have been encouraged and some discouraged by modest follow-up studies, but there are no adequate recent follow-up efforts. Nor are there studies using the control groups necessary to differentiate the effects of institutional treatment

[40] Donald A. Bloch, Marjorie L. Behrens, and others, A Study of Children Referred for Residential Treatment in New York State (New York: New York State Interdepartment Health Resources Board, 1959), pp. 8 ff. and 65.

[41] Ibid., pp. 77–79.

from normal maturation or to take account of initial intake rules and selectivity.

Facilities under the New York State Division for Youth. New York State's institutional and treatment resources are currently being expanded by another agency, the New York State Division for Youth, which succeeded the State Youth Commission in 1960. The program reflects public interest in offering preventive resources for those defined as "on the threshold of delinquency" as well as concern with diversification of facilities for adjudicated delinquents and young offenders. There was particular interest in "work camps" and in forestry camps at the time the legislation was discussed. (The State Department of Corrections has been developing a small forestry program for those beyond juvenile court age.)

A period of exploration and study led to the creation of two parallel programs which are now beginning modestly (capacity about 250) but are expected to expand gradually to a capacity of about 1,000. Both are addressed to the 15–17 year age group:

(1) *Opportunity centers:* for voluntary enrollment of youth with parental consent, on referral from a voluntary or public agency.

(2) *Rehabilitation centers:* for court-referred youth who will be referred as a condition of probation—but who must be accepted by the center's director.

Under these two general heading the division means to create comparable facilities: Highfields-type programs, to be called START Centers (Short-Term Adolescent Resident Training), capacity 20; forestry-work camps, capacity 60; Youth Division homes (much like the British urban probation hostels) from which boys will go to school or work, capacity 20; aftercare services; reporting centers. Rigorous research evaluation is intended.

Three START-rehabilitation centers are under way, as are four camps and two homes. Initial developments have been encouraging: qualified staff have been attracted and experimentation and research begun.

Obviously, New York State planning for institutions should and must take into account training schools, Youth Division facilities, and voluntary institutions. Combined they contain the elements of a well-diversified system. Separated they perpetuate confused images and a disfunctional hierarchy.

It is no longer sufficient to seek to provide more institutional space, increase clinical staffs, ensure improved personnel qualifications, and enrich general program content. All of these are essential to many institutions, but they will remain insufficient unless they are part of an even broader effort to (a) reexamine the place of institutions in total community strategy; (b) ensure diversified resources, each of which has a program appropriate to the range of needs expressed in the delinquencies of specified groups of children; (c) develop continuity between all institutions and related community-based services.

Do we use institutions too much? It is not known conclusively whether institutions are used too much. Since voluntary institutions in New York State control their own intake, they tend to feel that children accepted by them belong there. Training schools do not control their intake and most superintendents state that from 5 to 20 percent of the children in their training schools should not be there. A variety of studies, surveys, and reviews do suggest that many committed children would do better in the community were there adequate services and treatment resources; many children are committed to institutions not equipped to help them or to meet their needs.[42]

None of this negates the fact that a total system of services for children in trouble must provide treatment facilities away from home for (a) those who must leave the community for a period of time for their own or community security; (b) those whose problems cannot be dealt with unless they are removed from precipitating factors in their families or environments (and for whom foster homes are not appropriate or available); (c) those believed most "reachable" and "rehabilitatable" through institutional peer-group experiences, intensive individual psychiatric in-patient treatment, specialized educational-vocational programs—or other resources

[42] Kahn, *For Children in Trouble;* also, Juvenile Delinquency Evaluation Project, *The Institutionalization of Young Delinquents,* pp. 1–7. Also, Kahn, *New York City Boys Committed to State Training Schools in 1957 and 1958.*

which can be best provided in institutions. Since institutionalization, no matter what its objectives, involves loss of freedom and a life apart from the community, it should be considered carefully and authorized only through appropriate legal process initiated in the courts or through voluntary parental decision.

Because the institutionalized child must eventually face the problem of return to the community, with all its associated complexities, it is probably correct to assume that given great care in the decision to commit and realistic appraisal of the difficulties, costs, and failures of institutional treatment, commitment rates would probably decline. Recent emphasis on institutions is readily explained only by community rage and desperation in the face of delinquency—not by the success of institutional care.

Do children remain in institutions long enough? Again, the answer is that we do not know. Since there are few adequate studies of institutional effectiveness, there is no way to decide whether commitment periods are too long or too brief. Current theory and practice shows wide diversity. The national average is 9.7 months (boys, 9.3 months; girls, 12 months). Some states have "solved" all of their problems of providing additional space merely by increasing turnover. Highfields reports considerable success with a four-month stay, and a British study notes that brief institutionalization may be more effective than long-term commitment for youth in the 16–21 age group. An experienced training school superintendent expresses interest in experimenting with a six-month commitment period. On the other hand, many superior European institutions retain their students until a full "course" of vocational-apprenticeship training has been completed, which often means three years!

Given the present state of knowledge and weighing all factors, including the disabling effects of long periods in a stigma-bearing facility, it is both unwise and uneconomical to assume that long periods of institutionalization or traditional periods ("two years," "a school year") are necessarily best. The coming experimentation with diversification of facilities certainly should include some programs offering only very brief stays, followed by intensive service in the community, if needed—while others offer longer institutionalization.

Toward real diversification. A first step for any state would be the decision to regard as parts of one system all the relevant components in its institutional network. New York has provided an illustration. As we have seen, the State Department of Social Welfare has adopted the objective of diversification and has made slow but steady progress. Resources being developed by the State Youth Division add to the range—but the planning and operations in these two units are not integrated. The state supports substantially the voluntary institutions but they are almost fully autonomous. By any appropriate yardstick, then, these institutions do not constitute one system: definition of intake criteria, control of intake, program planning, interfacility transfers, locus of decisions about institutional functions or emphases.

Unless a unified system is created and more systematic diversification is planned, current frustration and rates of failure are bound to continue, since the competition for space in the small specialized centers will go on and allocation of resources will not necessarily be made in terms of the wisest possible criteria. Continuation of present institutional distinctions probably also involves a degree of avoidable waste, since there is perhaps not enough variation in lengths of commitment and not enough experimentation with brief stays; most important, many of the large institutions are attempting to conform to the expensive model of a controlled residential milieu whose major treatment resource is a well-staffed clinic offering individual psychotherapy. Some committed delinquents need this, but not all.

Apart from the solution of organizational obstacles to diversification (interdepartmental, public-voluntary, etc.), the pace of diversification must also be determined by the level of knowledge and experience. For adequate planning in this field assumes considerable knowledge of (a) the relevant dimensions from which institutions are to be viewed (i.e., the variations between them which are relevant to their effects) and (b) the kinds of case diagnoses or formulations which will assist in the assignment to particular institutions. In technical language, sound diagnostic and treatment typologies are essential. *If the institution is to provide a "specific" treatment, it is appropriate to ask what kind of "prescription" a given institution meets.* At present, the response is usually made in quite generalized terms. Knowledge at this point, which draws on a variety of experiences, experiments, and innovations, suggests that the following (which involve some overlapping) may be some of the relevant factors (dimensions) which would enter into differentiation between institutions in a diversified system:

(1) degree of security and custody
(2) size
(3) age ranges served
(4) extent of use or "neutralization" of peer-group development
(5) degree of emphasis on individual psychotherapy in an institution-based clinical facility
(6) whether open to members of one sex or coeducational
(7) whether work experiences are available in the institution or neighboring community
(8) extent of emphasis on intrapsychic and/or interpersonal problems, as compared with general value orientation, sound attitudes, and behavior
(9) extent of use of group therapy
(10) nature of educational and vocational offerings and their intensity
(11) length of stay
(12) medical treatment, if any, including extent of use of drugs

The specification of these and other dimensions is only a first step. There remains the task of combining them in various ways so as to emerge with a group of institutions not so large and expensive as to be impossible of attainment but adequate to serve effectively the entire range of committed children.

Clearly, then, diagnostic classification systems (typologies) are also required, since without them there is no basis for experimentation with combinations of the institutional dimensions suggested, nor for identifying the range of children for which a given institutional type may be appropriate. Here, too, there is much work to be done. Current experience suggests that the following may be some of the factors in a diagnostic typology relevant to choice of institutions:

(1) age
(2) degree of physical health or handicap
(3) psychiatric diagnosis, if any
(4) nature of relationships with parents and siblings

(5) specific social background and milieu

(6) nature of relationships with peers

(7) extent of destructive, aggressive, or self-destructive behavior, demonstrated or potential

(8) intelligence

(9) academic status, with particular reference to learning retardation and/or particular talents or abilities

(10) nature of relationships with adults in the neighborhood—outside of the immediate family

(11) "leverage" for intervention and change

This is by no means a full listing. There is need for creative work to suggest ways of combining elements such as these into a limited number of "types." California Youth Authority and Department of Correction research staffs have been giving this subject concentrated attention recently. Long descriptive summaries about children, which do not arrive at an appropriate case formulation, do not advance the task of matching child and institution and testing relative institutional effectiveness with various types.

Disposition as a technical problem. As a diversified institutional system is developed by a state, it will become increasingly difficult for the individual judge to make a wise choice among available facilities. Even where fully qualified for the task (and this cannot be assumed, generally, since it requires other than legal training), the judge should not and could not devote his time and energies to keeping abreast of the institutional programs and populations at any given time. Yet, without completely current information, the wise assignment of an individual child cannot be made.

Thus the logic of the Youth Authority position would seem to be reinforced. Without adopting the full plan, as originally proposed or as enacted in five states,[43] New York State (or any other state) might simply develop the practice of having all children who are committed assigned to the Department of Social Welfare, or an equivalent state agency, which would then—according to established diagnostic and classification criteria—choose the specific treatment program. This kind of plan has already developed in many places.

The question to be answered is whether or not such a plan inter-

[43] Bertram M. Beck, *Five States* (Philadelphia: American Law Institute, 1951).

feres too much with judicial responsibility. It is difficult to see how perpetuation of a system of relatively uninformed assignment (where, in effect, a child is usually sent to what the judge regards as the "best" of the institutions with space available at the time of commitment) may be called responsible action.

It is, however, possible to argue that the decision to institutionalize rather than to discharge or to place on probation involves a degree of deprivation of freedom and should be made by the judge. If one takes this position it follows that to make such a decision a judge requires a good probation case study and skill in conducting a disposition conference. Given the judge's decision to commit, however, the *choice* of facility should be turned over to those responsible for the entire institutional system, those who already have the right, following commitment, to transfer a child from one facility to another, even up to his twenty-first birthday if necessary.

There are those who hold that the judge's role is adjudication and that, given a strong probation program or a local "treatment authority," the judge could delegate *all* disposition decisions to technically specialized personnel. While this position has considerable merit in the abstract, the local "treatment authority" or outstanding probation structure on which it must be based does not exist in many places. Centralized classification of *committed* delinquents is a necessity, but the choice between institutionalization and a community-based program should at this time probably continue to be made by the judge.

A diversified system assumes maximum disposition flexibility. This would seem to bring into question California's recent action to limit delinquents who are violators of the criminal law to Youth Authority facilities while less-serious, first offenders may be committed only to county resources.[44] And, as indicated in an earlier chapter, it certainly reveals to be shortsighted New York's 1962 decision to exclude "children in need of supervision" from training schools, while permitting them commitment to voluntary institutions and those facilities under the State Division for Youth.

Since a very large portion of the children eventually committed

[44] Report of the Governor's Special Study Commission on Juvenile Justice, *Recommendations for Changes in California's Juvenile Court Law* (Sacramento: California State Printing Office, 1960).

come through detention facilities, the assignment of liaison teams by a Department of Social Welfare or other responsible department would, in effect, provide a diagnostic-classification facility with relatively small added expense and would avoid subjecting a child to two successive periods of observation and classification. A state would continue to require diagnostic-classification centers for those who do not come via well-equipped detention. Each facility would still require an orientation plan appropriate to its own program and necessary for both sound induction into a program and selection of appropriate group and class assignments. The staff in any facility should be in a position to initiate reassignments.

The voluntary institutions as part of a system. For New York State and other states with substantial voluntary institution development, an obvious and difficult question remains: Should not the planning for diversification and for assignment through diagnostic-classification centers also encompass the voluntary agencies? The answer is in the affirmative on almost every possible score: The inclusion of voluntary facilities gives the system necessary range and some of its best resources; it is inefficient and uneconomical for a state to plan independently of the voluntary agencies and vice versa; voluntary institutions receive a very substantial portion of their operating budgets through public subsidy and will require further public subsidy to improve aftercare and for many of their future capital improvements.

It is public policy in New York State and elsewhere to assign children, when practicable, to institutions under the auspices of their own religious faith. Some voluntary facilities are thus needed. It is also public policy to encourage the diversity, flexibility, and experimentation made possible by voluntary programs. None of this should be affected, or need be, by inclusion of voluntary institutions within state planning and referral systems. The New York State Board of Social Welfare already receives appropriate staff reports and has the responsibility of certifying the quality and value of any new or continuing institutional program under voluntary auspices from the perspective of the need for service. Such certification represents a minimum exercise of responsibility for the children committed by the courts and the minimum accountability for the use of state subsidy. A state can hardly be expected to exercise responsibility for a social welfare program, particularly one in which it invests heavily, without inspection, standard setting, and coordination. The task is only partly completed, however, unless allocation of children is centralized and the specific responsibilities of voluntary institutions in the total system more sharply defined.

Voluntary groups can always exercise initiative in proposing new facilities and should be expected to assume some portion of capital costs and to demonstrate sufficient philanthropic investment to justify voluntary auspices and state subsidy. In addition, state planning should include the policy (as it has in the past) of approaching voluntary groups and asking them to organize, with state backing, specialized facilities which they seem particularly equipped to plan and operate.

Given this kind of relationship, it would not be difficult to develop, for the use of staff responsible for diagnostic classification, criteria for assignment to voluntary institutions. The institutions could retain the right to specify intake policy, but would do so in relation to an over-all state plan if subsidy was to continue. Under any circumstances, such a plan could lead to clear definition as to what is, and what is not, within the responsibility assumed by the voluntary group—and would show clearly what a state had outlined as its own direct care program; state subsidy to voluntary agencies would be justified for specific services deemed necessary to the total network.

Such an integrated public-voluntary system could be developed into a diversified state-wide panoply of treatment resources away from home, planned on the basis of knowledge and needs and revised as knowledge and needs change. A modern program for children in trouble cannot do with less.

Part C

A SYSTEM OF SERVICES

CHAPTER XII

ACCOUNTABILITY AND INTEGRATION OF SERVICES IN AN ERA OF SPECIALIZATION

THIS DISCUSSION has moved from the philosophy and components of a community system of services to the implications for specific agencies and institutions. It has examined agency and institutional provision for case finding and for treatment—with attention to all the intervening processes. Assumed throughout and described to a limited extent is the integration of the separate efforts in a context of community accountability. This notion requires further definition and the mechanisms for its implementation are yet to be specified.

First, let us recall the problems here addressed. Efforts to deal with children in trouble are not nearly effective enough; exploration soon reveals that the resources committed to the effort are inadequate in quantity and in quality. As one seeks potent remedies, it is necessary to go beyond the question of the adequacy of individual programs, the sufficiency of resources in a given category, or even the qualifications of a given staff. Clearly, there are also problems relevant to the system of community services as a *system*. The following overlapping generalizations are central:

    a) *Cases are found, but opportunities are lost.* "Services rendered" are too often considered as "needs met." Case finding may be followed by the minimum of service prescribed by an agency's function; by unskilled service or a failure to follow up consistently—based on a limited concept of agency re-

446 A SYSTEM OF SERVICES

sponsibility; by the dropping of cases because of resource lacks.

b) *Far too much agency service and action is not based on adequate case appraisal or diagnosis.*

c) *Agencies often "drift" into case dispositions or make plans for services which are known to hold little promise of effectiveness.* Conflicting philosophies and objectives operate at the level of case disposition, and punitive impluses often outweigh treatment strategy. Knowledge is in some instances limited; in others adequate staff is not available to make plans anchored in available knowledge. Resources may be in short supply.

d) *Agencies are often in competition with one another for treatment resources; staff members within an agency are often in competition.* Referrals are often made by "shopping," not through wise apportionment of available resources.

e) *Agency service efforts in the individual case are not adequately integrated.* Far too often agencies work with portions of families and segments of individual problems, and their efforts are unrelated except in the most superficial sense. Cases are "lost" in the gaps between agencies and services which do not "mesh." The complexity of many of the case problems, their family and community ramifications, is such that only the systematically interrelated efforts of the appropriate agencies will make an impact.

f) *The sum total of agency prerogatives and rights and their implementation are such as to leave major gaps in the community pattern of services.*

g) *The deep and basic deficiency in the total community program, viewed as a whole, is in responsibility and accountability.*

Of necessity, our efforts to specify the elements of a total community approach and to suggest philosophy and method which might be appropriate are general. A given community must translate guidelines, principles, and a large number of action proposals into priorities, specifics, next steps. Moreover, a given community requires mechanisms and structure for constant evaluation of its achievements and for review of policies and strategy in the light of changing problems, changing knowledge, and experience. Therefore, it becomes necessary, in the final phase of this present undertaking, to discuss community provision for planning, coordination, evaluation, and research.

Available experience suggests that the provision must be on several levels. First, there is the problem of ensuring the integration of services for the individual case in the context of the philosophy of accountability already discussed. Then there is the coordination and planning relevant to the neighborhood or the city subdivision. Finally, there is the provision for community-wide planning and coordination and the relationship of community-wide provision to the neighborhood structure, on the one hand, and to city and state structures on the other.

THE CONTEXT OF THE PROBLEM

The sociologist would define much of what is here under discussion as a problem in bureaucracy. In a complex, industrial society, and particularly in its urban areas, the nature of population concentrations, the wide ramifications of needs, the multiplicity of skills required and services offered all lead social welfare programs to that inevitable formal organization (technically, "bureaucracy") which is characteristic of most organizations in the modern world. Wilensky and Lebeaux have reminded us that "red tape, buck passing, inaction, inflexibility," which are ways in which the layman would characterize many of the service problems, are actually pathological manifestations of some of the most basic and valuable features of modern formal organization. In their attempts to achieve efficiency, reliability, continuity, precision, and fairness, organizations are inevitably and increasingly characterized by *specialization* (within agencies and as between agencies); *hierarchy* (the distinction between workers and supervisors is especially important for present purposes); an emphasis on *rules* (activities are routinized where possible and all relationships are formalized); *assignment of roles to specialists* on the basis of assumed technical qualifications; and *official designation of areas of jurisdiction* for the several roles.[1]

These are necessary features of social organization in our age, but they were unknown in the days of mutual self-help in simple, agricultural communities, nor were they in evidence in many of the

[1] Harold L. Wilensky and Charles N. Lebeaux, *Industrial Society and Social Welfare* (New York: Russell Sage Foundation, 1958), Chapter X.

social welfare programs which developed earlier in the history of the industrial revolution, when religious and humanitarian impulses, and not technical training or scientific knowledge, were the basis for action, and when specialization was almost unnecessary and unknown. Even today, there is far less bureaucratization in rural areas or in some of the smaller religious charities which have not professionalized and which have limited themselves to small subpopulations. Those who would solve the problems created by the pathologies of bureaucracy by harking back to the "good old days" ignore the facts of modern life, however. While some islands of simple and informal organization may continue to exist in social welfare, the matter of size alone—size of client groups, size of agencies, size of staff—demands formal organization for the bulk of public and voluntary provision. Solutions are needed for the problems which seem inevitably to arise, but it is fantasy to assume that social welfare alone, of all areas in modern life, will avoid this normal development.

Many specific problems already identified as present in individual programs dealing with children in trouble—or in the total pattern of services—are recognizable as manifestations of broader problems described by observers of social welfare bureaucracy. To the client, of course, they often appear as "obstacles and impediments."

Thus, the pattern of social work supervision may decrease the caseworker's initiative and independence just where it is most needed. Moreover, stress on eligibility and intake rules may keep services from people on irrelevant technicalities, or discourage those who are poorly motivated or not socially equipped to deal with the requirements. A high degree of specialization may lead to formulation of job requirements which eliminate most of those available for the jobs—and leave programs unstaffed. Or it may narrow the service given to that range sanctioned by the specialty, despite the needs of the case or the abilities and inclinations of the practitioner. Specialization, too, may leave gaps in service, may leave some client groups or social groups or geographic groups unserved, or may segment the client. Specialization of some kinds ("delinquents") also adds to stigmatization of some clients. A given service tends to define in quite specific ways how a client should behave (the reciprocal of the professional's role); people who do not fit into the mold may be dismissed as too poorly motivated to benefit from the service. Considerable assignments of resources are made to keep records and to provide formal devices (conferences, etc.) for communication between personnel within agencies; the investment represents a serious problem since it decreases the time available for direct work with clients; moreover, the communication routines and records often become ends in themselves, while the organizational machinery serves to decrease the sense of urgency in serving people. The greatest hazard, in brief, derives from the tendency to envisage the organization and its preservation as ends in themselves while the original objectives of service and help may become lost.[2]

Some of these problems are obviously outside of the scope of the present work. Some are alluded to (Ch. X) in connection with developments on the forefront of practice which address themselves to the correction of professional concepts and methods obviously unequal to some of the tasks posed. Another group of problems would be faced directly if there could be adequate provision for evaluation, planning, coordination, service integration, and case accountability.

The generalization of these problems both for social welfare as a whole and for all large-scale organizations serves an additional purpose, however. The analysis suggests that just as many of the defects of current programs are best understood as consequences of what might be called the ever-threatening psychopathology of bureaucracies, so must a substantial part of the solution be sought through organizational measures. This discussion addresses itself, therefore, to *organized means* for ensuring accountability and service integration.

On first impulse, one might be tempted to eschew more organization as both costly and likely to create its own complications, and instead to seek solutions through an appeal to professional ethics. This has a measure of validity. The true professions have codes of service which stress concern for the client. A major tenet in the social work ethic, for example, involves a stress on the identification and meeting of client needs. Social workers are much preoccupied with improving services, upgrading their skills, adding to their knowledge, breaking through unnecessary "red tape." Identification

[2] *Ibid.*

with the professional association and its ethics often supersedes the limited perspective of the local agency.

On the other hand, professionalization, not unlike formal organization, does encourage specialization; formalization of relationship; control of spontaneous emotional responses to people's problems; and emphasis on roles, qualifications, techniques, and procedures. Thus, while all that is possible should be done by educators and professional associations to solve some of the problems described through an emphasis on professional ethics and codes of service, organized solutions must be sought simultaneously.

ACCOUNTABILITY AND SERVICE INTEGRATION

The agencies here in focus are instruments of public policy and social control. Their staff members are employed to achieve objectives defined in statutes, charters, and statements of purpose. The evidence is abundant and disturbing to the effect that where the objectives sought are not achieved, and this is quite often the case, the costs are high in destruction, waste, misery, and tragedy. In this context, the probation officer, medical social worker, social investigator for the welfare department, teacher—or any of the others who might be mentioned—may not be regarded as individual practitioners whose actions and practices affect only themselves. They represent agencies carrying well-defined community responsibility and must, each of them, come to appreciate that failure to exercise that responsibility has serious community consequences. The term "responsibility" thus may describe community allocation of function to a given agency or service and agency allocation of role to a specific practitioner—as well as the acceptance of such allocation by agency or individual practitioner.

It is helpful to consider devices for protecting or following the implementation of that responsibility with particular reference to the individual case. The concept of *accountability devices and instruments* may be useful in this regard. Put in slightly different phrasing: The case accountability device is a system or method designed to implement community responsibility by ensuring the continuity of work with the individual case until a point is reached at which community policy calls for case closing. (Implied, of course, is some assurance that the agency which maintains the contacts meets professional standards; this is a function of a variety of departments and of the planning machinery, perhaps, but is a burden too huge for any accountability system.)

An accountability system, by definition, must involve both some infringement on agency prerogatives and some increased invasion of an individual's privacy and of the confidential status of material about him known to social welfare agencies and others. Therefore, one would not wish a case accountability system so comprehensive that it would apply to all those who make use of social welfare, health, and educational services (i.e., most people). A "police state" atmosphere would not advance our objectives. Rather, there is need to define when and how a community should follow closely the service to members of the "high hazard" group in "clear and present danger" and how their rights are to be protected in the process. There is far less of a problem in the inclusion of those already subject to authoritative action because of their delinquency, neglect, or unlawful behavior as determined through court adjudication.

An acceptance of the accountability notion and the recognition that a major source of service failure is the fragmentation of services, fragmentation of clients, and loss of clients in the gaps between programs lead one to the view that *service integration* must be planned simultaneously with the creation of devices for case accountability.

It is helpful to differentiate between coordination in relation to the programs, policies, objectives, and plans of agencies, on the one hand, and coordination of the work *on the individual case,* on the other. The latter process, best identified as integration of services, involves ways of ensuring the meshing of resources and services for the individual client. It also includes concern for the consistency of approach and policies of various agencies or parts of agencies as experienced by the person for whom the service is designed.[3]

[3] Citizens' Committee for Children of New York City, Inc., *The Planning and Coordination of Services for Children and Youth in New York City* (New York, 1959), p. 10. Also see *Report of the Working Party on Social Workers in the Local Authority Health and Welfare Services* (London: Her Majesty's Stationery Office, 1959), pp. 33–35.

Coordination devices, invented in the nineteenth century and introduced widely by the charity organization movement, had the potential for case accountability and the integration of services, but they were addressed to the problems of another era. Thus, the social service exchange long served the primary function of detecting those who sought and obtained relief in more than one agency. This problem has ended with the growth of public welfare. The social service exchange still makes it possible for an agency to know the names of other agencies which have had contact with a family; however, registration is selective and some communities have abolished the exchange because they did not consider it helpful or because the ethics of registration without permission seemed questionable. In addition, the volume of work, the inability to separate good leads from poor ones on a social service exchange slip, and uneven levels of staffing have limited the extent to which the exchange is regarded as useful. In some instances case summaries are requested; this may lead to some meshing of efforts. In even fewer instances, records are read or an exchange slip leads to telephone conferences or to actual full-dress interagency conferences. These may foster considerable integration of effort but generally are seen as time-consuming and costly. It is doubtful that the exchange will ever become a potent service integration instrument unless it becomes more selective or is tied somehow to a system of case accountability. We shall return to this matter shortly.

The first charity organization societies of the 1880s were actually created in order to attain service integration (they did not, of course, use the phrase) where there seemed to be chaos. They soon discovered that the need for adequate relief and qualified service was greater than the demand for service integration, and they became today's family service societies. Several decades later, their heritage was seen in the community council movement, but here the major emphasis was on coordination on the level of agencies, not individual cases. Nonetheless, from time to time councils have sought to encourage case integration by promoting interagency understanding and communication, facilitating case conferences between two agencies working on a case, and conducting the kinds of workshops and institutes which lead to mutual clarification of function and greater readiness to work together. Most recently some councils have experimented with the new form of case conference described below or have initiated valuable projects.

The agency "merger" movement has also been in a sense a step toward case integration although actually a variety of motives are involved. Family agencies and children's agencies tended to join together after World War II. It was clear that efforts to maintain a family may be made more consistently and with greater skill before child placement begins; a protective unit requires close ties to a child placement service; etc. Attendance bureaus have joined with guidance and psychology programs to form more complete pupil personnel departments. Children's and family courts have been joined in one structure. There have even been a few instances in which child guidance clinics have become associated with in-patient treatment facilities.

Obviously the merger has important potential in case integration. The judge sitting in the children's case should have the family court record on the family. Without too much effort the psychologist should be able to review the experience of the attendance officer, and so on. Mergers appear to have achieved the desired effect where they were real, rather than mere paper actions, where staffs in the several components were on equivalent levels of status and skill, and where the programs were not so large as to demand formal integrating devices within the agency. The merger has obvious limits, however: one cannot achieve case integration in a large urban area by putting all the agencies under one organizational title and administration.

The case conference. While the older and earlier devices have not been adequate in their original forms, they have inspired recent developments which are encouraging. Central to these developments is a *new form of multiagency case conference* which serves both as an accountability device and an instrument for case integration. Cases are carefully selected for presentation because they represent "multi-problem" situations, a number of agencies are involved, and adequate progress has not been made. Agencies are represented by personnel on a supervisory and/or administrative level (augmented, perhaps, by the worker directly responsible for the case).

This form of case conference involves a sharing of information and evaluations, culminating in a new case diagnosis or evaluation, as well as in an action plan mutually arrived at. Professional confidentiality of material revealed in the conferences is ensured through agreement. Particularly crucial is the agreement generally made as to which agency is to "take the lead" with the family and how the others are to support the effort (case integration). Furthermore, a "reporting back" date is set for review of progress and the making of further plans (case accountability). Once the case thus comes into the center of community attention, it is not so readily "lost."

From time to time this kind of practice has grown up in a community without much publicity or reporting, but it has had special attention in a number of communities in recent years as a way of dealing with families considered particularly difficult. Thus, to illustrate rather than to enumerate all developments, the Montclair Council of Social Agencies organized a case conference committee several years ago, one of several such in New Jersey, and emphasized "reporting back"; it stated that positive results could be documented. The Roxbury Family Project, working for several years in a Boston neighborhood, developed a similar plan. Oakland County, Michigan, is said to find a case conference "very effective." [4]

The St. Paul, Minnesota, Family Centered Project promoted service integration through a continuous "workshop" for the special staff members assigned part-time by the agencies for purposes of the project. Because the project was a demonstration and research endeavor and staff were in a sense "loaned," if only part-time, it did not change the basic community pattern. The service integration emerged, in this instance, as a by-product of a joint study effort directed at the problem of designing treatment methods effective with so-called multiproblem families. A *Casework Notebook* produced by the project defines the case conference as "the best device we have for joint planning." This project stressed that case conference effectiveness depends on the caseworker and his immediate supervisor; while policy agreements may be reached on the administrative level, or in interagency councils, service integration re-

[4] "Progress Report of the Roxbury Family Project" (Boston: United Community Services, 1957, mimeographed). Also, *Mobilizing against Delinquency and Neglect*, a report of a conference of Michigan Probate and Juvenile Court Judges at Kalamazoo, December 13, 14, 15, 1958 (Michigan: The Conference, n.d.), pp. 7–8.

quires at least one meeting of those who will work together on the case.[5]

A more limited device which is described as very effective is the case review committee in the Philadelphia schools. Top administrators of special services (medical services, pupil personnel and counseling, special education, etc.) are joined by experts where needed to confer on the most seriously disturbed and potentially dangerous young people in school. While the conference may decide on school exclusions or may initiate commitment, school transfers and special programs are also possible. Unlike some of the other case committees, the Philadelphia plan is not tied to ongoing treatment decisions and does not involve reporting back to review progress and make new plans.

Los Angeles reports that during 1958–59 there were 49 case coordinating committees associated with local community coordinating councils. During the one year, the committees considered 314 new cases and 476 ongoing, approximately half involving a focus on children under 14.[6] In a current Madison, Wisconsin, project a "case conference demonstration" is being used for general coordination and planning purposes and to create a climate for use of such conferences as part of normal service.

In England, most local authorities (93 percent) have some kind of coordinating machinery and half use the case conference device —mainly in the instance of work with children. There is emphasis on neglectful families. Younghusband's definition and advice is applicable on this side of the Atlantic as well:

A case conference provides a setting for a limited number of workers directly involved in the case under consideration to assess the need, work out a plan of concerted action, and carry it out in cooperation with each other and with the person or family under discussion. . . . [It] should

[5] Ludwig L. Geismar, "The Family-Centered Project of St. Paul" (St. Paul: Family Centered Project, 1957, mimeographed); Malcolm B. Stinson, "The Family-Centered Project of St. Paul: An Experience in Community Organization," a paper presented at the National Conference of Social Welfare, 1956 (mimeographed); Charles J. Birt, "Family-Centered Project of St. Paul," *Social Work*, I, No. 4 (October, 1956), 41–47; Family Centered Project of St. Paul, *Casework Notebook* (St. Paul: Greater St. Paul Community Chests and Councils, Inc., 1957), p. 131.

[6] Welfare Planning Council, Los Angeles Region, *Los Angeles and the New York City Youth Board* (Los Angeles, 1960, mimeographed), p. 107.

be attended only by officers [involved] in the case under discussion, one of whom should take the chair.

She comments further that "the main problem is not so much multiplicity of visiting as multiplicity of independent and uncoordinated visiting." [7]

Case conferences have been used in New York City in a number of special projects. In 1957 the Welfare Department pioneered with what became known as the Borough Committees of the Mayor's Interdepartmental Committee for Multi-Problem Families. Administrative or supervisory personnel from public departments (Education, Buildings, Health, Hospitals, Police, Welfare, two courts, Housing, Mental Health Board, Youth Board) met monthly in each borough both to promote interdepartmental coordination in general and to ensure integration of services in the cases at hand. They constituted a permanent committee. All of the departments listed could refer cases. A conference sought to develop a plan of action for the particular case, to devise ways of cutting "red tape" and modifying directives where it seemed essential for the case being reviewed or for similar cases, and to designate the agency which would assume primary responsibility for service. Monthly reports of progress were required as a means of ensuring continued service integration as well as accountability. The total volume was small since only one case was discussed per meeting, but the effect on services and policies was said to be broader. While the plan was given up in the light of subsequent developments, its strength seemed to be primarily in the area of policy and program coordination. Unlike the practitioner case conference, the administrator and executive conference identifies action to be taken in definition of roles, filling of service gaps, and untangling of "red tape." It is not an efficient way to deal with many cases individually—since the direct-service practitioner must follow through with the cases.

In 1958, taking account of expressed concern at the fragmentation of services as well as the gaps between agency services and the frequency with which cases are "lost," the Youth Board developed an experiment in one of its Referral Units. Under the plan, a highly

[7] *Report of the Working Party on Social Workers in the Local Authority,* p. 34. Also, Gordon Rose, "Coordinating Committees," *Case Conference* (England), IV (1957), 41–46, 75–77, 111–14.

resistive, multiproblem family was selected for review and the project staff convened a meeting of an appropriate *ad hoc* committee which included representatives of all agencies, public or voluntary, currently or previously in contact with the family (usually four to ten in number). Prior to the meeting, the project staff prepared and circulated an up-to-date case summary. The Youth Board case conferences sought to attract the staff members directly concerned with the case, even though administrators were also welcomed.

At the meeting proper, the representative from each of the agencies reviewed his agency's experience with the family and the total group then explored the situation, pooled evaluative judgments, and developed a plan and reasonable goals with the family. Although the initial picture of a case as it emerged in a conference was often discouraging, the "pooled" thinking tended to discover positive factors and to suggest possible "leverage." One agency was eventually requested to assume the lead in work with the family and to integrate the services of the others. Follow-up reporting was scheduled for a date three months after the meeting. So gratifying was the experience during the first year that the Youth Board determined to assign similar activity to all of its Referral Units. Preparatory meetings with all interested agencies met enthusiastic responses.[8]

While the Youth Board experience with the case conference is substantially encouraging, organizational aspects have not been solved. A small community might achieve service integration and accountability through a "coffee-time" conference. Large cities need to staff many cases. What volume is possible? How are cases to be selected? Given considerable volume, what administrative devices are needed to implement accountability?

As will be seen (Ch. XIII), the unclear status of the Referral Units in recent years and their staffing difficulties have precluded the development of large-scale case conference machinery. In addition, the limited development of New York's "multiproblem" register has precluded its use for case selection. Yet the Youth Board conference experience suggests that it would not be at all unreasonable to expect a coordinating agency in a large city to use its machinery to organize and staff a network of case conference groups along the

[8] Helen W. Hallinan, "Coordinating Agency Efforts in Behalf of the Hard-to-Reach Family," *Social Casework*, XL, No. 1 (January, 1959), 9–17.

lines of the Youth Board pattern. Twenty-five or thirty such groups would be required for New York City, and they would staff two or three new cases each week and hear reports on cases previously staffed. This would bring about two or three thousand new cases into the accountability network a year—a reasonable total if the conferences are reserved for situations involving child neglect or delinquency, for cases with ramifications in a variety of agencies, for cases of considerable family disorganization and evidence that routine handling will not do.

Since the case conferences would generally not involve the same practitioners at each meeting, this kind of plan would not impose too heavy a burden on any staff member. It would depend in New York City on using Referral Unit staff resources or comparable staff to select the cases, prepare the conferences, and follow through. Other cities would need proportionately fewer conference groups. Organization of conferences on the basis of a neighborhood or city subdivision would seem desirable. Oakland, California, has set up a conference group for each of five high school districts and finds that both service integration and program coordination are possible. The Roxbury Family Project, which investigated the matter, stressed that coordinators and resource personnel involved in case conference procedures make their optimum contributions if they are "neutral," that is, if they do not have a direct service function.

Registers. The problems of case selection and administrative controls for this kind of machinery remain. A small community does not find it difficult to develop an accountability card index which is an integral part of a case conference system. It comes into play at the point of case finding.[9] There must be some work done in advance to arrive at mutual agreement as to cases to be added to the register and scheduled for conference. (Among the possibilities, to illustrate: all cases of alleged neglect, all cases in which a child is temporarily separated from his parents, all adjudicated delinquency cases under certain types of circumstances, public welfare cases with certain interagency ramifications.) Following conferences and mutual planning, a simple process of notation of "return dates" would be adequate—and would provide for the preparation of follow-up conferences at appropriate times.

[9] *Mobilizing against Delinquency and Neglect,* pp. 7–8.

The large-city roster is a more complex matter. Thus, despite frequent announcements of intent, the New York City Youth Board has not been able to use its roster for accountability purposes or for any other ongoing administrative operation even though some research use has been possible. Part of the problem is that of criteria for listing: cases have been placed on the roster on the basis of intra-familial relationship patterns and parental attitudes, the outgrowth of Youth Board interest in the Glueck prediction work. However, the core accountability notion would be better served and the roster kept within manageable limits if a committee of experienced practitioners were to formulate criteria relative to problems, behavior, and, most important, the community agencies' experiences with the family.[10]

Having solved the problem of criteria, the large city will have to use an electronic system to keep its roster usable and flexible. Cases could easily be coded by "conference group" (i.e., neighborhood), basic characteristics, agency ramifications. An electronic system could help select cases for conferences in the terms of predetermined priorities, while agencies themselves could add cases to the agenda in the light of their experience. The register could also provide, at appropriate times, suitable rosters of cases to be followed up, rosters of unreported cases, rosters of cases closed by an agency while core problems remained, and so on. Its costs, while important, would be small when weighed against current futile, uncoordinated, and pro-

[10] As the result of an analysis of the caseload of one of its units working with particularly resistive cases, the Youth Board decided to define a multiproblem family as one in which there is failure of three of the following five types: "(1) The functional failure of the mother, (2) the functional failure of the father, (3) the failure of siblings to function adequately within the family, (4) the failure of parents to function adequately in their marital roles and (5) failure in terms of total environment, including financial dependency and poor housing." Outlined in a New York City Youth Board Research Department mimeographed staff document entitled "The Multi-Problem Register" (1958). Obviously there are families who do not meet the "three factors" criteria who should be included in an accountability register, and some who do show the three factors could be "low priorities" in case conferences. Criteria based on community experience in intervening with a family would seem more appropriate.

Bradley Buell, who developed his reporting card and register for research purposes, stresses its administrative potential in Bradley Buell, Paul T. Beisser, John M. Wedemeyer, *Reorganizing to Prevent and Control Disordered Behavior.* A reprint from *Mental Hygiene,* XLII, No. 2 (April, 1958), 155–94.

longed services. Economies might eventually emerge if the social service exchange were properly to curtail its own activities in the light of the existence of the register. The community might, in fact, choose to place the register under social service exchange auspices and to merge it with the exchange. This is a matter of administration and financing, rather than a substantive issue.

The point is raised as to whether the use of a register does not abuse the client's confidence or stigmatize him. In some cases there is no question at all about the community's right to use a register as an instrument of intervention, since there has been either an adjudication which places the family or child under court supervision or protection or because the service is an outgrowth of a statutory charge to work with relief recipients (public welfare cases) or to help enforce the compulsory education law (many school-referred cases). Where the community's rights are not clear, discussion of the social service exchange and/or register should, under any circumstances, be a normal part of agency intake. The client accepts or rejects the register when he uses the service (or the decision may be deferred for reasons relevant to the case). Where the client cannot move voluntarily and children are endangered, the community may need to exercise its police power, which includes registration as part of the protective investigation process.

In fact, one may say of accountability devices generally what has been said of the register: if one limits cases listed to those which need to be in the forefront of community concern because of hazard, "clear and present danger," and complexity of interrelated problems, most cases will in fact present a legitimate basis for the partial invasion of privacy which is involved. Where such basis does not exist technically and the client rejects voluntary service, the protective services machinery may be called into action. If there is no legal basis for protective action and the client does not wish the service, his privacy should be safeguarded, despite the convictions of some professional workers that there are hazards involved—at least unless the predictions are validated by identifiable and justiciable "acting out."

"Intensive" workers. Accountability devices and service integration measures should ideally affect the practice of all agency staff members. A number of special studies and projects also have sug-

gested the possibility of a degree of specialization with some families found to require particular and concentrated attention. Agencies often have several staff members particularly suited for intensive, rehabilitative work on the basis of understanding, experience, and skill. Why not reduce their caseloads, increase their prerogatives, and stress the integration of their work with other agencies?

Recommendations for this work in a British study of *The Neglected Child* are also supported by American experience:

(a) Caseloads should be small, consisting of not more than twenty-five families for each worker. With a larger number than this, the families that are passing through a crisis of some kind cannot be given sufficiently close attention unless other cases are neglected.

(b) One worker should have responsibility for the whole family and for helping it in all its difficulties. Specialist workers will often have to be called in to deal with particular problems, such as poor physical or mental health. But one worker, from whatever service, must have full responsibility for the family, and others should visit only when necessary and only after first consulting with the worker in charge.

(c) Help of this comprehensive kind must be available to a family as soon as its problems grow too complex to be dealt with by the functional services.

(d) Those offering this help must be allowed to work in the same district for long enough to become well-known and trusted by the families they visit.

(e) There must be close coordination of all services, based on fairly frequent discussions both between those directing the services and (more important) between those actually visiting the same families. It matters little whether this is achieved through formal committees, over a cup of tea in the town hall canteen, or in other ways.

(f) When the immediate crisis is over and families once more begin to lead a fairly normal life, it must be possible for someone to keep in touch with them for long enough to prevent a relapse.

(g) People of the right character and experience should be chosen to undertake this personal service, and they should be encouraged to work in an independent and experimental manner and to develop new methods. This is the most important condition of all.[11]

Perhaps, after a family comes into focus, the first attempts might be on the basis of careful integration between agencies. For it is not the multiplicity of visits per se but uncoordinated work which is so undesirable.

[11] D. V. Donnison, *The Neglected Child and the Social Services* (Manchester: Manchester University Press, 1954), pp. 117–18.

If this produced no improvement, one of these specially chosen workers would take full responsibility for the family after discussion between all the services concerned. Other visitors would not abandon the family altogether but would henceforth visit as little as possible and take no action without first consulting the person in charge. Which service would be chosen to assume responsibility for any given family would depend on which worker appeared to be in the best position to help. In most cases there would be several visitors already calling on the family; by discussion between them it could be decided who was likely to exert the most influence (owing to personality, function, pressure of work, or any other reason). That person would be put in charge and asked to report progress at intervals to other organizations interested in the case.

In this way most of the conditions necessary for effective personal service would be achieved without radical change. Families . . . would merely find that one worker, whom they already knew and trusted more than others, was giving them more attention and was taking responsibility for matters upon which they had previously received calls from many people. Every organization would make its contribution. The distribution of casework would be decided not by theoretical arguments about the value of the different services, but by practical demonstration of their success in individual cases. No service would be condemned to limit itself henceforth to a narrow range of duties; each would be encouraged to think in terms of the whole family, and to gain a wider understanding of family problems. Good workers need no longer waste years of their time in dealing with the symptoms of trouble; they would be given a chance to tackle its underlying causes.[12]

Several British health and social services have, in fact, assigned "intensive" workers. The St. Paul project, which defined its special staff members as "general family practitioners," sought coordination of treatment (what we have called service integration) by assigning them responsibility for working with families "to bridge . . . them over to a more productive use of community resources"; developing better interagency collaboration in behalf of families; using their observations in order to contribute to community planning and social action.[13]

[12] Ibid., pp. 121–23. Also see Samuel Mencher, "The Relationship of Voluntary and Statutory Welfare Services in England" (Unpublished D.S.W. Dissertation, New York School of Social Work, Columbia University, 1959), p. 132.

[13] Bradley Buell and his colleagues in Community Research Associates have pioneered in epidemiological studies and experiments in service integration and accountability in several parts of the country. See Reorganizing to Prevent and Control Disordered Behavior. Also, Community Research Associates, Inc., The Prevention and Control of Disordered Behavior in San Mateo County, California

In the St. Paul project, in New York's Neighborhood Services Center, and in many special units for multiproblem families throughout the United States, the case is transferred to a special unit and then assigned to an "intensive" worker who carries a variety of the ramifications. We have yet to experiment systematically with intensive workers who remain within their agencies and are unassigned to special projects—but whose job assignments permit the special intensive work on a selective basis. The California Youth Authority is launching intensive community treatment of delinquents along these lines.

Accountability and agency prerogatives. A community cannot develop service integration and keep families in focus via accountability machinery unless there is some surrender of agency prerogatives. Individual agencies alone cannot make final determinations about cases to list—or about when cases may be dropped. A conference should be able to decide who takes the lead, even if there is not unanimity. Community reports must be free to compare agencies on their "sticking" and "holding power."

All of this can be made possible by democratically conducted community planning and coordination machinery—with local, neighborhood subdivisions in large cities. The agencies involved are either public services or voluntary programs supported by community chests or individual, tax-deductible contributions. In either instance it is legitimate to expect that an agency will cooperate with the community network, making its views known, participating in decisions, and supporting plans which are made. The *social* services are not the domain of individual entrepreneurs; those which act as such are hardly responsible in the sense in which the term is here employed.

In fact, once an agency accepts the philosophy here outlined, it will find its own ways of going even beyond the registers, conferences, and intensive units described. For example, a school system

---

(New York, 1954); *The Prevention and Control of Indigent Disability in Washington County, Md.* (New York, 1954); *The Prevention and Control of Dependency in Winona County, Minnesota* (New York, 1953). Also, C. Howe Eller, Gordon H. Hatcher, Bradley Buell, *Health and Welfare Issues in Community Planning for the Problems of Indigent Disability,* reprint from *Journal of Public Health,* Vol. XLVIII, No. 114 (November, 1958); Bradley Buell, *Is Prevention Possible?* reprint of a paper presented at the National Conference of Social Welfare (New York: Community Research Associates, Inc., 1959).

may develop a cumulative record system (or cumulative records plus confidential guidance files) to ensure continuity of service to a child from term to term, once his difficulties have identified him as requiring special help. The register must be in competent hands lest a child be stigmatized and forced into an unchangeable mold. The child health station offers similar opportunities to public health nurses and medical social workers.

Or, to illustrate further, a housing authority social service program might assign staff or obtain the help of public or voluntary casework services to maintain close contact with that "small hard core" of public housing tenants who require support and help lest their inadequacies produce new problems—and lead to even further family disorganization.[14] The Neighborhood Improvement Program of New Haven, Connecticut, places a casework unit which concentrates on multiproblem families within a public housing project. Within the unit are recreational and community organization personnel as well, offering a rounded program to casework clients and to the project as a whole.

THE NEIGHBORHOOD BASE

Staff members from a variety of agencies, responsible for cases in a given neighborhood, must eventually find ways to mesh their efforts. Any case integration system must therefore be brought down to the neighborhood level in some fashion. And this is just as well, since intensive knowledge of a locality is usually a prerequisite to successful service. This suggests the hypothesis that it may be useful to tie accountability and service integration provision to some kind of structure of neighborhood organization.

The Chicago Area Project, the model for many others, has had more than twenty-five years of experience and reports positive results.[15] Its program in the neighborhood tends to lead to recreation provision, general community self-improvement endeavors, direct work with gangs—but not to service integration or accountability. On

[14] Elizabeth Woods, *The Small Hard Core* (New York: Citizens' Planning and Housing Council, 1957).

[15] Solomon Kobrin, "The Chicago Area Project—a 25-Year Assessment," *Annals of the American Academy of Political and Social Science*, CCCXXII (March, 1959), 19–29. Also, Anthony Sorrentino, "The Chicago Area Project after 25 Years," *Federal Probation*, XXIII, No. 2 (June, 1959), 40–45.

the other hand, the South Central Youth Project, in a blighted Minneapolis area, arrived at the agency case conference structure and assignment of one responsible worker per case as its major working method, but concluded in its report that "more community forces should be involved." [16]

Given agreement to explore local organization in relation to service integration and accountability, several structural approaches would seem to be relevant. Any of these would require innovation and change, since much local organization in the youth field is concerned only with the provision of leisure-time and recreational resources. A proposal that there be some local ties to central planning and coordination bodies would win agreement in the abstract, but there would remain the need to define the realistic parameters of local initiative in fields in which decisions are made on city-wide or county bases. The question of the best possible relationships between social agencies, volunteer service groups, citizen self-help activities, and local planning bodies would still remain. Should a local action group ever be involved in case accountability? What of the possible therapeutic aspects of local self-help, alluded to briefly in an earlier chapter?

A search does not yield ready answers. Many patterns are obviously being considered, however, as urban areas seek to fill a vacuum created by the breakup of neighborhoods and the changes in urban political machines which in one sense provided for a degree of accountability of a sort. Many of the larger urban areas are, in fact, in transition in their patterns of neighborhood organization, as they take account of urban renewal, the problem of racial integration, and population mobility. Some special neighborhood organizations, created in order to deal with delinquency, are carrying out broad local improvements on the assumption that grass roots activity of this kind decreases antisocial orientations in the total community, creates needed services, and offers sound role models for youth.

This is, then, an area for tentative exploration and testing despite its urgency and substantive importance. The remainder of this section is devoted to brief mention of a variety of interesting develop-

[16] Gisela Konopka, "Coordination of Services as a Means of Delinquency Prevention," *Annals of the American Academy of Political and Social Science,* CCXXII (March, 1959), pp. 30–37.

ments. All aspects of local organization not immediately relevant are bypassed.

Oakland's "associated agencies." Oakland, California, in a plan under way since 1957, has created a coordination-service integration structure on a local basis by dividing the city into five high school districts. The executive of the program is based in the city manager's office and is called the "juvenile control coordinator." Costs are shared by the Board of Education and the City Council. Policies are made by an executive committee consisting of the executives of the agencies involved (schools, recreation, police, probation, Youth Authority, welfare, health). Each agency is represented on a coordinating committee, which is city-wide, and on the local district units. There is thus provision for joint planning, program coordination, and local case integration.

The heart of the program is the twice-monthly local district meetings which serve to ensure service integration and reporting back and to initiate new policies and provision needed to deal with emerging problems. All reports are positive. The effectiveness with which the agencies deal with local "emergencies" such as gang fights, as well as with individual cases, is impressive.

Coordinating councils. At one time the delinquency field was especially concerned with promoting the local coordinating council, a device for periodic meetings of local agencies or responsible local citizens concerned with delinquents. The movement's main development has been on the West Coast. Councils have lay and professional participation, generally combining both, and include a range of organizations, from law enforcement bodies to civic groups, schools, churches, and social agencies. They sometimes develop surveys or initiate activity to provide new resources. At other times they serve as informal centers for service integration. They are considered more effective in small communities and do not seem to meet an urban area's need for formally organized service integration and accountability involving large caseloads. Particularly lacking is a specification of roles appropriate to laymen and roles which should involve professional staff in order to protect confidentiality and ensure qualified help.[17]

[17] See Herbert A. Bloch and Frank T. Flynn, *Delinquency: The Juvenile Offender in America Today* (New York: Random House, 1956), pp. 526–27.

The New York City police-inspired precinct Youth Councils are like similar councils elsewhere. Theoretically, each police precinct (of which there are 78) has a council, but approximately one quarter are active. Local professionals, civic leaders, church leaders, and merchants join together to support PAL fund raising and to devise programs to meet special needs. The council is a means to organize some activity and occasional coordination, but is not structured either for accountability or integration. On occasion, it may have a vital, energetic program. The police are currently assigning professional staff to revitalize the councils but there is no city-wide policy guidance in relation to many areas in which other public and voluntary agencies also have youth councils and neighborhood organizations.

Washington, D.C., has given a larger task to its more than twenty boards set up in natural neighborhood areas, under the leadership of the Commissioner's Youth Council. Prevention, coordination, and some case integration tasks are undertaken by each local group.

New Jersey has juvenile conference committees in almost forty areas, having created them after a 1953 directive from its Supreme Court to local juvenile courts. A Monmouth County plan, which originated in 1945, was the model. Committee members are court-appointed; the committees are designed to encourage the locality to come to grips with delinquency, particularly in the early stages. According to a recent report, thousands of citizens have actually served on committees. As New Jersey has sought to strengthen all of its services to youth in trouble it has had to look at the conference committees and to recognize that they have sought to carry out case evaluation, treatment planning, and case supervision, often in open committee, without diagnostic understanding or appreciation of what the experience could mean to participants, and without adequately qualified personnel. On the other hand, the committees have led to some effective screening and informal handling of cases which might otherwise have gone to court. They have channeled much constructive citizen interest in community services. As needed probation services and court intake structures expand adequately in New Jersey and as community social agencies offer alternative forms of informal help, it would seem likely that the direct case handling by conference committees would end and that these would become juvenile court advisory committees and local citizen committees concerned with planning. By their nature, they cannot adequately undertake service integration, which should be a function of an operating staff.[18] The generalization applies to similar activities in many states.

The Baltimore area projects represent an intermediate type of development. They are, in effect, local community centers set up under the Welfare Department. The local community supplies all the needs of the project, but the Welfare Department adds clinical staff and a coordinator who encourages local organization to deal with local problems.

Precinct youth councils, juvenile conference committees, parent-youth aid committees, and their thousands of equivalents throughout the country are excellent recruitment grounds and orientation centers for "big brothers" and "big sisters" who may supplement professional helping services in valuable ways and who may act in lieu of such services for children referred through professionally qualified channels.

LENA. The Lower East Side Neighborhoods Association in New York City (LENA) is an elaborate and unusually imaginative effort in an area with a population of over 200,000. It was created in 1955, at a time of rapid neighborhood change, in response to local violence. It now joins together in a vigorous, effective, and in some ways unique organization five local neighborhood councils (four of which it initiated), community members, professional members, and 90 community organizations, from banks and trade unions to settlements and churches. Much of the work is carried on in divisions which have their parallels in the local councils: housing, health, education, youth, community arts, intergroup relations. Work is carried on in such a way as both to raise the tone and quality of community life and to deal with dangerous deviance. For example, the community arts program seeks through a summer concert program, dramatics, and a variety of offerings in the arts, plus a local "talent hunt," to enrich daily experience and to create pride in neighborhood—thus striking at one of the roots of its problem. Energetic self-help efforts are directed at problems and gaps in health, education, housing. Sys-

[18] State of New Jersey, Youth Study Commission, *Helping Youth in Trouble* (Trenton, 1957), pp. 61–75.

tematic work is done to increase contacts between diverse ethnic and social groups and to improve relationships.

There is much concentration on the youth. Neighbors, settlements, churches, schools, public departments are heavily committed to a two-pronged approach which includes a rich recreation and sports program (teams, leagues, competition, instruction, trips outside the area) and youth services. The neighborhood councils have their youth councils with similar emphasis and all give priority to grass roots volunteer-neighbor involvement and to youth participation and initiative. At the same time, a tightly coordinated network of area teams, consisting of professionals in local agencies, representatives of public departments, and neighbors, keeps its fingers on the pulse of youth gangs, meets immediately on call, and intervenes rapidly at the first signs of tension. Where constructive programs are possible, they are initiated; mediation is often undertaken; however, if danger threatens, the forces of the law are called into action at once.

Although more systematic testing of effectiveness is planned under the Mobilization for Youth project, being developed in a section of the LENA area, participants are convinced that the program has had considerable impact. Intergroup relations have been improved in the area, public services and housing have been brought more into harmony with need, closely coordinated agency programs— particularly social-athletic and social services—have ensured more complete coverage and have served many who were previously unreached. Particularly dramatic have been the successes in recent summers in heading off threatening gang violence and bringing together previously unfriendly groups.

While this description does not do full justice to LENA, it may serve as a backdrop for noting the extent to which an enthusiastic local self-help effort may both increase agency coordination on a neighborhood basis and approximate a system of accountability. As the result of the explorations and plans of local councils and LENA divisions, and as a natural by-product of the experiences which professionals and board members have in serving together in these activities, the public-voluntary coordination has been much enhanced. Public services in particular have often found new ways to adapt to local priorities and needs. At the same time, it has become routine, to take another illustration, for local settlements so to schedule their social and athletic programs as to provide the best possible neighborhood coverage for the entire week. Joint activities are common.

This total atmosphere, plus the activity of the area teams, increases the sense of accountability which is so important. Sometimes it is provided formally, as when LENA's Youth Service director helped meet a school suspension crisis by assuming responsibility for a group of 120 youngsters designated by the school officials as requiring concentrated attention. Local social service, medical, psychiatric, and educational help was rallied. At the same time, the district's best teachers cooperated in a Foster Teacher Plan to give special attention to a group of children with intense emotional difficulties.

Informal accountability and service integration develops particularly through the work of the area teams which keep attuned to the pulse of the youth gang situation and plan how to act in relation to specific individuals and gangs. This informal but intensive follow-through is most impressive when contrasted with the anonymity and "crisis service" of the typical area. In a sense it becomes an urban neighborhood re-creation of the small town primary group relationships on which social control is based. Youth perceive that significant adults (parents, neighbors, church, social agency, police) know and care about what they do and will intervene if unlawful action is threatened. Unfortunately, not every urban area has the continuity and concentration of agencies and churches of the LENA area—nor is it possible always to create such primary group controls.

Whatever the success of local organization (and it should have enthusiastic support), it will be necessary to ensure full coverage and to take account of intracity mobility through the establishment of some combination of formally organized case conference committees, "intensive" workers, and accountability registers or rosters. Perhaps there is a systematic way to relate these to a local neighborhood organization without violating confidentiality. A neighborhood service center may offer some possibilities.

Neighborhood service center. Early in its history, the New York City Youth Board experimented with a neighborhood "Department Store of Services," housing one of its Referral Units and also representatives of such public services as welfare, health, housing, employment, etc. The objective was facility in reaching the client, increased availability to him, and ease in referral by the Referral Unit, rather than service integration. Others have proposed local neighborhood service centers for some areas of large cities with services such as family casework, group work, work with gangs, day care, homemakers. Some would add a mental hygiene clinic, employment center, and legal aid and housing services. If this cross between a settlement and multifunction treatment center were created, it should obviously include integration and accountability devices of the sort already discussed. It should certainly encompass information and advice functions and a good referral service. The existence of a physical center would also facilitate its relationship to a "grass roots" self-help organization as well.

New York City has resumed experimentation with such an approach in a pilot Interdepartmental Neighborhood Services Center created in the spring of 1960 on a directive from the mayor. Unlike the earlier "Department Store of Services," which concentrated on case finding, information, steering, and referral, the new unit, in an area of high rates of social breakdown, actually seeks to provide well-integrated team services and accountability focused on families and their members. It includes a modest community organization program. Service units of six workers each are assigned by two city departments (Education, Health) and the courts. In addition, the Youth Board assigns two Referral Units.

Defined as within the scope of the program are the so-called multi-problem or hard core families, but it has been difficult to develop clear criteria for referral in the absence of a roster of the sort described. Case characteristics stated in Glueck "delinquency prediction" terms, rather than service ramifications of the case, were initially the basis for the referral system. Later, complex cases not worked with elsewhere on an intensive basis were accepted; the bulk come from schools and the Welfare Department.

The cornerstone of the plan is the designation of one rehabilitation caseworker per case (an "intensive" worker in the sense used above), even though the family may be on the rosters of such departments as welfare, schools, courts, and health. Although on the payrolls of various departments as probation officers, attendance teachers, youth guidance technicians, or social investigators, the Center's staff members become "general" social caseworkers. Only the minimum of core statutory responsibilities remains vested in the originating agencies (such as Department of Welfare relief eligibility or probation reporting responsibility), while the Center worker assumes the task of providing a broad range of "reaching out," supportive, protective, and rehabilitative services. Some of this help is very concrete and some is treatment through a relationship, in an effort to get a family back on its feet. Health consultation and guidance in access to the services of other city bureaus (housing, licenses, etc.) are provided by specialists although there is evidence that health ramifications of cases are so extensive as to demand a more complete health plan.

A specialist is also assigned to a community organization program which has very modest objectives. The intent is to provide a bridge between the "below par" families and their neighborhood by involving them in local activities of a constructive sort and exposing them to more stable people. Local resources which they require are developed (for example, exchange of baby sitting). The thought is that this type of community organization support of the casework may help make more normal the environment to which children are exposed and may generally strengthen family life.

Initial response to the program has been encouraging. Of some interest is the fact that this particular three-year experiment is being conducted with some staff on the case-aide level and some who have full graduate social work training. All are experienced. In-service training and psychiatric consultation buttress the practice. A caseload of fifteen families per worker (several members may be seen regularly) is being experimented with; this permits one interview with a family member and two collateral contacts per week. The unit may serve 350–400 families at one time when fully staffed. Case turnover is very slow since extensive service is needed.

One might venture the suggestion that the creation of a neighborhood services center which also encourages local self-help activity and, inevitably, is staffed for intake provides an obvious opportunity to experiment with a broader "open door" citizens' advice and steering service (Ch. IV). This would be a particularly strategic development should the three-year experiment be deemed successful and permanent operation and expansion be decided upon.

Hyde Park Youth Project. Many of the elements already described were also joined together in Chicago's three-year action research program known as the Hyde Park Youth Project.[19] Under the sponsorship of the city's Welfare Council and supported by a foundation grant the project undertook the following:

(1) services to individual "behavior problem" children and their families

(2) work with street clubs, corner groups, and street gangs

(3) help to citizen groups and institutions in an effort to understand and alleviate community conditions considered the source of delinquency

(4) coordination of all of this at the neighborhood level

(5) research and description designed to make the experience transferable

The project was concentrated in a changing area of approximately two miles which included the University of Chicago. Its own staff was supplemented by a considerable amount of added support by "cooperating" agencies which accepted referrals or concentrated project cases into specific caseloads. The philosophy of reaching out was similar to that of the New York City Youth Board, the St. Paul project, and others. Great emphasis was placed on service integration and on bringing the program to the neighborhood level.

Rigorous measurement of total effectiveness against "controls" was not undertaken, but a variety of studies based on observation, judgments, and ratings were in a positive direction. The project's staff and sponsors urged that Chicago's Commission on Youth Welfare develop the type of program demonstrated in Hyde Park in selective areas of the city and that this long-term endeavor be publicly financed.

Forms of local organization. To some extent, the question of whether and how case finding and accountability should be tied to neighborhood organization must depend on the form which neighborhood organization takes. New York City, for example, is actually organized in many ways and on many levels by local settlements and centers, health councils, school-based councils, block organizations, precinct coordinating councils, neighborhood improvement groups, tenant organizations, parent organizations, social agency councils,

[19] Charles H. Shireman, *The Hyde Park Youth Project* (Chicago: Welfare Council of Metropolitan Chicago, 1959, mimeographed).

474 A SYSTEM OF SERVICES

the Youth Board, the urban renewal agency, the Commission on Human Rights. The pattern varies from area to area, functions both overlap and leave large gaps, and there are few means to interrelate these many efforts. Several of the larger agencies see themselves as potentially able to coordinate local organization but none actually does. The Community Council lacks resources for direct operations but has served as a clearance and service center for some of the many small, local groups.

It occasionally has been proposed that the schools serve as major local coordinating agencies in the delinquency field—a role which would appear possible in relatively small communities. Schools have sometimes also taken initiative in promoting local neighborhood self-help efforts, as in the instance of New York where the school-community relations program has given a rather open-ended charge to its staff of school-community coordinators (teachers with relevant background). They have joined existing local councils or health councils and have represented the perspective of the schools, have created school-centered councils in order to increase and channel community interest in school problems, and have created block organizations. Recently they have done much to facilitate racial integration in schools. The premise is that citizen involvement in school and community problems is constructive and should be promoted. While many of these projects are noteworthy, community interests will ultimately require a somewhat more rational structure. The schools will want to relate their neighborhood activity directly to school programs while other provision is made for the sponsorship of general self-help developments.

Another type of local self-help effort with special focus on delinquency is represented by past efforts under the New York City Youth Board, through its Department of Borough Planning and Community Coordination. Trained community organizers in borough offices served as borough coordinators. They had assistants and clerical help. Within the structure there were actually two types of relatively separate efforts: (a) Borough committees, made up of citizens of considerable prestige, served as advisors to the borough office in its relationship to the Youth Board's city-wide planning and coordination machinery. These committees had no administrative functions or prerogatives; the projects they suggested were considered centrally. (*b*) A local community organization program involved staff support and/or service to a variety of kinds of local and neighborhood councils and their youth councils as well as a program of frequent area meetings (in a variety of patterns) to tap neighborhood needs and problems and initiate community actions. These neighborhood councils and area meetings have been the center of substantial activity, the kind of local council organized depending in each instance upon the specific interests and resources of the particular community.

While the Youth Board program is in transition, a very similar pattern of organization and vital activity is found in many other communities under the voluntary auspices of local community planning councils. New York's pattern developed as the consequence of a vacuum left by a Community Council with limited resources. Basic questions are raised about publicly conducted local community organization in the Youth Board pattern since a local neighborhood organization must, perforce, direct its attention to public departments and local government from time to time. Are not staff limited by their status as public employees? Is such a structure not subject to political manipulation at some point in the future? The Youth Board's answer and the response of all those who see local organization as a legitimate public function was that councils which are organized by professional staff (whatever the salary source) are automonous councils. Moreover, public employees have knowledge of and easy access to public departments. Many of the concerns of local councils need to be addressed to such departments.

While the preponderance of opinion would tend at present to oppose publicly operated neighborhood organization, conclusive evidence as to alleged dangers does not exist. Urban renewal, public housing, and public intergroup relations programs are making more public resources available for such work. Some of these funds may be expended through voluntary contracts, as when a local community council accepts a contract associated with urban renewal. Other funds will be expended publicly. Perhaps attention should be directed at providing necessary safeguards for public operation and at ensuring the coordination of local organization in appropriate fashion.

POSSIBLE PATTERNS

As large cities make their decisions about responsibility for local organization and the coordination of such organization, they should simultaneously consider provision for local accountability–case integration and its possible ties to self-help and to coordination structures. This chapter has illustrated a variety of tendencies. For the present, *several lines of experimentation* rather than final decisions would seem to be in order.

(1) Creation of public units (such as the Referral Units in New York) as centers of accountability and service integration. These units would organize case conferences. They would require central registers. They should be decentralized.

(2) Creation of accountability–service integration units under voluntary auspices, tied to broader local self-help activities, on the pattern of LENA. The LENA area teams are especially suggestive.

(3) Continued separation of the three levels of function: service integration and accountability, local self-help, city-wide coordination. This would be the "most natural" pattern and would continue present systems. It would not eliminate the urgent need to rationalize and simplify the relationships of city-wide planning and coordinating bodies to local self-help organizations.

(4) Continued experimentation with neighborhood-based treatment services staffed by "intensive" workers, on the pattern of the Interdepartmental Neighborhood Services Center. Experimentation in the use of community organization techniques as an adjunct to the casework should also continue. In addition, it would be useful to experiment with assignment of an "advice bureau" role to such centers. There is need for more rigorous criteria for assignment of cases to special units and intensive workers under this and other patterns of organization.

The leadership in such experimentation and planning must come from planning and coordinating bodies on several levels. Some of the possibilities are discussed in the next chapter.

CHAPTER XIII

COORDINATION AND PLANNING

SOME of the weaknesses in community services may be met through *improved handling of the individual case* within a given service or through *integration of the services of two or more agencies* in their relation to the individual case. Other "soft spots" in the system may be eliminated through the development of *accountability machinery* of the kind already described. However, the problems of an era of specialization, large-scale organization, social instability, and professional innovation also require something more: *adequate coordination and planning on several levels.*

While this volume addresses itself to the specific requirements of an urban area, the present chapter must turn initially to statewide planning and coordination structures. It may then focus on the problem of planning and coordination at the city level.

First, however, some additional concepts require specification.[1] *Planning,* as the word is employed here, is the process concerned with evaluating alternatives, developing proposals and timetables for the *future,* and indicating the methods and stages for implementing proposals. It involves formulation of criteria or goals relevant to choices to be made. It requires research and fact finding as well as decisions about goals, values, pace, and priorities.

Coordination, on the other hand, deals with the meshing of agencies, programs, services, and activities in order to accomplish basic objectives. Each agency or unit requires information about

---

[1] This section draws at several points on Herbert A. Simon, Donald W. Smithburg, Victor A. Thompson, *Public Administration* (New York: Alfred A. Knopf, 1950).

the activities, areas of responsibility, and policies of the others so that actions and plans may be appropriately dovetailed. Adequate coordination is based on communication, interpretation, and interchange as well as provision for negotiation, settling differences, and arriving at agreements relating to policy or procedures. At times, where differences of opinion exist about objectives or methods, and where the differences involve mutually contradictory courses, coordination may demand devices (hearings, policy decisions by those in authority, agreements for test periods, etc.) to ensure that some common course is adopted by all concerned.

For present purposes, it is helpful to differentiate between coordination relating to *agency programs*, policies, objectives, scope, and plans, on the one hand, and coordination of work *on the level of the individual case*, on the other. The latter phenomenon has already been referred to as *service integration*.

When a great many planning activities are carried on by different groups, there is need for *coordination of planning* to minimize inconsistencies, contradictions, and costly duplication, as well as to define roles and responsibility. A major objective in adequate coordination of long-range planning is the formulation of acceptable, coherent over-all goals, which become the point of departure, in the particular field, for those undertaking major responsibility in specific subareas.

STATE-WIDE STRUCTURES

The field of services to delinquents and other children in trouble has become increasingly concerned in the past decade with the need for adequate state-wide coordination machinery. Less attention has been given to long-range planning. The urgency of adequate provision was highlighted by the U.S. Senate delinquency subcommittee and by the 1960 White House Conference on Children.[2] Each legislative year brings changes in some states, so that no published work can be complete and up to date. Trends may be noted and alternatives posed, however.

[2] Subcommittee to Investigate Juvenile Delinquency, Committee on Judiciary, U.S. Senate, *New York Programs for the Prevention and Treatment of Juvenile Delinquency*, Hearing of December 4, 1957 (Washington, D.C.: Government Printing Office, 1958), pp. 33–50, and *Juvenile Delinquency*, Report of June 15, 1960 (Washington, D.C.: Government Printing Office, 1960), pp. 96–122.

The state welfare department. While a considerable proportion of the professional literature urges that a state's department of public welfare take on the major coordination role in relation to delinquency, three major public patterns are actually discernible in practice : (1) state coordination and planning in the hands of a public welfare department (approximately 13–15 states); (2) coordination and planning assigned to special youth commissions or committees, created by legislative enactment and/or gubernatorial appointment (7–8 states, totals depending on definitions); (3) coordination and planning by a youth authority or one of its derivations (7 states). Impressive, if piecemeal, contributions to planning and some limited coordination have also been effected by voluntary state-wide citizen machinery—initially, the groups established to follow up the 1950 White House Conference on Children and more recently, in several states, the Citizen Action programs. In many states the leadership-coordination task is divided—or not assigned.[3]

The American Public Welfare Association states very clearly the claim of a state public welfare department:

State government should place responsibility in a single state agency which it can hold responsible for planning, for facilitating coordination, and for seeing that needed services are made available either under its own or other auspices. The state welfare department is most advantageously situated to accept this responsibility. In carrying out this assignment, it is essential that the department work cooperatively with other organizations and agencies having appropriate functions in the field and that it contribute in every possible way to the strengthening of their programs. This is especially true in relation to juvenile courts which have a major and essential responsibility in the treatment of juvenile delinquents.[4]

[3] We do not attempt here to deal with assignment of responsibility for direct services for children referred by the courts or with the many programs listed by state welfare departments for prevention, control, and treatment of delinquency. All but five state departments have legal authority for some control or treatment functions. For results of a Children's Bureau questionnaire survey see Helen R. Jeter, *State Agencies and Juvenile Delinquency*, Juvenile Delinquency Facts and Facets, No. 12, U.S. Department of Health, Education, and Welfare (Washington, D.C.: Government Printing Office, 1960). See Appendix IV for a state-by-state listing. Also, in the same series, see Bjarne Romnes, *Coordination of the National Effort for Dealing with Juvenile Delinquency*, Juvenile Delinquency Facts and Facets, No. 7 (1960).

[4] American Public Welfare Association, "Public Welfare Services and Juvenile Delinquency," a Policy Statement adopted December 16, 1958, p. 2.

The case for this policy proposal is quite clear. Delinquency is considered to be symptomatic of deprivations and disturbances affecting an individual's total life-situation. Prevention and treatment require a broad range of services "which in most respects are concerned with the same problems that are dealt with by public welfare agencies in all of their areas of responsibility. These include economic dependency, family breakdown, desertion and abandonment, domestic discord, parental neglect and abuse, behavior problems and emotional disturbances." Moreover, a state public welfare agency has an existing structure in every locality of a state, is already in touch with large segments of the most vulnerable part of the population, and is always "deeply involved in community organization for developing needed services for families and children." To place responsibility elsewhere is to encourage duplication and fragmentation.[5]

Of some interest is the fact that this point of view envisages that the state public welfare department will have both operating responsibilities (which in turn may include direct administration of services, standard setting, supervision, licensing, consultation) and planning-coordination responsibilities. The department will also encourage, and perhaps provide staff services for, creation of a "statewide structure for broad citizen involvement in planning, decision-making and coordination of programs." Citizen social action will be welcomed.[6]

This general perspective has considerable support and is implemented in a number of states in varying degrees depending on state standards for services to children and the salience of the delinquency problem. Various professional groups and individuals on the national and state scenes, too, have resisted organization of services for delinquents apart from their broader child welfare or public welfare context.

The influence of the approach may be illustrated with reference to Pennsylvania. Within the State Public Welfare Department an Office for Children and Youth operates certain institutions and facilities directly, reimburses localities and voluntary agencies for institutional and child welfare services, and carries on a program of standard setting and licensing. Responsibility for prevention and

[5] *Ibid.*, p. 3.　　　　　　　　　　[6] *Ibid.*, p. 5.

treatment of delinquency is in a Bureau of Youth Services located within this department. The bureau operates the state institutions, supervises the other institutions, seeks to build up services for prevention and control (work with gangs), and subsidizes training of probation and police staff. Its consultation, research, and planning activities are modest but are expected to expand.[7]

Many similar functions are assigned to the Youth Rehabilitation Section of Idaho's Division of Mental Health, Maryland's Bureau of Child Welfare under the Department of Public Welfare, and Washington's Division of Children and Youth Services in a Department of Institutions. In addition to statistics systems, research, consultation, training, administration of institutions and forestry camps, and responsibility for aftercare activities which tend to characterize these agencies, they also have community services bureaus. The latter offer consultation to localities and may also, in some instances, become actively involved in upgrading individual agencies, supporting citizen action programs, or operating local community services.

Why, then, specialized coordinating agencies to deal with services to delinquents and young offenders? The answers are as often historical, political, and pragmatic as they are principled and substantive. (1) It is frequently possible to rally citizen and legislative interest around one problem, particularly an alarming, urgent, and unpleasant problem, where an ongoing program which has many facets cannot command attention or funds. (2) It is sometimes necessary to create a new structure for planning and coordination in order to ensure an energetic and creative staff and citizen board, where an ongoing department is bogged down in its traditions and long-accumulated limitations and roadblocks. (3) Sometimes the problem is so large and so urgent as to demand the creation of a body which will give it substantial and concentrated attention. (4) Even a public welfare department does not encompass all facets

---

[7] Government Consulting Service, Institute of State and Local Government, University of Pennsylvania, *Coordination of the Program of Institutional Care of Juvenile Delinquents in Pennsylvania* (Philadelphia, 1955, mimeographed), Sec. II, p. 5. Also, Community Services Branch, Division of Juvenile Delinquency Service, Children's Bureau, "Directory and Description of Statutory State Agencies Combating Juvenile Delinquency" (Washington, D.C.: Department of Health, Education, and Welfare, 1958, mimeographed), and current reports of the Pennsylvania department.

of a program for delinquents. Education, health, and mental health agencies in a state also conduct crucial programs. A case may therefore be made for a structure independent of any of these departments.

Thus, despite the strength of the public welfare position, one should not question alternative structures merely on the grounds that they are not state public welfare departments. The real issue is whether these alternative structures have adequate relationships to the welfare department and to other departments and whether they ensure implementation of the crucial functions. The American Public Welfare Association, in fact, recognizes this alternative in its statement:

Specifically in states where specialized correction or youth-serving agencies or authorities have already been created and are dealing effectively with parts of the total program, the public welfare department should not duplicate such services but should work with them in full cooperation.[8]

A youth authority. The Youth Authority Plan is frequently mentioned as an alternate coordination structure, concentrating on juvenile delinquency and youth crime. Its history, implications, and strengths are reviewed in a number of readily available sources.[9]

What has become known as the youth authority movement arose as a reaction to an exposé of New York City practices in dealing with offenders in the 16–21 age group. The American Law Institute drafted a model statute after considering a report and recommendations from New York's Community Service Society. As the result of a variety of local circumstances and a decade of crusading by John R. Ellingston of the American Law Institute, a number of states adopted youth authority plans and others were influenced in various aspects of their programing and administration of services. California led the way with its Youth Authority in 1941. Other plans (many since revised) were adopted by Minnesota (1947), Wis-

---

[8] "Public Welfare Services and Juvenile Delinquency," p. 6.

[9] Bertram M. Beck, *Five States* (Philadelphia: American Law Institute, 1951); Herbert A. Bloch and Frank T. Flynn, *Delinquency: The Juvenile Offender in America Today* (New York: Random House, 1956), pp. 487–507; Sol Rubin, "Changing Youth Authority Concepts," *Focus*, XXIX (May, 1950), 77–82, and *Crime and Juvenile Delinquency* (New York: Oceana Publications, 1958), Chapter VII. Also see the brief summaries in the "Directory and Description of Statutory State Agencies Combating Juvenile Delinquency."

consin (1947), Massachusetts (1948), Texas (1949), Arizona (1951), Kentucky (1952), Illinois (1953), the federal government (1956).

The states listed deviated considerably from the model act and developed wide variations in the programs implemented. For the most part, for example, youth authorities affect juvenile delinquents rather than youthful offenders, who were the original objects of interest. The "typical" authority, if there is one, accepts court-ordered commitments (usually juvenile court) for terms which are indeterminate—after court adjudication and court decision as to whether probation or another community-based decision is desirable. Committed children and youths are then sent to a reception-diagnostic-classification facility which makes a treatment plan. The authority has, or should have, access to a diversified group of treatment institutions. Authorities have pioneered in the use of conservation camps, following the California lead. In addition, most of the authorities have functioned in what is usually called the "prevention" area, although the specific programs show considerable variation. Several have undertaken training responsibilities, administrative research, and long-range planning.

Beck has acknowledged the extent to which youth authority programs have improved services to delinquents, but he has also asked whether all states need such a plan. The separate elements —commitment to one agency; central diagnosis and screening; indeterminate sentences; operation of new treatment facilities—do not require a new agency as such. In fact, Bloch and Flynn, as well as Beck, cite instances in which all of these have developed without an authority: Virginia has committed to a state department rather than one institution since 1922; New York and New Jersey have diagnostic centers; many states have forestry camps. While granting the advances a new agency may make because of enthusiasm, support, and publicity, they ask whether one should pay the price of separating out services to delinquents from the general field of child welfare when there is general conviction as to the need for a full range of child welfare services for effective prevention and treatment.[10]

[10] Beck, *Five States;* Bloch and Flynn, *Delinquency.* The Massachusetts commission is cited by Bloch and Flynn, p. 499.

The California Youth Authority, the oldest and most widely known of the authorities, has a program of diagnosis and treatment (reception centers, camps, institutions), administration, research, field services (probation, parole), prevention, education, and some coordination.[11] It is a major agency of state government, responsible for more than a dozen institutions–camps–reception centers and ten branch offices. Over 15,000 children are in its care in institutions and on parole, and an experimental community treatment program is being launched. The board itself is responsible for acceptance and rejection of cases; initial classification and assignment to institutions; release on parole; suspension, revocation, and restoration of parole; and final discharge of wards. The authority director is board chairman; in his capacity as director he administers the facilities and "prevention" work. Included in the latter is consultation to localities on probation services, juvenile detention, and county camps (there is a generous state-aid program). In addition, a field staff assists localities which wish to initiate broader prevention services. The authority has carried out many kinds of training courses and institutes for probation officers and law enforcement personnel. It has an outstanding research program.

Recent California legislation has joined the Youth Authority with the Corrections Department in a new, larger unit. California also has an active and effective Governor's Advisory Committee on Children and Youth, which brings citizen opinion to bear on planning, provides informal interdepartmental coordination, and also deals with child welfare and mental health issues beyond the range of the authority.

The Massachusetts Youth Services Board was created in 1948 in order to place responsibility for custody, diagnosis, care, and treatment of juvenile delinquents in a single specialized agency. The board consists of three members appointed by the governor. Its chairman is also director of a Division of Youth Services which has been placed in the State Department of Education since 1952 but is "not subject to its control." As new facilities have been de-

[11] Testimony of Harold Butterfield, deputy director, California Youth Authority, in *Institutions for Rehabilitation and Treatment of Juvenile Delinquency*, Hearing before the Subcommittee to Investigate Juvenile Delinquency, Committee on Judiciary, U.S. Senate, March 4, 1958 (Washington, D.C.: Government Printing Office, 1958), pp. 4–25.

veloped, they have been assigned to this division, which now administers a state-wide parole service, detention and reception centers, and state training schools (called "industrial schools"). Juvenile courts commit adjudicated delinquents to the board, which then selects specific facilities. The court continues to decide between community-based dispositions and adjudication.

Since 1953 a Bureau of Delinquency Prevention and Research, under the Division of Youth Services, has been developing a variety of consultation, survey, and training services. As is generally the case with such programs in many states, efforts are made to encourage local initiative and planning. State consultants make broader knowledge and experience available. The creation of local youth commissions and coordinating bodies is encouraged. A small staff of professionally qualified "detached workers" is available for "loan" to localities to cope with special problems and to conduct demonstrations. The board is also the channel to localities for a state-aid program involving the creation of school guidance and counseling programs.

The overburdened board has great difficulty in meeting its case disposition responsibilities, and it requires expansion. The history of the program would seem to provide no special evidence as to the validity of joining this role to that of providing leadership to local prevention efforts and stimulating state-wide planning and coordination. Since the delinquency program "umbrella" is inevitably limited and since this official state program, apparently, does not rally sufficient voluntary initiative, there is also an active state-wide Massachusetts Committee on Children and Youth, now in its third year. Within the state administration there is an Interdepartmental Committee on Children and Youth.

The modified structures which have been developed in Wisconsin and Kentucky also offer interesting ways of achieving some of the youth authority advantages while ensuring the sound relationship of the youth authority program to the public welfare structure. As the result of a series of events related to special conditions in the state, the Wisconsin statute was revised at an early date, leaving the youth authority functions divided between the Division of Children and Youth and the Division of Correction—both of which are parts of the State Department of Social Welfare. Related functions are placed under the Division of Mental Hygiene. In Kentucky, the Youth Authority as such became a Welfare Department division. The Bloch-Flynn evaluation is convincing: "The Wisconsin plan, which provides integrated services for delinquents within the framework of an omnibus department of welfare, seems most suitable *when the reorganization of state services for those of juvenile court age is required*" [italics added].[12]

The Wisconsin community organization program is deserving of special mention because of its substantial development.[13] It began in 1949, taking its cue from the Social Security Act provision for subsidy to states "for developing state services for the encouragement and assistance of adequate methods of community child welfare organization in areas predominantly rural and other areas of special need." The state statute stresses coordination of planning in education, recreation, health, welfare; development and strengthening of preventive programs; establishment of councils and a variety of other local coordination structures. Professionally qualified community organizers have been provided, and the well-led Division of Children and Youth has deployed them in district areas (each covering fifteen counties) and as specialist consultants in a central office. As have other states, Wisconsin has developed through this agency improved statistical reports, consultation and training for law enforcement officials, a degree of improved case finding in the schools, youth participation, extension of recreation facilities, and more public information activity.

For purposes of the present discussion, special note is made of the field assistance to local communities and its emphasis on planning and coordination. White House Conference recommendations have been followed up. Another unique feature is the program of local community surveys supported by Division of Children and Youth staff services and the cooperation of other state agencies, if the

[12] Bloch and Flynn, *Delinquency*, p. 500.

[13] Although the Wisconsin program is probably one of the most elaborate, other authority states also include community organization. For example, the Illinois Youth Commission has expanded its community services of late to include consultation and local surveys and has created eight district offices with a coordination function. See Illinois Youth Commission, *Biennial Report 1955–1956* (Springfield: The Commission, 1957). Also, Romnes, *Coordination of the National Effort*.

community meets conditions relative to an official request from a county board or a city council, broad community participation and involvement, distribution of the report, and acceptance of responsibility for follow-up. The program has proven to be an excellent, yet economical, way of ensuring citizen involvement in programs and a planning-coordination instrument which is quite effective in most communities in which it has been employed.[14]

In the past several years the Minnesota program has evolved in a unique direction. Its youth authority, the Youth Conservation Commission, had carried out a program of case assignment, training school and camp administration, and limited work in probation and prevention. In 1960 a unified Corrections Department joined the youth program with the previous adult institution program and the independent adult probation and parole agency. The new department is responsible for all these plus jail inspection and consultation. State subsidy permits probation and parole expansion to all counties through state aid or state operations in localities. Plans are under way to expand community organization and training activities. The department is organized in three divisions, Adult Corrections, Youth Conservation, and Administrative Services—but there is considerable across-the-board policy making and planning. The Youth Conservation Commission continues to sit on institution assignment and release.

These brief reviews of several youth authority programs point to a program in transition. On the one hand, authorities have become arms of state government, administering training schools, camps, staff training, research, and community prevention services. On the other, they continue as "boards" which accept cases on court commitment and are responsible for the choice of specific facilities, for release on parole, and so on. Each of these functions requires examination.

[14] The community services program of the Division of Children and Youth, State Department of Social Welfare, is described in a series of brochures, reports, and mimeographed documents distributed by the Division at Madison, Wisconsin. Also see Children's Bureau, U.S. Department of Health, Education, and Welfare, *Public Child Welfare in Wisconsin*, Child Welfare Report No. 7 (Washington, D.C.: Government Printing Office, 1957), and Fred DelliQuadri, "New Ways of Looking at Community Organization for Child Welfare," in National Conference on Social Welfare, *Planning Social Services for Urban Needs* (New York: Columbia University Press, 1957), pp. 56–64.

To the extent that youth authorities are operational agencies, the authority concept per se is not relevant or functional. It may be a device for initial rallying of support and funds, but there is no special value to the authority per se. Indeed, as in the instances of California and Massachusetts, the authority chairman becomes an administrative officer of a state agency. There is then every reason to unify the program with broader governmental units. California and Minnesota have now chosen the corrections "axis" for such unification, while Wisconsin places delinquency services in public welfare. Massachusetts uses education as the administrative "home" for its authority but true unification has not yet taken place.

Similarly, the "board" role of authorities may be in transition. It is certainly a major step forward when courts give up the attempt to decide from among the elements of an institution network and relegate the task to a board whose members visit the institutions frequently and are informed as to their facilities. Further progress has been made when authorities create diagnostic centers and rely heavily on their case analyses and proposals. Is it not reasonable to predict that the next and logical step may be to define the choice of facility and the decision to release as a purely technical task, assigned to diagnostic center staffs? It may be some time before this final step is taken both because states lack adequate diagnostic resources and because there is a desire to have nontechnical involvement in decision making. The process is nonetheless under way. In several of the states board members are now either too burdened to review and challenge most records or have high respect for technical recommendations; boards change only a small proportion of actions proposed by the staff.

Should authorities eventually transfer their disposition responsibilities to technical staffs, there will remain the need for a "public presence" which will periodically review disposition patterns in the light of public objectives. This, however, would be an advisory body, comparable to advisory welfare committees or institution visiting committees. There would be no reason for it also to assume administrative responsibility for institutions, probation, and so on. In fact, as youth authority administrative operations take the form of a typical state department, one public advisory group could fulfill several functions.

There is need for additional study of the so-called prevention activities of several youth authorities. Although not proposed in the initial statute, most of the authorities have developed programs which encompass surveys and self-surveys; community organization to increase local participation in surveys and in the implementation of recommendations for new facilities or for new ways of working; creation of local councils and coordinating bodies; consultation to the localities; educational programs of a variety of kinds. There may be modest grant-in-aid funds too. These efforts sometimes concentrate on the improvement of services for delinquents, but are more often based on the philosophy that delinquency is best prevented by "the betterment of all facilities for all children." [15]

As authorities and state governments look ahead, they will want to consider whether the delinquency problem is the best point of departure for their efforts at encouraging local initiative, planning, and coordination in health, education, welfare, corrections, and recreation. To some extent the answer will depend on where the authority is placed in state government. Under the Wisconsin plan, for example, the community services program has a broad public welfare basis. To some extent, too, the evaluation will depend on what other provision there is in the state for broadening the perspective. As noted, several youth authority states also have statewide citizens' committees on children and youth. Many other states also count on such committees to relate government action to citizen priorities and concerns.

Commission on children and youth. The assignment of major coordination responsibility to a public welfare department would seem to be the most advantageous way to obtain optimum integration of a substantial number of services vital to effective treatment. Assignment to a youth authority provides for the possibility of intensive and concentrated, but perhaps separate, institutional treatment facilities for delinquents. Each may undertake planning within its defined scope. However, the attainment of coordination and planning on even a broader front, plus the stimulation and support of citizen involvement and action, is perhaps more effectively handled by a state-wide committee or commission with official or semiofficial status, free of service responsibilities, and with some

[15] Beck, *Five States,* p. 129.

form of relationship to or the participation of key state commissioners.

Such nonoperating agencies or boards received particular stimulation through the nationally promoted follow-up effort after the 1950 White House Conference on Children. There was further encouragement through the 1960 Conference. Many of the programs obtained official or semiofficial status. One might illustrate with reference to such statutory bodies as the Tennessee Commission on Youth Guidance, the Florida Children's Commission, the Louisiana Youth Commission, the Mississippi Children's Code Commission, the New Mexico Council on Children and Youth. Each of these has its own special history and characteristics, but such functions as the following are found in a number of the programs: study, planning, advice, evaluation, consultation, coordination, legislative drafting, organization of citizen action in the localities. The concern is generally broader than juvenile delinquency. Unlike youth authorities and state agencies, the commissions or councils do not operate training schools or other diagnostic and treatment facilities.

The Louisiana State Youth Commission, which may be taken as an illustration, has statutory status, having been created by legislation in 1950 as the successor of an earlier Juvenile Court commission which found its charge too narrow and its resources too limited. The commission consists of nine members appointed by the governor. It has an executive secretary and a very small office staff. It is defined as "advisory, investigatory, consultative" but not as administrative. It is authorized to collect facts and make studies of conditions affecting children and youth, to keep abreast of developments, to provide for a mutual exchange of ideas and information, to conduct hearings, to make recommendations, and to coordinate the services of state agencies serving children.

Since the Louisiana commission is not an administrative body, it must emphasize advisory, investigatory, and consultative operations. Its coordination must be severely limited although it may encourage exchange of information and cooperative activities. To some degree it is able to initiate concerns in operating departments; it sits in at interdepartmental committee meetings but does not convene them.

Local governmental bodies and citizen groups and state-wide

voluntary groups may ask for consultation from the commission or may follow through vis-à-vis legislative or local bodies to obtain implementation of its legislation. Unlike many other state bodies, it is not itself staffed to initiate citizen action or to organize any large-scale citizen study of youth and child welfare problems.

Maryland's program, by contrast, is a nonstatutory one and does ensure far more citizen involvement. The related statutory agency is a Child Welfare Bureau in the Department of Public Welfare, organized into a Division of Training Schools (for consultation, not administration) and a Division of Consultant and Prevention Services. Consultation is technical, emphasizing probation, police, court services. The nonstatutory Maryland Commission for the Prevention and Treatment of Juvenile Delinquency (now Commission for Children and Youth) was appointed by the governor in May, 1956, after a state-wide governor's conference and is composed of forty-four citizens from a wide variety of backgrounds, as well as directors of state departments directly concerned with children and chairmen of affiliated local commissions. The chairman of the Youth Participation Committee, sponsored by the commission, is a member. Approximately half of the commission is lay, half professional. Staff services are provided by the State Department of Public Welfare through the Division of Consultant and Prevention Services.

The Maryland commission sees itself as a vehicle for citizen planning and action and seeks to "make more possible the coordinated efforts of agencies and individuals concerned with children and their families." The approach is broad:

The Commission was established with the conviction that if the community makes it possible for children—all children—to grow up with greater psychological and physical security than many of them are now privileged to enjoy, juvenile delinquency will be substantially reduced; as will the tragedies which come in the wake of it. This conviction has become even more firm as the Commission moved forward. Therefore, the approach taken is a broad one concerning itself not only with specific measures pertaining to delinquency treatment, but also with most of the crucial areas which touch and affect the lives of Maryland's children.[16]

[16] Maryland Commission for the Prevention and Treatment of Juvenile Delinquency, *Summary of Organization and Program* (Baltimore, 1957, mimeographed), p. 1. Also, *The Time for Action Is Now* (Baltimore: The Commission, 1957); National Committee for Children and Youth, *Patterns of Or-*

A group of thirteen program committees has served as the source of action proposals and has given detailed attention to the recommendations of the well-attended annual governor's conferences, which include considerable youth participation. The committees are assigned such subjects as community organization, family life, health, education, employment, police, juvenile courts, aftercare, etc. Six action committees are part of the permanent structure and are concerned with the formulation of annual recommendations for action by the executive committee and the commission, and with implementation.

Increasingly, the commission has stressed broad citizen participation in the governor's conferences, the establishment of local commissions (half the state is covered at this writing), and the sponsorship of local conferences. It is felt that this approach ensures widespread interest, the pinpointing of the most vital problems, and the necessary support for legislation growing out of the commission's program.

Consideration of this kind of program would suggest that its educational and social action potentials are perhaps its greatest strength. More systematic fact finding and long-range planning requires a research staff and formal relationship to administrative agencies. Coordination, on a level beyond that of interchange and the important informal accomplishments which derive through joint participation in meetings and conferences for formulation of program recommendations, must develop in a coordination structure of administrative personnel who address specific problems.

California has developed its Governor's Committee on Children and Youth as an effective device for tapping citizen opinion and achieving informal interdepartmental coordination. It tends to function in an area broader than the Youth Authority. This citizen group is composed of prominant members of several professions and active lay leaders. It is called upon by the governor from time to time to provide advice relative to special or continuing problems of children and youth in the state. It often coopts members to special subcommittees for basic study of major problems. The over-all committee and its subcommittees frequently obtain special foundation

ganization of State Committees for Children and Youth (Washington, D.C.: Government Printing Office, 1962).

grants for basic research. State-wide and local conferences may be called to tap public opinion and proposals—as many as eighteen in a year. Studies of youth services in given localities may be encouraged. In addition, the committee makes recommendations on pending legislation.

The vitality of this advisory committee is noted in its scope and achievements. A random list would include reference to its systematic state-wide surveys of services to children and youth in preparation for the last White House Conference on Children, its studies—with foundation assistance—of major child welfare problems such as adoption and detention, its comprehensive delinquency prevention program prepared at the governor's request in 1960, its continuous community-wide interpretation, the excellent participation of representative citizens in many local meetings, and its effect on pending legislation.

Since interdepartmental coordination of services to children and youth is an important concern in any state, it is interesting to note the extent to which the operational pattern of the governor's advisory committee makes a contribution in this realm. The total budget of the advisory committee is spent for travel allowances for citizen members, and staffing is the responsibility of cooperating departments. Each department assigns a senior staff person to a Staff Committee and the chairmanship rotates annually. The Staff Committee meets in advance to prepare the agenda for the citizen group and assembles again after each meeting to follow through on decisions. Responsibility is assigned to the departments as appropriate, and they commit whatever staff resources are required. If necessary, interdepartmental *ad hoc* subcommittees are created for study, policy clarification, and action. The directors of the various departments are themselves ex officio members of the governor's advisory committee and each senior staff representative develops a reporting practice appropriate to his department. Since departments and governor both receive committee recommendations and considerable interpretation at several staff levels and through citizen leadership it is not surprising to note the high degree of success in effecting executive action and the drafting of legislation by the administration.

The New Jersey Youth Study Commission, which recently completed its task, lacked many of the elements in the above programs but illustrates a unique fact-finding and research structure. The Jersey body was created in 1954 as a Juvenile Delinquency Study Commission and was renamed Youth Study Commission in 1957 to take account of the range of interests which inevitably developed through conscientious pursuit of its charge to conduct studies, recommend legislation, and publish reports relative to juvenile delinquency and ("as . . . related thereto") health, recreation, and education. It was composed of two members from the New Jersey State Senate, two from the Assembly, eight citizens at large, and the Commissioner of Education, ex officio. Appointments were made by the governor and the presiding officers of both legislative houses.

In the tradition of English legislative commissions, a tradition well over one hundred years old, the Jersey Youth Study Commission conducted hearings continuously in various parts of the state, drawing upon the experience of lay citizens and professionals and sometimes calling upon outside experts as well. With the aid of a small but outstanding research staff, which helped to define the focus of the hearings and to locate appropriate witnesses, it published comprehensive and sophisticated annual reports, based on the hearings, its own deliberations, and relevant research literature. It made specific action recommendations to the legislature each year. In addition, its reports represented outstanding planning documents, suggesting policy direction and priorities.[17] In completing its assignment, it recommended a broader and more permanent coordinating structure.

Utah, which has a Committee on Children and Youth, created early in 1961 a unique new agency, the State Council on Criminal Justice Administration, "to observe the criminal law in action" and to report its findings and recommendations. Existing agencies may not be relieved of statutory duties by this new body, which is specifically limited to consideration of basic principles and administrative processes.

The plan grew out of concern in the state with prison disturb-

---

[17] State of New Jersey, Youth Study Commission, *Helping Youth in Trouble: Second Report and Recommendations* (Trenton, 1957), and *New Ways to Reach Unreached Youth: Third Annual Report and Recommendations* (Trenton, 1958).

ances, the inadequacies in the juvenile court system, poor coordination between law enforcement and other services, and the general need to strengthen prevention and control programs. It was devised by an *ad hoc* legislative committee after careful study.

Evaluation of this device is, of course, not possible at this stage but it would seem to have the potential of the New Jersey Youth Study Commission and the advantage of a stronger charge and permanency. Ex officio members represent key public and private groups (supreme court, attorney general, legislative council, public welfare commission, board of corrections, state bar, state medical association, state social welfare conference, peace officers' association). In addition, the governor appoints six members. The council is both informed and in a position to channel its findings. Staffing, of course, is important.

Another kind of contribution in the area of study and citizen action is represented by the Citizen Action Program initiated by the National Council on Crime and Delinquency (NCCD).

NCCD Citizen Action Program. The NCCD Citizen Action Program, financed originally by the Ford Foundation for the period 1955–59 and recently renewed, began with the recognition that most communities do not have adequate juvenile courts; many delinquents are detained in jails rather than detention facilities; youths are often committed to inadequate training schools where probation would be the more appropriate disposition but is not available; most courts lack adequate diagnostic clinics; prisons are often obsolete and parole policy outdated. Modern knowledge and skill too often are not being applied to delinquency and crime, personnel are not provided, and funds are not voted. Legislation is often out of date and a handicap.

Our progress depends on public understanding, public leadership, and public action. Without public support, professional workers will remain severely limited in their efforts to control delinquency, family breakup, and crime.

In the past, wherever appreciable progress was achieved in correctional services, it was responsible citizen action that was the spark plug. Citizen action was largely responsible for developing the idea of probation, for promoting the juvenile court movement, for selecting qualified judges and correctional administrators.

Where the community is uninformed and does not understand the nature of the problem and the remedy, professional leadership may become stagnant and the result is a destructive treadmill of arrests, sentences, and indiscriminate imprisonment.

The Citizen Action plan is basically simple. A national Citizens Council and the central staff of the NCCD have sought to identify states most in need of action, yet having the potential for citizen activity, and have attempted to stimulate leadership in these states and to reinforce their action programs through consultation and help. In the meantime, broad public interpretation has been sought nationally through newspapers, magazines, radio, and television. Staff services are provided in the states from two sources: project personnel and specialist consultants on the NCCD staff.

The core of the action program in each state is a state council of approximately fifteen outstanding citizens from industry, business, and the professions. Much of the impressive success of the program in the early years is, in fact, associated with the ability of the project to attract top state leadership from these fields—many of them individuals never previously connected with programs for offenders—and to stimulate them to a point where visits, study, and consideration have convinced them of the ultimate economy and effectiveness of increased public investment in these programs and high standards of service. By virtue of their community stature, these councils have been effective in relation to legislation and appropriations.[18]

Programs were developed in eight states during the first five years: Michigan, Washington, Montana, Texas, Oklahoma, Ohio, West Virginia, and Indiana. They have in common the following:

Each state council works with judges, bar associations, and correctional administrators and technicians, to:
  1. examine and evaluate specific ways in which the state deals with the offender from first contact to disposition and treatment;
  2. recommend innovations and improvements, assigning each recommendation a priority according to its urgency;
  3. inform the public in every way it can, so that deficiencies are considered openly, widely, and realistically;

[18] In relation to the above and what follows see National Council on Crime and Delinquency, "Citizen Action Program," a brochure prepared by Lucy Freeman (1955). The quotation is from p. 9. Subsequent detail is reported in articles in the NCCD News, issues from 1958 to 1962.

4. act to get public and private individuals and groups to work for the recommended improvements.[19]

The actions, legislation, reforms, and special projects adopted vary with the state. Some councils have concentrated on the delinquents, others on adult offenders. Some have given more attention to prisons, others to community services. The Michigan council began with a demonstration of what a well-staffed probation department could do in an adult court and then undertook, at the request of a legislative committee, a comprehensive review of children's services in probate courts. One of the first significant actions of the Washington council in 1957 was the passage of constructive prison-industry legislation and of more adequate corrections budgets. The use of probation as a disposition was liberalized. Next, with the help of local citizens committees, the Washington council conducted probation and detention surveys in thirty counties, with resultant local improvements and a state-wide move for state subsidies to local juvenile probation services.

In Montana, the council chose to concentrate, first, on juvenile delinquency, but turned its attention to the state prison after a riot and played a major role in setting the direction of much-needed reform. The council has systematically studied various aspects of the state correctional picture in close cooperation with the bench, the bar, professional groups, civic groups, and official groups, depending on the issue. It has reported frequently to the public and has had wide attention.

The Texas council began successfully by "selling the idea" of a state parole system and, then, the sponsorship of a minimum program for young offenders: buildings, rehabilitation services, parole. Oklahoma began with a broad survey of the total correctional system, at the request of the legislature, and employed a group of experts for the task. The final report had widespread attention. Major reform proposals are now before the legislature.

Both Washington and Ohio have conducted impressive citizen information programs and the latter initiated a training institute for juvenile court judges.

The Indiana group has placed particular stress on community services, especially probation, as opposed to the increase of institu-

[19] N.P.P.A. News, XXXVIII, No. 1 (1959), 1.

tional space. The first major action in West Virginia followed a state prison scandal, which allowed opportunity for investigation and sound planning.

On the basis of its 1960 grant from the Ford Foundation, the NCCD is moving its program into a number of additional states and seeking ultimate self-support for it. At the present writing Citizen Action Programs exist in thirteen states. The expansion will undoubtedly involve new patterns of organization and the ultimate creation of state groups which, in combination, could be effective nationally as well.

Clearly, the Citizen Action Program is one which would serve well the situation in many states. It seems able to play a planning role as well as an action role since it may undertake comprehensive surveys, at legislative invitation, and may stimulate local surveys and planning. Its validity is not affected by the type of official structure which exists in the state. On the other hand, unlike some of the official structures described, it is not in a position to make a major contribution to the coordination of ongoing operations or to service integration. Its scope is relatively narrow.

A state plan. What, then, does the examination of state measures suggest? First, the coordination function, when broken down further, is really several functions, each suitable for its own mechanisms. There is need for a structure to coordinate program and policy of operating departments; this is a function of the executive arm of government. On the other hand, citizen leadership opinion should contribute in some way to policy formulation both in the executive branch and in operating departments. An appropriate advisory body with a clear charge might be constituted by either the chief executive or a legislative body. There is also a forum function whereby people in all parts of a state may communicate needs and views both to government and to the citizen policy advisory arms. Planning and research may be related to each of these in a variety of ways.

It would thus seem that official and unofficial bodies are needed and that there should be clarity about their differences. Too many of the existing arrangements blur such differences and leave gaps either in coordination, planning, or citizen action.

Second, the distinctions between direct service and operational coordination are significant and one should not ignore the consensus that high level coordination is most effective when carried out as a function of an agency of the executive branch which is not at the same time responsible for direct services—and thus not adequately "neutral" about issues which arise. In fact, all direct service operations as well as state aid to localities for special services (except perhaps demonstrations, experiments, and local coordination and planning) should be assigned to operating departments, not to the coordinating machinery.[20]

Third, there is no disagreement that even if it is found desirable to focus certain services and even some coordination of services primarily on delinquency, *other coordination machinery and planning machinery must relate the delinquency program to children's programs, more broadly defined.*

Fourth, coordination and planning require research and evaluation of both the short-term spot kind and the more basic kind. Competent professional staffing is essential for this purpose, as it is for the administrative, community organization, and social action phases of the work.

If a state were beginning *de novo* and sought to provide all necessary elements, one would be tempted to suggest the following—with full recognition that the total "package" has been tried nowhere and that the evaluations of the pieces are far from comprehensive:

a) A coordinating device within the executive branch of state government and involving the active participation of the commissioners or their committee of alternates sitting as the equivalent of a "family and children's cabinet."

b) A youth commission or its equivalent, made up of citizens,

[20] See the following two publications from the New Jersey State Youth Study Commission, *Twenty-ninth Public Hearing, May 25, 1960,* and *What Kind of Permanent Youth Agency for New Jersey, a Summary of Testimony* (Trenton, 1960, mimeographed). Note, too, that the coordination plan may be made without attempting to choose, for all purposes, among the alternatives of a state-administered program for all children and youth, a partially state and partially locally administered program, a state-administered program for delinquent children and youth. U.S. Children's Bureau, *Proposals for Drafting Principles and Suggested Language for Legislation on Public Child Welfare and Youth Service* (Washington, D.C.: Department of Health, Education, and Welfare, 1957).

not of public officials, with an advisory and investigatory charge. It would stress policy and long-range planning recommendations and would channel reports to the executive or to the legislative branch and to the public at large.

c) A planning, coordination, research, and evaluation staff to service these two bodies and to ensure liaison between them.

d) A citizen forum structure on a state-wide basis, which might also sponsor local conferences and forums from time to time with a view to locating problems, defining priorities, and assembling citizen proposals. Reports might channel to the youth commission although opinions on legislative and executive issues should also be routed to governor and legislature.

Since few states begin with a blank slate, it is assumed that there will be many variations on this pattern and experimentation with other approaches to the definition and allocation of functions. Differences in the size and complexity of states will also call for modifications and other approaches. Comparative study in the future would be instructive and helpful.

A slightly more detailed but nonetheless brief look at New York State's planning and coordination machinery may serve as a way of illustrating the possibilities and implications in more detail.

PLANNING AND COORDINATION IN NEW YORK STATE

In 1960 New York State abolished its Youth Commission, transferred major functions to a newly constituted Youth Division in the governor's office, and assigned operational responsibilities to it. The Youth Commission had been a "temporary body" from 1945 to 1956 when it was reorganized and made "permanent" by statute. It had been created initially as a response of the legislature to the wartime delinquency rise and was charged, in rather broad terms, with the task of stimulating localities, guiding them, and helping financially in the development of programs for coping with delinquency. Under the original plan, the commission was composed of both lay members and the heads of all state departments involved in youth programs. The 1956 legislation created a "commission within the executive department which shall consist of the chairman and eight other members who are not holders of public office." The chairman was to be a paid, full-time official. A separate interdepartmental committee of the Youth Commission was created at the same time and was given a quite broad assignment to initiate policies relative to youth, to advise on matters brought to it by the commission chairman, and, generally, to advise the commission and help achieve its objectives.[21]

The statute's statement of the New York State Youth Commission role allowed a variety of emphases and directions:

. . . to recommend and put into effect those measures most suitable to supplement and aid in coordinating the work of existing religious and social institutions for the prevention of delinquency and youth crime, and the advancement of the moral, physical, mental and social well-being of the youth of this state, and to encourage the municipalities of this state to undertake increased activities in this field by assistance and financial aid as provided in this article.[22]

The spirit of the program was reflected in the following excerpt from the 1957 report of the chairman, Mark A. McCloskey:

The Commission's small staff goes unendingly from county to county through the State bringing the technical skills and knowledge of the State's formula of financial aid. The staff strives to build sound public attitudes; helps with the improvement of existing services; helps build new services as the communities recognize their need; helps communities to realize that coordinated effort multiplies the strength of their work, and helps them to understand that isolated effort in a job of his kind is never so effective as combined operations. Success in our effort will only come from the closest working cooperation of State and municipal, public and private undertakings.

The financial aid provision, a unique pioneering feature in a state program, represented the Youth Commission's major leverage and set much of the direction for its program. It was continued when the commission gave way to the Youth Division. While the details of the financial formula are not immediately relevant, it may be helpful to note that the state reimburses localities for expenditures for recreation programs, youth services, and youth bureaus which meet statutory requirements, at a level equal to half of the local expenditure—within certain limits defined by the size of the locality and its youth population. The subsidy system

[21] New York State, Chapter 636 of the Laws of 1956, as Amended, Sec. 410–426; Article 19-A of the Executive Law.

[22] Ibid., Sec. 411.

includes special incentives for the creation of what is judged to be a "coordinated program for youth guidance in an area or areas with a high delinquency rate." Under the provision, the state aid appropriation totals $3,500,000 at this writing. This is apart from funds for the "rehabilitation" and "opportunity" centers. New York City has tended to receive slightly more than half of the state grant over the years. The system of state financial aid has achieved its purpose of stimulating local expenditures as well as giving state aid to major programs. The matching feature has tended to result in responsible planning and modest proposals.

In analyzing its charge, the Youth Commission listed four major functions: to encourage coordination at the local level, to carry on educational activities, to conduct basic research in the causation of delinquency and the effectiveness of programs, to encourage municipalities to develop youth programs through technical aid and financial help. The commission was staffed by a small headquarters group of administrative personnel and specialists, two area directors, and nine field representatives, and also had authority to grant funds in support of local programs. Given access to such resources, most of the communities in the state sought technical and financial help in the development of local youth programs. The coordination, education, and research tasks were by no means ignored by the commission, but they were secondary to its concentration on the development of subsidized youth bureaus, youth service projects, and recreation projects. A number of these programs, in turn, developed coordination, research, and education on the local level.[23]

Brief definitions of the latter terms will suggest the scope and nature of the program. A *youth bureau* is, in a sense, a local equivalent of the parent state body. A full youth bureau program would include: early case finding and treatment; expansion of services (ranging from recreation to psychotherapy); public education to stimulate citizen action and support; administrative research related to identifying areas needing service and the service needed, as well as evaluating results; encouraging coordination and service integration, involving both public and voluntary services. The New York City Youth Board, which is a youth bureau, is described later

[23] New York State Youth Commission, *Program for Youth* (Albany, 1959).

in this chapter. As of the present writing, there are ten others. The bureaus have undertaken the activities listed with varied degrees of emphasis and "with varying degrees of success." [24] Youth bureaus received approximately 5 percent of the total state grant in 1961.

Youth bureaus organize a variety of programs within the scope of their charge and tend to do broad local planning. *Youth service projects* may be organized in a community whether or not a bureau exists; they are defined as "any experimental plan or organized activity, other than a youth bureau or a recreation project." To illustrate: Onondaga County reorganized the Juvenile Aid Bureau under this provision and added two deputies, partially paid for by the Youth Commission grant. Another project permits employment in the county of a supervisor and field workers to work with youth groups who "are potential delinquents but who cannot nor will not associate with established community agencies or programs."

Syracuse, too, reorganized its Juvenile Aid Bureau under the Youth Service Projects provision, while Madison County created a psychological service in its schools and Poughkeepsie organized a community center in a housing project, with the participation of Vassar College which used the center for student training. Fallsburgh and Woodbridge organized a remedial reading project. Until the creation of the New York State Community Mental Health Program, many localities received financial help toward the development of child guidance services through Youth Service Projects. Such projects accounted for about 43 percent of the total state grant in 1961 (66 percent of the grant to New York City and 15 percent of the grant upstate, local expenditures not included). The presence of a youth board or its equivalent has proven necessary in the past to generate the kinds of self-examination and planning which result in youth service projects. Youth Commission field staff have undertaken the function more actively in recent years.

While until quite recently it asked for help for only a limited number of youth service projects, the upstate area has eagerly sought state help in expanding *recreation*, an area of service readily grasped, widely appreciated, clearly visible, and not requiring unavailable staff. Municipalities representing well over 90 percent of

[24] *Ibid.*, p. 23.

the state's population conduct state-aided recreation programs. The Youth Commission stated its own perspective: "Although recreation cannot, by itself, be considered a delinquency prevention program, it is one of many services essential for creating a healthy community environment in which youth can grow and mature." The commission developed an elaborate program of grants-in-aid, technical consultation, publication of helpful guides, distribution of educational films, development of training opportunites, and cooperation in establishment of standards of performance and leadership. Programs are operated by recreation committees, municipal boards, recreation commissions, school systems, and other agencies.[25] Recreation projects accounted for over half of the total state grants-in-aid in 1961 (over 30 percent of the total grant to New York City and close to four fifths of the upstate grant, local expenditures not included).

Beyond the program of local support, the Youth Commission prepared displays and exhibitions for fairs and conferences, undertook education through publication of pamphlets and a free film loan service, made use of radio and television to interpret its philosophy and program, encouraged town meetings on youth and numerous informal reviews of needs and services, and sponsored training for law enforcement officers. Its chairman and members were called upon for advice on legislation and other matters by the office of the governor from time to time.

In 1960, for reasons not relevant to issues here under discussion, the Youth Commission was abolished and there was created, in its stead, a Youth Division in the governor's office and a Council on Youth. The director of the Division for Youth became the administrative officer responsible for carrying through all of the original Youth Commission responsibilities and also for developing and operating the system of "opportunity centers" and rehabilitative facilities for youth in the 15–17 age group, described in Chapter XI. Thus, the State Department of Social Welfare continued its training school and aftercare services, the State Department of Correction continued to supervise and to subsidize expansion of local youth probation services, and a new agency also began to operate facilities closely related to each of these and to the Department of Education as well. The new Council on Youth was to become an

[25] *Ibid.*, pp. 39–43.

advisory, study, and review body whose approval was required by the director as he exercised the original Youth Commission grant-in-aid powers.

All of these developments, which certainly add to resources and facilities in very significant fashion, do not yet solve the planning and coordination problem.

On the positive side, grants for youth bureaus, recreation projects, and youth service projects have impact on planning and coordination locally, and may have more as the Youth Division sets direction and priorities in the light of broad considerations. The structure also allows for an influential citizen group which may speak to the governor, the legislature, and citizens at large about public policy for youth. The relatively broad Youth Commission interpretation of areas of concern and support, for example, encouraged the notion that decreased delinquency is dependent on improved community and family life—and that services for delinquents must be quite extensive and varied, as varied as services for all children. The citizen board has devoted considerable time and effort since its reconstitution in 1957 as a permanent body to becoming acquainted with needs, problems, services; it is in a position to exert far more influence in the direction of policy leadership and innovation than it has in the past. In effect, it is constituted so as to permit it some of the initiative and range of the NCCD Citizen Action Program, despite its official character and responsibility for grants-in-aid as a Council on Youth.

The Youth Commission (and now the Youth Division) has undertaken several brief surveys and studies, including a useful survey of experience with the use of curfews. It has prepared and circulated a manual on Police Juvenile Aid programs and a guide for school personnel in early detection and treatment of maladjusted children. From time to time it has assembled useful statistical data about delinquency rates and institutionalization. It has not, however, carried out any basic research which might shed light on policy but is currently planning rigorous studies of its opportunity-rehabilitation centers. Nor has it attempted the kinds of administrative studies relevant to long-range planning—that is, projections as to the amount of institutional space to be needed in the coming decade.

Of some concern too is the fact that the plan does not meet one of the other state needs, the need for *operational* coordination. In fact, creation of the Youth Division further fragmented operations. There is no definite operational coordination charge or structure. An Interdepartmental Health Resources Board demonstrated some years ago how effective such a body can be, but its scope was subsequently limited.

What, then, of the forum function? In 1956 a "temporary commission," which superseded the Youth Commission during a delinquency "crisis," held well-attended regional meetings while its staff carried out studies. The process was capped by a state-wide conference. The Youth Commission itself gave leadership to a similar process in preparation for the 1960 White House Conference on Children and Youth. The Youth Division is now charged with follow-up on that conference. In addition, many of the youth bureaus conduct local conferences, meetings, and forums. The previous chapter described the New York City Youth Board's community program.

The New York State program thus provides for many of the coordination and planning functions listed in the previous section but would seem to need to undertake some sorting out and redefinition. Although the opportunity-rehabilitation services are essential innovations, they should obviously be joined with the Social Welfare Department facilities when the pioneering, innovation, testing phase has passed. Until this occurs they inevitably must continue to divert the Youth Division somewhat from its basic coordination and planning task. Located as it is in the governor's office, the Youth Division is ideally situated for such a role, but will have to reorient its staff services for it. Consultation to localities is valuable and important, but there is also need for administrative research which projects trends and needs, evaluates programs, tests effectiveness—all oriented to posing policy issues and to making long-term plans.

Given movement in this direction, the Youth Council's role will gain new importance. It will be ideally constituted in an advisory role to help develop policies and plans, to react to division reports and studies, to respond to new community needs. Currently the statute makes it an advisory body to the director; it should probably have a more direct channel to governor or legislature.

The Youth Division has a variety of channels to local citizens through its youth bureau programs. The Council on Youth should perhaps establish some systematic way of tapping local opinion. It is already planning to conduct regional hearings and state-wide meetings as White House Conference follow-up.

Finally, to cover all dimensions, the state will have to implement a regular plan of interdepartmental coordination. As the Youth Division gives up direct services, it should be in a position to staff a vital interdepartmental committee which should be convened by the governor at a cabinet level and might operate routinely as a committee of deputies. There are beginnings in this direction.[26]

CITY-WIDE PLANNING AND COORDINATION

It is possible to support the generalization that six of every ten cities have some sort of coordinating structure for the control and treatment of delinquency—but only if one stretches the definition. Larger cities have substantially greater rates of coverage, according to a survey by the American Municipal Association; but the count includes both welfare and community councils, official direct-service programs, advisory bodies, and a program as elaborate as that of the New York City Youth Board. There is no one pattern, and there should not be.[27]

For lack of nationwide, systematic, comparable data, it is impossible to say much about the variety of coordination patterns. The one available survey merely illustrates several types. Mention has already been made of parts of several municipal programs in connection with neighborhood organization and accountability. The New Jersey Youth Study Commission reports a variety of devices in use in New Jersey communities: (a) children's and special service bureaus, such as the bureaus in Jersey City and Passaic which are school-administered services to coordinate school efforts with police case finding and treatment; (b) municipal youth guidance councils; (c) case conference committees; (d) councils of social agencies.[28] One interesting pattern is represented by Detroit's Mayor's Committee on Children and Youth, which functions as a community "sounding board," as an advisory board, and as a group which contributes, on one level, to planning. This committee of

[26] A much-expanded planning role is emerging through an interdepartmental committee as we go to press.

[27] J. L. Levin, *How Cities Control Juvenile Delinquency* (Washington, D.C., and Chicago: American Municipal Association, 1957).

[28] *New Ways to Reach Unreached Youth*, p. 10.

fifty has twenty-three members appointed by public and voluntary organizations and twenty-seven by the mayor. An administrative committee (board) is appointed by the mayor and may, in turn, set up working committees which draw upon qualified citizens from the city at large. An executive secretary, who is a city employee, heads a small technical staff. The quarterly meetings of the total committee consider both matters on which advisory action is needed and proposals requiring mutual action and support by the organizations represented in the committee membership. The committee reviews studies and reports which provide the background for action.[29]

In 1954 the mayor of New Haven, Connecticut, appointed a Commission on Juvenile Delinquency which began with a period of orientation and study, divided itself into nine subcommittees for more intensive study and formulation of specific recommendations, transmitted the recommendations and a general report, and then, convinced that continued citizen involvement was essential, sounded the call for a Citizens' Action Committee.

San Diego, California, has placed a comprehensive, city-wide effort in its Social Service Department. The program includes a variety of case finding efforts to locate deviant children, parent discussion groups, group guidance with teen-agers which is directed at street clubs and neighborhood groups, short-term family counseling in the neighborhood, and general public education about delinquency.

Lincoln, Nebraska, had a relatively inactive community council when a local foundation created the Lincoln Youth Project. In addition to assisting in the establishment of a needed youth employment service, organizing a youth council, and surveying recreational programs and facilities, the project set up a research-demonstration program in "reaching out casework" which sought to promote a new kind of service and increase service integration. The experiences of this program and subsequent supplementary research and data analysis provided the basis for a series of reports published between 1957 and 1959, evaluating existing services, outlining needed services, and urging adequate standards. Particular emphasis was placed in these reports on a coordinated community program; case finding, adequate police, court, and clinic services; child protective services.

[29] *How Cities Control Juvenile Delinquency*, pp. 28–29, 46.

Action to implement the various proposals is under way and a Lincoln Citizens' Committee for Children has been created as an action–coordination–fact-finding group.[30]

St. Louis has an active, staffed Metropolitan Youth Commission which initiates citizen action, studies, planning, and coordination. A U.S. Children's Bureau listing also calls attention to the following specialized, large-city agencies for delinquency control: the Los Angeles County Department of Community Agencies; the St. Petersburg, Florida, Juvenile Welfare Board of Pinellas County; the recently created Chicago Commission on Youth Welfare; the Cincinnati, Ohio, Citizens' Committee on Youth; and the Commissioner's Youth Council in Washington, D.C.

From 1954 to 1957 the Philadelphia Youth Services Board had an advisory and coordination function, but the need for direct services led to expansion in the form of a Youth Services Division in the Welfare Department, guided by a Youth Conservation Commission.

There are at least fourteen municipal youth commissions or their equivalent.[31] They tend to concentrate on the improvement of public services to delinquents and the development of demonstrations and projects. They have emphasized work with gangs, "reaching out" to multiproblem families, case conference machinery, special employment programs for youth. Some have initiated coordination.

Community welfare councils, traditionally, "have continued to provide a channel for operating agencies and interested organizations to share ideas, coordinate programs, raise professional standards and interpret services and problems to the community at large." [32] Despite impressive records of accomplishment in the coordination realm in specific instances, they are more effective with voluntary agencies than with the public programs which provide the bulk of services. They are best at specific projects, rather than at long-range operational coordination which may infringe on agency prerogatives. Many would now change the emphasis "to include re-

[30] *Community Organization through Citizens' Action in Lincoln, Nebraska* (Lincoln: Lincoln Youth Project, 1959).

[31] Welfare Planning Council, Los Angeles Region, *Los Angeles and the New York City Youth Board* (Los Angeles, 1960), pp. 7–12.

[32] Harold Gustafson, "Emerging Concepts in Community Welfare Organization," *The Social Welfare Forum, 1960* (New York: Columbia University Press, 1960), pp. 154–65.

search and planning on the larger social welfare issues." [33] But it is not certain that they have the needed standing, resources, or access to power. Of interest is the fact that several quite strong welfare councils have sought to initiate youth commissions because of the advantages of official status and ability to combine lay and professional leadership.[34]

It seems reasonable to conclude this section with the notation that municipal coordination must be approached pragmatically. A few obvious principles may serve as a point of departure. Examination in some depth of one ambitious effort (the New York City Youth Board) does permit a few additional suggestions.

NEW YORK CITY YOUTH BOARD

New York City's size and resources are matched only by the scale and scope of its task. If it would plan and coordinate, it must suit its machinery to its unique circumstances. Since the New York City Youth Board has set the pace nationally in a variety of areas, its development and program deserve relatively full treatment. The detached worker program and borough and neighborhood organization programs have already been discussed in proper context. The Youth Board's contribution to planning and coordination, as well as its limitations in these fields, demands examination here. As will be seen, the agency must make certain choices between direct service and coordination. The city has begun to face the issue of adequately relating Youth Board program planning and coordination activities to the planning and coordination of all services for children and youth in New York City.[35]

The New York City Youth Board was created as an agency in the office of the mayor by a local resolution in July, 1947. It was set up to qualify as a youth bureau under the State Youth Commission Act of 1945. As was true of the state agency, the Youth Board's status was

---

[33] *Ibid.*   [34] *Los Angeles and the New York City Youth Board.*

[35] For detail, see *The Planning and Coordination of Services for Children and Youth in New York City* (New York: Citizens' Committee for Children of New York City, Inc., 1959). The following publications of the New York City Youth Board will be of particular interest to readers (authors not specified): *New Directions in Delinquency Prevention, 1947–1957; Reaching the Unreached* (1952); *How They Were Reached* (1954); *Reaching the Group* (1956); *Reaching the Unreached Family* (1958). In addition see *Youth Board News* (monthly).

uncertain as long as the state program was a temporary one. Steps toward fuller incorporation into city government, including civil service status for staff, followed the legislation making the state program permanent. The resolution conferred five powers and duties upon the Youth Board:

a. To coordinate the activities of public, private and religious agencies devoted in whole or in part to the welfare and protection of youth;
b. To make studies and analyses of the problems of youth guidance and the prevention of juvenile delinquency;
c. To seek to remove the causes of juvenile delinquency through the means available to City Departments and private agencies;
d. To collect, correlate and disseminate information, statistics and data on the subject of juvenile delinquency and the methods of removing the causes of juvenile delinquency;
e. To approve applications of City agencies for the maintenance of youth projects under the State law.

An Executive Order issued by the mayor in September, 1957, added to this general authority of the Youth Board a specific grant of coordinating responsibility to the board's Executive Director.

The New York City Youth Board consisted initially of thirteen members, six representing city departments and seven appointed by the mayor, who was also empowered to designate one member as chairman. The membership was subsequently increased to twenty-eight, of whom eighteen are private citizens appointed by the mayor on a staggered membership plan. The other ten are the heads of city departments having important youth services or special responsibilities in the field of delinquency.

The Youth Board has qualified for maximum state reimbursement by developing what the state law describes as a "coordinated program for youth guidance in an area or areas with a high delinquency rate." Its budget is over five million dollars, with the state contributing almost 45 percent (the city having exceeded, in its own expenditures, the maximum for state matching). One of the unique features of the Youth Board program has been its authorization to expend the bulk of its funds through contracts with public and voluntary agencies. Contracts permit expansion of existing programs and creation of new services—all designed to meet the needs uncovered in Referral Unit efforts to obtain needed treatment or services and in the fact finding of the Youth Board staff and advisory committees.

Thus the creation of the Youth Board began an era of stepped-up public subsidization of voluntary agency programs in new fields in New York City: recreation, group work, child guidance, vocational guidance, family casework.

The nature of the state's reimbursement pattern has significantly affected the scope and emphasis of the New York City Youth Board's program. Although the Board of Estimate resolution did not focus the Youth Board's efforts upon the neighborhoods with high delinquency rates to the exclusion of others, the board in defining its own program very early limited its operations to these areas (now twenty-two in number). This concentration has been explained as a means of securing the greatest impact upon delinquency with limited funds; it also enabled the city to obtain the maximum state contribution to the board's work. Besides this geographic focus, recently relaxed somewhat in connection with neighborhood organization, the board decided early in its life to confine its program to services to children living in the community in their own homes, to give preference to projects serving youth directly rather than indirectly, and to work as far as possible through existing agencies and facilities rather than through the creation of new ones.

The scope of the program. The Youth Board program began in the summer of 1948. Although its basic character has been set for over a decade, there has been subsequent modification involving a gradual shift in the Referral Unit function; considerable expansion of the work with gangs; much increased emphasis on coordination, planning, neighborhood organization; transfer of mental health programs to the subsequently created Mental Health Board; transfer of one program to the Welfare Department.

Prior to analysis of the planning and coordination program of the Youth Board, it may be helpful to outline the service and contract programs, which draw the bulk of the resources.

a) Recreation projects conducted by the Board of Education and the Police Athletic League, on a contract basis, account for over one quarter of the annual Youth Board budget. The bulk of the program is assigned to the afternoon, evening, weekend, and summer recreation centers in the schools and to the community centers in housing projects which, in turn, are operated either by voluntary agencies or the school system; but several PAL centers have been expanded and improved and its summer play street program expanded. The premise is that mass recreation facilities belong in a delinquency prevention program.

b) Over 10 percent of the budget is devoted to *group work* contracts with voluntary settlements and centers which then accept referrals of Referral Unit cases and seek to "reach out" to groups which do not ordinarily make use of their programs. Group work involves considerably more individualization and higher staff standards than mass recreation.

c) The program of detached workers, the *street club project* of the Council of Social and Athletic Clubs, is a direct Youth Board operation. As the community has become increasingly concerned with gang conflict in recent years, the program has risen in importance. Its budget is close to one and one-half million dollars annually, constitutes over a quarter of the whole, and is second in size only to the recreation program.

d) *Referral Units* established by the Youth Board for case finding, brief service, referral, and identification of resources in short supply in "high delinquency" areas were school-based for over ten years. They are now Youth Board operated and in transition. Referral Units account for almost 10 percent of Youth Board appropriations.

e) Prior to the establishment of the Community Mental Health Board, approximately 13 percent of the budget was expended through contracts with voluntary agencies for casework and child guidance *treatment* upon Referral Unit request. "Youth Board" caseloads were created and new staff employed. More recently the contracts have emphasized family service to multiproblem families. Family agencies hold contracts either on a fee-per-interview basis or an annual caseload basis, accounting for almost 11 percent of the budget.

f) A casework treatment program for multiproblem families, *Services for Families and Children*, which pioneered in "reaching out" methodology, was originally a cooperative Youth Board–Welfare Department enterprise, but was fully transferred to the Welfare Department late in 1957 and was then absorbed by a revised program.

g) The recently developed and expanding program of *borough planning offices and assistance to neighborhood councils* now receives almost 15 percent of Youth Board funds but is in transition.

h) *Research, administration, in-service training*, and the *planning and coordination* operations described below account for about 12 percent of the budget.

i) At various times the Youth Board has included in its program subsidization for expansion of *court diagnostic* and *treatment clinics* (taken over by the Community Mental Health Board), *group therapy contracts* (taken over by the Community Mental Health Board), contracts for *vocational guidance programs* which emphasize "reaching out" techniques (continuing), the *Three-Schools* demonstration of school-based clinical services (completed), a *central registration project* for accurate study of delinquency statistics (converted into a more modest index), *free summertime transportation for children* to beaches, etc. (continuing).

In general, contracts account for over half the annual budget, direct services for close to 30 percent, administration for over 10 percent, and city-wide planning, coordination, and related services for another 10 percent.

This summary of program would hardly be complete without mention of the substantial impact of the Youth Board program and philosophy on agencies and professional persons in New York City and throughout the country. There is of course no way to separate those general trends of which the Youth Board is a part from the developments which would not have taken place without the Youth Board's stimulation and support. One can only cite the substantial demands made on staff for conference papers, panel participation, workshop leadership, consultation. The board's publications are in demand throughout the world. Even its terminology has been influential. Certainly, all who are involved in helping delinquents and their families are aware, in a way seldom articulated before 1947, of the agency's responsibility vis-à-vis clients not immediately prepared to fit into a traditional pattern of taking service. The emphasis on the consideration of social dimensions in diagnosis and treatment has been given urgency and clear purpose. Experimentation with unorthodox patterns of service and professional role-definitions has been encouraged, particularly in the Street Club programs and the "reaching out" casework efforts. In addition, the Youth Board program has emphasized early case finding, has clarified the technical problems of successful case referral, and has contributed to the needed expansion of programs and to the increased volume of services.

Moreover, it seems reasonable to add, in a period of considerable public outrage at delinquents and their conduct, that the very existence of the Youth Board and its wide range of programs provided an outlet for constructive community action where there might otherwise have been only emotionalism and punitive policy. While one may differ with specific policies and actions,[36] a total appraisal would describe Youth Board services and influence as constructive, valuable, and effective. For purposes of the present chapter, the specific planning and coordination role demands more intensive examination.

Planning and coordination. Under the charge "to coordinate the activities of public, private and religious agencies devoted in whole or in part to the welfare and protection of youth," the board gave the following restricted interpretation to its responsibilities until 1955: "The agency would perform coordinating functions through its relationships with its contract agencies, through its advisory committees and through Board activities, but would not enter actively into over-all coordination of community activities, except through representation by staff and Board members on committees under auspices of other agencies and professional organizations." [37] The resulting activities were significant if limited in scope. In fact, criticism of the Youth Board's program has often centered upon the sizable proportion of its energies devoted to direct operations that continue long past the demonstration stage and the consequent underemphasis of the planning, coordinating, and standard setting through which some believe it could make its greatest contribution. However, in the Youth Board's view, the major portion of its program, including direct operations, has been aimed at actual coordination. For example, the Referral Units provided the machinery for helping school personnel identify maladjusted youngsters and potential delinquents and for follow-through on referral to appropriate treatment resources. Contract arrangements were made to permit expansion of voluntary services specifically geared to accept these referrals. The Council of Social and Athletic Clubs, now a major

[36] See *Planning and Coordination,* Report C.   [37] For detail, *ibid.*

direct operation, was created in an effort to provide essential coordination in the approach to working with street gangs found to be
necessary after unsuccessful earlier experience in contracting for
this type of service with voluntary agencies.

1. Increased interest in planning: Several reviews urged that the
Youth Board undertake *community-wide planning,* whereas its previous planning had been limited to its own programs. In an official
evaluation, the then deputy mayor said:

In addition to a broadened research perspective, I therefore believe the
Youth Board needs a small unit of full-time experts who can bring various
special skills to the problems of coordination and long-range planning.
This team would be responsible for smoothing working relationships with
other agencies and for the development of over-all operations plans with
the Youth Board members and Executive Director. It would be well to
involve in planning the chiefs of the Board's operating divisions, and perhaps private agency representatives as well. But the pressing need is for
additional personnel who can look beyond day to day problems and have
no direct responsibility for operations, no commitment to a particular
aspect of today's problem.

In the several years which followed, a considerably increased budget was used in part to develop the borough and neighborhood organization machinery (Ch. XII). Planning and coordination operations developed slowly and became the province of the Youth Board
director and his top staff, while the Youth Board as board continued
to devote itself to direct services and to contracts. Advisory committees, composed of lay and professional members, were appointed
in the areas of child welfare and family services, jobs, group work
and recreation, work with volunteer organizations, problems of
changing neighborhoods, problems of protective and correctional
services, religious groups, and work camps.

A series of crises demonstrated that there was not yet adequate
provision for planning and coordination: large numbers of children
were suspended by the schools without joint planning with the many
agencies affected; detention and institution space proved wholly insufficient; needed diagnostic facilities were not available and the
ramifications affected many services; and so on.

Nor was the expanded program of borough committees and neighborhood organizations pointed to the requirements of a planning
structure. The concept was that a borough committee would offer

advice to the borough office but could initiate projects through city-wide "channels." It was unrelated, in any formal sense, to ongoing borough administration or to area meetings and neighborhood council programs. Thus, while the borough structure gave substantial support to neighborhood community organization and gave the Youth Board "listening posts" in major localities, it was not a long-range planning body. (Changes are now being made.)

Then, as a result of the community concern over particularly violent outbreaks of juvenile delinquency during the summer of 1957, the Youth Board was given clear authorization (although its statutory charge has always been broad) to assume through its Executive Director a larger role in the coordination of the community's delinquency-control efforts. An Executive Order made the board's Executive Director the "coordinator" of the city's antidelinquency program. He was charged with uniting the efforts of public and voluntary agencies for the more adequate provision of social services in "potentially hazardous areas." All municipal agencies were directed to cooperate with him, thus conferring upon him a measure of the mayor's authority over the other municipal departments concerned. The Youth Board also received additional state and city funds to strengthen its own programs. To strengthen the director's role and to place him on a par with department heads, he was named Commissioner of Youth Services and Executive Vice President of the Youth Board in December, 1958.

2. *Evolution of the role:* A more detailed review of developments from the fall of 1957 is already available.[38] Relevant to long-range issues are the following:

a) The Youth Board intensified the activities of city-wide advisory committees and created a standing committee of city-wide voluntary coordinating agencies and fund-raising bodies.

b) Borough and neighborhood activity was stepped up and local "town meetings" held.

c) Social services, employment programs, and gang programs were expanded in high-hazard areas (and, again, in subsequent "crises").

d) The Youth Board reached an agreement with the Community Council specifying that the latter was responsible for the over-

[38] *Ibid.*

all, broader aspects of planning and coordination of welfare and health services while the Youth Board's planning and coordination would be directed mainly "to the hard core or multiproblem family, the high-hazard areas, for the prevention, reduction and control of juvenile delinquency."

The latter definitions were soon dropped. The general weakening of the Community Council, for reasons not here relevant, resulted in a vacuum which the Youth Board filled to a degree through a variety of *ad hoc* project committees involving religious leaders, mass media, employer and labor groups, educators, and so on.

The Youth Board director, in his capacity of commissioner, moved into City Hall to advise the mayor. His new role there had elements of two types of role: use of a City Hall base to lead an antidelinquency campaign; coordination of the entire social welfare effort on behalf of children. Thus he developed plans to screen and serve suspended pupils. At the same time, a program of maximum summer coverage of services ("summer vigilance") was evolved, to meet the expected delinquency increase, and has been repeated annually. Finally, the director undertook a series of tasks as trouble shooter and representative of the mayor in regard to a wide range of social welfare situations and budgetary demands on the city. Meetings which might lead to new programs or to coordination of efforts were also begun.

Between 1959 and 1962, when he retired and was replaced in his Youth Board executive role, but not as commissioner, the Commissioner of Youth Services undertook a large trouble-shooting role in the youth services field, particularly in relation to delinquency, aided by the Youth Board Central Planning Unit and research staffs—i.e., the Youth Board coordination machinery. He initiated some operational coordination through the device of commissioner cabinet meetings, called with the authority of the mayor. The degree of cooperation and participation varied with the urgency of the matter and the degree of the mayor's concern and backing. At the same time, the Youth Board per se continued its major concern with direct services, contracts, and borough programs. Direct services were decentralized through the borough offices. Coordination and research were central office functions. In his role as Executive Vice

President of the Youth Board, the Commissioner of Youth Services directed that program. As commissioner, he reported to the mayor, not to the Youth Board, in relation to planning and coordination.

This "case history" of the Youth Board coordination and planning effort would seem to hold certain general lessons:

a) An agency which grants funds for services and which conducts a case finding and referral program *is* in a strategic position to coordinate operations related to its own area of service and to promote service integration. Thus, the present case conference program and the as-yet-undeveloped use of the multiproblem family register for accountability purposes are appropriate functions for an agency such as the Youth Board.

b) When a long-range planning effort bases itself on the initiative of advisory committees composed of personnel whose primary ties are to other programs, it tends to generate useful, vital, but unrelated projects. Basic long-range planning requires a technical planning staff with considerable initiative and a citizen-based policy board. The Youth Board itself might have played the latter role but, as indicated, its commissioner members are oriented to their program needs and its citizen members are not personally related to enough of the program. Moreover, it is burdened with the statutory responsibility of administering grants to agencies through "contracts."

c) As soon as a delinquency program which is community-based turns to problems of prevention and long-range planning, it must deal with public welfare services, family agency services, education, recreation, health—and many aspects of child welfare. Local neighborhood self-help activity becomes important. It is questionable, as a matter of community policy, to seek to encompass so wide a range of services under a delinquency program "umbrella" for purposes of planning and coordination, even though financing may be facilitated thereby.

d) It is exceedingly doubtful that the selfsame person should seek to function successfully as director of a series of direct-service programs related to delinquency, a program of grants-in-aid and contracts to public and voluntary agencies, a series of mechanisms for service integration and accountability—and at the same time coordinate all child care services in the role of commissioner, in the mayor's office. One role or the other will be played down; the role conflicts will probably decrease the effectiveness of all roles.

Other cities considering their own patterns will find interesting the Los Angeles appraisal which recorded the program and method contributions of the Youth Board but which argued against duplicating the Youth Board plan. Stating that each locality must develop its own structure, Los Angeles noted that its organization is on a county, not city, basis and lacks the strong private and sectarian agency development which characterizes New York. It favored creation of a Youth Commission to coordinate planning and operations as well as a citizen policy advisory body. No direct services except for research would be assigned to this machinery.[39]

THE SEARCH FOR A PLANNING AND COORDINATION STRUCTURE

The analysis would seem to suggest a well-defined, if narrower, role for the Youth Board or its equivalent. As a planning, coordination, and accountability instrument of community policy relative to *delinquency*, it might continue to implement a program of contracts. Its board requires both sound staff work and full policy discussions of its own in order to relate the system of allocations to broader community strategy, new needs, coordinated operations. At the same time, the Youth Board's direct operations should probably concentrate on case finding, service integration, and accountability (Referral Units, case register, case conferences). Direct service operations of other kinds should be for purposes of demonstration and training so as not to interfere with the coordination-accountability role. Thus, the Street Club Project should ultimately be housed elsewhere if an appropriate base can be found. The Youth Board's research program should involve administrative studies vital to its functions and evaluative studies of its demonstration experiments.

The borough and neighborhood efforts would be most appropriate as devices for tapping citizen opinion and sentiment, channeling local project suggestions, and promoting education. Members of the Youth Board itself should participate in or have ties to the borough committees, to make the latter effective. In turn, Youth Board borough and neighborhood efforts should be related to and

[39] *Los Angeles and the New York City Youth Board.*

even be incorporated into a broader program of neighborhood organization, preferably under voluntary auspices. If public funds are required for staff services, it would seem wiser to expend them through a Community Council than through a public network of neighborhood councils and borough offices. By definition, neighborhood organization, in a democracy, should be free to direct its pressures to city government, as needed; staffing by public employees complicates the process. Separate auspices for neighborhood organization and case conferences would not preclude experimental ties between the two.

Although this kind of refocus is not proclaimed as the Youth Board direction, it would seem to be implied in the city's decision late in 1961 to define the Youth Board's coordination role as lying in the delinquency sphere—while the office of administration develops machinery for public planning and coordination of family and children's services in general. The latter designation follows a long period of analysis, discussion, and experimentation in New York City, in the course of which claims for the role were advanced in various forms by the Youth Board, the Commission on the Foster Care of Children, the Community Mental Health Board, and the Community Council.[40]

Analysis of the total New York experience of the past two decades would seem to suggest the following:

a) City-wide planning and coordination of services to families and children requires a cabinet committee or its equivalent, directly responsible to the chief executive. It should be presided over by the chief executive or his deputy—i.e., by an official who outranks a departmental commissioner. It requires a research staff and other staff to implement its role of study, planning, and operational coordination. Only interdepartmental coordination based on the commissioner level will truly permit significant operational coordination. Only a staff based in the city administration can undertake significant planning.

b) While coordination bodies may be needed in a variety of fields (delinquency, recreation), the over-all body should have a broad charge in the family and children's field.

c) There is also need for a citizens' planning commission, an ad-

[40] Reports A, B, and D in *Planning and Coordination.*

visory group concerned with policy and planning priorities. It should have close liaison to the cabinet-level body and be served by the planning-coordination staff. It should report periodically to the chief executive and the public in addition to expressing itself on ongoing policy and planning priorities and issues. It should be in a position to initiate and receive the reports of evaluation and research.

This proposal is based on the assumption that it is appropriate for department heads, sitting as a "cabinet" under a top municipal official, to deal with major policies and to use committees of alternates or deputies for handling details of implementation or program development. This approach has been successful in many places.

The question then arises, why would such a body not be able to do the *whole* job; why an additional body, a commission?

Response with reference both to city and state levels would be similar. The coordination through cabinet, staff, and top-official chairman has an inevitably serious handicap which derives from the necessary concern and orientation of each commissioner toward his own program, his problems in meeting his department's budget, and his healthy reluctance to raise questions about the services of other departments. Somebody not responsible for execution of any one part should see the whole, be free to ask questions about any of the parts, note the gaps and weak spots, and be able to make objective and disinterested recommendations.

In addition, it is necessary to face the fact that department heads are members of the "administration," politically speaking, and are under administration discipline in many areas. They are often not free to air differences about policy or practice. They are certainly not in a position to report vital issues and recommendations to the public unless a mayor or governor chooses that they do so. However, the function of reporting to the public on crucial matters so that sound policy direction may crystallize, *even if contrary to current administration policy*, is an important part of the job to be done. Thus, although a cabinet is strongly recommended for the things it will be able to do best, there is need, too, for the planning commission.

From this perspective New York City would appear to have gone part way. The city's administrator has the function temporarily, and his office may convene the commissioners and deputies. A study to develop over-all structure is under way. The Youth Board role, if logically developed, would now seem much clearer. Unclear, as yet, is how and where the citizen advisory function in the form of a planning commission will be discharged. It would seem possible to assign this through a change in role and status of one of several existing advisory bodies (Foster Care, Mental Health, Youth Board, Welfare, etc.), each of which would require a broadening of concern, separation from any operational department, and assignment of membership in individual, not representative, capacities. Another possibility is the creation of a new over-all citizen body while existing ones continue with their tasks in specific spheres.

The limitations of the New York City Community Council do not make a third alternative realistic for New York, but there are some communities in which the planning council function is well discharged by a welfare planning council. A precondition is that the council be a *community* body—neither public nor voluntary—be much more than an instrument of social agencies, and have broad citizen support. Given such a situation, the council might then also serve to coordinate public and voluntary agency operations and planning as well. The existence of such a body does not, however, obviate the need for the public cabinet and interdepartmental structure. The scale, scope, costs, and ramifications of public operations are such that no outside body could conceivably discharge the task.

A final note about planning: Much of this chapter would seem to stress planning *for*, while our political philosophies and social ethic give priority to planning *with*. Consumers of all services, agency clients, and youth all have their contributions to make.[41] In part, this is the case for a public planning structure: in a representative government, a public body reports and is ultimately accountable to the supporters and consumers of service, who are one, for what is done. In part, too, this is the case for neighborhood organization, local self-help agencies, youth councils, and community planning bodies. These too are channels for all the people and make it possible for them to react, challenge, initiate, and support services.

[41] Nelson N. Foote and Leonard S. Cottrell, Jr., *Identity and Interpersonal Competence* (Chicago: University of Chicago Press, 1955), Chapter V.

EPILOGUE:
THE UNTRIED WEAPON

ONE DOES NOT have to travel very far or very long to encounter a newspaper headline or a political speech urging more punitive policy toward young offenders and their parents. Those who would call them children and families "in trouble" are branded as mollycoddlers. The slogans are well known: "We need to go back to the woodshed!" "This is the time for large fines and jail sentences to bring irresponsible parents to their senses!" "The children's courts and treatment agencies don't work. Those hoods will understand only firmness."

Occasionally, community members who favor individualized rehabilitative measures for offenders begin to wonder about their position. Advocates of a scientific approach feel uncomfortable, for they know that news stories report serious offenses by youths on probation or on parole from training schools or treatment institutions. Periodically, a criminal court judge may call attention to the earlier children's court record of a vicious offender. Should one, then, give up humane and scientific objectives? Is the philosophy launched by the juvenile court movement a bad dream now to be forgotten?

The readers of previous chapters will know the answer. First, it is clear that individualization and humanitarian concern, treatment, and rehabilitative effort are not less firm or protective of the community than are other measures. In fact, they promise greater protection. To put the offender away "in cold storage" is only to ensure a repetition and intensification of his antisocial outbursts when he must eventually be released.[1]

But even the premises of those who attack rehabilitative approaches are false. Individualized treatment has not failed. This is far from the time to give up the hope that scientifically selected measures will work and that public policy supporting such measures will yield results. For the fact is that *systematic, comprehensive rehabilitation based in validated knowledge has not yet been tried.*

In the face of clear evidence of failure after centuries of trying to control crime through retaliation, brutality, and punishment, our society has yielded to some humanitarian and scientific concepts. As one major result, a new kind of philosophy pervades laws governing the offenses of children and youths. Special police juvenile units are to be created. Children are not to be jailed with adults. Detention facilities should be equipped for social and clinical study to guide the judge's disposition plan. Children's court procedures are to be directed toward understanding and helping. Probation counseling is to become a treatment medium. Institutions are to be charged with responsibility for changing basic behavior patterns and are no longer to limit themselves to mere custody. Some children in trouble are to be dealt with in clinics, group programs, schools, and a variety of kinds of training facilities appropriate in the light of their situations and needs.

However, our public has been ambivalent about these measures. Even some of the responsible professionals have not been sure about the whole. Each of these institutions has been permitted or has achieved only partial development of a role suitable to a rehabilitative program—and all facilities are in short supply. Knowledge and skill are incomplete in important respects; yet there has been only limited support for filling in major knowledge gaps and for the needed substantial improvement in methods of intervention. Finally, even where a good facility is available, it is rare to discover that related facilities which must articulate with it at various stages of the rehabilitative work are of equal caliber.

In short, an integrated system of high quality services is required

---

[1] For an earlier formulation of the theme, see Alfred J. Kahn, "The Untried Weapon against Delinquency," *Federal Probation*, XXII, No. 3 (September, 1958), 11–15.

to apply a scientifically based rehabilitative program. Such a system does not exist today.

The previous chapters have documented all of this in relation to juvenile delinquency, a field in which treatment objectives are widely enunciated. We have reviewed the incomplete development of the children's court movement, for example, as well as the major problems relative to roles, procedures, and professional qualifications. We have noted that most of the country has yet to create modern detention facilities—and that juvenile police programs need substantial strengthening. Or, to take another illustration, we have estimated the gap between the philosophies, staffing, and resources of training schools—and the demands made upon them by the total system of services.

Particularly lacking, in fact, is general acceptance of the concept that only a *system of services* can be effective. The implications for case accountability, service integration, coordination, and planning are only beginning to be considered. For this reason, the author has chosen to emphasize functions to be fulfilled, roles to be played, the need for agency flexibility in contributing to an organized, goal-directed, community pattern of case finding and intervention.

No. Well-planned, organized, and staffed scientific rehabilitation has not yet been tried; but our philosophies and our knowledge demand that it should be. Earlier chapters have sought to elaborate the implications.

There are, fortunately, some encouraging notes. *The States Report* to the 1960 White House Conference on Children found that "more and more, treatment and training are being substituted for punishment." [2] Many cities and states are giving high priority to coordination and service integration. There are fragments of evidence that well-staffed programs which are geared to changing behavior patterns, value systems, or personality structures of youths can achieve their objectives. Scattered throughout the country are exciting and effective institutions, good probation departments, strong police juvenile units, model detention facilities, excellent clinics, and other related facilities. While few of these have done enough to test results rigorously, there is sufficient positive evidence to justify invest-

[2] Golden Anniversary White House Conference on Children and Youth, *The States Report on Children and Youth* (Washington, D.C., 1960), pp. 78 ff.

ment in expanding these programs and appraising their effectiveness.

At the same time, the basic theorizing and research is yielding new and helpful understanding of the delinquencies and neglects and is inspiring encouraging departures in modes of intervention. It begins to be possible to talk of a diversified network of services in which differentiations are made in the light of knowledge of the sources of individual deviation and the maximum leverage for change. Paralleling this, leading service agencies are now staffed by well-equipped professionals, and professional schools know, far better than they did a decade ago, how to train for the task. The time for large-scale recruitment and general upgrading of these services seems to be at hand.

Why, it will be asked, should the taxpayer and voluntary contributor finance all of this? The fact is that equivalent expenditure will be made in one way or another. When the community is aroused by an increase in delinquency, more policemen are put on the streets, more detention beds provided, more institutional space built. The choice is between financing, on the one hand, an elaborate network for apprehension, formal processing, and custody—with the accompanying costs of the continued antisocial behavior of those temporarily graduated from the system—and, on the other hand, paying enough to permit a real effort at finding and redirecting those in trouble relatively early in their histories. While the initial expenditures for the latter approach may be large, the success of the effort would mean long-range savings in the traditional costs. It has already been shown that many treatment services such as probation are more economical than the custody which makes no pretense at changing behavior, but which cannot be avoided if we intervene too late.

Thus, positive developments coexist with attacks on the system; the call for resources and staffing is paralleled by proposals for further retreat. And between the advocates of both views is the large citizenry whose silence is interpreted as apathy. Only firm public policy and support will tip the balance; as the policy vacuum is filled and sound direction is set the process of creating strong community programs will be accelerated. Is the American public prepared to affirm that this *is* the time to begin?

INDEX

Criminal Justice Administration, Utah Council of, 494-95
Criminal, the Judge and the Public, The (Alexander and Staub), 39
Curfew, 218
Custody, and schools, 197-98, 203-4; and training schools, 396, 398

Deaf and Hard of Hearing, New York City Schools for, 167
Decisions, brief screening, 98-100; *see also* Evaluation, case
De Francis, Vincent, 329
Delaware, 291
Delinquencies, 25-32; concepts of, 5, 32-44, 360; statistics of, 10-11, 29, 33-34; prediction of, 86-90, 157, 459, 471; and special schools, 197-205; and police, 206-29; and court, 230-76; and detention, 277-311, 393-96
Delinquency, *see* Delinquencies
Delinquency Prevention and Research, Massachusetts Bureau of, 485
Delinquent Boys (Cohen), 37
Des Moines, 291
"Detached workers," 376-85, 387
Detection, 209-11
Detention, 12, 31, 73, 243, 277-311; and rehabilitation, 50, 51; philosophy, criteria, and program, 279-91; regional, 291-93; problems of, 293-96; at Youth House, New York City, 296-311
Detention of Children in Michigan (Norman), 293
Deterrence, 46, 208-9
Detroit, 359, 377, 507-8
Deutsch, Albert, quoted, 395
Diagnosis, 15-16, 20, 34-36 *passim*, 446, 488; and family service agency, 125-27; and police, 219-20; and institutionalization, 436-38; *see also* Family, in diagnosis and treatment
Discipline, in training schools, 403-4
"Disordered behavior," 135-36
Disposition of cases, 16-17, 100-3, 438-40, 446, 488; court, 254-56, 257, 260-61
Diversity, in community services, 56-60; in educational offerings, 153-57; in institutional systems, 417-25

Domestic Relations Court, New York City, 339
Donnison, D. V., quoted, 461, 462
Doorways, to a court, 248-52; *see also* Intake
Drugs, 383
Durkheim, Emile, 40

Early Identification and Prevention Program, 195-96
Education, 146-63, 409-10; *see also* Schools
Education, New York City Board of, 305, 512
Education, New York State Department of, 430
Educational and Vocational Guidance, New York City Bureau of, 167, 174-83, 191-97, 200-2 *passim*
Effectiveness of efforts, 10-13
Ego, 358, 361-62
Ellingston, John R., 482
Emotional neglect, 318
Empey, LaMar, 265-66
Employment placement services, 391
Enforcement, a police function, 208-9; law, 328, 342-43, 346
England, 321-24, 371-73, 455-56, 461-62; multiproblem families in, 366, 367; institutions in, 405, 435; treatment in, 423-24
Erickson, Erik, 40
Erie County, New York, 345
Ethics, of "reaching out," 374
Ethnic factors, 360
Evaluation, case, 98-105, 111, 131; and public welfare departments, 139-40; and police, 211-15, 224-25, 226-28; and court, 241-42, 254; in probation, 257-60; and detention, 279-80; and neglect, 327-32
Experimentation, in treatment, 389-92

Fallsburgh, New York, 503
Family, in diagnosis and treatment, 50-53, 358-59, 364-65; service agencies, 77-78, 119, 120-28, 453; and neglect, 325; the multiproblem, 365-74 *passim*, 459n, 513
Family Centered Project (St. Paul), 359, 367-69 *passim*, 373, 385, 454-55, 462-63 *passim*
Family Court, New York, 103, 247, 276, 308